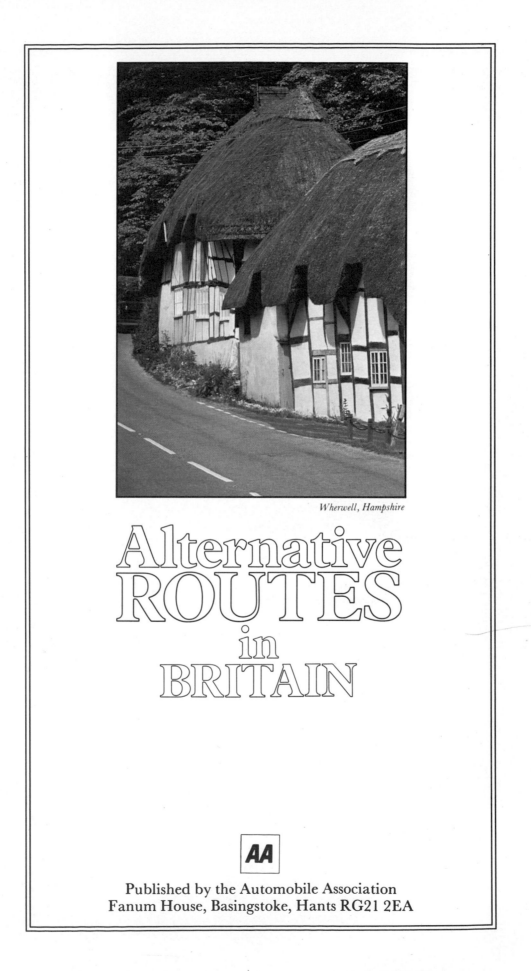

Wherwell, Hampshire

Alternative ROUTES in BRITAIN

AA

Published by the Automobile Association
Fanum House, Basingstoke, Hants RG21 2EA

Produced by the Publications Division of the Automobile Association
Editor   Julia Brittain
Art Editor   Dave Austin
Assistant Editors   Michael Cady, Richard Powell
Editorial Contributors   Bryn Frank, Barbara Littlewood, Stan Liversedge,
Philip Llewellin, Ian Nairn, Rebecca Snelling

Routes compiled by the Publications Research Unit of the Automobile Association

Original photography by Martyn J Adelman, Robin Fletcher, S & O Mathews,
Colin Molyneux, Richard Surman, Trevor Wood, Jon Wyand
Text illustrations by Kuo Kang Chen
Wildlife illustrations by Don Cordery
Picture research by Sally Howard
Index compiled by Roger Prebble
From an original design concept by Keith Russell

Maps produced by the Cartographic Department of the Automobile Association
Based on Ordnance Survey Maps, with the permission of the Controller of
HM Stationery Office. Crown Copyright reserved

Typeset, printed and bound in Great Britain by
Morrison & Gibb Ltd, London and Edinburgh

The contents of this book are believed correct at the time of printing. Nevertheless, the publisher can accept no responsibility for errors or omissions or for changes in the details given

ISBN 0 86145 063 9

Published by
The Automobile Association
Fanum House, Basingstoke, Hampshire RG21 2EA

090606

Penshurst, Kent

Contents

Route Finder

This cast-iron pump has graced Chipping Campden's High Street since 1832

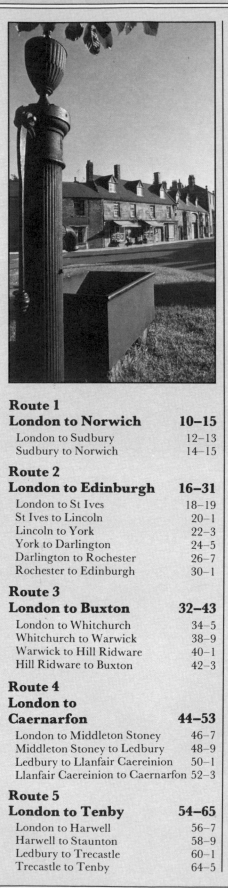

Route 1
London to Norwich   **10–15**
London to Sudbury   12–13
Sudbury to Norwich   14–15

Route 2
London to Edinburgh   **16–31**
London to St Ives   18–19
St Ives to Lincoln   20–1
Lincoln to York   22–3
York to Darlington   24–5
Darlington to Rochester   26–7
Rochester to Edinburgh   30–1

Route 3
London to Buxton   **32–43**
London to Whitchurch   34–5
Whitchurch to Warwick   38–9
Warwick to Hill Ridware   40–1
Hill Ridware to Buxton   42–3

Route 4
London to Caernarfon   **44–53**
London to Middleton Stoney   46–7
Middleton Stoney to Ledbury   48–9
Ledbury to Llanfair Caereinion   50–1
Llanfair Caereinion to Caernarfon   52–3

Route 5
London to Tenby   **54–65**
London to Harwell   56–7
Harwell to Staunton   58–9
Ledbury to Trecastle   60–1
Trecastle to Tenby   64–5

Route 6
London to Bude   **66–75**
London to Newbury   68–9
Newbury to Frome   70–1
Frome to Halberton   72–3
Halberton to Bude   74–5

Route 7
London to Plymouth   **76–85**
Epsom to Petersfield   78–9
Petersfield to Blandford Forum   80–1
Blandford Forum to Newton Poppleford   82–3
Newton Poppleford to Plymouth   84–5

Route 8
London to Bournemouth   **88–93**
London to Overton   90–1
Overton to Bournemouth   92–3

Route 9
London to Eastbourne   **96–103**
London to Tunbridge Wells   98–9
Tunbridge Wells to Eastbourne   102–3

Route 10
Birmingham to Norwich   **104–13**
Birmingham to Lubenham   106–7
Lubenham to Warboys   108–9
Warboys to Mildenhall   110–11
Brandon to Norwich   112–13

Route 11
Birmingham to Scarborough   **114–23**
Birmingham to Wymeswold   116–17
Wymeswold to Lincoln   118–19
Lincoln to Humber Bridge   120–1
Humber Bridge to Scarborough   122–3

Route 12
Birmingham to Glasgow   **124–37**
Birmingham to Chapel-en-le-Frith   126–7
Chapel-en-le-Frith to Horton in Ribblesdale   128–9
Horton in Ribblesdale to Kirkoswald   132–3
Kirkoswald to Carronbridge   134–5
Carronbridge to Glasgow   136–7

Route 13
Birmingham to Aberystwyth   **138–43**
Birmingham to Knighton   140–1
Knighton to Aberystwyth   142–3

Route Finder

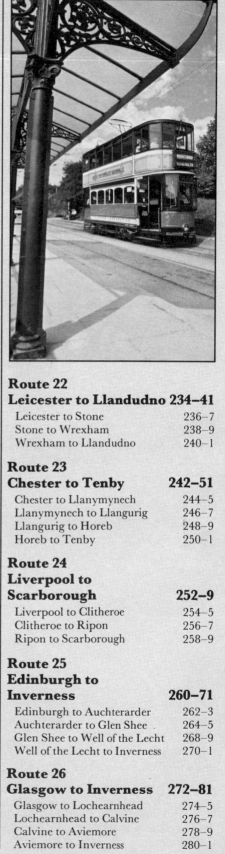

Many of the splendid old vehicles at the Crich Tramway Museum near Matlock are still in working order

Planning your Routes

This book of planned alternative routes in Britain is designed to help those who want to travel about the country without relying on major trunk roads and motorways. The routes are for everyone who likes to get off the beaten track and explore the lanes, by-ways, villages and towns of lesser-known Britain.

All kinds of journeys can be planned with the aid of this book. Twenty-six long-distance routes are described in detail, and the key map opposite shows how these cover the country. Thirty-two more routes can be compiled simply by linking parts of the basic routes: instructions for following these are given on pages 282–3. Most of the routes run from large centres of population to holiday areas, and were selected on the basis of routes most frequently requested by AA members. (It should be noted that some of the minor roads included in the routes are unsuitable for caravans.)

Alternative Routes in Britain can also be used to plan shorter trips, whether as an afternoon's outing or as an entertaining way of making a necessary journey. As the key map shows, the network of basic routes covers the length and breadth of Britain, and the index lists every place described in the book, so it is simplicity itself to join or leave a route wherever you wish.

Each of the twenty-six basic routes opens with a pictorial map and an introduction, to give a general picture of the route and what you can expect to find along the way. A mileage chart gives distances between selected towns on each route. The routes are then broken down into sections, each averaging fifty or sixty miles' driving and occupying two facing pages. Each of these double-page spreads is self-contained, providing all that you need to follow your chosen route with confidence – a detailed map, pictures of places that you will pass, and a commentary describing many fascinating things to see on the way and giving full route directions. (The abbreviation 'SP' is used in the text to denote 'signposted'.) Sometimes the routes pass within a mile or two of a stately home, castle or village of special interest, and a number of recommended detours are included. The route directions and descriptive text for such places appear in smaller type, boxed off from the main text.

All this information packs every section of each route with interest. There may not be time to visit every place mentioned, but from the details given you can make your own selection.

The routes in the book pass through many outstandingly beautiful and interesting stretches of countryside, such as national parks, ranges of hills, moors and forests. Fourteen special picture essays are devoted to the best of these, bringing out their characteristic features, explaining something of their history and wildlife, and suggesting places to visit.

Other special features concentrate on the destinations of the routes. Each includes a town plan, a brief introduction to the town, its history and places of interest – all you need to round off the journey.

A note on places open to the public

Many historic buildings, museums and other places of interest are featured in this book. An asterisk following the name of such a property in the text indicates that it will be found in the list of opening details given on the introductory pages of the route concerned. Places are listed in the order in which they appear in the text and, unless otherwise stated, are open all day every day of the week throughout the year.

Although the opening times given are believed to be correct at the time of printing, such details are always subject to change, sometimes at short notice. To be certain of avoiding disappointment, visitors are advised to check times by telephone.

Places that are open by appointment only, only occasionally open, or for which no accurate details are available, have been omitted from the lists in this book. The mention of a house or other property in the text therefore does not necessarily mean that it is open to the public.

Churches may generally be visited at all times; some are kept locked, but the key can usually be obtained without difficulty. Often a notice in the church porch will say where it is.

Planning your Routes

The key map shows the 26 routes that are described in detail in the book. Parts of these basic routes can be linked together to form 32 additional long-distance routes as described on pages 282–3. The map also shows the locations of the 14 countryside features highlighting areas of special scenic interest.

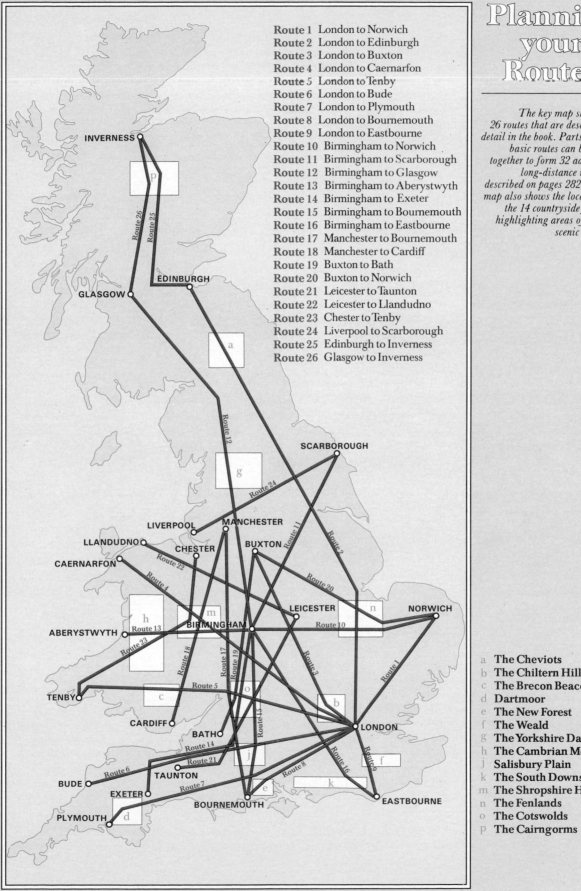

Route 1   London to Norwich
Route 2   London to Edinburgh
Route 3   London to Buxton
Route 4   London to Caernarfon
Route 5   London to Tenby
Route 6   London to Bude
Route 7   London to Plymouth
Route 8   London to Bournemouth
Route 9   London to Eastbourne
Route 10 Birmingham to Norwich
Route 11 Birmingham to Scarborough
Route 12 Birmingham to Glasgow
Route 13 Birmingham to Aberystwyth
Route 14 Birmingham to Exeter
Route 15 Birmingham to Bournemouth
Route 16 Birmingham to Eastbourne
Route 17 Manchester to Bournemouth
Route 18 Manchester to Cardiff
Route 19 Buxton to Bath
Route 20 Buxton to Norwich
Route 21 Leicester to Taunton
Route 22 Leicester to Llandudno
Route 23 Chester to Tenby
Route 24 Liverpool to Scarborough
Route 25 Edinburgh to Inverness
Route 26 Glasgow to Inverness

a   The Cheviots
b   The Chiltern Hills
c   The Brecon Beacons
d   Dartmoor
e   The New Forest
f   The Weald
g   The Yorkshire Dales
h   The Cambrian Mountains
j   Salisbury Plain
k   The South Downs
m   The Shropshire Hills
n   The Fenlands
o   The Cotswolds
p   The Cairngorms

Using the Maps

Each section of every route has its own specially drawn map, which appears beside the route commentary. All the strip maps should be read from the foot of the page upwards, and each includes a north point, for easy direction-finding, and a scale. The main route is shown by a bold purple line.

ROUTE MAP SYMBOLS

- ☀ AA viewpoint
- ⛪ Abbey or cathedral
- ✈ Airport
- ⛷ Artificial ski slope
- ✕ Battle site
- 🐦 Bird park
- ♜ Castle
- ⚓ Coastal launching site
- 🦋 Country park
- 🏏 County cricket
- 🌲 Forest drive
- ✳ Garden
- ✕ Gliding centre
- ⚑ Golf course
- 🏛 House or stately home
- 🏡 House with garden
- ▲ Hill with spot height
- 🐎 Horse racing
- 🏭 Industrial interest
- ℹ Information centre
- ℹ Information centre – summer only
- LC Level crossing
- 🚨 Lighthouse
- 🚶 Long-distance footpath
- 🏁 Motor-racing circuit
- 🏺 Museum or collection
- 🍂 Nature trail
- Ⓟ Picnic site
- • Other place of interest
- 🏛 Prehistoric site
- 🚂 Preserved railway
- 🍺 Pub or other landmark
- ♜ Ruined abbey or cathedral
- 🎣 Sea angling
- 🐴 Show jumping or equestrian centre
- ⚡ Surfing
- 🐾 Wildlife park
- 🎡 Windmill
- 🐾 Zoo

To make the routes simple to follow, the emphasis is on roads, towns and villages adjacent to the route, but all primary routes and sizeable towns are included over the entire strip-map area to show how the alternative route is linked with towns which lie within a few miles of it. This makes it easy to leave or join a route wherever you wish.

Names of towns, villages and places of interest in rural areas are printed in black on the maps where they are described in the text. Some places of interest which lie near the route but are not described are also marked on the maps. A number of these places (named in blue type) are described on other routes in the book and can be found by referring to the index.

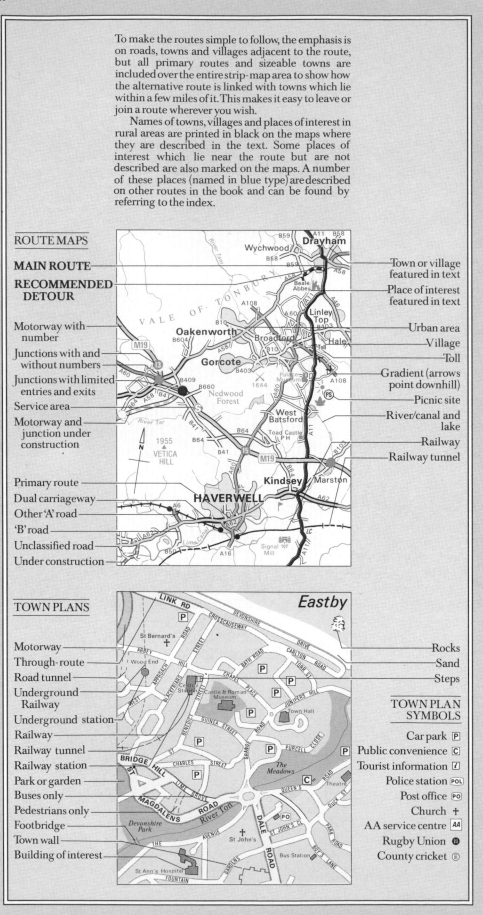

ROUTE MAPS

- MAIN ROUTE
- RECOMMENDED DETOUR
- Motorway with number
- Junctions with and without numbers
- Junctions with limited entries and exits
- Service area
- Motorway and junction under construction
- Primary route
- Dual carriageway
- Other 'A' road
- 'B' road
- Unclassified road
- Under construction

- Town or village featured in text
- Place of interest featured in text
- Urban area
- Village
- Toll
- Gradient (arrows point downhill)
- Picnic site
- River/canal and lake
- Railway
- Railway tunnel

TOWN PLANS

- Motorway
- Through-route
- Road tunnel
- Underground Railway
- Underground station
- Railway
- Railway tunnel
- Railway station
- Park or garden
- Buses only
- Pedestrians only
- Footbridge
- Town wall
- Building of interest

- Rocks
- Sand
- Steps

TOWN PLAN SYMBOLS

- Car park Ⓟ
- Public convenience Ⓒ
- Tourist information ℹ
- Police station POL
- Post office PO
- Church ✝
- AA service centre AA
- Rugby Union 🏉
- County cricket 🏏

Foreword

by Ian Nairn

Broad Street, Ludlow

An acknowledged expert on Britain's architecture, Ian Nairn has always had a passionate interest in the country's out-of-the-way places. Through his television appearances, books, and articles in the 'Sunday Times', he has encouraged thousands of others to explore lesser-known Britain.

Rediscovering Britain

The idea for this book came from the many route requests received by the AA from people who want to make the most of their motoring. People who had-to make long journeys, but who wanted to avoid traffic jams and motorway monotony, preferring to spend their time rediscovering Britain.

That's been my attitude for years. Ever since, as a child during the war, I used to curl up in my father's Austin Ten, chocked up in the garage for the duration. Not with a book, but with a road atlas. And not to look at trunk roads, but at B-roads, unclassified roads, small towns like Hexham and Hungerford, Oswestry and Midhurst.

One day, I said to myself, I'll find out about all that. Now, forty years later, I have, and it has been a revelation. If this book helps anyone else to do the same, I'll be delighted. Because in terms of scenery and townscape Britain is the most varied country I know.

Looking at the routes selected by the AA, one thing hits me immediately. The 'alternative' equivalents to the M1 and Spaghetti Junction are roads studded with small towns of great character: places like Cirencester and Ludlow. Cirencester is fascinating not only for its medieval church and market place; underneath all this is a complete Roman town to an entirely different plan. And Ludlow, for my money, is simply the best country town in Britain. For its site, above the Teme and opposite a green cliff. For the castle, and the church, which has the best misericords in Britain – a complete sculpture book of medieval life. For the totally genuine, well-kept elegance of Broad Street. And for the people, a happy mixture of Midland common sense and Welsh fantasy.

As you will discover in the pages that follow, Britain is packed with splendid, unspoilt towns and villages like these. They're all there, away from the motorways. I confess that I hardly ever use motorways, for I want to be able to stop and wander away from the road when and where I like; to see the *real* countryside and the marvellous towns and villages that might never have come my way if I'd stuck to the main roads.

Inevitably most of these routes are on numbered roads, though I hope that having acquired the taste for alternative motoring you will find your own unclassified alternatives to the alternatives. When stuck in a traffic jam, just turn left out of it and see where it gets you – otherwise what is the point of travelling at all?

ROUTE 1

London to Norwich

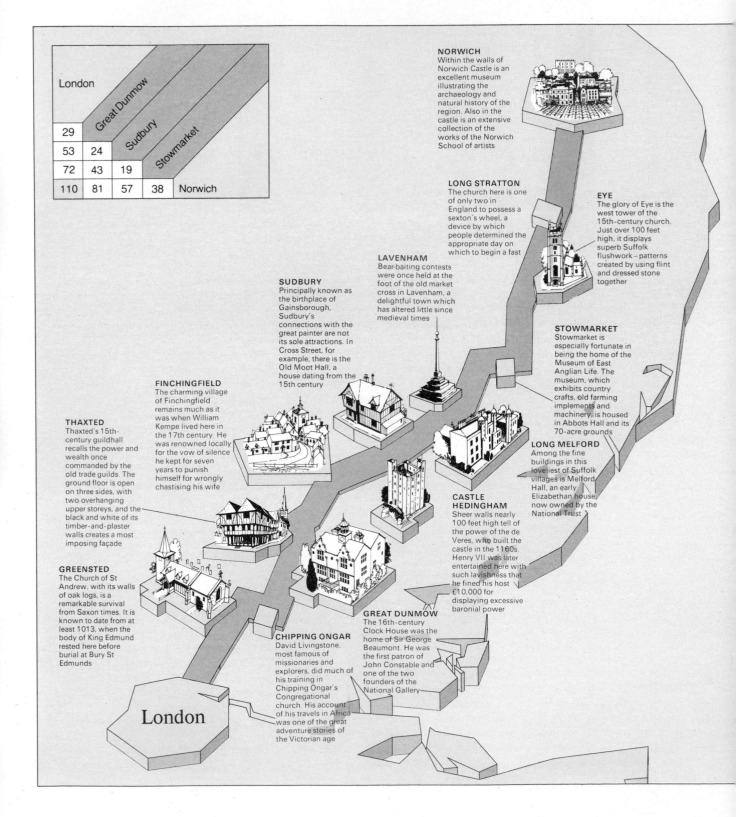

London				
29	Great Dunmow			
53	24	Sudbury		
72	43	19	Stowmarket	
110	81	57	38	Norwich

NORWICH
Within the walls of Norwich Castle is an excellent museum illustrating the archaeology and natural history of the region. Also in the castle is an extensive collection of the works of the Norwich School of artists

LONG STRATTON
The church here is one of only two in England to possess a sexton's wheel, a device by which people determined the appropriate day on which to begin a fast

EYE
The glory of Eye is the west tower of the 15th-century church. Just over 100 feet high, it displays superb Suffolk flushwork – patterns created by using flint and dressed stone together

LAVENHAM
Bear-baiting contests were once held at the foot of the old market cross in Lavenham, a delightful town which has altered little since medieval times

SUDBURY
Principally known as the birthplace of Gainsborough, Sudbury's connections with the great painter are not its sole attractions. In Cross Street, for example, there is the Old Moot Hall, a house dating from the 15th century

STOWMARKET
Stowmarket is especially fortunate in being the home of the Museum of East Anglian Life. The museum, which exhibits country crafts, old farming implements and machinery, is housed in Abbots Hall and its 70-acre grounds

FINCHINGFIELD
The charming village of Finchingfield remains much as it was when William Kempe lived here in the 17th century. He was renowned locally for the vow of silence he kept for seven years to punish himself for wrongly chastising his wife

LONG MELFORD
Among the fine buildings in this loveliest of Suffolk villages is Melford Hall, an early Elizabethan house, now owned by the National Trust

THAXTED
Thaxted's 15th-century guildhall recalls the power and wealth once commanded by the old trade guilds. The ground floor is open on three sides, with two overhanging upper storeys, and the black and white of its timber-and-plaster walls creates a most imposing façade

CASTLE HEDINGHAM
Sheer walls nearly 100 feet high tell of the power of the de Veres, who built the castle in the 1160s. Henry VII was later entertained here with such lavishness that he fined his host £10,000 for displaying excessive baronial power

GREENSTED
The Church of St Andrew, with its walls of oak logs, is a remarkable survival from Saxon times. It is known to date from at least 1013, when the body of King Edmund rested here before burial at Bury St Edmunds

GREAT DUNMOW
The 16th-century Clock House was the home of Sir George Beaumont. He was the first patron of John Constable and one of the two founders of the National Gallery

CHIPPING ONGAR
David Livingstone, most famous of missionaries and explorers, did much of his training in Chipping Ongar's Congregational church. His account of his travels in Africa was one of the great adventure stories of the Victorian age

London

LOVELY old villages and quiet country roads through gentle rural landscapes are the unifying features of this route to the 'capital' of East Anglia. Throughout Essex, Suffolk and Norfolk bustling villages and remote farms are linked by a complex network of minor roads and lanes that still offer motorists the pre-war luxury of being more or less the only vehicles in sight. The villages themselves – many of them showpieces of English vernacular architecture – are set like jewels against green backdrops that have inspired some of Britain's best-loved painters.

East London falls away as the route follows the River Roding upstream through Chipping Ongar into the part of Essex called the Rodings. A good many of the cottages in southern Essex are weatherboarded, a practice that was introduced into the eastern counties during the 18th and 19th centuries as an alternative to the traditional plaster or brick. The weather-boarded colonial buildings that are typical of the east-coast states of North America are a perfection of this style of architecture and were introduced by colonists from the south-eastern counties of England.

Beyond Great Dunmow the route passes through the tiny hamlets of Bran End, Duck End and Oxen End to reach Great Bardfield, one of the most beautiful villages in Essex. Its treasures include a 14th-century church with a superb rood screen, and, just beyond the village, a brick-built tower windmill. Windmills are a traditional part of the East Anglian scene, and at one time there were hundreds of them. Built principally to grind the corn from the fertile wheatlands of Suffolk and Essex, many of them were still working after the Second World War. Now, however, most of those which survive are sadly dilapidated, but a few have been renovated or converted into unusual houses. Finchingfield, the next village, also has a windmill and it too is a place of outstanding beauty and charm. Its village green and pond, set amid lovingly preserved cottages, have long been a favourite subject of photographers, and the timber-framed guildhall is an ideal setting for a small local museum.

The Norman keep at Castle Hedingham, built of Barnack stone, looks over a sleepy village that was once a place of considerable importance, for the castle was the principal residence of the powerful earls of Oxford. At Sudbury, the birthplace of the painter Thomas Gainsborough, the route crosses the River Stour. Although Gainsborough is primarily thought of as a portrait painter, he had a tremendous feeling for landscape, as can be seen in his exquisite painting *Mr and Mrs Andrews*, in which the scenery is taken directly from the area around Sudbury. He said of his native countryside that there was not 'a picturesque clump of trees, or even a single tree of any beauty' that he had not committed to memory. As the river makes its way eastwards to the sea it passes through scenery that has been immortalized by John Constable, England's greatest landscape painter. Constable, who was born 50 years after Gainsborough, wrote enthusiastically about Gainsborough's landscapes and they undoubtedly influenced his own work.

North of Sudbury are two villages, Long Melford and Lavenham, whose fame is justifiably international. They grew in the 14th century during the great wool boom, and attracted large numbers of Flemish cloth-workers and weavers. The wealth brought by the wool trade enabled the merchants to build themselves houses of exceptional beauty and churches that are among England's greatest architectural treasures.

PLACES OF INTEREST: OPENING DETAILS

Finchingfield
FINCHINGFIELD GUILDHALL AND MUSEUM open Easter, then end May to Sep Sun and Bank Holidays, pm only

SPAINS HALL open May to end Jul Sat, Sun and Bank Holidays, pm only

Castle Hedingham
CASTLE open May to end Sep Tue, Thu and Sat, pm only; open Bank Holidays all day

Sudbury
GAINSBOROUGH'S HOUSE open all year daily (except Sun am, Mon and 25-26 Dec)

Long Melford
MELFORD HALL open Apr to end Sep Wed, Thu, Sun and Bank Holiday Mon, pm only

Lavenham
GUILDHALL open Mar to Nov daily (except Fri in Mar and Nov)

Stowmarket
MUSEUM OF EAST ANGLIAN LIFE open Apr to end Oct: Mon to Sat all day, Sun pm only

Many of these rich merchants are commemorated in their churches by exquisite brasses and other memorials which are remarkable examples of the medieval craftsman's art.

The East Anglian custom of colour-washing plastered buildings is beautifully illustrated in these and other villages on this route. Traditional colours tended towards pastel hues of ochre, yellow and buff, with pink in some areas, but nowadays the range is much greater and some village streets are as varied in colour as a child's box of paints. Hand-in-hand with the plasterwork goes pargeting – decorative plasterwork that is confined almost exclusively to East Anglia. It was developed in the 16th century simply as a way of enlivening flat areas of plaster, and by the 17th century it had become an art form. Many East Anglian timber-framed houses were built to be plastered, but where the timbers were designed to be exposed the oak has faded to a delightful silvery-grey.

With the decline of the wool trade in East Anglia during the late 16th century the wool towns and villages also declined. For the most part they were isolated from later innovations, particularly those resulting from the Industrial Revolution, so their houses were not altered or rebuilt, and they stand now as living history, preserved much as they were in their heyday.

From Sudbury the route continues through the rich claylands of 'high Suffolk', passing through villages like Chelsworth, Bildeston and Hitcham, which are set in a landscape of waving corn punctuated by majestic oak trees.

Stowmarket is the largest town on the route. As a result of modern development it has lost a great deal of its former charm and character; however, it is the home of the Museum of East Anglian Life – a marvellous collection of craft tools and agricultural bygones, many of which were in daily use until little more than 30 years ago.

A little way beyond Earl Stonham, the route joins the A140, which betrays its Roman origins by running all the way to Norwich in a series of straight stretches. It passes through, and close to, villages usually ignored by tourists but which preserve cottages and churches of great charm and interest.

Norwich would make a worthy end to any journey. It has a breathtaking array of superb churches, a Norman castle that is now a museum packed with exhibits ranging from gaily painted dragons once used in parades to dioramas of East Anglian natural history, and streets that are lined with every architectural style from medieval to Victorian Gothic. Perhaps of more immediate interest to weary travellers, Norwich also has comfortable hotels, guest-houses and restaurants as good as anywhere in England.

LONDON TO CHIPPING ONGAR

The route starts from the roundabout junction of the A406 North Circular Road and the A104 at Waterworks Corner, Woodford. Follow signs for Chelmsford and the A12, then take the left-hand lane and at the next roundabout take the first exit, the A113 (SP Chigwell). This road runs along the Roding valley, leaving London behind and soon reaching Chigwell. Beyond the modern development at the southern end of the village lies the old part, set on the crest of a hill. The church is on the left, and contains a fine brass to its remarkable vicar, Samuel Harsnett. In 1692 he founded the grammar school, next to the church. He eventually rose to become Archbishop of York.

About 2½ miles beyond Chigwell, the A113 runs through the pleasant village of Abridge, situated in the broad Roding valley, its pastures bordered by willow and poplar trees. At Passingford Bridge roundabout, turn left (SP Ongar) with the A113, continuing up the valley for 4½ miles, then joining the A128 at Marden Ash.

GREENSTED CHURCH

A few hundred yards past this junction, a detour may be made by turning left on to an unclassified road leading to Greensted church, which has one of the oldest wooden naves in the world. The church is about 1 mile from the main road on the right. It is tiny, and the nave is built of rough-hewn oak logs, with latticed dormer windows and rambler roses round its porch. Founded in the 7th century by the Celts, it was enlarged by the Saxons in the 9th century. The funeral procession carrying the body of St Edmund, an East Saxon king martyred by the Danes in 1013, is said to have stopped here on its journey to the king's last resting place at Bury St Edmunds.

The main route follows the A128 into Chipping Ongar, a large village with pretty white weatherboarded buildings whose charm is somewhat marred by the amount of traffic roaring through its main street.

CHIPPING ONGAR TO GREAT DUNMOW

At the roundabout near the end of the village, take the second exit, the B184 (SP Fyfield, Great Dunmow). Between Fyfield and Great Dunmow you are in Rodings country. There are eight of these villages, and the route goes through three of them. Four miles beyond Fyfield the route turns right on to the A1060 to reach the first, Leaden Roding, a pretty little cluster of cottages. Shortly past its church, turn left (SP Great Dunmow), again on the B184, noticing as you do so the sign to 'the Easters'. These are two villages called High Easter and Good Easter, popular at Easter when people try to have greetings cards postmarked from them. The route continues through Aythorpe Roding and High Roding and, just past the Kicking Dicky pub, turns left into Great Dunmow, passing the oddly named Dunmow Flitch Bacon Company premises. The tradition of the Dunmow Flitch began in the reign of Henry III when Robert Fitzwalter offered a flitch (side) of bacon to the first married couple who could prove that they had never quarrelled. Dunmow is a lively country town, full of interesting streets and ancient buildings.

GREAT DUNMOW TO SUDBURY

From the town centre follow signs for Great Bardfield and Finchingfield on the B1057, turning right opposite the Saracen's Head Hotel into Old Market Place and down a narrow hill, at the foot of which stands a pretty row of cottages leading to the church.

One of the
gargoyles on the
church of St John
the Baptist

THAXTED

...continuing northwards from Great
...nmow on the B184 a detour may be made
...Thaxted, rightly one of the most celebrated
...lages in Essex. It remains an unspoilt
...twork of delightful streets and old houses.
...he foundation of its prosperity was the
...tlery trade, and it was the cutlers who
...gan to construct the church in the 14th
...ntury. It contains a fine 15th-century brass
...a parish priest, Robert Wedow, and all
...und the outside are gargoyles of nightmar-
...h vitality. The cutlers also built the beautiful
...mbered guildhall at the foot of the hill.

...From Thaxted take the unclassified road
...hich leads eastwards off the B184 at the
...uthern end of the village. This road leads
...rough Little Bardfield, a peaceful village set
...nid rolling fields, to rejoin the main route at
...reat Bardfield, turning left on to the B1057.

The B1057 runs through Bran End and
later enters Great Bardfield, where there is a
fine windmill, one of only a few that remain
in a part of the country where they were once
the characteristic feature. From here the
route continues along the B1057 to the
famous picture-postcard village of Finchingfield. Its rows of old cottages overlook a neat
green complete with a village pond and
plump white ducks. Above the cottages
stands the fine 15th-century guildhall,*
which now houses a small local history
museum. Beside it is the church, with its great
Norman tower. Among the interesting features inside is a monument to William Kempe
who, for shame at having spoken a 'hasty'
word to his wife, is said to have kept a vow of
silence for seven years. His house, a magnificent Elizabethan mansion called Spains
Hall,* is set in rolling parkland, and lies on a
minor road (SP Spains Hall, Helions Bump-
stead) just outside the village off the B1057
Haverhill Road.

Leave the village by the B1053 (SP
Wethersfield, Braintree), and at Wethersfield
take the unclassified road on the left by the
church to the unassuming little village of
Sible Hedingham, where the route turns left
(SP Haverhill) on to the A604, and then very
shortly right on to the B1058 (SP Castle
Hedingham, Sudbury).

Castle Hedingham, 1 mile further on, is yet
another enchanting village, with narrow
streets, antique shops, craft market, pubs and
restaurants. It was once famous for a distinctive type of pottery called Hedingham ware,
now much prized by collectors. The massive
castle* from which the village takes its name
can still be seen. Built in the 12th century by
the powerful de Vere family, earls of Oxford,
it is one of the best preserved Norman keeps
in the country. The parish church has a
Tudor tower and porch, but its interior,
apart from the superb medieval hammer-
beam roof in the nave, is strikingly and
unmistakably Norman.

Continue along the B1058 towards
Sudbury, turning left on to the A131 at
Bulmer Tye and crossing the Suffolk border
to enter Sudbury. From here the town's
appearance is not inviting, but it is more
attractive than it seems – and than its
occurrence in Dickens' *Pickwick Papers* under
the name of Eatanswill would suggest. It was
the birthplace of the painter Sir Thomas
Gainsborough, and there is a statue of him,
palette in hand, in front of St Peter's Church
in the town centre. His birthplace is now an
art gallery and museum.* Near the statue is a
remarkable corn exchange – a Victorian
extravaganza surmounted by stooks of corn
and figures of reapers.

*Finchingfield's cottages, grouped informally round the green and the sturdy old church, date from many periods and combine to
create one of the loveliest villagescapes in England*

SUDBURY TO HITCHAM

LONG MELFORD

From Sudbury, a detour on the A134 (SP Bury St Edmunds) leads to Long Melford, one of the longest 'street' villages in England. The main street, stretching for almost two miles, is lined with lovely old houses and punctuated by the stately Elizabethan hall,* which contains superb collections of Chinese porcelain, furniture and a number of Old Master paintings. At the northern end of the village is the magnificent 15th-century church, particularly noted for its Lady Chapel, dating from 1496, and for its interesting monuments and brasses.

Melford Hall

The main route leaves the centre of Sudbury by the A134 (SP Colchester), shortly branching left on to the B1115 (SP Stowmarket). After about 4 miles, at the junction with the B1071, turn right to remain with the B1115 for Monks Eleigh and Stowmarket.

LAVENHAM

By branching left at this junction you can make a detour along the B1071 to Lavenham, an old wool town which is one of the chief glories of Suffolk. The road enters the town past the magnificent church, whose 141-foot-high flint tower dominates the town from its hilltop site. In the church is the tomb of Thomas Spring, one of the wealthy clothiers who provided funds for the building. By turning right at the bottom of the hill and then left up Lady Street you will reach the old market place with its splendid timbered guildhall,* which is now a museum. This is Lavenham's most famous building, but the market place and the streets around it are all packed with delightful and well-preserved buildings of many periods.

Leave Lavenham by the A1141 (SP Hadleigh) to rejoin the route at Monks Eleigh.

Just before Monks Eleigh the main route (B1115) bends sharply left before turning right on to the A1141 Hadleigh road. Pass through Monks Eleigh and at the end of the village, on a sharp right-hand bend, carry straight on, joining the B1115, which runs through Chelsworth and Bildeston, both pretty villages in the Brett valley. Bildeston was a flourishing cloth market in the 16th century, and it retains an attractive little market square. Hitcham, a few miles further on, has associations with a learned 19th-century vicar, John Henslow. He was a naturalist and a friend of Charles Darwin, and angered his farmer-parishioners by introducing botany as a subject for study in the local schools. There is a memorial to him in the church.

...ibits in the Museum of East Anglian Life at Stowmarket include elevators, harvesters, a remarkable variety of ploughs and a restored smithy

...TCHAM TO EARL STONHAM

...Hitcham turn sharply right with the ...115 and continue to Stowmarket. The ...n has had two phases of rapid expansion, ...first as a result of the canal age in the late ...h and early 19th centuries when the River ...pping, which runs into the Orwell at ...wich, was made navigable; the second ...ase has occurred in recent years, and as a ...ult the old market town has not retained ...ch of its former character. It is, however, ...home of the fascinating Museum of East ...glian Life,* set in the 70-acre grounds of ...bots Hall. The museum has a marvellous ...lection of items relating to the rural life and ...ditional crafts of the region. There is a fine ...en-air section where you can see an old ...ithy, a water-mill and a timbered, aisled ...mhouse dating from the 14th century. ...ollow signs through Stowmarket for the ...120 (SP Yoxford) and join this road by ...ning left, 1¼ miles beyond the level ...ssing, at a T-junction. The route passes ...ough Stowupland to reach Earl Stonham, ...n turns left (SP Norwich) on to the A140 ...swich to Norwich road.

...RL STONHAM TO NORWICH

...yond Earl Stonham the road runs through ...reat expanse of open countryside and you ...n see for miles on either side across the flat ...st Anglian fields. In winter, when there is ...en a piercing east wind, the prospect can be bleak, but in summer the landscapes are superb. For most of its distance the road strikes across country in an almost straight line, travelling due north along the course of an old Roman road.

EYE

About 9 miles from Earl Stonham, at a crossroads, a detour can be made by turning right on to the B1117 for Eye, a delightful little town of narrow streets and old grey houses. The first really noteworthy building is the remarkably ornate Victorian Gothic town hall, but it is the church that is most often admired, chiefly for its lovely, slender tower, more than 100 feet high and dating from the 15th century. Eye also boasts a 16th-century guildhall and the ruins of a Norman castle, founded by William Mallet, who came over with William the Conqueror and was killed whilst fighting against the great East Anglian hero, Hereward the Wake.

THORNHAM PARVA

From the same crossroads a second detour can be made by taking the unclassified road on the left to the little hamlet of Thornham Parva, about ½ mile from the main road, where a tiny, thatched church stands amid fields. Even its tower bears a cap of thatch, and inside is a masterpiece of medieval painting, a crucifixion dating from the 14th century, which was found by chance among junk sold at a farm auction in 1927.

The main route continues along the A140 through Scole, crossing the River Waveney, which marks the border between Suffolk and Norfolk. The 17th-century White Hart Inn here is a reminder of the days when this road was used by stage-coaches travelling between Norwich and Ipswich, and Scole was an important posting stop between the two. Two-and-a-half miles beyond Scole lies Dickleburgh, and 7 miles past it the route reaches the aptly named 'street' village of Long Stratton. To the right as the road enters the village is the church, which has a distinctive East Anglian round tower and is remarkable for its rare sexton's wheel. With this wheel, the medieval devout could play a sort of religious roulette to determine when to start a 365-day fast of bread and water. Cords were attached to the wheel to represent the feast days sacred to the Virgin; the sexton spun the wheel and the would-be faster caught one of the strings at random and thus knew when to start his year of fasting.

Still following the A140, the route passes Swainsthorpe's attractive Dun Cow Inn, built in the late 17th century. Swainsthorpe village is set off the main road and once boasted two parish churches. Nothing survives of St Mary's, but St Peter's, with its handsome round tower, still stands. At Harford Bridge the route crosses the River Yare and shortly enters the outskirts of Norwich. (For details and a town plan of Norwich, see p. 113.)

ROUTE 2   406 MILE

London to Edinburgh

FORESTS, fens, wolds, moors and mountains – these are some of the natural features which make this route highly rewarding and dramatically varied. Architectural wonders include Cambridge, perhaps the most beautiful university city in the world; four cathedral cities, all of which preserve their medieval street patterns, and dozens of interesting villages, from homely groups of cottages in the Home Counties to stern moorland settlements in the Border country.

London's suburbs soon seem far behind as the route runs through Epping Forest. Distinctive East Anglian architecture, typified by half-timbering and beautiful decorative plaster-work known as pargeting, makes its first appearance around Bishop's Stortford. From Newport the route follows the River Cam to skirt the magnificent city to which it gave its name. Cambridge was a strategic river crossing in prehistoric times, was given a boost by the Romans, and began its rise to lasting and universal fame with the establishment of the first colleges in the 13th century. The Via Devana, a Roman road, is followed for a few miles beyond Cambridge, but shortly the route turns northwards through St Ives to join the A1 below Stilton.

Beyond Stilton, the route continues through Peterborough and the flat landscapes of the Fens to reach Lincoln. The city stands on the limestone ridge that stretches all the way from Leicestershire to the Humber estuary, and its unique Newport Arch is a reminder that it has been an important place since Roman times. From the city the route runs alongside a canal built by the Romans, and shortly enters the rich farming country of the Trent valley. Leaving the Trent at Gainsborough, the route continues across the Isle of Axholme to reach the serpentine meanders of the Ouse estuary at Goole before continuing to York, one of the most stunningly well-preserved of all British cities. Its walls, standing on Rom foundations, encircle a town that retains its medieval str pattern almost intact and is a veritable treasure-chest buildings from all ages.

From Easingwold the route runs along the edge of Howardian Hills to Thirsk, where views to the east take in North York Moors, with the Hambleton Hills in the fo ground. Crossing the River Tees at Croft, the route pa Darlington, scene of some of the earliest experiments in railw development, and then Durham, whose collection of arc tectural treasures is grouped within a loop of the River Wea

On the other side of the Tyne is the Roman town of C stopitum and Hadrian's Wall, one of the most impressive fe of military engineering in Europe. Roman Dere Street car the route into the wild countryside of the Northumberla National Park and through Rochester – the site of *Bremeniun* Roman military outpost. Settlements in this region, the scen bloody border conflicts for many centuries, and perpetually the mercy of long, harsh winters, are often little more th hamlets clustered close together round ancient farmsteads.

Jedburgh, set in incomparable Lowland scenery, is the f Scottish town on the route. Skirting the Eildon Hills, the rou then follows the River Tweed through Melrose to Galashie passing close to Abbotsford House, home of Sir Walter Sco whose novels capture the unique atmosphere of the Lowla countryside. Gala Water is followed to the Moorfoot Hi where the route crosses into the recently formed region Lothian. Edinburgh Castle, set on a dramatic rocky pinnac looks over a city that has been Scotland's cultural a administrative hub since 1437 and which preserves one of t finest Georgian townscapes in Europe.

PLACES OF INTEREST: OPENING DETAILS

Bishop's Stortford
RHODES MEMORIAL MUSEUM AND COMMONWEALTH CENTRE open all year daily (except Sun and Bank Holidays)

Stansted Mountfitchet
WINDMILL open Apr to Oct first Sun in month and every Sun in Aug, pm only; also open Bank Holiday Sun and Mon (except Christmas), pm only

Saffron Walden
AUDLEY END HOUSE open Apr to Oct daily (except Mon, Maundy Thu and Good Fri)

Duxford
DUXFORD AIRFIELD open Mar to end Oct

Cambridge
COLLEGES open most days throughout year, but with some restrictions during term time

St Ives
NORRIS MUSEUM open all year: Tue to Fri am and pm, Sat am only; also open Sat pm and Sun pm May to Sep (closed Bank Holidays)

Lincoln
LINCOLN CASTLE open all year (except Christmas), Mon to Sat all day; also open Sun Apr to Oct, pm only

Gainsborough
OLD HALL open weekdays all year (except 25-26 Dec and 1 Jan), pm only; also open Sun pm Easter to Oct

Epworth
OLD RECTORY open Mar to Oct: Mon to Sat am and pm, Sun pm only

York
YORK HERITAGE CENTRE open all year (except 25-26 Dec and 1 Jan): Mon to Sat all day, Sun pm only

NATIONAL RAILWAY MUSEUM open all year (except 24-26 Dec, 1 Jan, Good Fri and May Day): Mon to Sat all day, Sun pm only

YORK CASTLE MUSEUM open all year (except 25-26 Dec and 1 Jan)

Beningbrough
BENINGBROUGH HALL open Apr to Oct, pm only

Darlington
NORTH ROAD STATION RAILWAY MUSEUM open all year: Mon to Sat all day, Sun pm only. Closed Sun Nov to Easter

Durham
GULBENKIAN MUSEUM OF ORIENTAL ART open all year: Mon to Sat am and pm, Sun pm only. Closed Sat and Sun Christmas to Easter

DURHAM CASTLE open first three weeks in Apr, then Jul to end Sep, Mon to Sat am and pm; open rest of year Mon, Wed and Sat, pm only

DURHAM LIGHT INFANTRY MUSEUM open all year: Tue to Sat all day, Sun pm only; also open Bank Holiday Mon

Corbridge
CORSTOPITUM ROMAN STATION open all year

Wall
CHESTERS ROMAN FORT AND MUSEUM open all year

Jedburgh
JEDBURGH ABBEY open all year (except 1½ days per week Oct to Mar)

CASTLE JAIL open Apr to Sep: Mon to Sat am and pm, Sun pm only

MARY QUEEN OF SCOTS HOUSE open Mar to Oct

St Boswells
DRYBURGH ABBEY open all year

Melrose
MELROSE ABBEY open daily all year

ABBOTSFORD HOUSE open Mar to Oct: Mon to Sat am and pm, Sun pm only

Edinburgh
HOLYROODHOUSE open all year daily (except Sun Nov to Apr and also for about four weeks in spring)

JOHN KNOX'S HOUSE open weekdays all year

EDINBURGH CASTLE open all year

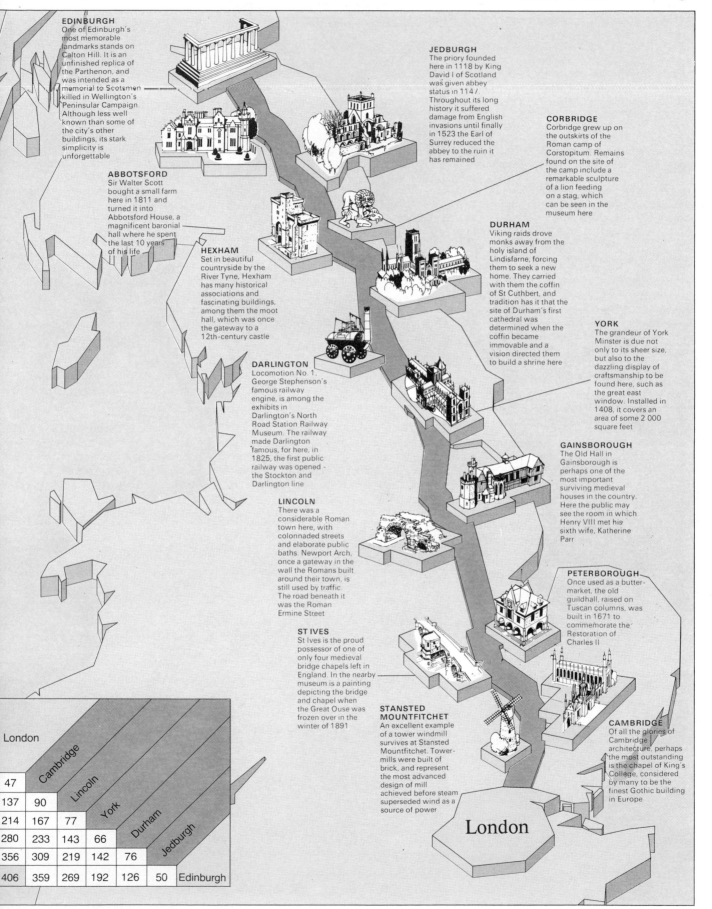

EDINBURGH
One of Edinburgh's most memorable landmarks stands on Calton Hill. It is an unfinished replica of the Parthenon, and was intended as a memorial to Scotsmen killed in Wellington's Peninsular Campaign. Although less well known than some of the city's other buildings, its stark simplicity is unforgettable

JEDBURGH
The priory founded here in 1118 by King David I of Scotland was given abbey status in 1147. Throughout its long history it suffered damage from English invasions until finally in 1523 the Earl of Surrey reduced the abbey to the ruin it has remained

CORBRIDGE
Corbridge grew up on the outskirts of the Roman camp of Corstopitum. Remains found on the site of the camp include a remarkable sculpture of a lion feeding on a stag, which can be seen in the museum here

ABBOTSFORD
Sir Walter Scott bought a small farm here in 1811 and turned it into Abbotsford House, a magnificent baronial hall where he spent the last 10 years of his life

HEXHAM
Set in beautiful countryside by the River Tyne, Hexham has many historical associations and fascinating buildings, among them the moot hall, which was once the gateway to a 12th-century castle

DURHAM
Viking raids drove monks away from the holy island of Lindisfarne, forcing them to seek a new home. They carried with them the coffin of St Cuthbert, and tradition has it that the site of Durham's first cathedral was determined when the coffin became immovable and a vision directed them to build a shrine here

YORK
The grandeur of York Minster is due not only to its sheer size, but also to the dazzling display of craftsmanship to be found here, such as the great east window. Installed in 1408, it covers an area of some 2 000 square feet

DARLINGTON
Locomotion No. 1, George Stephenson's famous railway engine, is among the exhibits in Darlington's North Road Station Railway Museum. The railway made Darlington famous, for here, in 1825, the first public railway was opened - the Stockton and Darlington line

GAINSBOROUGH
The Old Hall in Gainsborough is perhaps one of the most important surviving medieval houses in the country. Here the public may see the room in which Henry VIII met his sixth wife, Katherine Parr

LINCOLN
There was a considerable Roman town here, with colonnaded streets and elaborate public baths. Newport Arch, once a gateway in the wall the Romans built around their town, is still used by traffic. The road beneath it was the Roman Ermine Street

PETERBOROUGH
Once used as a butter-market, the old guildhall, raised on Tuscan columns, was built in 1671 to commemorate the Restoration of Charles II

ST IVES
St Ives is the proud possessor of one of only four medieval bridge chapels left in England. In the nearby museum is a painting depicting the bridge and chapel when the Great Ouse was frozen over in the winter of 1891

STANSTED MOUNTFITCHET
An excellent example of a tower windmill survives at Stansted Mountfitchet. Tower-mills were built of brick, and represent the most advanced design of mill achieved before steam superseded wind as a source of power

CAMBRIDGE
Of all the glories of Cambridge architecture, perhaps the most outstanding is the chapel of King's College, considered by many to be the finest Gothic building in Europe

London

London						
	Cambridge					
47		Lincoln				
137	90		York			
214	167	77		Durham		
280	233	143	66		Jedburgh	
356	309	219	142	76		Edinburgh
406	359	269	192	126	50	

LONDON TO BISHOP'S STORTFORD

This route starts at Woodford Green, 13 miles north-east of central London on the A104 (formerly A11). Soon leaving London's urban sprawl behind, the route runs northwards along the A104 (SP Epping) and then crosses the county boundary into Essex before entering Epping Forest. This 6000-acre expanse of woodlands, ponds and open heath was a royal hunting-ground for more than 600 years, and deer still roam the dense glades of beech and hornbeam, sometimes wandering within sight of the road.

Keep forward on the A104 (SP Epping) at the first roundabout in the Forest, and in 1¾ miles, at the roundabout by the Wake Arms pub, take the second exit, the B1393 (SP Epping). This road leads out of the Forest and through Epping. In 3 miles, at the motorway junction roundabout, take the first exit, the A414, to skirt Harlow, following the A414 at the next three roundabouts. At the fourth, take the third exit, the A1184 (SP Bishop's Stortford). The route soon crosses the River Stort to enter Hertfordshire, and runs through Sawbridgeworth to Bishop's Stortford, following the A1184 (SP Newport) at the roundabout on the south side of the town.

RHODES MEMORIAL MUSEUM

From this roundabout a very brief detour along South Road (the first exit) leads to the house* where Cecil Rhodes was born in 1853. The son of the local vicar, Rhodes went to South Africa as a youth of 17 and later became one of the most remarkable Victorian empire-builders, giving his name to Rhodesia. The house has a series of rooms illustrating Rhodes's story from his birth until his death in 1902, when he was buried in the Matopo Hills near Bulawayo. Personal relics include a cigarette case, a snuff-box and the uniform he wore as Honorary Colonel of the Diamond Field Horse. He is commemorated by a tablet in St Michael's Church.

Follow the A1184 into Bishop's Stortford, swinging left over the railway bridge and then keeping forward on to the B1383 (SP Newport) at the traffic lights. At the roundabout on the far side of the town take the second exit (SP Newport).

BISHOP'S STORTFORD TO SAFFRON WALDEN

The road from Bishop's Stortford to Stansted Mountfitchet is overlooked by the brick tower and huge sails of a windmill* built in 1787. It was rescued from dereliction in the early 1960s and is now cared for by volunteers known as 'The Stansted Millers'. Its machinery and furnishings are still intact. Keep forward through Stansted, passing an ornate cast-iron drinking fountain and several picturesque thatched cottages. The route soon passes a sign for Ugley – the butt of many jokes about the Ugley Women's Institute – and crosses the M11 beyond Quendon.

Although it is right on London's doorstep, the former royal hunting-ground of Epping Forest is one of the most unspoilt tracts of woodland in eastern England

The road continues northwards to Newport, an enchanting village with many beautiful buildings. Bow windows, weatherboarding and projecting upper storeys abound, and there are some good examples of pargeting – ornamental plasterwork on the outsides of buildings, an East Anglian speciality. The most eye-catching building the right of the road, is a timber-framed ho known as Monk's Barn. It dates from the 1 century and has an oriel window abov wooden panel carved with figures depict the Virgin Mary and angels.

Just over a mile beyond Newport turn ri on to the B1052 for Saffron Walden, one of most attractive old towns in eastern Engla It takes its name from the autumn-flower saffron crocus that was cultivated here o commercial scale from the Middle Ages u the 18th century. It was used to make dye a perfume, condiments and medicines. 1 splendid church, rebuilt between 1470 a 1540, looks down on the remains of a Norn castle, while many of the town's fir buildings flank Church Street. To the wes the town stands Audley End House,* Jacobean masterpiece built at the start of 17th century and substantially altered by John Vanbrugh a century later. The orn interior contains many excellent paintin and a miniature railway runs through extensive grounds.

SAFFRON WALDEN TO ST IVES

Signs for Cambridge take the route ou Saffron Walden along the B184, which clir very gently and skirts the village of Gi Chesterford. At Stump Cross roundab the route joins the A1301 (SP Cambrid and continues north-westwards, runn parallel to the course of the River Cam. A 2¼ miles, at the next roundabout, the ro keeps straight ahead for Great Shelford a Cambridge.

Decorative plasterwork, or pargeting, is typical of East Anglia. This example is in Church Street, Saffron Walden

King's College, Cambridge. Pinnacles and a cupola crown the gatehouse, built 400 years after the college was founded

DUXFORD AIRFIELD

At this roundabout you can make a detour to the left, along the A505 (SP Royston), to Duxford Airfield,* 2 miles away. The former Battle of Britain base now houses most of the Imperial War Museum's collection of aircraft, tanks and other large exhibits, together with the Duxford Aviation Society's civil aircraft. Second World War aircraft include a P51 Mustang and a B17 Flying Fortress, while among the more recent models are a Hawker Hunter and Britain's prototype Concorde. Elsewhere, visitors can see miniature submarines and a Russian T34 tank.

Approaching Cambridge the main route passes through Stapleford, Great Shelford and Trumpington, where the church on the Grantchester road has a brass commemorating Sir Roger de Trumpington. It dates from 1289 and is said to be the second oldest memorial of its type in England.

The centre of Cambridge can be avoided by following signs for Bedford, then Huntingdon, to leave by the A1307.

CAMBRIDGE

For a detour into Cambridge itself, follow signs for the city centre. Long ranked among the most beautiful and interesting cities in Europe, Cambridge's roots go back to Roman times, more than 1000 years before the university tradition was started with the foundation of Peterhouse College in 1284. There are now 30 colleges,* almost half of them founded at least 500 years ago. St John's, Trinity, King's and others dominate the ancient heart of Cambridge with their magnificent architecture. Built around large courtyards, they have grounds that run down to a lovely stretch of the Cam, known as the Backs, where punts glide on summer days.

The city has no fewer than ten museums, plus many other places of interest, but if you want to stop for just an hour or so, concentrate on King's College and its near neighbour, Trinity College. King's, founded by Henry VI in 1441, stands beside a magnificent chapel built during the next 70 years. It has all the lofty grandeur of a small cathedral and houses Rubens' great painting *The Adoration of the Magi*. Trinity College, founded by Henry VIII, has a chapel whose memorials to past students include one commemorating Sir Isaac Newton. He gained a BA in 1665 and became a Fellow of Trinity two years later.

Leave the city on the A1307 (SP Huntingdon) which follows the arrow-straight line of a Roman road. On the outskirts of Cambridge it passes Girton College, built in 1873 for the university's female students. Beyond the college the road becomes the A604. After skirting Fenstanton, follow signs for St Ives at the A1096 junction. In 1½ miles, at a new roundabout, the A1096 keeps forward to join the new St Ives by-pass, soon crossing the Great Ouse.

ST IVES TO PETERBOROUGH

ST IVES

In ½ mile, at the next roundabout, a detour can be made into St Ives itself by taking the first exit. This is the St Ives of nursery-rhyme fame – recalling the days when people travelled for many miles to the important annual fair, held here from 1110. The history of the town and the Fens is told in the Norris Museum* in the Broadway. St Ives has interesting buildings of many periods, and the Great Ouse here is spanned by a 15th-century bridge which has one of only four medieval bridge chapels in England. Oliver Cromwell lived in the town from 1631 until 1636, and his statue stands in Market Hill.

The main route continues on the St Ives bypass, turning left at a roundabout on to the A1123 (SP Huntingdon). After 2 miles turn right on to the B1090 (SP Abbots Ripton). The road soon passes RAF Wyton, where a twin-engined Canberra bomber stands near the main gates.

On reaching the A141, turn right then left to continue on the B1090 to Abbots Ripton, a lovely little village where dormer windows peep out beneath roofs of thatch. Follow the B1090 as it crosses the railway line and immediately swings right (SP The North). The road runs along rising ground at the edge of the Fens. The combination of fen and woodland shelters many rare kinds of wildlife, which are preserved and studied at several nature reserves in the area.

The route climbs gently to Walton Hill – less than 150 feet above sea level, but high ground by local standards and a good viewpoint. Follow the B1090 down to its junction with the A1, where you should turn right on to the dual carriageway.

A typical East Anglian landscape of wide skies, cornfields and poppy-studded verges on the road to St Ives

STILTON

In 5 miles a short detour can be made turning left to the village of Stilton – n exactly the home of the famous cheese, for was always made in Leicestershire, but this certainly the place responsible for its fam There is a 'Stilton Cheese' hotel in the villa but it is a newcomer. The place that w astute enough to buy up vast supplies of t cheese to serve to its customers as a speciali was the Old Bell Inn, a fine 17th-centu stone building. In the days when the Gre North Road went straight through the villa centre, the Old Bell was a busy staging po for coaches travelling up and down t country, so the fame of 'Stilton' cheese spre far and wide, and attracted the attention diary-keeping travellers like Daniel Defoe.

Past Stilton, the A1 reaches a rounda where the route takes the third exit Yaxley) for the 6-mile run along the A15 Peterborough, passing numerous brickw – a thriving industry in this part of the w

The 16th-century customs house, to by a lantern to guide shipping, overl the River Nene as the route enters the of Peterborough, a place of importa

This imposing classical gatehouse is all that remains of Folkingham's early 19th-century prison, known as the House of Correction. It was built within the earthworks of a castle which previously stood on the site

since before Roman times. Its greatest glory is the cathedral, begun in 1118 after a fire destroyed the Saxon church. It has a west front of quite exceptional grandeur. Inside, large mirrors mounted on wheels enable the superbly painted 13th-century ceilings to be clearly seen. A plain grey stone in the north aisle marks the burial place of Catherine of Aragon, the first of Henry VIII's six wives, who died in 1536 at Kimbolton Castle. Mary, Queen of Scots, was also buried in the cathedral after her execution at nearby Fotheringhay, but her remains were moved to Westminster Abbey in 1612. Cathedral Square is overlooked by the guildhall, built in 1671 to commemorate the Restoration. It is embellished by the coats of arms of several local dignitaries of the period.

PETERBOROUGH TO LINCOLN
Leave Peterborough on the A15 (SP Sleaford) and follow it across farmland as flat as a billiard-table. The route crosses the River Welland to enter Lincolnshire, keeping forward with the A15 at the roundabout and passing through Market Deeping. The south side of the church tower here has a sundial bearing the words 'The Day is Thine'. On the north side, away from the sun, another dial reads 'The Night Cometh'. Behind the church is the oldest inhabited rectory in England, dating from the 13th century.

The road runs northwards through Bourne, known to generations of motor-sport enthusiasts as the home of the ERA and BRM racing cars. The little market town is reputed to have been the birthplace of Hereward the

Wake. North of Bourne, the A15 begins to climb very gently, giving extensive views eastwards over the fenlands towards Boston, Spalding and the Wash. Folkingham, where the A15 swings hard right, is a very attractive village with a broad, grass-flanked main street and buildings roofed with red pantiles. The sternly classical gatehouse of the House of Correction, built in 1825, is an eye-catching feature. Continue through Osbournby to Silk Willoughby, passing the handsome 17th-century manor house. The village is dominated by the fine steeple of its 14th-century church. Inside is a wonderfully well preserved Norman font, and the church is a treasure-trove of the woodcarver's art. The screen is richly carved with animals, and there is an immense wooden eagle lectern with decorative carving on the base to match that of the Jacobean pulpit. On the wall hangs an unusual 17th-century Italian painting worked on a base of agate.

As you enter Sleaford, turn right and then left (SP Lincoln) over a level crossing, then in the main street turn right on to the A153 (SP Horncastle). This runs past Sleaford's 12th-century church, noted for its ancient stone spire and the beautiful tracery of its windows. Nearby stands Carre's Hospital, a group of attractive stone almshouses founded by a local knight in 1636. Three miles beyond Sleaford, the route leaves the A153, keeping straight ahead on to the B1188 (SP Lincoln). Curving gradually towards the north-west, the road runs through a number of sleepy old villages before Lincoln's magnificent cathedral appears in the distance.

LINCOLN TO GAINSBOROUGH

The B1188 ends at a roundabout outside Lincoln; follow signs here for the city centre.

Lindum Colonia, as the Romans called it, grew wealthy on the medieval wool trade and, in a later century, on the proceeds of the Industrial Revolution, leaving a legacy of many beautiful buildings of differing periods. Lincoln's magic is best appreciated by walking up to the cathedral from the High Street. The street crosses the River Witham by High Bridge, which still has a row of 16th-century buildings on the downstream side, and passes under a handsome Tudor arch known as the Stonebow. The city council still meets in the guildhall above the arch. Timber-framed buildings add a dash of 'magpie' charm before the walk enters The Strait, where the stone Jew's House dates from the 12th century. Aaron the Jew's House, higher up Steep Hill, dates from the same period and is believed to be the oldest building in England still used as a dwelling. The 14th-century Exchequer Gate, at the entrance to the cathedral close, looks westward past a beautiful Tudor building to the castle.* Much of the castle's original Norman work survives, though the low tower called Cobb Hall dates from the 14th century. It was built as a place of punishment, and public executions took place on its roof until little more than a century ago. The great walls of the castle protect two Norman towers built upon artificial mounds or mottes. Lincoln Castle was deeply involved with King John's quarrel with the barons, and this accounts for one of

Remarkably well preserved Norman carvings embellish the west front of Lincoln Cathedral. Above the doorway are seated figures of the Apostles

Old buildings of stone, red brick and half-timbering line aptly named Steep Hill in Lincoln. The street stands in the part of the city known as 'above hill'

the cathedral's treasured exhibits: the fi existing copy of Magna Carta. The cathe itself dates from the same period, though magnificent west front and twin west to are survivals of an even earlier cathedral of which was destroyed by an earthquak 1185. The cathedral contains much beau medieval glass, particularly in the tran windows, which are known as the 'De Eye' and the 'Bishop's Eye'. (For Lincol also p. 120.)

The A57 (SP Worksop) takes the route of Lincoln past the city's race-course. It runs alongside the Fossdyke Navigatio canal dug by the Romans more than years ago to link the Witham to the T Follow the road through Saxilby and 2 r later keep straight ahead on to the A156 Gainsborough). This road heads northw to Torksey, where the scanty remains castle overlook the broad, meandering wa of the Trent. The river provides water fo power stations whose clustered cooling to rise far above the flat landscape.

Rich farmland flanks the road as it tinues northwards along the Trent valle Gainsborough, where the route turns le to the A631 (SP Bawtry).

GAINSBOROUGH

A brief detour can be made into the to centre to visit the Old Hall,* a delight blend of 15th-century stonework, mell brick and timber-framing. The timber great hall is particularly fine, and the buildi incorporates a medieval kitchen. Henry VI is said to have met his last wife, Katheri Parr, at the Hall in 1540. It was later used a meeting place by the religious dissenters w became known as the Pilgrim Fathers.

GAINSBOROUGH TO GOOLE

Follow the A631 out of Gainsborough over the Trent, then take the A161 Goole) at the second roundabout on the of Beckingham. Three waterways are cr in the next few miles: the Chesterfield C the River Idle and the oddly named War Drain. This area, known as the Isl Axholme, is a little higher than the surro ing countryside and was indeed an isl surrounded by marshes, until complex tems of canals and ditches drained the F

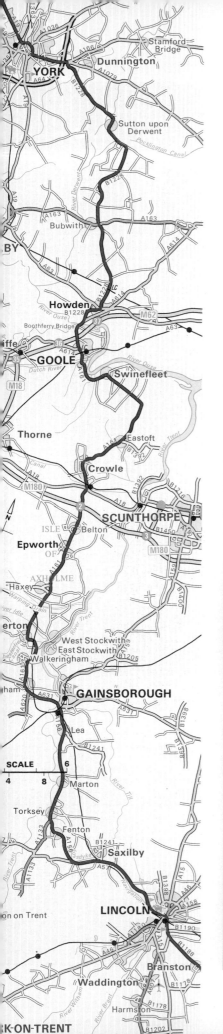

Passing through Misterton and Haxey, the route runs on to Epworth, the birthplace of John and Charles Wesley (1703–91 and 1707–88). Their father took over the living in 1696, but his political views became so controversial that a mob set fire to the rectory 13 years later. John was rescued just before the roof caved in. He went on to become the founder of Methodism, preaching from his father's tomb in St Andrew's churchyard and from the ancient market cross in the town centre. His younger brother became a prolific writer of hymns, contributing much to the Methodist cause. The Old Rectory* at Epworth still stands, off the main road to the right. It was rebuilt a year after the fire, then restored in 1957, and is now a Wesley museum. The family lived here until 1735.

The A161 continues northwards from Epworth through Belton. Follow signs for Goole to cross the M180 and several waterways before turning right then left at the A18 junction to pass through Crowle. Scunthorpe and the long, low line of the Lincolnshire Wolds can be seen on the right, but the road zig-zags across a landscape that is astonishingly flat, never rising more than a dozen feet above sea level. Deep ditches flank the road as it heads towards Swinefleet, where it follows a huge meander of the tidal River Ouse to reach Goole. Although they are 50 miles from the open sea, Goole's busy docks are used by substantial ships which can be seen from the road as it runs into the town. Coal and textiles from the industrial towns of Yorkshire were responsible for the growth of Goole's docks following the completion of the Aire and Calder Navigation in 1826.

GOOLE TO YORK

Bear left into the town centre and at the end of the main street, just beyond the grammar school, turn right on to the A614 (SP Hull). The route crosses Boothferry Bridge – a notorious bottleneck before the M62 was built – and almost immediately turns left on to the B1228 (SP York). Just over one mile later, at a crossroads, turn right (SP Howden) and keep forward on to the A63 past Howden's splendid church, most of which dates from the 14th century. Only the nave, transepts and tower are still in use, but the ruins of the lovely octagonal chapter house and the chancel can still be seen.

In $\frac{1}{4}$ mile turn left on to the B1228 (SP Bubwith) and follow the road across the plain, with the Yorkshire Wolds rising gently in the east. Keep straight on 6 miles later to cross the A163, and at the T-junction 7 miles further on, turn left (SP York). The road soon crosses the Pocklington Canal – dug to link Pocklington with the River Derwent – and passes through Sutton upon Derwent and Elvington. Four miles beyond Elvington, turn left on to the A1079 and take the second exit at the roundabout to enter York.

Commemorative plates from Methodist chapels throughout the United States and Canada are displayed on a 17th-century dresser in the Old Rectory at Epworth, the former home of John and Charles Wesley

YORK TO THIRSK

York is one of Britain's most priceless jewels. Doing full justice to its astonishing wealth of historic treasures can keep even the most energetic and enthusiastic visitor busy for two or three days. The York Heritage Centre,* housed in a former church in Castlegate, is the perfect starting point for anyone setting out to explore the city. Audio-visual and other imaginative displays relate York's story since pre-Roman times.

The city itself is packed with vivid reminders of every stage in its development. The remarkable Multangular Tower, west of Museum Street, still has Roman masonry 19 feet high. Remains of the Viking city, known as *Jorvik*, were uncovered in Coppergate in 1973. Clifford's Tower and the Twelfth-century House, off Stonegate, are links with the Normans, and the heart of the city, which covers 260 acres, is almost completely surrounded by 13th-century walls. Other features bring the story up to the 19th century, when George Hudson – 'The Railway King' – helped to make the city one of the most important rail centres in Britain. Appropriately, York is now the home of the superb National Railway Museum.* Among its exhibits is *Mallard*, the streamlined locomotive that reached a record-breaking 126 mph in 1938.

Some of the city's old streets are closed to traffic and have retained much of their bustling, medieval atmosphere. Stonegate and The Shambles, where upper storeys lean within a handshake of each other, are perhaps the finest examples, and in the Castle Museum,* housed in what was originally an 18th-century prison, are three full-sized reconstructions of cobbled streets along which visitors can stroll between quaint old buildings. Also to be seen here is the cell where the highwayman John Palmer, better known as Dick Turpin, spent his last night before being hanged in 1739. His grave can be seen in St George's churchyard, not far from the museum. Contrary to popular legend, Turpin never did create his famous alibi by speeding to York on Black Bess. The ride was actually accomplished 60 years earlier by another highwayman, William Nevison, who died on the gallows in York 55 years before Turpin's execution.

The Minster that so magnificently dominates the city is one of the finest buildings in Europe and is the largest Gothic church in England. Built on the site of a Saxon church, it dates from the start of the 13th century and took 250 years to complete. Memorable features include what is believed to be the oldest stained glass in England – it dates from about 1150 – and a stone choir screen with statues of all the rulers of England from William the Conqueror to Henry VI. In

The most famous of York's old streets, The Shambles, still preserves much of its medieval character

A white horse cut into the Hambleton Hills is a striking landmark near Thirsk

1967, craftsmen strengthening the base of the 20,000-ton central tower unearthed many substantial traces of the Roman and Saxon past. Their finds prompted the establishment of the fascinating Undercroft Museum, housed in the Minster.

The A19 (SP Thirsk) takes the route out of York past Bootham Bar, one of the series of fortified gateways in the medieval walls. Leaving the city, this road follows the Ouse valley for a short distance, then skirts Skelton before reaching Shipton.

BENINGBROUGH HALL

From Shipton a detour may be made left to Beningbrough Hall,* a classically handsome mansion completed in 1716 and owned by the National Trust since 1959. The Hall contains many beautiful examples of the woodcarver's art, including elaborate chimneypieces and a wonderfully delicate oak staircase. The principal rooms house a collection of 100 portraits from the National Portrait Gallery.

Continue from Shipton up the A19 to Easingwold. The broad Vale of York contrasts with the steep-flanked North York Moors ahead, and the Pennines can be seen away to the left. Follow the A19 (SP Thirsk) through Easingwold, with the white horse high up on the escarpment a major landmark ahead. Carved into the slope by a local schoolmaster and his pupils in 1857, the horse is 228 feet high, 314 feet long and, on a clear day, is visible from Leeds, 40 miles away.

Gliders can often be seen soaring over the grassy airfield on the plateau immediately above the horse.

Follow the A19 and then the A170 into Thirsk, an old town whose cobbled market square, to the left, is overlooked by such inns as the Three Tuns and the Fleece, which date from the colourful heyday of the stage-coach.

THIRSK TO DARLINGTON

Leave the town on the A168 (SP Northallerton). Like Thirsk, Northallerton recalls the stage-coach era. It also has memories of Robert the Bruce, the Scottish warrior-king, who razed the town to the ground in 1318. As the A167 (SP Darlington) takes the route out of the town, the line of the North York Moors can be seen gradually falling away to the right.

At Croft-on-Tees the road swings right and left, crossing the Tees and one of its tributaries, the River Skerne. Charles Lutwidge Dodgson (1832–98), better known as Lewis Carroll, the author of *Alice in Wonderland*, lived in Croft rectory as a child. His father was vicar here for 25 years. Continue up the A167, joining the A66 for Darlington, where the route takes the ring road (SP Durham). After looping to the east of the town centre the road continues northwards.

NORTH ROAD STATION RAILWAY MUSEUM

Immediately before going under a railway bridge, the route passes the end of McNay Street on the left. The street leads to the historic North Road Station,* built by the Stockton and Darlington Railway Company and opened in 1842. It is now a museum whose most treasured exhibit is Locomotion Number One, the engine that inaugurated the world's first passenger line in 1825 and made the name of its designer, George Stephenson, a household word.

DARLINGTON TO DURHAM

Continuing northwards from Darlington up the A167, cross the A1(M) and pass Newton Aycliffe and Ferryhill, then cross the Rivers Wear and Browney beyond Sunderland Bridge. The centre of Durham can be by-passed by keeping forward on the A167 at the roundabout 1 mile later, continuing for 2¾ miles to another roundabout where you take the first exit, the A691 (SP Consett).

DURHAM

A detour can be made into the city centre by taking the A1050 for Durham at the first roundabout. The road into the city runs close to the Gulbenkian Museum* – part of Durham University's School of Oriental Studies – which houses Britain's finest collection of oriental art and archaeological relics.

Durham is an ancient city of great charm and character, watched over by the massive towers of a cathedral that many consider to be the most outstanding example of Norman architecture in the world. It stands in the heart of the city on a steep hill almost islanded by the Wear and now virtually traffic-free. The great cathedral was started by Bishop William of Calais in 1093, but its central tower was added in the 15th century after the original had been struck by lightning. The main door has a 'sanctuary knocker', a reminder of medieval times when fugitives could obtain temporary freedom from arrest in the cathedral precincts.

Many of the buildings near the cathedral now form part of Durham University, founded in 1832 and the oldest in England after Oxford and Cambridge. They include the Norman castle,* which was the palace of the 'prince-bishops' until the 19th century. The A691 (SP Consett) leads out of the city, passing the Durham Light Infantry Museum,* whose exhibits trace the regiment's history back to 1758.

DURHAM TO HEXHAM

Leaving Durham's outskirts behind, the A691 runs north-westwards, up a wood-dappled valley framed by hills that rise to almost 1000 feet, and passes through Lanchester, where a Roman altar stone stands in the porch of the Norman church.

At the traffic lights in Leadgate turn left on to the A692 (SP Consett). The route swings right and crosses the railway bridge, then immediately turns right on to the A691 (SP Shotley Bridge). This road passes through Blackhill, reaching almost 900 feet before plunging down into the deep valley of the Derwent. At Shotley Bridge, turn left on to the B6278 (SP Stanhope) and in 2 miles turn right on to the A68 (SP Corbridge). Down to the west of the A68 is the Derwent Reservoir. Held back by a long, grass-covered dam, this man-made lake was formed in the late 1960s and covers 1000 acres. The reservoir is popular with anglers and sailing enthusiasts, and there is a country park and a nature reserve on its shores.

The A68 switchbacks through woodlands before dropping into the Tyne valley near Riding Mill. At the new roundabout just beyond a railway bridge take the first exit, the A695 (SP Riding Mill).

A 13th-century carving in the chancel of Durham Cathedral

The Roman arch in Corbridge church

After 3 miles a detour can be made Corbridge by turning right on to the B65 Cross the Tyne and enter the town, wh recorded history begins with the Roman f of Corstopitum. Corbridge later surviv Viking raids and became a place of so importance in the Middle Ages. It is stil delightful place, clustered round St Andre Church, the oldest parts of which are Saxe Its most remarkable feature, far older th the building in which it stands, is a Rom gateway from Corstopitum that must ha been dismantled and moved to the villa when the church was built in the 8th centu Equally unusual is Vicar's Pele, a squa tower in the south-east corner of the chur yard. It was built early in the 14th century a fortified residence for the parish priest a was used as such for about 300 years. Chu and tower overlook the market place, wh the dukes of Northumberland are co memorated by a cross and a fountain.

Signs for the Corstopitum Roman Stat on the edge of Corbridge take the dete westwards along an unclassified road wh leads up the beautiful Tyne vall Corstopitum stands at the point where D Street, the main Roman highway into So land, was crossed by another ancient ro known as Stanegate. The base was establis towards the end of the 1st century AD, an large area has been excavated. Finds ma during the excavations are on display in site's museum.* Hexham can be reach from Corstopitum by continuing along same unclassified road up the Tyne valley the T-junction either turn left to see Hexh or turn right to rejoin the main route.

A typical North Country scene near the village of West Woodburn, set in the valley of the River Rede. In the background are the conifer plantations on Chesterhope Common

The main route continues on the A695 to Hexham. Set on a hill laced with narrow streets, Hexham is watched over by an abbey church every inch as impressive as many cathedrals. It was founded in AD 674 by St Wilfrid, Bishop of Hexham. This early church was built with stone brought from Corstopitum. The crypt survives, and is probably England's finest example of a Saxon crypt. The rest of the church was rebuilt later, after being devastated by Danish raiders and marauding Scots. Inside is the headless cross from the grave of an 8th-century bishop. It stands near the long flight of stone steps that leads to what was originally the monks' dormitory. Many other notable features include a 7th-century Saxon chalice and a huge Roman gravestone, almost 2000 years old, on which the carved figure of a standard-bearer rides triumphantly over a cowering enemy. Another ancient treasure is the Frith Stool, a stone chair dating from Saxon times. It is thought to have been used at the coronations of Northumbrian kings.

On the far side of the main square, beyond a small, covered market, stands the moot hall which, from 1112 to 1545, was the residence of the archbishops of York when they visited the town as 'Lords of the Liberty and Regality of Hexham'. Behind it stands the Manor Office, dating from 1330 and said to be the first building in England specifically constructed as a prison. It was used as such for almost 500 years.

HEXHAM TO ROCHESTER

From Hexham follow signs northwards on the A6079 for Otterburn and the A68, crossing the Tyne then turning left (SP Carlisle) on to the A69 at the roundabout. In ¾ mile the route turns right on to the A6079 (SP Otterburn, Rothbury) and follows the Tyne valley through Wall, the last settlement to the south of the great defensive system built by the Emperor Hadrian in the 2nd century AD.

CHESTERS ROMAN FORT

At the crossroads beyond Wall a brief detour to the left leads along the B6318 to the Roman fort at Chesters,* one of the finest sites on Hadrian's Wall, and the best surviving example of a Roman cavalry fort. The areas that have been excavated include barracks and stables, the headquarters building and the commandant's house. The fort, rectangular with rounded corners, was protected by stone walls five feet thick which rose above a ditch and were pierced by six gateways. The remains of an elaborate bath house can be seen between the fort and the North Tyne's western bank, where substantial traces of a Roman bridge have survived.

Part of the bath house at Chesters

Five miles beyond Wall the route turns left on to the A68 (SP Jedburgh) and, following the line of Roman Dere Street, climbs into the wild border hills. Long switchback straights with numerous blind summits take the road up to almost 1000 feet before it drops to West Woodburn and then runs along the boundary of the Northumberland National Park.

After crossing the River Rede the route turns left at the point where it is joined by the A696, and continues through Rochester and past Redesdale Army Camp. (Route continues on p. 30.)

THE CHEVIOTS

As well as being one of the finest examples of military engineering in Europe, Hadrian's Wall marches across some of the most spectacular landscapes in northern England

RISING to 2674 feet at the summit from which they take their name, the Cheviot Hills form an impressive and evocative natural barrier between England and Scotland. The border zig-zags over such peaks as Peel Fell, Leap Hill, Greyhound Law and the Cheviot itself, and there are superb views from the point where it is crossed by the A68 at Carter Bar, almost 1400 feet above sea level. Much of the range on the English side of the border is in the Northumberland National Park; officially designated as such in 1956, the park covers 398 square miles.

This magnificently wild and windswept tract of high ground sprawls south-westwards from the A697 as it runs to and through Wooler, an excellent base from which to explore the range. Rothbury, another good centre, stands on the River Coquet which rises right on the border between Carter Bar and the Cheviot. Although flanked on one side by a military training area, the narrow road along upper Coquet Dale passes through some of the finest Cheviot scenery. The headwaters of the Coquet are overlooked by Roman camps built to guard Dere Street. Roman, prehistoric and medieval remains – forts, cairns, ancient trackways, standing stones and 'pele' towers – are dotted all over the hills.

Like much of the Pennines, which roll southwards beyond the Tyne valley, the Cheviots are rounded hills. They were created millions of years ago when volcanic action forced granite and lava up through the earth's crust. The relentless Ice Age glaciers created the smooth contours of today. Forests now swathe large areas, leaving the rest as open moorland where hardy, short-legged Cheviot sheep graze and defy the elements.

Isolated farm-buildings like these near Westnewton shelter from the worst of the elements in the Cheviots' gentle folds

HADRIAN'S WALL guards the southern approaches to the border's high, rolling hills just as the Cheviots form a natural bulwark between England and Scotland. Even today, crossing the wall can make travellers appreciate that they are entering a unique part of Britain.

The wall is a remarkably eloquent tribute to the Romans' genius and ranks high among the world's most outstanding military monuments. The need to delineate the empire's northern boundary was appreciated towards the end of the 1st century AD, when the legions withdrew from Scotland. It was the Emperor Trajan who established the 'Stanegate' system of military posts between Carlisle and Corbridge – but Hadrian thought a physical barrier was needed to deter the northern barbarians.

Work started in AD 122 and the wall eventually extended for 73 miles, from Wallsend-on-Tyne to Bowness-on-Solway. There were 17 forts, about five miles apart, each of which housed either 500 foot-soldiers or 1000 cavalry, and additional troops were stationed in smaller forts, set at intervals of one Roman mile. Look-out towers were also built between each 'milecastle'. At least 13,000 men were deployed along the wall, but it was abandoned when the Roman forces were transferred to Europe to defend the heart of the Empire at the end of the 4th century.

Below: The fort at Housesteads is on best preserved along the wall. Its stone were originally over 12 feet high and e barracks, workshops and a hospital

F ORESTS are relatively recent additions to the Cheviot landscape. Seven of them combine to form the 145,000-acre Border Forest Park which reaches 1975 feet on Peel Fell. Waymarked walks, picnic places, visitor centres, day-permit trout fishing and campsites enable the park to be enjoyed to the full. There is also a memorable forest drive, 12 miles long, between Kielder and the A68 near Byrness.

Work on what is now the largest man-made forest in Britain was started by the Forestry Commission in 1926. Half the trees are sitka spruce, which reach heights of about 75 feet before being felled. Norway spruce, Scots pine and Japanese larch are prominent among other species. The forests produce more than 100,000 tons of timber a year, mainly for the building and paper-making industries.

Sheep are by no means the only animals living on the hills. Shaggy-coated wild goats with spectacularly long, curved horns roam the moorland, where fortunate visitors may also see such rare birds of prey as the hen harrier and osprey. The Forestry Commission woodlands have attracted many new species to the area since the First World War. More than 2000 roe deer live in and near the conifer forests, the planting of which has resulted in a dramatic increase in the numbers of short-eared owls. Red squirrels can still be found in the old woodlands, and otters inhabit many of the region's riverbanks.

OODYBUSH EDGE, Foulplay
ve, Bloody Moss and other grim
-names are reminders that the
ot Hills have a turbulent
y. Until the 17th century they
plagued by raiding bands of
rs' or 'moss-troopers' from both
of the border.

jor battles were also fought,
as the one at Otterburn in 1388.
ttish army under the Earl of
las was marching home after
g as far south as Durham. They
ed near Otterburn, but were
ked at sunset by a much larger
led by Sir Henry 'Hotspur'
. Douglas organized a daring
er-attack, but was killed before
emies were defeated. Hotspur
his revenge in 1402 when many
were slaughtered at Homildon
north-west of Wooler.
e bloodiest encounter in the
ot area was the Battle of
en, fought near Branxton in
where the Scots under James
avily outnumbered the English.
King was among the 15,000 who
however, and Flodden is still
ed as the worst defeat in
sh history.

Left: a highly romanticized engraving of the Battle of Otterburn
Below: the cross which marks the site of the Battle of Flodden Field

ROCHESTER TO JEDBURGH

The route continues into the heart of the Cheviot Hills and soon enters the Border Forest Park, whose millions of trees produce more than 100,000 tons of timber each year. Picnic areas, nature trails and a forest drive flank the road as it runs towards the Catcleugh Reservoir, well over a mile long. Beyond it, the road sweeps up to the Scottish border at Carter Bar, almost 1400 feet above sea level. Snow fences do their best to protect the road from winter blizzards, but patches of snow often linger late into the year on the northern side of the pass. From the crest there are magnificent views over southern Scotland, and the triple-peaked Eildon Hills above Melrose are notable landmarks.

Beyond Carter Bar the A68 descends into Scotland in a series of sharp bends, then sweeps down into the valley of the Jed Water, which runs past wooded sandstone cliffs as it nears Jedburgh, one of the several small, neat border towns whose names appear frequently in the pages of Scottish history. Its spectacular ruined abbey,* founded by King David I of Scotland in 1118, looks down on to the road. In its heyday the abbey witnessed the coronation of Malcolm IV in the 12th century and the marriage of Alexander III in 1285. The great building was badly damaged during an Anglo-Scottish battle in the 16th century. A 19th-century jail, now used as a museum,* stands on the site of Jedburgh Castle. The house* where Mary, Queen of Scots, stayed in 1556 can also be visited.

JEDBURGH TO MELROSE

Follow the A68 (SP Edinburgh) out of Jedburgh. Views to the right of the road are soon dominated by the 150-foot-high Waterloo Monument, built by the Marquess of Lothian to commemorate Napoleon's defeat in 1815. Shaped like a gigantic pencil, the monument stands on the 744-foot-high summit of Peniel Heugh.

The A68 soon turns right to cross the River Teviot then continues through hilly country before descending into the Tweed valley at St Boswells. A village green complete with cricket pitch gives St Boswells a surprisingly English air. To the north of the village, set in a great loop of the River Tweed, are the lovely ruins of Dryburgh Abbey,* whose church is the burial place of Sir Walter Scott. At the end of the next village, Newtown St Boswells, turn left on to the A6091 (SP Galashiels). The road skirts the steep northern flanks of the Eildon Hills and then enters Melrose, an attractive little town on the south bank of the Tweed. Its abbey,* like its counterpart in Jedburgh, was founded by David I and suffered considerably during the long series of wars between Scotland and England. The abbey was rebuilt in 1385 but destroyed again in the 1540s and has remained a memorable ruin. The Eildon Hills provide a perfect backcloth for its beautiful arcades, flying buttresses and window tracery, all carved from rich, red sandstone. Among the gargoyles on the roof is one depicting a pig playing the bagpipes.

MELROSE TO EDINBURGH

Leave Melrose on the A6091 (SP Galashi and, continuing westwards along the Tw valley, keep forward at the second of roundabouts outside the town.

ABBOTSFORD HOUSE

For a short detour to Sir Walter Scott's home take the first exit, the B6360 (SP Abbotsford at this roundabout. This part of the Bord country inspired many of Scott's historic novels, which epitomize the romance an drama of Scotland's turbulent history. H began building Abbotsford House,* his la home, in 1820, replacing the modest far where he had lived for the previous nine year It developed into a very impressive residenc complete with 'baronial' turrets, towers an battlements. The house has remained virt ally unchanged since Scott died here in 183 and contains his library of 20,000 books well as weapons used in the border wars.

The main route follows the A6091 over River Tweed and at the roundabout t right on to the A7 to enter Galashiels, a b little town set in the steep-sided valley of Gala Water, and noted for its tweed woollen industry. The route through town centre passes a striking war memc that features a 'border reiver' on horseba Follow the A7 (SP Edinburgh) round to right on the far side of the town centre, cr ing the Gala Water and then swinging lef the last part of the journey.

High, steep hills and patches of woodl flank the road as it follows the Gala W towards its source and reaches almost 900 at Middleton Moor, on the northern edg the Moorfoot Hills; Arthur's Seat, the lated hill that is one of Edinburgh's grea landmarks, can soon be seen in the distanc the route skirts Gorebridge, Newtongra and Dalkeith. The A7 is clearly signposted the way into the capital.

Although it is now a roofless ruin, the magnificent Nor abbey at Jedburgh is still one of the finest buildings in Border country

EDINBURGH

Watched over by its crag-perched castle, Edinburgh is really two cities in one. The original city developed along the line of the 'Royal Mile' that runs eastwards from the castle to the Palace of Holyrood-house,* passing such buildings as St Giles' Cathedral and the home of John Knox,* the great 16th-century religious reformer. Commendably careful planning preceded the city's expansion northwards towards the end of the 18th century. The result, a Scottish answer to the classical elegance of Bath, is epitomized by Charlotte Square, planned by Robert Adam in 1791. It stands close to the western end of Princes Street, which runs eastwards towards Calton Hill, passing the ornate memorial to Sir Walter Scott. The famous shopping street is overlooked by Edinburgh Castle.* There has been a castle here for over 1000 years, but the earliest part of the present building dates from the 12th century.

Edinburgh Castle looks over some of the most elegant streets in Britain

Edinburgh

ROUTE 3   174 MILE

London to Buxton

CHILTERN beechwoods, limestone hills, Midland plains and windswept moorlands are the outstanding landscapes on this route from one of the world's largest and most cosmopolitan capitals to a small town that is the unofficial capital of Derbyshire's Peak District.

Market gardens and open countryside begin remarkably close to central London, and by the time it has reached Chalfont St Giles the route is running through scenery that is truly rural in character. When John Milton came to the village in 1665 to escape the plague that was raging through London it must have seemed an isolated, remote place. It was here, in a cottage that is now a museum to his memory, that the poet completed *Paradise Lost* and began work on *Paradise Regained*.

Following the little River Misbourne, the route continues to Amersham, a cluster of houses and venerable old cottages set in the beech-hung landscapes of the Chiltern Hills. Rolling Chiltern scenery continues to Wendover, which also boasts a wealth of lovely domestic architecture as well as a number of quaint old coaching inns. Beyond Aylesbury the Chilterns give way quite suddenly to gently undulating countryside and unassuming Buckinghamshire farmland. Whitchurch and Winslow, set in the wide vale between Aylesbury and Buckingham, both have fine examples of timber-framed and brick-built houses.

The River Great Ouse, which flows through the unspoilt heart of Buckingham, marks the county boundary with Northamptonshire as the route nears the hillside town of Brackley. Banbury, a few miles further on, lies in Oxfordshire and, like Brackley, is a mixture of quaint, narrow streets and elegant thoroughfares with classical buildings of golden stone.

Distant views over the Avon valley open up at Warmington, a beautiful Warwickshire village with many stone-built houses, overlooked from the west by Edge Hill. At the foot of the scarp, which overlooks Shakespeare country some miles to the north-west, is the site of the Battle of Edgehill. This was the first major battle of the Civil War. The King's initial position, on the wooded ridge of Edge Hill itself, was a strong one, but he made the mistake of moving his troops down to fight the Roundheads on the plain, and consequently suffered heavy losses. Yet the Parliamentarians did not succeed in stopping the King's march towards London as they had intended.

Crossing the line of the Roman Fosse Way, the route soon reaches Warwick. Magnificent castles, steeped in legends and memories of ancient political struggles, are the outstanding features of both Warwick and Kenilworth, the next town on the route. Many of the murky deeds of medieval times were transformed into glittering romance in the novel *Kenilworth* by Sir Walter Scott, who stayed in Kenilworth in 1821.

Making its way through the flat farmland that lies between the great industrial conurbations of Coventry and Birmingham, the route passes several villages with fine old half-timbered buildings, then joins the A5 for a while before turning north to reach Lichfield, a town with distinguished literary connections. Samuel Johnson was born here in 1709 in a ho which was completed only a year before his birth, and whic preserved today almost unaltered. Johnson received his e education in Lichfield, and returned to the town through his life, often with his friend and biographer, James Boswell Lichfield's beautiful cathedral there is a memorial to poetess Anna Seward, known as the 'Swan of Lichfield'. knew Johnson, and Boswell used some of her reminiscence his *Life of Samuel Johnson*.

Across the River Trent is Abbots Bromley, famous for ancient Horn Dance. The origins and function of the dance obscure, but it is thought to be connected with hunting rig which the villagers once enjoyed in nearby Needwood For Skirting Bagot's Park, the route continues to Uttoxeter, wh also has connections with Dr Johnson.

From Uttoxeter the route continues, never far from the Ri Dove, through Rocester to Ellastone. As the route approac Mayfield views of distant hills open up, and soon the roa crossing open moorland divided by drystone walls. The vill of Waterhouses lies on the boundary of the Peak Dist National Park – 540 square miles of magnificent scenery t ranges from soft green landscapes and delightful river vall in the south to rugged gritstone peaks like Kinder Scout to north of Edale. Crossing the River Hamps at Onecote, route continues through Warslow to Longnor, a lovely villa set between the Rivers Manifold and Dove. From Glut Bridge it is only a few miles, past the incongruous 'moonsca of a limestone quarry, to the quietly refined charms of Buxt

---

PLACES OF INTEREST: OPENING DETAILS

Chalfont St Giles
MILTON'S COTTAGE open Feb to end Oct: Tue to Sat am and pm, Sun pm only. Also open weekends in Nov

Aylesbury
BUCKINGHAMSHIRE COUNTY MUSEUM open all year daily (except Sun, Good Fri, 25-26 Dec and 1 Jan)

Winslow
WINSLOW HALL open Jul to Sep daily (except Mon), pm only

Stowe
STOWE HOUSE LANDSCAPE GARDENS open end Mar to end Apr and Jul to Sep, pm only

Farnborough
FARNBOROUGH HALL open Apr to Sep Wed and Sat, pm only

Warwick
WARWICK CASTLE open all year (except 25 Dec)

LORD LEYCESTER'S HOSPITAL open all year daily (except Sun, Good Fri and 25 Dec)

WARWICK DOLL MUSEUM, OKEN'S HOUSE open all year

Kenilworth
KENILWORTH CASTLE open all year

Kingsbury
KINGSBURY WATER PARK open all year (except Christmas)

Fazeley
DRAYTON MANOR PARK AND ZOO open Easter to Oct

Lichfield
JOHNSON BIRTHPLACE MUSEUM open all year Mon to Sat (except most Bank Holidays); also open Sun May to Sep, pm only

HANCH HALL open Apr to Sep Sun pm only; also Easter, Spring and Summer Bank Holiday Mon and following Tue, pm only

Alton
ALTON TOWERS open Easter to mid Oct

Buxton
MUSEUM AND ART GALLERY open all year Mon to Fri

BUXTON
The splendid Crescent at Buxton, built by the Fifth Duke of Devonshire, includes the Natural Baths, constructed on the site of baths built by the Romans many centuries earlier

LONGNOR
In the square of this little town, set amid dramatic Peakland countryside, is an impressive market hall dating from 1873

ALTON TOWERS
Charles Talbot, Fifteenth Earl of Shrewsbury, created these 600 acres of exotic parkland in the early 19th century. The classical colonnade is just one of many unusual follies in the park

UTTOXETER
As a boy, Dr Samuel Johnson once refused to tend his father's bookstall in Uttoxeter. A plaque now marks the spot where, as an old man, Johnson stood for several hours in the rain as an act of penance for his youthful disobedience

ABBOTS BROMLEY
Every September hundreds of people visit Abbots Bromley to see the famous Horn Dancers. The reindeer horns used in the dance have never left the village since Anglo-Saxon times, and the tradition of the Horn Dance may go back even further

LICHFIELD
The three graceful spires of Lichfield Cathedral tower above a delightful close of medieval houses, creating a peaceful oasis in the heart of the city

KENILWORTH
The imposing ruin of Kenilworth Castle still vividly imparts a sense of the power and wealth it knew when Richard Dudley entertained Elizabeth I here with 17 days of music and feasting

DRAYTON MANOR PARK
160 acres of parkland here include a zoo where visitors can see big cats, monkeys, reptiles and birds. The park also offers a miniature railway, a jungle cruise and a 'Lost World', complete with life-size replicas of dinosaurs

BUCKINGHAM
In 888 Alfred the Great divided England into shires, choosing Buckingham as the county town of the shire which bears its name. A gilded swan, the emblem of Buckinghamshire, is still a feature of the town hall's clock-tower

BANBURY
The present Banbury Cross dates only from 1859; the original was destroyed by the Puritans in 1602. The ride to the cross described in the popular nursery-rhyme was probably a May Day ceremony

WARWICK
14th-century Warwick Castle is a splendid survival of medieval England. Sir Walter Scott called it 'that fairest monument of ancient and chivalrous splendour which yet remains uninjured by time'

WINSLOW
Winslow Hall is thought to have been designed by Sir Christopher Wren. If this is so, the hall is one of the few domestic buildings attributable to the architect of St Paul's Cathedral in London

WENDOVER
Situated in the beautiful Chiltern Hills, Wendover retains several old houses, Georgian and earlier, and as its centrepiece boasts a clock-tower of 1842

FARNBOROUGH HALL
Built soon after 1684 by the Holbech family, Farnborough Hall stands on a high natural terrace overlooking a valley, a perfect setting for one of the most spectacular pieces of landscape gardening in the country

STOWE
The founding of Stowe School in 1923 saved Stowe Park from demolition. The magnificent Georgian mansion is the work of great architects such as Adam and Vanbrugh, whilst the grounds were landscaped by Kent and Capability Brown, among others

AYLESBURY
This old county town is known far and wide for a traditional Buckinghamshire industry – the breeding of Aylesbury duck for the table

CHALFONT ST GILES
The blind poet John Milton came to Chalfont St Giles in 1665 to escape the plague which ravaged London. The brick-and-timbered cottage where he lived is now a museum devoted to his life and work

AMERSHAM
The old town of Amersham is centred on its 17th-century market hall. The beautifully panelled meeting room, overlooked by the arms of Charles II, is set on open arches and reached by the original stairway

London

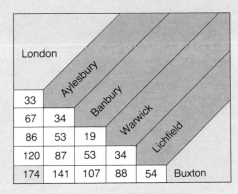

London					
33	Aylesbury				
67	34	Banbury			
86	53	19	Warwick		
120	87	53	34	Lichfield	
174	141	107	88	54	Buxton

London

LONDON TO AMERSHAM

The route begins at the junction by Hanger Lane Underground station, 7 miles west of central London at the point where the A40 intersects with the A406 North Circular road. Follow signs for Oxford, driving westwards on the A40 and skirting Perivale, where the sparkling white-and-green Hoover factory – an outstanding example of 1930s industrial architecture – stands surrounded by lawns on the right. Very soon the countryside begins to open out, with several garden centres and nurseries to emphasize the out-of-London feeling – in fact, it is possible to be in open country on this road within 20 minutes of leaving the West End.

Northolt Aerodrome, an RAF installation, lies to the right just before the A40 crosses the viaduct over the Colne valley to enter Buckinghamshire. Follow signs for Gerrards Cross and the A40, branching left to avoid the M40 motorway, and at the roundabout take the fourth exit to continue on the A40. After 1½ miles, at Tatling End, turn right on to the A413 (SP Amersham). The road is dual carriageway at first, but the surroundings are wholly rural. The A413 skirts the smart village of Chalfont St Peter, then passes a turning to Chalfont St Giles on the left.

> **CHALFONT ST GILES**
> It is a very short detour to the village, which has a small green and several 16th- and 17th-century cottages. The most notable is Milton's Cottage,* where John Milton finished writing *Paradise Lost* and began *Paradise Regained*. The blind poet fled here in 1665 to escape the plague which was raging in London. The house has a charming garden, and inside is a collection of Milton mementoes, including rare editions of his works.

Continue along the A413, following the valley of the little River Misbourne as it weaves its way through a landscape dotted with typical Chiltern beechwoods. After 3 miles the road passes through Amersham Old Town. The main part of Amersham, very much a product of the commuter age, lies on a hill to the north, but the old town is still most attractive. Its wide main street has an exceptional variety of architecture – red brick, white or yellow stucco, black-and-white half-timbering. The most distinctive building is the 17th-century market hall, which stands on open arches opposite the Crown Hotel, an old coaching inn. Amersham church contains many fine monuments and some 17th-century stained glass.

Long considered an architectural eyesore, the Hoover factory at Perivale is now regarded by many as one of the outstanding industrial buildings of its period

ERSHAM TO WENDOVER

...tinue from Amersham along the A413
...Great Missenden). About a mile out of
...town, to the left, lies the Palladian
...sion of Shardeloes. It is not open to the
...lic, though several public footpaths lead
...ugh the fine park, which was landscaped
...Humphry Repton in the late 18th century.

LITTLE MISSENDEN

...st off the main road to the left, 1½ miles
...rther on, is Little Missenden, a quiet and
...ral village whose cottages cluster around
...e manor house and church, parts of which
...re Saxon in origin. Inside are remarkably
...ell preserved fragments of 13th-century
...all paintings, including a representation of
... Christopher.

*...ittle Missenden's handsome red-brick manor house
dates mainly from the 17th century*

...ntinue along the A413 for about 7 miles,
...n turn right (SP Aylesbury) at the
...unction on the outskirts of Wendover, an
...ractive town of red brick and Suffolk-pink
...cco, set amid densely wooded hills. Go
...vn the High Street (part of the ancient
...per Icknield Way) and turn left (SP
...lesbury) by the Victorian clock-tower.

...NDOVER TO WHITCHURCH

...st of Wendover, and clearly visible from
... road, is Coombe Hill, topped by a
...morial to 148 dead of the Buckingham-
...re regiments who fell during the Boer War.
...yond Coombe Hill lies Chequers, the
...ntry home of the prime minister.
...The route continues along the A413 to
...lesbury. Follow signs to the town centre,
...n turn left (SP Buckingham, A413). The
...proach to the town is dominated by the
..., modern offices of the County Council.
...e best of Aylesbury lies in its centre, the old
...vn, which stands on a hill and has winding
...eyways and passages in dramatic contrast
...he efficient ring road. One narrow passage

This impressive mullioned window has lit the King's Head Inn at Aylesbury for 500 years

shelters the late medieval King's Head Inn,
whose windows still contain some of their
original glass. Cromwell stayed here in 1651,
and since 1926 the historic inn has been in the
care of the National Trust.

Near the top of the hill is St Mary's
Church, its medieval tower crowned by a
curious little spirelet. Inside is an exquisitely
carved 12th-century font. As the county
town, Aylesbury is the site not only of the
elegant 18th-century County Hall but also of
the Buckinghamshire County Museum,*
which is housed near the church in the former
grammar school of 1720.

As you come out of the town, follow signs
for Buckingham and the A413. From the
A413 between Aylesbury and Buckingham

there are views across the flat Vale of
Aylesbury, strikingly different from the
beech-clad slopes of the Chilterns. On one of
the low hills that characterize this part of the
route is the village of Hardwick, just off the
main road to the right and distinguished by
its limestone church tower. In the churchyard
is a communal grave containing over 200
skeletons, discovered at nearby Holmans
Bridge in 1818 and thought to be relics of the
Civil War battle fought there in 1643.

The route continues through Whitchurch,
a village with many attractive houses of stone
or red brick, some of them thatched. The
village was once important for its castle,
traces of which are still to be found on a hill to
the left. (Route continues on p. 38.)

THE CHILTERN HILLS

Hᴵɢʜ Wʏᴄᴏᴍʙᴇ, in the heart of the beech-clad Chilterns, has long been acknowledged as the chair-making 'capital' of England. For many years this was essentially a rural craft practised by men who worked individually or in pairs. Trees were felled and rough-cut by 'pit sawyers' while 'benchmen', 'bottomers', 'bodgers' and others prepared the various components. Although the term is now anything but complimentary, the original 'bodgers' were highly skilled craftsmen who specialized in producing legs for chairs.

The modern chair-making industry in the Chilterns – and the area's furniture industry as a whole – owes a great deal to Samuel Treacher, a farmer from High Wycombe who started making complete chairs at the end of the 18th century. Beech is particularly suitable for making chairs because of its close, straight grain and inherent strength. The museum on Castle Hill, High Wycombe, has many exhibits relating to the Chilterns' furniture-making traditions, and some chairs are still hand-made by craftsmen in the area.

Mᴏʀᴇ ᴛʜᴀɴ 60 square miles of beechwoods help make the Chiltern Hills one of the loveliest and most romantic parts of the Home Counties. The woodlands are particularly delightful in springtime, when fresh, light green leaves burst from their buds and grassy glades become bright with carpets of nodding bluebells. But the beech is at its most memorable in the autumn, when its leaves are transformed into a glowing palette of rich browns, reds and golds.

The hills themselves rise from the Thames valley at Goring and run in a long, gentle arc to the downs above Dunstable and Luton. They are part of the chalk formations that run right across England from Dorset to the Wash. Although their highest point is less than 900 feet above sea level, the hills form a very definite and delightful natural barrier between the London area and the broad, clay-covered plains of central England. They

rise gently beyond the capital and its suburb but the escarpment is impressively steep an has many splendid viewpoints. Names such Beacon Hill are reminders of fires that once blazed warnings or were lit to celebrate victories and royal jubilees.

Several main roads pierce the hills, radiating out from London like the spokes wheel, but the Chilterns are characterized a tangled skein of narrow, leafy lanes which climb the ridges and wander along tranqui valleys. The Hambleden valley, running d north from the Thames at Mill End, is particularly attractive. Framed by wooded hills, it shelters the villages of Hambleden, Skirmett, Fingest and Turville, and is overlooked by the old windmill on Turville Hill. As in other parts of the Chilterns, flint dug from the chalk combine with mellow brick, timber and a few thatched roofs to create buildings of great traditional charm.

Chiltern beechwoods supply timber that is transformed into beautiful chairs by craftsmen like Stuart Linford (inset), seen here in his workshop near High Wycombe

MEMORABLE VIEWPOINTS
[pro]vided by the steep chalk
[escarp]ment of the Chilterns. One of
[the high]est is Coombe Hill, between
[Prince]s Risborough and Wendover.
[It is 8]48 feet above sea level and was
[given] to the National Trust by Lord
[Lee of] Fareham in 1912. Britain's first
[public] nature trail was opened on the
[hill ex]actly 50 years later. On the
[summ]it stands a monument
[comm]emorating local men who died
[in the] South African wars. Wooded
[Haddington] Hill, at 857 feet the highest
[point] in the Chilterns, is just over two
[miles] away, beyond Wendover.
[Bea]con Hill, crowned with Iron
[Age] earthworks, reaches 760 feet
[above] Wendover and is also
[protec]ted by the National Trust. It
[overlo]oks the Pitstone windmill,
[which] dates from 1627 and is believed
[to be] the oldest in Britain. The hill
[above] Aston Clinton was a famous
[motor]-hillclimb course in the 1920s.
[A re]gular competitor was Lionel
[Marti]n, an engineer who decided to
[call hi]s cars Aston Martins following
[nume]rous successes there.
[An]cient crosses are carved into the
[chalk] slopes above Chinnor and

Princes Risborough, while a turf-cut
lion 140 yards long looks over the
plain from Dunstable Down. It marks
the site of Whipsnade Park Zoo, and
is a landmark for many miles around.

Visitors with time to spare are
catered for by several waymarked
nature trails and 1500 miles of public
footpaths. They include the eastern
part of the Ridgeway Path which
runs from Overton Hill, near
Marlborough, to the summit above
Ivinghoe. The path takes in sections
of the Icknield Way, a prehistoric
trade route at the foot of the
Chiltern escarpment.

Apart from the Thames, the
Chilterns' most important waterway
is the Grand Union Canal.
Completed early in the 19th century,
it links London to Birmingham and
emerges from the hills near
Berkhamsted. The summit locks at
Dudswell are on the outskirts of the
town. This gap in the hills was also
exploited by George and Robert
Stephenson when they built the first
railway into London.

---

*Views from Coombe Hill take in most of the
Chilterns' west-facing escarpment*

FAMOUS PEOPLE

*One of the most flamboyant figures in British
political history, Benjamin Disraeli lived at
Hughenden Manor for more than 40 years*

*Left: John Milton lived at
Chalfont St Giles during
London's Plague*

MANY NOTABLE FIGURES
from the pages of English history
have links with the Chilterns.
Edmund Burke (1729–1797), one of
the greatest political thinkers and
orators, is buried in Beaconsfield
church. Benjamin Disraeli was born
at Bradenham in 1804 and lived at
Hughenden Manor from 1848 until
his death in 1881. He is buried in the
church on the estate.

Great Hampden was the home of
John Hampden (1594–1643), an
MP whose refusal to pay the Ship
Money tax introduced by Charles I
helped trigger off the Civil War, in
which Hampden died. He is buried
at Great Hampden and there is a
roadside memorial to him nearby.

Chalfont St Giles, on the eastern
edge of the hills, is where John
Milton completed *Paradise Lost* and
started *Paradise Regained* while the
plague was ravaging London in
1665. His cottage is now a museum.
The neighbouring village of
Jordans is the burial place of
William Penn (1644–1718), the
Quaker who gave his name to the
American state of Pennsylvania.
Lord Cardigan, leader of the
Charge of the Light Brigade at
Balaclava, was born at Hambleden

*Above: Rare editions of 'Paradise Lost'
are among the mementoes in Milton's
Cottage at Chalfont St Giles*

---

in 1797. The chest he took to the
Crimea can be seen in the church.

Chequers, north-east of Princes
Risborough, has been the prime
minister's official country residence
since 1922, when it was given to the
nation by Lord Lee of Fareham.

WHITCHURCH TO BRACKLEY

The A413 soon reaches the small market town of Winslow, passing 18th-century Winslow Hall* on the right. The large, imposing building is attributed to Sir Christopher Wren. The town itself is enhanced by thatch, new and old, toning attractively with the red brick, and sometimes complemented by decorative brickwork. Winslow has several old inns and a handsome church. Turn right in the town, following the clearly signed A413, and pass the tiny market square.

From Winslow the route runs on to Buckingham. Follow signs here for the A422 (SP Brackley). The White Hart Hotel, right by the busy crossroads, is a good example of the buildings put up in Buckingham after a great fire that swept through the town in 1725, destroying over a third of the houses. Many other buildings in the town centre date from the 18th century, but Buckingham still has the air of 'a good old town' as Samuel Pepys, the famous diarist, described it when he came here in 1668. It is certainly old, having been selected as the county town in the year 888, when King Alfred first divided England into shires. Aylesbury eventually took over this role, since it was more centrally placed in the county, but traces of Buckingham's former authority remain. The clock-tower of the town hall is still topped by a gilded swan, the county emblem, and the old jail recalls an 18th-century landowner's attempt to restore Buckingham's former status as the seat of justice in the county.

STOWE

About 2½ miles west of Buckingham on the A422 you can make a detour to Stowe by turning right on to an unclassified road (SP Dadford, Silverstone). About a mile along this country lane is the entrance to Stowe Park.* Vanbrugh, Robert Adam, Capability Brown and William Kent are among the great names who had a hand in the design of the mansion and grounds of Stowe, creating between them a true showpiece of 18th-century architecture and landscape gardening. The grounds are spectacular, with lakes, grottoes, temples and an elegant covered bridge. A 13th-century church is all that is left of Stowe village, which stood here before work began on the park in 1713. For a time the seat of the dukes of Buckingham, Stowe House is now a well-known public school.

Carry on along the A422, crossing the county boundary into Northamptonshire to reach Brackley. This spacious hillside town, with its clean stone buildings, has a wide main street that is perfectly appropriate to an 18th-century coaching town. The oldest building in Brackley is the Norman chapel of the Hospital of St James and St John, which has been known as Magdalen College School ever since Fellows of Magdalen College, Oxford used the building as a refuge during the Great Plague. The Hospital was founded by the Earl of Leicester in the mid 12th century, and became a school 400 years later. The route turns left at a T-junction on to the A43 (SP Oxford) then right by the tall, elegant 18th-century town hall to continue on the A422 (SP Banbury).

CKLEY TO BANBURY

ond Brackley the road runs through hinghoe and Middleton Cheney, whose rch lies off the main road to the right. Its f treasure is some beautiful stained glass Burne-Jones, William Morris and other ninent Victorian artists.

he A422 takes the route all the way to bury. The busiest part of the town can be passed by following signs for Birmingham Warwick.

BANBURY

In place of Banbury's medieval cross stands a 19th-century replica. The statues of Queen Victoria, George V and Edward VII were added in 1914

Bakers in Banbury still use a 300-year-old recipe to produce the cakes that are named after the town

o see more of Banbury, keep straight on for e town centre, where attractive old houses d inns line narrow medieval streets. A one-ay system leads to Banbury Cross, a ictorian replica of the original of nursery-ayme fame, which was destroyed in 1602 by e Puritans. Banbury was notorious for its uritan zeal, commemorated, along with the ill-famous Banbury cakes, in an old saying oting Banbury for its 'cheese, cakes and al'. Turn right by the cross and go past the npressive golden ironstone Whateley Hall otel, on the left of the road. Opposite, and uilt in the same golden stone that glows in e slightest hint of sunlight, is St Mary's hurch, a late 18th-century replacement, in e neo-classical style, of an even finer church at was blown up in 1792. The people of anbury gained a reputation for wanton estruction of historic buildings: the castle, o, was blown up at their insistence. At the ot of the hill, turn left at the traffic lights on e A41 (SP Birmingham, Warwick) and ep straight on for Warwick.

BANBURY TO WARWICK

About 3 miles out of Banbury the A41 leaves Oxfordshire and enters Warwickshire. Approaching Warmington, the route passes a sign for Edge Hill where, on 23 October 1642, the Battle of Edgehill – the first major battle of the Civil War – took place.

Warmington's fine church, 14th-century with some Norman features, stands right beside the main road on a hill, offering panoramic views of the countryside and overlooking Warmington village, which sits snugly in the hollow below. Having run high along a ridge from Banbury, the road begins to descend towards the wide Avon valley.

This peaceful Warwickshire landscape was the setting for the Battle of Edgehill in the Civil War

FARNBOROUGH HALL

A mile past Warmington is an unclassified road on the right for Avon Dassett and Farnborough Hall, offering a pleasant detour. The Hall,* about 2 miles from the main road, is a late 17th-century ironstone mansion whose elegant interior is a fine example of the rococo style. The tranquil landscaped gardens have terraced lawns, a small lake, and a classical pavilion and temple.

On a hill to the right as the A41 continues to the edge of Warwick is a small, round 16th-century beacon tower, set in Burton Dassett Country Park. A fire on its top was the first in a chain which conveyed news of the Battle of Edgehill to London.

WARWICK TO KENILWORTH

At the major junction south of Warwick, where trunk routes and the A41 are signposted to the left, take the second exit at the roundabout, the A425 for Warwick. (To by-pass the town, take the A41. At the next two junctions follow signs for Coventry and the A46, and at the third branch left on to an unclassified road for Leek Wootton.)

Trees line the road as it approaches the elegant bridge which takes the route across the River Avon into Warwick. On the right is an attractive park, while to the left is the imposing castle.* Shortly the route passes its main gate. Warwick Castle is one of the most impressive medieval fortresses in the country, rebuilt in the 14th and 15th centuries on a site which had been fortified first by Aethelfleda, the daughter of King Alfred, and then by William the Conqueror. The interior was rebuilt during the 17th century. The castle contains an excellent collection of paintings, and is set amid fine landscaped gardens where peacocks roam.

Much of medieval Warwick was burnt down in 1694, and the town's largely Georgian streets, planned after the fire, are elegant and unspoilt. Among the buildings to escape the blaze was Lord Leycester's Hospital,* at the western end of the High

One of Europe's finest examples of medieval military architecture, Warwick Castle overlooks the peaceful waters of the Avon

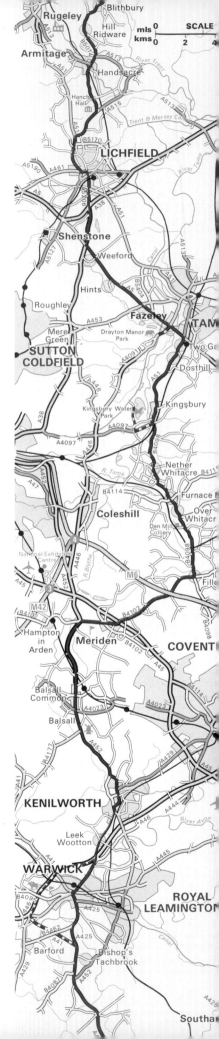

et. Built in 1383, it is still a 'hospital', or
shouse, for retired servicemen. Its 12th-
ury chapel is built above the old West
e of the town. Another early building,
er the castle, is 16th-century Oken's
se in Castle Street, which now houses a
nating museum of dolls.* Much of St
y's Church had to be rebuilt after the fire,
the sumptuous 15th-century Beauchamp
pel survived. In it stand the elaborate
ble tomb of Richard Beauchamp and
ral other interesting monuments.

eave Warwick on the A429 (SP
entry, Kenilworth) and at the by-pass
tion roundabout take the first exit to join
nclassified road (SP Leek Wootton). Pass
ugh the village of Leek Wootton and in
iles keep forward on to the A452 to enter
ilworth. The King's Arms in the town is
re Sir Walter Scott is said to have begun
novel *Kenilworth*. The parish church has a
tifully carved Norman doorway, be-
d to have been taken from Kenilworth
ey, whose ruins can still be seen to the
h of the church. To the north-west of the
n centre, beyond the abbey, is the
lstone shell of Kenilworth Castle.* The
dy keep dates from the 12th century,
st the great banqueting hall was built by
n of Gaunt during the 1390s.

NILWORTH TO FAZELEY

ve Kenilworth by the A452 Birmingham
, crossing a small river. In 3 miles, at the
idabout, keep forward with the Birming-
road to pass through Balsall and Balsall
mon. After 3½ miles, at the next rounda-
, take the third exit, the B4102, for
iden. In 1¼ miles, at the roundabout at
edge of Meriden, take the second exit (SP
ngley), and 4½ miles later, at Fillongley
sroads, turn left on to the B4098
gsbury and Tamworth road. Fillongley
mentioned in *Domesday Book*, and has
cally attractive Warwickshire red-brick
ses and a parish church with a great 14th-
ury tower. In 2¾ miles, at the T-junction
beyond the Dan Mill Colliery at Over
tacre, turn left on to the B4114 and in
ile, at Furnace End crossroads, keep for-
d on to the B4098 (SP Tamworth).
ow the road through Nether Whitacre to
edge of Kingsbury, taking the second exit,
A51, at the roundabout there.

KINGSBURY WATER PARK
t this roundabout the Kingsbury Water
ark* is signposted off to the left along the
4097. The park offers picnic areas, sailing
cilities, an adventure playground, lake-
de walks, a pool for model boats and an
hibition of wildlife in the area.

---

ut 4 miles beyond Kingsbury the main
e turns left (SP Brownhills) on to the A5,
former Roman Watling Street, continu-
through Fazeley, an important focus of
Midland canal system.

*Quaint old houses huddle beneath Lichfield Cathedral's
magnificent west front, which is adorned by 113 statues*

DRAYTON MANOR PARK
Turn left in Fazeley on to the A4091 (SP
Coventry) for a detour to Drayton Manor
Park,* 1 mile away. Drayton Manor was built
in the 1820s for the father of Sir Robert Peel,
the 19th-century MP for Tamworth who
reorganized the London police force, bringing the nicknames 'peelers' and 'bobbies' into
the language. The house no longer exists, but
the 160-acre park includes a large zoo, a
garden centre, amusements, 'jungle cruises'
and the 'Lost World' with its collection of life-
sized model dinosaurs.

FAZELEY TO LICHFIELD

The next village, 3 miles further on, just off
the A5, has the intriguing name of Hints: it
may be derived from *hynt*, the Welsh for
'course' or 'way', possibly indicating that the
village stood on one of the old drove roads.
At a major roundabout 2 miles past it, take
the third exit, the A38 (SP Lichfield) and in
1¾ miles, at the next roundabout, take the
second exit to follow the A5206 into Lichfield.

The first views of Lichfield from almost any
direction are dominated by the cathedral's
three spires, known as the 'Ladies of the
Vale'. The first cathedral here was built in
AD 700 as the mother church of the entire
Midland kingdom of Mercia. Traces of a
later, Norman, cathedral can still be seen, but
much of the building we see today dates from
about 1330. The cathedral was very badly
damaged in the Civil War, and much restoration and rebuilding has been carried out
over the centuries since. Apart from the three
elegant spires, the most striking feature of the
cathedral's exterior is the richly adorned west
front. The interior, gloomy but graceful, has
some fine furnishings in the High Victorian
style, such as the brass and iron pulpit and the
lovely chancel screen. The windows of the
exquisite Lady Chapel contain fine 16th-
century Flemish glass, and in the south
transept stands a bust of Dr Samuel Johnson,
Lichfield's most famous son, the compiler of
the first English dictionary. The Johnson
Birthplace Museum,* by the market place, is
a tiny house with several storeys and a
dramatically steep stairway. Here the great
man was born in 1709. Close by the house
stands his statue, together with that of James
Boswell, his companion and biographer.

Lichfield is still a most attractive – and
surprisingly compact – cathedral city, and
retains much of the elegance of the stage-
coach era. The George Hotel and the Angel
Croft are fine 18th-century buildings that
were once coaching inns. The last stage-coach
left here for London on 11 April 1838.

LICHFIELD TO HILL RIDWARE

Leave Lichfield by the A51 (SP Rugeley),
and at the roundabout ½ mile beyond the
outskirts of the city turn right on to the A515
(SP King's Bromley). After 1½ miles turn left
on to the B5014 (SP Handsacre, Armitage).
On the left just past this junction Hanch
Hall* can be seen from the road. Parts of the
house are several centuries old, but the best of
it dates from the time of Queen Anne.

At Handsacre, where views of Rugeley's
massive power station appear to the left, turn
right, crossing the Trent and Mersey Canal
and following the B5014 (SP Uttoxeter). This
road soon crosses the Trent and comes to the
village of Hill Ridware. A pub sign in the
village shows the elaborate Chadwick Arms,
commemorating a distinguished local family
to whom there are memorials in the parish
church of nearby Mavesyn Ridware.

HILL RIDWARE TO UTTOXETER

From Hill Ridware the B5014 runs on through Blithbury, where an unusual pub sign depicts the 'Bull and Spectacles'. After 3 miles the road leads into Abbots Bromley's long village street, lined with red-brick houses, some of them Georgian. Several of these are now part of a girls' public school, which was originally two schools – St Mary's, on a bleak hilltop to the left of the road, and St Anne's on the right. Great trees and attractive gardens surround the school buildings. On the village green is a 17th-century butter-cross and nearby stands the timber-framed Goat's Head Hotel. The village is particularly well known for its Horn Dance; performed every year in early September, the custom is many centuries old, and probably of pagan origin. People come from miles around to see the antics of men wearing brown, green and yellow costumes and deer antlers, a boy with a bow and arrow, jesters and a 'maid'.

Above: Abbots Bromley's 17th-century butter-cross is overlooked by the timbered Goat's Head Hotel, which is probably a century older

Right: The antlers used in the famous Horn Dance are thought to be as old as the dance itself

Continue north towards Uttoxeter, keeping forward on to the B5013 at the end of the village and turning right on to the A518 after 5 miles. In Uttoxeter's market place is an old lock-up – now a confectionery kiosk – bearing a memorial to Dr Samuel Johnson.

UTTOXETER TO WARSLOW

From the town centre follow signs for the A50 and Stoke, and shortly turn right on to the B5030 (SP Ashbourne). Past Uttoxeter there is an enticing hint of higher ground to the right of the road, a foretaste of the Derbyshire hills. Bear right to enter Rocester, pleasantly situated between the Rivers Churnet and Dove. Approaching the village, you cannot miss the huge JCB excavator factory on the left, home of the great yellow monsters seen on construction sites. The works are set amid attractive landscaped gardens surrounding an artificial lake.

ALTON TOWERS

A left turn at this point offers a detour to Alton Towers,* clearly signposted along the B5031 via Denstone and Alton village. The fairy-tale mansion of Alton Towers itself is now little more than a shell, having been uninhabited for 60 years, but it is set in attractive wooded grounds with winding paths, temples, summer-houses, an extravagant conservatory and a pagoda, as well as many exotic trees and shrubs. These combine with a model railway, a cable-car and other family amusements to make up one of the most popular leisure parks in the Midlands.

The main route follows the B5030 (SP Ellastone) through Rocester village. Ahead rise high hills, and to the right flows the River Dove, which follows the road to Ellastone. A footpath runs from the village's 18th-century bridge along an attractive stretch of the river, which marks the Derbyshire–Staffordshire border. Ellastone was the model for Hayslope in George Eliot's classic novel *Adam Bede*. The novelist's father lived and worked here as a young carpenter.

Continue along the B5032 to Mayfield, where several Victorian mills stand beside the River Dove. Turn left on to the A52 (SP Stoke, Leek), and at the junction where the A52 turns left for Stoke, continue on the A523 Leek road.

Within a short distance the road is running through open moorland country with dry-stone walls and few trees – quite different from the Dove valley. Shortly the route drops into

houses, right on the edge of the Peak
ct National Park. The village is set on
River Hamps, whose unusual name
s 'summer-dry'. Here the river meets
tone for the first time, often disappearing
what locals call 'swallet holes' or 'shack
to run underground.

out 3 miles past Waterhouses, turn right
the B5053 (SP Longnor). This road
s uphill to almost 1250 feet before
nding to Onecote, where there is an
ctive Georgian church, then continues
the high, bleak country of Butterton
through a stretch of countryside known
y as Lousybank. From the hilltops there
xcellent views over farmland and moor-
owards even more windswept heights in
istance. The road drops to Warslow, an
ctive village of Peakland stone set amid
ees.

ECTON AND THE MANIFOLD VALLEY
detour can be made to Ecton and the
anifold valley by following the sign for
on at the eastern end of Warslow village.
rn right here to drive down a steep, narrow
e which leads into a delightful tucked-
ay valley entirely surrounded by steep hills
a kind of natural amphitheatre. Another
y narrow lane and footpath lead up the
posite side of the valley to 'the Top of
on', from where there are superb pano-
ic views of the Manifold valley and the
s around it. Like the Hamps, the River
anifold is 'summer-dry'. A sceptical Dr
nson once refused to believe that the
anifold flowed underground in the porous
estone, and the fact had to be demon-
ated to him by means of marked corks.

SLOW TO BUXTON
B5053 leads on from Warslow to
nor. Sheltered by spectacular hills and
s, this large gritstone village is a maze of
streets and paths between the houses.
e are neat, painted iron railings outside
of the cottages, scrubbed stone steps,
lots of trees, and, surprisingly for so
a place, a market hall. On its façade are
ds of the tolls once paid by farmers – for
y pen of sheep sold, 4d; for every basket
gs, 1d.

the B5053 continues towards Buxton,
are dramatic views on every side before
oad dips steeply down towards Glutton
ge, crossing the River Dove to enter
yshire.

short distance beyond Glutton Bridge
udden appearance of Buxton Quarry, to
ight, is quite a shock after the spectacular
rland scenery of the last few miles. The
e that is quarried here is not generally
to build houses, but rather for road
ding, in animal feed and for unromantic
nical processes that have little to do with
e beautiful hills.

n reaching the A515, turn left (SP
on). This fast, well-surfaced road takes
oute the last few miles to its destination.

BUXTON

At over 1000 feet, Buxton is
England's highest town.
Conventionally regarded as the
capital of the Peak District, it
actually stands outside the
boundaries of the Peak District
National Park, but it is a fine
touring centre for a most
appealing part of Derbyshire.
Within a few miles of the town
are several of Derbyshire's
prettiest limestone dales; the
Blue John Caverns at Castleton;
charming Peakland villages
such as Ashford in the Water
and Hartington; the exquisite
church at Tideswell and much
more.

Buxton's facilities for the
modern visitor carry on a
tradition which goes back to
Roman times when people first
came to 'take the waters'. The
original 18th-century Pump
Room is now an information
centre, though Buxton is still a
spa: about 250,000 gallons of
warm mineral water are
pumped here daily. Like many
other spa towns, it is geared to
elegant entertainment, and has
pleasant gardens, golf-courses, a
museum and art gallery,* and
Victorian hotels in the grand
style, as well as a beautifully
restored opera house.

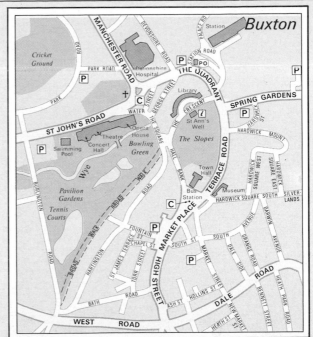

*Right: Buxton's elegant Crescent,
designed by John Carr, was built at
the end of the 18th century*

*Below: The opulent Edwardian
Opera House now plays an important
role in the Buxton Festival*

ROUTE 4

260 MILE

London to Caernarfon

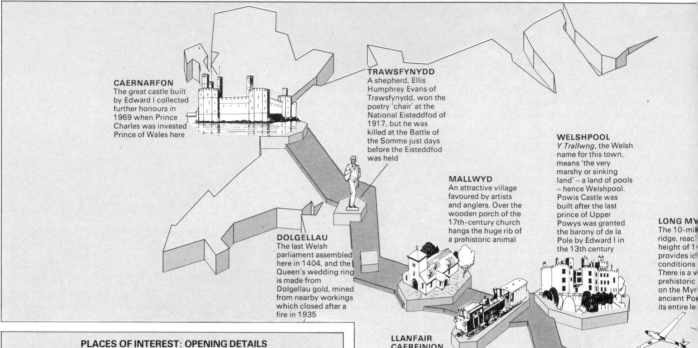

CAERNARFON
The great castle built by Edward I collected further honours in 1969 when Prince Charles was invested Prince of Wales here

TRAWSFYNYDD
A shepherd, Ellis Humphrey Evans of Trawsfynydd, won the poetry 'chair' at the National Eisteddfod of 1917, but he was killed at the Battle of the Somme just days before the Eisteddfod was held

WELSHPOOL
Y Trallwng, the Welsh name for this town, means 'the very marshy or sinking land' – a land of pools – hence Welshpool. Powis Castle was built after the last prince of Upper Powys was granted the barony of de la Pole by Edward I in the 13th century

MALLWYD
An attractive village favoured by artists and anglers. Over the wooden porch of the 17th-century church hangs the huge rib of a prehistoric animal

LONG MY
The 10-mi ridge, reac height of 1 provides id conditions There is a v prehistoric on the Myr ancient Po its entire le

DOLGELLAU
The last Welsh parliament assembled here in 1404, and the Queen's wedding ring is made from Dolgellau gold, mined from nearby workings which closed after a fire in 1935

LLANFAIR CAEREINION
The terminus of the Welshpool and Llanfair Light Railway was first opened in 1903, but closed in 1956. Happily visitors can again travel by steam as the line was reopened in 1963 by a private company

LUDLOW
This pleasant and historic town is a good centre from which to explore the Welsh Marches, and there is much to see in Ludlow itself. The Feathers Hotel of 1603 is famed for its elaborately carved woodwork

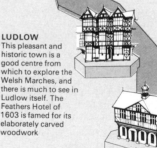

T C
The 'g scann aviatio share hill w of an

LEOMINSTER
Formerly used as a butter market, Leominster's old town hall was moved to its present site in 1855, when a second town hall, in the Italianate style, was built to replace it

EASTNOR
Although in appearance me Eastnor Castle begun in 1812. obelisk in the p commemorates son of Lord So who died fighti the Napoleonic

PLACES OF INTEREST: OPENING DETAILS

Beaconsfield
BEKONSCOT MODEL VILLAGE trains run frequently Easter to Oct daily (weather permitting). Gardens open all year (except Christmas holiday)

High Wycombe
WYCOMBE CHAIR AND LOCAL HISTORY MUSEUM open all year daily (except Wed, Sun and Bank Holidays)

HUGHENDEN MANOR open Apr to Oct Wed to Sun and Bank Holiday Mon, pm only. Mar and Nov Sat and Sun, pm only

West Wycombe
WEST WYCOMBE PARK AND CAVES house and grounds open Jun Mon to Fri; Jul and Aug daily (except Sat), pm only. Caves open Mar to end Sep daily, pm only; end Sep to end Feb Sat and Sun, pm only

Long Crendon
COURT HOUSE upper storey open Wed, pm only; Sat and Sun all day

Rousham
ROUSHAM HOUSE open Apr to Sep Wed, Sun and Bank Holidays, pm only. Gardens open daily all year

Chastleton
CHASTLETON HOUSE open all year: weekdays (except Wed), am and pm; weekends pm only

Ashchurch
DOWTY RAILWAY PRESERVATION SOCIETY open Sat and Sun all year, pm only

Eastnor
EASTNOR CASTLE open Sun end May to end Sep, also Wed and Thu in Jul and Aug, and Bank Holiday Mon

Leominster
LEOMINSTER AND DISTRICT FOLK MUSEUM open Apr to Oct: weekdays am and pm, Sun pm only

Eye
EYE MANOR open end May to mid Sep Wed, Thu, Sat and Sun, pm only. Also every pm in Aug

Ludlow
LUDLOW CASTLE open all year

Stokesay
STOKESAY CASTLE open Apr to Oct daily (except Tue)

Welshpool
POWIS CASTLE open Easter weekend, then May to end Sep Wed to Sun and Bank Holiday Mon, pm only

POWYSLAND MUSEUM open all year daily (except Sun), am and pm; Sat pm only. Closed Wed Oct to May

Llanfair Caereinion
WELSHPOOL AND LLANFAIR LIGHT RAILWAY open weekends Easter to Oct and daily Jun to Sep

Caernarfon
CAERNARFON CASTLE open all year

HE first 'modern' route between London and North [Wal]es, the A5, was built by the great engineer Thomas Telford [in th]e early years of the 19th century. Its southern sections were [ac]tually side-stepped by the M1 and M6 motorways, but [Telf]ord's highway over the border and through the mountain [pass]es of Snowdonia is still used by streams of frustrated nose-[to-ta]il motorists during the summer months.

[T]he excellent alternative described here follows a re-[mar]kably direct line north-westwards from London, avoiding [the] notorious bottlenecks to such an extent that it never so [muc]h as crosses the A5. Apart from being a thoroughly [prac]tical route, it runs through a rich variety of landscapes, [pass]es through many attractive villages and country towns, [and] provides places of interest from caves associated with black [mag]ic to the tunnels of a mountain railway.

[T]he route leaves the enormous sprawl of Greater London as [it cr]osses the River Colne to enter the soothing landscapes of [Buc]kinghamshire. Beyond the Chiltern 'capital' of High [Wy]combe – whose ancient coaching inns preserve vivid [mem]ories of mud-spattered coaches, portly red-faced landlords [and] weary passengers refreshed by steaming mugs of mulled [ale] – is the village of West Wycombe. It is one of only three [villa]ges completely owned by the National Trust and is justly [fam]ous for its lovely old buildings. It is also known for the [acti]vities of Sir Francis Dashwood and his Hell Fire Club. The [hel]lish goings-on that caused such a stir in 18th-century [soci]ety may well have been little more than indulgent drinking [sess]ions, but visitors to the great hollow ball on the church [tow]er or the caves in West Wycombe Park can give themselves [tin]gling thrills by imagining all sorts of unsavoury rites.

[A]t Thame the route begins its journey across the Cotswolds. [The] singular beauty of Cotswold architecture is due principally [to t]he fossil-packed oolitic limestone from which whole villages [and] small towns were built.

[T]ewkesbury is the first town on the route to illustrate the [chan]ge in architecture from Cotswold stone to the black-and-white buildings so typical of the West Midlands. From Tewkesbury the route leads under the southern brow of the Malvern Hills, a wedge of ancient rock that separates two great bands of sandstone.

The route then travels through a whole string of small towns – Ledbury, Leominster and Ludlow – that have preserved their timeless atmosphere and fine buildings in a countryside of verdant foliage and rich, red soil. A few miles north of Ludlow is what must surely be one of the most charming and romantic of all British castles, Stokesay, and beyond that are the heather-clad slopes of the Long Mynd, formed from some of the oldest rocks in the world.

Wales is entered just beyond Chirbury, and from there it is only a short distance, through Welshpool and Mallwyd, into the wild mountains of North Wales. First come the Arans, and then, beyond Dolgellau, the formidable Rhinogs, whose glowering slopes are now partly covered by the regimented firs of the Coed-y-Brenin forest. This stretch of the route (the A470) is called Sarn Helen, a name that Welshmen frequently gave to old Roman roads. Beyond Trawsfynydd, at Tomen-y-Mur, there are remains of a 1st-century Roman fort.

After crossing the Festiniog Railway the route snakes up through the beautiful Pass of Aberglaslyn. The trackbed and tunnels of another light railway, the Welsh Highland, can be clearly seen along here. The line was a financial failure and eventually closed in 1937, although the Welsh Highland Railway Society hopes to re-open the track from Porthmadog to Beddgelert in the foreseeable future. Beddgelert is in the very heart of Snowdonia and makes an ideal centre from which to explore all the majestic peaks and glittering lakes. On the route from Beddgelert to Caernarfon, the star-shaped Snowdon range rears up in all its fierce glory to the east.

The towers and roofs of Caernarfon snuggle between the mountains and the Menai Strait and look across to the Isle of Anglesey, which, because of the acres of wheat that grew there, was once known to Welshmen as *Mona* – the Mother.

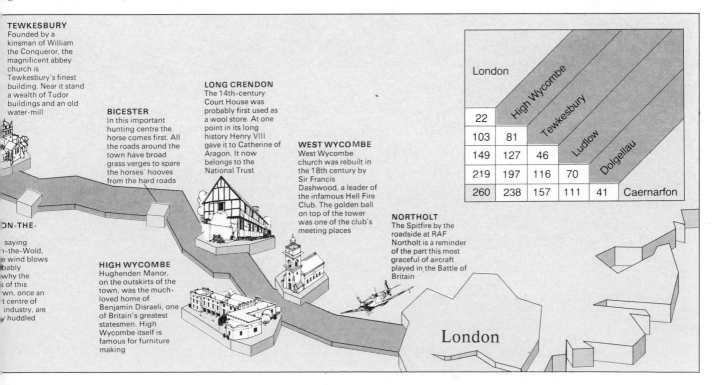

TEWKESBURY
Founded by a kinsman of William the Conqueror, the magnificent abbey church is Tewkesbury's finest building. Near it stand a wealth of Tudor buildings and an old water-mill

BICESTER
In this important hunting centre the horse comes first. All the roads around the town have broad grass verges to spare the horses' hooves from the hard roads

LONG CRENDON
The 14th-century Court House was probably first used as a wool store. At one point in its long history Henry VIII gave it to Catherine of Aragon. It now belongs to the National Trust

WEST WYCOMBE
West Wycombe church was rebuilt in the 18th century by Sir Francis Dashwood, a leader of the infamous Hell Fire Club. The golden ball on top of the tower was one of the club's meeting places

NORTHOLT
The Spitfire by the roadside at RAF Northolt is a reminder of the part this most graceful of aircraft played in the Battle of Britain

HIGH WYCOMBE
Hughenden Manor, on the outskirts of the town, was the much-loved home of Benjamin Disraeli, one of Britain's greatest statesmen. High Wycombe itself is famous for furniture making

[...ON-THE-...]
[...saying ...-the-Wold, ...e wind blows ...bably ...why the ...s of this ...wn, once an ...t centre of ...industry, are ...y huddled]

London

	High Wycombe	Tewkesbury	Ludlow	Dolgellau	
22					
103	81				
149	127	46			
219	197	116	70		
260	238	157	111	41	Caernarfon

London

LONDON TO HIGH WYCOMBE

The route begins at the junction by Hanger Lane Underground station, 7 miles west of central London at the point where the A40 intersects with the A406 North Circular road. Follow signs for Oxford, driving westwards on the A40.

After 6 miles the route passes RAF Northolt, where a Spitfire is parked near the main gate. At the roundabout 2½ miles beyond the airfield, keep forward, crossing the viaduct over the Colne valley, then branch left (SP Gerrards Cross) to avoid the M40. At the roundabout, take the fourth exit to remain on the A40. Clusters of trees flank the road as it skirts Gerrards Cross and heads towards Beaconsfield.

This Spitfire stands outside RAF Northolt, which was part of London's defences during the Battle of Britain in 1940

The old part of Beaconsfield flanks the A40 and has a wealth of 16th- and 17th-century buildings that once echoed to the clatter of stage-coaches on the route between Oxford and London. In the newer part of the town, to the north of the A40, is Bekonscot Model Village,* where visitors look like Gullivers in a colourful Lilliput as they wander among the landscape of tiny buildings, airport, docks and miniature railway.

Continue on the A40 along a stretch of road which was the haunt of Claude Duval, the 17th-century highwayman noted for his gallantry to beautiful women. Soon the route

enters High Wycombe, a bustling to famous for its furniture industry since 17th century. It nestles in a valley beneath Chiltern Hills, whose beech trees have provided a perfect raw material for craftsmen. The story of the furniture indu is told in the Wycombe Chair and L History Museum* on Castle Hill. The ma place is overlooked by an 18th-cent guildhall and by the Shambles, which bears a plaque listing the tolls paid stallholders.

FRIENDS' MEETING HOUSE, JORDANS

Between Gerrards Cross and Beaconsfield, ¾ mile past the Bell House Hotel on the left, is a right turn on to an unclassified road (SP Jordans) which offers a detour along wooded Potkiln Lane to the Friends' Meeting House, 1 mile away. The building dates from 1688 and overlooks a graveyard where William Penn, the Quaker who founded Pennsylvania, is buried. The nearby Mayflower Barn has timbers said to have come from the ship that carried the Pilgrim Fathers to North America in 1620.

HUGHENDEN MANOR

A detour along Valley Road (SP Grea Missenden, A4128) leads northwards t Hughenden Manor,* on the edge of the tow Benjamin Disraeli, one of the greatest figur in British political history, bought th Hughenden estate for £35,000 in 1848 an lived in the manor until his death in 1881. Th house dates from about 1800 but was com pletely remodelled by his wife. It contain many relics of the statesman's personal an political life, and the study has remained as was on the day of his death.

HIGH WYCOMBE TO THAME

Continue along the A40 (SP Oxford), pas through High Wycombe's suburbs, then right on to the A4010 (SP Aylesbury) before the A40 enters West Wycombe.

Gravestones of William Penn and his family stand beside the Friends' Meeting House at Jordans. Portraits and other mementoes of famous Quakers are a feature of the interior

WEST WYCOMBE

By continuing along the A40 for a few hundred yards you can make a detour to West Wycombe, a village entirely owned by the National Trust. It has an abundance of beautiful old buildings – and a host of somewhat lurid memories. Despite its sedate appearance, this place has been linked with tales of orgies and black magic since the days of Sir Francis Dashwood. Born in 1708, he travelled throughout Europe as a young man and became notorious for his adventures and practical jokes. Returning to the family seat at West Wycombe, he founded the infamous Hell Fire Club whose meeting places included the golden ball on top of St Lawrence's Church and the caves in the hill below.* Nearby is the Dashwood Mausoleum, a hexagonal folly built by Sir Francis in 1762. He was also responsible for rebuilding the family home, West Wycombe House,* which stands in grounds studded with classical temples. The house contains many art treasures, some dating from Roman times, and is particularly noted for its magnificently painted ceilings.

The A4010 runs northwards along a soft-profiled Chiltern valley to the outskirts of Princes Risborough. Here the hills fall away to left and right, and the great plain of central England stretches away into the distance. At the Black Prince Hotel on the near side of Princes Risborough bear left on to the B4444 (SP Thame) and follow signs for Thame until the route meets the A4129 in open country

beyond the town. It then curves gently westwards to Thame, there swinging right to run along the wide High Street, where thatched and timber-framed cottages rub shoulders with classical Georgian houses. The route turns right on to the B4011 (SP Bicester), passing Thame's parish church, which contains beautiful effigies of a 16th-century nobleman and his wife.

THAME TO MIDDLETON STONEY

The B4011 climbs gently from the Thame valley and enters Long Crendon, a village of great charm and character. Picturesque buildings, many of them timber-framed, thatched and colour-washed, line the High Street, off the main road to the right. At the far end of the street, next to the church, is the quaint 14th-century Court House,* which was probably used at one time as a wool store.

Continue along the B4011, gradually climbing to a point beyond Oakley that is just over 400 feet above sea level and offers extensive views over the southern Midlands. The route passes a large army camp and in 2½ miles turns left on to the A41 and carries on into Bicester. The A41 follows the line of Roman Akeman Street, which ran through the Roman settlement of Alchester, to the south of Bicester. On the far side of the town centre, with its spacious market place, turn left (SP Oxford) and in ½ mile turn right on to the A4095 (SP Witney). After 1 mile the route keeps forward on to the B4030 (SP Enstone) to reach Middleton Stoney 2 miles later.

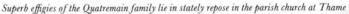

Superb effigies of the Quatremain family lie in stately repose in the parish church at Thame

Tweed has been manufactured for over a century at this imposing Victorian mill in Chipping Norton

MIDDLETON STONEY TO CHIPPING NORTON

At Middleton Stoney turn right and left to cross the A43. In 3¼ miles follow the B4030 to the left and cross the Cherwell.

ROUSHAM HOUSE
Immediately after crossing the river, a lane on the left leads to Rousham House,* ½ mile away. This fine example of Jacobean architecture was built in 1635 and enlarged by William Kent a century later. Kent, one of the greatest English landscapers, also created a wonderland of temples, statues, waterfalls and hanging woods along the western bank of the Cherwell. The house became a Royalist stronghold during the Civil War.

Continue westwards along the B4030, and at the traffic lights turn right then immediately left (SP Enstone) to cross the A423. A feature of the next village, Middle Barton, is the model landscape and railway behind a shop on the left of the road, almost opposite the post office. In 4½ miles, at the edge of Enstone, turn right on to the A34 (SP Stratford), then 3 miles later turn left on to the A44 (SP Evesham) for Chipping Norton.

Like many Cotswold towns, Chipping Norton prospered with the growth of the wool trade in the Middle Ages. It is still a busy little place, with many charming buildings of rich, pale-gold stone. Near the 14th-century church is a row of almshouses, built in 1640, with 'Remember the Poor' carved over the gateway. The main street is dominated by the handsome market hall of 1842. The A44 turns left then right (SP Stow) through the town and passes a splendid Victorian tweed mill with a lofty chimney.

CHIPPING NORTON TO TEWKESBURY

Four miles beyond Chipping Norton, by the Cross Hands pub, the route turns left on to the A436 (SP Stow).

ROLLRIGHT STONES
It is worth turning right just before the pub on to an unclassified road to visit the Rollright Stones, the 'Stonehenge of the Cotswolds', 2¼ miles away. The main group, known as the King's Men, is a stone circle 100 feet in diameter and was erected during the Bronze Age, between 1800 and 550 BC. The solitary King Stone is on the opposite side of the road, while another cluster of stones known as the Whispering Knights stands in a nearby field. They are the remains of a prehistoric burial chamber that was originally completely covered over with earth.

CHASTLETON HOUSE
Just over a mile further along the A436 detour can be made to Chastleton Hous along an unclassified road on the right. T Jacobean mansion retains much of its origin furniture, and other treasures include a Bi given by Charles I to the priest who pray with him before his execution in 1649.

The A436 drops into the valley of the R Evenlode before climbing again to Stow the-Wold. 'Stow' was the Saxon word 'meeting place', and roads do indeed verge on the town from all points of compass. Most of the stone buildings, and immense market square, date from the when this little town boasted the r prosperous wool market in England. fewer than 20,000 sheep were sold during annual fair when Daniel Defoe, traveller author of *Robinson Crusoe*, visited Stow du the 17th century.

Turn right on to the A429 (SP Stratf on the far side of the town centre, then aft few hundred yards turn left on to the A Evesham road and immediately left agai join the B4077 (SP Tewkesbury). The r runs through the delightful stone villag Upper Swell, complete with watermill Norman church, and continues thro beautiful Cotswold country, with part larly fine views from the top of Stanway before it twists down the steep western flan the hills to the Gloucestershire plain. Jus to the right at the foot of the hill is Stan village, which has a handsome manor h and an ancient tithe barn.

At the roundabout beyond Stanway, the A46 to join the A438 (SP Tewkesbu At Teddington Hands roundabout, stay the A438 and go through Ashchurch, hom the Dowty Railway Preservation Socie collection of steam locomotives, rolling s and other railway exhibits.* After 1 mile road crosses the M5 to enter Tewkesbury.

This historic town has a great dea delight the visitor. Many interesting buildings line the streets, from the Royal

A memorable townscape at Tewkesbury, where black-and-white cottages huddle beneath the abbey's fine Norman tower

Pole Hotel, a coaching inn mentioned by Charles Dickens in *Pickwick Papers*, to Old Baptist Chapel Court, a 15th-century house later used as a chapel. The town's greatest glory is its magnificent abbey church, founded in 1092. The abbey was closed by order of Henry VIII in 1540, but the townsfolk paid the king £453 to retain the great church with its medieval glass and superb Norman tower. Inside is the tomb of George, Duke of Clarence, said to have drowned in a butt of malmsey wine in the Tower of London in 1477.

TEWKESBURY TO LEDBURY

Follow the A38 (SP Worcester) out of Tewkesbury, crossing the Avon, and in ½ mile turn left on to the A438 (SP Ledbury) to cross the Severn. Views ahead are soon dominated by the long, steep chain of the Malvern Hills. Three miles after passing under the M50, the A438 turns right and immediately left to cross the B4208, then climbs to cross the southern end of the Malverns. Beyond the crest, the grey towers of Eastnor Castle* catch the eye. Although it looks medieval, the castle was built during the last century. The reception rooms contain a fine collection of armour, tapestries and paintings.

The A438 swings right by the castle gates, then climbs to a junction with the A449, where you turn left (SP Ross). Follow the A449 into Ledbury and turn right on to the A438 (SP Hereford), which brings you into the main street. The heart of Ledbury is its market place, watched over by the black-and-white herringbone-patterned market house supported on 16 oak pillars. Gabled Ledbury Park and 16th-century inns such as the Feathers Hotel typify the wealth of old architecture in the town, while St Michael's is one of the finest parish churches in Herefordshire.

The fairy-tale turrets of Eastnor Castle belie its true age, for it was not built until the 19th century

LEDBURY TO LUDLOW

Leave Ledbury by turning left with the A438 (SP Hereford) just before the railway bridge. Four miles beyond the town, at the crossroads by the Trumpet pub, turn right on to the A417 (SP Leominster) and follow the road north-westwards, crossing the A4103 and the A465. Running through fertile farmland grazed by Hereford cattle – a breed noted for the quality of its beef – the route skirts the wooded slopes of Dinmore Hill, crosses the River Lugg and joins the A49, turning right for Leominster.

'Lemster' is an ancient market town where narrow streets laid out in the Middle Ages contrast with broad thoroughfares created by tidy-minded 18th-century planners. One of them, Etnam Street, has a folk museum* whose exhibits illustrate many facets of Leominster's history. The most memorable building is the large priory church, dedicated by Robert de Bethun, Bishop of Hereford, early in the 12th century. It stands on the site of a 7th-century church founded by Merewald, King of Mercia. In the north aisle stands a huge, wheeled ducking-stool. The last recorded use of such an instrument of punishment in England was at Leominster in 1809 when a woman was paraded through the town and ducked in the River Kenwater.

Leave the centre of Leominster on the A49 (SP Shrewsbury) and in ½ mile keep forward on to the B4361 (SP Richards Castle).

A detail of the Feathers Hotel, the finest of Ludlow's many examples of Tudor 'magpie' architecture

---

EYE MANOR

Just under 3 miles later, in Luston, a short, signposted detour on the right leads to Eye Manor,* built in 1680 by Ferdinando Gorges, a man who made his fortune in the slave trade between West Africa and Barbados. The house has superbly ornate plastered ceilings, and its other attractions include a collection of beautifully costumed dolls.

Two miles beyond Luston bear righ[t] Ludlow) and keep straight on throug[h] village of Richards Castle. The pre-Con[quest] stronghold from which it took its name high on a hill a mile to the left of the near the medieval church. Wooded create a real 'border' atmosphere as the continues towards Ludlow, with Titter Clee Hill – its summit topped by the 'golf balls' of a radar station – domin[ates] views to the north-east. Turn left wit[h the] B4361 to complete the run to Ludlow.

Set on a steep hill above the River T[eme] Ludlow grew up under the protection great fortress, now an impressive ruin, was started towards the end of the century and became one of the most im[port]ant border strongholds. It was from L[udlow] Castle* that the young sons of Edward the famous 'Princes in the Tower' – set o[n] their ill-fated journey to the Tower of Lo[ndon] during the Wars of the Roses. Two cen[turies] later, the Great Hall was the setting fo[r the] first production of *Comus*, a masque writt[en by] John Milton while staying at the castle. ruins now provide a superb setting for air plays at the two-week Ludlow Fes[tival] held every summer. The festival also inc[ludes] concerts in the impressive parish ch[urch] whose tower gracefully dominates the The church is the burial place of Housman, the 'Shropshire Lad' poet.

LUDLOW TO LLANFAIR CAEREINIO[N]

Signs for the A49 and Shrewsbury tak[e the] route out of Ludlow and along the val[ley of] the River Onny. Cross the river at On[ibury] and continue to Stokesay, whose pictur[esque] 'castle',* off the main road to the left, is a fortified manor house. The oldest part from the 12th century, and there ar[e no] better examples of this type of bui[lding] anywhere in Britain. The nearby churc[h] dates from the 12th century, but was damaged during a Civil War skirmi[sh in] 1646. Rebuilt in 1654, the church has q[uaint] box pews and even quainter canopied p[ews in] the chancel. The religious texts painte[d on] the walls date from the same period.

The great whale-back of the Long M[ynd] rising to 1695 feet, overlooks the route runs through Craven Arms and in 1¼ turns left on to the A489 (SP Newt[own]. Gliders launched from the top of the Mynd's steep western face can often be soaring high above the tranquil b[order] landscape as the road continues up the valley to Lydham. Here the route turns (SP Welshpool) and ¾ mile later veer[s] running along the valley of the Cam[lad to] Church Stoke. Turn right on to the A49[0 (SP] Welshpool) in Church Stoke and follo[w the] road through Chirbury. Three miles turn right (SP Welshpool) and drop into the Severn valley, crossing the rive[r and] then, 1 mile later, turning right for Wels[hpool] on to the A483.

One of the earliest fortified houses in England, Stokesay Castle is remarkably well preserved. The gabled and half-timbered gatehouse is a later addition, probably dating from the 16th century

POWIS CASTLE

After crossing the old Montgomery branch of the Shropshire Union Canal, the road passes a turning on the left which offers a detour to Powis Castle.* This great red sandstone fortress was spared by the Parliamentarians during the Civil War, and has some fine plasterwork and panelling dating from the late 16th century. Terraced gardens laid out in the 18th century complement the building to perfection, and magnificent woodlands lie between it and Welshpool.

The Shropshire Union Canal runs beside the A483 into Welshpool. The town has played its part in the turbulent past of these border lands, and exhibits relating to its history are preserved in the Powysland Museum.* Most buildings in Welshpool are Georgian, but some older half-timbered ones survive, as well as the splendid Victorian railway station.

At the traffic lights in the centre of Welshpool turn left on to the A458 (SP Dolgellau) and in ½ mile, at the roundabout by the new Welshpool and Llanfair Light Railway terminus, take the first exit. The A458 follows the course of the narrow-gauge railway line, opened in 1903 but never a great commercial success. It closed in 1956, but has been restored by enthusiastic amateurs and is now a popular tourist attraction. The headquarters of the line* can be seen on the left as the road skirts Llanfair Caereinion.

A return to the age of steam with the French-built locomotive 'Sir Drefaldwyn' on the Welshpool and Llanfair Light Railway

LLANFAIR CAEREINION TO MAENTWROG

The A458 turns left, 1½ miles beyond Llanfair Caereinion, to cross the Afon Banwy. High hills overlook the route as it runs on along the Banwy valley into the wild heart of Wales and enters the county of Gwynedd and the Snowdonia National Park 7 miles beyond Llangadfan. The scenery becomes increasingly splendid as the road drops to the tiny village of Mallwyd, where you turn right on to the A470 (SP Dolgellau) by the Brigands' Inn. The name recalls the notorious Red Brigands of Mawddwy, who terrorized the area for many years in the 16th century before being hunted down after killing a judge. A bow-drawing brigand is the symbol of the Meirion woollen mill, just over 1 mile beyond the inn on the left, where traditional Celtic cloths are made. The road skirts the southern foothills of the Arans, the highest peaks in Britain south of Snowdon, and climbs steeply to almost 1200 feet before plunging down to Dolgellau, with views of the great mass of Cader Idris ahead and to the left.

Dolgellau's position on the Afon Wnion, in the midst of some of the most dramatic scenery in Wales, accounts for its popularity as a hiking and touring centre. Quaint, twisting streets packed with stout granite houses lead up from the river, which is spanned by an old seven-arched bridge. The town can be a busy place at peak times, though the new bypass will keep through traffic out of the centre.

Follow the A470 (SP Porthmadog) beyond Dolgellau, soon swinging northwards up the

The Meirion Mill is among Gwynedd's newer woollen mills, but the industry itself is more than 1000 years old

dramatic valleys carved by the Mawddach and its fast-flowing tributary, the Eden. Waterfalls race through the trees of Coed-y-Brenin – 'The King's Forest' – where gold mines were worked from Roman times until shortly before the Second World War.

COED-Y-BRENIN VISITOR CENTRE
Two miles beyond Ganllwyd a short, signposted detour to the left leads to a Forestry Commission visitor centre in the heart of the dense woodlands, while a little further along on the right is a picnic site and a forest trail.

The road suddenly emerges from the forest into a wild landscape of scattered boulders and stunted trees with the Rhinog peaks rising to the left. It soon skirts Trawsfynydd village notable for its statue of Humphrey Evans. Hedd Wyn, to give him bardic name, was a shepherd-poet who the coveted 'chair' at the National Eisted in 1917, but he had been killed in action a Battle of the Somme a few days ear Beyond Trawsfynydd, a large nuclear po station on the left makes a stark and expected landmark. Keeping forward to the A487, the route sweeps down into lovely Vale of Ffestiniog at Maentwrog.

MAENTWROG TO CAERNARFON

Still following signs for Porthmadog, cros river, then turn right on to the B4410 Rhyd) by the Oakley Arms Hotel. The r climbs steeply through trees and rhodo drons, passing a small lake before going u the narrow-gauge track of the Festi Railway. Past Rhyd, the route begins its l winding descent to the flat, reclaimed l surrounding the lower Afon Glaslyn. T right on reaching the A4085 (SP Caernar in Garreg. This village has an eye-catc war memorial designed by Sir Clc Williams Ellis, the architect best knowr the Italianate village of Portmeirion, 3 r to the south-west.

Scenery of increasing splendour takes route to the deep and wooded Pas Aberglaslyn, where it turns right on to A498 (SP Beddgelert). The track of the sh lived Welsh Highland Railway can be see the far bank of the rushing river. Beddg nestles in a majestic ring of high, crag-top

Spectacular views in the heart of the Snowdonia National Park are one of the highlights of the route around Beddgelert

mountains and takes its name from Gelert, a faithful hound said to have been slain by his master, Llewelyn the Great, who mistakenly thought the beast had killed his baby son. The tale was actually invented by a 19th-century innkeeper with a keen sense of publicity. He was also responsible for the 'grave' of the dog, which stands in a field south of the village.

Cross the bridge in Beddgelert and turn left (**SP Caernarfon**). The A4085 skirts the southern slopes of the Snowdon massif and soon passes the Beddgelert Forest. A Forestry Commission picnic area, clearly signed to the left, is also the starting point for three waymarked walks through the woodlands. The little village of Rhyd-Ddu, 1 mile further on, is the starting point for one of the most

popular walks to the summit of Snowdon. It involves a round trip of about eight miles and takes the average walker some five hours to complete. Beyond, the impressive bulk of 2290-foot-high Mynydd Mawr towers above the placid waters of Llyn Cwellyn as the road passes the Snowdon Ranger youth hostel. This is the departure point for another well-trodden route up Snowdon.

Beyond the village of Waunfawr, where derelict slate workings can be seen on the slopes to the right, there are views over the Menai Strait to Anglesey as the route drops down to Caernarfon. The road passes the excavated remains of *Segontium* – a settlement founded by the Romans around AD 78 – before continuing into the town centre.

CAERNARFON

Like Conwy, 25 miles away, Caernarfon boasts the almost miraculously well-preserved defences of a classic medieval fortress-borough. The castle* escaped destruction by the troops of Owain Glyndwr in 1401 and demolition by order of Parliament in 1660, and is now the biggest single tourist attraction in Wales and one of the finest castles in Britain. To the north and east, the 13th-century town walls embrace a network of narrow streets that conceal antique shops and ancient taverns.

In the square at the castle's feet stands a fine statue of First World War prime minister David Lloyd George, who was MP for the Caernarfon constituency for 54 years until he retired and became the first Earl of Dwyfor in 1944.

Right: Sir William Orpen's portrait of Lloyd George

Below: The Afon Seiont and the Menai Strait form a fine natural moat round two sides of Caernarfon Castle

ROUTE 5

London to Tenby

A kaleidoscope of scenery, several great rivers, and an exciting cross-section of Britain's architectural heritage are the outstanding visual features of this alternative route from London to one of the most attractive seaside resorts in Wales.

The route slips through the mesh of suburbs and dormitory towns that surround London to emerge into the green landscapes of the Thames valley beyond Windsor. Indeed, the Thames is the thread that links the first part of the journey westward. Broad and bright with boats at the start of the route, the river sweeps past elegant towns like Henley and Marlow, famed for their handsome bridges and appealing old buildings.

At Henley the route leaves the Thames for a while – to rejoin it at Wallingford – and cuts across the southern slopes of the Chilterns. This escarpment of beech-clad hills forms the central part of a great wedge of chalk which stretches all the way from the Dorset coast to East Anglia. Beyond Wallingford the route

heads into southern Oxfordshire and the Cotswolds, pass two striking and very different monuments to man's build and engineering skills: the first is the power station at Did whose great cooling towers are one of the Thames valley's c landmarks; the second is the magnificent tithe barn at G Coxwell, built of the honey-coloured stone that typi Cotswold architecture. For many miles the route pa through towns and villages that are composed almost enti of this enduring and delightful material.

The Thames is encountered once more at Lechlade, whe is already a swift-flowing little river, having emerged from quiet source south of Cirencester and wandered eastwa through meadows and tiny villages to be gradually enlarged other streams and rivulets.

A long stretch of Roman road (now the A417) carries route from Cirencester to Birdlip, where the road plumm

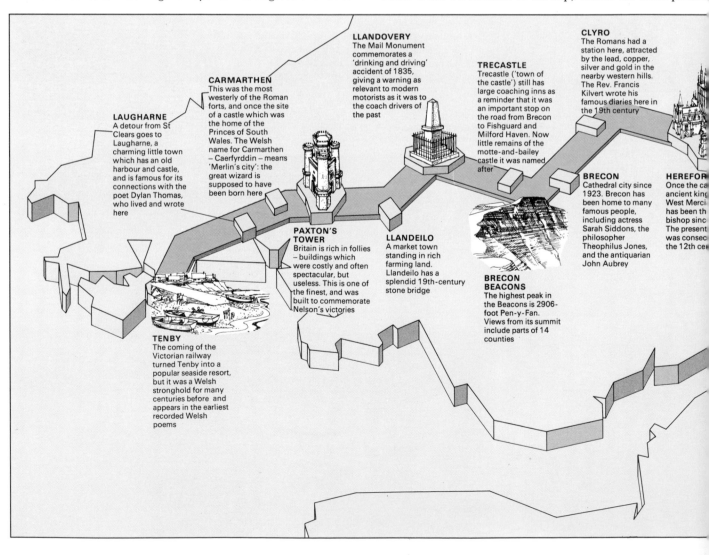

LLANDOVERY
The Mail Monument commemorates a 'drinking and driving' accident of 1835, giving a warning as relevant to modern motorists as it was to the coach drivers of the past

CARMARTHEN
This was the most westerly of the Roman forts, and once the site of a castle which was the home of the Princes of South Wales. The Welsh name for Carmarthen – Caerfyrddin – means 'Merlin's city': the great wizard is supposed to have been born here

LAUGHARNE
A detour from St Clears goes to Laugharne, a charming little town which has an old harbour and castle, and is famous for its connections with the poet Dylan Thomas, who lived and wrote here

PAXTON'S TOWER
Britain is rich in follies – buildings which were costly and often spectacular, but useless. This is one of the finest, and was built to commemorate Nelson's victories

LLANDEILO
A market town standing in rich farming land. Llandeilo has a splendid 19th-century stone bridge

TENBY
The coming of the Victorian railway turned Tenby into a popular seaside resort, but it was a Welsh stronghold for many centuries before and appears in the earliest recorded Welsh poems

TRECASTLE
Trecastle ('town of the castle') still has large coaching inns as a reminder that it was an important stop on the road from Brecon to Fishguard and Milford Haven. Now little remains of the motte-and-bailey castle it was named after

BRECON BEACONS
The highest peak in the Beacons is 2906-foot Pen-y-Fan. Views from its summit include parts of 14 counties

CLYRO
The Romans had a station here, attracted by the lead, copper, silver and gold in the nearby western hills. The Rev. Francis Kilvert wrote his famous diaries here in the 19th century

BRECON
Cathedral city since 1923. Brecon has been home to many famous people, including actress Sarah Siddons, the philosopher Theophilus Jones, and the antiquarian John Aubrey

HEREFOR
Once the ca ancient king West Merci has been th bishop sinc The present was consec the 12th ce

m the Cotswolds into Gloucester and affords stupendous
ws across the Severn plain to the Welsh border country.
rm stone gives way to striking black-and-white architec-
e, seen at its best on this route in Gloucester and Ledbury,
d the River Severn forms a natural frontier between England
d the Welsh Marches. Another great river, the Wye, is joined
Hereford, and both route and river curl round the Black
untains to cross the Welsh border just beyond Whitney.

Wales is a country of mountains and valleys; this is
matically illustrated as the route nears Brecon. To the south
e the astonishing peaks of the Brecon Beacons, the highest
untains in Britain south of Snowdonia, and to the north and
st are the steep, shadowy valleys that cut deep into the bleak
ss of Mynydd Eppynt.

Two more rivers accompany the route towards its desti-
ion. From Brecon to Trecastle the Usk is never far from the
d, and from Llandovery to Carmarthen the A40 follows the
le flood plain of the Tywi. This is a landscape of lush
adows, slate-roofed farms, and market towns whose modest
ses are often enlivened by washes of pastel colours. Around
nby the countryside becomes much flatter and less
matic, and somehow feels less Welsh. This is not entirely
sory, for much of southern Pembrokeshire was taken over
English and Flemish settlers during medieval times, and is
l sometimes referred to as 'Little England beyond Wales'.

PLACES OF INTEREST: OPENING DETAILS

Cookham
STANLEY SPENCER MEMORIAL GALLERY open Easter to Oct daily; Nov to Easter Sat and Sun

Didcot
GREAT WESTERN SOCIETY open Apr to Oct Sun and Bank Holiday Mon. Steam days first and last Sun each month and some Bank Holidays

Great Coxwell
TITHE BARN open all year

Buscot
BUSCOT PARK open Apr to end Sep Wed to Fri, also second and fourth Sat and following Sun in month, pm only

Gloucester
BISHOP HOOPER'S LODGING open all year Mon to Sat (except Bank Holidays)

Ashleworth
TITHE BARN open all year

Hereford
OLD HOUSE open all year Mon to Fri am and pm, Sat am, Sun pm (closed Sun Oct to Mar)

CHURCHILL GARDENS MUSEUM open all year, pm only

HEREFORD WATERWORKS MUSEUM, BROOMY HILL open Apr to Sep first Sun in month; also Sat and Sun during Jul and Aug, pm only

BULMERS RAILWAY CENTRE open Apr to end Sep, pm only

Swainshill
THE WEIR GARDENS open Apr to mid May daily (except Sat and Good Fri), pm only; and May to Oct Wed and Bank Holiday Mon, pm only

Brecon
BRECKNOCK MUSEUM open all year Mon to Sat

Abergwili
CARMARTHEN MUSEUM open all year Mon to Sat

Tenby
TENBY CASTLE open all year

TUDOR MERCHANT'S HOUSE open mid Apr to Sep Mon to Fri am and pm, Sun pm only

ST CATHERINE'S ISLAND open Whitsun to end Sep

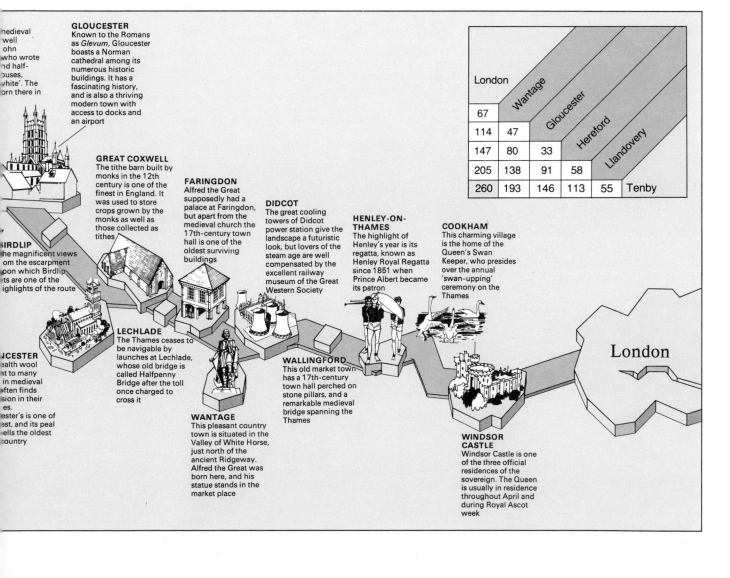

GLOUCESTER
Known to the Romans as *Glevum*, Gloucester boasts a Norman cathedral among its numerous historic buildings. It has a fascinating history, and is also a thriving modern town with access to docks and an airport

London	Wantage	Gloucester	Hereford	Llandovery	
67					
114	47				
147	80	33			
205	138	91	58		
260	193	146	113	55	Tenby

GREAT COXWELL
The tithe barn built by monks in the 12th century is one of the finest in England. It was used to store crops grown by the monks as well as those collected as tithes

FARINGDON
Alfred the Great supposedly had a palace at Faringdon, but apart from the medieval church the 17th-century town hall is one of the oldest surviving buildings

DIDCOT
The great cooling towers of Didcot power station give the landscape a futuristic look, but lovers of the steam age are well compensated by the excellent railway museum of the Great Western Society

HENLEY-ON-THAMES
The highlight of Henley's year is its regatta, known as Henley Royal Regatta since 1851 when Prince Albert became its patron

COOKHAM
This charming village is the home of the Queen's Swan Keeper, who presides over the annual 'swan-upping' ceremony on the Thames

IRDLIP
he magnificent views om the escarpment pon which Birdlip ts are one of the ighlights of the route

LECHLADE
The Thames ceases to be navigable by launches at Lechlade, whose old bridge is called Halfpenny Bridge after the toll once charged to cross it

CESTER
ealth wool t to many in medieval ften finds ion in their es. ester's is one of est, and its peal ells the oldest country

WANTAGE
This pleasant country town is situated in the Valley of White Horse, just north of the ancient Ridgeway. Alfred the Great was born here, and his statue stands in the market place

WALLINGFORD
This old market town has a 17th-century town hall perched on stone pillars, and a remarkable medieval bridge spanning the Thames

WINDSOR CASTLE
Windsor Castle is one of the three official residences of the sovereign. The Queen is usually in residence throughout April and during Royal Ascot week

London

nedieval well ohn who wrote nd half- uses, white'. The orn there in

LONDON TO MARLOW

To begin this route from the London area, make your way to Chiswick flyover, 6 miles west of central London on the A4 and the North and South Circular roads. Take the M4, crossing the Chiswick flyover and following the motorway as it crosses the Grand Union Canal and then falls to pass the lake-dappled acres of Osterley Park, a National Trust property on the left. There is always a chance of seeing Concorde among the jets thundering in and out of Heathrow, a mile south of junction 4, and soon views of Windsor Castle dominate the skyline to the left as the motorway skirts Slough.

Leave the M4 at junction 7 (SP Slough West, A4) and at the A4 roundabout turn left for Maidenhead. As the A4 crosses the Thames, you will see, to the left, one of Isambard Kingdom Brunel's enduring masterpieces – the bridge he built in 1838 to carry the Great Western Railway's line to Bristol. It features the widest and flattest brick arches in the world. Each of them spans 128 feet, and has a rise of only 24 feet. Immediately after crossing the river, turn right on to the A4094 (SP Cookham).

Running parallel to the river, the Cookham road soon passes Boulter's Lock, one of the many Thameside beauty spots immortalized in Jerome K. Jerome's hilarious book *Three Men in a Boat*. From the lock there are fine views up Cliveden Reach to the wooded grounds of Cliveden, one of the most

beautifully sited of all the National Trust's properties. The towers of the great 19th-century house can be seen above the trees as you cross open country before reaching picturesque Cookham, whose timber-framed buildings include an inn believed to date from the early 15th century.

Cookham was the birthplace of Sir Stanley Spencer (1891–1959) who featured the village in some of his paintings. Many of his works, together with other exhibits relating to his life, can be seen in the Memorial Gallery* on the corner of the High Street. His famous *Last Supper* hangs in the 12th-century church. Cookham is the home of Her Majesty's Swan Keeper. Dressed in splendid scarlet livery, he supervises the traditional 'swan-upping' ceremony in July, when cygnets on the Thames are marked to identify their owners. The ceremony is the subject of one of Spencer's best-known paintings.

The wooded Chiltern Hills roll gently northwards as the A4094 crosses the Thames and runs into Bourne End. Keep left to join the A4155 (SP Marlow), with huge, open fields sweeping away to the right as the road heads westwards once more. At the Marlow by-pass roundabout take the second exit to enter Marlow, one of the most attractive towns on the lower Thames. Its broad main street runs down to a delightful little suspension bridge. The poet Shelley lived in West Street with his wife Mary while she was writing *Frankenstein* in 1817–18.

A detail from Stanley Spencer's painting 'Christ Preaching at Cookham Regatta', one of the works in the Stanley Spencer Memorial Gallery in Cookham. The artist was born in the village in 1891

RLOW TO HARWELL

e A4155 (SP Henley) climbs gradually be-
d Marlow to run through Medmenham,
ose Dog and Badger pub is said to date
n 1390. Trees flank the road as it follows
river round to Henley-on-Thames. The
te turns right on to the A423 (SP Oxford)
he outskirts of the town, whilst a detour
the centre can be made by turning left.

HENLEY-ON-THAMES

he one-way system brings you into New
treet, passing Brakspear's famous and long-
stablished family brewery. Opposite stands
e Kenton Theatre of 1805, the fourth oldest
England. New Street runs down to the
hames, spanned by an 18th-century bridge
hose keystones are carved with figures of
ld Father Thames and the goddess Isis.
cross it stands the riverside boathouse of the
enley Rowing Club. Known as 'Leander',
e club was founded in 1839, the year of the
rst Henley Regatta. Now a world-famous
cial and sporting occasion, the regatta takes
ace during the first week of July.

*Bricks took four days to fire in temperatures as high as
950°C in Nettlebed's bottle-shaped brick kiln*

The Fair Mile, a long, straight road with
young trees along its broad verges, takes the
A423 away from Henley towards Nettlebed
Woods, where rhododendrons grow among
the trees, adding dashes of exotic colour in
early summer. Nettlebed itself has a tall,
beautifully restored brick kiln, the only
survival of a centuries-old industry in the
village. Shaped like a bottle, it was built
about 300 years ago and used until 1927.
Previous kilns at Nettlebed made 35,000 tiles
for the building of Wallingford Castle in the
14th century.

The road climbs to almost 670 feet at
Gangsdown Hill before sweeping down to the
Thames again at Wallingford. This old
market town is reached by a narrow medieval
bridge whose 19 arches span a total of 900
feet. The remains of Wallingford Castle,
demolished by order of Oliver Cromwell in
1652, can be seen on the western bank of the
river just above the bridge. Beside the road to
the left stands St Peter's Church, which has
an unusual and graceful openwork spire,
built in the late 18th century.

The town gained borough status in 1155
and has many attractive old buildings,
including the 17th-century town hall, where
paintings by Gainsborough and the original
town charter, granted by Henry II, may be
seen. Several 16th-century buildings are
survivors of the great fire that ravaged
Wallingford in 1675.

The A4130 (SP Didcot) takes the route out
of Wallingford towards the huge cooling
towers of Didcot power station. Didcot was a
sleepy little village until Brunel's broad-
gauge Great Western Railway arrived in
1841. Vivid memories of the GWR's history
are kept alive by the Didcot-based Great
Western Society. Its headquarters* are
situated behind the station – now used by
125-mph inter-city expresses. The old locomotive depot here houses many GWR relics,
including numerous engines. The oldest, built
in 1857, was in regular service until 1945.

Continue along the A4130 (SP Wantage)
and on the far side of Harwell turn right on
to the A417 (SP Wantage). Harwell is the
home of the Atomic Energy Research
Establishment, which stands in open country
to the south-west. The village stands amid
many acres of orchards, a delight in spring,
when the blossom is out. In summer some of
the produce is for sale, either on a 'pick-your-
own' basis or at roadside stalls.

*The immense cooling towers of Didcot power station, rising abruptly from the flat Thames valley, provide a striking contrast
with the orchards of nearby Harwell at blossom-time*

Henley's numerous buildings of special
chitectural and historical interest include
e 14th-century timbered Chantry House,
side the parish church, and Speaker's
ouse, which was the home of William
nthall, Speaker of the House of Commons
m 1629 until 1640. He was among those
ho signed Charles I's death warrant.

HARWELL TO CIRENCESTER

From Harwell the A417 continues to Wantage, overlooked by the Berkshire Downs. Here Alfred the Great was born in AD 849. In the square, surrounded by many Georgian buildings, stands an impressive statue of the Saxon warrior-statesman who drove the Danes from Wessex. His right hand rests on the handle of a huge battle-axe, while the left holds a scroll. (For Wantage see also p. 171.)

Follow the A417 (SP Faringdon) out of Wantage. Running north-westwards, it crosses the broad vale that takes its name from the great white horse that prehistoric men carved into the chalk downs 5 miles south-west of Stanford in the Vale. The road runs up to a T-junction overlooked by a wooded hillock on which stands the Folly, a 140-foot-high brick tower built by Lord Berner in 1935 to alleviate unemployment in the area. Turn left at this junction on to the A420 and in ½ mile turn right (SP Faringdon) and follow the A417 (SP Lechlade) through the town, just by-passing the centre. (For the centre of Faringdon see p. 170.)

GREAT COXWELL

Travellers with time to spare could make a brief detour to Great Coxwell, off the A420 (SP Swindon) to the south-west of Faringdon. It is a beautiful little village with thatched cottages, a 12th-century church and a magnificent stone tithe barn* built around 1250 by Cistercian monks. The tranquil atmosphere epitomizes the quiet charm of rural England, and has hardly changed in centuries.

The wooded acres of Buscot Park* roll away to the left of the A417 as the route continues towards Lechlade. The great house, built in 1780, stands among attractive Italianate water gardens. Spoilt by an over-zealous Victorian renovation, the house was carefully restored to its original state in the 1930s. Buscot's treasures include a remarkable series of paintings by Sir Edward Burne-Jones, the leading pre-Raphaelite artist. Just over a mile beyond the entrance to the park, Buscot Old Parsonage, built in 1703, makes an attractive landmark on the right.

Christ with St Mary Magdalen: a detail of Fairford's exquisite glass. The priceless windows were hidden away during the Civil War and the Second World War

The Thames, now only 15 miles from its source and not much more than a stream, is crossed for the last time just before the route enters Lechlade. Follow the A417 (SP Cirencester) through Lechlade, a pleasant little town with Georgian buildings of stone and mellow brick lining the streets, and overlooked by the elegant spire of the 15th-century church.

Between Lechlade and Cirencester lies Fairford, whose church is famous for its unique collection of 28 stained-glass windows dating from the 15th and 16th centuries. The first depicts the Garden of Eden while the last in the sequence, at the western end of the nave, portrays the Last Judgement with hideous demons claiming the souls of sinners.

Continue through Ampney St Peter and Ampney Crucis to the edge of Cirencester. At the by-pass roundabout, take the third exit for the A417 Gloucester road. Alternatively take the second exit (SP Town Centre) for a detour to this captivating country town, enriched over the centuries by Roman magnificence and by the prosperity brought by the medieval wool industry. (See p. 227.)

CIRENCESTER TO STAUNTON

The A417 from Cirencester to Gloucester follows a line plotted by Roman surveyors and marched by Roman legions. Perfectly straight for mile after mile, it spears north-westwards across the rolling Cotswold uplands, climbing to almost 1000 feet at Birdlip, on the edge of the escarpment. The road swings round to the right in the village and there are soon magnificent views to the left, over the broad Severn valley to the Malverns

*Air Balloon
near Birdlip,
called the Anne
n until the
, when one of
wfangled hot
lloons landed
y*

AIR BALLOON

the distant peaks of Wales. The A417
s hard left at the roundabout by the Air
oon pub, then swoops down to
cester, dropping almost 800 feet in little
e than two miles. Gloucester can easily be
assed but it is an attractive and interest-
place to explore, and on this route you are
mmended to go through the city centre.

riginally known as *Glevum*, Gloucester
established as a base for the Roman
sion of South Wales in the 1st century
Traces of the neat 'grid-iron' pattern
ured by Roman planners can still be seen
e heart of the ancient city, and the main
ts are still called Northgate, Eastgate,
hgate and Westgate. It is a fine place to
ore on foot, because many surprises await
walker. The façade of the 15th-century
Inn, in Northgate Street, conceals what
robably the finest open-galleried inn

courtyard in England, whilst the modern
frontage of a seed and bulb shop in Westgate
Street covers the timber-framing of the old
Judge's House, which was the garrison
commander's headquarters during the siege
of Gloucester in 1643.

Bishop Hooper's Lodging, a timber-
framed medieval building in Westgate Street,
contains a fascinating folk museum* whose
exhibits include such diverse things as an
1860 washing-machine, coracles, a complete
wheelwright's shop, and the city's great
South Gate, badly damaged during the Civil
War siege. Also preserved is the base of the
stake at which Bishop John Hooper was
burned to death in 1555 when Queen
'Bloody' Mary was persecuting the Protes-
tant clergy. A statue in St Mary's Square,
west of the magnificent and graceful
cathedral, marks the spot where Hooper died
for his faith. (For Gloucester see also p. 184.)

Leave the centre of Gloucester on the A40
(SP Ross) and in 1 mile turn right (SP
Ledbury) to rejoin the A417.

ASHLEWORTH QUAY

At Hartpury a detour can be made by turning
right on to an unclassified road to
Ashleworth. Ashleworth Quay, beyond
Ashleworth village, is a peaceful spot on the
banks of the Severn where a fine old house, a
small church, a 15th-century National Trust
tithe barn* and a tiny pub look over the river
to the tree-topped slopes of Sandhurst Hill.

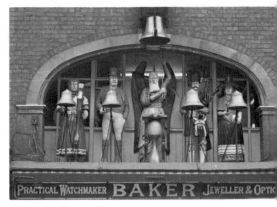

*Bell-ringing figures of Old Father Time and four
characters symbolizing Wales, Scotland, England and
Ireland stand in an alcove above one of the shops in
Southgate Street, Gloucester*

The main route continues along the A417,
turning left in Staunton, 3 miles past
Hartpury. As the road nears the M50 there
are views straight ahead to the great steep-
sided ridge of the Malvern Hills. Although
their highest point is only 1394 feet – little
more than an undulation by Welsh and
Scottish standards – the Malverns tower
above the surrounding countryside with all
the grandeur of mountains. A lofty obelisk on
high ground to the left of the range is a
notable man-made addition to the landscape.
Erected in 1812, it is 90 feet high and stands in
the grounds of Eastnor Castle.

mous views open up over the Vale of Gloucester and the National Trust property of Crickley Hill as the route snakes down the Cotswold edge near Birdlip

LEDBURY TO HEREFORD

Having crossed the M50, follow the A417 to the delightful old town of Ledbury, birthplace of John Masefield (1878–1967), who became Poet Laureate. The Feathers Hotel is among the most attractive of the long main street's many eye-catching buildings. A few yards away stands St Katharine's Hospital, founded in 1232 by Hugh Foliot, Bishop of Hereford, for 'wayfarers and the poor'. The timber-framed market house, built in the 17th century, still has sternly worded notices, more than 150 years old, that warn people not to disturb the business of the corn market. Ledbury's greatest treasure is Church Lane, a narrow, cobbled and traffic-free street that runs between medieval buildings to the 13th-century church.

Follow the main road through Ledbury, then turn left on to the A438 (SP Hereford) just before the railway bridge on the far side of the town. Hop-fields and a few old oast-houses flank the road as it runs westwards through rich farming country and crosses a medieval bridge over the River Lugg at Lugwardine, close to the outskirts of Hereford. The 'wardine' part of the village's name is not uncommon on the Welsh border and is the Anglo-Saxon term for an enclosed farmstead.

The building of an inner ring road for through traffic has enabled the centre of Hereford to regain a good deal of atmosphere. Some of the streets have been made into pedestrian precincts, and one of them, Church Street, leads from the main shopping area to the great cathedral,

Overlooked by the massive sandstone tower of the cathedral, the Wye at Hereford is spanned by a 15th-century bridge

...ord Cathedral's chained library contains nearly 1500 ...es, and is the largest of its kind in the world. Seventy ...books were printed before 1500, including two printed ...illiam Caxton

...h has watched over the city since the 12th ...ury. Hereford's importance as a religious ...re goes back to the Saxon era, however, ...the city had a bishop in the 7th century. ...sures to be seen inside the cathedral ...de the remarkable Mappa Mundi – a ...of the world drawn around 1290 – and ...Stephen's chair, said to be the oldest ...in England. Some of the books in the ...ed library are older still; they include ...Anglo-Saxon Gospels, written in Latin ...e 9th century. Each book is attached by ...in to rods on the bookcases.

...est of the cathedral is Castle Green, a ...eful park with extensive views of the ... The bridge a few hundred yards ...ream dates from 1490, and one of its ...es was broken by Hereford's defenders ...the city was attacked by a Scottish army ...645, during the Civil War. One of the ...s most attractive buildings is the Old ...se,* at the junction of High Town and St ...n's Street. A plaque in Gwynne Street ...rds the birthplace of Nell Gwynne, whose ...dson became Bishop of Hereford.

...e city has several museums and art ...ries, among them the Churchill Gardens ...eum* on Aylestone Hill. A traditional ...fordshire cider mill stands in the ...nds, and there are panoramic views over ...ity and surrounding countryside. Lovers ...team-power are catered for at the ...fordshire Waterworks Museum* at ...my Hill on the town's western outskirts, ...at the Bulmers Railway Centre* where ...world's largest producers of cider have ...al immaculate locomotives.

HEREFORD TO TRECASTLE

Leave the city on the A438 (SP Brecon), which runs along the broad valley of the meandering Wye, with isolated hills to the north and a long, wooded ridge rising steeply beyond the far bank of the river. The Weir Gardens,* 5 miles beyond Hereford on the left, are a National Trust property on the edge of the Wye, offering enchanting views of the surrounding landscape. Nine miles later, approaching Willersley, turn left, still on the A438 (SP Brecon) and enter Wales 1¾ miles beyond Whitney. The scenery suddenly becomes much wilder and more dramatic, with the Black Mountains and Brecon Beacons rising impressively on the opposite side of the valley.

Four miles beyond Whitney is Clyro, a pleasant little village backed by high, rolling hills, and famous for its links with the Rev. Francis Kilvert. He was the local curate from 1865 until 1872, and wrote diaries which vividly evoked rural life on the Welsh border in Victorian times. They were turned into a highly praised television series in the late 1970s. There is a memorial to Kilvert in the church. He is also commemorated by a plaque on his home, Ashbrook House, which stands beside a stream opposite the Baskerville Arms. Clyro Court, south of the village, was the Baskerville family home for many years and was visited by Sir Arthur Conan Doyle.

The A438 crosses the Wye at the edge of Glasbury, then swings right and leaves the river behind as it heads for Bronllys. One-and-a-half miles beyond Bronllys keep forward to join the A470, entering the Brecon Beacons National Park a few miles later.

BRECON

To see Brecon, you will need to turn right off the by-pass for the town centre. Clustered round the confluence of the rivers Honddu and Usk, Brecon is an old-established market town with narrow streets and several character-packed buildings. The point where the rivers meet is overlooked by the remains of a Norman castle that was partially destroyed during the Civil War. Much of the damage was done by the people of Brecon, who did not want it to become a stronghold for either Royalists or Parliamentarians.

The Brecon Beacons dominate the view to the south, and a model showing their geological structure is one of many exhibits in the Brecknock Museum.* It is housed in the former County Hall, a Victorian building inspired by the temples of ancient Greece.

Decorated 'love spoons' like these examples in the Brecknock Museum were traditionally carved by young Welshmen for their sweethearts

The A40 (SP Llandovery) leaves Brecon and heads west up the Usk valley to Trecastle, where the tree-crowned motte of a Norman stronghold stands to the right of the road. (Route continues on p. 64.)

The hill-fort of Pen-y-Crug, north-west of Brecon, offers splendid views over the Brecon Beacons National Park. The Beacons are the highest mountains in Britain south of Snowdonia, soaring to 2906 feet at the top of Pen-y-Fan

THE BRECON BEACONS

VIVIDLY likened to the crest of an immense wave, petrified at the point of breaking, the Brecon Beacons tower majestically above the River Usk as it flows through Brecon town. They are the highest mountains in Britain south of the Snowdonia National Park and reach 2906 feet at the summit of Pen-y-Fan. Its neighbour, Corn Du, is only 43 feet lower. Pen-y-Fan is a magnificent viewpoint from which Cader Idris, the Malverns, Devon and Somerset can all be seen on a clear day.

Although they give their names to the 519-square-mile Brecon Beacons National Park, these 'table-topped' mountains form only the central part of an impressive chain. It runs right across the park from the Llandovery–Llandeilo road to the English border, almost 50 miles away. The northern boundary is marked by the valleys of the Usk, Llynfi and Wye, and the park's other boundary skirts the heads of the industrialized valleys of South Wales.

It is a landscape of magical contrasts and ever-changing moods. The steep-scarped mountains are wild moorland – the haunt of curlew, snipe, merlin, kestrel and buzzard – but wooded valleys cut deeply into their relatively gentle southern slopes. Thousands of acres of common land are roamed by sheep and ponies, but plump beef and dairy cattle graze the patchworked pastures of the lush Usk and Tywi valleys. Rushing rivers and several spectacular waterfalls contrast with the placid waters of Llangorse Lake and more than a dozen reservoirs.

The few small towns are rich in rural character and seem a world away from their counterparts beyond the mountains. They have memories of battles between the Welsh and the Norman invaders, of Owain Glyndwr's bid for Welsh independence at the start of the 15th century, and of the days when they were on the main stage-coach route between England and the Irish ferries.

The Romans reached this part of Wales and built a five-acre fort, known as Y Gaer, on the Usk between Brecon and Sennybridge. Their highways are now 'green roads' used by walkers and pony-trekkers whose leisurely progress enables them to appreciate the park's beauty and character to the full.

The great sandstone crest of the Brecon Beacons forms a dramatic backcloth to slate roofs of Brecon town

Much of Llanthony Priory now stands a beautiful ruin, but part is used as a parish church and the west range is still inha[bited]

STONE circles, burial chambers, hill-forts, Roman camps and medieval strongholds are scattered all over this part of Wales, but the park has two notably evocative ruins that should not be missed.

Carreg Cennen Castle, 3 miles south-east of Llandeilo, may lack the majesty of the great fortresses built by Edward I in North Wales, but the setting is superb and few castles can equal its atmosphere. Reached through a farmyard, the old stronghold stands on the brink of a dramatic 300-foot cliff looking down to the little Afon Cennen and across to the forbidding ridge of the aptly named Black Mountain. The castle that originally stood on this site was probably built by a Welsh prince called Rhys ap Gruffydd in the 12th century, but the present structure dates from the late 13th and early 14th centuries. It changed hands many times during the long struggle between the Welsh people and the Norman–English invaders, and in 1403 was captured for a while by Wales's last great nationalist leader, Owain Glyndwr. Its effective role was ended during the Wars of the Roses, when it was surrendered to the Yorkists, who partly demolished it so

Carreg Cennen Castle stands on a precipitous limestone cliff and is one of the most romantic ruins in Wales

that it could no longer be a refuge for those who 'lived by robbery and the spoiling of our people'. There is one great mystery about Carreg Cennen: it is the eerie cave that is situated at the end of a passage built into the side of the cliff and approached from the inner ward. Many theories have been put forward as to the possible use of the cave, including well, storehouse and hiding-place, but none of them is supported by hard fact and it is pleasant to speculate on other, less mundane possibilities.

Natural sculpture in Dan-yr-Ogof Caves

Scwd-yr-Eira Falls on the Afon Hepste

ther gem is **Llanthony Priory,**
lovely Vale of Ewyas on the
eastern border between Hay-
ye and Abergavenny.
was founded in the early 11th
ry by a Norman knight called
m de Lacy who, while out
ng one day, was so taken by the
of the setting that he decided to
the rest of his days here as a
t. A religious order gradually
up, and the beautiful priory
h whose ruins can be seen today
uilt at the turn of the 12th
ry. Giraldus Cambrensis, a
-travelled Norman–Welsh cleric
hronicler, described Llanthony
place truly fitted for
mplation'. The resident monks
ess enthusiastic and likened the
people to wolves. The priory
osed by order of Henry VIII in
but there is a postscript to its
In the early 19th century the
y and its grounds were bought
poet Walter Savage Landor,
reamed of turning it into a
l estate. Despite considerable
on his part the plans came to
ng and he eventually moved
d, from where he wrote these
about Llanthony:

thee by the streams of yore,
ant streams I love thee more.

Llangorse Lake, five miles east of
Brecon, has a shoreline nearly four
miles long and is the largest natural
lake in South Wales. In recent years it
has become a popular water sports
venue, but its reed-fringed banks still
shelter a tremendous variety of
wildlife. A dug-out canoe was found in
the lake in 1925 and is preserved in
Brecon's Brecknock Museum.
Although it is of a type used since
prehistoric times, the canoe has been
dated to the 8th century and was
probably used by a fisherman

THE belt of limestone near the
national park's southern border is
riddled with caves which form a
secret world hidden far beneath the
mountains. The greatest of them all is
Ogof Ffynnon Ddu – Cave of the
Black Spring – near Abercraf. It is
the deepest and longest cave system
in Britain, extending over more than
20 miles and reaching a point 850 feet
below its entrance. Another notable
cave is Agen Allwedd, with more
than nine miles of passages below
Craig Cilau, south-west of
Crickhowell. A roadside parking area
overlooks dramatic Porth-yr-Ogof as
it swallows the Afon Mellte
downstream from Ystradfellte.

The exploration of such caves
should be left to experts, but more
than a mile of the beautiful Dan-yr-
Ogof show caves near Abercraf are
open to visitors. They were originally
explored by coracle in 1912.

The southern part of the park also
has some superb waterfalls, notably in
the valleys below Porth-yr-Ogof. The
loveliest of them all, reached by a
two-mile walk, is Scwd-yr-Eira on the
Afon Hepste. The 90-foot-high
Henrhyd Fall, three miles from Seven
Sisters, is a reminder of what the
valleys of South Wales were like
before the Industrial Revolution.

TRECASTLE TO CARMARTHEN

Six miles beyond Trecastle, in the deep and wooded gorge of the Afon Gwydderig, the road passes a small monument 'erected as a caution to mail-coach drivers to keep from intoxication'. It was raised after an accident in 1835, when the drunken driver of the Gloucester–Carmarthen stage plunged off the road, having suddenly encountered a cart while 'going at a full speed or gallop'.

The A40 follows the Afon Gwydderig into Llandovery, where the river meets two others, the Afon Bran and the Afon Tywi – hence the name of Llandovery, which means 'church amid the waters'. The ruined keep of its medieval castle overlooks the livestock market, which has played a key role in local life for many generations. The town certainly dates back at least to Roman times, for its church stands within the ramparts of a Roman fort, to the north-east.

The A40 (SP Llandeilo) swings hard left just beyond the town, crosses the Tywi and runs towards Llandeilo through the rich dairy pastures that flank the river, the longest in Wales. The A40 changes direction again in Llandeilo, another attractive little market town where the Tywi is spanned by a fine 19th-century bridge. Inside the church are parts of two Celtic crosses. Turn right (SP Carmarthen) to skirt the private grounds of Dynevor (or, more correctly, Dinefwr) Castle, home of a family whose ancestors were rulers of South Wales in the Middle Ages.

The road continues above the Tywi towards Carmarthen, and is overlooked from the south by Paxton's Tower. Its builder, Sir William Paxton, was a Scot who bought a large estate near Carmarthen after making a fortune in India, where he was Master of the

A detail from a stone frieze in the Carmarthen Museum, part of an elaborate memorial to Sir Thomas Picton

Calcutta Mint. In 1802 he stood as the Whig candidate for Carmarthen, failing to win the seat despite spending vast sums of money on such things as 11,070 breakfasts and 39,901 dinners, more than 20,000 bottles of wines and spirits, and 25,275 gallons of beer!

Abergwili, 13 miles beyond Llandeilo and 2 miles from Carmarthen, is the site of the Carmarthen Museum.* Housed in the former palace of the bishops of St Davids, the excellent and wide-ranging collection includes a Roman-period gold necklace and pendant, huge gravestones from the dawn of the Christian era, Victorian clothes and part of a stone frieze depicting the death of a local hero, General Sir Thomas Picton, at the Battle of Waterloo. The frieze spent more than a century in the garden of a cottage near Carmarthen.

Founded by the Romans to command the upper tidal reaches of the Tywi, and known to them as *Moridunum*, Carmarthen became a flourishing port from which local goods, including gold from the Dolaucothi mines, were shipped to Europe. Trading links with the sea ended shortly before the Second World War, but the town's mayor still holds

Set in a commanding position overlooking the Tywi valley, Paxton's Tower was built in the 19th century by a flamboyant and wealthy Scotsman to commemorate Nelson's victories

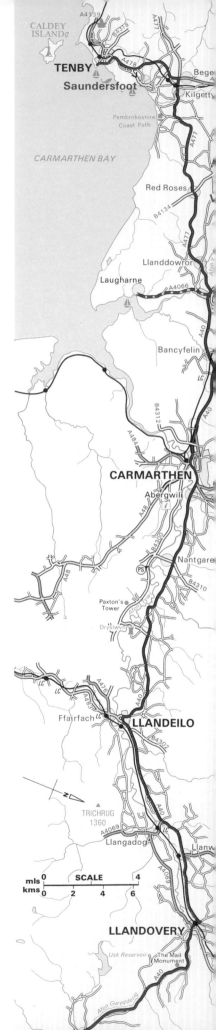

...tle of Admiral of the Port. Like the ...ns, the Normans who conquered south-...Wales at the end of the 11th century ...ciated the strategic importance of ...arthen, and founded a castle on a hill ...oking the river. Its gatehouse, together ...a short section of wall, still stands in a ... of Nott Square. Other buildings of ...st in the town include the excavated ...ns of the Roman amphitheatre, and the ...h of St Peter is well worth a visit.

...ARTHEN TO TENBY

... Carmarthen on the A40 (SP St ...), and at the roundabout on the St ... by-pass take the first exit on to the ... for Tenby.

LAUGHARNE

...n St Clears a detour may be made along ... A4066 to Laugharne (pronounced ...n'), 4 miles away on the Taf estuary. The ... town has a 13th-century castle, but is ...fly famed for its connections with the poet ...an Thomas. He first moved here in 1938, ... not until 1949 did he move to his best-...wn home, the Boat House, built on stilts ...e end of a path now called Dylan's Walk. ...as in Laugharne that much of his best ...k, including *Under Milk Wood*, was written ...d in the pubs here that he indulged the ... of drinking which contributed to his ...ic death in 1953 at the age ...9. He died in New York, ...is buried in Laugharne ...rchyard.

...Taf estuary, Laugharne. ...he left, the Boat House, ... of Dylan Thomas

...A477 for Tenby runs through a land-... of low but steep and wooded hills, ...al of this part of Wales, before turning ...n to the A478 (SP Tenby) at the ...dabout just beyond Kilgetty. Hills sud-... give way to views over Carmarthen Bay ... route continues to its destination.

TENBY

The ancient heart of Tenby – already a Welsh stronghold long before the Norman Conquest – was for centuries protected by sturdy walls, built over 600 years ago and still standing. The five-arched main gate in South Parade is remarkably well preserved, though the 13th-century castle* is now in ruins.

Below the castle is the picturesque little harbour. Tenby was a busy local port from the Middle Ages, and to this period of prosperity belongs St Mary's Church, the largest medieval parish church in Wales. One of Tenby's most delightful buildings is the Tudor Merchant's House.* Situated in Quay Hill, a narrow street which runs down to the harbour, the 15th-century building belongs to the National Trust.

No longer alive with the bustle of coastal traders, Tenby's harbour is now geared to the demands of the holidaymaker. Among the attractions are sailing and sea-fishing, and there are boat trips out past St Catherine's Island,* with its Victorian fort – now a small zoo – to Caldy Island, where there is a Cistercian monastery. The monks farm the island and make perfume.

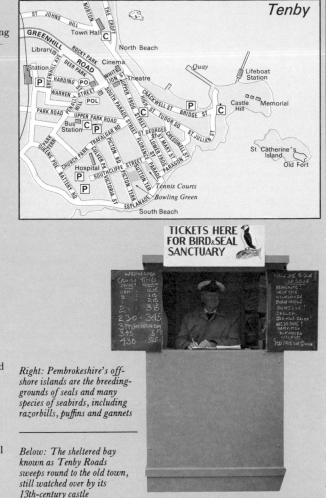

Right: Pembrokeshire's off-shore islands are the breeding-grounds of seals and many species of seabirds, including razorbills, puffins and gannets

---

Below: The sheltered bay known as Tenby Roads sweeps round to the old town, still watched over by its 13th-century castle

ROUTE 6

London to Bude

T HIS route makes use of a river, a motorway and a railway to chart a quiet and little-known course from the nation's capital into the West Country.

The river is the Thames, which from very early times has provided a natural route corridor westwards from London. But because the Thames valley is so winding, modern trunk roads have tended to avoid it, leaving it relatively quiet. The motorway is the M4, the building of which has meant that the old Great West Road, the A4, has been freed of the heaviest traffic. The railway is Brunel's main line to Exeter and Plymouth, which parts company with main roads at Hungerford and does not rejoin them until Taunton.

From London the route leads up the Thames valley, touching the river at Windsor, Maidenhead, Marlow and Henley. It then cuts across the southern tip of the Chilterns to Goring. The Thames crossing from Goring to Streatley has

been important since prehistoric times, for the river was ea ford at this point, and the ancient Icknield Way and Ridg paths converged here.

The route climbs steeply out of the Thames valley crosses a shoulder of the Berkshire Downs before descendi Newbury. Between Newbury and Hungerford the A4 along the Kennet valley, with both the river and the Ke and Avon Canal running near to the road. At Hungerfo leaves the A4, heading towards the Vale of Pewsey, a greer pleasant land between the Hampshire and Berkshire Dow is a natural through-route, and was first used as such by Rennie in the 18th century for his Kennet and Avon C and again, a century later, by Isambard Kingdom Brun his railway. The advent of the railways sounded the death for canals, but the peaceful towpaths and old locks o Kennet and Avon, left to decay for a number of years

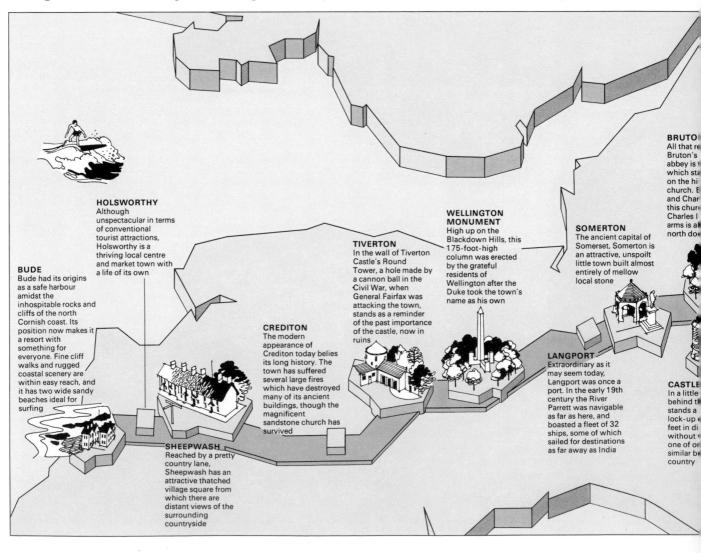

BUDE
Bude had its origins as a safe harbour amidst the inhospitable rocks and cliffs of the north Cornish coast. Its position now makes it a resort with something for everyone. Fine cliff walks and rugged coastal scenery are within easy reach, and it has two wide sandy beaches ideal for surfing

HOLSWORTHY
Although unspectacular in terms of conventional tourist attractions, Holsworthy is a thriving local centre and market town with a life of its own

SHEEPWASH
Reached by a pretty country lane, Sheepwash has an attractive thatched village square from which there are distant views of the surrounding countryside

CREDITON
The modern appearance of Crediton today belies its long history. The town has suffered several large fires which have destroyed many of its ancient buildings, though the magnificent sandstone church has survived

TIVERTON
In the wall of Tiverton Castle's Round Tower, a hole made by a cannon ball in the Civil War, when General Fairfax was attacking the town, stands as a reminder of the past importance of the castle, now in ruins

WELLINGTON MONUMENT
High up on the Blackdown Hills, this 175-foot-high column was erected by the grateful residents of Wellington after the Duke took the town's name as his own

LANGPORT
Extraordinary as it may seem today, Langport was once a port. In the early 19th century the River Parrett was navigable as far as here, and boasted a fleet of 32 ships, some of which sailed for destinations as far away as India

SOMERTON
The ancient capital of Somerset, Somerton is an attractive, unspoilt little town built almost entirely of mellow local stone

BRUTO
All that re Bruton's abbey is t which sta on the hi church. B and Char this churc Charles I arms is a north do

CASTLE
In a little behind th stands a lock-up feet in di without one of or similar b country

y being restored by a dedicated group of enthusiasts.
om Rushall to Westbury the route runs under the chalk
of Salisbury Plain. Then comes a belt of limestone that is a
ward extension of the Cotswold stones, jutting into which
e Mendips – composed of a much harder limestone. This
is so difficult to work that it is not often used for building,
when it is it takes on a distinctive lavender colour.
yond Castle Cary the route crosses the Polden Hills, whose
on the landscape is much greater than their modest
t would suggest; the sides are steep and the whole green
work of the Somerset Levels can be seen from the hilltops.
any of the buildings in this area are roofed in pantiles,
ly thought of as a feature of eastern England. At first they
imported from the Low Countries and distributed up the
r river valleys from Bridgwater, but from the 18th century
rds they were actually made in Bridgwater.
e hills are left behind for a while as the route skirts the
of Taunton, and then begin again in earnest with the
down Hills, from where on clear days there are views
the Bristol Channel to the distant Welsh mountains.
now on the route is in the heart of the West Country: mile
mile of tumbled hills, tiny towns and villages with, even
very few visitors compared to the north and south. In fact
Devon is probably the biggest area of unknown, unspoilt
tryside in England. From here any number of roads can be

taken to the coasts of north or south Devon, whilst the main route can be followed across the heaving clay lands of western Devon to Bude, with its surfing beaches, cliff walks and magnificent Atlantic seascapes.

PLACES OF INTEREST: OPENING DETAILS

Windsor
WINDSOR CASTLE open all year, but state apartments closed mid Mar to Apr. Castle is always subject to closure at short notice

GUILDHALL open Apr to Sep, pm only

Eton
ETON COLLEGE: SCHOOL YARD AND CLOISTERS open weekdays pm only, but am during school holidays. CHAPEL open daily pm only, but am in school holidays (closed Sun during school holidays)

Stonor
STONOR HOUSE AND PARK open Apr to end Sep Wed, Thu, Sun and Bank Holidays, pm only

Longleat
LONGLEAT HOUSE open all year

Nunney
NUNNEY CASTLE open all year

Castle Cary
MUSEUM open Apr to Oct daily (except Sun)

Tiverton
TIVERTON CASTLE open Easter then mid May to mid Sep daily (except Fri and Sat), pm only

TIVERTON MUSEUM open all year daily (except Sun and Bank Holidays)

Bickleigh
BICKLEIGH CASTLE open Easter to Sep Wed, Sun and Bank Holiday Mon; also Jul to first week in Sep daily (except Sat), pm only

BICKLEIGH MILL CRAFT CENTRE AND FARM open all year (except 25 Dec to 5 Jan). Jan to Mar pm only

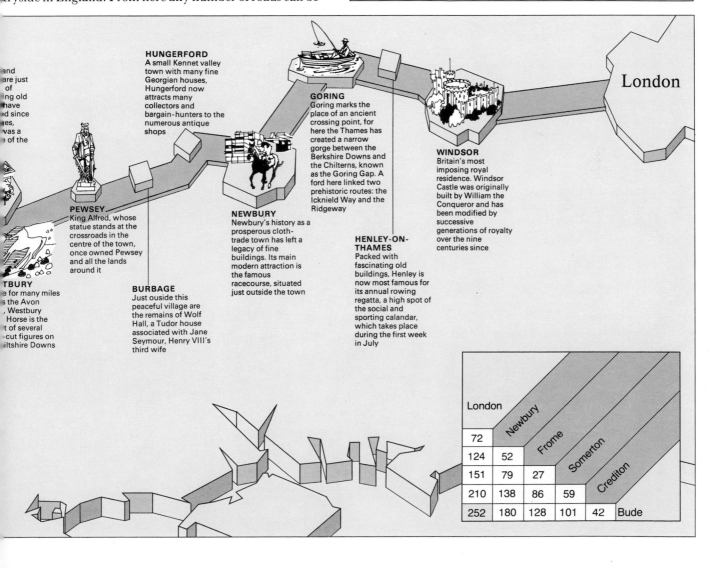

London					
72	Newbury				
124	52	Frome			
151	79	27	Somerton		
210	138	86	59	Crediton	
252	180	128	101	42	Bude

LONDON TO WINDSOR

The route starts at the roundabout beneath Chiswick flyover, 6 miles west of central London at the junction of the A4 and the North and South Circular roads. Follow the A4 (SP The South-West, Slough), passing the main entrance of Heathrow Airport after 7½ miles. At the next roundabout take the first exit, the A3044 (SP Staines), and shortly, at another roundabout, take the third exit, the B3378 (SP Colnbrook). At the Punch Bowl Inn in Poyle, turn left on to an unclassified road, and in ¾ mile, at the roundabout, take the third exit (SP Datchet), passing Wraysbury Reservoir on the left, then bearing left in Horton to pass the Queen Mother Reservoir on the right. The green, landscaped banks, often dotted with grazing sheep, give just a taste of the countryside: indeed, parts of this road might well be a real country lane many miles from London.

When you reach the B376 bear right for Datchet, where you take the B470 (SP Windsor), turning left over the level crossing, then right to drive alongside the Thames before crossing it to enter Windsor. To the left lies Home Park, part of the extensive grounds of Windsor Castle, while in the distance on the right is the 15th-century splendour of Eton College chapel. The main route turns right (SP Maidenhead, Riverside) on entering Windsor, avoiding the main tourist areas.

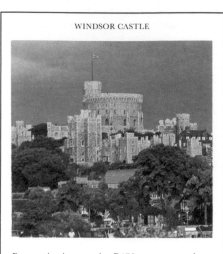

WINDSOR CASTLE

By continuing on the B470 you can make a detour, driving up the hill round the castle* and passing its entrance. The state apartments and the Queen's dolls' house are very popular with visitors, and St George's Chapel is famous for its exquisite fan-vaulting. The chapel contains the tombs of several monarchs, including Henry VIII and Charles I. Further along the High Street, on the left, stands Sir Christopher Wren's Guildhall* of 1689. A stroll down the hill and across the bridge over the Thames will bring you into the quaint streets of Eton, home of Britain's most famous public school.*

WINDSOR TO HENLEY

Leave Windsor on the A308 Maiden[head] road. After 4 miles pass underneath th[e] and immediately after it turn right on [the] B3028, a leafy lane which leads to the [pretty] village of Bray. Jesus Hospital, on the lef[t, a] delight: 17th-century almshouses and c[hapel] are charmingly set around a beautifully flower-filled garden.

Continue through Bray and out to[wards] Maidenhead, turning left on to the A[4,] following signs through Maidenhe[ad to] Marlow and the A308. Maidenhead is a[ ] return to suburbia, but soon the ro[ad is] winding through the edge of the Ch[iltern] beechwoods. At the roundabout 4 [miles] beyond Maidenhead, take the second ex[it for] Bisham, passing the National Sports C[entre] at Bisham Abbey on the left before [going] through the village with its attr[active] Georgian cottages and 12th-century chu[rch.]

Soon the route enters Marlow and c[rosses] the suspension bridge, overlooking a foa[ming] weir. Beside it is the Compleat Angler [Hotel,] famed for its connection with Izaak Wa[lton,] after whose classic book it is named[. Go] straight on up the main street and turn l[eft by] the Crown Inn (once the town hall) on [to the] A4155 (SP Henley).

The route runs through fine wo[oded] country above the Thames, passing thr[ough] the hamlet of Medmenham, which [ ]

The Thames at Marlow is spanned by an elegant Regency suspension bridge and overlooked by the graceful 19th-century spire of All Saints' Church

connections with Sir Francis Dashwood and the 'Hell Fire Club' – otherwise known as the 'merry monks of Medmenham'. Their notorious meetings took place in the former St Mary's Abbey, which stood on the river bank.

HAMBLEDEN

About 2 miles past Medmenham a detour may be made by turning right to Hambleden, a lovely brick-and-flint village nestling in the beechwoods. The large church is mainly 12th-century, and has a font thought to date back to Saxon times. At the centre of the village is the old pump, still in working order.

Following a great loop of the river, the route reaches the outskirts of Henley-on-Thames. Turn right as you enter the town on to the A423 (SP Oxford), though the town centre, richly endowed with historic buildings, is well worth a visit (see p. 57).

HENLEY TO NEWBURY

STONOR HOUSE AND PARK
Climbing into the Chilterns from Henley on the Oxford road, the route passes a turning on the right which offers a detour to Stonor House and Park,* 3 miles away. The estate has been in the same family for some 800 years, and the house incorporates some of the earliest domestic architecture in the county. It contains some very fine furnishings and works of art.

The road reaches its highest point past Nettlebed (see p. 57), then marvellous views open up as it descends towards the Thames again. At Crowmarsh Gifford, turn left on to the A4074 Reading road, and after 1 mile turn right on to the B4009 Goring road, which gives fine views stretching both ways along the Thames valley.

In Goring, turn right over the railway and go down into the village, crossing the river by the old mill. Behind it is the church, whose bell, dated 1290, is one of the oldest in England. To the right as you cross the river is Goring Lock, which serves a constant stream of river traffic in fine weather.

Across the river, and in Berkshire, lies Streatley, Goring's sister village. Lovers of fine cheese know it for Wells Stores (just to the left at the traffic lights), which stocks around 150 different kinds of cheese, specializing in English and French varieties.

The route carries straight on at the traffic lights, following the B4009 (SP Newbury), twisting and turning across the downs and through the sleepy thatched villages of Aldworth, Hampstead Norris and Hermitage to reach Newbury. At the large roundabout on the edge of the town, take the fourth exit, the A4 (SP Hungerford). (For the town centre see p. 171.)

Set on a most attractive stretch of the Thames, Goring Lock in summer is always busy with pleasure craft

NEWBURY TO WESTBURY

Now that the M4 carries most of the heavy traffic, the A4 is once again a pleasant, quiet country road, giving a clear run from Newbury along the Kennet valley to Hungerford. Here the route turns left by the Bear Hotel on to the A338 (SP Salisbury) and into the centre of Hungerford: a handsome, relaxed main street without a single jarring note. There are several fine Georgian town houses of limestone, although the limestone quarries are some 50 miles away. The stone was shipped here from Bath along the Kennet and Avon Canal, which runs beneath the bridge. A short stroll along the towpath leads past quaint old cottages to Hungerford Lock. Anglers are often to be seen along this stretch; Hungerford has been proud of its fishing ever since John of Gaunt granted the town fishing rights in the 14th century. Nowadays the antiques business flourishes in Hungerford: there are over 20 antique shops of all sizes and specializations, and an antique market too – worth stopping for a browse if time permits.

Follow the A338 out of Hungerford, weaving between the Berkshire and Hampshire Downs. East Grafton is a cheerful village with a green; 2 miles later, at the edge of Burbage, go straight on at the crossroads to join the B3087 for Pewsey.

Despite its small-town amenities – banks, varied shops and a railway station – Pewsey's charming streets of cottages clustered around the infant River Avon give it a distinctly

Hungerford's antique market is a treasure-trove of bygones, from bric-a-brac to exclusive collectors' pieces

village-like atmosphere. Turn left by the statue of King Alfred to leave Pewsey by the A345 (SP Upavon), and after 3 miles, at the roundabout by the Woodbridge Inn, go forward on to an unclassified road (SP Rushall). At the end of Rushall village turn right on to the A342 (SP Devizes), and 4½

miles later take a left turn to join the B[...] (SP Westbury).

This road skirts the village of Urch[...] where delightful cottages and a churc[...] grouped around the village pond. The [...] century manor house (now a colle[...] further education) was once owne[...] William Pitt the Elder, the 18th-ce[...] prime minister. The next village, East[...] features several elaborately timbered h[...] and ½ mile further on is the busy main str[...] Market Lavington. One mile past i[...] B3098 crosses the A360 and cont[...] through a chain of villages along the sp[...] line at the edge of Salisbury Plain. In [...] them, Edington, there is a startling sur[...] The parish church, just off the road t[...] right, has all the scale and ambition of a [...] cathedral. Unusually, it was built i[...] 1350s, the years of the Black Death, an[...] rare and interesting combination o[...] Decorated and Perpendicular styles. [...] reason for this unexpected display in a [...] Wiltshire village is that William of Edi[...] became Bishop of Winchester in 1345 [...] this magnificent church was part of a m[...] tery which he founded in the place whe[...] was born.

A mile past Edington the road [...] through the old village of Bratton, overl[...] by Bratton Castle, a large hill-fort d[...] from the Iron Age. The lane which lead[...] from Bratton is also signposted to Wes[...] White Horse, which can soon be seen fro[...]

The poet George Herbert was married in 1629 in Edington's priory church. The building is a unique masterpiece of medieval craftsmanship

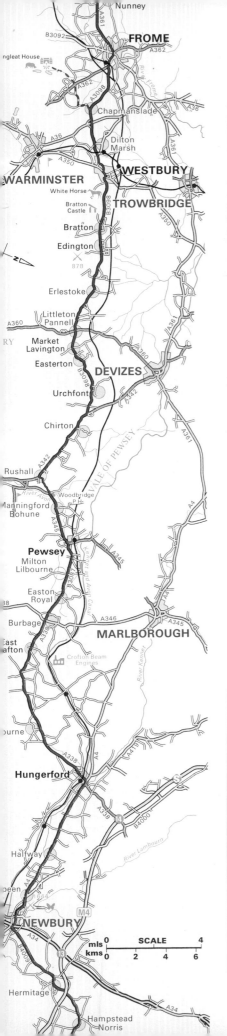

A lane in Bratton village leads up to the Westbury White Horse, cut into the chalk hillside in 1778

road if you look back towards Bratton. Set at the top of the scarp, the chalk figure displays all the elegance of the Georgian era in which it was cut – though a white horse is believed to have occupied this site since King Alfred's victory over the Danes nearby in AD 878.

Similarly Georgian is Westbury, with its little market square, stone-built classical town hall and small town houses. At the centre of the town, take the left fork on to the A350, and in $\frac{1}{4}$ mile turn right on to the A3098 (SP Frome).

WESTBURY TO FROME
As the route continues from Westbury, the feel of the West Country begins to take over as the Somerset border approaches and chalk downs give way to limestone country.

The A3098 runs on to Frome (pronounced 'Froom'), where the route turns right on to the A362 for the town centre. Frome's prosperity was at its height in the 18th century, and though it may now seem an unprepossessing place at first sight, it is full of unexpected small surprises and well worth exploring. The hillside on which the town stands makes an impressive setting for St John's Church, and the narrow alleyways around it provide glimpses of many attractive and tucked-away corners of this interesting town. Cheap Street, for example, has quaint overhanging houses and a central watercourse, and the Blue House almshouses by the bridge over the River Frome have an unusual stone façade carved with statues of charity figures. The building dates from 1726.

LONGLEAT
About 3 miles past Westbury, at Chapmanslade, a detour may be made by following signs along an unclassified road on the left to Longleat,* 4 miles away. The splendid early Renaissance house was completed in 1580 and occupies the site of an Augustinian priory. Robert Smythson was the master mason responsible for much of what can be seen today. The house contains a wealth of period furniture and works of art, displayed in rooms decorated with Italian marble, painted and gilded ceilings and marquetry doors. The Bishop Ken's Library is little altered since the 1690s, and contains a first edition collection of Shakespeare. The grounds, landscaped by Capability Brown, now include a well-known safari park, most famous for the 'Lions of Longleat'. The Marquess of Bath, owner of Longleat, pioneered the idea of safari parks and other family entertainments as a means of financing stately homes.

FROME TO SOMERTON

Leave Frome by the A361 Glastonbury road, and in 3¼ miles, by the Theobald Arms pub, bear left on to the A359 (SP Bruton, Yeovil).

NUNNEY

At this fork in the road a short detour may be made by turning right to Nunney, where there is a stout little 14th-century castle* whose moat is said to be the deepest in England. The notorious Judge Jeffreys is reputed to have held court at the George Inn.

Nunney Castle was begun in 1373 by Sir John de la Mare, whose effigy can be seen in the nearby village church. The castle's four imposing towers are surrounded by a moat believed to be the deepest in the country

Bruton, the next town along the A359, has the first of a grand succession of Perpendicular churches on this route. This one has the bonus of a Georgian chancel with pretty rococo plasterwork. A dovecot crowns the bare hill behind the church, as stark as Glastonbury Tor. Opposite the western entrance to the churchyard is Bow Bridge, a very old packhorse bridge barely three feet wide.

From Bruton continue along the A359 and in 3¾ miles turn right on to the A371 for Castle Cary, turning left 1 mile later for the town centre. Castle Cary is quite the opposite of Bruton – a handsome, no-nonsense place with a Victorian market hall, housing an interesting museum,* and a tiny windowless lock-up, built in 1779, in the square behind it. Follow signs for the B3152 and Shepton Mallet, heading north-west from the town centre, and in ¼ mile branch left on to an unclassified road (SP Somerton). After ½ mile turn right at the crossroads, then in ¾ mile left on to the B3153. This road follows the Brue valley, crossing the A37 and passing through Keinton Mandeville, birthplace of the famous actor-manager Sir Henry Irving.

The B3153 leads to Somerton, the ancient capital of Wessex and still one of the best small towns in the West Country. It is a real country town, with everything where it should be: market square complete with market cross, market hall, a fine church and handsome Georgian houses; everything old and nothing olde. Somerton was the birthplace of Ina, an ox-drover who became king of the West Saxons and was the first king to hold all southern England under one rule.

He was noted for his humanitarian laws his reign was cut short when, filled shame and despair at the outbreak of wa returned to his former peasant way o abandoning his kingdom.

SOMERTON TO HALBERTON

The B3153 continues from Somerto Langport. At the edge of the town forward at the crossroads on to the A372, in ½ mile bear left under the railway br following the A378 into the main s Langport grew up around a Saxon for the River Parrett – noted, incidentally, f eels. In the early 19th century, when the was navigable as far as Langport, the had a fleet of 32 ocean-going ships, so which travelled as far as India. Traces o old quays they used can still be seen. Langport see also p. 233.)

Continue towards Taunton on the A crossing the River Parrett and contin westwards to Curry Rivel, which has a l late medieval church, set at the end pleasant green. There is also a fascin basket shop, displaying many fine exam of this traditional Somerset craft, v locally grown willows. Turn left in the vi on to the B3168 (SP Hambridge, Ilmin Pleasant stone cottages see you out of C Rivel into rich agricultural land. through Hambridge and Puckington, re the River Isle and turn right on to unclassified road (SP Ilton, Chard, Tau by a white house called the Old Way C When you reach the A358, turn right Taunton, Ashill), then 2 miles beyond A turn left on to an unclassified road Fitzpaine, Bickenhall).

Somerton's 17th-century market cross forms part of a strikingly attractive townscape of local blue lias stone

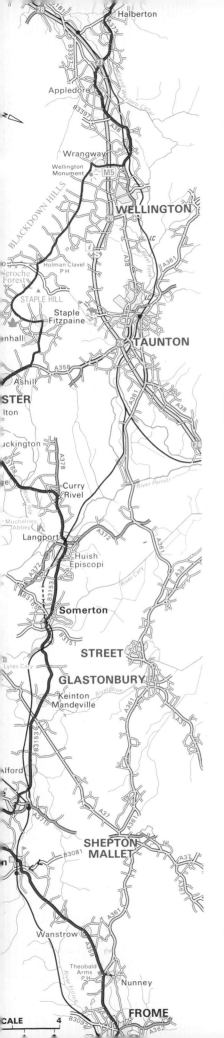

This winding lane leads to a T-junction, where you turn left for Staple Fitzpaine, whose church tower, amid a clump of chestnut trees, shows the way into the village. At the crossroads in Staple Fitzpaine, turn left (SP Combe St Nicholas, Chard), passing the church and a row of 17th-century cottages, with the manor house nearby. A mile beyond the village the road begins to climb through woodland into the Blackdown Hills, reaching a T-junction where the route turns right (SP Churchingford, Wellington), continuing to ascend to nearly 1000 feet close to the summit of Staple Hill. Cross the B3170 to enter Neroche Forest, and at the crossroads turn right past the Holman Clavel Inn.

Following signs for Wellington, the route runs through a stately avenue of beeches, turning the way into a great wooded hall. Rhododendrons grow in the hedgerow, and the banks are full of wild flowers in spring and summer. The road follows the top of the Blackdown Hills for several miles.

> ### WELLINGTON MONUMENT
> The best views are from the Wellington Monument, signposted along an unmetalled road to the right, and well worth the short detour. The tall stone monolith was erected by the people of Wellington in 1817 to commemorate the fact that the first duke took his title from their town. From here breathtaking views span 180 degrees northwards. Even parts of Exmoor can be seen on a clear day. A plaque beside the monument points the direction of various places that can be seen from here, and gives distances.

Dramatically situated on a spur of the Blackdown Hills, the Wellington Monument can be seen for many miles and commands panoramic views over much of Somerset

A mile past the monument turning, the route turns sharply right (SP Wrangway, Wellington), with more fine views as it leaves the hills and passes through the farming hamlet of Wrangway. Cross the M5 and keep forward at the crossroads, then in $\frac{1}{4}$ mile turn left on to the A38 (SP Exeter). Soon the route enters Devon, crossing the M5 again and coming to a large roundabout, where you take the second exit, the A373 (SP Tiverton, Barnstaple). The last village before Tiverton is Halberton, set in a loop of the Grand Western Canal. Inside the Perpendicular church is a complete rood screen, running right across nave and aisles.

HALBERTON TO CREDITON

From Halberton follow the A373 into Tiverton, which is worth a good deal of exploration. Again there is a show Perpendicular church; its Greenway Chapel is the most ornate of all, its exterior and that of the south porch richly carved. Some of the carvings show merchant ships such as were engaged in the medieval wool trade, for John Greenway, who built the chapel, was himself a wool merchant. St Blaise, patron saint of wool-combers, is among the saints to whom the chapel is dedicated. To the north of the church are the ruins of the castle,* which dates from 1106 and contains fine furniture and paintings as well as a clock collection. The museum,* too, is well worth a visit to see its varied local domestic, agricultural and transport exhibits. Tiverton traded in local stone and limestone, and the building of the Grand Western Canal in 1814 linked it with the lime-kilns near Lowdwells, some 11 miles away. This stretch of the canal has recently been restored and passengers can make the trip through rolling Devon countryside by horse-drawn barge.

Traffic in Tiverton is often slow-moving, but westwards from here to the coast are roads as open as any in England. The route from Tiverton is first a valley, then a hilltop journey to Crediton. Take the A396 Exeter road from Tiverton and after 4 miles, when you reach the Fisherman's Cot Hotel at Bickleigh Bridge, turn right on to the A3072 (SP Crediton).

BICKLEIGH MILL FARM AND CRAFT CENTRE
About a hundred yards across the bridge on the Exeter road is Bickleigh Mill Farm,* well worth a detour. An old farmstead at the edge of picturesque Bickleigh village has been preserved as a living museum of the agriculture and country life of bygone days. Nearby is Bickleigh Mill,* where the old mill machinery has been restored and a working craft centre established. Here visitors may see potters, spinners, weavers and other traditional craftsmen at work.

BICKLEIGH CASTLE
A few hundred yards from the bridge on the Crediton road, a second detour is possible by turning left for Bickleigh Castle.* The mighty sandstone gatehouse and the chapel, with its fine font, are Norman, and the other buildings mainly late Tudor. A particularly attractive feature is the 18th-century wrought-iron gate.

The A3072 leads to Crediton, where the route turns right on to the A377 (SP Barnstaple). Crediton was a bishopric before Exeter (from 909 to 1050) and the church, though much later, is huge and impressive; the clerestory windows are indeed on a cathedral scale. Crediton was the birthplace, in 680, of St Boniface, who converted large areas of Europe to Christianity, bringing unity to lands long divided by tribal feuds. He was for 300 years patron saint of England, and is still patron saint of Germany.

CREDITON TO BUDE

From Crediton travel west on the A3 Copplestone, where there is an old cro feet high, carved over 1000 years ago. over the railway and then bear left on t A3072. Four miles beyond Bow, cros infant River Taw and bear right Hatherleigh), continuing through the lightful thatched village of Sam Courtenay, nestling in a hollow. Jacobstowe bear right on to the B: following signs for the A386 and Hather a pleasant hillside town on the River The route turns left just before Hather on to the A3072 (SP Holsworthy).

SHEEPWASH
At Highampton it is worth turning right fo detour to Sheepwash, a peaceful and lit known Devon village with a delightful squa of thatched buildings and fine views over rolling countryside all around.

Follow the A3072 to Holsworthy. It is a idea to drive through the town centre the market place with its individual, idi cratic shops, and to enjoy the atmospher completely unspoilt West Country t Holsworthy is Saxon in origin, and its held every July, is a tradition dating fro 13th century. From Holsworthy the A (SP Bude) continues towards the Co border. The landscape is sterner and bl now, with the tower of Pancrasweek ch on a hill to the right in complete accord.

An ancient castle, a working water-mill, delightful old cottages and this five-arched medieval stone bridge all combine to make Bickleigh one of the most rewarding historic villages in

LAUNCELLS

Just north of the road on this last stretch between the Tamar and the coast is Launcells church, a typical Cornish delight, snug in its valley and full of richly carved medieval benches. At the east end are some fine 15th-century tiles.

The main road skirts Stratton, a nest of quaint, narrow streets leading up to the church. Turn left when you reach the A39 and, in less than ½ mile, right on to the A3072 to complete the journey.

Bude grew up as the only sheltered harbour on a long strip of exposed and windy coast where shipwrecks occurred all too frequently. But, unlike sailors of old, today's surfing enthusiasts thrive on such conditions, and Bude's copious sands and Atlantic rollers have made it one of the best surfing centres in Britain. The rugged cliffs around it, crossed by the Cornwall Coast Path, are fine walking country. The town itself has developed over the past century into a cheerful summer resort and a local centre with plenty of life of its own all the year round.

Long rollers sweep in from the Atlantic at Bude, creating ideal conditions for surfing. Undeterred by the English climate, many intrepid surfers now practise this most exhilarating and exacting of sports throughout the year

ROUTE 7   244 MILE

London to Plymouth

THIS alternative route strikes out of London in a southerly direction, takes a deep breath on Epsom Common and gets its first real taste of country air at Box Hill. The evergreen bush from which the hill takes its name is native to the chalk downs of southern England, but is now much more widespread, having proved to be an ideal hedging plant.

Next comes a series of picturesque Surrey villages called the Tillingbourne villages because they are all set on the little river of that name. Shere, with half-timbered buildings like 17th-century Old Prison House, is perhaps the most attractive, but all of them – Abinger Hammer, Gomshall and Albury – have something to please the eye and excite the imagination.

The route then takes the A3 through southern Surrey and into Hampshire just beyond the Devil's Punch Bowl – an extraordinary bite taken out of the greensand ridge. From Liphook to Petersfield the road runs through the quiet

woodlands that make up much of Hampshire and are so o overlooked by those eager to reach the well-known bea spots. Petersfield is an attractive old town with at least peculiar story attached to it: it is said that during the time o great plague every house on one side of the street was infe and shut, while the houses on the other side were entirely fr the disease.

The Meon valley, deep in the Hampshire chalk countr joined at West Meon. The valley is famous for its wild flo and its ancient churches – especially those at Warnford Corhampton. The route then cuts across the Itchen valle Eastleigh to reach the historic town of Romsey. A little lat dips into Wiltshire for a while, only to return to Hamps along the Avon valley, passing Breamore House, with its Sa church, beautiful old carriages and fascinating country museum, on the way.

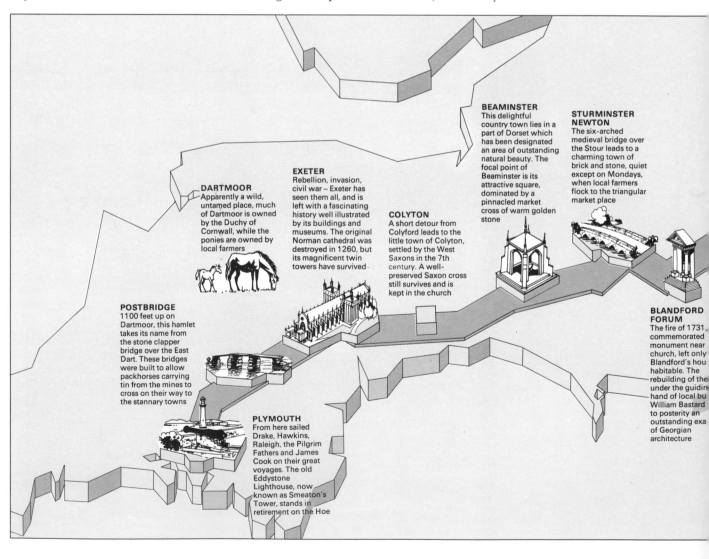

BEAMINSTER
This delightful country town lies in a part of Dorset which has been designated an area of outstanding natural beauty. The focal point of Beaminster is its attractive square, dominated by a pinnacled market cross of warm golden stone

STURMINSTER NEWTON
The six-arched medieval bridge over the Stour leads to a charming town of brick and stone, quiet except on Mondays, when local farmers flock to the triangular market place

DARTMOOR
Apparently a wild, untamed place, much of Dartmoor is owned by the Duchy of Cornwall, while the ponies are owned by local farmers

EXETER
Rebellion, invasion, civil war – Exeter has seen them all, and is left with a fascinating history well illustrated by its buildings and museums. The original Norman cathedral was destroyed in 1260, but its magnificent twin towers have survived.

COLYTON
A short detour from Colyford leads to the little town of Colyton, settled by the West Saxons in the 7th century. A well-preserved Saxon cross still survives and is kept in the church

BLANDFORD FORUM
The fire of 1731, commemorated monument near church, left only Blandford's hou habitable. The rebuilding of the under the guidin hand of local bu William Bastard to posterity an outstanding exa of Georgian architecture

POSTBRIDGE
1100 feet up on Dartmoor, this hamlet takes its name from the stone clapper bridge over the East Dart. These bridges were built to allow packhorses carrying tin from the mines to cross on their way to the stannary towns

PLYMOUTH
From here sailed Drake, Hawkins, Raleigh, the Pilgrim Fathers and James Cook on their great voyages. The old Eddystone Lighthouse, now known as Smeaton's Tower, stands in retirement on the Hoe

...om Fordingbridge leafy lanes lead to sleepy Cranborne,
... comes the wide, undulating road for Blandford Forum.
... landscape becomes much more open as the route skirts the
... spaces of the ancient royal hunting-ground of Cranborne
...se. Rich in prehistoric remains, the Chase became well
...wn in archaeological circles in the 19th century, when
...ral Pitt-Rivers conducted a series of excavations here on
...h much modern archaeological fieldwork is based.
...landford Forum, with its fine array of Georgian architec-
..., marks the half-way stage of this route and the beginning of
...West Country. It is also the beginning of Hardy country.
...y of the windswept hills and heaths and unspoilt villages
...g the route between Blandford and the coast are featured,
...n disguised by fictional names, in Thomas Hardy's novels.
...rom Blandford to Seaton the route leads along a succession
...uiet country lanes, from which, at field gates and hill
...mits, there are wide panoramas of hills and farms, with
...sional glimpses to the south of the blue sparkle that can
...r be the sea. The next large place is Exeter.
...urely one of the most frequently by-passed cities in the
...ntry, Exeter has an exceptionally rich historical tradition
...repays many hours of exploration. Apart from having one
...e finest cathedrals in England, it also has ancient buildings,
...rb museums and the biggest variety of shops in the West
...ntry. Beyond Exeter the route plunges off across Dartmoor.

It actually takes little more than an hour to cross the moor, but
its feeling of remoteness is more striking than almost anywhere
else in southern England.

Plymouth is set at the mouth of the River Tamar to the
south-west of the moor, and is one of the gateways to Cornwall.
It can also be said to be a gateway to the world, for from here
many explorers set out to discover lands that, only a few
hundred years ago, were considered to be either impossibly
remote or even mythical.

PLACES OF INTEREST: OPENING DETAILS

Godalming
BOROUGH MUSEUM
open all year Tue, Fri
and Sat, pm only

Bishop's Waltham
BISHOPS' PALACE
open all year, but
closed Mon (except
Bank Holidays) and
Sat

Romsey
BROADLANDS open
Apr to end Sep;
closed Mon except
Aug, Sep and Bank
Holidays

Breamore
BREAMORE HOUSE
AND MUSEUMS
open Apr to end Sep
Tue to Thu, Sat, Sun
and all Bank
Holidays, pm only

Cranborne
CRANBORNE
MANOR GARDENS
open Apr to Oct first
Sat and Sun in
month, Bank
Holidays and some
other weeks
advertised locally

Exeter
GUILDHALL open all
year Mon to Sat
(except when used
for meetings)

MARITIME MUSEUM
open all year

UNDERGROUND
PASSAGES open all
year Tue to Sat,
pm only

Yelverton
BUCKLAND ABBEY
open Good Fri to end
Sep Mon-Sat am and
pm, Sun pm only; Oct
to Easter Wed, Sat
and Sun, pm only

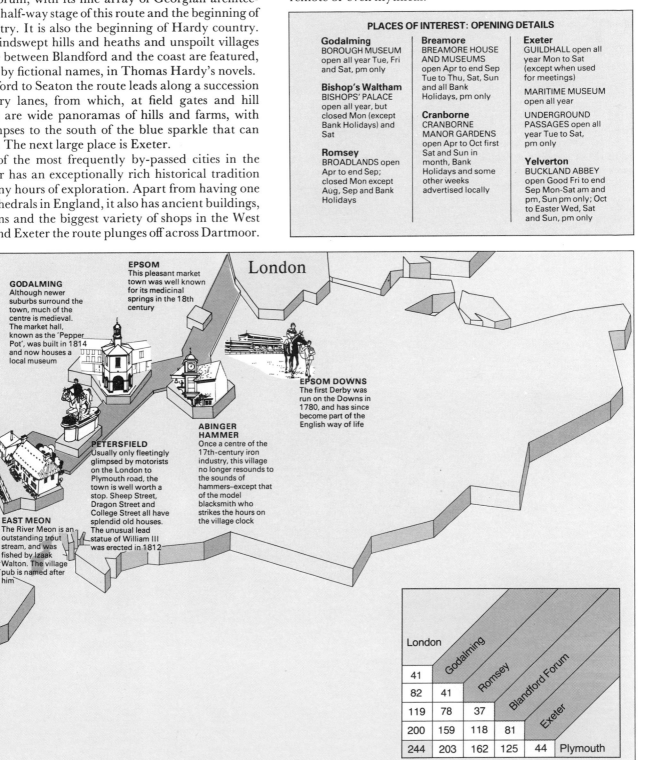

London

EPSOM
This pleasant market town was well known for its medicinal springs in the 18th century

GODALMING
Although newer suburbs surround the town, much of the centre is medieval. The market hall, known as the 'Pepper Pot', was built in 1814 and now houses a local museum

EPSOM DOWNS
The first Derby was run on the Downs in 1780, and has since become part of the English way of life

PETERSFIELD
Usually only fleetingly glimpsed by motorists on the London to Plymouth road, the town is well worth a stop. Sheep Street, Dragon Street and College Street all have splendid old houses. The unusual lead statue of William III was erected in 1812

ABINGER HAMMER
Once a centre of the 17th-century iron industry, this village no longer resounds to the sounds of hammers–except that of the model blacksmith who strikes the hours on the village clock

EAST MEON
The River Meon is an outstanding trout stream, and was fished by Izaak Walton. The village pub is named after him

...gnificant
...ilt in the
... but
...or are
...ns of an
...urch

London					
41	Godalming				
82	41	Romsey			
119	78	37	Blandford Forum		
200	159	118	81	Exeter	
244	203	162	125	44	Plymouth

EPSOM TO DORKING

The route begins in Epsom, 13 miles south-south-west of central London on the A24. Follow signs to Dorking, driving out across Epsom Common. Off to the right are the Wells, source of the medicinal waters which became known as Epsom salts and made Epsom a popular 18th-century spa.

Continue along the A24 through Ashtead and then turn left on to the Leatherhead bypass (SP Dorking), following it until you turn left with the A24. A pleasant stretch of dual carriageway runs along the wooded Mole valley; after 1 mile turn left on to the B2209 to Mickleham, a collection of lovely old houses and a Norman church. Continue along a tree-shaded lane, passing Juniper Hall, where a group of French aristocrats fled to escape the Revolution. One of them was General d'Arblay, who met the novelist Fanny Burney here. They were married in the village church at Mickleham in 1793.

BOX HILL

Box Hill is soon signposted to the left, and demands a detour. A narrow unclassified road snakes up the hill amid a wonderful spectrum of different greens and golds. A short walk along the road beyond the car park at the top is a must, for the view is breathtaking and stretches for many miles.

The main route continues along the B2209, rejoining the A24 at Burford Bridge, the scene of Nelson's final farewell to his neglected wife in 1800. Turn left for Dorking, and in 1½ miles turn right at the roundabout on to the A25,

Sweeping views over Dorking from the top of Box Hill

which leads into Dorking High Street. On the left is the White Horse Hotel, parts of which are 400 years old. Dorking has many good shops, including fine antique shops in West Street and South Street. At the junction where these branch off the High Street is a quaint old fingerpost incorporating a pump. The route bears left here; follow signs for Guildford, bearing right and shortly turning left at the mini-roundabout.

DORKING TO GODALMING

Continue through Westcott and Wotton, where author and diarist John Evelyn (1620–1706) was born and is buried. His famous *Diary* was found in an old clothes-basket at Wotton over 100 years after his death. Opposite the lush green in Abinger Hammer, the next village, is a timber clock-tower. On the hour a model blacksmith strikes the bell with his hammer, and a motto reads 'By me you know how fast to go'.

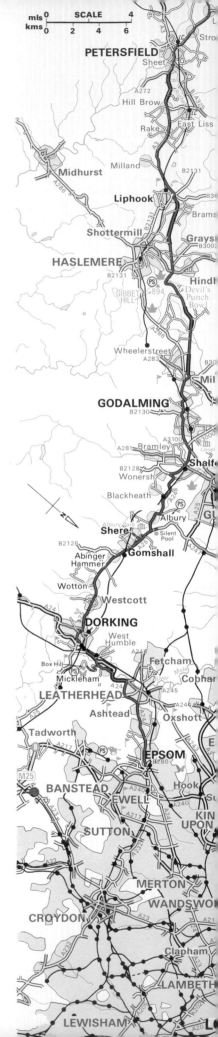

...e string of pleasant Surrey villages ...nues with Gomshall. A mill here is ...ioned in *Domesday Book*, with an annual ...f 40d.

...e of the treasures of ...re church is this tiny ...h-century bronze ...ue of the Madonna ...Child

...ERE

...st Gomshall an unclassified road on the left ...ers a very short detour to Shere. Timber-...med buildings abound, and a church has ...od here since long before the Norman ...nquest, though the present building dates ...m about 1190. Outside the north wall are ...ces of the cell where, from 1329, Christine ...rpenter, Anchoress of Shere, chose to shut ...self away for several years.

...e straight on through the village and ...tly turn left to rejoin the A25, then turn ...n to the A248 (SP Godalming).

SILENT POOL
...detour may be made here by continuing for ...st a few yards along the A25 and turning ...ght to the Silent Pool, a pleasant wooded ...auty spot, where a local girl is said to have ...owned herself in shame after King John saw ...r bathing naked.

The A248 takes you past a very ornate Victorian church, then skirts Albury Park on the left. Amid the park's stately trees stands a second, Saxon, church – now disused and partly ruined. The village of Albury also stood here until the 1840s, when a new squire drove the villagers away from their cottages near his manor to the present site of the village, on the main road.

Continue along the A248 through Chilworth, then at the T-junction turn right to cross Shalford Common, for many years the site of a famous fair. Turn left at the mini-roundabout and then right on to the A248 (SP Godalming). Cross the River Wey and at the T-junction turn left on to the A3100 for Godalming, whose lofty lead-covered church spire guides you for the last mile or two.

Follow the one-way system, bearing right, and then turn left into the High Street, which is packed with all kinds of interesting old buildings. At the top is the 'Pepper Pot', the odd little town hall of 1814, surmounted by a clock-tower and now housing a museum.*

GODALMING TO PETERSFIELD
Continue along the A3100 to Milford, where you turn left on to the A3 (SP Petersfield). This gives a clear run through open country, sweeping round the great wooded combe known as the Devil's Punch Bowl.

Follow the A3 through Liphook, whose 17th-century Royal Anchor Hotel, despite its modern trimmings, stands as a reminder that this was the old coaching route from London to Portsmouth. Continue through wooded country to Petersfield.

Elaborately patterned brick chimneys tower above the road in the Victorian village of Albury

PETERSFIELD
You can make a detour to the demure little town centre by turning left and then right, opposite the Red Lion Inn, into the High Street. At the end is the market place, dominated by an equestrian statue of William III and overlooked by St Peter's Church, which contains some exquisite Norman work.

PETERSFIELD TO ROMSEY

Leave Petersfield by the A272, following signs for Winchester. At Langrish, turn left on to an unclassified road for East Meon. The village centre is off to the left. Here old cottages of many styles – thatched, flint-and-brick, timbered and tile-hung – sit beside a stream crossed by several small bridges. The pub is called the Izaak Walton, after the author of *The Compleat Angler*, who used to fish here.

Carry on past the little flint church, through open downland country to West Meon. Turn left on to the A32 Fareham road, passing through Warnford, where watercress beds thrive in the pure water of the River Meon. The road winds back and forth over the river to Corhampton, where the route turns right on to the B3035 for Bishop's Waltham. The tiny church at this junction has an unusual carved Saxon sundial in the outside wall by the doorway.

An undulating road leads from here to Bishop's Waltham, where the great crumbling ruin of the 12th-century Bishops' Palace* can be glimpsed from the roundabout. To the left is the town centre, a nest of narrow streets and quaint little shops. Take the A333 (SP Eastleigh, Winchester), and at Lower Upham turn left on to the B3037 (SP Eastleigh). At Fair Oak turn left and in ¼ mile right to continue along the B3037. Railways and station dominate the approach to Eastleigh: the now sprawling town grew up as a railway village around the station for much smaller Bishopstoke. Turn left after crossing the railway, then right (SP Romsey) opposite the station. Follow signs straight on to the edge of Chandler's Ford, where the route turns left at the T-junction and immediately right into Castle Lane. A straight road leads into open country again, meeting the A27 at a T-junction, where you turn right towards Romsey. After 1½ miles, on a left-hand bend, turn right on to an unclassified road (SP Whitenap), which gives a short cut into Romsey itself.

The tranquil atmosphere and old-world charm of East Meon can hardly have changed since Izaak Walton fished here more than 300 years ago

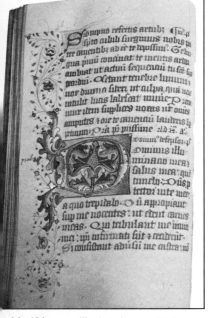

...quisite 15th-century illuminated manuscript, known ...Romsey Psalter, is on display in Romsey Abbey

...e Norman abbey alone would make this ...esting country town worth a stop. It was ...d from destruction, at the Dissolution of ...Monasteries, by the townspeople, who ...ght it from Henry VIII for £100; the deed ...e is on display in a glass case. The abbey ...wo famous pieces of Saxon sculpture, and ...ors go not only to see these ancient ...ures but also to visit the grave of Earl ...ntbatten of Burma. Broadlands,* the ...ntbatten family home, is just outside the ... A former occupant of the house was ... Palmerston, the 19th-century prime ...ster nicknamed 'Firebrand'.

...SEY TO CRANBORNE
... Romsey follow signs for Salisbury, ...ing the River Test and turning right on ...he A27, which takes the route to ...eparish. At the end of this village turn ...n to a single-track road (SP Downton), ...n ¾ mile cross the A36, following signs to ...ynch, where you turn right and shortly ...again (SP Downton), joining the B3080. ...the river in Downton is an old mill, ...site the large creeper-clad tannery. A ...w green fringed with thatched cottages ...hes from the Avon up to the main road, ...A338. Turn left (SP Fordingbridge), ...wing the Avon valley down to Breamore.

BREAMORE HOUSE
...amore House* stands in a commanding ...sition at the edge of the downs to the right, ...d a detour to it and the adjacent carriage ...d countryside museums can be made by ...ning right in Breamore. By the gates is a ...xon church, which celebrated its millen- ...m in 1980. Parts of it, including several ...dows and an archway which still carries ...ved Anglo-Saxon script, remain much as ...y were 1000 years ago.

Continue along the A338 to Fordingbridge, where you turn off for the town centre. Cross the medieval bridge and take the left fork (SP Damerham, B3078). The church is off this road to the left, reached through an avenue of limes. Its north chapel has an intricately carved roof, dating from the 15th century.

Carry on along the B3078, eventually dropping into the wooded hollow which cradles Cranborne. The large and impressive church – once an abbey – tells of the former importance of this quiet red-brick village. Monks from here built the magnificent abbey at Tewkesbury. The wall paintings above the nave date from the 13th century.

CRANBORNE TO BLANDFORD FORUM
Turn right on to an unclassified road (SP Salisbury) at the end of the beech hedge which screens the manor house, set amid fragrant, typically English gardens.* A sign at this junction reads '6d Handley' – short-hand for a nearby village, Sixpenny Handley. After 1 mile, at the next T-junction, turn right on to the B3081 (SP Shaftesbury). The road later crosses the unmistakably Roman line of Ackling Dyke, marching dead straight across country from Badbury Rings to Old Sarum. At the roundabout ¼ mile past it, turn left on to the A354.

This road skirts Cranborne Chase, an ancient hunting-ground characterized by scattered beechwoods and vast skyscapes. The first outpost of Blandford Forum is Blandford Camp, a windswept army instal-lation on a hill to the left. Descending all the time now, the route runs through Pimperne and into Blandford. Head for the town centre,

A plaque in this classical portico commemorates the rebuilding of Blandford Forum after a disastrous fire

a handsome main street with a uniform, planned appearance, as if all the buildings were designed together as a complete townscape. This is in fact exactly what happened, for in 1731 a great fire devastated the town and it had to be systematically rebuilt. The classical portico by the west door of the church was built to house a pump, which it was hoped might prevent another such disaster. One of the few buildings to survive the fire is the curious Old House, in The Close, a Renaissance building with a steeply pitched roof.

This quaint old forge with its higgledy-piggledy roof stands beside the road in Pimperne

BLANDFORD FORUM TO BEAMINSTER
Leave Blandford by the A350 (SP
Sturminster Newton, Shaftesbury), following
the Stour valley for about 2 miles. Turn left at
the traffic lights on to the A357 (SP
Sherborne), crossing a narrow stone bridge
which bears a plaque threatening anyone
who damages the bridge with transportation
for life. Several such plaques can still be seen
at various places in Dorset.

Past Durweston the route climbs up the
valley side, with views across the river to
peaceful Stourpaine in the meadows beyond.
Continue through Shillingstone to
Sturminster Newton, where an attractive old
mill sits upstream from the six-arched stone
bridge which leads into the busy little market
town, off the main road to the right.

Continue along the A357 to Lydlinch, and
on Lydlinch Common turn left on to the
A3030 (SP Sherborne). Just past the wood

One of the four angels depicted in lovely medieval stained glass in Lydlinch church

An attractive mill stands beside a foaming weir on the River Stour near Sturminster Newton

Stock Gaylard Park, where fallow deer
e among the oaks. At the end of the park,
left again on to the B3143 (SP
hester, King's Stag). The killing of a
e hart in defiance of Henry III gave the
village of King's Stag its name, and the
is depicted in old tiles on the floor of
by Glanvilles Wootton church. Past
am village, turn right at a crossroads on
he B3146 (SP Glanvilles Wootton,
borne), and follow the lane sharply
d to the right. After 1¼ miles turn left on
unclassified road (SP Minterne Magna,
dlemarsh). Carry straight on at the
roads and almost immediately turn left
e T-junction on to the A352. Follow this
for some 2 miles between steep wooded
and through Lyon's Gate, then on a left-
bend turn right (SP Evershot).

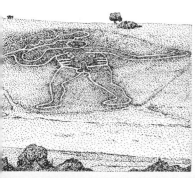

CERNE ABBAS
etour here takes you on for 2¾ miles along
A352 through Minterne Magna to Cerne
bas. Cut into the chalk hillside to the left as
approach Cerne Abbas is the famous
nt. The figure is thought to date back to
nan times, and has for many centuries
n associated with fertility rites.

The Evershot road turns sharply left and runs
along an 800-foot-high ridge, with the upper
reaches of Blackmoor Vale spreading out
below to the right. Between the turnings to
Hilfield and Batcombe, an ancient stone
pillar stands on the right-hand verge. This is
Cross-in-Hand, its origin unknown, though it
is said by gypsies to be a wishing-stone. It was
known to Thomas Hardy, and the heroine of
Tess of the d'Urbervilles swears an oath on it.

Cross the A37 at Holywell by turning right
and immediately left for Evershot, whose
village street is a delight. Lines of cottages
with mullioned or bow windows lead up to
the church, topped by a spiky little spire.

Carry straight on for Beaminster, and in 3½
miles cross the A356 on to the B3163. Soon
the buildings of Beaminster appear below and
the road sweeps down to them between high
walls of mellow stone. Turn right on to the
A3066 at the T-junction and go up the hill
and through the market place. Beaminster
has suffered three bad fires over the centuries,
but the church survived and its tower, of
richly carved golden stone, is one of the finest
in Dorset.

BEAMINSTER TO NEWTON POPPLEFORD
Follow the A3066 Crewkerne road through
the town centre and in ¼ mile turn left on to
the B3163, which switchbacks through pleasant country to Broadwindsor. Keep forward
at the first crossroads in Broadwindsor, and at
the second crossroads, below the church, look
out for a cottage which bears a plaque
commemorating a visit by Charles II in 1651.
Cromwell had ordered a manhunt after the
King's escape from the Battle of Worcester,
and here the fugitive hid, only narrowly
escaping a party of Roundhead soldiers who
stayed here the same night.

At this junction, take care to turn left on to
the B3164 (SP Axminster). Now comes one of
the most rewarding parts of the journey. The
mass of Pilsdon Pen, at 908 feet the highest
hill in Dorset, towers to the right and soon the
road is climbing its flanks. As you round the
southern end of the hill an unbelievable view
opens up to the left, right across the great
green bowl of Marshwood Vale to the sea
several miles away. The rich dairy-farming
country below is the home of local cheeses,
including the much-prized Blue Vinny.

The road begins to descend, though the
country is still windswept and lofty, and the
stern and lonely Rose and Crown Inn at
Birdsmoor Gate might almost be somewhere
on the Yorkshire Moors. Turn left here on to
the B3165 and drive through Marshwood,
the last Dorset village. As you approach the
Devon border, there are views far across the
Axe valley to the right, and then left towards
the sea as well. Skirt Raymond's Hill, and at
Hunter's Lodge crossroads turn right on to
the A35 and after a few yards left on to an
unclassified road (SP Combpyne, Rousdon,
Seaton). Cross Trinity Hill and at Rousdon
turn right on to the A3052 (SP Exeter), dropping into the Axe valley to reach Colyford.

COLYTON
A possible detour here is to Colyton, 1 mile
north of Colyford. Its winding, narrow streets
are packed with attractive stone and colour-
washed cottages and shops, and the church
has a pretty octagonal lantern-tower. Inside
the spacious, airy church are elaborate 17th-
century tombs of members of the Pole family,
and a very well-preserved Saxon cross, found
in pieces built into the tower wall.

Press on along the A3052 towards Exeter,
later descending a steep hill into Sidford and
then striking inland through Newton
Poppleford on the River Otter, with its
gleaming white cottages.

NEWTON POPPLEFORD TO EXETER

The route continues westwards from Newton Poppleford to skirt Woodbury Common and descend, with views stretching ahead, to Clyst St Mary. At the first roundabout take the A376 (SP Exeter), and at the second roundabout either take the M5 west to the next junction, by-passing Exeter, or make a detour by following signs into the city centre.

EXETER

Many drivers will have by-passed Exeter at one time or another, but few stop to explore. However, there is much to see. The Maritime Museum,* on the Exe just off the Torbay road, is a great novelty: a huge collection of boats from all over the world is on display, and primitive-looking Arab dhows rub shoulders with Peruvian canoes and brilliantly painted Portuguese fishing vessels.

Exeter is an excellent shopping centre, and sandwiched between modern chain stores in the High Street are fine old buildings such as the ancient Guildhall* and some 16th-century timber-framed houses. Behind the high street is the tranquil Close, where shops, offices and hotels are grouped around the cathedral with its twin towers and sumptuously sculptured west front. (For further details and a town plan of Exeter, see p. 155.)

From the city centre, head along Fore Street for the twin Exe bridges. Having crossed the river, take the second exit, the B3212 (SP Moretonhampstead).

EXETER TO PRINCETOWN

The main route leaves the motorway at junction 31 and takes the A30 (SP Okehampton), turning off on to the A377 (SP Exeter). At the roundabout, take the first exit on to an unclassified road (SP Moretonhampstead). This road runs alongside the A30 to a T-junction where you turn left on to the B3212 for Moretonhampstead.

The most outstanding features of Moretonhampstead's almshouses are the massive granite pillars which support the upper floor

---

Past Longdown, the inhospitable contours of Dartmoor can be seen for the first time. But the moor's eastern fringes are threaded with delightful wooded valleys, and the road follows the River Teign along one of them – a beautiful gorge, dense with trees. Cross the river at Steps Bridge, where there is a tourist information office and a nature trail. Weaving steadily upwards through the trees, the route comes out into more open country and the tower of Moretonhampstead church appears on the skyline. Refusing to be hurried, the B3212 winds back and forth until eventually it reaches this stern moorland town. On the right as you enter it is the attractive portico of the almshouses, dated 1637; the sturdy little granite church stands on a windy hill behind. In the church porch are memorials to two French military officers, prisoners of the Napoleonic Wars, who died here whilst on parole from the prison across the moor at Princetown.

The road winds on (SP Princetown) from Moretonhampstead and soon the cosier landscape of the moor's edge gives way to the real thing. All around lie rolling hills with a meagre covering of scrub and bracken, and the bare contours of the skyline are interrupted only by the occasional granite tor.

Pass the Warren House Inn, in a desolate spot frequented mainly by travellers and, of old, by tin-miners who worked in these uninhabited spaces. It is said that the peat fire in the inn has been burning continuously for 130 years. At Postbridge the road crosses the East Dart River, spanned by an ancient clapper bridge to the left of the road.

t Two Bridges, turn right on to the B3357
a few hundred yards, crossing the West
t, again with an old bridge – this time a
horse bridge – to the left. Shortly past it,
left (SP Plymouth) along the B3212 to
cetown, perhaps the most grim of English
ns. Everything seems gloomy, grey and
t. The solemn church tower, visible from
y miles away, stands over a memorial to
Thomas Tyrwhitt, who began quarrying
ite and growing flax on Dartmoor in the
18th century. He could not tempt
kers to this inhospitable place, so he built
prison here and filled it with French
oners-of-war from the overcrowded
on ships in Plymouth harbour.

NCETOWN TO PLYMOUTH
Princetown the lower land west of the
r comes into view and you can see the sea
n. Dousland and Yelverton herald the
of the moor, and a more civilized
scape returns: neat sheep shut in tidy
n fields, and buildings a little more
orative than the sterner ones of the
dswept moorland. At Yelverton roun-
out take the first exit, the A386, which
all the way to Plymouth.

BUCKLAND ABBEY

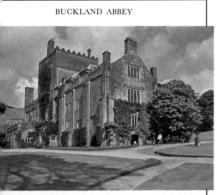

lere a detour can be made to Buckland
bbey* by turning right off the A386 just past
e Yelverton roundabout and following signs
Crapstone, where you bear left. The abbey,
idden away in a tree-filled hollow, was
onverted to a residence by Sir Richard
renville, the famous seafarer and captain of
e *Revenge*, who sold the abbey to Sir Francis
rake in 1581. It is now a National Trust
roperty, housing a museum which includes
ementoes of the two great sailors. To rejoin
e Plymouth road from here, take the un-
assified road immediately opposite the
bbey gates (SP Plymouth, Roborough),
hich leads back to the A386.

verton is not strictly at the western limit of
tmoor, for the first few miles of the
nouth road are still within Dartmoor
ional Park, but the feeling of remoteness
gone. No sooner does the road leave the
r than it starts its plod through
nouth's sprawling outskirts. Continue
g the A386, following signs for the
yport and city centre.

PLYMOUTH
Plymouth is a planned, modern city,
rebuilt as a result of war damage. The
bombed ruin of 15th-century St Andrew's
Church in the centre of a traffic roundabout is a sad sight, but Plymouth is keen
to salvage what it can of the past, and the
area around the Hoe, where Drake
finished his game of bowls as the Armada
approached, is still attractive. From here
there are wide views across the great
harbour where, in both war and peace, so
much of Britain's history has unfurled.

*Plymouth's New Customs House watches over Sutton
Harbour, where fishing boats moor at quays which have
witnessed the safe return from sea of famous voyagers
from Sir Francis Drake to Sir Francis Chichester*

DARTMOOR

One of the Bronze Age huts at Grimspo[und]

SPINE-chilling legends of the supernatural, superb views, 'picture postcard' villages and a wealth of prehistoric remains are just four facets of Dartmoor's bewitching character. Ringed by Bovey Tracey, Ivybridge, Tavistock and Okehampton, the moor is the greatest expanse of wilderness left in southern England. Its wild beauty and rich traditions were formally acknowledged in 1951 when the 365-square-mile Dartmoor National Park was established. Its symbol is the sturdy Dartmoor pony, mentions of which date back to before the Norman Conquest.

The moor is basically a great fist of river-carved granite clenched defiantly above the surrounding shales and sandstones. Most of the land is more than 1000 feet above sea level and punctuated by rocky outcrops, known as 'tors', sculpted into weird shapes by wind and weather over the ages. High Willhays, in the north-west corner of the moor, rises to 2038 feet and is the highest point in England south of the Pennines. Its neighbour, Yes Tor, is only 8 feet lower, and the ridge formed by the two summits is dubbed the 'Roof of Devon'. This part of the moor is a military training area where visitors should not stray when warning flags are flying.

Great expanses of heather carpet the open moorland, but the sheltered valleys of the Teign, Bovey, Dart and other rivers are green with hardy oakwoods. At Dartmeet, Postbridge and elsewhere the rivers are spanned by ancient granite slabs, known as 'clapper' bridges.

Widecombe in the Moor is probably the best-known of Dartmoor's villages. Its fame is due to the song about Uncle Tom Cobley and his friends riding to Widecombe Fair on a borrowed mare. Tom Cobley was a landowner from Spreyton who died around 1800 and lies in an unmarked grave in the village churchyard. The 'Thomas Cobley' headstone there commemorates his nephew.

TIN has been mined in the West Country since the Bronze Age, when it was mixed with copper to form the alloy which gave the period its name. Dartmoor's tin deposits were, however, not worked on a large scale until the 12th century, when the ore was 'streamed' from the area's numerous rivers. Mine shafts were not sunk until much later.

During the Middle Ages Dartmoor was one of Europe's richest sources of tin, and the miners jealously guarded their rights by drawing up their own laws and establishing their own 'parliament'. At that time Plympton, Tavistock, Ashburton and Chagford became 'stannary' towns – *stannum* is Latin for tin. Lydford Castle, on the moor's western edge, was specially built in 1195 as a prison for those who broke the tinners' laws. It rapidly gained a reputation for harsh punishment, so that at one time it was said that offenders were hanged in the morning and tried in the afternoon. Among those incarcerated there was Richard Strode, MP for Plympton, who incurred the miners' wrath during Henry VIII's reign.

There was another tin boom during the 16th century, and the ore has been mined in th[e] Country ever since, some[times on] a large scale and sometim[es in] little more than an optim[istic] exercise.

Remains of about 50 b[lowing] houses, the buildings in w[hich] the ore was smelted, have [been] found on the moor. Two [fine] examples can be seen at [Black] Tor Falls, on the River M[eavy] near Princetown. After t[he 18th] century tin began to be e[xtracted] from underground mines [and] the blowing houses fell in[to] disuse to become romant[ic] and, at first sight, enigma[tic] ruins. There are old min[e] shafts near the Warren [...]

Hound Tor, near Manaton, is one of many dramatic outcrops of weathered granite that punctuate Dartmoor's skyline

This thatched cottage at Buckland in the Moor is built of granite, which has been used as a building material on the moor since prehistoric times

EXPLORERS armed with large-scale maps swiftly appreciate that Dartmoor has one of the greatest concentrations of prehistoric remains anywhere in England. Man is believed to have inhabited the area 10,000 years ago, but most of the antiquities date from the Bronze Age, which lasted from around 1400 BC until around 500 BC.

Granite provided Bronze Age settlers with one of the world's most durable building materials. They used it for their huts, for the walls that encircled their villages and livestock enclosures, for their burial chambers and for the rows of standing stones whose purpose was probably religious.

The most notable of the villages is Grimspound, south of the B3212 between Moretonhampstead and Postbridge, where the remains of 16 huts can be seen inside a four-acre enclosure. These dwellings, like those at Broadun Ring and elsewhere, originally had roofs of poles which radiated out from a central post and were covered with turf or thatch.

The valleys of the Meavy, Plym and Dart are rich in burial chambers and hut circles. But the best-known Bronze Age burial is Spinster's Rock, at Drewsteignton, where three granite uprights support a capstone. Cairns and standing stones flank the B3357 at Merrivale and a remarkable row of standing stones, just over two miles long, extends from the Erme valley to Green Hill.

's *clapper bridge*

(between Moreton-
d and Postbridge),
miners planted crops
aped like the symbols
g cards.

ostbridge, where the
apper' bridge enabled
len packhorses to cross
Dart dry-shod, stands
Crockern Tor. From
1749 this hill was the
Dartmoor tinners'
nt'. There were 96
– 24 from each of the
ary towns – and during
their deliberations
they sat on granite
boulders beneath
the moorland sky.

Near the centre of this double row of stones at Merrivale are the remains of a round barrow surrounded by a stone circle

ROUTE 8

118 MILE

London to Bournemouth

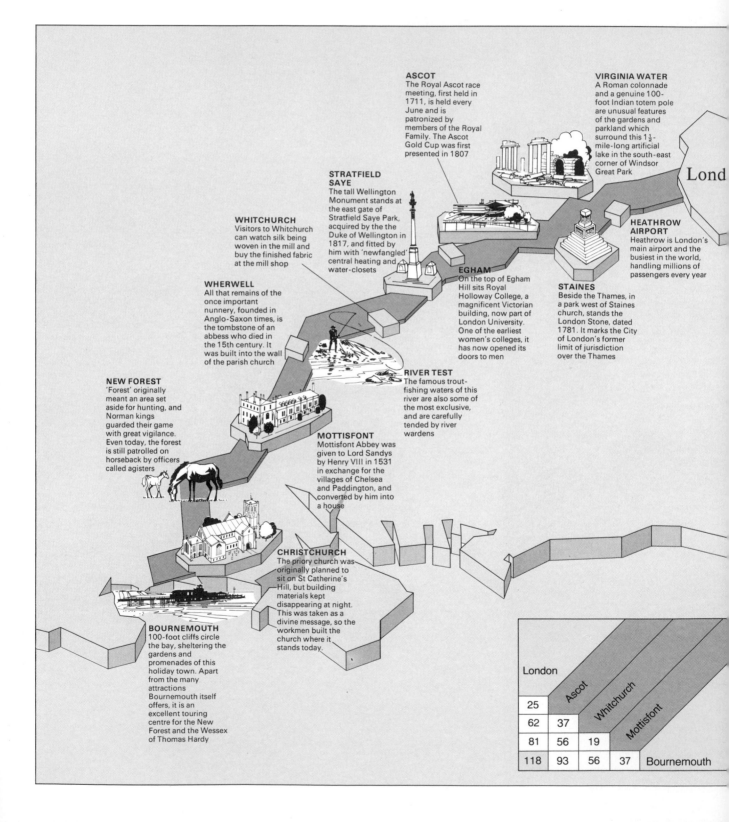

ASCOT
The Royal Ascot race meeting, first held in 1711, is held every June and is patronized by members of the Royal Family. The Ascot Gold Cup was first presented in 1807

VIRGINIA WATER
A Roman colonnade and a genuine 100-foot Indian totem pole are unusual features of the gardens and parkland which surround this 1½-mile-long artificial lake in the south-east corner of Windsor Great Park

Lond

STRATFIELD SAYE
The tall Wellington Monument stands at the east gate of Stratfield Saye Park, acquired by the the Duke of Wellington in 1817, and fitted by him with 'newfangled' central heating and water-closets

HEATHROW AIRPORT
Heathrow is London's main airport and the busiest in the world, handling millions of passengers every year

WHITCHURCH
Visitors to Whitchurch can watch silk being woven in the mill and buy the finished fabric at the mill shop

EGHAM
On the top of Egham Hill sits Royal Holloway College, a magnificent Victorian building, now part of London University. One of the earliest women's colleges, it has now opened its doors to men

STAINES
Beside the Thames, in a park west of Staines church, stands the London Stone, dated 1781. It marks the City of London's former limit of jurisdiction over the Thames

WHERWELL
All that remains of the once important nunnery, founded in Anglo-Saxon times, is the tombstone of an abbess who died in the 15th century. It was built into the wall of the parish church

NEW FOREST
'Forest' originally meant an area set aside for hunting, and Norman kings guarded their game with great vigilance. Even today, the forest is still patrolled on horseback by officers called agisters

RIVER TEST
The famous trout-fishing waters of this river are also some of the most exclusive, and are carefully tended by river wardens

MOTTISFONT
Mottisfont Abbey was given to Lord Sandys by Henry VIII in 1531 in exchange for the villages of Chelsea and Paddington, and converted by him into a house

CHRISTCHURCH
The priory church was originally planned to sit on St Catherine's Hill, but building materials kept disappearing at night. This was taken as a divine message, so the workmen built the church where it stands today.

BOURNEMOUTH
100-foot cliffs circle the bay, sheltering the gardens and promenades of this holiday town. Apart from the many attractions Bournemouth itself offers, it is an excellent touring centre for the New Forest and the Wessex of Thomas Hardy

London				
25	Ascot			
62	37	Whitchurch		
81	56	19	Mottisfont	
118	93	56	37	Bournemouth

OURNEMOUTH, with its gentle climate, enticing sands
memories of Victorian seaside holidays, is closer to London
any other south-western resort. However, the principal
don–Bournemouth trunk route is not a pleasing appetizer
the delights to come. For much of its length it is an
spiring journey along miles of motorway, and where the
d is not motorway, drivers using the route at the height of
season will often find themselves trapped in hot, frustrating
ic jams. This is especially so on the notorious Winchester
pass. When it was built it was more than adequate for its
pose; today it simply cannot cope with the volume of traffic.
mittedly one stretch of the route runs through the New
est, but it is used almost entirely by traffic eager to get
ewhere else. It is therefore decidedly not peaceful, and
way it conscientiously avoids the best parts of the Forest.

his alternative route escapes all that flurry and fuming by
ting a course through the fine scenery and quiet country-
which lies slightly north and west of the main trunk route.

he Great West Road and the A30, built on the course of the
nan road to the West Country, carry you out of London
ards the ancient woodlands of Royal Berkshire, past
oric Runnymede and genteel Virginia Water – both of
ch are excellent places to stroll along grassy paths in the
t and sound of water.

he route then skirts Windsor Great Park, a great tract of
ded countryside originally set aside as a royal hunting
erve by the Norman kings, and stretching from Windsor
ost to Bracknell. The sandy soils of eastern Berkshire and
h Hampshire were once cloaked by dense and continuous
ds, and though much of this natural cover has gone to make
for ever-growing towns and villages, the route is
ctuated by stretches of shady woodland almost as far as
ngstoke. In parts, the soil is very acid, ideal for the pines
rhododendrons which can sometimes seem so alien in the
ly deciduous South Country.

ratfield Saye House will be an essential stop for those
rested in military history. The house itself, which was built
e reign of Charles I, is not outstanding, but it contains a
que collection of paintings, furniture and effects connected
the first Duke of Wellington, the hero of Waterloo. The
nds of the house form an extensive park.

asingstoke marks a subtle change in scenery as sand and
give way to chalk downs. Hardly more than a generation
the change in soil would have been much more evident, for
large arable fields on the hill slopes were then sheep-
ped turf, and on market days Basingstoke's old streets (now
ed under a modern concrete precinct) echoed to the sounds
eating and the calls of shepherds.

st east of Overton is the source of the River Test, and from
the route is never more than a mile or so from the river for
stance of some 30 miles, passing through a string of river-
villages which are small, quiet and, without exception,
uresque. Fed by pure streams from the surrounding chalk
nlands, the river is ideal for trout, and it is famous for its
rb (and expensive) game fishing. Watercress also flourishes,
there are many commercial cressbeds in the area.

eligious houses were invariably founded in areas of
quil beauty, and the Test valley is no exception. Wherwell
ey, founded in the 10th century, has long since disappeared
but name, but a good deal of Mottisfont Abbey can still be
, although much of the building dates from the 18th
ury – 500 years later than the original priory church.

PLACES OF INTEREST: OPENING DETAILS

Stratfield Saye
STRATFIELD SAYE
HOUSE
open end
Mar to end Sep daily
(except Fri)

Mottisfont
MOTTISFONT ABBEY
open Apr to end Sep.
grounds Tue to Sat,
house Wed and Sat,
pm only

Christchurch
RED HOUSE
MUSEUM AND ART
GALLERY open all
year daily (except
Mon and 25 Dec);
Sun pm only

Crossing the Test at Mottisfont, the route follows a little-used, but clearly defined, unclassified road – crossing a couple of 'A' roads to Salisbury and the West – and enters the New Forest at its north-eastern corner. Many little roads lead from the route into the Forest, which, despite the fact that parts of it are thronged with visitors in high summer, still retains much of its wild, primeval character. The route shows the Forest in several of its different moods and facets – ranging from stands of immense oaks and beeches through gentle meadows to areas of desolate gorsey heath.

Saxon kings hunted in the area before William the Conqueror set aside the Forest's thousands of acres as a royal hunting-ground, and deer were pursued by royalty across the heaths and through the woodlands up until the reign of James II. It was not until Queen Victoria's time, however, that royal rights over the deer were finally relinquished.

By the Middle Ages, partly because of the royal protection of game, growing numbers of deer and domestic animals were beginning to threaten the Forest. They prevented natural regeneration by eating the succulent green shoots and saplings. As a result, the first of several tree-growing acts was passed towards the end of the 15th century, when timber was the most important of all raw materials. Areas of woodland were enclosed for the first time, enabling young trees to become firmly established. Fast-growing trees, such as the Scots pine, were introduced towards the end of the 18th century. During the Second World War, when the Forest produced more than 400,000 tons of timber, it was frequently the target for German incendiary bombs.

About two-thirds of the land has been under Forestry Commission control since 1924 and it remains one of southern England's most important sources of wood for building, fencing and many other purposes. The Forestry Commission, working in conjunction with old-established authorities, has also done much to make the New Forest an exciting and beautiful place for visitors, and there are many points along this route which offer peaceful places for picnics and walks.

The final stretch of the route drops down from the Forest to Fordingbridge, and from here to the coast follows the River Avon (another famous fishing river) along its broad, flat valley. The alternative route intersects with the main trunk route at Ringwood, but thanks to a newly built and busy 'A' road along the western side of the Avon the parallel 'B' road to the east is uncluttered and peaceful. It reaches the coast at Christchurch, from where the A35 runs the last few miles into Bournemouth.

Bournemouth is journey's end, and it has more than enough attractions of its own for most people, but it can also be used as a base from which to explore the surrounding countryside. To the east stretch the New Forest and the coastlands of the Solent; to the north are Cranborne Chase and the Wiltshire Downs, and to the west is Poole's huge natural harbour, and beyond it the beautiful Isle of Purbeck.

LONDON TO ASCOT

The route begins at the roundabout beneath the Chiswick flyover, 6 miles west of central London at the junction of the A4 and the North and South Circular roads. Follow the A4 (SP The South-West, A30), which runs beneath the towering concrete structure carrying the elevated section of the M4 motorway. A wide, straight dual carriageway soon speeds you out of London, alternately between neat rows of suburban villas and an assorted 20th-century jazz of factories and offices. At the end of the Hounslow by-pass take the A30 (SP Staines), which branches off the A4 here. The road runs directly beneath one of Heathrow Airport's main incoming flight paths, so be prepared for planes whistling by, only a few feet above you, on their way in to land.

Past Heathrow, a few tidy fields and market gardens hint that the worst of Greater London is behind. The A30 here follows the course of the main Roman road from London to the West: hence its unwavering straightness. The Roman route crossed both the Thames and the Colne at Staines, and a market town grew up near the point where the rivers meet. Staines today is not without interest, but it is a busy place and is easily by-passed by following signs for Basingstoke to continue along the A30.

RUNNYMEDE

At the large roundabout by the Runnymede Hotel a detour may be made to Runnymede by turning on to the A308 (SP Windsor). This road runs through pleasant riverside meadows, and a car park on the right is conveniently situated for a stroll by the river or up the path to the Magna Carta memorial, erected to commemorate the place where King John signed Magna Carta in 1215. A memorial to President John F. Kennedy, assassinated in 1963, stands on nearby Cooper's Hill.

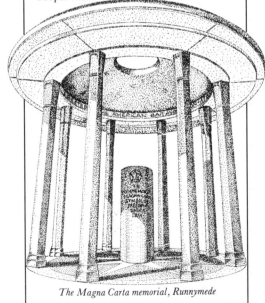

The Magna Carta memorial, Runnymede

The rolling wooded landscapes of Windsor Great Park provide a perfect setting for Virginia Water. The beautiful 1½-mile-long lake was constructed for the Duke of Cumberland in the mid 18th century. A much later addition is the colourful totem pole (detail, right) which stands on the shore. This was brought from British Columbia in 1958

The main route continues westwards along the A30 (SP Basingstoke), by-passing Egham. At the top of the next hill you will glimpse Royal Holloway College on the left. This extraordinarily ornate Victorian building, now part of the University of London, was one of the first women's colleges in the country when it was completed in 1887. Its design is modelled on that of the romantic chateau of Chambord on the River Loire.

The road now begins to weave through pleasant wooded country as it skirts Windsor Great Park. A worthwhile stop is at Virginia Water, where a car park is signposted to the right. In the grounds around the large man-made lake you can see a real Indian totem pole, from British Columbia, or a Roman colonnade which was shipped stone by stone from Leptis Magna in North Africa. These classical ruins were a gift to the Prince Regent in 1816, intended for the portico of the British Museum, but were rebuilt at Virginia Water 10 years later.

A quarter of a mile past the car park, leave the A30, turning right on to the A329 (SP Ascot, Bracknell). Follow this road through Ascot. Many of the buildings along the main street are associated with the famous race-course, which lies to the right. Queen Anne

founded the race meeting in 1711, an retains its place as the most opulent prestigious social and sporting event of year. It takes place in June.

ASCOT TO EVERSLEY

The A329 takes the route on to Brack With no warning at all, woodland sudd gives way to something very different: crete in abundance and a maze of rou bouts and dual carriageways. However route is well signposted, and if you fc signs on to the A3095 for Crowthorne you succeed in picking your way through jumbled townscape of assorted per shapes and building materials – for b means all of Bracknell is newly develc The town centre has several 17th-cen buildings, and a little way to the south o town is Caesar's Camp, a hill-fort dating the Iron Age.

From Bracknell the A3095 runs thr Crowthorne Wood – an example of Forestry Commission's efforts to preserv wooded character of the area – and Crowthorne, where the route takes a turn (SP Eversley, Finchampstead). Crowthorne station on the left and go str on at the roundabout on to the B3348 to

Wellingtonia Avenue. The majestic symmetry of the two ranks of immense pines, with the straight road between meeting the sky in the distance, is breathtaking. At the end of the avenue to the left are Finchampstead Ridges, 60 acres of variegated woodland owned by the National Trust and offering fine views over the Blackwater valley and beyond.

Continue to the war memorial and go straight on, still following the B3348.

FINCHAMPSTEAD CHURCH
Just past the junction a right turn offers a signposted detour to Finchampstead church. A narrow lane leads into the sleepy little village, whose church is perched on a prehistoric earthwork. Its chancel and nave are Norman, and the brick tower dates from the 18th century.

The main route continues on the B3348 to Eversley. Turn left by the Tally Ho pub on to the A327, crossing the Blackwater River to pass through Eversley. Charles Kingsley, author of *The Water Babies*, was rector of Eversley and is buried in the churchyard.

EVERSLEY TO OVERTON
Shortly past Eversley, leave the A327, keeping forward on to an unclassified road, then at the crossroads turn right (SP Bramshill,

Heckfield). The route runs through more trees, continuing forward to join the B3011. Keep forward at the crossroads on to the A32, following it to the Wellington Monument. This stands at the eastern entrance to Stratfield Saye Park, which has been the seat of the dukes of Wellington since it was bought by the 'Iron Duke' with money voted to him by Parliament after his heroic victory at the Battle of Waterloo. At the monument turn left on to the A33 towards Basingstoke.

STRATFIELD SAYE HOUSE
To visit Stratfield Saye House,* turn right by the Wellington Arms at Stratfield Turgis and follow signs to the visitors' entrance. The house dates from the reign of Charles I, and contains some fine furniture and a collection of paintings and memorabilia of the first duke. In the grounds is the grave of Copenhagen, the duke's favourite horse. There is a pleasant walled garden, and plants and produce are often on sale to visitors.

The main route continues to Basingstoke, like Bracknell a new town and littered with roundabouts, but again signposts are a salvation. At the ring road roundabout take the A339 Newbury road, then follow signs to the B3400 for Whitchurch to reach Overton.

A series of bronze busts, including one of Napoleon, is a feature of the gallery at Stratfield Saye House. Gold leaf embellishes the walls, which are hung with numerous old prints, and the beautiful carpet was specially woven in Madrid

OVERTON TO STOCKBRIDGE

The route continues through Overton, a name familiar to readers of Richard Adams's novel *Watership Down*, which is set in this area. Between Overton and Whitchurch you pass Laverstoke Mill, where the paper for Bank of England notes was made. Follow the B3400 (SP Andover) through the little town of Whitchurch, passing the parish church, which contains an interesting carved Saxon gravestone over 1000 years old, discovered only in 1868 when the church was being restored. At Hurstbourne Priors turn left on to the B3048 (SP Longparish), which takes you through a string of appealing thatched villages along the River Test.

Turn right and left to cross the A303 and continue on the B3048 to Wherwell, a village which repays exploration. Just before you reach the village shop (quaintly called the '20th-Century Stores'), a quiet lane on the left, lined with thatched cottages, crosses a tributary of the Test and leads to the churchyard. The present church is 19th-century, but a much older one, part of Wherwell's former abbey, stood on this site. Some very interesting ancient carvings, including part of a Saxon stone cross and an effigy of a nun, are preserved in the church.

Continue along the village street and keep forward on to an unclassified road (SP Fullerton). When you reach the A3057 turn left for Stockbridge. The road rejoins the Test 2 miles later and follows it into Stockbridge, where you should take the Romsey road, still

Timber-framing and thatch at Wherwell, one of several lovely Test valley villages on this route

---

Those lucky enough to hold angling rights on the River Test can store their tackle in unusual thatched huts like this one near Mottisfont. The nets strung across the river are for catching eels

the A3057. Stockbridge's broad main s lies off the route to the right, and has se antique and craft shops which make a stop worthwhile.

STOCKBRIDGE TO FORDINGBRIDG

From Stockbridge the A3057 rises into rolling farmland well above the Test, drops into King's Somborne whose attra village street, complete with stream and is tucked away to the left. Three and a miles past King's Somborne take a right on to an unclassified road (SP Mottis Cross the river and ascend into the vil whose church, on the left, is a gem. It fine Norman chancel arch and a good d original 15th-century stained glass. F the main street through the village and r a bend, then turn left on to an unclas road (SP Awbridge, Broughton).

MOTTISFONT ABBEY

By keeping forward for a few yards at junction you reach the entrance to Mottisf Abbey* on the right. This is a National Tr property well worth a stop if you have ti The grounds, with their spreading lawns a majestic copper beeches and cedars, tomize the English country garden, and River Test flows through the midst to co plete the picture. Most of the house itself built in the 18th century, but it incorpora an Augustinian priory, founded in 1201, pa of which can still be clearly seen. drawing-room has famous *trompe-l'oeil* pa ings by Rex Whistler.

The main route follows the unclassified road described above to a T-junction, where you turn left on to the B3084 (SP Romsey). Half a mile past Dunbridge take a right turn on to an unclassified road (SP Awbridge, West Wellow), and at the next junction turn left, then right (SP West and East Wellow). Continue along a densely wooded lane and cross the A27 on to another unclassified road. Turn right on to the A36 and almost immediately left (SP Bramshaw), crossing a cattle grid which indicates that you have just entered the New Forest.

This part of the Forest is a delight: there are cottages and hamlets, lush grass verges and hedges, overhanging trees and groups of inquisitive, neat ponies browsing by the roadside. Continue through Bramshaw, crossing the B3079, and when you reach the B3078 turn right for Fordingbridge. The landscape changes quite suddenly, and from here to Fordingbridge the Forest shows a wilder face: thorny scrubland and barren, windswept spaces stretch in all directions from the ridge along which the road runs. On the outskirts of Fordingbridge, turn left on to the A338 (SP Ringwood), by-passing the town centre.

FORDINGBRIDGE TO BOURNEMOUTH

The A338 takes you on an attractive journey along the wide flood plain of the Avon valley – sometimes the road runs right beside the river – to Ringwood. At Ringwood, first follow signs to the town centre, but instead of going into it take the B3347 Sopley road at the mini-roundabout. Still following the Avon, the road runs within a few feet of Tyrrell's Ford, so called because Sir Walter

Tyrrell is said to have fled this way after he killed William Rufus in the New Forest on 2 August 1100. The route continues along the B3347 through the attractive village of Sopley and at the roundabout outside Christchurch takes the third exit, the A35, for Bournemouth.

CHRISTCHURCH

Christchurch is by-passed by the A35, but it is a town not to be missed. A detour can be made by turning left at the roundabout ½ mile along the A35. Follow the main street to a mini-roundabout, from where a one-way system of narrow streets leads past the Red House Museum and Art Gallery* to the splendid priory. The town grew up between the Rivers Avon and Stour around the priory, founded in about 1100. Legend has it that during the construction of the priory church a vital roof beam was cut too short by mistake. The builders went home despondent, but returned the next day to find the beam mysteriously set in its place. This 'miraculous beam' can still be seen to this day.

Just past the priory, the one-way system passes near to the quay, haunt of numerous sailing enthusiasts and fishermen. Beyond the fleet of small boats in the harbour stretches the peninsula of Hengistbury Head, reached from the Bournemouth side of the estuary.

The main route follows the A35 for the last stretch – in fact, you are in Bournemouth as soon as you cross the Stour, though you must thread your way through a mile or two of seaside-town sprawl to reach the centre, with its pleasant parks and excellent shopping area. Fine beaches, many kinds of entertainment and a mild climate complete the picture – a true 'all-round' resort. (For details and a town plan of Bournemouth, see p. 187.)

Surrounded by gardens and appealing old houses, the priory church is the only survivor of the monastic buildings at Christchurch

THE NEW FOREST

WILLIAM THE CONQUEROR 'created' the New Forest in 1079. He did not plant trees, but set aside an area stretching from the Wiltshire Downs to the Solent and from the Avon valley to Southampton as a royal hunting-ground Today the Forest is not quite so large, but it still covers over 100 square miles and comprises a unique mixture of heaths, commons and majestic woodlands.

Many of the Forest's finest trees can be seen along the Ornamental Drive that links Brockenhurst with the A31 Ringwood to Cadnam road. Superb examples of introduced trees, such as giant redwoods from California, can be seen in the Bolderwood Arboretum, and native species are seen at their most splendid in Mark Ash Wood.

...lade in one of the
...ancient and ornamental'
...ls. Although the unique
...of the stands of beech
...ad been appreciated
...19th century, they were
...lly protected until 1971

...er, like these two does,
...mon sight in the Forest

TRADITIONS rooted as deeply as the trees themselves still play an important part in the New Forest's day-to-day life. Many date from Norman times, when local people were granted rights to make limited use of the royal hunting-grounds.

Common of Mast allows pigs to feed during the 'pannage' season – between September and November – when acorns and beech mast lie thick on the ground. Common of Tubary permits turf or peat to be cut, and Common of Marl involves a primitive type of fertilizer dug from marl pits. About 80 commoners still receive logs under the Common of Fuelwood, but the timber must be burned in the recipient's own home. More than 300 graze livestock under the Right of Pasture, granted because fences and hedges would have interfered with free-running deer and their hunters.

The Verderers' Court, another Norman institution, still keeps a watchful eye on the Forest's welfare. Every two months it meets in the lovely old Queen's House at Lyndhurst, the 'capital' of the New Forest. The court's duties include appointing 'agisters' – horsemen who patrol the woods and heaths to protect wild and domestic animals. Their formal uniform includes a peaked riding hat bearing the verderers' stirrup insignia. There are also forest keepers whose office dates back to the reign of King Canute. In the days when the Forest was a royal hunting ground the Verderers administered the harsh Forest laws. These included execution or maiming for poachers, and blinding for peasants who disturbed the deer.

HABITATS ranging from bogs to the 'ancient and ornamental woodlands' enable the New Forest to support an exceptionally rich variety of flora and fauna. Rare plants include the marsh gentian and bog orchid, and the wild gladiolus – found nowhere else in Britain – grows in glades and on the edges of the woodlands. Birds likely to be seen include the lapwing, curlew, snipe, buzzard, kestrel and sparrow-hawk.

About 2000 cattle are grazed by commoners, but they are outnumbered two-to-one by the famous New Forest ponies. James I is believed to have had one for his children to ride and they are now popular in many European countries. Regular sales are held near Beaulieu Road station. The ponies wander everywhere and are often seen ambling through the Forest's picturesque villages. But they should not be fed, because titbits encourage them to frequent the forest roads and cause accidents.

Fallow, sika, roe and red deer are the largest of the Forest's many wild animals. Red and roe deer are native to Britain, but the fallow was introduced by the Romans and the sika originally came from Japan. Two escaped from the estate at Beaulieu in 1904 and were later joined by another pair that were released to keep them company. There are now a large number in the southern part of the Forest, but they are exceptionally shy and usually only emerge from cover at night.

The wild gladiolus is extremely rare and was given protection in 1975 under an Act of Parliament that makes its removal an offence

A male silver studded butterfly. This species is commonly found on the dry heathlands of the Forest from mid June to August

Among the exhibits in Bucklers Hard Maritime Museum is this figurehead from HMS *Gladiator*. Launched in 1788, the *Gladiator* was one of many ships that rolled off the Bucklers Hard slipway into the Beaulieu River during the 18th century

ROUTE 9

70 MIL

London to Eastbourne

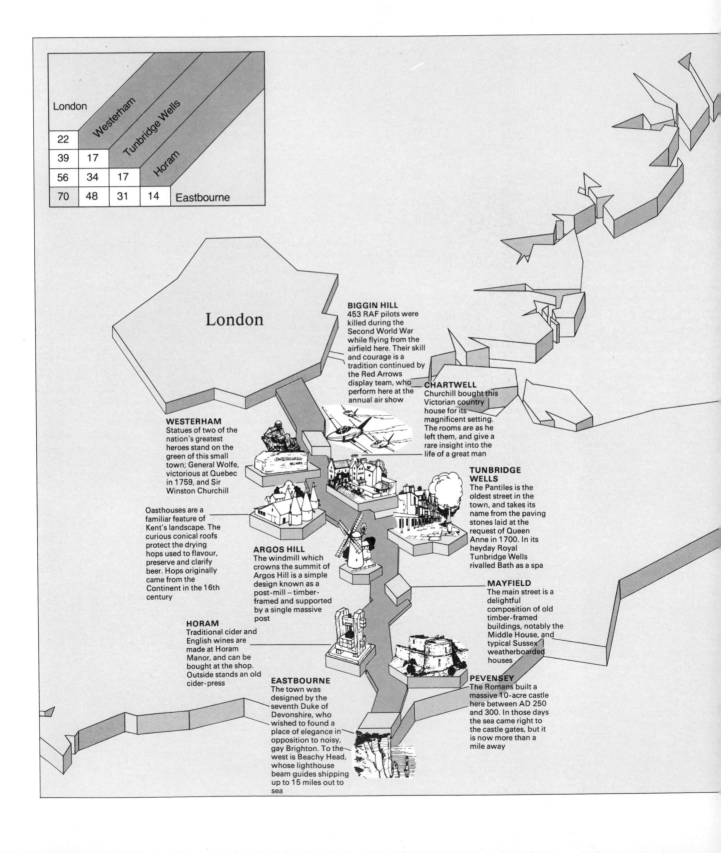

London				
22	Westerham			
39	17	Tunbridge Wells		
56	34	17	Horam	
70	48	31	14	Eastbourne

London

BIGGIN HILL
453 RAF pilots were killed during the Second World War while flying from the airfield here. Their skill and courage is a tradition continued by the Red Arrows display team, who perform here at the annual air show

CHARTWELL
Churchill bought this Victorian country house for its magnificent setting. The rooms are as he left them, and give a rare insight into the life of a great man

WESTERHAM
Statues of two of the nation's greatest heroes stand on the green of this small town; General Wolfe, victorious at Quebec in 1759, and Sir Winston Churchill

Oasthouses are a familiar feature of Kent's landscape. The curious conical roofs protect the drying hops used to flavour, preserve and clarify beer. Hops originally came from the Continent in the 16th century

ARGOS HILL
The windmill which crowns the summit of Argos Hill is a simple design known as a post-mill – timber-framed and supported by a single massive post

TUNBRIDGE WELLS
The Pantiles is the oldest street in the town, and takes its name from the paving stones laid at the request of Queen Anne in 1700. In its heyday Royal Tunbridge Wells rivalled Bath as a spa

MAYFIELD
The main street is a delightful composition of old timber-framed buildings, notably the Middle House, and typical Sussex weatherboarded houses

HORAM
Traditional cider and English wines are made at Horam Manor, and can be bought at the shop. Outside stands an old cider-press

EASTBOURNE
The town was designed by the seventh Duke of Devonshire, who wished to found a place of elegance in opposition to noisy, gay Brighton. To the west is Beachy Head, whose lighthouse beam guides shipping up to 15 miles out to sea

PEVENSEY
The Romans built a massive 10-acre castle here between AD 250 and 300. In those days the sea came right to the castle gates, but it is now more than a mile away

THOUGH this is the shortest route in the book, it
des in its length at least three striking changes of scenery,
l of England's best-loved historic houses, and a wealth of
cular architecture.

ose who do not know the counties to the south and east of
on may think that they consist almost entirely of chunks of
nuterland', separated by countryside that is enlivened
by regimented orchards and huge fields of vegetables.
this is clearly not so is demonstrated by this route, which is
ne of many that could be made through what, for better
rse, is known as the 'Garden of England'.

e route begins in Bromley, an easy-to-reach borough on
inge of London, and rapidly leaves the densest concen-
ns of suburbs behind to emerge on the windswept
lands of the North Downs. This is the first of the
ctive landscapes that are crossed on the route's journey
rds the sea.

pping steeply to Westerham, the road presently climbs
more to cross the woodlands of the Chart and then
ds again to the western part of the Vale of Kent. This is
eart of the Garden of England, and away to the east
h many acres of market gardens, orchards and hop-fields,
riving on the rich Wealden soils. Penshurst and
lingstone, two villages of exceptional charm and beauty
valleys of the rivers Eden and Medway, owe some of their
cter to the 19th century. A good many of Penshurst's
nt-looking timbered and tile-hung cottages are in fact
l reconstructions by Victorian architects and craftsmen,
he castle which looks over Chiddingstone's genuinely
nt houses is a 19th-century version of Gothic architecture.
Chiding Stone, a large sandstone block from which the
e is said to take its name, stands behind the main street.
ing wives were supposedly brought to it to be scolded.

ose who prefer airy hills to fertile lowlands will soon be
ed as the route rises once more on to the tree-clad
tone slopes of the Weald. When the Romans arrived in
ountry much of the Weald was covered by an almost
etrable forest – which they called *Anderida* – and even
centuries later it could not be safely negotiated without
pert help of professional guides. Gradually, however, the
was cleared, partly by sheep, who nibbled the saplings
revented the natural regeneration of the trees, and partly
demands of industry and building.

ch of the timber was made into charcoal for use in the
ng processes of the Wealden ironworkings; and many of
eat trees can still be seen today, incorporated into the
mbered buildings with which this region is so richly
ed. That there are so many fine timbered houses in these
es is due mainly to the seemingly limitless supplies of
but it may also have something to do with the system of
tance introduced by Germanic settlers who arrived after
oman withdrawal. Their land was left to be divided
g all the children – not only the eldest. This tradition,
lingered for centuries, goes some way to explaining why
are far more small farms and manor houses in the
en counties than in other parts of the country.

vards the end of the 17th century tiles became more
y available, and many of the old half-timbered houses
aced with hung tiles as additional weatherproofing. A
ry later, houses began to be faced with imported
ods – and today weatherboarding is the hallmark of
Kentish vernacular architecture.

PLACES OF INTEREST: OPENING DETAILS

Westerham
QUEBEC HOUSE
open Apr to Oct daily
(except Thu and Sat),
also Sun only in Mar,
pm only

CHARTWELL open
Mar to Nov Tue to
Thu, pm only; Sat,
Sun and Bank
Holiday Mon all day;
garden and studio
Apr to mid Oct, same
times

Hever
HEVER CASTLE AND
GARDENS open Apr
to Sep Tue, Wed, Fri,
Sun and Bank
Holidays, pm only

Chiddingstone
CHIDDINGSTONE
CASTLE open Apr to
Oct Tue to Fri, pm
only; Sat, Sun and
Bank Holiday Mon, all
day

Penshurst
PENSHURST PLACE
open Apr to early Oct
daily(except Mon and
Fri), pm only.

Heathfield
HEATHFIELD
WILDLIFE PARK open
all year (except 25
and 26 Dec)

Pevensey
PEVENSEY CASTLE
open all year

OLD MINTHOUSE
open all year Mon to
Fri all day, Sat am
only; also all day Sun
mid Jul to Sep

Eastbourne
ROYAL NATIONAL
LIFEBOAT MUSEUM
open Easter to Sep

TOWNER ART
GALLERY open all
year (except Good
Fri, 25 and 26 Dec),
Mon to Sat am and
pm, Sun pm only

EASTBOURNE
CIRCULAR REDOUBT
open May to Sep
daily, Oct to Apr Mon
to Fri

WISH TOWER:
COASTAL DEFENCE
MUSEUM open
Easter to Sep

Stone from the sandstone belts and bricks made from Wealden clays are also important features of the buildings of this area. There are a great many different textures and colours, reflecting the subtle differences in the character of the raw materials. Other famous architectural features of the south-east are the yeomen's houses, with their overhanging jetties, and catslides – large expanses of tiled roof stretching from roof level almost to the ground.

The route travels through this intriguing mix of history and geology to Tunbridge Wells, which is about half-way along the route. On the way it has passed mansions like Hever Castle and Penshurst Place, which were chosen as homes by noble and important people because of the beautiful countryside, and also because of their proximity to London. Sir Winston Churchill, General Wolfe of Quebec, Sir Philip Sydney and Anne Boleyn all had their homes on or near this route, and their houses – rich in historic memories and treasured belongings – are now open to the public.

Tunbridge Wells did not exist until the middle of the 17th century. It owed its discovery and growth to Dudley, Lord North, who noticed a pool of discoloured water in the Wealden woodlands while returning from an unsuccessful rest cure at Eridge Castle in 1606. He tried the waters, found them beneficial, and by the 1630s the waters were being taken by great numbers of the nobility and by royalty. At the beginning of the 19th century, though it was a fashionable spa, Tunbridge was still little more than a village, but a tremendous amount of residential expansion took place after 1830. Today the town is popular with London's commuter population.

Continuing across the Weald, the route touches the eastern part of Ashdown Forest near Mayfield. This is the largest remnant of the forest of *Anderida*. At Hailsham begins the third of the outstanding landscape types on this route – the Pevensey Levels, a flat coastal plain made up of sedimentary materials and stretching from Eastbourne to Bexhill.

Eastbourne is situated at a point where the three principal landscapes of this route meet. To the north-east are the sandy soils of the Pevensey Levels; the town itself stands on a bed of greensand, and stretching eastwards from the Hampshire border is the rolling glory of the South Downs, culminating in the towering chalk cliffs of Beachy Head.

BROMLEY TO WESTERHAM

The starting point of this route is Bromley, 13 miles south-east of central London on the A21. From Bromley market place follow signs for Sevenoaks and the A21, driving down the High Street. Just past Bromley South station, turn right (SP Hayes, B265), then very shortly left into Hayes Road. In ½ mile, at the T-junction, turn right (SP Hayes, Keston), to join the B265.

Now the gradual change from metropolis to countryside begins: trees soften the landscape and a few market gardens and fields give a foretaste of Kent, the 'Garden of England'. Cross the A232 on Hayes Common, then pass through Keston and shortly turn right on to the A233 for Westerham. Just past Leaves Green, the route passes Biggin Hill Airport, one of the airfields from which the Battle of Britain was fought in 1940. A host of light aircraft can usually be seen lined up beside the road on the left, and there is a public viewing area.

The A233 runs through Biggin Hill village and later, at the foot of a steep, attractively wooded hill, crosses the ancient Pilgrims' Way, which runs right along the North Downs. In complete contrast, less than 1 mile later, the road crosses a recently opened section of the M25 London orbital motorway.

The A233 meets the busy A25 by the green in Westerham, and here the route turns left. An attractive town at the edge of the North Downs, Westerham is chiefly noted as the home of two great men, both commemorated by statues on the green. At the top is James Wolfe, the English military commander who defeated the French at Quebec in 1759. He was born and brought up here, and his home,

Quebec House,* lies to the east of the town on the A25. Many relics are on display there. The other statue is of Sir Winston Churchill, who lived for the last 40 years of his life at nearby Chartwell. At the far corner of the green is Westerham's church, parts of which date back to the Early English period. A fine 14th-century timber spiral staircase leads up to the bell-tower.

WESTERHAM TO PENSHURST

Drive along the A25 for ¼ mile and turn right on to the B2026 (SP Edenbridge). The route climbs to cross an area of heath and woodland called the Chart, then turns left on to an unclassified road (SP Chartwell), passing the house where Churchill lived.* Many Churchill memorabilia are preserved at Chartwell, including a number of Sir Winston's paintings. Visitors can stroll through the gardens, which give magnificent views over the Vale of Kent to the Weald beyond, and can see the high wall round the kitchen garden, built by Churchill himself.

Continue along this lane, and in 2 miles turn left on to the B269 (SP Tonbridge, Edenbridge), keeping forward at Four Elms crossroads to join the B2027 for Bough Beech.

HEVER CASTLE

After 1 mile a detour may be made to Hever Castle,* signposted to the right. Hever was the home of Anne Boleyn, and was visited by Henry VIII. He later took over the 13th-century moated castle and gave it to Anne of Cleves, his fourth wife. Yet despite its royal connections, the castle was forgotten and fell into disrepair, to be restored to its former magnificence only this century when the wealthy American Astor family bought it.

main route continues along the B2027 to
h Beech, where it turns right then left
the railway bridge.

CHIDDINGSTONE

rtly past here a second detour can be
de by turning right on to an unclassified
d which leads to the National Trust village
hiddingstone. Ahead at the crossroads is
ddingstone Castle,* complete with turrets
battlements and a lake popular with
lers. Turn left into the village, whose little
et offers a backward glimpse to Tudor
es. Some of the timber-framed houses are
erved almost exactly as they were in the
n century.

---

main route follows the B2027 to
dingstone Causeway. Shortly past
urst station turn right on to the B2176,
passing some of the oast-houses which
re in so many pictures of Kent. Some are
n use, some have been converted into
commuter residences and others left to
, but they are still very much a trade-
of this corner of England.

the T-junction turn right (SP Penshurst,
ridge Wells) into Penshurst. To the left
green sweep of Penshurst Park, where
ful trees are scattered around the lake,
on Penshurst Place* comes into view. It
e and very well-preserved 14th-century
r, although the part visible from this
is mainly a later addition. The visitors'
nce, through a gate by the village
h, leads to the original manor with its
ous medieval hall. In 1552 the house was

*Penshurst churchyard is reached through a cluster of
half-timbered cottages known as Leicester Square*

---

given by Edward VI to Sir William Sydney,
grandfather of the Elizabethan poet and
statesman Sir Philip Sydney, and it remained
the seat of the Sydney family for some 200
years. The creeper-clad Leicester Arms Hotel
in the village is named after Sir Philip's
brother Robert, who was created Earl of
Leicester in 1618. In Penshurst church is a
fine modern stained-glass window commemorating the institution of its first parish
priest by St Thomas à Becket.

---

*Although they are seldom used for drying hops now,
oast-houses are still a familiar feature of Kent's landscape*

PENSHURST TO TUNBRIDGE WELLS

Turn right in Penshurst on to the B2188 for
Tunbridge Wells, then at the T-junction 1
mile past Fordcombe turn left on to the A264
(SP Tunbridge Wells) and at the next T-
junction left again for Tunbridge Wells.

HIGH ROCKS

An unclassified road to the right on Rusthall
Common (SP High Rocks) offers a detour
down a narrow, steep lane to High Rocks.
Huge blocks of weathered sandstone rise
among oaks and rhododendrons to create a
weird and fantastic world of curious shapes
and gloomy grottoes. Paths and bridges have
been constructed to make the extraordinary
rock formations easy to explore, and the area
is also popular with trainee climbers.

Continue along the A264 into Tunbridge
Wells. No visitor should miss the Pantiles, the
Regency arcade built for fashionable
Londoners who came here to take the waters.
The mineral springs at Tunbridge Wells were
discovered in 1606. News of their beneficial
properties soon reached royal ears, and
Queen Henrietta Maria came here in 1630 to
recuperate after the birth of Prince Charles,
later King Charles II. She camped on the
Common, for the colonnade of the Pantiles
was not built until later in the 17th century.
The Pantiles still makes a perfect pedestrian
shopping area, inviting visitors to browse in its
elegant boutiques or take a break in one of the
teashops, just as it offered rest and refreshment
to the smart city-dwellers of two and three
centuries ago. (Route continues on p. 102.)

THE WEALD

CONVENIENT sources of raw materials, excellent communications, power provided by swift-flowing streams and rivers – all these combined to make the Weald the greatest industrial area in England for many hundreds of years. Wealden iron was known to the Romans, but it was not until the 16th and 17th centuries that the industry reached its peak. Cannon and shot were the most important products, but the railings and ornamental gates for St Paul's Cathedral in London were wrought at Lamberhurst in the 18th century.

Until the end of the 15th century the production of iron was a tremendously laborious and wasteful business, demanding huge amounts of charcoal to smelt tiny quantities of iron, and repeated hammering of the metal to remove the waste material (which included a great deal of unsmelted iron and was often re-used in later centuries). However, in about 1490 blast-furnaces were introduced from the Continent and caused a boom in production, although the process still demanded mountains of charcoal.

By the late 16th century over 7000 men were employed in the Wealden iron industry, and in 1574 the Admiralty remarked that so many trees were being devoured to make cannon for naval ships that there was a real danger no timber would be left to build the ships themselves. At Ashburnham – the last works to close, in 1828 – 250 tons of timber were needed to produce just 13 tons of pure iron.

The ore came mainly from 'bell pits' scattered throughout the Weald. Miners sank a vertical shaft, about six feet in diameter, then opened out a bell-shaped chamber when they reached the iron, generally no more than 20 feet below the surface.

At the peak of production the Weald was loud with the sound of hammering and bright with the glare from furnaces, but none of the forges or furnaces now survive. The Wealden iron industry began to decline in the 18th century, partly because the local fuel was running out, but mainly because another fuel, coal, attracted the industry to the North Country. The most prominent visual reminders of the industry are the hammer-ponds (like the Furnace Pool at Horsmonsden) which were created to store water for turning the mill wheels that powered the furnace bellows and the huge trip-hammers. Cinders and slag made excellent road surfaces, and may still be found along a few unfrequented country lanes.

FRAMED by the North and South Downs, the Weald runs right across West and East Sussex to the far side of Kent. It forms part of the 'Garden of England' and is almost too English to be true. It is the sort of country that a film director would choose to portray all the most typical aspects of English life.

Low, wooded hills run down to fertile valleys where plump cattle graze beneath the trees. Orchards are heavy with blossom in late spring and early summer. Picturesque oast-houses, many tastefully transformed into homes of great character and charm, thrust their conical heads above acre after acre of hops. There are ruined castles and elegant mansions – many of them open to visitors – windmills and follies, formal gardens and tracts of open country where signs warn motorists to beware of ponies and deer.

With few exceptions, the Wealden buildings are every bit as beautiful as the landscape itself. Some are picture-postcard studies in timber-framed black and white. Others feature pale and weathered stone, reminiscent of the Cotswolds, or mellow brick. In many cases, visual appeal is enhanced by weatherboarding or hanging tiles. Biddenden, Petworth, East Grinstead, Goudhurst, Penshurst and Royal Tunbridge Wells – a fashionable spa in Regency times – are just six of the many places with architecture to delight the stroller. One of the greatest treasures is Chiddingstone, a tiny gem of a village whose Tudor buildings are protected by the National Trust.

One of the most famous ironmasters was 'Mad Jack' Full an eccentric 19th-century squire MP who is buried beneath a loft rather sinister pyramid in Bright churchyard (above). According local legend he was entombed sit upright, wearing a top hat and clutching a bottle of claret. The countryside around Brightling is dotted with follies that were buil 'Mad Jack'.

Left: Furnace ponds like the one at L Beeding are evocative reminders of the Wealden iron industry

Oast-houses like the one near Chiddingstone (left) were built to dry hops, which are used to clarify, preserve and flavour beer. The hops are ready for harvest in late summer, and during Victorian times it became traditional for London's Cockneys to make extra money by working in the hop-fields, as is depicted in the illustration above, taken from the 'Illustrated London Almanack' of 1870

[SM]UGGLERS once roamed the [Weald] in huge bands as contraband – [chiefl]y tea, coffee, brandy and silks – [m]oved inland from quiet [harbo]urs on the coast. The illicit [trade w]as at its height in the 18th [centur]y when the 'owlers' – so called [becaus]e they used owl-like noises as [warnin]g cries – fought pitched battles [with e]xcisemen. The notorious [Hawk]hurst Gang, led by a smuggler [called] Arthur Gray, could muster [more t]han 300 horsemen plus many [more r]uffians on foot.

[The] gang was later commanded by [Thom]as Kingsmill, who came from [Goudh]urst, and the Star and Eagle [th]ere – connected to the church [by a tu]nnel – was one of their bases. [Sprays], a neighbouring house of [glowi]ng brick, was a convenient [look-o]ut post in the main street. [Larg]e profits were made by the [smugg]lers and by the local people [who ai]ded them, but in the eyes of [law-ab]iding citizens the owlers [were n]othing more than mercenary [cut-thr]oats who terrorized the [counte]ryside.

The Star and Eagle at Goudhurst [was a r]endezvous for smugglers in the [18th cen]tury

The Hawkhurst Gang was finally broken up in 1747 when the people of Goudhurst, led by an ex-soldier called Thomas Sturt, decided to band together in an attempt to keep the smugglers out. When he heard that

the village was to be defended against him, Kingsmill contemptuously announced that he would raze the village to the ground, and even informed the villagers when they could expect him to arrive.

When the gang attacked they found the streets booby-trapped with concealed trenches, snipers on every vantage point and the church turned into a fortress. The smugglers retreated, leaving several of their fellows dead and many more wounded, but Kingsmill himself escaped. He was finally brought to justice two years later and hanged at Tyburn after having been caught robbing a coach. His body was subsequently brought back to Goudhurst and hung in chains outside the village.

Not all of the smugglers were murdering louts, and some had respectable daytime occupations. The tale is told of a Sussex vicar who pretended to be ill and cancelled Sunday services because his church was being used as a temporary warehouse for contraband. The tradition of turning a blind eye was immortalized by Rudyard Kipling in his poem 'A Smuggler's Song':

Five and twenty ponies
Trotting through the dark –
Brandy for the parson,
'Baccy for the clerk;
Laces for a lady, letters for a spy,
And watch the wall, my darling,
while the Gentlemen go by!

TUNBRIDGE WELLS TO MAYFIELD

Leave Tunbridge Wells by the A267 Eastbourne road. The land drops sharply away to the right, giving more of the open views which are typical of this undulating route. Frant is the first Sussex village, with an interesting church off to the left as you enter the village. The interior is a reminder that you are in the Sussex Weald, once famed for its iron-working industry: the pillars, gallery balustrade and window tracery are all of Sussex iron. The unusual churchyard gate is hexagonal – almost like a bandstand – and has an interior weather-vane on the ceiling, attached to the one outside on the roof. From the church an attractive street of cottages leads to the spacious green.

The route continues along the A267 towards Mayfield, dipping and rolling along through the Sussex countryside, more open and less intimate than that of Kent. To the right of the road less than 2 miles beyond Frant is tree-clad Saxonbury Hill, the site of an Iron Age camp whose defensive ditch can still be clearly distinguished. A later addition to the hilltop is a folly, a round tower dated 1828 and complete with arrow-slits. About 3 miles further on, the route passes Argos Hill, topped by a picture-book windmill above the trees. To the left are more fine views, with the Norman tower and tall spire of Wadhurst church in the distance.

MAYFIELD TO HORAM

Mayfield is a most picturesque Wealden village, its houses and shops variously half-timbered, tile-hung and weatherboarded, giving the village a wealth of local charm. The convent school in the main street incorporates what remains of an ancient palace of the Archbishops of Canterbury, including a wonderfully well-preserved 14th-century hall, now the convent's chapel. Mayfield's connection with the Archbishops of Canterbury dates back to the 10th century and to St Dunstan, who was a blacksmith in Mayfield. Legend has it that when he was visited at his anvil one day by the devil, he grasped the devil's nose with a pair of red-hot tongs. The incident is depicted on the elaborate village sign in the main street, along with the 'maid's field' which is thought to have given the village its name. The sign won second prize in a nationwide village-sign competition in 1920. The church is dedicated to St Dunstan, who built the first church on this site. Two unusual cast-iron grave slabs – one with several characters cast back to front – in the floor of the nave testify to Mayfield's former iron-working days.

Leave Mayfield centre on the A267, and on a right-hand bend shortly past the Mayfield Inn branch left on to an unclassified road. An attractive country lane leads down into the upper reaches of the Rother valley and climbs again through pretty woodland. When you reach the A265, turn right on to it and in ¼

mile turn left on to the B2203 (SP Horam, Hailsham, Eastbourne). Heathfield Park, former home of General Eliott, later Lord Heathfield, defender of Gibraltar, lies to the left behind a long stone wall. The Gibraltar Tower is a folly in the park, built to commemorate Eliott's military successes in the 1780s. The grounds are now a wildlife park* whose attractions include vultures, ostriches and chimpanzees. Queen Victoria's Royal Pavilion houses a museum of agricultural archaeology.

The B2203 leads through the edge of Heathfield to Horam, passing the Runt-in-Tun pub, whose name might appear to be gibberish without the accompanying sign showing a pig in a barrel. The name is a pun on that of nearby Runtington Manor Farm.

HORAM TO EASTBOURNE

At Horam, turn left on to the A267. Just past the junction is Horam Manor, the head-quarters of the Merrydown Wine and Cider Company. An old wooden cider-press stands by the road and there is a shop where visitors can buy English wines and cider.

Four miles past Horam turn left (SP Hellingly Hospital, Horsebridge) and at Lower Horsebridge left again on to the A271, then cross the Cuckmere River and turn right on to the B2104 (SP Hailsham). Continue through Upper Horsebridge to Hailsham, a busy little market town and shopping centre, and leave on the A295 Eastbourne road. In just under ½ mile turn left on to the B2104 (SP Pevensey); this road is less likely to attract the nose-to-tail queues which can so easily spoil the last few miles of a holiday journey. Past Hailsham, the landscape changes dramatically after what has been a very up-and-down drive. To the right is the outline of the South Downs, plunging to the sea at Beachy Head. Away to the left stretch the flat, damp plains of the Pevensey Levels, once completely covered by the sea.

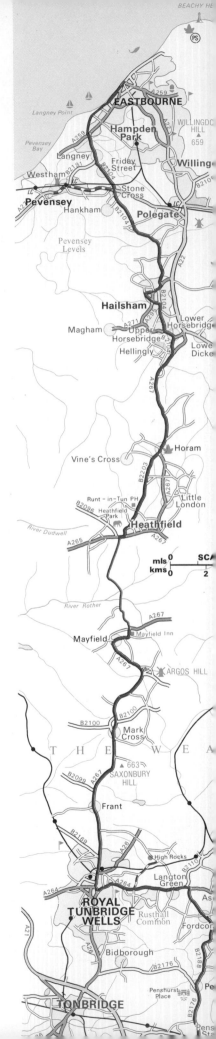

PEVENSEY

...vensey, 2½ miles east of the B2104 along the ...7, was a historic place even when the ...ormans landed, and they incorporated part ...the 3rd-century Roman fort which was ...eady there into their castle.* The Normans ...d a mint at Pevensey, and the building now ...own as the Old Minthouse,* built some 300 ...ars later, occupies the same site. For a long ...e Pevensey was one of the chief ports of ...ssex, but the silting of its harbour and the ...clamation of the marshes led to its decline, ...ough boats of up to 60 tons could reach it ...til the 16th century. Today, Pevensey is ...re than a mile from the sea.

...he last few miles the route runs through ...ourne's seaside-town sprawl, but ...g crossed the A27 and passed through ...y Street (where the route joins the ...1) and the modern estates of Langney, it ...reaches the seafront.

EASTBOURNE

Eastbourne combines all the conventional pleasures of the seaside with an atmosphere of great elegance, as well as many unexpected delights of its own.

The elegance of the place is due to a gentleman whose statue stands in Devonshire Place. He was William Cavendish, later the Seventh Duke of Devonshire, who turned the town into a genteel watering place in the 19th century when sea-bathing became fashionable. A wealthy landowner with an eye for business, he laid out the smart squares and crescents and built the grand hotels which attracted the gentry of a century ago, giving the town a dignity it has never lost. The 3-mile-long seafront is still lined with restrained, colour-washed buildings, some featuring tile-hung gables or ironwork balustrades to give the flavour of Sussex.

Eastbourne's unique attractions include, first and foremost, the dramatic cliffs of Beachy Head, where the South Downs drop abruptly to the sea, offering superb walking country with spectacular views. In the town itself you will find the country's first lifeboat

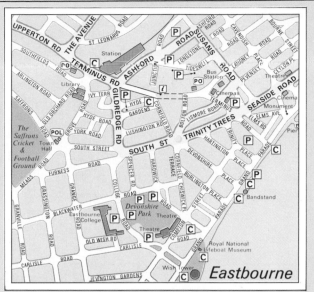

Eastbourne

museum;* a huge bandstand arena which can accommodate audiences of up to 3500 people; and the Towner Art Gallery* – a Georgian house containing a collection of paintings of local interest as well as a wider range of 19th- and 20th-century works. The historically minded will not want to miss Eastbourne's reminders of the Napoleonic Wars: two fortresses, built in the early 19th

century when it was feared that Napoleon might invade England. One is the Redoubt, on Royal Parade, now housing a museum of the military history of Sussex.* The other, the Wish Tower, is one of many Martello towers built along this part of the coast for the same reason. It also houses a museum,* with an exhibition illustrating defence methods and armaments of the Napoleonic period.

ROUTE 10

181 MIL

Birmingham to Norwich

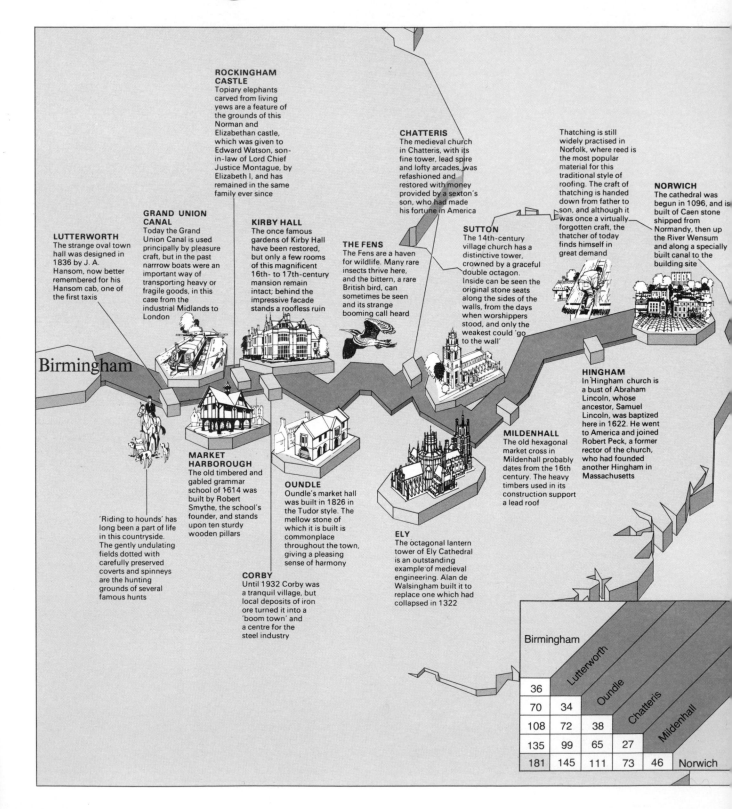

ROCKINGHAM CASTLE
Topiary elephants carved from living yews are a feature of the grounds of this Norman and Elizabethan castle, which was given to Edward Watson, son-in-law of Lord Chief Justice Montague, by Elizabeth I, and has remained in the same family ever since

CHATTERIS
The medieval church in Chatteris, with its fine tower, lead spire and lofty arcades, was refashioned and restored with money provided by a sexton's son, who had made his fortune in America

Thatching is still widely practised in Norfolk, where reed is the most popular material for this traditional style of roofing. The craft of thatching is handed down from father to son, and although it was once a virtually forgotten craft, the thatcher of today finds himself in great demand

NORWICH
The cathedral was begun in 1096, and is built of Caen stone shipped from Normandy, then up the River Wensum and along a specially built canal to the building site

GRAND UNION CANAL
Today the Grand Union Canal is used principally by pleasure craft, but in the past narrow boats were an important way of transporting heavy or fragile goods, in this case from the industrial Midlands to London

KIRBY HALL
The once famous gardens of Kirby Hall have been restored, but only a few rooms of this magnificent 16th- to 17th-century mansion remain intact; behind the impressive facade stands a roofless ruin

SUTTON
The 14th-century village church has a distinctive tower, crowned by a graceful double octagon. Inside can be seen the original stone seats along the sides of the walls, from the days when worshippers stood, and only the weakest could 'go to the wall'

LUTTERWORTH
The strange oval town hall was designed in 1836 by J. A. Hansom, now better remembered for his Hansom cab, one of the first taxis

THE FENS
The Fens are a haven for wildlife. Many rare insects thrive here, and the bittern, a rare British bird, can sometimes be seen and its strange booming call heard

Birmingham

HINGHAM
In Hingham church is a bust of Abraham Lincoln, whose ancestor, Samuel Lincoln, was baptized here in 1622. He went to America and joined Robert Peck, a former rector of the church, who had founded another Hingham in Massachusetts

MILDENHALL
The old hexagonal market cross in Mildenhall probably dates from the 16th century. The heavy timbers used in its construction support a lead roof

MARKET HARBOROUGH
The old timbered and gabled grammar school of 1614 was built by Robert Smythe, the school's founder, and stands upon ten sturdy wooden pillars

OUNDLE
Oundle's market hall was built in 1826 in the Tudor style. The mellow stone of which it is built is commonplace throughout the town, giving a pleasing sense of harmony

'Riding to hounds' has long been a part of life in this countryside. The gently undulating fields dotted with carefully preserved coverts and spinneys are the hunting grounds of several famous hunts

ELY
The octagonal lantern tower of Ely Cathedral is an outstanding example of medieval engineering. Alan de Walsingham built it to replace one which had collapsed in 1322

CORBY
Until 1932 Corby was a tranquil village, but local deposits of iron ore turned it into a 'boom town' and a centre for the steel industry

Birmingham	Lutterworth	Oundle	Chatteris	Mildenhall	
36					
70	34				
108	72	38			
135	99	65	27		
181	145	111	73	46	Norwich

STARTING in the heart of the industrial Midlands, this route travels eastwards through Birmingham's suburbs to reach open country beyond the hilltop town of Coleshill. From Nuneaton, with its memories of the novelist George Eliot, the route makes its way through Lutterworth into the fox-hunting country around Market Harborough. Hounds and riders have been chasing foxes across the Leicestershire countryside since the 18th century, and the names of some of the packs are now world-famous. Hunting became such an all-consuming passion among the local gentry that they planted groups of trees – as cover and breeding places for the foxes – which have grown to create a landscape that is both attractive and highly distinctive. The route continues to Corby, hardly more than a village until the 20th century, but now an industrial sprawl surrounded by the livid scars of opencast mining. Oundle – little more than ten miles further on – seems worlds apart. Here handsome old houses and a famous public school stand near the tranquil waters of the River Nene.

Beyond Clopton and the Giddings are the vast levels of the Cambridgeshire Fens, stretching to distant horizons and dominated by arrow-straight drainage channels and church towers thrusting into enormous skies. Until the Fens were drained during the 17th century this was a land apart, virtually inaccessible and with a fiercely independent population who made their homes on the islands of gravel and clay which rose from the surrounding lakes and marshes.

Rheumatism and malaria (in England called the ague) were serious drawbacks to life in these strange lands, but the advantages – limitless supplies of fish and wildfowl, and distance from the interfering outside world – attracted monks as well as the fenmen. The remains of one of their abbeys can be seen on this route at Ramsey, and Chatteris, on the other side of Nene Fen, is one of the fenland towns that is built on what was once an island.

After crossing the Old Bedford River – created during the 17th-century land drainage scheme and running across country without a bend for 21 miles – the route reaches Ely and the tremendous lantern-tower of its abbey church.

Wicken Fen, to the south of Soham, is one of the few remaining areas of undrained fen, standing several feet above the surrounding countryside. As the fens around were drained to expose the rich peat soil, the peat itself began to dry and sink, leaving Wicken Fen, which formed the common for the village of Wicken and was never drained, remaining high and wet.

Beyond Mildenhall the route leaves the Fens and crosses another of East Anglia's distinctive landscapes – the Breckland. This great tract of wind-blown sand and gravel covers nearly 400 square miles and is Britain's nearest equivalent to a desert. It was not always as desolate as it appears today. Until the 13th century the area was well populated, but the inhabitants created a dustbowl by destroying the heathland vegetation which had consolidated the thin soil. Overwhelming disaster struck in about 1300 when a great sandblow covered some parts of Breckland to a depth of three feet. Where cultivation was carried out the plough turned up thousands of flints – hence the name, the broken or 'breck' land.

Until the 18th century, when trees began to be planted as wind-breaks and boundary markers, the sands of the Breckland were frequently blown uninterrupted for miles by the notorious East Anglian winds, and it was not uncommon for whole villages to be inundated by drifts. In 1922 the Forestry Commission began to plant conifers around Thetford on a

large scale, and extensive areas have also been set aside as army training grounds and air force bases, but in several areas the heathland flora and fauna that is special to Breckland has been left virtually undisturbed, and is a happy hunting-ground for botanists, naturalists and those who simply enjoy beautiful open country.

To the east of the route from Brandon to Mundford are Grime's Graves, where Neolithic man dug deep into Breckland in search of the flints from which he made his weapons and tools. Over 350 partly filled-in mine shafts have been discovered in the area, and one of them has been excavated and roofed with concrete so that visitors can go down to explore the ancient workings.

Flint is still worked at Brandon. It is used in the pottery industry, for the firing mechanisms of reproduction flintlock guns and for the flushwork that graces many East Anglian buildings. East Anglia has a shortage of usable building stone, but a wealth of flint, so it was natural for builders to make use of this hard material. The flints were 'knapped' or split apart and used with their flat, dark sides facing outwards; indeed, the use of flint in parts of East Anglia became an art form. Norwich has some particularly fine examples of flushwork patterns. Flints for use in churches and important buildings were finely worked and squared, but some of the more modest buildings incorporate into their walls huge, roughly broken flints. Round church towers built of flint are a familiar landmark throughout East Anglia. There are over a hundred in Norfolk alone, the reason for their appearance being that flint is unsuitable for quoins – the stout rectangular stones necessary to construct the corners of square towers.

The route skirts Breckland's vast 'battle area', where whole villages have been abandoned and given up to military use, and makes its way to Norwich through the quiet and unspoilt countryside along the upper reaches of the River Yare.

Norwich, the capital of East Anglia and the destination of this route, is unique in being the only provincial city in England to have produced a 'school' of painters. Many of their pictures, including an unrivalled collection of watercolours and oils by the group's most important painter, John Sell Cotman, now hang in the Norwich Castle Museum. The thirty or so artists associated with the School captured on paper and canvas the huge skies and gentle landscapes which are the outstanding features of the latter part of this route.

106 *Route 10*

BIRMINGHAM TO NUNEATON

If you are setting off from the Bull Ring at the centre of Birmingham, follow signs for the A47 (East) and Nuneaton. If it is more convenient you can join the route from the A4040 ring road or from the roundabout adjacent to junction 5 of the M6 at Castle Bromwich (motorway access to it from south only). The A47 leads for several miles through rather featureless suburbs to the roundabout at the edge of Castle Bromwich, where you should take the first exit. In ½ mile, at the next roundabout, take the third exit, the A452, which runs for 3¾ miles alongside the M6 then reaches another roundabout where you take the first exit, the B4114. After crossing the motorway, suburbs give way to green fields and the route crosses the River Cole before passing through Coleshill, whose huge power station dominates views to the left as the route continues across the Tame valley. About 2 miles beyond Shustoke, at Furnace End crossroads, turn right with the B4114 (SP Nuneaton), then in 4 miles, at Church End, turn right on to the B4112 (SP Ansley). Keep forward through Ansley for Nuneaton, and at the roundabout take the second exit. The nearby village of Astley, signposted off to the right, was the family home of Lady Jane Grey, the 'Nine Days Queen'.

As you come into the suburbs of Nuneaton, keep forward on to the B4102. Soon you will see signs for Arbury Hall.* The entrance to this astonishing 18th-century Gothic mansion is on the right, guarded by a gatehouse like a miniature castle. The house stands on the site of an Augustinian priory, and retains some features of the 16th-century mansion which replaced it after the Dissolution of the Monasteries. The interior is just as elaborate as the exterior, with fan-vaulted ceilings, decorative panelling and elaborate chimney-pieces. Fine furniture and china are on display in the house, and the paintings include one of a lady-in-waiting to Queen Elizabeth I sometimes claimed to be Shakespeare's enigmatic 'dark lady' of the Sonnets. Arbury's 17th-century stable block houses a museum of veteran cycles.

Just outside Arbury Park is South Farm, the birthplace in 1819 of Mary Ann Evans – better known as George Eliot, the author of such classic Victorian novels as *The Mill on the Floss*, *Silas Marner* and *Middlemarch*. As a child, she often accompanied her father on his rounds as agent for Arbury Hall and later used much of what she had seen in her books.

NUNEATON TO LUTTERWORTH

To by-pass the centre of Nuneaton, turn right ½ mile past the entrance to Arbury Hall into Heath End Road (SP Coventry, B4112). After 1 mile keep right, and at the roundabout junction with the A444 take the first exit (SP Lutterworth). At the next roundabout take the second exit, still following the B4112, into Avenue Road, and in ½ mile, at the

This curiously placed wooden dog looks across the street facing Lutterworth's 19th-century town hall

centre of Attleborough, turn right, kee forward 1 mile later, where the road fork to the B4114 (SP Lutterworth, Rugby). 1¾ miles, where the road forks again, bea to continue along the B4114, following s for the A46. The road soon crosses the and in ¾ mile reaches a crossroads whe keeps forward for Lutterworth. At roundabout take the third exit, the B (SP Lutterworth). This peaceful, stra road leads through open country, cros two Roman roads – the Fosse Way afte miles then, 3¾ miles later, at a roundab Watling Street (now the A5). Take second exit here, the A427 (SP Lutterwo Market Harborough), passing Bittes Aerodrome on the left.

Follow signs for Market Harbor through Lutterworth, a little town w may well once have been a more thri centre than it seems today, though its st have character and its buildings are interesting than they may at first appea neo-classical town hall, for example, is usual in being oval in shape, and a pla informs you that it was designed in 183 the J. A. Hansom who gave his name t Hansom cab, the forerunner of the mo taxi. Half-hidden behind the town hall real old-fashioned sweet shop and on th just below is a traditional draper's shop. butcher's, too, is no chain store, b thatched, half-timbered building at the end of the market place. The large p

Gaily painted narrow-boats on the Grand Union Canal near North Kilworth. Once the busiest canal network in the country, the Grand Union linked London with Birmingham, Leicester and Nottingham

church, dating from the 13th and 14th centuries, was well known to John Wycliffe, who made the first English translation of the Bible. He was rector here from 1374 until his death ten years later. He and his followers, called Lollards, were considered heretics, and his bones were later exhumed, burned and thrown into the nearby River Swift. The charming row of old half-timbered cottages beside the church has been carefully restored and would grace any town.

LUTTERWORTH TO LUBENHAM

As you leave Lutterworth on the Market Harborough road, the A427 turns left off the A426 to cross the M1, continuing through Walcote to North Kilworth.

NORTH KILWORTH CHURCH

A short detour can be made to North Kilworth church, reached by turning right (SP South Kilworth) in the village, then left a few hundred yards later. The chancel is fine Early English work, and you can still see a pane of the old east window bearing an inscription written with a diamond by William Belgrave in 1665: 'Fear God, honour ye King. He who giveth to the poor lendeth to the Lord.' The 14th-century west tower has a peal of five bells, though the church history notes that 'The rising bell at 5am and the dinner bell at 1 o'clock are no longer rung, nor is the Pancake Bell on Shrove Tuesday.'

Shortly past North Kilworth the road crosses the Leicester section of the Grand Union Canal and continues into Husbands Bosworth. This place took the first part of its unusual name ('husband' here meaning 'farmer') to distinguish it from Market Bosworth – scene of the famous battle where Richard III was killed – which lies some miles to the north. It is an outstandingly attractive little red-brick town with a real country atmosphere, and a stroll round its streets is refreshing before you press on along the A427 towards Market Harborough.

This is hunting country, as is evident in the numerous spinneys and coverts – small patches of woodland maintained by the hunting squires to ensure a good supply of foxes – shown on large-scale maps: Tallyho Covert, Long Hold Spinney, Gumley Covert; the names speak for themselves. Whatever the rights and wrongs of foxhunting, these rolling, spacious landscapes make an unforgettable impression.

The A427 runs through the pretty village of Theddingworth, whose unusual cottage industry was once the weaving of silk plush for covering hats. Several miles to the south is the famous battlefield of Naseby, where Oliver Cromwell's forces defeated the Royalists in 1645. Lubenham, the next village, has an attractive 13th-century church whose dignified Georgian interior features a three-decker pulpit and box pews.

LUBENHAM TO CORBY

From Lubenham the A427 continues to Market Harborough, a bustling and lively town, its architecture appealing, especially in the High Street and the square, which is dominated by the fine steeple of St Dionysius' Church. Created a market town by Henry II, Market Harborough has retained much of its charm despite modern development. Its best-known building is the old grammar school, a quaint timbered house set on pillars and featuring decorative plasterwork reminiscent of Suffolk 'pargeting'. In the High Street is the Three Swans, a pub with a marvellous 18th-century inn sign of wrought iron.

The Three Swans Inn, Market Harborough

The splendid 14th-century broach spire of Market Harborough's church overlooks the quaint old grammar school, which dates from 1614

Follow the A427 (SP Corby) through the town centre and continue towards Corby, crossing the border into Northamptonshire. The countryside is more hilly here and it seems odd that a steel town should be set among such green fields.

ROCKINGHAM CASTLE

Just before the route enters Corby, you can turn left at the roundabout on to the A6003 (SP Oakham) for a detour to Rockingham Castle* and Park, just over 1 mile away on the left. The castle was for centuries a royal hunting lodge for Rockingham Forest, which once covered much of Leicestershire. Although the castle dates from Norman times, the 11th-century keep was destroyed during the Civil War, when the Roundheads captured the castle from the Royalists. Of the Norman castle, the great hall, gatehouse and moat remain, but much of the present house is Elizabethan. Charles Dickens was a frequent visitor here, and used Rockingham as the model for Chesney Wold in *Bleak House*. The novel contains a vivid description of the gallery. The castle is set on high ground overlooking the River Welland, with views over four counties, and the gardens include a famous yew walk of topiary elephants.

The main route follows the A427 (SP Oundle) through Corby, passing the British Steel works, gaunt, angular and massive. Ironstone deposits around Corby turned it almost overnight from a peaceful village into a boom steel town and more recently into a topic of bitter controversy when the British Steel Corporation announced that the works there would close down.

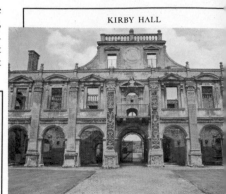

KIRBY HALL

Past the steelworks, an unclassified road the left offers a detour to Kirby Hall.* road turns left in Weldon village then, miles later, sharp right. The hall is on the le Now partly ruined, it dates from the late 16 century, when it belonged to the Lo Chancellor of England, Sir Christoph Hatton, who was a favourite of Elizabeth Tucked away in a secluded hollow of the hi Kirby Hall is a harmonious house of mell stone, with two great double bow-windo gracing the south front. The drive leads p the west front, where the formal gardens ha recently been restored, and through a dou archway into the beautifully symmetric enclosed courtyard. The arcaded loggia a the walls of what were once 'lodgings' guests are richly carved and ornamented, b this part is now only a shell. The lofty gr hall, with its barrel-vaulted ceiling, galle and tall windows, is still intact, as are so other rooms, but the furnishings are gone.

DEENE PARK

Further along the same lane is Deene Par another beautiful 16th-century mansion pale stone, set in a charming village. Sir 1514 Deene Park has been the home the Brudenell family, whose most fam member, Lord Cardigan, led the Charge the Light Brigade at Balaclava in 1854.

CORBY TO WARBOYS

The A427 briefly joins the A43 Stamford at Weldon, then turns right to con eastwards through the pretty stone villag Upper and Lower Benefield to Oundl outstandingly attractive town on the F Nene, with a well-known public school. main route turns right here on to the (SP Thrapston, Kettering).

OUNDLE

To the left is Oundle's pleasing main str lined with old stone houses and leading p the imposing 19th-century buildings of school, on New Street, into the market pla here there is a handsome town hall and a f 13th-century church whose spire domina the town. There are now two schools Oundle, Laxton Grammar School and famous public school. Both were founded the 16th century by William Laxton, Oundle grocer who rose to become Lo Mayor of London. The two schools separa in the 19th century.

The A605 heads southwards from Oundle, leaving the town by a narrow stone bridge over the Nene and passing Oundle Marina. After 3 miles turn left on to the B662 (SP Huntingdon), continuing through the village of Clopton and turning left 2½ miles beyond Clopton church on to the B660 (SP The Giddings). This road soon passes through Winwick – associated with Sir Thomas Malory, author of *Morte d'Arthur,* who was lord of Winwick manor. Great Gidding is the next village, and there are two other Giddings – Little and Steeple – away to the right. Continue following signs for Ramsey, and 1 mile beyond Glatton turn left and right to cross the busy A1.

The B660 continues through Holme and towards Ramsey; east of the A1 the Fens begin, and the road is bordered by the ditches so typical of fenland landscapes. On the left just past Holme is Holme Fen, where there is a nature reserve with a nature trail which provides a fine introduction to fenland flora and fauna. In 1851 a huge iron post was sunk into the ground of Holme Fen, to measure the peat's rate of shrinkage after the draining of nearby Whittlesey Mere. This completed the drainage of these fens, and over the next 100 years the land level around the post dropped by an amazing 12 feet.

The route continues across the fens, running for long stretches as straight as an arrow, but punctuated suddenly by sharp right-angled bends as the road follows some old field boundary or changes direction to avoid a dyke. When you reach the B1040, turn right at the T-junction and in ½ mile cross a dyke and immediately turn left for Ramsey. For a short stretch the road runs alongside one of the great 18th-century drainage dykes, New Dyke, then veers right into Ramsey. This small town once had an important Benedictine abbey, founded in AD 969. Scarcely anything of its former splendour remains except the fine 15th-century gatehouse* which is in the care of the National Trust. At the T-junction in the town centre turn right (SP Warboys, St Ives), following the B1040 through the town and climbing to 100 feet, indeed a hill in these flat East Anglian landscapes, before reaching Warboys.

Summer wild flowers add a bright splash of colour to the fenland landscape near Ramsey

WARBOYS TO ELY

At Warboys turn left by the clock tower (SP Fenton, St Ives) and in ½ mile left again on to the A141 (SP March). The road into Chatteris is attractively lined with a double row of poplar trees, reminiscent of many roads in France. In Chatteris the road bears left (SP March) and then joins the A142; turn right on to it (SP Cambridge, Ely). This is an old military road, known as Ireton's Way because it was built by General Ireton, one of Cromwell's commanders.

Just before reaching the village of Mepal (pronounced to rhyme with 'steeple'), the road crosses first the Old Bedford River, then the New Bedford River or Hundred Foot Drain, two of the great achievements of the 17th-century Dutch engineer Cornelius Vermuyden. He was commissioned by the then Earl of Bedford and his associates to reclaim thousands of acres of unusable land by diverting the waters of the River Ouse, which regularly flooded the countryside, into two great 'drains', the Old and New Bedford Rivers. The Earl and his companions who 'adventured' on this scheme are commemorated in such place-names as 'Adventurers' Fen' and the 'Bedford Levels', as this area of the Fens is called.

South of Mepal is the village of Sutton, known as Sutton-in-the-Isle because of its position in the Isle of Ely. The magnificent

Red brick and Barnack stone harmonize perfectly to give a pleasing villagescape at Sutton-in-the-Isle

church tower, its double octagon echoing that of Ely cathedral 5 miles to the east, rises like a beacon from the flat fenlands around it. The church was built in the 14th century by two bishops of Ely, and their coats of arms feature in the roof vault of the south porch.

Late afternoon sunshine enhances the golden stone of Ely Cathedral's great west tower. It was once even taller than its present 215 feet, for until 1801 it was topped by a lead spire

In Sutton the A142 turns left be continuing into Ely, the cathedral city of Fens. In medieval times this was an islan high ground, surrounded by impenetr marshes which made it a secure base for Saxon hero Hereward the Wake in campaign against the Norman invaders you come into the city, turn left on to the A then right, following signs for the cathe car park. This road leads past the car par a junction with the A142 where you sho turn right (SP Newmarket).

The building of Ely Cathedral began in early Norman period, but the great octag crossing tower, which is its most remark feature, and the elaborately carved L Chapel date from the 14th century. It magnificent building, and, compared v the little market town that it dominate vast and almost intimidating structure stands on a pleasant green, and the 1 century Bishop's Palace stands to the rig the west front.

From 1636 to 1647 Ely was the hom Oliver Cromwell, who for a time wa 'farmer' or collector of cathedral tithes. house stands next to the parish church. town itself has some very pleasant buildi both in the market place and in the str leading from it.

ELY TO MILDENHALL

Leave Ely on the A142 Newmarket r shortly crossing the River Great Ouse continuing through Stuntney to Soh Surprisingly for such a small place, Soh once had a cathedral. Founded in the e 7th century, it was destroyed by the Da and never rebuilt, but Soham's church, v its imposing Perpendicular west tower fine angel roof, is a more than adeq replacement. Soham is very close to Wic Fen, one of the few areas of fenland that been preserved in its original state, just a was before drainage and reclamation.

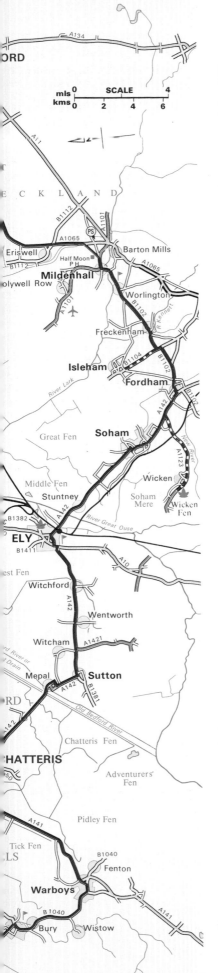

For a detour to Wicken Fen,* turn right 1 mile beyond Soham on to the A1123 (SP Stretham). The lane to the Fen leads off to the left at the western end of Wicken village. It is the habitat of many species of insect, bird and plant life, some of them extremely rare: there are for example over 700 kinds of butterflies and moths. The Fen is maintained by the National Trust and is used as an open-air laboratory, but may be visited by the public.

The main route continues along the A142 to Fordham, where it turns left on to the B1102 (SP Mildenhall). After 1½ miles the B1102 meets the B1104, turning left and, ¼ mile later, right for Freckenham.

ISLEHAM

By continuing northwards on the B1104, you can make a detour to Isleham, 1¾ miles away, to see the superb 14th-century parish church. The first of its many interior features of interest is the angel roof. There are ten full-size figures of angels with outstretched wings, bearing emblems of the crucifixion such as the nails, the crown of thorns, and a sponge on a reed. On the crossbeams are thirty winged angels' heads. There are also some fine funeral effigies, mostly of members of the Peyton family, one of whom gave the roof in 1495, and some marvellous brasses, particularly that in the north aisle to Thomas Peyton and his two wives. Also in this village is a small Norman chapel, now used as a barn – all that remains of a Benedictine priory, built in the 11th century as the offshoot of a French abbey, but suppressed as early as 1414.

The main route follows the B1102 through Freckenham and Worlington to Mildenhall, a delightful old Suffolk village. In the market place stands the original market cross, built of timber and topped by a lead roof. Like Isleham and Soham, Mildenhall has an outstandingly lovely church, where each of the hammer beams supporting the nave roof has been carved in the shape of a winged angel. The roofs of the aisles are remarkable, too, particularly that of the north aisle, where the carvings include St George and the dragon, and Abraham and Isaac. The church dates from the 13th century. Considerably older is the Mildenhall Treasure – a quantity of priceless 4th-century Roman silverware ploughed up here in the 1940s and now a prized possession of the British Museum.

Leave Mildenhall on the A1101 (SP Bury St Edmunds) and in ½ mile, at the Half Moon pub, turn left on to an unclassified road which leads to the A1065; turn left on to this road (SP Brandon) and continue through pleasant, shady woodland that is part of Thetford Forest – a more familiar and immediately appealing countryside than that of the Fens. In between the plantations of woodland lies the Breckland, now a wide heath, owing to sheep and rabbits which destroyed the vegetation. Devastating sandblows resulted, occasionally severe enough to bury whole villages.

The water pump at Wicken Fen – the only one of its kind still in use – plays an uncharacteristic role. Such drainage mills were generally used to dry out the fens; this one pumps water into the nature reserve, keeping it damp enough to support species of flora and fauna that lived in the fens before they were drained

BRANDON TO HINGHAM

The A1065 leads to Brandon, a pleasant little country town which has long been a centre for flint-knapping, the old East Anglian craft of shaping flints for building. The chippings are either sold for use as gun flints or dispatched to the Potteries to be ground up and used as a strengthening agent or in glazes.

SANTON DOWNHAM

For a detour to the Breckland village of Santon Downham, go forward at the cross-roads on to the B1107 (SP Thetford) and in 1 mile fork left on to an unclassified road (no sign) which brings you down a wooded lane into the village. Buried by sand in the 17th century, the village was rebuilt by the Forestry Commission, who have their district headquarters here. There is a big timber-treatment plant, and much of the conifer seed used in plantations up and down the country is extracted and processed here. There is also a tourist information office where visitors can obtain details about the forest and the Breckland. To reach the office, turn left by the little Norman church, and left again into the car park, which is also the start of a well-marked forest trail.

The main route, still the A1065, swings left at the crossroads into Brandon's main street, then goes over a level crossing and immediately bears right (SP Swaffham). Entering Norfolk as it leaves Brandon, the road runs through large belts of woodland, a most attractive part of the route, and there are many opportunities to pull off the road and enjoy a quiet stroll or a picnic.

GRIME'S GRAVES

Just past a large picnic site, at Emily's Wood, 2 miles from Brandon level crossing, an unclassified road on the right offers a detour to Grime's Graves.* Follow this lane for 1¼ miles, then turn right on to a signposted track. Grime's Graves are not graves at all, but ancient flint mines excavated by Stone Age man some 4000 years ago. The shafts go down more than 20 feet through the chalk to the flint layer beneath, and galleries radiate out horizontally at the bottom, scarcely wider than foxholes. Although most of the shafts now appear merely as shallow depressions in the ground, having long since been filled in, one of them has been opened up and visitors can go down. They were rediscovered in the 19th century by a clergyman. Animal bones and deer antlers have been found in the mines, as well as numerous bones sharpened for use as picks. A prehistoric stone figure of a fertility goddess has also been discovered here.

The main route continues through Mundford and 3½ miles further on turns right on to the B1108 (SP Watton). The road takes you through Bodney and past Bodney Army Camp, with a rash of Ministry of Defence warning signs; the Breckland is much used as a military training area. Pass through Watton, a market town with a large RAF station, and continue on the B1108 through a landscape of tidy fields to Hingham, a village of elegant Georgian houses which is of considerable historical interest, particularly to American visitors. In 1622, Samuel Lincoln, the son of a long-established

Hingham family, was baptized here. La[ ] was apprenticed to a Norwich weave[ ] emigrated to the New World in 1637, [ ] his apprentice with him. One of the [ ] direct descendants was Abraham Li[ ] the first president of the United States. [ ] north aisle of Hingham's 14th-ce[ ] church is a bronze bust of the great [ ] donated by the American people an[ ] veiled by the US ambassador in 1919.

HINGHAM TO NORWICH

After Hingham the B1108 winds th[ ] peaceful, wooded country, passing th[ ] the tiny village of Kimberley, a clus[ ] thatched 'model' cottages around a g[ ] The church contains some magni[ ] stained glass, some of it 15th-century E[ ] and some Flemish. The latter, togethe[ ] the exquisite 16th-century German gl[ ] the east window of Hingham church[ ] donated in the early 19th century by [ ] Wodehouse of Kimberley House, [ ] stands in parkland to the east of Kimber[ ] has been the home of the Wodehous[ ] many centuries, and several memoria[ ] members of the family are a featu[ ] Kimberley church.

Continue through Barford, set on the [ ] Tiffey, which joins the Yare near here [ ] way to the sea at Great Yarmouth. [ ] B1108 takes the route all the way [ ] Norwich, passing the campus of [ ] University of East Anglia – one of the [ ] universities (see p. 221) – before crossin[ ] ring road to reach the city centre.

Traces of one of Europe's oldest industries can still be seen at Grime's Graves, where a series of shallow depressions in the ground marks the site of over 350 Neolithic flint mines

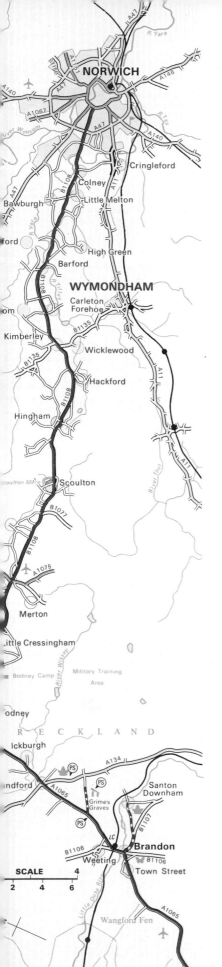

NORWICH

The unofficial capital of East Anglia, Norwich combines all the grandeur of a cathedral city steeped in history with the unpretentious charm of a busy country town. There has been a settlement here since the Dark Ages – possibly earlier – and by the time of the Anglo-Saxons there was already a thriving town. The Normans built the castle* and the cathedral, and Norwich prospered both as a market centre and as a port, trading with Holland and other countries across the North Sea.

It is still a flourishing regional capital, and from the visitor's point of view it has everything. Whilst close enough to the Norfolk Broads and the coast to be a convenient holiday centre, it is in itself an exciting place to stay. Not only has it an excellent market and good shops, but there are also scores of little side streets, alleyways, and old courts to explore as well as the magnificent cathedral, the castle and several interesting churches. The city's varied and well-planned museums* include a museum of church art and craftsmanship, housed in St Peter Hungate Church,* and the fascinating Strangers' Hall,* a 15th-century house which has been imaginatively turned into a museum. Antique markets and craft fairs are held from time to time, and for the evenings there are plenty of restaurants, cinemas, concerts and two theatres.

Above: A selection of dolls dating from the 18th century onwards is among the exhibits in the Toy Room of Strangers' Hall. Other rooms in the museum are beautifully furnished period pieces, including 17th-century bedrooms and a Regency music room

Right: A browse round Norwich's excellent shops would not be complete without a visit to the Royal Arcade. This masterpiece of the Art Nouveau style was designed by George Skipper in 1899, and stands on the site of a former coaching inn

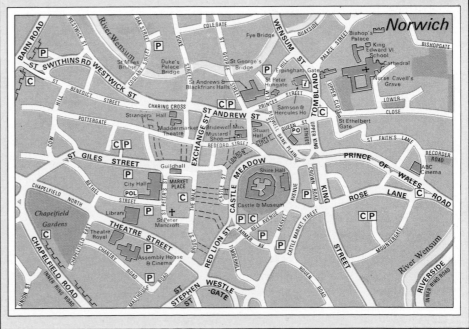

ROUTE 11   179 MILE

Birmingham to Scarborougl

FROM Birmingham this route threads across the fox-hunting country of the East Midlands, marches up the line of the Roman Ermine Street to the River Humber, then crosses the chalklands of the old East Riding to reach the historic seaside town of Scarborough.

The route soon shakes off Birmingham's suburbs to enter the soft landscapes of the East Midlands. It crosses the A5 (built on the line of Roman Watling Street), and one of the many canals that encircle Birmingham, to reach Tamworth, dominated by its imposing Norman castle.

Between Tamworth and Ashby-de-la-Zouch the countryside is dotted with pretty villages whose names – Stretton en le Field, Appleby Magna and Appleby Parva – are lasting reminders of the Norman barons and their clerks who adapted the original English names to their native language when they settled these areas after the Conquest.

To reach Melton Mowbray the route curves up into Nottinghamshire and passes to the north of the outcrop of ancient rock that is Charnwood Forest. A good many of the 18th- and 19th-century brick houses in this part of the country are roofed with Swithland slates, which were quarried on the eastern side of Charnwood and are distinguishable from the more common Welsh slates by their different colour and the way in which they are graded in size from eaves to ridge – larger at the bottom, smaller at the top.

Beyond Rempstone the route enters Leicestershire once more to reach Melton Mowbray. The town is famous for its pork pies, Stilton cheese, and for its associations with fox-hunting. It was in Leicestershire, more than any other county, that fox-hunting gained the status and aura that it has never lost. The sport became popular during the 18th century because deer, the huntsman's traditional quarry, declined in numbers as the countryside lost its natural tree cover through the demands of agriculture and industry. The landed gentry looked for something else worthy of the chase, and the fox, quick-witted and resourceful, was the obvious choice. The fox-hunting craze had a considerable impact on the landscape. Coverts and spinneys were planted to provide shelter and breeding places for the foxes, and fields were bounded with hawthorn hedges that could easily be cut back to allow hunters to clear them at full gallop. From Melton to Belvoir (which gave its name to one of the great hunts) the countryside is dominated by symmetrical clumps of trees and neat hedges.

The Nottingham and Grantham Canal joins the route as it continues into Grantham, with its majestic church and old coaching inns. From here the route heads towards Lincoln along the western edge of the limestone ridge which stretches in a long, thin line from the Leicestershire border all the way to the Humber. Red brick gives way to stone houses roofed with bright red pantiles, recalling those seen earlier in villages like Waltham on the Wolds. The pantiles, which give such a distinctive look to the buildings of the eastern counties, were first imported from the Netherlands in the 17th century.

The beautiful grey stone of Lincolnshire was quarrie places like Ancaster, to the east of the route beyond Bark and used not only to build local houses (whose size reflec wealth brought to this area by the wool trade), but als some of the most splendid churches and cathedrals in Eng Several of the villages on the way to Lincoln, notably Ful whose lovely green is situated just off the route, have exce examples of limestone buildings.

From Lincoln the route follows the course of the Ro Ermine Street, which linked London to Lincoln and Yor the limestone ridge of the Lincolnshire Cliff as fa Redbourne, where it veers off to Brigg.

The rolling countryside of the limestone belt changes ar Brigg to flat, rich farmland that was once marshy fen. Be Elsham the route rises once more on to the northern extre of the Lincolnshire Wolds before descending to the great ri of the River Humber and crossing it by the magnificent suspension bridge.

From the Humber the route follows the eastern edge c Yorkshire Wolds to Beverley, whose wealth of fine buildi crowned by the Gothic glory of the Minster. The land bet Beverley and Great Driffield is dead flat and is, like mu Lincolnshire, reclaimed fenland. Gradually, however, route rises on to the chalk uplands of the Wolds, which w bleak and barren tract of country until a far-sighted philanthropic landowner, Sir Christopher Sykes of Sledr encouraged their cultivation at the end of the 18th centur Staxton the route drops down into the Vale of Pickering b passing through Seamer to reach Scarborough and the ru coasts of North Yorkshire.

PLACES OF INTEREST: OPENING DETAILS

Tamworth
TAMWORTH CASTLE MUSEUM open all year (except 25 Dec and Fri Oct to Mar), Mon to Sat all day, Sun pm only

Ashby-de-la-Zouch
ASHBY-DE-LA-ZOUCH CASTLE open all year daily (except Wed and Thu)

Hathern
WHATTON HOUSE GARDENS open Easter to end Sep Sun and Bank Holiday Mon, pm only

Melton Mowbray
MELTON CARNEGIE MUSEUM open all year (except Good Fri, 25 and 26 Dec) Mon to Sat all day, Sun pm only

Belvoir
BELVOIR CASTLE open end Mar to end Sep Wed, Thu, Sat, Sun, Good Fri and Bank Holiday Mon, pm only; Sun only in Oct, pm only

Grantham
GRANTHAM MUSEUM open all year (except Sun, Bank Holidays and library holidays)

Belton
BELTON HOUSE PARK AND GARDENS open end Mar to Oct

Lincoln
LINCOLN CASTLE open all year (except Christmas) Mon to Sat all day; also Sun Apr to Oct, pm only

GREYFRIARS CITY AND COUNTY MUSEUM open all year (except Good Fri, 25 and 26 Dec) Mon to Sat all day, Sun pm only

USHER GALLERY open all year (except Good Fri and Christmas) Mon to Sat all day, Sun pm only

Elsham
ELSHAM HALL COUNTRY PARK open all year (except Good Fri and 25 Dec), pm only

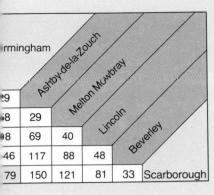

Birmingham	Ashby-de-la-Zouch	Melton Mowbray	Lincoln	Beverley	
9					
8	29				
8	69	40			
46	117	88	48		
79	150	121	81	33	Scarborough

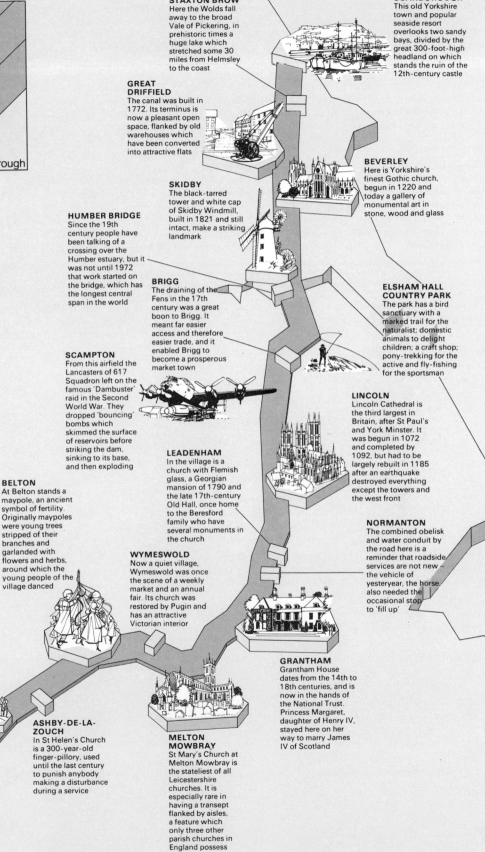

STAXTON BROW
Here the Wolds fall away to the broad Vale of Pickering, in prehistoric times a huge lake which stretched some 30 miles from Helmsley to the coast

SCARBOROUGH
This old Yorkshire town and popular seaside resort overlooks two sandy bays, divided by the great 300-foot-high headland on which stands the ruin of the 12th-century castle

GREAT DRIFFIELD
The canal was built in 1772. Its terminus is now a pleasant open space, flanked by old warehouses which have been converted into attractive flats

BEVERLEY
Here is Yorkshire's finest Gothic church, begun in 1220 and today a gallery of monumental art in stone, wood and glass

SKIDBY
The black-tarred tower and white cap of Skidby Windmill, built in 1821 and still intact, make a striking landmark

HUMBER BRIDGE
Since the 19th century people have been talking of a crossing over the Humber estuary, but it was not until 1972 that work started on the bridge, which has the longest central span in the world

ELSHAM HALL COUNTRY PARK
The park has a bird sanctuary with a marked trail for the naturalist; domestic animals to delight children; a craft shop; pony-trekking for the active and fly-fishing for the sportsman

BRIGG
The draining of the Fens in the 17th century was a great boon to Brigg. It meant far easier access and therefore easier trade, and it enabled Brigg to become a prosperous market town

SCAMPTON
From this airfield the Lancasters of 617 Squadron left on the famous 'Dambuster' raid in the Second World War. They dropped 'bouncing' bombs which skimmed the surface of reservoirs before striking the dam, sinking to its base, and then exploding

LINCOLN
Lincoln Cathedral is the third largest in Britain, after St Paul's and York Minster. It was begun in 1072 and completed by 1092, but had to be largely rebuilt in 1185 after an earthquake destroyed everything except the towers and the west front

LEADENHAM
In the village is a church with Flemish glass, a Georgian mansion of 1790 and the late 17th-century Old Hall, once home to the Beresford family who have several monuments in the church

NORMANTON
The combined obelisk and water conduit by the road here is a reminder that roadside services are not new – the vehicle of yesteryear, the horse, also needed the occasional stop to 'fill up'

BELTON
At Belton stands a maypole, an ancient symbol of fertility. Originally maypoles were young trees stripped of their branches and garlanded with flowers and herbs, around which the young people of the village danced

WYMESWOLD
Now a quiet village, Wymeswold was once the scene of a weekly market and an annual fair. Its church was restored by Pugin and has an attractive Victorian interior

TAMWORTH
Tamworth Castle displays a mixture of architectural styles ranging from the 10-foot-thick walls of the original Norman keep to the beautiful Tudor workmanship of the banqueting hall

GRANTHAM
Grantham House dates from the 14th to 18th centuries, and is now in the hands of the National Trust. Princess Margaret, daughter of Henry IV, stayed here on her way to marry James IV of Scotland

ASHBY-DE-LA-ZOUCH
In St Helen's Church is a 300-year-old finger-pillory, used until the last century to punish anybody making a disturbance during a service

MELTON MOWBRAY
St Mary's Church at Melton Mowbray is the stateliest of all Leicestershire churches. It is especially rare in having a transept flanked by aisles, a feature which only three other parish churches in England possess

Birmingham

BIRMINGHAM TO ASHBY-DE-LA-ZOUCH

Follow signs from central Birmingham for the A38 (SP The North), sweeping past the West Midlands County Council's office block on an elevated section of the inner ring road. Bear left (SP Middle Ring Road) at the start of the A38(M) urban motorway and at the roundabout take the second exit, then keep left (SP Aston). At Aston clock tower bear right, and in 1½ miles, at the roundabout beneath 'Spaghetti Junction', take the fourth exit, the A38 (SP Lichfield). Dual carriageway speeds you through Birmingham's suburbs and out through open country for several miles. At the roundabout north of Sutton Coldfield, leave the A38 and take the third exit, the A453 (SP Tamworth). Continue towards Tamworth, crossing the A5 by turning right and left at the edge of Mile Oak.

Follow the road round to the left on the outskirts of Tamworth, where the River Tame is overlooked by a castle of dark stone. Tamworth's traditions as a market town go back more than 1000 years: it was once the capital of the great Saxon kingdom of Mercia, which stretched right across the Midlands to the Welsh border. Street markets are still a colourful part of local life, and the traditional stalls in Market Street and elsewhere contrast with their modern counterparts in a roofed shopping precinct. Market Street also has a delightful little town hall built in 1701 by Thomas Guy, the benefactor who gave his name to Guy's Hospital in London. The upper part of the building looks down on a statue of Sir Robert Peel, the 'father' of Britain's police force. He was Tamworth's MP from 1833 until 1850, when he died after being thrown from his horse in Hyde Park.

Tamworth's town hall overlooks a statue of Sir Robert Peel, the 19th-century prime minister who was the town's MP for 17 years. His 'Tamworth Manifesto' pioneered the reform of the old Tory Party, which later became the Conservative Party

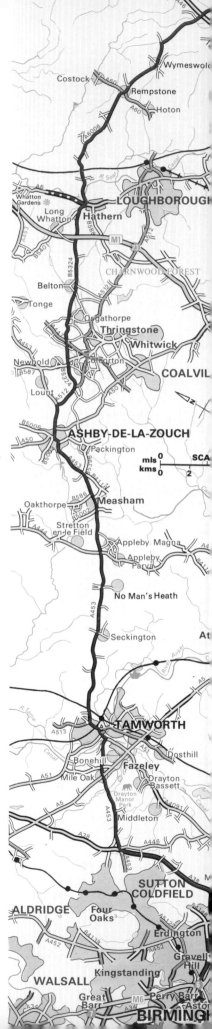

...ment erected near Tamworth Castle in 1913 ...orates its founding 1000 years earlier by ...eda, the 'Lady of the Mercians'

...e castle* stands on a site originally ...ed in AD 913 by Aethelfleda, the ...or daughter of Alfred the Great. Parts of ...orman stronghold which was built after ...Conquest by Robert de Marmion, ...m the Conqueror's Royal Champion, ...and. Unlike many basically medieval ...s, Tamworth is not a ruined shell. Inside ...lendid Tudor banqueting hall. Period ...ure and painted oak panels are features ...er rooms, and the castle also houses a ... museum whose exhibits include ...ur, costumes and Saxon coins minted in ...wn during the reign of King Offa, who ... palace here as early as AD 781.

...ow the A453 Nottingham road out of ...orth and into the soft farming country ...s so typical of the Midlands. The road ...and falls in a series of long, gentle ...ations to reach No Man's Heath, where ...gn outside the Four Counties Inn ...ates the fact that the boundaries of ...rdshire, Derbyshire, Leicestershire and ...ickshire meet nearby. Six miles later, ...g passed through the large mining ...e of Measham, the route enters Ashby-...Zouch.

...e town takes its unusual name from a ...h nobleman, Alain de Parrhoet la ...e, who acquired the manor in about ... The castle,* now in ruins, grew from ...orman manor house, and in 1464 passed ...he hands of William, Lord Hastings, ...rd IV's Lord Chamberlain. The lofty ...ngs Tower, linked to the kitchen's cellar ...n underground passage, is his most ...g memorial. Hastings was executed in ...after falling foul of Richard III, but the ... remained in the family. They later ...d host here to royal visitors including ... VIII, James I and Charles I. Mary, ...n of Scots, also stayed here in 1569 and

1586, during her long years as a prisoner. Ashby featured prominently in the Civil War and withstood a 15-month siege before surrendering to Parliamentary forces in 1646. The castle was 'slighted' two years later to render it useless for military purposes. Heraldic glass from the castle's chapel can still be seen in the east window of St Helen's Church, and also in the church is the only known surviving finger pillory, used on those who dared to misbehave in church. (For Ashby see also p. 236.)

ASHBY-DE-LA-ZOUCH TO WYMESWOLD
Leave the town on the A453 (SP Nottingham) and in 1¼ miles turn right on to the A512 (SP Loughborough). Follow this road for another 1¼ miles, then turn left on to the B5324 for Rempstone. A small but eye-catching brick building on the junction bears the words 'This hospital and school was founded and endowed by the Rt Hon. and truly charitable Thomas Lord, Viscount Beaumont, of this place. This hospital was removed to another site the same year.' Coleorton Hall, the Beaumont family seat until 1934, stands in private grounds to the left of the road. The hall was visited by many famous figures from the world of literature and the arts in the 19th century, when Sir George Beaumont entertained such friends as Wordsworth, Byron and Constable. The

B5324 runs north-eastwards through rolling countryside to skirt Belton, a village complete with traditional maypole and market place, recalling the days when it was the site of a famous horse fair. The road then passes under the M1 to meet the A6.

WHATTON HOUSE GARDENS
At this junction a short detour to the left, along the dual carriageway, leads to Whatton House,* on the left, where 25 acres of gardens may be visited. There is a water garden, a dogs' cemetery, a Chinese garden and an unusual Dutch garden. But even more curious is the 'Bogy Hole', a strange garden ornament built in the last century.

The main route turns right and immediately left to cross the A6 and joins the A6006 for Rempstone, where thatched cottages catch the eye beyond the junction with the A60. Wymeswold, the next village, also has several attractive buildings scattered along its main street, notably the brick manor house on the left. St Mary's Church, with gargoyles glowering down from its fine Perpendicular tower, was restored and furnished in the 19th century by Augustus Pugin, the architect best known for his work on the Houses of Parliament. To the east of the village can be seen two old drove roads, with typically wide verges – a legacy of the days when Wymeswold had a weekly market.

A Chinese garden adorned by all kinds of exotic curios is among the unusual features of Whatton House Gardens

WYMESWOLD TO GRANTHAM

The A6006 continues to Melton Mowbray, an old market town that became the 'capital' of English fox-hunting in the 19th century. One of the greatest social centres in England during the season, Melton attracted nobility, business tycoons and upper-crust politicians, who were entertained in mansions known as 'hunting boxes'. Champagne flowed and many wild escapades were woven into the town's folklore. One involved a party of revellers who quite literally 'painted the town red' in 1837, concentrating on the 17th-century White Swan Inn.

The story of Melton's two most famous products – Stilton cheese and pork pies – is told in the Melton Carnegie Museum.* There is a link between the two, because whey left over from the cheese-making process is an ideal food for pigs.

In Burton Street stands St Mary's Church, Melton's most prized possession. With its fine tower and exceptionally large transepts, it looks more like a small cathedral than the parish church of a market town. Treasures inside include an effigy of a crusader clad in remarkably detailed chain mail, and a beautiful figure known as the Alabaster Lady, whose head rests on a pillow supported by two angels.

The A607 (SP Grantham) takes the route on through Thorpe Arnold, a village of rustic brick cottages clustered round an attractive church. A slab in the north aisle is believed to mark the grave of John de Wodeford, a 14th-century lord of the manor who lived to be 107. Old milestones with cast-iron faces appear on

This 14th-century alabaster effigy of a lady is among the historic treasures in St Mary's Church, Melton Mowbray

the roadside as the A607 swings northwards and climbs gently into the rolling Wolds. Brick suddenly gives way to delightful stone as the route enters Waltham on the Wolds, a charming village that could have been transplanted from the Cotswolds. Weathered red pantiles roof many of the buildings, while others nestle beneath cosy coverings of thatch. The name of the Granby Inn recalls the Marquis of Granby, who founded the Belvoir Hunt in 1730.

Three famous hunts – the Quorn, Cottesmore and Belvoir – meet near Melton Mowbray, and hunting scenes such as this feature prominently in the Melton Carnegie Museum

BELVOIR CASTLE

As the A607 approaches Grantham, passing under the A1, the 282-foot high spire of St Wulfram's – one of the most impressive parish churches in England – soars majestically above the town. The great church, one of only two in England dedicated to St Wulfram, dates from the 12th century, although the superb tower and spire were not added until the 14th. Some of the stained-glass windows, fitted between 1969 and 1974, are striking examples of modern art. A room above the south porch houses a library of chained books that was given to the church during the reign of Elizabeth I.

One of St Wulfram's neighbours is 15th-century King's School where the name of its most famous pupil, Sir Isaac Newton, is carved on a window ledge. Sir Isaac was born near Colsterworth, south of Grantham, in 1642. Tribute is paid to him by a statue outside the museum,* which also has exhibits linked with Newton's life. Castlegate, between the museum and the church, has what is probably Britain's most unusual inn sign – a beehive, complete with bees, outside the door.

GRANTHAM TO LINCOLN

The A607 (SP Lincoln) takes the route northwards out of Grantham and passes through a series of picturesque stone-and-pantile villages with spired churches.

BELTON HOUSE
Belton, just to the right of the main road 3 miles from Grantham, is the neat little 'estate' village for Belton House,* which stands in 600 acres of parkland. Built in 1685, it has been the home of the Brownlow family ever since. Its treasures include paintings, silver, tapestries, Grinling Gibbons carvings and mementoes of the Duke of Windsor who, during his brief reign as Edward VIII, made Lord Brownlow his lord-in-waiting. The estate also has an adventure playground, nature trails, a miniature steam railway and a museum devoted to horses.

After skirting Barkston, bear left at the junction with the A153 and continue on the A607 towards Lincoln through a landscape of gentle undulations and low, wooded ridges. A reminder of the days when horsepower involved horses, not internal combustion engines, stands on the left of the road in Normanton. It is a combined obelisk and water conduit, engraved with the distances to Grantham, Lincoln and London. The road crosses the A17 at Leadenham (see p. 215) and climbs to follow a long limestone ridge, with a string of villages just off to the left. Two miles beyond Waddington, at Bracebridge Heath, the route turns left to join the A15 and continues along it into Lincoln.

he main route follows the A607 all the way Grantham, but a well-signed detour to the t enables it to take in Belvoir (pronounced eaver') Castle.* This has been the seat of the kes of Rutland for almost five centuries, d it was the first earl who began, in the 16th ntury, to turn the castle from a fortress into stately mansion. Successive houses on the e were gutted by Civil War damage and by e, and the present castle dates from about 30. Set on a wooded hill commanding wide ws over the lovely Vale of Belvoir, it houses asures that include paintings by Holbein, ynolds and Gainsborough.

The detour returns to the A607 through oolsthorpe and Denton, by which time the ute has crossed the county boundary from icestershire into Lincolnshire.

Museum of the Horse in the grounds of Belton House includes not only a selection of splendid antique carriages but also live horses to pull them

LINCOLN TO BRIGG

Lincoln's triple-towered cathedral – the third largest in Britain after St Paul's and York Minster – appears to float above the city with all the majesty of a great galleon under full sail. It is one of the most spectacular sights in the country. Work started within ten years of the Battle of Hastings, and the building was completed in 20 years, only to be shattered by an earthquake in 1185. However, the great west front and its twin towers survived and were incorporated into the new building. The interior is every bit as magnificent as the exterior – a priceless repository of stained glass, carved wood and beautiful stonework. A sculpted figure of the Lincoln Imp, the most notorious character in the city's folklore, grimaces down from its perch on a pillar high above the angel choir.

The cathedral's site, on a ridge above the River Witham, was already fortified before *Lindum Colonia* became the base for Roman rule over eastern England. The most remarkable reminders of the Roman period are the Newport Arch – the only Roman gateway in Britain still used by traffic – and the Fossdyke Navigation, an 11-mile canal between the Witham and the Trent.

Like the cathedral, the castle* was built soon after the Norman Conquest. From the bailey rise the main keep and the Observatory Tower, an excellent viewpoint.

By the gate of RAF Scampton stands a Lancaster bomber together with some of the Tallboy bombs it carried during the Second World War

A ridge high above the River Witham is the perfect site for Lincoln's majestic cathedral, the third largest in the country

Many aspects of the city's long history are displayed in the Greyfriars City and County Museum,* while the nearby Usher Gallery* has a good collection of paintings and *objets d'art*. One of the gallery's rooms is devoted to Alfred, Lord Tennyson, the 19th-century poet. His statue stands at the eastern end of the cathedral. (For Lincoln see also p. 22.)

Leave Lincoln on the A15 (SP Scunthorpe), which leads out into the open, rolling country of Lindsey, the old name for north Lincolnshire, and still one of the county's administrative divisions. The A15 here is Ermine Street, one of the main Roman arteries, which ran from London to Lincoln and on to York. It is remarkably straight, like all Roman roads, and runs almost due north from Lincoln, following the line of a long, narrow limestone ridge known as the Cliff: hence farm and hamlet names such as Saxby Cliff and Owmby Cliff. Place-names ending in '-by' and '-thorpe' are very common in Lincolnshire. The suffix is of Danish origin, and a legacy of the Danish invasion of Lincolnshire in the 9th century.

Five miles from Lincoln, the road deviates from its ruler-straight course in a huge but gentle bend to avoid the main runway at Scampton airfield, the most famous of all the RAF's wartime bomber bases. It was from here, on the night of 16 May 1943, that the Lancasters of the elite 617 Squadron, commanded by Wing Commander Guy Gibson, took off for Germany on the 'Dambuster' raid. It was a spectacular success – two of the dams were destroyed and one badly damaged – but 53 of the 133 air crew were killed. Gibson was awarded the Victoria Cross, but he too lost his life 16 months later.

Cross the A631 at the Caenby Corner roundabout. After 5½ miles the A15 parts company with Ermine Street and strikes north-eastwards to Redbourne, the first village on the road since Lincoln, though

is a whole chain of villages to the west of
oute. A handsome stone gateway on the
 leads into Redbourne Park, an estate
passed to the Dukes of St Albans in the
century. The first of the line was a result
arles II's affair with Nell Gwynne, and
er of her children is said to be buried in
grounds of the disused 15th-century
h. Stocks stand in the former smithy
site the churchyard entrance, and a
 horse prances on an anvil on the roof of
uaint old building.
llow the A15 northwards through the
ng village of Hibaldstow, soon passing a
 plant where sugar beet is processed;
 join the A18 (SP Grimsby) and continue
igg. Approaching the town, the road
es the New River Ancholme. Firmly
sed by artificial banks for much of its
h, this channel runs perfectly straight for
 after mile across the fertile fens, carrying
 waters which once flooded these lands
 to the Humber estuary. Brigg was one of
many settlements which grew up on
ds of higher ground in the sodden
nds. It is probably a settlement of some
uity – indeed, an ancient boat possibly
g from prehistoric times was discovered
by – but most of Brigg's buildings are of
9th and 20th centuries, for it came into
vn as a market town only after the fens
 drained.

GG TO HUMBER BRIDGE
e roundabout in Brigg, take the first exit,
A18, and in 1 mile branch left on to the
6 (SP Barrow upon Humber).

WRAWBY
s well worth making a brief detour here by
ntinuing along the A18 into Wrawby. A
e on the right, ½ mile beyond the medieval
rch, leads to a brick-and-timber windmill
lt around 1780 and restored to full work-
 order almost 200 years later. It is the last
rking example of the hundreds of post-mills
t once ground corn from the rich farm-
ds between the Humber and the Wash.

hills dappled with trees contrast with the
enland around Brigg as the B1206 runs
rds Elsham, crossing the M180 South
berside motorway. Elsham Hall
try Park,* in an attractive lakeside
g to the right 1¼ miles beyond Elsham
n, offers something for everyone. Its
erous attractions include an art gallery
 craft shop, fly-fishing, carp-feeding, a
 trail and pony-trekking.
3½ miles keep forward on to the B1218
Barton-upon-Humber) and continue for
es to reach Barton, where there is a fine
n church. At the T-junction turn left on
 A1077 Scunthorpe road, bearing left ¼
 later. In ¾ mile, at the roundabout, take
hird exit, the A15, which leads across the
ridge. (The toll charge for private cars,
 time of going to press, is £1.00.)

Schemes to cross the Humber estuary,
well over a mile wide at this point, were
first discussed in the 19th century. In 1872,
for instance, there was talk of driving a
railway tunnel between Barton and
Hessle. A bridge was proposed in the
1930s, but it was not until 1969 that
governmental approval was given.
Work on the new bridge started in 1972,
but suffered several setbacks, ranging
from political controversy over the
huge cost of the project – estimated
to be £77 million – to gale damage
and industrial mishaps. The bridge,
completed in 1981, has a main span
of 4626 feet – the greatest in the
world, beating the Verrazano
Narrows bridge in New York
by 366 feet.

HUMBER BRIDGE TO BEVERLEY

The bridge takes you to the western outskirts of Hessle. From here, follow signs for Beverley, later joining the A164 and passing Skidby, where an attractive windmill, built in 1821 and still operational, crowns a low outlier of the Wolds.

The A164 runs on into Beverley, whose minster, grander than some cathedrals, ranks with the finest examples of medieval architecture in Britain. It contains the tomb of St John of Beverley, an 8th-century Bishop of York who founded a monastic settlement on the site. This was destroyed by Vikings, but a succession of later buildings attracted many pilgrims after John was canonized in 1037. The present church, built between 1220 and 1420, features an astonishing wealth of beautifully carved wood and stone. Outstanding craftsmanship can be admired in the choir, around the altar and along the north aisle where musicians, weird creatures and other figures line the wall at eye level. The 14th-century Percy tomb is another outstanding example of elaborate stonework.

Medieval stained glass has been preserved in the great east window while its counterpart at the other end of the church depicts, among others, rulers of the ancient kingdom of

Christ and the 12 disciples are among the carved figures that adorn Beverley Minster's exquisite north porch

Skidby windmill is the only surviving example of a working tower-mill in north-eastern England

Northumbria. Military chapels in the south transept house regimental colours, war memorials and a striking monument to Major-General Barnard Foord Bowes. He was killed at Salamanca, during the Peninsular War, and the memorial is carved with an array of cannon, cannon-balls, a ramrod, powder scoops and swords.

Elsewhere in Beverley, such quaint street names as Wednesday Market, Toll Gavel and North Bar Within complement the exceptionally rich character of an enchanting old town. Noteworthy buildings include the 18th-century Guildhall, St Mary's Church and the North Bar, built of brick in 1409 and the last of the town's five ancient gateways. Beverley also has a wealth of classically elegant houses from the 18th and early 19th centuries. Some of the best examples flank the cobble-edged North Bar Without as the route continues on the A164 (SP Driffield).

BEVERLEY TO GREAT DRIFFIELD

North of Beverley, the Yorkshire Wolds rise gently to the west, but the road itself runs through a landscape as flat as a bowling-green and no more than 20 feet above sea level in places. The A164 skirts the village of Leconfield, where a footpath to the left of the road leads across fields to a moat, half a mile round – all that remains of a manor house which once belonged to the influential Percy family, Earls of Northumberland. By-passing the tiny villages of Scorborough and Beswick, each complete with manorial hall and Victorian church, the road passes through Watton. Down a lane to the right in this

e are the remains of Watton Priory, a
century nunnery. The only building
urvives is the partly 15th-century prior's
ng, now a private house, but the plan of
obey has been excavated to reveal that
uilding was clearly divided into western
astern halves so that nuns and canons
be completely segregated.

e route continues through Hutton
swick – really two villages, Hutton to the
and Cranswick to the south, each with
n green.

eat Driffield, 3 miles further on, is the
yled capital of the Wolds. It grew from
all village to a thriving market town
ds the end of the 18th century, after the
ing of the Driffield Canal in 1767
utionized local transport. The water-
tranquil terminus behind the station is
ightful spot, no longer busy with laden
s but still complete with its old crane.
nearby buildings that were originally
warehouses have been tastefully con-
d into flats, helping to retain the
cter of the area.

AT DRIFFIELD TO SCARBOROUGH
oute runs up Driffield's main street, then
right on to the B1249 for Scarborough
e junction beyond the parish church.
splendid road runs for 14 miles over the
wolds, dipping in and out of pleasant

The canal basin at Great Driffield has been given a new lease of life. Its grain warehouses have been imaginatively converted into pleasant flats, and the old crane which once unloaded barges has been carefully preserved

South Bay, Scarborough. Beyond it rises Castle Cliff, a 300-foot-high promontory once used by the Romans as a signalling station

little villages. Langtoft is attractively set in a hollow of the wolds – a site which has more than once brought tragedy to the village during rainstorms, when water has poured off the surrounding hills and flooded the village to a depth of several feet. At a crossroads 2½ miles beyond Foxholes, the next village, the road reaches 527 feet, the highest point on the entire route. Just over 1 mile later, at the top of Staxton Brow, a picnic area provides sweeping views over the broad Vale of Pickering to the North York Moors National Park beyond. At the foot of the 1-in-6 hill turn right on to the A64 and follow it east-wards to the roundabout, taking the first exit to continue along the A64 towards Scarborough. Stone-and-pantile cottages line the road through Seamer, where the A64 turns right and takes the route the rest of the way into Scarborough.

The town, overlooked by the hilltop ruins of a 12th-century castle, claims to have been Britain's first seaside resort. Castle Cliff, a formidable headland, towers above two bays whose sands, safe bathing and rock pools have attracted visitors for more than 200 years. Elegant buildings from Georgian and Victorian times share the town with bingo halls and funfairs, and pleasure craft mingle in the harbour with businesslike fishing boats and coastal traders. (For further details and a town plan of Scarborough, see p. 259.)

ROUTE 12   342 MILE

Birmingham to Glasgow

THIS route begins in England's second largest city, crosses the rich farming lands of the Trent and the Dove, and then climbs on to the Pennine Chain – accurately described as the 'backbone' of England – to reach Robert Burns' beloved Lowlands and Glasgow, the biggest city in Scotland.

Quiet farmland begins, and the suburbs of Birmingham are left behind, as the route leaves Sutton Coldfield and makes its way to the beautiful cathedral city of Lichfield. The title 'Ladies of the Vale' describes not only the graceful magnificence of Lichfield Cathedral's three spires, but also the countryside which they overlook; the fields watered by the Trent, Dove and their tributaries form some of the richest dairy pastures in the country.

Between Yoxall and the Dove stretches the area called Needwood Forest – although the oak trees for which it was once famous are now more likely to be seen incorporated into half-timbered buildings than growing in leafy glades. The last sizeable remnants of the forest were swept away during the 17th century to make way for parkland and pasture.

Beyond the Dove the road climbs towards Ashbourne and the Peak District. The route to Buxton follows, for part of its length, the line of a Roman road across windswept hills whose limestone has been used for centuries to build the local houses and the drystone walls that march up hill and down dale for mile after mile. The stone has also been used for far more mysterious purposes – to the east of the route, half-way between Ashbourne and Buxton, is the great stone circle of Arbor Low. The stones are set within a bank and ditch, so that from the air the monument looks very much like an enormous clock face.

Past Buxton, the 'capital' of the Peak District, the route runs through the village of Dove Holes towards the moorlands around Hayfield, where the 2088-foot summit of Kinder Scout rises to the east. Its daunting gritstone slopes were the scene of an extraordinary demonstration in 1932, when thousands of people turned out for a 'mass trespass' designed to force landowners to allow access to the high moorlands of the Pennines. Some of the leaders of the demonstration were imprisoned, but the protest eventually led to the National Parks Act, and, in 1965, to the completion of the Pennine Way from Kinder up to the Cheviots on the Scottish border.

Glossop, with its monuments to the 19th-century cotton boom, is the next town, after which the route passes through a string of villages whose weavers' cottages and mill chimneys are reminders that the Pennines have been producing sheep and woollen cloth since the Middle Ages.

Beyond the glowering slopes of Blackstone Edge and the mill town of Hebden Bridge the route approaches Haworth across landscapes that will forever be associated with the Brontë family and their novels. From Haworth the route continues to Skipton and the beautiful Yorkshire Dales. Ribblesdale is followed through Settle and up to the moorlands around Ribblehead, after which the route runs along Widdale to reach the little Wensleydale town of Hawes.

From the lonely Moorcock Inn the route follows the Eden across bleak Mallerstang Common to Kirkby Ste and stays with the river through the beautiful Eden valley as Kirkoswald. Hadrian's Wall is crossed at Newtown Scotland is entered not far from Gretna Green – famous scene of many a clandestine marriage.

Dumfries is the first town on the route with strong I connections, and his shadow falls over much of the rest c journey. Nithsdale, whose fine river scenery is typifi Auldgirth where the waters drive through a magnificent below the 18th-century bridge, is followed all the way to Cumnock. To the east stretch the rolling Lowther Hills a the west is 2298-foot Blackcraig Hill.

After Galston, a lace-making centre which attracted I and Huguenot settlers in the 17th century, comes Moscow mystifying name of this otherwise undistinguished pla compounded by the fact that it stands on a stream calle Volga. Moorland and open scenery reach almost to Glas doorstep. Despite the city's reputation, it has a wealth c buildings, parks and museums and is surrounded by marve scenery on all sides.

PLACES OF INTEREST: OPENING DETAILS		
Wall ROMAN REMAINS open all year Wed to Sat all day, Sun pm only	**Skipton** SKIPTON CASTLE open all year (except Good Fri, 25 and 26 Dec) Mon to Sat all day, Sun pm only	LINCLUDEN COLLEGE open all year ELLISLAND FARM open all year
Sudbury SUDBURY HALL open Apr to Oct Wed to Sun and Bank Holiday Mon, pm only	CRAVEN MUSEUM open all year: Apr to Sep Mon, Wed, Thu and Fri all day, Sat am and pm, Sun pm only; Oct to Mar Mon, Wed, Thu and Fri pm	**Carronbridge** DRUMLANRIG CASTLE open Easter then Sat, Sun, Wed, and Thu in May and Jun and Bank Holiday Mon, pm only; Jul and Aug daily
Parsley Hay ARBOR LOW STONE CIRCLE open all year	only; Sat am and pm GEORGE LEATT INDUSTRIAL AND FOLK MUSEUM open most Suns and Bank Holidays, pm only	**Wanlockhead** MUSEUM OF SCOTTISH LEAD MINING open Easter to end Sep
Uppermill SADDLEWORTH MUSEUM open all year Sat, Sun and Wed, pm only	**Appleby** APPLEBY CASTLE open Easter, then May to end Sep	**Mauchline** BURNS MEMORIAL TOWER open most o the year
Oxenhope KEIGHLEY AND WORTH VALLEY RAILWAY open weekends Sep to Jun and daily in Jul and Aug	**Temple Sowerby** ACORN BANK GARDENS open Apr to end Oct daily (except Mon)	**Glasgow** TRANSPORT MUSEUM open all year Mon to Sat all day, Sun pm only
Haworth HAWORTH PARSONAGE open all year (except last 3 weeks in Dec) Mon to Sat all day, Sun pm only	**Annan** KINMOUNT GARDENS open Apr to end Sep **Dumfries** BURNS HOUSE open	ART GALLERY AND MUSEUM, KELVINGROVE PARK open all year Mon to Sat all day, Sun pm only (closed 25 Dec and 1 Jan)
Keighley CLIFFE CASTLE open all year (except Good Fri, 25 and 26 Dec)	all year: end Mar to end Sep Mon to Sat am, Sun pm; Oct to end Mar Mon to Sat am and pm	BOTANIC GARDEN open all year (main glasshouse pm only)

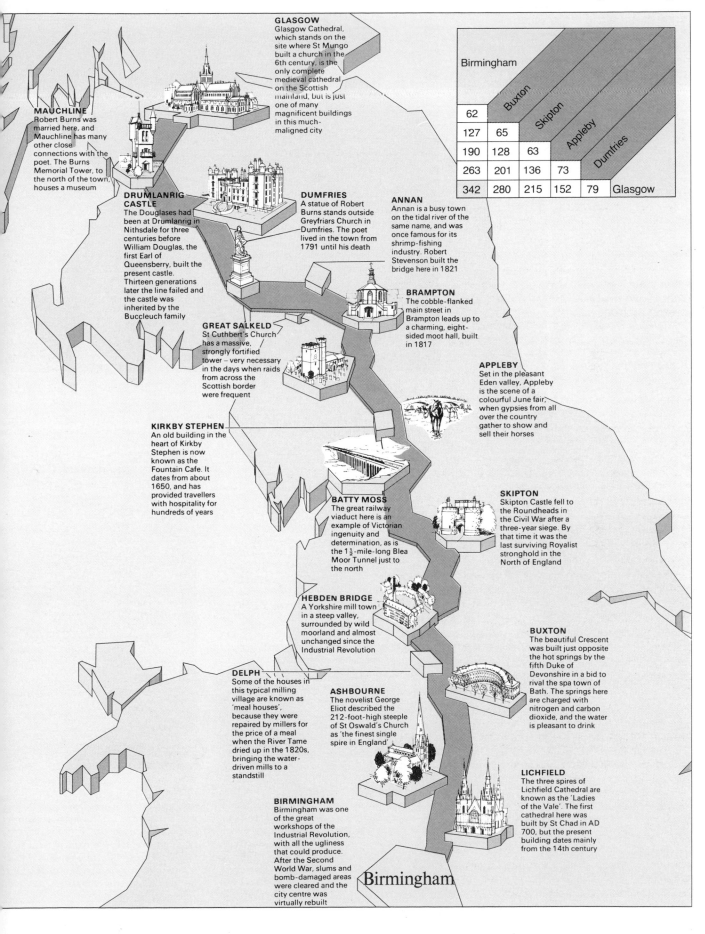

GLASGOW
Glasgow Cathedral, which stands on the site where St Mungo built a church in the 6th century, is the only complete medieval cathedral on the Scottish mainland, but is just one of many magnificent buildings in this much-maligned city

MAUCHLINE
Robert Burns was married here, and Mauchline has many other close connections with the poet. The Burns Memorial Tower, to the north of the town, houses a museum

DRUMLANRIG CASTLE
The Douglases had been at Drumlanrig in Nithsdale for three centuries before William Douglas, the first Earl of Queensberry, built the present castle. Thirteen generations later the line failed and the castle was inherited by the Buccleuch family

DUMFRIES
A statue of Robert Burns stands outside Greyfriars Church in Dumfries. The poet lived in the town from 1791 until his death

ANNAN
Annan is a busy town on the tidal river of the same name, and was once famous for its shrimp-fishing industry. Robert Stevenson built the bridge here in 1821

BRAMPTON
The cobble-flanked main street in Brampton leads up to a charming, eight-sided moot hall, built in 1817

GREAT SALKELD
St Cuthbert's Church has a massive, strongly fortified tower – very necessary in the days when raids from across the Scottish border were frequent

APPLEBY
Set in the pleasant Eden valley, Appleby is the scene of a colourful June fair, when gypsies from all over the country gather to show and sell their horses

KIRKBY STEPHEN
An old building in the heart of Kirkby Stephen is now known as the Fountain Cafe. It dates from about 1650, and has provided travellers with hospitality for hundreds of years

BATTY MOSS
The great railway viaduct here is an example of Victorian ingenuity and determination, as is the 1½-mile-long Blea Moor Tunnel just to the north

SKIPTON
Skipton Castle fell to the Roundheads in the Civil War after a three-year siege. By that time it was the last surviving Royalist stronghold in the North of England

HEBDEN BRIDGE
A Yorkshire mill town in a steep valley, surrounded by wild moorland and almost unchanged since the Industrial Revolution

DELPH
Some of the houses in this typical milling village are known as 'meal houses', because they were repaired by millers for the price of a meal when the River Tame dried up in the 1820s, bringing the water-driven mills to a standstill

ASHBOURNE
The novelist George Eliot described the 212-foot-high steeple of St Oswald's Church as 'the finest single spire in England'

BUXTON
The beautiful Crescent was built just opposite the hot springs by the fifth Duke of Devonshire in a bid to rival the spa town of Bath. The springs here are charged with nitrogen and carbon dioxide, and the water is pleasant to drink

BIRMINGHAM
Birmingham was one of the great workshops of the Industrial Revolution, with all the ugliness that could produce. After the Second World War, slums and bomb-damaged areas were cleared and the city centre was virtually rebuilt

LICHFIELD
The three spires of Lichfield Cathedral are known as the 'Ladies of the Vale'. The first cathedral here was built by St Chad in AD 700, but the present building dates mainly from the 14th century

Birmingham

Birmingham				
62	Buxton			
127	65	Skipton		
190	128	63	Appleby	
263	201	136	73	Dumfries
342	280	215	152	79	Glasgow

BIRMINGHAM TO LICHFIELD

To leave Birmingham follow signs for the A38 (SP The North) from the city centre, but bear left (SP Middle Ring Road) at the beginning of the A38(M) Aston Expressway. At the roundabout take the second exit, then keep left (SP Aston). At Aston clock tower bear right and in 1½ miles, at the roundabout beneath 'Spaghetti Junction', take the A5127 for Sutton Coldfield. Follow it through the suburbs of Gravelly Hill and Erdington, and so out of Birmingham.

Seven miles from Birmingham is the Royal Town of Sutton Coldfield. Sutton was an important market town in the Middle Ages and still retains several of its ancient buildings. The town owes much to John Veysey, who was born in Sutton and became Bishop of Exeter in 1519. A great benefactor, he paved the streets of his native town and built houses, bridges, a school and a market hall. He lived to be 102, and is buried beneath his effigy in the parish church.

The A5127 (SP Lichfield) continues northwards from Sutton through open country, keeping forward to cross the A5 – the famous Roman road, Watling Street – at a large roundabout ½ mile past Shenstone.

WALL

A few hundred yards beyond the roundabout an unclassified road to the left offers a detour to Wall. Now little more than a village, it was once the sizeable Roman town of *Letocetum*, a posting station on the Roman road. The remains of the bath house are among the most complete in the country, and there is an interesting museum.*

Continue to Lichfield, where the route passes under the railway bridge and keeps forward at the first roundabout. In ¼ mile, at the next roundabout, take the second exit, the A51 (SP Stone). As you drive northwards along the A51, which by-passes Lichfield centre, the 'Ladies of the Vale' – the three spires of Lichfield's Early English cathedral – are clearly visible beyond the roadside trees to the right. (For central Lichfield see p. 41.)

LICHFIELD TO ASHBOURNE

At the roundabout ½ mile beyond Lichfield's outskirts turn right on to the A515 (SP Ashbourne), dropping gently into the Trent

valley and passing through picturesque King's Bromley. In the 11th century this village was the home of Lady Godiva, famous for her daring ride through Coventry, and her husband Leofric, Earl of Mercia. Cross the Trent at Yoxall Bridge, and continue through Yoxall, with its attractive brick and half-timbering. Past Yoxall, the A515 runs through the area known as Needwood Forest before dropping down to the River Dove and crossing it to enter Derbyshire. Off to the left at the next junction is magnificent Sudbury Hall* (see p. 237).

At the T-junction just past the Sudbury junction, turn left on to the A50 (SP Stoke) and in 1 mile turn right (SP Ashbourne) to pick up the A515 again. Continue for 9 miles to Ashbourne, the Gateway to the Peak District. Attractive old buildings hug the hillsides of the town, and across the valley stands St Oswald's Church, where Charles I attended a service after his defeat at Naseby in 1645. A church has stood on this site since Saxon times, but the present building is mainly 13th-century. On Shrove Tuesday an extraordinary game of football is played in Ashbourne in which the rival teams, each hundreds strong, play from opposite banks of the river and the goals are some 3 miles apart.

ASHBOURNE TO CHAPEL-EN-LE-FRITH

Following the A515 for Buxton, turn left to cross the river, then right into Church Street. The route passes beneath the unusual inn sign for the Green Man and Black's Head, which spans the road on a gantry, then turns left up the hill. Leaving Ashbourne, the A515 climbs steeply to the hillcrest, where Derbyshire's beautiful dales unfold before you. Soon you enter the Peak District National Park, and

An unusual shrouded effigy of Thomas Beresford a wife is a feature of Fenny Bentley church. Their 2 children are depicted on the sides of the tomb

Derbyshire limestone accounts both for the mellow buildings of villages like Fenny Bentley and for the scenery which surrounds them

the road winds through the attractive v of Fenny Bentley. Just off to the left village church, which has a fine 16th-ce carved screen. An unusual feature o interior is a macabre shrouded effigy, c in alabaster, of Thomas Beresford ar family, who lived in the nearby 15th-c manor house. Thomas Beresford and ei his sons fought under Henry V at the Ba Agincourt in 1415.

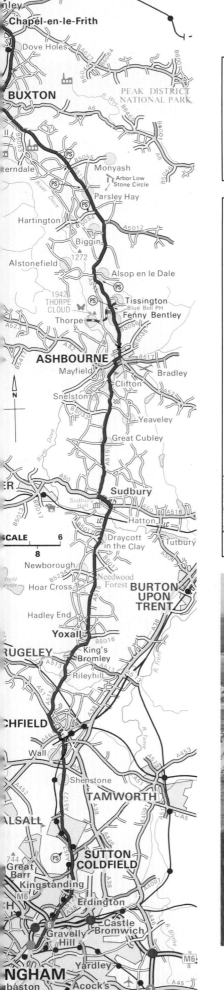

DOVEDALE

One mile beyond Fenny Bentley, at the crossroads just past the Blue Bell Inn, a detour may be made by turning left to see the superb scenery of Dovedale, perhaps Derbyshire's most famous beauty spot. Here the Dove runs through a narrow limestone gorge overlooked at its foot by Thorpe Cloud, from whose top there are magnificent views of the whole area.

TISSINGTON

Alternatively, a right turn at the same crossroads offers a detour to the picturesque village of Tissington, one of the Derbyshire well-dressing villages. Every Ascension Day five wells here are decorated with flowers, moss, feathers and other materials which are intricately worked into colourful pictures of saints or Bible scenes.

From here to Buxton the landscape is a powerful one of bare hills and isolated farmsteads. A mile east of the oddly named hamlet of Parsley Hay is the stone circle of Arbor Low.* Crowning the hill are 46 stones, set here some 4000 years ago.

A maze of drystone walls criss-crosses fields on both sides of the road, and suddenly a huge limestone works brings an abrupt reminder of man's activity on the approach to Buxton, which nestles in the valley ahead, its rooftops visible through the trees.

Besides its excellent situation amid some of Derbyshire's finest scenery, Buxton has been noted since Roman times for its mineral springs. Like other spa towns, it has many elegant buildings including the splendid Crescent, built in the 1780s by the Fifth Duke of Devonshire, who also built the Devonshire Hospital, originally a riding school. Its huge dome was constructed over the area where the Duke exercised his horses. (For more details and a town plan of Buxton, see p. 43.)

Follow signs to the A6 (north) through the market place, then turn right at the traffic lights and go under a bridge before turning left to leave by the A6 (SP Stockport, Manchester). The road passes through the village of Dove Holes to reach the small gritstone town of Chapel-en-le-Frith, whose name means 'chapel in the forest'. A chapel was originally built here in 1225 by the foresters of the Peak, and the present parish church stands on the same site.

The limestone country of central Derbyshire is not all unspoilt hills and dramatic gorges. The Buxton area has many limestone quarries, giving rise to 'moonscapes' such as this one at Hind Low

CHAPEL-EN-LE-FRITH TO UPPERMILL

From the centre of Chapel, turn right (SP Glossop) following the A624 past the huge Ferodo works. Pass underneath the railway viaducts and in ½ mile turn right with the A624 to continue to Hayfield, a largely 19th-century weaving community which is a good centre for hiking in the Peak. The massive plateau of Kinder Scout, 2088 feet high, rises to the east of the village.

Bear right, following the A624 (SP Glossop) across open, bracken-clad moorland with superb hill views, eventually to pass the lonely Grouse Inn and descend to the edge of Glossop, where you keep left on to the A6016 (SP Manchester). After 1¼ miles turn left at a T-junction on to the A57 (SP Manchester).

Pass underneath the Dinting railway viaduct and after 1¼ miles bear left over the River Etherow. Continue up the hill to the traffic lights, then turn left with the A57 (SP Manchester). In ¾ mile turn right on to the A6018 (SP Ashton-under-Lyne), and in 2¾ miles, at Stalybridge, turn right on to the B6175 (SP Mossley). Gradually climbing up the valley side, this road skirts Mossley and crosses the A635 before dropping to cross the River Tame, then climbs again to join the A670 (SP Huddersfield).

Continue on the A670 to Uppermill, where many of the houses are typical weavers' cottages of gritstone, with distinctive large mullioned windows, built when workers had to rely on natural light. The small but fascinating museum* in Uppermill is worth a visit for its displays of old machinery and other exhibits relating to the textile industry.

A wages tray – the forerunner of the wage-packet – in Uppermill museum. Millworkers' wages were counted out into numbered metal cups, one for each employee

UPPERMILL TO HEBDEN BRIDGE

Immediately beyond the railway bridge at Uppermill, turn left on to the A6052 (SP Rochdale). Follow this road to its junction with the A62, where you turn right then left for Delph. Bear left at the end of this attractive village and continue on the A6052 to Denshaw. At the mini-roundabout by the Junction Inn, take the third exit (SP Halifax) to join the A672.

Much of the old town of Hebden Bridge is unchanged since the Industrial Revolution, when its mills were driven by fast-flowing Hebden Water and Colden Water

Now the climb 'over the tops' begins, and the route is soon crossing appropriately named Windy Hill and Bleakedgate Moor to enter West Yorkshire. After passing under the M62, the road starts the long descent to Ripponden, giving dramatic moorland views. To the north-west, Blackstone Edge rises to over 1500 feet, dividing West Yorkshire from Lancashire.

In Ripponden, continue straight across the traffic lights on to the A58, following it to the busy town of Sowerby Bridge. Cross the River Calder and shortly, by the church, turn left (SP Todmorden, Burnley, A646). At the T-junction ½ mile later turn left again on to the A646 (SP Burnley). From Sowerby Bridge, road, railway and canal run parallel along the narrow Calder valley to Hebden Bridge, a pleasant mill town with distinctive, many-storeyed buildings crowded cheek by jowl into the valley, typifying the early effects of the Industrial Revolution in Yorkshire.

HEBDEN BRIDGE TO SKIPTON

Turn right in Hebden Bridge on to the A6033 (SP Keighley, Haworth). Across the valley to the left, Heptonstall is clearly visible on the horizon. This was the original weaving community, until the coming of mechaniz-ation drove the industry down into the valleys where there were rivers to power the mill wheels. Unusually, Heptonstall has two churches sharing the same churchyard: Victorian Gothic and ruined 15th-century Perpendicular stand side by side. Open country and dramatic views to the left characterize the long climb out of Hebden Bridge, then the road crosses Oxenhope Moor and descends to Oxenhope.

KEIGHLEY AND WORTH VALLEY RAILW

A sign to the left in Oxenhope offers a de to the Keighley and Worth Valley Railw The beautifully preserved locomotives coaches run between Keighley Oxenhope, taking in the famous Br village of Haworth. An exhibition of roll stock is housed in the engine shed Oxenhope, and more engines and carri can be seen at Haworth station.

HAWORTH

A second detour can be made from the vil centre by following signs left along uncl fied roads to Haworth. At the top of this s hillside village is the parsonage* where Brontë family – the three novelist sisters their brother, Branwell – grew up after t father became rector here in 1820. All of t except Anne are buried in Haworth chu and their family vault is commemorated memorial chapel built in 1964.

Carry on along the A6033, and in 2 miles turn right (SP Keighley), then in ½ mile turn left on to the A629 and continue to Keighley, where you stay with the A629 (SP Skipton). Despite modern development, Keighley retains its light and very broad main street, with many elegant buildings. High up to the left as you leave the town on the A629 is Cliffe Castle,* a Victorian mansion in attractive grounds, which houses Keighley's museum and art gallery. The exhibits include three reconstructed craftsmen's workshops, including one of a clog-maker.

The A629 for Skipton runs along Airedale, passing through Steeton and crossing the Aire by an attractive medieval bridge at Kildwick. The church here is known as the 'Lang Kirk of Craven', being nearly 170 feet long and only 50 feet wide. From here the road follows the Leeds and Liverpool Canal to Skipton.

Skipton's name is said to be derived from 'sheep town', and it still has one of the busiest sheep markets in Yorkshire. The town centre is superb, with a wide and architecturally varied main street leading up to the Perpendicular church. Nearby is the imposing gateway of Skipton Castle,* one of the best-preserved castles in the country. It has six 14th-century round towers and a delightful inner courtyard. The Craven Museum,* near the town hall, contains a fascinating local collection relating to geology, archaeology and industrial history, whilst the George Leatt Industrial and Folk Museum* is housed in a delightful old mill on a site where milling has been done since the 12th century. (For Skipton see also p. 256.)

SKIPTON TO HORTON IN RIBBLESDALE

Leave Skipton on the A65 (SP Settle) continuing up Airedale to Gargrave, an attractive little town set in a cleft of the Pennines. The Victorian church contains fragments of several Saxon crosses. Here too is the family grave of the MacLeods, where Iain MacLeod, the Conservative chancellor of the exchequer who died in 1971, is buried.

Leaving the Aire behind, the A65 continues through Hellifield and into Ribblesdale, winding through constantly changing moorland scenery with spectacular panoramas. After passing through the charming village of Long Preston it is possible to see right across Ribblesdale to Burn Moor.

Settle, Ribblesdale's main town, is a popular touring centre within easy reach of the astonishing limestone scenery around Malham, to the east, and Clapham and Ingleton to the north-west. In the handsome little town centre is Folly House, so called because the man who built it in 1679 did not have enough money to finish the job – hence the elaborate front and plain back. Magnificent views of the surrounding countryside can be had from Castleberg Crag, which towers 300 feet above the town. Just outside Settle turn right on to the B6479 (SP Horton in Ribblesdale) to continue along Ribblesdale. This road skirts Langcliffe and Stainforth, then passes a steep lane on the left which leads to Little Stainforth across a 17th-century packhorse bridge preserved by the National Trust. Below it is Stainforth Force, a picturesque cataract on the River Ribble. (Route continues on p. 132.)

A spur of the Leeds and Liverpool Canal leads right into the centre of Skipton. The canal, the longest single inland waterway ever opened in Britain, follows the Aire valley for this section of its winding journey across the Pennines

THE YORKSHIRE DALES

SPREAD out between Skipton and Teesdale, which forms the boundary between Yorkshire and County Durham, the Dales run deep into the heart of the central Pennines. Pastures enclosed by mile after mile of drystone walls patchwork the lower parts of the valleys, while above them loom impressive crags and great sweeps of unfenced moorland roamed by Swaledale and Dalesbred sheep.

The Dales are linked by narrow roads that climb steeply to provide stirring views over the 'backbone' of northern England. One of the most impressive of these roads reaches more than 1800 feet between Kettlewell and Hawes before plunging down into the shelter of Wensleydale. Another memorable by-road, overlooked by the ridge of Great Whernside, zig-zags up to more than 1600 feet on its way

north-eastwards from Kettlewell. Indeed, it is almost impossible to find a road that does not leave scenic images etched deeply into the mind's eye. There is much to delight visitors in general. Villages and towns of local stone, ruined castles and abbeys, ancient lead mines, clear rivers, cliffs, caves and waterfalls wait to be explored and enjoyed.

Mickle Fell, in the north-west corner of the region, is the highest peak at 2591 feet – but more than 20 others top 2000 feet. Among the most distinctive are Ingleborough Hill (2373 feet) and the 2273-foot bulk of Pen-y-ghent. Together with Whernside (2419 feet) they are the main landmarks on the annual 'Three Peaks' race for fell-runners. Others, only a shade less energetic, follow the Pennine Way footpath from dale to dale.

WATERFALLS, cliffs and ca are spectacular features of the Yorkshire Dales and do much to make this one of the most visuall rewarding parts of Britain. Mall Cove, a mile from Malham villa certainly ranks high among England's most dramatic natura wonders. A majestic limestone c curved like a section of a giants' amphitheatre, it towers almost feet above the source of the Rive Aire. Gordale Scar, also near Malham, is an awe-inspiring go formed when the roof of an underground river cavern colla Huge 'pavements' of weathered limestone punctuate the moors a Malham, running eastwards to Kilnsey Crag in Wharfedale.

The action of running water limestone has riddled the Natio Park with caves and immense potholes. The greatest of them a Gaping Gill, north of Clapham. huge cave could contain York Minster and has an entrance

STONE WALLS marching up hill and down dale for mile after mile, and isolated barns like the one near Keld pictured below, are distinctive features of the Dales.

One of the best and most rewarding ways to see the secret heart of the Dales is to walk part of the 250-mile Pennine Way. It starts near Edale, in Derbyshire, and heads northwards to Kirk Yetholm, on the Scottish side of the Cheviot Hills. The 4-mile stretch between Muker and Keld, over Kidson Hill, is one of the most beautiful on the entire route, and – unlike some sections – is suitable for 'casual' walkers in fine, settled weather. A delightful alternative, avoiding the steep climb from Muker, is to follow a parallel path beside the Swale and its waterfalls.

er 365 feet high through which
g torrents of water cascade.
f the caves are for experts only,
ne are open to visitors. These
e White Scar Cave, near
n, and the Stump Cross
s between Grassington and
y Bridge.
able waterfalls include
rth Force, High Force,
ton Force and Caldron Snout.
aw Force, near Hawes, falls 98
d is claimed to be the highest
drop waterfall in England.
is derived from the Old Norse
or a waterfall.

*Situated on a dramatic moorland
ween Wensleydale and Swaledale to
h of Hawes, the Buttertubs are a
extraordinary holes carved into the
e by water. Their name is derived
e old belief that they were dug by
to cool and harden butter that had
m on the way to market*

*Clumps of sycamores dot the slopes
sleydale near Hawes*

The Dipper

T HIS enchanting little bird can
often be seen bobbing up and down
on stones in the rushing streams of the
Dales. It usually flies low and fast
over the water, and is unique among
perching birds in that it wades along
the bed of streams and can feed
underwater.

Ramsons

G ROWING in large numbers
alongside shady roads and in damp
woodlands, the ramson, which is also
known as the wood garlic, lends a
distinctive visual character to many
parts of the Dales in May and June.
It has a pungent garlic smell, and in
ancient herbalist lore was considered
to have health-giving properties.

C ASTLES were established to
guard many of the Yorkshire Dales in
the troubled Middle Ages, when gaps
in mountain ranges were open
invitations to raiding parties and
armies. The first one in Skipton was
built by Robert de Romille shortly
after the Norman Conquest. Three
hundred years later it was rebuilt by
Lord Robert de Clifford and later

proved strong enough to keep out
Parliamentary forces during a
lengthy Civil War siege. It was then
restored by Lady Anne Clifford. She
also restored 15th-century Barden
Tower, now a picturesque ruin near
Bolton Abbey, in lower Wharfedale.
  Bolton Castle, in the tiny village of
Castle Bolton, looks southwards over
the lovely heart of Wensleydale. It
was built towards the end of the 14th
century by Richard Scrope, Lord
Chancellor of England, and cost him
£12,000 – a vast amount of money in
those days. The ill-fated Mary,
Queen of Scots, was held prisoner
there for six months in 1568. Like its
counterpart at Skipton, the castle was
besieged by Parliamentary troops
during the Civil War. It was
surrendered to them after the
starving defenders had been reduced
to eating their horses.
  In the north-eastern part of the
Dales there are splendid medieval
strongholds at Richmond,
Middleham and Barnard Castle.
Middleham was owned by the
powerful Nevilles for 200 years until
Richard Neville, known as 'Warwick
the Kingmaker', died in battle during
the Wars of the Roses.

*Left: Bolton Castle was built at a time
when considerations of comfort had become
as important as defence*

HORTON IN RIBBLESDALE TO HAWES

Soon the road reaches Horton in Ribblesdale, set in the valley between two of Yorkshire's famous 'Three Peaks': Ingleborough to the west and Pen-y-ghent to the east. A bridleway leads from the village up through stern moorland to the Pennine Way, whilst north of Horton are several outstanding potholes, such as Alum Pot and Hull Pot. The route crosses the river and continues up Ribblesdale, surrounded by rolling hills. At the head of the valley, approximately 5 miles north of Horton, turn right on to the B6255 (SP Hawes). The railway viaduct facing you at this junction spans the hollow of Batty Moss with 24 great arches. This section of the line – a continuous climb from Settle to Blea Moor – is known as the 'Long Drag'. Just north of the viaduct the line disappears into the 1½-mile-long Blea Moor Tunnel. This great feat of late Victorian engineering cost many lives. Over 100 victims of accidents and the harsh working conditions are buried nearby at Chapel le Dale.

About a mile along the B6255 is an isolated house, Gearstones, once an inn on the cattle droving route. Here hundreds of beasts were gathered for the twice-yearly sales. The road climbs to 1400 feet, winding through unforgettable, heather-clad scenery before the descent into Widdale. Nine miles beyond Gearstones, turn left on to the A684.

HAWES

Just off the route to the right at this junction is Hawes. It has been a market town for almost 300 years, and the Tuesday market is still a great attraction to tourist and Dalesman alike. Hawes is also an important Wensleydale cheese-making centre; the green flanks of Wensleydale are ideal pasture land. The mild, crumbly white cheese is now internationally famous, and an unusual blue-veined variety is also to be found here.

HAWES TO APPLEBY

Drive westwards along the A684 Sedbergh, Kirkby Stephen) for 5½ miles turn right at the Moorcock Inn on t B6259 (SP Kirkby Stephen). After 3 mil road crosses the border into Cumbria runs across the wild emptiness of Maller Common, following the ancient drove from Scotland to cattle fairs at such pla Gearstones and Malham. The River accompanies the road to Kirkby Ste and continues near it for many more About 1 mile north of Outhgill, on the the road, lies the picturesque rui Pendragon Castle, which legend fanc insists was built by the father of King A Uther Pendragon.

On reaching Kirkby Stephen, turn rig to the A685 (SP Brough). The market to Kirkby Stephen is full of architectural est, ranging from the Victorian tempe hall to the building dating from around which is now the Fountain Café. On on of the cobbled market square, behin imposing entrance called the Cloisters merly the butter market), stands the church, known as the 'Cathedral of the I It dates mainly from the 13th century. I is an interesting carved Saxon stone dep the Devil in chains, and a modern eng glass window which portrays the st of St Stephen.

Surrounded by sheep-cropped fields criss-crossed by drystone walls, this typical Dales farmstead is overlooked by 2273-foot-high Pen-y-ghent, one of Yorkshire's 'Three Peaks'

Gypsies and tinkers from all over Britain meet in Appleby for the annual horse fair, the largest of its kind in the world. This colourful spectacle takes place on the second Wednesday in June, and the travelling people set up camp on Fair Hill

Follow the A685 through Kirkby Stephen and in ¼ mile turn left on to the B6259 (SP Warcop). The countryside is quietly rural along this narrow hedge-fringed country lane, dramatically different from the bleak and lonely fells. Warcop is a charming tucked-away stone village, and is the scene, every summer, of a rush-bearing festival, dating from the days when earthen church floors were strewn with rushes for warmth. About 1½ miles beyond Warcop turn left on to the A66 for Appleby.

APPLEBY

Set in a loop of the River Eden, Appleby is one of the most attractive towns in the North Country. To visit it, turn left off the A66 (SP Town Centre) at the start of the by-pass. Cross the sandstone bridge and go up Boroughgate, whose cottages and ancient buildings – including the 17th-century moot hall, where the borough council still meets and the information office is housed – are set back from the road behind wide, green verges. Lined by pleasant lime trees, Boroughgate leads up the hill to Appleby Castle,* a venerable borderland fortress with a Norman keep. The grounds house a collection of rare breeds of farm animals. The church, at the bottom of Boroughgate, was rebuilt in the 12th century after being destroyed by Scottish raiders. From Appleby town centre follow signs for Penrith to rejoin the A66.

APPLEBY TO KIRKOSWALD

North-west of Appleby the A66 gives a clear run along the Eden valley. Much of this road is Roman in origin, and Kirkby Thore, off to the right, was the Roman fort of *Bravoniacum*. The next village on the route is Temple Sowerby, a pleasant place with sandstone houses, two greens and a little church which stands well back from the road. Half a mile past the village turn right on to the B6412 (SP Culgaith).

ACORN BANK GARDENS
A clearly signed road to the right, about 200 yards from this junction, offers a detour to the gardens of Acorn Bank,* noted especially for its display of spring bulbs. There is also a fine walled garden and a fragrant herb garden.

The B6412 leads by a series of twists and turns to Culgaith and then runs a straighter course to Langwathby, where you turn left on to the A686. Here there is a large village green and a church, rebuilt in 1718, which contains some 17th-century armour. At the end of the village turn left again to cross the River Eden by a single-track bridge controlled by traffic lights. In ½ mile turn right on to the B6412 (SP Lazonby, Great Salkeld), continuing northwards through Great Salkeld. The ivy-clad church here has a 14th-century tower fortified against Scottish raids, and a sumptuous Norman south doorway. Two miles later, at the T-junction near the Midland Hotel in Lazonby, turn right on to the B6413 (SP Kirkoswald, Brampton), shortly re-crossing the River Eden.

Next in this string of small Cumbrian villages is Kirkoswald. The southern approach to it is particularly pleasing: a steep village street, a tiny square to the left, a couple of cosy pubs. St Oswald's Church is built in a hollow, probably because pre-Christians worshipped a well there: indeed, a spring still runs beneath the nave. Kirkoswald also has a ruined 13th-century castle, though only its dungeons and one turret remain.

KIRKOSWALD TO ANNAN

Continue along the B6413, crossing after 5 miles the burn called Croglin Water, which rises in the heart of the bleak moorland country lying to the east of the road as it runs through Croglin, Newbiggin and later Castle Carrock to Brampton, a little-known but thriving market town, full of local charm. Two special attractions are the octagonal moot hall and the even older building (now a shoe shop) where Bonnie Prince Charlie received the surrender of Carlisle during the 1745 rebellion.

Cross the A69 in Brampton, keeping forward on to the A6071 (SP Longtown), which crosses the line of Hadrian's Wall at Newtown. At Longtown, the last village in England on this route – although it has a distinctly Scottish feel – turn right on to the A7, cross the River Esk, and then turn left to pick up the A6071 again, following signs for Gretna and Glasgow. Three miles beyond Longtown, turn right (SP Annan, Dumfries) on to the A74 dual carriageway.

GRETNA GREEN
For a detour to Gretna Green, keep forward at this junction to cross the A74 and join the B721, then branch right on to an unclassified road. Until 1856, Scottish law allowed any couple to be married simply by declaring, in front of witnesses, their wish to become man and wife. Gretna Green was the first place across the border, so here English runaway couples – often those whose parents disapproved of the match – came to be married secretly by local blacksmiths and other tradesmen. Now the two smithies are geared to parties of tourists, with joke marriage certificates, postcards and a little museum.

Follow the A74, crossing the Scottish border at the River Sark bridge, and in ½ mile bear left with the A75. This road runs straight along the flat lands bordering the Solway Firth to Annan. Occasionally, to the left, there are views across the fields to the Solway Firth, while to the right it is hard to ignore the bulk of Chapel Cross nuclear power station. Stay with the A75 through Annan, a shrimp-fishing port for hundreds of years, and once an important shipbuilding centre where some of the great tea-clippers were constructed.

ANNAN TO DUMFRIES

About 4 miles beyond Annan, to the left of the A75, are the gardens of Kinmount House,* spectacular when the rhododendrons and azaleas are in bloom. There are signposted woodland walks, and a picnic area.

Surrounded by flat dairying land, which is among the most fertile and prosperous in Scotland, the A75 continues through Carrutherstown to Dumfries, whose ancient streets are set within a loop of the River Nith. Sometimes referred to – like its football team – as 'Queen of the South', Dumfries is the gateway to Burns country. Robert Burns, whose poetry so often takes second place to the legend which grew up around him, died here in 1796, and lies buried in an elaborate mausoleum in St Michael's churchyard. His house in Burns Street is now a museum.* The poet was often in the audience at the elegant 18th-century Theatre Royal, and spent many an evening in the Globe Inn and the Hole i' the Wa', which can still be visited. Another literary figure associated with Dumfries is J. M. Barrie, best known as the author of *Peter Pan*, who was a pupil at the Academy here.

An elegant statue of Robert Burns stands in front of Greyfriars Church in Dumfries, the town where the po[et] spent the last five years of his life

Dumfries was created a royal burgh [by] William the Lion in 1186. In 1306 Rober[t] Bruce stabbed his rival, the Red Com[yn,] representative of the English king, in the Greyfriars monastery. He then claimed [the] Scottish throne and struck the first b[low] against Edward I that was to lead to the W[ars] of Independence. In his first victory [he] captured the castle, whose site at Castled[ykes] is marked by a memorial stone.

Follow signs for Kilmarnock and cross [the] Nith to leave Dumfries by the A76.

DUMFRIES TO CARRONBRIDGE

LINCLUDEN COLLEGE
On the outskirts of Dumfries, signposted [down] the road to the right through a housing estat[e,] lie the ruins of Lincluden College,* a 12t[h-]century Benedictine nunnery. Some of th[e] buildings, of a later date, are beautif[ul] examples of the Decorated style of archite[c-]ture, and the little church contains som[e] interesting tombs. The setting is delightf[ul] woodland at the point where Cluden Wat[er] joins the River Nith.

As the A76 runs up Nithsdale, the wild hill[s] the Forest of Ae rise in the distance to the e[ast.]

ELLISLAND FARM
About 6 miles from Dumfries, down a track [to] the right, is Ellisland Farm,* rented by Bur[ns] for three years. He wrote many songs an[d] poems here, but the farm was not successf[ul,] and the poet and his wife left it in 1791 to liv[e] in Dumfries. Parts of the farmhouse are muc[h] as they were when Burns lived there.

Sheltered by bleak fells rising to 2000 feet, the isolated hamlet of Castle Carrock is set amid rolling farmland

Thornhill, 8 miles beyond Ellisland, has been called the prettiest small town in Scotland. The wide main street is enhanced by grass verges, and attractive lime trees line the road. The shops, hotels, cottages and grander Victorian and Edwardian houses are built mainly of warm red sandstone. In the village centre is a tall column, topped by the winged horse emblem of the Queensberry family who built Drumlanrig Castle.

Lime trees planted by the Sixth Duke of Buccleuch in the 19th century complement the mellow stone cottages that line Thornhill's main street

DRUMLANRIG CASTLE

The castle* lies just over 3 miles further along the A76 beyond Carronbridge. To reach it, turn left off the A76 opposite a right turn for Holestane, approximately 1½ miles north of Carronbridge. A long drive enhances this imposing late 17th-century building, seat of the Dukes of Buccleuch. The interior is an Aladdin's cave of treasures, among them paintings, silver, Louis XIV furniture and a chandelier that was a wedding gift from Charles II to the Duke of Monmouth. In the park stands a ruin known as Tibber's Castle.

CARRONBRIDGE TO SANQUHAR

The A76 continues through Enterkinfoot and along Nithsdale, which is much narrower now, with high moors close to the road. Road, river and railway run beside each other along the valley towards Sanquhar.

WANLOCKHEAD
In Mennock, a mountain road on the right (B797) leads to Wanlockhead, Scotland's highest inhabited village, at the northern end of the Mennock Pass. In the village is a fascinating museum* relating the village's long history of gold, silver and lead mining. As well as the indoor museum, there is a 1½-mile-long walkway which leads visitors round several old lead-mining installations such as smelting sites, tramways and mine-head pumps. Less than 2 miles further along the pass is the village of Leadhills, where in 1741 the local miners founded the first subscription lending library in Britain.

The main route follows the A76 to Sanquhar. An obelisk at the approach to the town associates it with the Covenanters, who refused in the 1680s to swear allegiance to the English king. Staunch defenders of Presbyterianism, they affixed the two 'Declarations of Sanquhar' to the old town cross, which was replaced by the present monument. Sanquhar has been a royal burgh since 1484, and it claims to have the oldest post office in Britain. It was to Sanquhar Castle – now a ruin, situated above the River Nith – that the First Duke of Queensberry moved soon after Drumlanrig Castle was finished. The cost of building Drumlanrig had nearly bankrupted him, and he spent only one night there.

SANQUHAR TO MAUCHLINE

Carry on along the A76 through Kirkconnel, a small industrial town at the edge of the Ayrshire coalfield. Road and railway follow the peaceful River Nith, and in the next village, New Cumnock, the Nith is joined by Afton Water, the subject of a poem by Burns: 'Flow gently, sweet Afton, among thy green braes'. Beautiful and isolated Glen Afton lies to the south of the village. Leaving the Nith behind, the A76 runs on to Cumnock, an industrial and market town among rolling green hills. Coal-mining has replaced a quainter industry for which Cumnock was once known – the manufacture of snuff-boxes. Cumnock was the home of the great socialist thinker and politician Keir Hardie, one of the founders of the Labour Party. He lived here when he was secretary of the Miners' Federation, and is commemorated by a bust outside the town hall. Leave Cumnock on the A76 (SP Kilmarnock), passing through Auchinleck, where James Boswell, companion and biographer of Dr Johnson, is buried in a mausoleum.

Mauchline, the next village, is famed for its associations with Burns. After his father's death in 1784, the poet farmed with his brother at Mossgiel, near Mauchline. He never successful as a farmer, but the yea spent at Mossgiel were probably his fines poet. Whilst living there, he fell in love Jean Armour, a local girl whom he marri Mauchline in 1788. The couple began married life here, in a house in Castle S now known as Burns House.

MAUCHLINE TO GLASGOW

By the A76 ½ mile north of Mauchline i Burns Memorial Tower,* which hous small museum of interesting memento the poet. Five miles from Mauchline, place called Crossroads, turn right on to A719 (SP Galston). Galston is a bustling semi-industrial town set amid the woodl of the upper Irvine valley. The local mi industry is now defunct, but mills still ope and the town is noted for its lace-mak Follow signs through the town for Edinb and the A71, then turn left on to the A719 Glasgow). The route passes near ru Loudoun Castle, to the right just nort Galston. Once one of south-west Scotla most impressive houses, it was virtu destroyed by fire in 1941.

The next hamlet along the A719 has intriguing name of Moscow, and 2 miles the road passes through Waterside, set little dip on Craufurdland Water. Abo miles beyond here, turn right at a T-junc on to the A77 (SP Glasgow), and follow wide road all the way into the city.

The Italian Renaissance building of the City Chambers overlooks the Cenotaph, designed by Sir John Burnet and harmonizing perfectly with the elegance of Glasgow's George Square

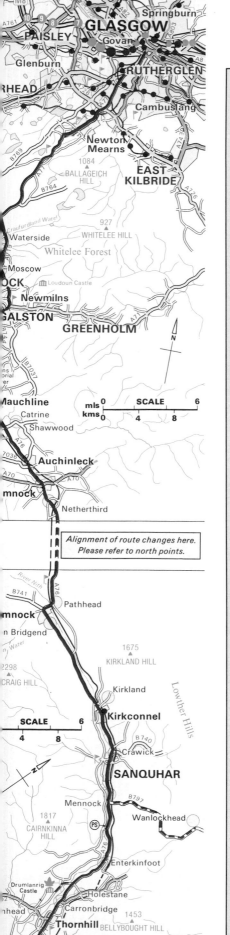

GLASGOW

Perhaps Britain's most underrated city, Glasgow – despite its reputation – is a place of great style, and represents fine architecture of many periods. Its chief treasure is the cathedral, more affectionately known as St Mungo's, after the nickname given to St Kentigern, who traditionally founded Glasgow. Part of the crypt of the original St Mungo's Church survives, but the present cathedral dates mainly from the 15th century.

In Albert Drive is the Museum of Transport,* where every imaginable kind of wheeled vehicle may be found, from trams to veteran bicycles. There are several other museums and galleries, among them the art gallery in Kelvingrove Park,* which holds the finest municipal collection in Britain. Off Great Western Road is the Botanic Garden,* where rare and exotic plants thrive in the controlled atmosphere of glasshouses; there are also 40 acres of outdoor gardens.

Quite apart from the attractions of Glasgow itself, the city lies on the edge of some of the loveliest countryside in Scotland: Loch Lomond is only about 40 minutes' drive away, and the Trossachs can be reached in about an hour. The coast at Ayr and Ardrossan is about the same distance.

Above: It is hard to believe that this astoundingly ornate building in Glasgow Green is in reality a factory. Richly decorated with mosaics and coloured brickwork, the Templeton Carpet Factory is the city's most striking example of Victorian industrial architecture

Right: A completely different 19th-century approach to architecture is the elegant library of the Glasgow School of Art in Renfrew Street. It was designed by the great Glasgow-born architect Charles Rennie Mackintosh (1868–1928), influenced by the Art Nouveau movement

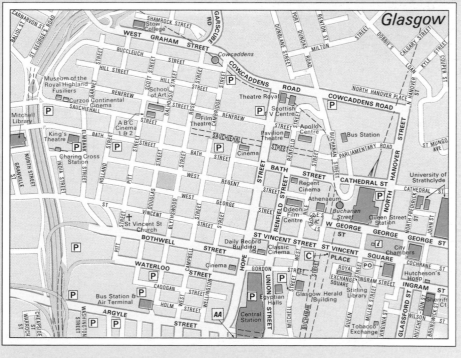

ROUTE 13

Birmingham to Aberystwyt

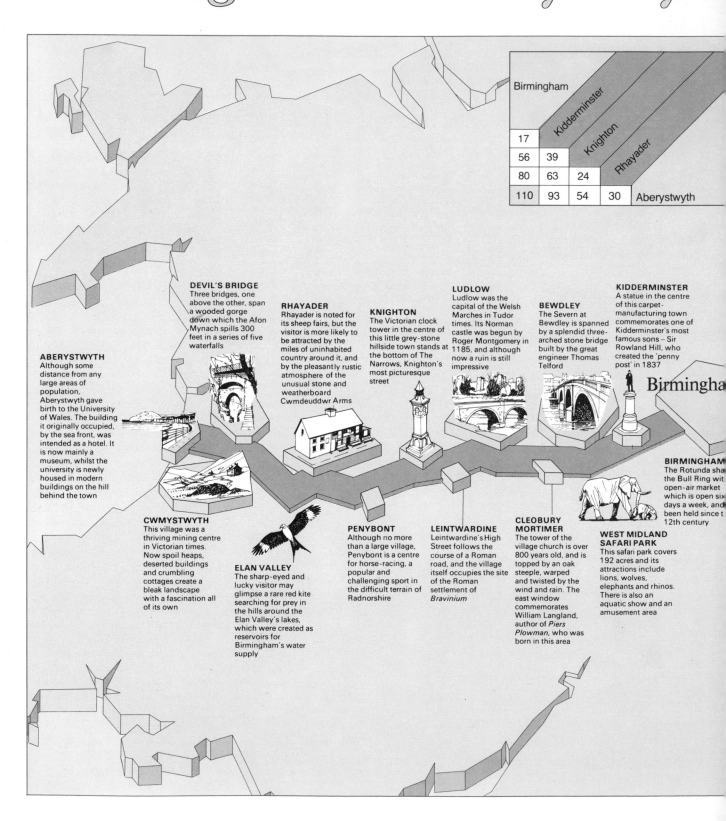

Birmingham				
17	Kidderminster			
56	39	Knighton		
80	63	24	Rhayader	
110	93	54	30	Aberystwyth

DEVIL'S BRIDGE
Three bridges, one above the other, span a wooded gorge down which the Afon Mynach spills 300 feet in a series of five waterfalls

RHAYADER
Rhayader is noted for its sheep fairs, but the visitor is more likely to be attracted by the miles of uninhabited country around it, and by the pleasantly rustic atmosphere of the unusual stone and weatherboard Cwmdeuddwr Arms

KNIGHTON
The Victorian clock tower in the centre of this little grey-stone hillside town stands at the bottom of The Narrows, Knighton's most picturesque street

LUDLOW
Ludlow was the capital of the Welsh Marches in Tudor times. Its Norman castle was begun by Roger Montgomery in 1185, and although now a ruin is still impressive

BEWDLEY
The Severn at Bewdley is spanned by a splendid three-arched stone bridge built by the great engineer Thomas Telford

KIDDERMINSTER
A statue in the centre of this carpet-manufacturing town commemorates one of Kidderminster's most famous sons – Sir Rowland Hill, who created the 'penny post' in 1837

ABERYSTWYTH
Although some distance from any large areas of population, Aberystwyth gave birth to the University of Wales. The building it originally occupied, by the sea front, was intended as a hotel. It is now mainly a museum, whilst the university is newly housed in modern buildings on the hill behind the town

Birmingha

BIRMINGHAM
The Rotunda sha the Bull Ring wit open-air market which is open si days a week, and been held since t 12th century

CWMYSTWYTH
This village was a thriving mining centre in Victorian times. Now spoil heaps, deserted buildings and crumbling cottages create a bleak landscape with a fascination all of its own

ELAN VALLEY
The sharp-eyed and lucky visitor may glimpse a rare red kite searching for prey in the hills around the Elan Valley's lakes, which were created as reservoirs for Birmingham's water supply

PENYBONT
Although no more than a large village, Penybont is a centre for horse-racing, a popular and challenging sport in the difficult terrain of Radnorshire

LEINTWARDINE
Leintwardine's High Street follows the course of a Roman road, and the village itself occupies the site of the Roman settlement of *Bravinium*

CLEOBURY MORTIMER
The tower of the village church is over 800 years old, and is topped by an oak steeple, warped and twisted by the wind and rain. The east window commemorates William Langland, author of *Piers Plowman*, who was born in this area

WEST MIDLAND SAFARI PARK
This safari park covers 192 acres and its attractions include lions, wolves, elephants and rhinos. There is also an aquatic show and an amusement area

LEADING west from the bustling centre of Birmingham,
 route soon skirts the Clent Hills, which give just a flavour of
 wild upland scenery that will be encountered in mid Wales.
lton Hill, at 1034 feet, is not only the highest of the Clents,
 also the tallest summit in the central Midlands. There are
ensive views from the hills, including, to the north of the
te, Wychbury Hill, which is crowned by an Iron Age hill-
. On the western side of the Clent Hills is the village of
gley. Although much of it now consists of modern housing, it
ains some of its old atmosphere and an 18th-century
nsion set in parkland dotted with follies.

'ast Kidderminster the route crosses the River Severn and
ers the handsome town of Bewdley, beyond which stretch
 woodlands and heaths of the Wyre Forest. Most of the
iving woodlands of this old royal hunting-ground lie to
 north of the route, but in former days it also ran southwards
the outskirts of Worcester. Between the 14th and 19th
turies most of the forest's acres were turned into coppices,
 many of the big oaks which stand today grew from ancient
pice stumps that have long since rotted away. Oak and
h dominate the parts of the forest that have not been
ited with conifers by the Forestry Commission, but there
 many other kinds of tree, including wild cherries, the
estors of our cultivated varieties. The forest is exceptionally
 in flora and fauna, especially around Dowles Brook, which
s into the Severn north of Bewdley.

fter passing through Cleobury Mortimer the route skirts
southern edge of the Clee Hills. Scarred though they are by
rrying for the hard black stone for which they are famous,
 nonetheless preserve some of their former grandeur and
rd stupendous views in all directions.

 long descent takes the route to Ludlow, perhaps the most
tanding of all the delectable border towns. From
twardine, eight miles west of Ludlow, the route follows the
er Teme across the Welsh border to Knighton. Quiet and
oilt, the town stands astride Offa's Dyke, which marked
border for hundreds of years after it was constructed in the
century on the instructions of King Offa of Mercia.

etween Knighton and Penybont are the rounded hills of
nor Forest. Divided by many small streams and rising to
 2000 feet at Black Mixen, this remote area was the haunt
olves until Tudor times. Penybont has been the scene of a
ving stock market since 1919, when it was decided that it
ld not be appropriate to drive cattle and sheep through
genteel streets of nearby Llandrindod Wells.

eyond Rhayader the route strikes into the huge landscapes
ntral Wales. The most common sounds on these immense
rland acres are the bleating of sheep, the mewing of drifting
zards and the murmur of running water. Birmingham's
tiable demands for water brought great changes to these
rland hills and valleys in the closing years of the 19th
ury. Four great reservoirs were constructed along the Elan
y, to the west of Rhayader, and transformed the area into
t is now often called the Welsh Lake District. In 1952
her huge reservoir, the Claerwen, was built even further in
heart of the moorland. Welcomed by many, these huge
ts of water were regarded with mixed feelings by
ralists, for the area is the last stronghold in Britain of the
kite and it was feared that the disturbance would finally
g it to extinction. Fortunately this has not happened, and
y visitors to mid Wales may catch a glimpse of this
nctive hawk as it circles high in the sky.

PLACES OF INTEREST: OPENING DETAILS

Bewdley
WEST MIDLAND SAFARI AND LEISURE PARK open mid Mar to Oct

SEVERN VALLEY RAILWAY open Mar to end Oct Sat and Sun; May to Sep usually daily; also all Bank Holidays

BEWDLEY MUSEUM open Mar to end Nov: Mon to Sat all day, Sun pm only

Foxwood
CLEE HILL BIRD AND ANIMAL GARDEN, open all year (except 25 Dec)

Devil's Bridge
VALE OF RHEIDOL LIGHT RAILWAY open Easter to Oct

Aberystwyth
NATIONAL LIBRARY OF WALES open all year Mon to Sat (except Christmas and Easter)

Under the waters of the Caban Coch Reservoir are the
remains of two houses that have connections with the poet
Shelley. He stayed at his cousin's house, Cwm Elan, in 1811,
and returned a year later, shortly after his marriage to Harriet
Westbrook, to stay at the neighbouring farm of Nant Gwyllt.
While in residence Shelley impressed the local inhabitants with
his eccentric behaviour, and on one occasion is said to have
launched a paper boat on the river which had a five pound note
for a sail and a cat for crew. Nant Gwyllt, whose walls can still
be seen when the waters are very low, was the setting for
Francis Brett Young's novel *The House under the Water* which is a
fictionalized account of the flooding of the valley. In all 18
cottages, several farms, a church and a Baptist chapel lie
submerged under the reservoirs.

The route follows the Elan, then the Ystwyth, to the old lead-
mining village of Cwmystwyth, from where it continues to
Devil's Bridge. Two stupendous waterfalls – the Mynach and
the Gyfarllwyd – together with a gorge spanned by a stack of
three bridges combine to make the scenery at Devil's Bridge
spectacular and unforgettable. George Borrow, who travelled
the length and breadth of Wales in the last half of the 19th
century, and recorded all that he saw and heard in his book
Wild Wales, wrote the following description of the scenery at
Devil's Bridge that still holds true today: 'Of all the falls the fifth
or last is the most considerable: you view it from a kind of den,
to which the last flight of steps, the ruggedest and most
dangerous of all, has brought you; your position here is a wild
one. The fall, which is split into two, is thundering beside you;
foam, foam, foam is flying all about you; the basin or cauldron
is boiling frightfully below you; hirsute rocks are frowning
terribly above you, and above them forest trees, dark and wet
with spray and mist, are distilling drops in showers from their
boughs.'

From Devil's Bridge the route descends into Aberystwyth,
never far from the steep, oak-clad slopes of Cwm Rheidol and
the little railway which travels up the valley from Aberystwyth
to Devil's Bridge. It is the only narrow-gauge railway owned
and operated by British Rail, and was opened in 1902 to carry
lead ore down from the mines. From its earliest days the
railway attracted tourists, and after the mines fell into disuse it
was tourist traffic which kept the line open. Even so, the line
was nearly closed in 1954, but concerted efforts kept the trains
running, and when British Rail completed the switch to
electricity and diesel in 1968, the steam engines on the Rheidol
ensured its success.

Set on a hillside flanking the mouth of the Afon Rheidol,
Aberystwyth is a seaside resort, a university town and an
administrative centre. It has all the attractions that might be
expected of a town with such a diversity of functions, plus a
unique and wholly Welsh charm.

BIRMINGHAM TO BEWDLEY

From central Birmingham take the A456 (SP Kidderminster, The West). This road soon becomes dual carriageway, carrying you swiftly out of the city and passing under the M5, following signs for Kidderminster all the way. The route shortly passes the Clent Hills, to the left, an attractive rural area surprisingly close to the city. Rising to 1034 feet at the summit of Walton Hill, the Clents are protected by the National Trust from encroaching urban development, and the country park here attracts many visitors from the industrial towns of the West Midlands.

Follow the A456 through Hagley and Blakedown to Kidderminster, a busy town where carpets have been manufactured for over 200 years. In the centre is a statue of the town's most famous son, Sir Rowland Hill. Born in 1795, he introduced the 'penny post' in 1837 and became the first Secretary to the Post Office 17 years later.

Continue along the A456 (SP Bewdley), leaving Kidderminster and soon passing the entrance to the West Midland Safari and Leisure Park* on the left. Almost 200 acres of parkland here are roamed by lions, giraffes, elephants, camels, tigers and other animals from all over the world. Monkeys, guinea pigs, ponies and other more domesticated creatures inhabit the pets' corner, while additional attractions include a boating lake for rowing and canoeing, and a miniature railway with a 'Wild West' locomotive, particularly popular with younger visitors.

The A456 passes beneath the viaduct carrying the Severn Valley Railway.* This runs from Bewdley station (to the left of the route) through $12\frac{1}{2}$ miles of picturesque Severn valley scenery to Bridgnorth. It is the best-known standard-gauge steam railway in the country, with a large collection of locomotives and rolling-stock.

Soon the route enters Bewdley, swinging right then left to cross the Severn over Telford's typically handsome stone bridge. Bewdley is an attractive town whose buildings span many periods and styles, from the

Pleasure craft on the River Severn at Bewdley, once a busy inland port. In the background is the handsome balustraded bridge built by Thomas Telford in the late 1790s

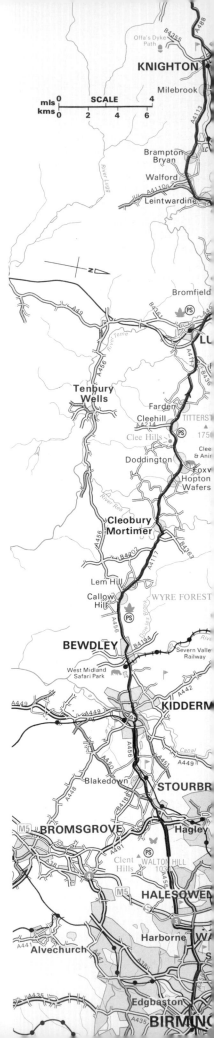

-century gabled post office to the classical
-century town hall. There is a small but
lent museum* in Load Street, where you
see exhibits of traditional local forestry
s, such as a charcoal-burner's wigwam
the Wyre Forest and bark-stripping
from the days when bark was used in the
ing industry here. Demonstrations of
local crafts are also held from time to
The museum is housed in the Shambles
old butchers' market – where arcades
a cobbled way behind the 18th-century
et hall. The route runs up Load Street,
follows the A456 to the right (SP
ury) behind the church and climbs
ly between rows of terraced cottages.

LEY TO LUDLOW

WYRE FOREST VISITOR CENTRE
ree miles from Bewdley, at Callow Hill, a
nposted detour to the right leads to the
restry Commission's picnic area and visitor
tre on the southern edge of the Wyre
rest. Listed as a royal hunting-ground in
mesday Book, the forest now covers about
0 acres. The picnic site is the starting point
three waymarked walks which vary in
gth from ¾ mile to 2 miles.

Enormous views over unspoilt countryside are characteristic of this route: here, looking eastwards from Clee Hill

nue along the A456 for 1 mile, then turn
on to the A4117 (SP Cleobury). A mile
the impressive Mawley Oak stands to
-ft of the road, facing a garage named
the tree. Believed to be almost 250 years
he tree is about 90 feet tall and has a
of 24 feet. Several large branches broke
1974, but local people succeeded in
g almost £350 to preserve the tree and
nt young oaks nearby.
ore the road runs down to Cleobury
imer there are good views of the Clee
which rise to 1772 feet at the northern-

most summit of Brown Clee, the highest point
in Shropshire. 'Clibbery' Mortimer itself is a
place of considerable charm and character
with lengths of raised pavement, dashes of
black-and-white architecture and a good deal
of mellow, Georgian brick. The town's name
recalls the powerful Mortimer family who
sailed to England with William the
Conqueror and became virtual rulers of
much of the Welsh Marches. It was they who
founded the parish church that overlooks the
curving, climbing main street. Its bulging
walls and twisted steeple were stabilized by
the indefatigable Telford in 1793.

Heading into hilly country that sets the
mood for the rest of the journey, the A4117
swoops down to Hopton Wafers before
climbing steadily to skirt the southern slopes
of Titterstone Clee Hill. To the right of the
route in the hamlet of Foxwood is the ten-acre
Clee Hill Bird and Animal Garden.* A
colourful variety of exotic birds from as far
afield as India, South America, Africa and
Australia share the grounds with wallabies,
llamas, four-horned St Kilda sheep and other
unusual animals.

A mile further on, an AA viewpoint
indicator stands to the left of the road, 1047
feet above sea level. Landmarks visible from
here on a clear day include the Sugar Loaf
near Abergavenny, the Black Mountains
beyond Hay-on-Wye and the 'whale-backed'
Malverns. Jones's Folly, a huge Victorian-
Gothic clock-tower, soars above the wooded
hills to the south-east of the viewpoint.

The road keeps climbing gradually, reaching the village of Cleehill at 1150 feet before
plunging down towards Ludlow, dropping

700 feet in 2 miles. Ludlow itself can be side-
stepped by joining the A49 (SP Shrewsbury)
at the by-pass roundabout, though the town
centre is really too good to miss (see p. 50).

LUDLOW TO KNIGHTON

The A49 runs from Ludlow along the broad
Teme valley to Bromfield, where the route
turns left on to the A4113 (SP Knighton) and
climbs to an acute bend called the Fiddler's
Elbow before dropping into Leintwardine.
This pleasant village stands on the line of a
Roman road and is overlooked by a sturdy
church tower clearly built with Welsh raids in
mind. Follow the main road through the
village, then cross the River Teme and in ½
mile turn right for Knighton, still on the
A4113. Brampton Bryan, the last English
village on this route, was the scene of a famous
siege in the Civil War. The ruins of its 14th-
century castle can still be seen, and the
present church was built in 1656 to replace
one damaged in the siege. Typical border
country, with high, wooded hills on both
sides, accompanies the route into Wales.

Knighton stands on the Welsh side of the
border and has an attractive 19th-century
atmosphere epitomized by the Victorian
clock-tower in the square. The town's history
goes back much further, however. The original Saxon settlement was taken over by the
Welsh in 1052, and subsequently by the
Normans. They built Knighton's first castle,
a wooden structure whose mound, still known
as Bryn y Castell, can be seen to the east of the
town. Earthworks to the west mark the site of
the first stone castle here, built in the 12th
century. (For Knighton see also p. 193.)

There are peaceful views down the Ystwyth valley as the route leaves Powys and heads towards Cwmystwyth

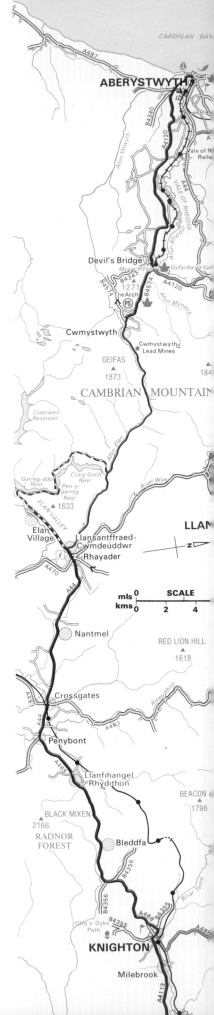

KNIGHTON TO RHAYADER

The route follows the A488 (SP Rhayader), which runs through the town then makes a winding ascent into the hills, reaching 1150 feet, and eventually wriggles down into the valley of the River Lugg. Swinging westwards, the road skirts the steep northern slopes of Radnor Forest, its rounded top crowned by a radio mast. Rising slowly but surely, the road reaches 1200 feet just beyond Bleddfa, whose village green, church and pub give it an atmosphere quite out of character with its name, which means 'place of wolves'.

Soon the Cambrian Mountains can be seen for the first time; then the route leads across an expanse of sheep-cropped common to Penybont, a village whose size belies its former importance. As a coaching stop and later a postal centre it was once an important settlement. Its role was gradually taken over by nearby Llandrindod Wells, but the inhabitants of that spa town wanted nothing to do with the area's cattle market, so it is held at Penybont to this day. Turn right here on to the A44 and in 2 miles cross the A483 at Crossgates to continue to Rhayader.

Sheltered by high hills and within easy reach of the spectacular Elan valley, Rhayader is a popular centre for touring and pony-trekking. It also has several craft workshops such as the Dragon Pottery in East Street. In the 19th century, Rhayader was the scene of the Rebecca Riots, the turnpike gates being smashed in protest at heavy tolls.

RHAYADER TO CWMYSTWYTH

At the crossroads in the town centre keep forward on to the B4518 (SP Elan valley) and in ½ mile, after crossing the River Wye, turn right on to an unclassified road (SP Aberystwyth – Mountain Road) to begin the most impressive part of the route.

ELAN VALLEY

A detour can be made here by keeping forward for a spectacular drive along the four Elan valley reservoirs, constructed at the turn of the century to supply Birmingham with water. Continue along the B4518 to Elan Village, where you keep straight on along an unclassified road (no sign). This leads past the Caban Coch dam and along the reservoir's northern edge. The new landscape created by the reservoirs is most memorable, with high moorland and forest sweeping dramatically down to tranquil waters. The Elan valley is said to have been a place of even greater beauty before it was flooded. The poet Shelley wrote enthusiastically of its scenery when he stayed here in 1811 and 1812 in a house now covered by Caban Coch Reservoir.

Follow the road round to the right at the Garreg-ddu viaduct, driving along the wooded eastern shore of Garreg-ddu Reservoir to cross Pen-y-garreg dam at the end. The road runs along the western side of Pen-y-garreg and Craig Goch Reservoirs, then crosses the Afon Elan and climbs steeply to meet another unclassified road. Turn left here to rejoin the main route.

Continue to the Powys-Dyfed boundary along the upper valley of the Afon Elan, which winds its way along a bed of pebbles. In contrast, the infant Afon Ystwyth on the other side of the boundary races down at the start of its journey to the sea, carving deep into the rock. Further on, the extensive remains of the Cwmystwyth lead mine add a dramatically unexpected dash of lunar desolation to the landscape. The workings date from Roman times, but the derelict workshops and precipitous tramways are silent monuments to Victorian miners. Several shafts remain open, making it wiser to view the site from the safety of the road than to attempt to explore it on foot.

MYSTWYTH TO ABERYSTWYTH
through the scattered and lonely hamlet
wmystwyth, then bear right on to the
4 (SP Devil's Bridge) to climb through a
plantation of conifers to the Arch, built
10 to mark George III's golden jubilee.
cnic area beside the Arch is also the
ing point for three waymarked walks up
miles long. Follow the B4574 down to
l's Bridge, and turn left there on to the
0 (SP Aberystwyth).

vil's Bridge is a popular beauty spot
e the Afon Mynach plunges down
acts through a rocky, wooded gorge.
ip of the falls is spanned by three bridges,
test Victorian, the earliest 12th-century.
nd has it that the lowest bridge was built
he devil to enable an old woman to
er a cow that had strayed across the
canyon. The devil made her promise
he could have the soul of the first living
ure to cross the bridge, but was foiled
she sent a dog across ahead of her.

ntinue along the A4120 past the ter-
s of the Vale of Rheidol Light Railway.*
is British Rail's only narrow-gauge line,
operated by the last steam locomotives
ir possession. It links Devil's Bridge with
past at Aberystwyth, and was opened in
to carry passengers, as well as lead and
re from mines lower down the valley.
line came perilously near to closure in
but is now firmly established as one of

Three bridges, stacked vertically one above the other, span the narrow gorge of the Afon Mynach at Devil's Bridge

Constitution Hill offers fine views over Cardigan Bay and Marine Terrace, which curves round to the headland crowned by the ruins of Aberystwyth's 13th-century castle

the most popular tourist attractions in mid Wales, running as it does through some of the area's finest scenery. The journey time is about an hour each way.

The A4120 descends gently from Devil's Bridge, giving dramatic views down into the deep Vale of Rheidol. Aberystwyth soon comes into sight, flanked by a hill whose summit is crowned with a cannon-shaped monument erected by a local landowner who fought at Waterloo. Join the A487 for the last stage of the journey.

The town is overlooked from the north-east by the impressive façade of the National Library of Wales.* It contains 5½ million books, and its treasures include the 12th-century *Black Book of Carmarthen* – the oldest manuscript in the Welsh language – and also a manuscript copy of the Canterbury Tales. On the opposite side of the town are the ruins of the medieval castle, set in pleasant gardens on a headland overlooking Cardigan Bay. Colour-washed Victorian and Edwardian buildings line the broad, curving promenade as it sweeps northwards from here to the foot of Constitution Hill, whose steep face is climbed by a funicular railway.

Beaches, hotels and fine scenery nearby have made Aberystwyth a popular summer resort, but this has never eclipsed its importance as a busy administrative and shopping centre, cultural and university town and the focal point for a wide area.

THE CAMBRIAN MOUNTAINS

UNLIKE the naked crags of Snowdonia and the sandstone crests in the Brecon Beacons National Park Cambrian Mountains are relatively green and smoot Most of the slopes are steep, but this is a landscape fo walkers and pony-trekkers rather than climbers. The are exceptions. Cader Idris and Aran Fawddwy, both almost 3000 feet high, have great walls of rock and a of scree that hug small, secluded lakes carved by glac during the Ice Ages.

What has often been dubbed the 'desert' of Wales southwards towards the Brecon Beacons from a line formed by the deep valleys joining Dolgellau, Bala a Llangollen. It includes the Berwyns and Plynlimon, which reach 2713 and 2468 feet respectively, but 200 feet is rarely exceeded elsewhere. Superb and typical views can be enjoyed from many vantage points, including the dramatic 'mountain road' that runs westwards from Beulah on the A483 to the valley of t sparkling River Teifi.

It is a part of Britain where people are heavily outnumbered by sheep, even in midsummer. Little t such as Tregaron, Lampeter, Llanidloes and Rhaya no more than villages by English standards – are ma centres of population and commerce. When he walk through the principality in the 19th century, gatheri material for his book *Wild Wales*, George Borrow me a local who proudly assured him that Tregaron was 'very good place' although 'not quite so big as Lond

...rs have contributed to the changes
... taken place in the Cambrian
...ins since George Borrow's time.
... Elan valley lakes – of which
...och (pictured above) is one – were
... opened in 1904, and provide water
...ingham. Llyn Brianne (pictured
... situated north of Llandovery, is the
...ke. It covers almost 14 square
...d supplies Swansea. The oldest
...is Lake Vyrnwy, north-west of
...ool, which was built between 1880
...0 to supply Liverpool. On either side
...mon are two other reservoirs –
...moch, and Clywedog, which has the
...'am wall in Britain

TREGARON BOG, a nature
reserve 3 miles north of the little
market town of Tregaron, is one of
the largest undrained bogs in Britain,
and was once a lake. It teems with
wildlife of all kinds, including curlews
and warblers in spring, and ducks
and snipe in winter. Its Welsh name,
Cors Goch, meaning 'red bog', is
derived from the fact that in winter
the stems and leaves of the cotton
sedge take on a distinct red tinge. In
high summer the bog is white with
the dainty tassels of the sedge.

WORKINGS abandoned long
ago are fascinating reminders of the
men who mined for precious metals in
the heart of wild Wales. The gold
deposits at Dolaucothi – a wooded
beauty spot between Llandovery and
Lampeter – were probably worked
before the dawn of history. But it was
the Romans who left their mark on
the site, building sophisticated
waterways to serve their opencast
workings and adits. Waymarked
trails guide visitors over the hillside.

To the north, silver and lead were
mined from prehistoric times until the
20th century. Cwmsymlog, north of
the A44 near Aberystwyth, was once
one of the 'Mines Royal' and
produced silver for Charles I and
other monarchs. Llywernog, on the
A44 11 miles east of Aberystwyth, has
a museum devoted to the great days
of silver and lead mining. The old
Bryn Tail mine, at the foot of the
Clywedog dam, has also been
restored.

Medieval miners had many strange
beliefs. Underground spirits were said
to guide good people to lead deposits
by knocking on the ground. Some
thought that the richness of the ore
depended on the sun's heat. Others
looked for barren slopes, because lead
deposits were said to give off gases
that inhibited plant growth.

*Right: Overshot water-wheels are among
the mining machinery displayed at the
19th-century Llywernog Silver-Lead Mine
near Ponterwyd*

MANY of the most scenic by-roads
and footpaths in the Cambrian
Mountains were once walked by
cattle, sheep, pigs, geese and even
turkeys as they were driven eastwards
as far afield as Hertfordshire, Essex
and Kent. The animals were usually
first fattened on the rich English
pasturelands and then sold at the
Michaelmas fairs. The drovers who
walked and rode with them played a
prominent role in the life of rural
Wales from medieval times until the
end of the 19th century.

Tens of thousands of animals
travelled to England every year.
There was roughly one drover for
every 30–35 cattle, and the men were
aided by nimble, heel-nipping corgi
dogs who kept the huge herds
together in open country. Many dogs
developed astonishing homing
instincts and frequently returned
several days before their masters after
cross-country trips of more than 200
miles. They were tough little
creatures, but the cattle had to be
shod for the journey and even geese
had their feet treated with a mixture
of tar and sand or pulverized shells. It
took them almost three weeks to
travel from mid Wales to Kent.

It was not safe to carry large sums
of money across the wild uplands of
Wales, so the drovers established their
own banks. One of the most
important of them, Banc-y-Ddafad,
was founded in Aberystwyth. It
issued its own distinctive bank-notes,
ranging from 10 shillings to £5.

Several of the drove roads
converged at Rhayader, which served
as a market centre for a very large
area of mid Wales. It is possible to
trace one of them eastwards to
Abbeycwmhir, and one leads
westwards, through what is now the
Elan valley group of reservoirs, across
the moorlands to Strata Florida.

The Red Kite

NOW confined to the lonely
moorlands of mid Wales, the red
kite was widespread throughout
Britain until the 18th century,
and was a common sight in the
streets of London during Tudor
times. Its numbers gradually
dwindled through loss of habitat,
changing agricultural practices
and a determined campaign by
gamekeepers. The kite's deeply
forked tail makes it easily
distinguishable from other birds of
prey, and although perhaps no
more than 30 breeding pairs
survive in the whole of Wales, it
can still occasionally be seen here.

ROUTE 14   164 MIL[

Birmingham to Exeter

BIRMINGHAM's tangle of factories, suburbs, canals, railways, roads and motorways falls gradually away beyond the 19th-century 'garden suburb' of Bournville, and this alternative route to the lush meadows and sparkling coasts of South Devon enters rural landscapes as it nears Alvechurch. It bypasses Redditch, a southerly outlier of the industrial West Midlands, and follows the Worcestershire–Warwickshire border through a countryside that has many fine examples of black-and-white timber-framed buildings.

The delightful village of Abbots Morton, just off the main route, is a living museum of vernacular architecture of all sorts. It even has a thatched letter-box. Many of the timbered buildings in the area are infilled with bricks from the Midland kilns, and these are frequently painted white to achieve the startling 'magpie' effect that is typical of the West Midlands. In complete contrast, many houses in south-western Warwickshire are built of thin slabs of pale lias limestone.

Next comes the Vale of Evesham, whose dark soils rival in fertility those of the Weald of Kent, and in springtime the huge orchards here are white with blossom. The Vale is not only famous for its orchards – all around Evesham there are fields of soft fruit, great beds of asparagus, and acre after acre of vegetables. Evesham itself stands in a mighty loop of the beautiful River Avon, and the route follows one of its tributaries, the Isbourne, to cross into Gloucestershire.

After passing through elegant Cheltenham the route climbs on to the Cotswold escarpment. From Leckhampton Hill, crowned by an Iron Age hill-fort, tremendous views may be obtained from the rocky pinnacle called the Devil's Chimney. There is another hill-fort at Crickley Hill, and even more spectacular views open up, across the Severn valley, as the route climbs Birdlip Hill.

Beyond Birdlip village the route continues to Stroud through rolling Cotswold scenery partly cloaked in beechwoods. It then follows the limestone country down through Nailsworth and past the stately homes of Dodington and Dyrham to descend to neat, flat farmlands beyond Keynsham.

At Chewton Mendip the route ascends on to the Mendip Hills, which are composed of a very much harder limestone than the Cotswolds. This rather desolate upland has been mined for lead and other minerals since at least as early as Roman times, and disused mine-workings combine with isolated stone farmhouses to increase the sombre atmosphere.

On the other side of the Mendips is the cathedral city of Wells, where the swans on the moat round the Bishop's Palace ring a bell when they wish to be fed. From Wells the route crosses the Somerset Levels to the Isle of Avalon. This mysterious and magical place, which was a real island surrounded by meres and marshes until the Middle Ages, is steeped in legend. It may have been a centre of worship for the prehistoric moon goddess, and it was thought to be one of the entrances to the Celtic Otherworld, but its best-known stories concern King Arthur, who is said to be buried in the grounds of

Glastonbury Abbey. Glastonbury Tor has its own leg[some of them connected with King Arthur, and on days the tor rises like a gigantic finger from surrounding seas it is not difficult to believe the myriad tales of fairies, g riders and magic.

The route leaves Glastonbury and Avalon, crossing was once a causeway across water, to ascend the flanks Polden Hills. This shoulder of high land cuts right acro Somerset Levels, and although it reaches no great heigh views from such summits as Walton Hill (to the east route) are extensive.

Shortly the route is on the Levels once more, here King's Sedge Moor – the scene of the Duke of Monm crushing defeat in 1685. Most of the Levels were drain agricultural use between the 10th and 14th centuries by from local abbeys, one of which was situated on the Athelney. It was at Athelney (just off the route, beyond B Bridge) that King Alfred made camp in 878 before so defeating the Danes in a battle that brought peace to En for a considerable time. It is also here that Alfred is suppo have burned the cakes.

From Burrow Bridge the route follows the valley of the Tone to Taunton, and then sweeps round the slopes Blackdown Hills to join the Culm Valley at Cullompton. here the route travels through a countryside of ric sandstone soils and picturesque old cottages of thatch an before entering the historic seaport of Exeter.

PLACES OF INTEREST: OPENING DETAILS

Evesham THE ALMONRY open Apr to end Sep daily (except Mon and Wed), pm only	**Dodington** DODINGTON HOUSE open Apr to Sep	**Street** SHOE MUSEUM open May to Oct M to Sat
Cheltenham PITTVILLE PUMP ROOM open all year: Mon to Sat am and pm, Sun and Bank Holidays pm only	**Dyrham** DYRHAM PARK open Apr to Oct daily (except Fri, and Thu Apr, May and Oct), pm only	**Burrow Bridge** BURROW BRIDGE PUMPING STATIO MUSEUM open all year Mon to Fri
ART GALLERY open all year daily (except Sun and Bank Holidays)	**Wookey Hole** WOOKEY HOLE CAVES AND MILL open all year (except 25 Dec)	**Taunton** TAUNTON CASTL AND COUNTY MUSEUM open all year (except Bank Holidays); closed
GUSTAV HOLST MUSEUM open all year Tue to Sat	**Wells** BISHOP'S PALACE open Easter, then May to Oct Sun (also open Thu, grounds only); and every day in Aug, pm only	Sun Apr to end Sep closed Sun and Mo Oct to end Mar
Stroud STROUD AND DISTRICT MUSEUM open all year daily (except Sun, 1 Jan, Good Fri and Christmas)		**Killerton** KILLERTON HOUS AND GARDENS house open Apr to end Oct; gardens open all year
Horton HORTON COURT open Apr to Oct Wed and Sat, pm only	**Glastonbury** GLASTONBURY ABBEY open all year SOMERSET RURAL LIFE MUSEUM open all year: Mon to Fri all day, Sat and Sun pm only	**Exeter** UNDERGROUND PASSAGES open a year Tue to Sat, pm only MARITIME MUSE open all year

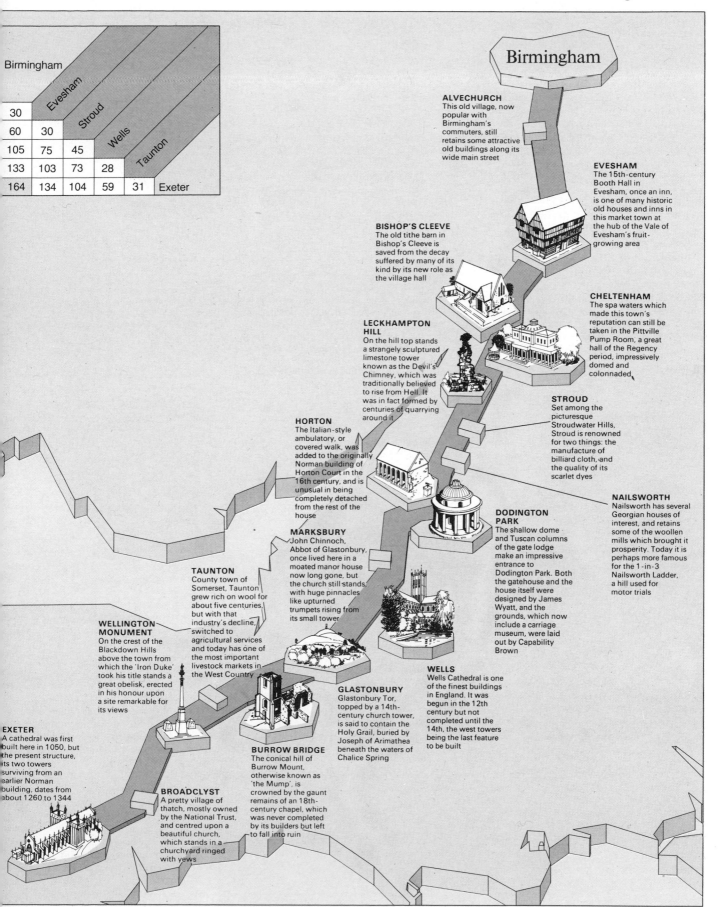

Birmingham					
30	Evesham				
60	30	Stroud			
105	75	45	Wells		
133	103	73	28	Taunton	
164	134	104	59	31	Exeter

Birmingham

ALVECHURCH
This old village, now popular with Birmingham's commuters, still retains some attractive old buildings along its wide main street

EVESHAM
The 15th-century Booth Hall in Evesham, once an inn, is one of many historic old houses and inns in this market town at the hub of the Vale of Evesham's fruit-growing area

BISHOP'S CLEEVE
The old tithe barn in Bishop's Cleeve is saved from the decay suffered by many of its kind by its new role as the village hall

CHELTENHAM
The spa waters which made this town's reputation can still be taken in the Pittville Pump Room, a great hall of the Regency period, impressively domed and colonnaded

LECKHAMPTON HILL
On the hill top stands a strangely sculptured limestone tower known as the Devil's Chimney, which was traditionally believed to rise from Hell. It was in fact formed by centuries of quarrying around it

STROUD
Set among the picturesque Stroudwater Hills, Stroud is renowned for two things: the manufacture of billiard cloth, and the quality of its scarlet dyes

HORTON
The Italian-style ambulatory, or covered walk, was added to the originally Norman building of Horton Court in the 16th century, and is unusual in being completely detached from the rest of the house

NAILSWORTH
Nailsworth has several Georgian houses of interest, and retains some of the woollen mills which brought it prosperity. Today it is perhaps more famous for the 1-in-3 Nailsworth Ladder, a hill used for motor trials

MARKSBURY
John Chinnoch, Abbot of Glastonbury, once lived here in a moated manor house now long gone, but the church still stands, with huge pinnacles like upturned trumpets rising from its small tower

DODINGTON PARK
The shallow dome and Tuscan columns of the gate lodge make an impressive entrance to Dodington Park. Both the gatehouse and the house itself were designed by James Wyatt, and the grounds, which now include a carriage museum, were laid out by Capability Brown

TAUNTON
County town of Somerset, Taunton grew rich on wool for about five centuries, but with that industry's decline, switched to agricultural services and today has one of the most important livestock markets in the West Country

WELLINGTON MONUMENT
On the crest of the Blackdown Hills above the town from which the 'Iron Duke' took his title stands a great obelisk, erected in his honour upon a site remarkable for its views

WELLS
Wells Cathedral is one of the finest buildings in England. It was begun in the 12th century but not completed until the 14th, the west towers being the last feature to be built

GLASTONBURY
Glastonbury Tor, topped by a 14th-century church tower, is said to contain the Holy Grail, buried by Joseph of Arimathea beneath the waters of Chalice Spring

EXETER
A cathedral was first built here in 1050, but the present structure, its two towers surviving from an earlier Norman building, dates from about 1260 to 1344

BROADCLYST
A pretty village of thatch, mostly owned by the National Trust, and centred upon a beautiful church, which stands in a churchyard ringed with yews

BURROW BRIDGE
The conical hill of Burrow Mount, otherwise known as 'the Mump', is crowned by the gaunt remains of an 18th-century chapel, which was never completed by its builders but left to fall into ruin

BIRMINGHAM TO REDDITCH

Leave central Birmingham on the A38 (SP The South-West), following it out through Edgbaston and passing the university, whose buildings are grouped around a prominent clock-tower. In the suburb of Selly Oak, turn left on to the A4040. This road leads through the well-heeled suburb of Bournville – a name synonymous with fine chocolate – where, in 1895, one of the country's first garden city estates was created by the Cadbury brothers for the employees of their chocolate factory. At Cotteridge keep forward to join the A441 for Redditch, following it along Pershore Road South, out through the suburbs and over the county boundary to enter Hereford and Worcester.

The route soon crosses the Worcester and Birmingham Canal and, at the roundabout 1 mile later, takes the first main exit to continue on the A441 to Alvechurch. Although Alvechurch has grown rapidly as a commuter village in recent years, its centre has retained its old-world charm and has some attractive buildings. However, only traces of a moat remain to testify to the village's former

importance in the days when the bishops of Worcester had a palace here.

After 3 miles of pleasant country, the vast new town developments of Redditch appear, but the route passes swiftly through this red-brick sprawl of a place by means of a new and efficient dual carriageway.

REDDITCH TO EVESHAM

At the roundabout at Crabbs Cross, take the second exit to continue along the A441 towards Evesham, passing through Astwood Bank. The road follows the county boundary for several miles, with views to the right over Hereford and Worcester and to the left over Warwickshire, taking in the parkland surrounding Ragley Hall (see p. 158).

WEETHLEY

Cross the A422, and 1 mile beyond the junction look out for a fingerpost to Weethley church, off to the right. If you follow this down the unmetalled lane, past some deserted farm buildings, you will come upon a small church, delightfully situated next to a duck-pond, and overlooking open farmland with distant views of the Cotswolds. On returning to the A441 and looking back to the right, the full beauty of the church's isolated position can be appreciated.

ABBOTS MORTON

Just over ½ mile beyond the turning to Weethley church you can make a second detour, to the old village of Abbots Morton. Turn right (SP Abbots Morton) opposite a thatched cottage topped by a bird of thatch, then after 1½ miles turn right again to reach the village. It consists almost entirely of attractive black-and-white timbered buildings. St Peter's Church, backing on to open fields at the end of the village, is well worth a visit; notice particularly the 15th-century roof beams and the Flemish stained-glass medallions in the east window.

Right: One of the medallions of 16th-century Flemish stained glass in the east window of St Peter's Church

Below: Ornamental timber-framing at Abbots Morton. The familiar black-and-white effect is a comparatively recent feature; until the 19th century the beams were usually left unpainted

The main route continues on the A441 to crossroads at the edge of Dunnington, wh[ere] it turns right on to the A435 for Evesha[m]. Around Harvington the famous orchards [of] the Vale of Evesham are much in evidence[, a] delight in spring, when they are a glori[ous] mass of blossom. One of the main reasons [for] this area's success in fruit and vegeta[ble] growing is its climate. Rainfall is unusua[lly] low and winters mild. Most of the holdi[ngs] are small, because of the ancient 'Evesh[am] custom' method of land tenure: a depart[ing] tenant is entitled to nominate his succe[ssor] and to claim compensation for any cr[op] growing. To the right of the road, an orch[ard]

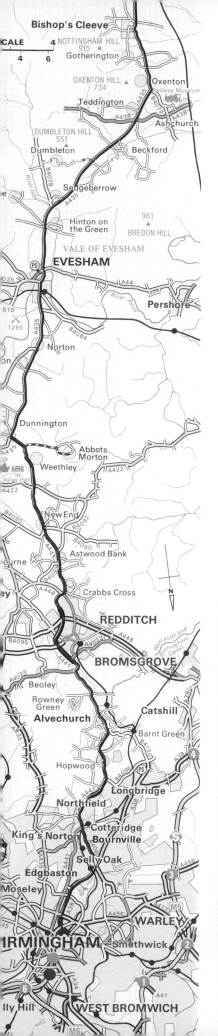

now grows on the site of the Battle of Evesham, where in 1265 Simon de Montfort's rebellion against Henry III was crushed and de Montfort himself was killed.

Evesham is all character and charm, a town packed with fine old buildings and set off to perfection by the tree-lined River Avon, which curls round three of its sides. The town grew up around its abbey, founded in AD 714 when, so the legend goes, a swineherd persuaded Egwin, Bishop of Worcester, to build it after he saw a vision of the Virgin Mary in the woodlands nearby. Egwin resigned his bishopric and became the first Abbot of Evesham. Most of the abbey buildings have long since disappeared, but the lovely abbey precinct survives, and is linked to the town by a picturesque half-timbered gateway known as the Norman Gate. The churchyard has the rare honour of being shared by two parish churches – All Saints and St Lawrence's – together with the lavish 110-foot-high bell-tower built by Clement Lichfield, Evesham's last abbot, not long before Henry VIII began his ruthless purge of the monasteries.

Practically every street in Evesham can boast splendid old buildings, such as 15th-century Booth Hall in the market place; graceful Dresden House, with its huge hood on iron brackets over the door; and the Georgian buildings in Vine Street. Also in Vine Street is the Almonry,* a 14th-century house associated with the abbey and now containing a museum of local history.

EVESHAM TO BISHOP'S CLEEVE

Leave Evesham by the A435 Cheltenham road, passing Abbey Park on the left before crossing the Avon by Abbey Bridge. The A435 continues across the Vale of Evesham, crossing the River Isbourne and passing the edge of Sedgeberrow on the left after 3 miles. At first the route is surrounded by flat fields of vegetables, then it passes between Dumbleton Hill and Bredon Hill and heads into Gloucestershire. The A435 (SP Cheltenham) keeps forward at Teddington Hands roundabout to cross the A438 and soon passes the 734-foot mass of Oxenton Hill on the left.

OXENTON

The village of Oxenton sits at the foot of the hill and is signposted to the left, offering a short detour to see the medieval church, situated at the end of a lane lined with delightful timbered cottages and farms. The road into the village passes a building called Pike House, which has a blocked-up window inscribed with 'Tolls to be taken at the gate' and a list of fees. Inside the unspoilt little church are several interesting features – especially the chancel floor, which is decorated with coloured tiles giving a curious three-dimensional effect.

The main route continues on the A435 through Bishop's Cleeve. This small town does not tempt the traveller to stop, although it does claim to have the oldest parsonage in Gloucestershire, and possesses a fine church which contains many interesting monuments.

Peaceful gardens sloping down to the Avon surround Evesham's Perpendicular bell-tower, a magnificent survival of the abbey and a lasting tribute to the skill and piety of its builder, Clement Lichfield, Evesham's last abbot

BISHOP'S CLEEVE TO BIRDLIP

PITTVILLE PUMP ROOM

At the edge of Cheltenham, 2½ miles from Bishop's Cleeve, the Pittville Pump Room* is signposted to the left. This is well worth visiting as one of Cheltenham's finest examples of Regency architecture, domed and colonnaded and placed in an appropriate setting of sweeping formal parkland. It was built as the centrepiece of the smart new spa quarter of Pittville, for which ambitious plans were drawn up in 1824 by the wealthy MP and banker Joseph Pitt.

Perched on the slopes of the Slad valley is the unspoilt village of Slad, the setting for Laurie Lee's 'Cider with Rosie'

Continue on the A435 into the town centre. Cheltenham epitomizes all that is graceful and stylish in English architecture. A great feeling of space and dignity is derived from the wide streets, sweeping crescents and well-proportioned squares that pattern this sophisticated spa town. The terraces and crescents of Lansdown and Montpellier are elegant in every detail, from the dainty ironwork of their balconies and porches to the attractive hexagonal pillar-boxes which stand on the pavements. The Rotunda, inspired by the ancient Pantheon in Rome, is only one of many examples of Italianate influence in the early 19th century.

Cheltenham's patronage of the Arts, which began with the educated and wealthy city-dwellers who came here in those early days of elegance, has continued ever since. The art gallery,* in Clarence Street, houses fine paintings, furniture and *objets d'art*, and there is a museum* relating to Gustav Holst, the composer, who was born here in 1874. The Cheltenham Music Festival was founde 1944 and has been honoured by first pe mances of many works by 20th-cen British composers including Benjamin Bri and Sir Arthur Bliss.

Leave the town centre by the A46 Stroud), and follow signs for Stroud for a 1 mile, then at the roundabout branch le to the B4070 (SP Birdlip). The route cli out of the town and then winds round edge of Leckhampton Hill, which is top by an Iron Age hill-fort and a curious pill rock known as the Devil's Chimney. T are magnificent views down to the right a road climbs steeply up the Cotswold e After 1 mile turn right on to the A436, th the roundabout by the Air Balloon pub forward to join the A417 (SP Cirence Birdlip). Soon, yet more spectacular v open up to the right over the lower Se valley and across to the Black Mountain South Wales. To the right is the s escarpment of Crickley Hill, which bel to the National Trust.

In ¾ mile, on entering Birdlip, turn rig a T-junction on to the B4070 (SP Stro then, just past the Royal George pub, left, still following signs for Stroud.

BIRDLIP TO NAILSWORTH

For about 3 miles the road runs along the of a ridge, shaded by glorious beechw which reveal glimpses of the Vale Gloucester through the trees to the r Continue for several miles to the villag Slad, where author Laurie Lee grew up. peaceful Slad valley is the setting of *Cider Rosie*, his evocative account of a Cotsw childhood in the 1920s.

The road continues along the side of valley and descends into Stroud. The was an important centre of the Cotswold industry for hundreds of years, and was noted for its scarlet dyes. Cloth produced was used for military uniforms in the

Broad pavements and pleasant gardens enhance Cheltenham's elegant Promenade. It was built in the 1820s, and the baroque Neptune fountain was added in 1893

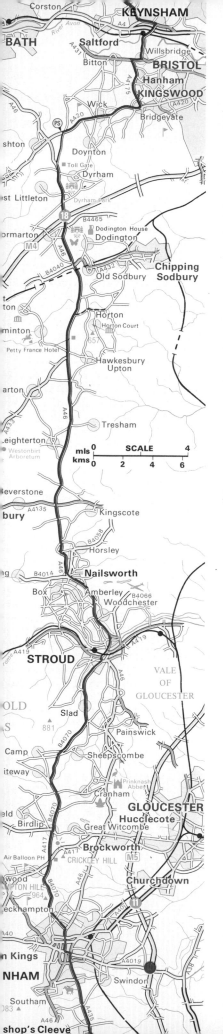

More than 30 vehicles vividly recalling the era of the stage-coach can be seen in the carriage museum at Dodington Park

when the British were famous for fighting in 'thin red lines' and had not appreciated the advantages of camouflage. Although scarlet tunics are no longer in demand, there are still some working mills producing high-quality cloth here, and Stroud's speciality now is the manufacture of baize for billiard-tables. The town has an interesting museum* where domestic and industrial exhibits rub shoulders with a life-sized model of a dinosaur.

Leave Stroud on the A46 (SP Bath), soon passing through Woodchester, also once a wool town of some importance. Continue for 2 miles to Nailsworth, a small town with steep streets and a number of attractive buildings, mainly Jacobean or Georgian. The well-known 1-in-3 hill called Nailsworth Ladder is used by the adventurous for motor trials.

NAILSWORTH TO KEYNSHAM
As the road climbs up from the valley the scenery opens out into rolling countryside criss-crossed by drystone walls.

HORTON COURT
About 11 miles past Nailsworth, and 1 mile beyond the Petty France Hotel, an unclassified road on the right (SP Horton) offers a detour to Horton Court.* Follow signs to Horton, turning left then sharp right to cross another unclassified road, and after ¼ mile, by Widden Hill Farm, turn right (SP Hawkesbury). Horton Court lies ½ mile along this road. Now in the care of the National Trust, this fine Cotswold house was built in 1521 for William Knight, who later became Bishop of Bath and Wells. The north wing of the house, however, is some 400 years older, and was a Norman great hall. In the early 18th century it was divided into two storeys, the upper one used first as a Roman Catholic chapel and then as a school.

Three miles beyond the Horton turning, the A46 passes the entrance to Dodington Park* on the right. Dodington was the home of the Codrington family, one of whose members, Sir Edward, served with Nelson at Trafalgar, and rose to the rank of Vice-Admiral and Commander-in-Chief of the Mediterranean fleet. The elegant Regency house, designed by James Wyatt, is approached by a long drive through parkland laid out by Capability Brown. As well as the attractions of the house and grounds, there is a fascinating carriage museum, with more than 30 different carriages; a large collection of model aeroplanes; a children's adventure playground and a farm.

The route crosses the M4 to continue along the A46, soon passing the third historic house in barely 6 miles. This one is Dyrham Park,* a late 17th-century mansion set in a beautiful deer park (see p. 209).

About 1 mile past the entrance to Dyrham, immediately beyond a house named Toll Gate, turn right on to an unclassified road (no sign). After 1½ miles, turn right again on to the A420 and continue through Wick to Bridgeyate. Turn left here on to the A4175, skirting the eastern edge of the built-up area around Bristol. At the T-junction turn right on to the A431, passing under a railway bridge and continuing to Willsbridge, where the route turns left to rejoin the A4175 (SP Keynsham, Bristol).

The large, distinctive red-brick building over to the right as the route approaches Keynsham is Fry's chocolate factory, built after the manner of Bournville. The road soon crosses the River Avon, and to the left the old stone bridge can still be seen. But Keynsham has little to interest the visitor today, having lost most of its old buildings and been taken over by light industry.

KEYNSHAM TO CHEWTON MENDIP

Follow signs through Keynsham for Wells (A39), cross the River Chew and shortly turn right on to the B3116 (SP Wells). After 3 miles, still following signs for Wells, turn right on to the A39 and continue to Marksbury, a village dominated by its large church whose four pinnacles are each topped by a weather-vane. Just beyond Marksbury bear left with the A39 (SP Wells) and pass through the villages of Farmborough, High Littleton and Hallatrow, their new estates gradually spreading over the countryside to cater for Bristol's ever-growing commuter population. Open country between the villages reveals views of the Mendips to the south-west.

At the T-junction with the A37, turn left (SP Yeovil, Wells) to pass through Farrington Gurney and cross the border into Somerset. Almost immediately the landscape changes to one of flat, small fields dotted with copses and threaded with drystone walls. Follow the A39 to Chewton Mendip, in the shelter of the Mendip Hills.

Chewton Mendip has a cheese dairy – one of only seven in the West Country still making traditional farmhouse cheddar cheese. To reach it, continue through the village, pass under a footbridge and turn right at the crossroads almost ½ mile later. The dairy is signposted to the right. In the mornings visitors may tour the working dairy, watching cheese being made as it has been for hundreds of years. Even some of the old equipment, such as the decorative presses making 'truckles' (small cheeses) is still in use.

CHEWTON MENDIP TO GLASTONBURY

As the route continues along the A39 towards Wells, the conical shape of Glastonbury Tor can be seen rising abruptly from the flat plain of Queen's Sedge Moor, beyond Wells.

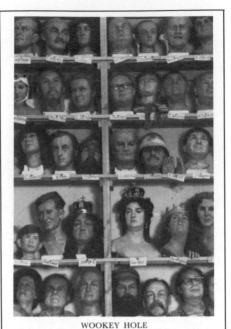

WOOKEY HOLE

At the edge of Wells, a detour can be made to the Wookey Hole Caves.* Turn right at a crossroads, then follow signs along unclassified roads. The great cavern, with its splendid stalactites and stalagmites, was hollowed out of the limestone by the River Axe which flows through it. Beyond it are many other underground chambers, some accessible to tourists and others only to expert potholers. The complex now includes a museum where there are finds from the period when the caves were inhabited, around 2000 years ago. Visitors can also see a store-room for Madame Tussaud's waxworks. The shelves are filled with rows of astonishingly lifelike waxwork heads, making a macabre sight. The store-room is housed in an old paper-mill, whose machinery has been restored to provide a working exhibition of paper-making.

Traditional farmhouse cheddar cheese in preparation at Chewton Mendip

Wells's glory is undoubtedly the Cathe Church of St Andrew. Its beauty is al unparalleled in Europe; notice particu the richly adorned west front, the century clock famed for the rotating figu mounted knights that appear as the strikes, and the chapter house with profusion of light and soaring arches. medieval ecclesiastical precinct in which cathedral stands has been the heart of since King Edward the Elder chose this new bishopric in AD 909. The surv buildings are all later, though the mo Bishop's Palace* dates from the 13th cen and is still inhabited today. In its garde the city wells, fed by subterranean str from the Mendips. The swans on the ring a bell at feeding time. Wells is so com that it can easily be explored on foot, a stroll round its ancient streets is one o highlights of the route.

From the market place follow 'thr traffic' signs, then take the A39 Glaston road. Soon after leaving Wells, Glaston Tor appears again to the left more cle and a pub called the Camelot Inn reminder of the Arthurian legends surround the area.

Steeped as it is in ancient legends, the of Glastonbury conjures up fairy-tale im of the Holy Grail and King Arthur. The goes that Joseph of Arimathea came having travelled many miles with the Grail, and rested on Wearyall Hill, t west of the town. When he stabbed his into the ground it promptly rooted flowered. Taking this as a sign from Joseph and his fellow disciples built Eur first Christian church, on the site of the pr abbey ruins. It is said that King Arthur Lady Guinevere were buried in this ch and Tor Hill is reputed to be the leger Isle of Avalon. Glastonbury Thorn, su grows in St John's churchyard today, is to be the tree which first flowered Joseph's staff. Recorded fact takes over legend in 688, when King Ine found Benedictine monastery here. For a long it was a wealthy and influential house, fell into ruins after Henry VIII's Dissol of the Monasteries. The abbey ruins* prise mainly 12th- and 13th-century b ings; the best preserved include the Ab Kitchen. The Somerset Rural Life Mus is housed in the abbey's stone tithe barr contains numerous relics from a by agricultural age.

GLASTONBURY TO BURROW BRID

Leave Glastonbury on the A39 Bridgwater, Street) passing the abbey on the left, and then the huge Mor woollen factory on the right. The A39 Taunton, A361) by-passes Street, wh famous for its long-established foot industry, and even has a shoe muse Follow the A39 through Walton and in

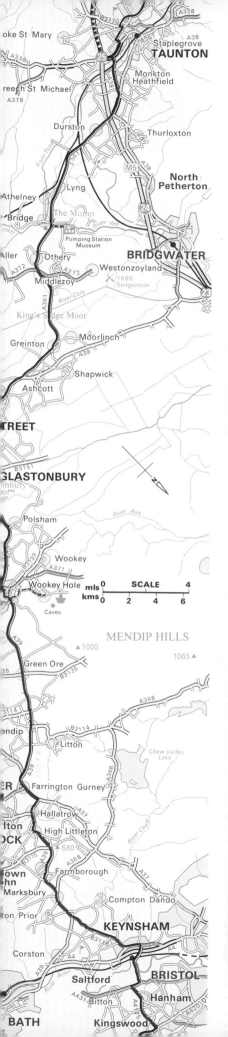

branch left on to the A361 (SP Taunton), crossing King's Sedge Moor. The land is drained by an efficient network of ditches and wide waterways, controlled by pumping stations. Pollarded willows lean over ditches and streams, their young shoots – called withies – being used in the local craft of basket-making. Two miles past Othery, at Burrow Bridge, the road passes the Mump, a curious conical hill which looks quite out of place in these low, level lands.

BURROW BRIDGE PUMPING STATION MUSEUM
Opposite the King Alfred Hotel at Burrow Bridge, an unclassified road on the right leads to a pumping station museum* on the River Parrett. Beautifully preserved Victorian steam pumping engines are among the items on display here.

The agriculture of bygone ages is brought to life in Glastonbury's Rural Life Museum, housed in the abbey's 14th-century tithe barn

BURROW BRIDGE TO TAUNTON

Continue from Burrow Bridge through Lyng and Durston, after which the route crosses the M5 and joins the A38, following it into Taunton. (By turning left at the roundabout shortly past Bathpool, it is possible to by-pass Taunton, joining the M5 ½ mile later and following it westwards to the next junction, then following signs for Wellington to rejoin the main route there.)

Taunton is the county town of Somerset, its prosperity dating back to the 13th century when it had the first wool mill in the West Country. It subsequently gained much wealth through the industry, and this enabled the beautiful church of St Mary Magdalene to be built. The present Perpendicular tower is in fact a Victorian replica, though you would not know it, so well does it blend in with the medieval building. Taunton's history is imaginatively portrayed in the Somerset County Museum, housed in the castle.* (For more details and a town plan of Taunton, see p. 233.)

TAUNTON TO CULLOMPTON

Leave Taunton on the A38 (SP Exeter), following signs for Exeter for about 6 miles. At the roundabout 1 mile east of Wellington, take the third exit (SP Willand) to enter the town. The people of Wellington have always been proud of the fact that the 'Iron Duke' took his title from their town, and in 1817 they built a 175-foot-high obelisk in his honour high on the Blackdown Hills to the south (see p. 73). No one seems to know the reason for the Duke's choice, and he is said to have been here only once. The town's importance lay in its weaving trade, which

The Church of St Mary Magdalene, Taunton

developed here in the 17th and 18th centuries. An interesting local industry associated with the cloth business is the growing of teasels, which are cultivated for use as a kind of comb to dress the cloth. 'Teasing' gives the fabric a certain type of finish which can be achieved by no other means, though modern mechanization has led to a decline in the cultivation of this unusual crop.

Less than 4 miles beyond Wellington the A38 crosses into Devon. The county sign is pale blue with a white galleon, signifying Devon's long association with the sea and voyages from Plymouth by many famous seafarers. Continue on the main road and in 4 miles, by the Waterloo Arms, branch left on

A long, colourful herbaceous border enhances the setting of 18th-century Killerton House

to the B3181 (SP Willand). The road ski Willand and crosses the motorway, passi through typical Devon countryside, rolli and green, to reach Cullompton. This is pleasant old country town whose most priz possession is St Andrew's Church, set back a close to the left of the main street. It ha 16th-century west tower of local red sar stone, carved with splendid gargoyles. Insi a beautiful, brightly painted rood scre runs across the width of the church. As Taunton, the wool industry was responsi for this magnificent display. The south a of the church is called the Lane aisle, af the wool merchant who built it in the ea 16th century. Its exterior features symb representing several local industries wh brought wealth to Devon, among them wool trade and tin-mining.

CULLOMPTON TO EXETER

The B3181 continues along the fertile Cu valley, never far from the motorway.

KILLERTON HOUSE

After 6 miles, a detour may be made to Killerton House* by turning right on to the B3185. The house and gardens are signposted on the left. The gardens, laid out by Si Thomas Acland after the Napoleonic Wars are a magnificent profusion of rare and exoti trees and flowering shrubs. The arboretum o the slope of Dolbury Hill becomes denser an more glorious as you climb. At the top of th hill – from where there are fine views over th Clyst valley to the south – is Killerton Clump the remains of an Iron Age fort. Hidden awa amongst the foliage is the Hermitage, delightful 19th-century folly in the form of tiny thatched cottage made from split tre trunks. Killerton estate extends for some 500 acres, of which the gardens account for 1 West of the house is the hamlet Columbjohn, the home of the Acland famil before they moved to Killerton House i 1778. Only the gatehouse remains of th original Elizabethan mansion here.

Killerton House, a fine 18th-century hous remained in the Acland family until 194 when it was given to the National Trust. now houses a museum of costume. Th collection ranges from the 18th century to th present day, and the costumes are displaye in various rooms furnished in keeping with th different periods.

The B3181 continues through Broadclyst. to the right in the village, by the stone c which stands amid old yews, is the 1 century Church of St John, approac through a double lychgate. Inside is a la Jacobean monument to Sir John Acland.

The B3181 goes on to Exeter, crossing motorway for the last time to pass thro Pinhoe, on the outskirts of the city. Aft mile, where the road forks, either bear left Through Traffic) to pick up the old by- for destinations further west, or keep righ to the B3212 for the city centre.

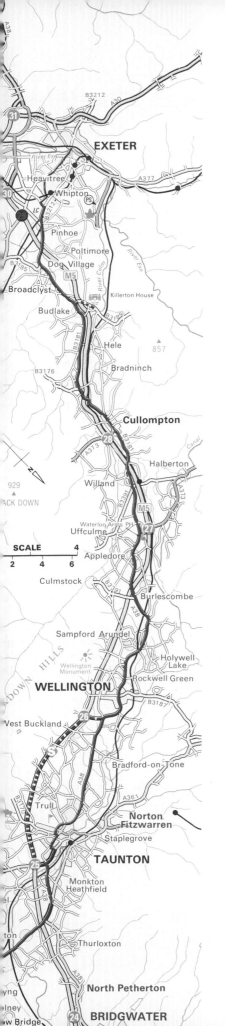

EXETER

Like so many English cities, Exeter has a long and interesting history and a thriving present. The Romans were responsible for walling the city and for its basic street plan, and when the bishopric was moved here from Crediton in 1050 the growth of the medieval town began. Much of the Exeter of the Middle Ages disappeared as a result of heavy bombing during the Second World War, but the cathedral remained standing amid the devastation. It was founded under Leofric, the first bishop, and although the present building dates from the 13th and 14th centuries, it incorporates two towers from the earlier Norman cathedral. The nave has the longest stretch of Gothic vaulting in the world, and on the north side is a charming minstrels' gallery featuring figures of angels playing musical instruments.

The city has several old buildings of rich, red sandstone, among them the ruins of Rougemont Castle, built by William the Conqueror and now surrounded by pleasant, shady gardens alive with birds and squirrels.

Another legacy of medieval times is Exeter's system of underground passages.* These were water conduits in the Middle Ages, and the houses above had holes in the floor so that water could be drawn up in buckets.

A detail of the exquisite carvings on the cathedral's 14th-century west front

Exeter was a thriving port until the late 13th century, when Countess Wear was built below the city, causing the Exe to silt up. However, the building of the Shipping Canal in 1564 (the first of its kind in England) revived the port. The city's long association with the sea is now reflected in the fascinating Maritime Museum.*

Standing in dramatic contrast to historic Exeter is the university, set on a hillside campus to the north of the city centre. The complex of buildings ranks among the most advanced modern architecture in the West Country, and includes the Northcott Theatre – the only full-time professional theatre in this part of England.

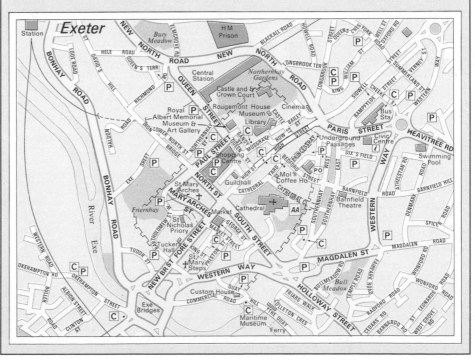

ROUTE 15   161 MILE

Birmingham to Bournemouth

PREHISTORIC monuments are the connecting theme for much of this route from the industrial Midlands to the South Coast. Belas Knap, high on the Cotswolds, is one of the best preserved chambered cairns in England and there are hill-forts overlooking the Vale of Gloucester near Cheltenham. Between the Thames and the English Channel is the chalk country of southern England, strewn with ancient monuments ranging from great stone circles to enigmatic earthworks.

From Birmingham the route follows the Warwickshire–Worcestershire border down to the ancient needle-manufacturing town of Studley. The line of Roman Ryknild Street is followed to Alcester, then the River Arrow accompanies the route past Ragley Hall and into Shakespeare country. 'Prinny' – the Prince Regent – stayed at Ragley Hall in the 18th century and suggested to the owner that the view from the mansion would be considerably improved by the addition of a folly. Hence Oversley Castle was built across the valley above the pretty little village of Arrow.

Much of the countryside in this area was once covered by the Forest of Arden, and Shakespeare, who knew the forest intimately, used it as a setting for *As You Like It*. Shakespearean connections are continued at Bidford-on-Avon, where the bard and a group of friends are said to have been challenged to a drinking bout one night; they came off worst, slept under a crab-apple tree, and in the morning Shakespeare vowed never to drink with the men of Bidford again.

Across the Avon is the Vale of Evesham with its acres of orchards, vegetables, soft fruit and glasshouses. Beyond Evesham, on the other side of Sedgeberrow, the route crosses into Gloucestershire and climbs on to the rolling limestone hills of the Cotswolds. Belas Knap, between Winchcombe and Cheltenham, is a marvellously preserved chambered cairn that was found, on excavation, to contain the bones of more than 30 people. One of its outstanding features is the drystone walling which forms its false entrance. This has been carefully restored and echoes the honey-coloured walls of the Cotswold villages and countryside that surround it.

As the route nears Cheltenham, tremendous views open up over the Vale of Gloucester. To the east, on the slopes of the Cotswolds' highest point, is the Iron Age promontory fort of Cleeve Hill, while to the north-west, on Nottingham Hill, is another hill-fort.

Beyond Cheltenham the route follows the River Churn to Cirencester. Safely tucked away off the main road along the river is a series of delightful and little-known villages like Cowley and Baunton, almost all of which have churches that are lovingly cared for and repay exploration.

The village of Down Ampney lies near the route between Cirencester and Cricklade. The composer Ralph Vaughan Williams was born here in 1872. His music – especially the lovely Third Symphony – captures the haunting and magical essence of the English countryside. Near Cricklade the River Churn enters the infant Thames, whose elusive source is situated away to the west near Cirencester. In spring summer the flat water meadows of the Thames and tributaries around Cricklade are rich with a dazzling displa wild flowers, both common and rare.

The route keeps to the western edge of the Marlbor Downs through Cricklade, Wootton Bassett and Calne be passing the amazing flight of canal locks on the outskir Devizes, then climbing to cross the grassy expanse of Salis Plain. In prehistoric times the Plain was densely populate is shown by the vast number of henge monuments, b chambers and mysterious earthworks. The chalk uplands natural causeways above the virtually impenetrable val and the thin soil was easy to clear and cultivate, makir natural for early men to congregate here.

Stonehenge, the most famous of the Plain's and monuments, is a lasting memorial to the dedication sophistication of these long-dead pastoralists. Huge stones the nearby downs were painstakingly cut and shaped be being erected, and at a later stage in Stonehenge's deve ment the smaller bluestones were laboriously carried her boat and trackway from distant Wales.

Barrows and earthworks can be seen along many parts o route to Salisbury, and on the city's outskirts is Old Sar itself of prehistoric origin. Subsequently occupied by Ror and, later, by Normans, it was a flourishing town medieval times. The population gradually moved to the ' town of Salisbury, leaving Old Sarum virtually dese However, until the passing of the Reform Bill in 1832 it voters continued to send two members to Parliament.

West of Salisbury the route crosses part of Cranborne C also rich in prehistoric remains, before turning southwar reach the River Allen and Knowlton. Here the ruins church stand within the circular embankment of a h monument – visible proof of the sanctity of this site thousands of years. From Wimborne Minster it is only a miles, across the River Stour and Canford Heath Bournemouth and the seaside.

PLACES OF INTEREST: OPENING DETAILS

Coughton
COUGHTON COURT open May to end Sep Wed, Thu, Sat and Sun, also Bank Holiday Mon and following Tue; also open Apr and Oct Sat and Sun, pm only

Arrow
RAGLEY HALL open Easter to Sep daily (except Mon and Fri), pm only

Middle Littleton
TITHE BARN open all year

Winchcombe
SUDELEY CASTLE open Mar to end Oct

BELAS KNAP LONG BARROW open all year

Calne
BOWOOD HOUSE open Apr to end Sep daily (except Mon), pm only

Salisbury Plain
STONEHENGE open all year

Salisbury
OLD SARUM open all year

MOMPESSON HOUSE open Apr to end Oct daily (except Thu and Fri), pm only

Wimborne Minster
PRIEST'S HOUSE MUSEUM open Apr to Sep weekdays

MODEL TOWN open Mar to end Nov

	Birmingham	Evesham	Cirencester	Salisbury	
	32				
	65	33			
	124	92	59		
	161	129	96	37	Bournemouth

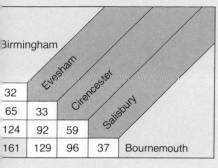

Birmingham

BIRMINGHAM
The Bull Ring is Birmingham's oldest inhabited area, and the new complex comprises 23 acres of shops and offices built on several levels

ALCESTER
Alcester Town Hall once stood on open stone arches. Each October the Manor Court meets here to elect the High Bailiff and fellow officials who have titles such as Ale Tasters and Bread Weighers

COUGHTON
It was in the gatehouse drawing room at Coughton Court that the conspirators involved in the Gunpowder Plot of November 1605 anxiously awaited the success or failure of their venture

WINCHCOMBE
The church at Winchcombe displays a startling array of gargoyles, grotesque stone figures which are also practical. They are water spouts which throw water running off the roof clear of the walls

EVESHAM
The Booth Hall, also known as the Tudor Round House, is a 15th-century half-timbered building which, despite its name, was never a booth (or market) hall but an inn

CIRENCESTER
The Parish Church of St John the Baptist is one of the finest 'wool' churches ever built by the rich merchants of the 15th century. Its most remarkable feature is the three-storeyed fan-vaulted porch which faces the market place

CHELTENHAM
The Cheltenham Gold Cup is one of the main steeplechasing events in the horse-racing calendar. The course is at Prestbury Park, to the north of the town

WOOTTON BASSETT
The town hall, half-timbered and supported by 15 stone pillars, was given to the town by Lawrence Hyde, first Earl of Rochester, in 1700

CALNE
Calne originally derived its wealth from weaving, but when the Industrial Revolution replaced the traditional cottage industry with mills Calne turned to bacon-curing, sausage- and pie-making, for which it has become famous

CAEN HILL
The Kennet and Avon Canal rises 230 feet over Caen Hill through a flight of 29 locks, built in 1810. Having been left to decline for a number of years, the locks are now being restored

OLD SARUM
Once a castle and a cathedral stood at Old Sarum, but a shortage of water, the exposed site, and bitter argument between church and state forced the clergy to found nearby Salisbury, where they built a new cathedral in 1220

SHREWTON
In the middle of Shrewton, by the stream which runs through the village, is an old domed lock-up known as the Blindhouse

SALISBURY
The hexagonal 15th-century Poultry Cross stands in a small square at the end of Butcher Row, and is the last of four market crosses which stood in Salisbury

COOMBE BISSETT
Just downstream from the road bridge is a three-arched medieval packhorse bridge. It has low, pointed arches and wooden railings, and still looks much as it did in the Middle Ages

BOURNEMOUTH
The mild climate at Bournemouth encourages outdoor activities. Sporting events held here include tennis tournaments, county cricket matches and league football, and there is every facility to enable visitors to play almost any sport of their choice

KNOWLTON
The early Christians often built their churches on sites sacred to ancient pagan religions. Knowlton church, now in ruins, stands in the centre of a ring laid out some 3000 years before the Normans built here

BIRMINGHAM TO ALCESTER

From the centre of Birmingham head south on the A41 (SP The South, Warwick), passing first St Martin's Church, gaunt and uneasy in the midst of all that concrete, and then the even more incongruous Old Crown, an inn dated 1386. Half a mile past it, at the crossroads, turn right on to the A435 (SP Alcester), then turn left at the T-junction to continue on the A435 out through the suburbs. At the roundabout by the Berkeley Shopping Precinct, take the third exit (SP Evesham), still following the A435, which now becomes a dual carriageway. Quite suddenly the route is running through open country, away from the urban landscape and crawling traffic.

Follow the A435 all the way to Studley, skirting Redditch on the right. At the roundabout as you enter Studley, keep forward with the main road, passing the modern red-brick factory of Studley Needle Industries, which reveals nothing of Studley's 300-year history of needle-making. It is now one of the largest needle-manufacturing centres in Europe.

Continue southwards along the A435. Two miles beyond the centre of Studley is Coughton Court,* its fairy-tale façade and turrets clearly visible from the road. This has been the family seat of the Throckmortons since the 15th century, and Coughton's

A magnificent early Tudor gatehouse with octagonal turrets and oriel windows leads into the courtyard of Coughton Court

The Avon at Bidford is spanned by an eight-arched stone bridge. It dates mainly from the 15th century, but some of the arches are thought to be even older

village pub is named after them. The family remained Catholics after the Reformation, and the house has priest holes to prove it.

Alcester is a pleasant little country town with an interesting assortment of buildings of many periods grouped around the 17th-century town hall, which lies off the main road to the left. The route skirts the town centre, taking the second exit, the A422 (SP Evesham) at the roundabout.

ALCESTER TO BIDFORD-ON-AVON

After ¾ mile, in the village of Arrow, the route keeps forward to join the A435, soon passing the imposing gates of Ragley Hall,* a 17th-century stately home which contains a fine collection of paintings, china and furnishings.

One mile further on bear left on to the B4085 (SP Wixford, Bidford), following the River Arrow. This is Shakespeare country, and the pub on the left as you enter Wixford proclaims hopefully that 'Shakespeare probably drank here'. A raised terrace of charming black-and-white cottages stands opposite. Continue along the B4085 to Bidford-on-Avon. At the T-junction turn right (SP Evesham, Broadway), then turn left at a roundabout (SP Broadway, Cleeve Prior) to continue along the B4085.

The town centre lies just to the left. The small square is fringed with cottages and shops, and at the end is the Old Falcon, an imposing stone house built of layers of blue lias and golden oolite stone which give a subtle striped effect. The same unusual mixture is a characteristic of several other buildings in Bidford, and complements the red brick to perfection.

RD-ON-AVON TO EVESHAM

the narrow 15th-century bridge over
von and in ½ mile turn right at a
ads (SP Marlcliff, Cleeve Prior). Neat
of vegetables line the road, for this is the
t-gardening country of the Vale of
am. Continue through Cleeve Prior –
stone cottages, church and manor
with finely manicured, topiaried
cluster about a village green – and in
s, at the crossroads, turn right on to the
(SP Offenham, Evesham, Fish and
r Crossing).

MIDDLE LITTLETON

his crossroads a detour can be made to
dle Littleton. Turn left down Arrow Lane
orth Littleton and keep right at each
tion, making a circuit around Middle
leton's great tithe barn.* Church, manor
se and tithe barn form an attractive group
ellow stone – no museum pieces, but used
y as they have been for many centuries,
ugh the 13th-century barn now shelters
ht modern tractors beneath its great stone
f. Turn right on to the B4085 to return to
crossroads, and turn left there to rejoin the
n route.

and river meet at the Fish and Anchor
nd the B4510 runs on among orchards
elds of soft fruit to Evesham. Many acres
overed by glasshouses filled with tender
g lettuces and other crops which add
t splashes of green to the landscape on
he dreariest winter days. At the edge of
am turn right on to the B4035 (SP
Centre), then bear right at the rounda-
(SP Worcester, A44). The street leading
e town centre has numerous green-
rs' shops displaying colourful and
dant heaps of fresh local produce.
en you reach the river, turn left at the
lights on to the A44 (SP Worcester).
road runs beside the Avon, with views
s it to the town centre. The abbey ruins
the opposite bank, and the magnificent
ndicular bell-tower can be clearly seen.
the town centre see p. 149.)

HAM TO CHELTENHAM

e next bridge turn left on to the A435
heltenham), following it for 3 miles to
berrow, where you turn left on to the
(SP Winchcombe). Cross the A438
miles and continue to Winchcombe,
rst Cotswold town on this route. In the
, turn right by the George Hotel on to
46 (SP Cheltenham). This old inn was
as a hostelry for pilgrims to the impor-
bbey at Winchcombe, which once stood
o the fine 'wool' church. The abbey was
lished by Lord Seymour of nearby
ey Castle,* who was the second hus-
of Katherine Parr, widow of Henry
There are many attractive old build-
Winchcombe, all tightly packed into a
scape of mellow stone.

*Lime trees and dormered cottages line the street leading
from Winchcombe to Sudeley*

*Framed by rolling Cotswold countryside, Sudeley Castle
once belonged to Richard III. The ruins of his apartments
can still be seen there*

BELAS KNAP LONG BARROW

As you leave Winchcombe the route passes a
left turning (SP Brockhampton,
Andoversford) leading to Belas Knap Long
Barrow.* This is a detour strictly for the
enthusiast, for although there are splendid
views over Sudeley Castle and Winchcombe
from the lay-by, 1 mile up the lane, where you
can park, it is fifteen minutes' energetic walk,
uphill, to Belas Knap itself. However, the
views on the way up are an ample reward,
and at the top you will see one of the finest
surviving chambered long barrows, 180 feet
long and with a false entrance at one end, as
well as three neolithic burial chambers.

Continue on the A46 towards Cheltenham,
climbing steadily up to the Cotswold edge.
On the left, rugged hills rise to 1083 feet – the
highest point in the Cotswolds – while to the
right the land drops sharply away, giving fine
views over the Vale of Gloucester.

A sprinkling of guest-houses and hotels
heralds the approach to Cheltenham, which
really begins at Prestbury. The race-course
here – home of the Cheltenham Gold Cup – is
the scene of champagne and feverish excite-
ment during Gold Cup week in March. Here
you can either turn left (SP Through Traffic)
to avoid the town centre, or carry on to see the
elegant spa (see p. 150). From Cheltenham
take the A435 Cirencester road, soon passing
the steep ridge of Charlton Kings Common
to the right.

CHELTENHAM TO CIRENCESTER

It is a pleasant journey along the valley of the River Churn from Cheltenham to Cirencester, with several attractive and unspoilt villages on or very near the route.

COWLEY

Four miles beyond Cheltenham you can make a detour to Cowley, off the main road to the right. The 19th-century manor house and adjoining 13th-century church, hidden behind a great yew hedge, are in a lovely setting, best appreciated by taking the first turning left past the main gates and driving along a lane which leads right round the grounds. Turn left by the Green Dragon pub to cross the River Churn, then turn right on to the A435 to rejoin the main route.

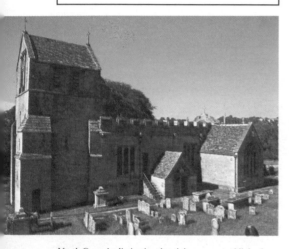

North Cerney's distinctive church has a rare saddleback tower and a Georgian gallery, reached by an external stone staircase

Continue towards Cirencester, later passing on the left Colesbourne Park, where many rare species of trees can be found. As the country becomes hillier and the valley narrower the fine Italianate mansion of Rendcomb College can be seen on a hilltop to the left. North Cerney is next, on the main road. This pleasant stone village, charmingly situated on the Churn and sheltered by the North Cerney Downs, is overlooked by its fine 12th-century church, which has an unusual saddle-back tower.

BAUNTON

Baunton is the last Churn valley village, and lies off the A435 to the left. Its church belonged to Cirencester Abbey, and has a large and well-preserved 14th-century wall painting of St Christopher.

Skirt the edge of Stratton, then turn left on to the A417 – the Roman Ermin Way. It is easiest to continue straight round the Cirencester by-pass, following signs to join the A419 for Swindon and Cricklade. Cirencester town centre is signposted to the right at the first roundabout if you wish to make a detour into this pleasant country town (see p. 227).

CIRENCESTER TO WOOTTON BASSETT

COTSWOLD WATER PARK

To the right, about 4 miles past Cirencester, is the Cotswold Water Park. Flooded gravel pits around the upper waters of the Thames are being put to good use here, and this is destined to become England's largest collection of man-made lakes. The park covers some 14,000 acres, and has facilities for water sports as well as providing a refuge for many species of water birds and other aquatic wildlife.

The female mallard lines her nest with her own down

DOWN AMPNEY

Further along the A419, off to the left, is Down Ampney, the village where the composer Ralph Vaughan Williams was born in 1872. One of his hymn settings is named after this pleasant Gloucestershire village. An exhibition of paintings by local artists is held at Down Ampney House every summer.

Continue through Latton, where an old village cross stands by the road, and leave the A419 (now dual carriageway) at the Cricklade exit (SP Cricklade, Wootton Bassett, B4041). Immediately the great Tudor tower of St Sampson's Church, Cricklade, comes into view, its height and hilltop site ensuring that it dominates the flat lands of the upper Thames. Drive into Cricklade – the only Thames-side town in Wiltshire – and turn left on to the B4041 (SP Wootton Bassett) at the T-junction by the brightly painted town clock. Down to the right the infant Thames skirts the town, and on its bank is a small, unassuming Norman church, which could hardly be more different from the grandiose building which first claims the visitor's attention.

PURTON STOKE

The hamlet of Purton Stoke, situated just to the right at a crossroads on the B4041 almost 2 miles south of Cricklade, must surely have been England's smallest spa. At the west end of the village street is a track (better walked than driven) leading past the tiny octagonal pump room built over a mineral spring known as Salts Hole. It is now derelict and sadly overgrown.

Continue to Purton, about 2 miles further along the B4041.

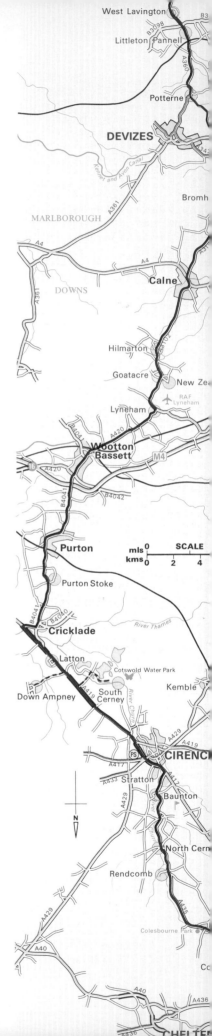

PURTON

not miss a short detour here to the old
̣tre of Purton village, reached by driving
ᶦght on into Church Street where the
ᶦn road swings to the right. Half a mile
ᶰg this road, turn left just past an immense
̣ne barn. Round the corner is quite a
̣prise: not only a fine church with two
̣ers, but also, between it and the barn, an
̣ractive stone manor house dating from
̣ut 1600. Several delightful houses and
̣tages, also of stone, are dotted along the
̣e as it sweeps right round the churchyard.

B4041 continues towards Wootton
̣tt, crossing the M4 motorway. Shortly
̣t, at a roundabout, keep forward to join
̣A420 which brings the route into
̣tton Bassett. Drive through the broad
̣busy High Street, where there are a
̣er of fine Georgian buildings. To the
̣ is the half-timbered town hall, dated
̣. Sheltered among the 15 stone piers
̣h support its upper floor are the old town
̣s and a curious little wooden fire engine.

̣TTON BASSETT TO
̣T LAVINGTON
̣y straight on along the A420 to
̣ham, where you should turn left on to
̣3102 (SP Calne, Hilmarton). Lyneham
̣ large RAF station, with the inevitable
̣ of unmistakably military housing. The
̣continues through Goatacre, skirting a
̣et with the unlikely name of New
̣nd. After Hilmarton the route strikes
̣ into more open downland country,
̣nding again to Calne, where you should
̣v signs to the A4 and then turn left on to
̣P Melksham, Marlborough). The short
̣ along the A4 takes the route past
̣e's most famous landmark: Harris's huge
̣rick factory, home of Wiltshire ham and
̣any other pork products. Shortly past it
̣right on to the A3102 (SP Melksham),
̣h later skirts the 1000-acre estate

surrounding Bowood House* (reached from
the A4 1 mile west of Calne), and after 3¼ miles
turn left on to the A342 (SP Devizes,
Melksham). All the time the steep scarp slope
of the Marlborough Downs rises over to the
left, extending long fingers of high ground
into the flatter lands beneath.

Carry on through market gardening
country to Rowde, where the route turns
right, by the Cross Keys pub, into Marsh
Lane, the B3101. A mile along this road is a
unique sight. A hump-back bridge crosses the
Kennet and Avon Canal not far from its
highest point, near Devizes, and a great
ladder of nearly 20 locks – part of a flight of 29
– stretches up the stepped hillside to the left as
far as the eye can see. Though most of them
have become disused and derelict, their
restoration is under way. Constructed in
1810, they make an impressive sight, and
mark a milestone of engineering history.

Shortly past the bridge, turn left on to the
A361 (SP Devizes), and after ¼ mile turn right
on to an unclassified road (SP Potterne). The
lane crosses pleasant countryside and enters
Potterne by a quaint, winding street complete
with village pump. At the top, turn right on to
the A360 Salisbury road. Opposite the junction is Potterne church, a simple yet strikingly
beautiful example of the Early English style.
Inside is a Saxon font which has a Latin
inscription from the Psalms round the rim.

Go down the hill, following the A360 and
passing Porch House, a most impressive
timber-framed building of the late 15th
century. Next to it is another attractive black-
and-white timbered house probably a century younger.

The A360 continues through Littleton
Pannell and into West Lavington, whose
pub sign carries a portrait of Sir Winston
Churchill. (Route continues on p. 164.)

̣ennet and Avon Canal crosses Caen Hill by a flight
̣ocks, one of the wonders of England's waterways.
̣tretch of the canal is currently being restored

SALISBURY PLAIN

Discovered by aerial photography in 1925, Woodhenge is an enigmatic monu- marked out today by concrete plinths which indicate the position of wooden p It is generally supposed that the six egg-shaped rings which comprise Wood the outline of what was once a large, roofed timber building. No-one is sure function it may have fulfilled, but a clue may lie in the fact that the long axes holes seem to be aligned towards the midsummer sunrise

RUNNING southwards from the Vale of Pewsey to the outskirts of Salisbury, and westwards from Tidworth to Warminster, Salisbury Plain is part of the chalk uplands that sweep from Dorset to the Wash and go on to form the Wolds of Lincolnshire and Yorkshire. Basically a rumpled plateau surrounded by steep slopes, the Plain averages just under 500 feet above sea level, but rises to 755 feet at Westbury Hill, a splendid viewpoint. The Plain is seen at its best in clear, sunny weather – ideally after rain has washed the air and clotted-cream clouds sail serenely against the bluest of backcloths.

Chitterne, Tilshead, Orcheston and a few other settlements nestle in the chalky folds, but there are many more villages and small towns at the feet of the escarpments and in the fertile valleys of the meandering Avon and Wylye. They include Edington, with its 14th-century priory church, and Urchfont, whose manor house was once owned by the 18th-century prime minister William Pitt the Elder. These and other communities developed where springs of sparkling water, filtered down through the chalk, emerged round the base of the plateau.

Roman legions once marched across the Plain, and it has been used as a military training area since the Napoleonic Wars, almost 200 years ago. Pioneering aviators were also attracted to this great expanse of open country. The airfield at Upavon, established in 1912, is one of the oldest in Britain. Large areas of the Plain are still used as a military training area, so walkers must watch out for red flags and other warning signs when exploring the ancient footpaths and bridleways.

SALISBURY PLAIN boasts a greater concentration of prehistoric monuments than any other part of Britain with the sole exception of Orkney. It is almost impossible to drive for more than ten minutes without passing close to burial mounds, forts, ridgeway tracks and other reminders of the earliest Britons.

According to legend, Stone-henge was transported from Ireland by Merlin, King Arthur's resident wizard. The truth is almost as extraordinary. The oldest parts of the huge Bronze Age religious site date from about 2700 BC. Additions and alterations were made until about 2000 BC when the so-called bluestones were arranged in their present positions. At least 80 bluestones, weighing up to four tons apiece, came from the distant hills of Pembroke-shire and are believed to have covered the distance of more than 200 miles on rafts and log rollers. Woodhenge, be Amesbury and Durring thought to be even old Stonehenge.

Iron Age settlers bui vantage points around plateau. They include Castle – an evocative si of Steeple Langford – a perched above the Wyl valley. Bratton Castle, impressive earthwork, the highest point of the above Westbury.

Stonehenge has mystified scholars and laymen alike for hundreds of years. It has attracted scores of legends, countless theories as to its purpose, and legions of eccentrics. At midsummer this most famous of prehistoric monuments is the focus of much activity, ranging from sedate processions of white-robed druids to impromptu festivals organized by hippies

EVER since prehistoric times, men have been unable to resist displaying their artistic talents on the steep flanks of chalk downs.

The northern edge of Salisbury Plain has three such carvings. The graceful white horse on Westbury Hill is the biggest in Wiltshire – 163 feet high and 175 feet from head to tail. It dates from 1778, but an earlier horse on the same site is said to have been cut into the turf in the 9th century to commemorate Alfred the Great's decisive victory over the Danes at nearby Edington.

Local folklore also tells how a man called 'Jack the Painter' was paid £20 to carve the white horse on the hill above the twin villages of Alton Barnes and Alton Priors. He took the money and bolted without cutting a single turf, but was eventually caught and hanged. The horse was cut, without further drama, in 1812. The third horse looks northwards over Pewsey. It dates from 1785 but was re-cut in 1937 to commemorate the coronation of George VI.

Soldiers who trained on Salisbury Plain during the First World War kept up the tradition. They carved huge regimental badges into the chalk slopes overlooking Fovant, a village a few miles south of the Plain.

The 'Bread Stones' (left) at Great Wishford record the changing price of dough. Cottages like those at Stockton (top) are a delightful feature of the Wylye valley. Enford (far left) is set in the tranquil upper reaches of the River Avon

E WYLYE VALLEY is a fine le of the sudden contrasts that ute so much to England's ape. Its rich blend of lush s and picturesque little s seems far removed from the carped plain that rolls away to th.

minster is one of the 'gateways' valley. The colonnaded Old tel and other handsome gs are reminders that this was e of the most flourishing corn-ol-markets in southern d. There are quaint old uses at Heytesbury and n, where thatched cottages also catch the eye. Codford St Peter should be visited for the carved, 9th-century cross in the church. Great Wishford's churchyard wall is set with plaques recording the price of bread since 1800. The prices are quoted in gallons, because bread used to be sold as dough ready for home-baking. One gallon cost 3s 4d in 1800. Inside the church is an 18th-century fire engine and a magnificently ornate Tudor tomb.

Wilton, at the point where the Wylye joins the Nadder, has been synonymous with carpets since the 17th century. Its great showplace, Wilton House, is the seat of the earls of Pembroke and was rebuilt by Inigo Jones after a fire in 1647. A feature of the lovely grounds is a Palladian-style bridge over the River Nadder.

Eight regimental badges, and the emblem of the YMCA, are carved into a chalk slope at Fovant, off the A30 between Salisbury and Shaftesbury

WEST LAVINGTON TO SALISBURY

From West Lavington the road begins to climb on to Salisbury Plain. Soon the landscape changes completely and you are surrounded by bare, open spaces and great, wide skyscapes. The only splashes of colour in this bleak and windswept country are provided by the red flags of artillery ranges and the columns of bright posts at tank crossings: the Plain is much used as a military training area. Tilshead, the first village, looks refreshingly cosy, with an Early English church and several thatched cottages, all built of flint and stone in a distinctive chequerboard pattern – a style typical of this area. Further on, the road passes Orcheston, set in a wooded hollow to the left. The village has two churches, and so does Shrewton, the next village, although, strictly speaking, one church belongs to the neighbouring hamlet of Maddington. At the road junction in Shrewton is a stout little lock-up, called the Blindhouse, whose walls and domed roof are built of solid stone blocks. Beside it, and through the main street, runs the River Till, which brought disaster to the village in 1841 when Shrewton and several nearby villages suffered terrible floods.

Some 2 miles past Shrewton the A360 makes a sudden right turn at a crossroads.

Approaching Salisbury, the earthworks of the city's predecessor, Old Sarum, can be seen across the Avon valley. In 1220 the clergy left this bleak hilltop site to found the new city of Salisbury in the valley below, and Old Sarum gradually fell into ruins

STONEHENGE

At this point you can make a detour to Stonehenge,* which lies straight ahead, 1½ miles away along the A344. The magical atmosphere of the place has undoubtedly lost something now that the site is fenced and equipped with tourist facilities. but Stonehenge is still Britain's most remarkable prehistoric wonder.

It was begun towards the end of the Stone Age with the construction of a bank-and-ditch earthwork, and the huge stones were brought here at later dates from the Marlborough Downs and the Preseli Hills in South Wales. The reason why this colossal task was undertaken is still a mystery. Sun-worship is a popular theory, no doubt because the central axis of Stonehenge is aligned with the point where the sun rises on midsummer's day. But the ceremonies enacted here each year by Druids can have little to do with the monument's original purpose, for Stonehenge was begun about 1500 years before the Druids came to Britain.

The A360 crosses the A303 trunk road at a roundabout known as Longbarrow Crossroads because a neolithic long barrow is nearby. It is part of the Winterbourne Stoke barrow cemetery, where there are 13 barrows of different types, some of them owned by the National Trust. This whole area is packed with prehistoric monuments of many kinds.

The A360 runs straight on to Salisbury. Look left as you pass the town sign to see the earthworks of Old Sarum* on a hill across the Avon valley. We may think of Salisbury as an

n, but from the Iron Age until the 13th
the settlement – complete with castle,
al, bishop's palace and city walls –
Old Sarum. Around 1200, the clergy
out to found Salisbury where it stands
Some of the stone from Old Sarum's
gs was used to build the new city, and
15th century Old Sarum was in ruins.
ue to Salisbury, following signs round
road for the A354 and Blandford.

SALISBURY

a detour into the city centre, ignore
gh-routes and follow signs at the first
dabout to the city centre. There are
al car parks, and Salisbury is well worth
ring on foot if you have time. The
dral and its Close are a must. The
nt, soaring cathedral spire, at 404 feet, is
ighest in England, and is a 14th-century
ion to an entirely Early English building
leted in 1258. The cloisters and chapter
were added later. The Close is a
ful setting for the Bishop's Palace (now
horisters' School) and the lovely build-
round it, including Mompesson House,*
1701. Parts of some other buildings are
st as old as the cathedral itself.
the north of the cathedral is the spacious
et place, with its avenue of trees and
y guildhall. Nearby, on the corner of
Street, is the hexagonal Poultry Cross,
ly survivor of four such medieval crosses
n once stood in Salisbury.
e city's 20th-century attractions include
ant shopping streets and an excellent
rn theatre.

URY TO BOURNEMOUTH

signs for Blandford to leave Salisbury
A354. Coombe Bissett is the first village
he last for some miles. Here the little
Ebble flows beside and beneath the
and a picturesque weatherboarded
ands among willows on its bank. To
is a narrow old packhorse bridge, and
g ground further along on the left is
man church.
here the road climbs up a small
approaching the rolling grasslands
echwoods of Cranborne Chase. This
e Salisbury Plain, is rich in prehistoric
ents, and 9 miles beyond Coombe
there are several round barrows in a
the left. Beyond them the route
a roundabout where you should turn
to the B3081 (SP Ringwood,
rne). After 3½ miles turn left and in ¾
a crossroads turn right on to the B3078
mborne).
the church tower of Knowlton comes
w. This is an interesting place with an
magical aura; the medieval village no
exists, but the ruined 12th-century
urch stands right in the middle of a
s pagan monument, a Bronze Age
The circular rampart and ditch can
seen, and there are other prehistoric
nd round barrows in the area.

Right: One of the carvings which embellish the Joiners' Hall in St Ann Street, Salisbury – the finest surviving example of over a dozen such guildhalls that once stood in the city

Below: Salisbury Cathedral was almost entirely built within 30 years of the laying of the foundation stone in 1227. The spire was added a century later

From here the road follows the valley of the River Allen through rolling farmland and into Wimborne, distinguished by the two stately towers of its minster. A nunnery was founded here in the 8th century, but it was destroyed by the Danes, and much of the present church is fine late Norman work. The west tower contains the famous Quarter Jack clock; on the outside is a little model grena-dier which strikes the quarter-hours. Near the minster is the small local history museum,* in the Priest's House, and the model town,* a 1-in-10 replica of Wimborne as it was in the 1950s, complete with miniature trees and gardens.

Leave Wimborne on the Bournemouth and Poole road, the A349, shortly crossing the River Stour. Do not be confused by the Poole town signs, but 1 mile further on turn left on to the A341 (SP Bournemouth). There is a last short stretch of open country as the route skirts Canford Heath, passing through the village of Canford Magna, before the out-skirts of Bournemouth begin. The final few miles can be slow, but have patience and head for the town centre, which is clearly sign-posted. There is no shortage of hotels in the town, and it is an excellent base for excursions to the New Forest and into Hardy country while at the same time possessing numerous attractions both man-made and natural to ensure an enjoyable holiday. (For details and a town plan of Bournemouth, see p. 187.)

This attractive old timbered barn stands beside the River Ebble to the right of the road in Coombe Bissett

ROUTE 16

209 MIL

Birmingham to Eastbourn

Birmingham, which had been a thriving manufacturing town since as early as the 16th century, reached the peak of its expansion during the Industrial Revolution, and owed a good deal of its prosperity and importance to the network of canals that was built around the city in the late 18th century. But the canals, quick and efficient though they were, could not compete with the railways that spread across the country during the mid 19th century. By the close of the century most of them had become weed-choked waterways strewn with decaying locks and rotting barges.

As this route travels southwards from Birmingham it crosses the Stratford-upon-Avon Canal, begun at Kings Norton in 1793. In 1802 this canal was connected to the Warwick and Birmingham Canal – later the Grand Union. By 1816 the whole 25-mile stretch from Kings Norton to Stratford was open and in use, but its brief heyday lasted only 40 years, after which time it became neglected and began to silt up. In 1960 a tremendous effort was made to save the canal, and in 1964 it was reopened for pleasure craft by the Queen Mother.

Beyond Wootton Wawen the route continues to Stratford through a landscape of gentle hills that were once covered by the Forest of Arden. The vast amounts of timber available in the region account for the numerous old timbered buildings that typify Shakespeare country.

Stratford-upon-Avon, and all the countryside and villages around, are soaked in Shakespearean associations and are visited by countless pilgrims from all over the world who come to pay tribute to the man who is generally described as the greatest playwright of all time. South of Stratford and the Avon is the countryside once known as Feldon which, in contrast to heavily wooded Arden, was composed of large fields and grassy meadows.

Meon Hill marks the beginning of the limestone country, and by Chipping Campden the route is in the Cotswolds. No other part of England has such a uniform beauty as these hills – nearly every church, house and wall is built of warm oolitic limestone, and at one time even the roads and pavements were made of the same material.

From Chipping Campden the route climbs across the high escarpment of the Cotswolds then descends to the valley of the Windrush at Bourton-on-the-Water, where the river is spanned by several delightful little bridges. Burford is also on the Windrush, and from here the route continues across the Oxfordshire countryside to the water meadows, reed-beds, willows and poplars of the upper Thames valley.

Beyond the Vale of White Horse the route climbs on to the Lambourn Downs and crosses the Ridgeway. This prehistoric trackway is now a long-distance footpath running from Avebury across the chalk country to the Thames at Streatley and then on into Buckinghamshire. Along its course, to the west of the route, are some of the finest prehistoric monuments in England, including the magnificent chalk-cut figure that gives the Vale of White Horse its name.

The open landscapes of the Lambourn Downs give wa rolling countryside of fields enclosed by flower-st hedgerows and copses as the route approaches Newbury, lies between the Hampshire and Berkshire Downs. C other side of Kingsclere the route travels along the edge Hampshire Downs, giving panoramic views across the n the county and away into Berkshire.

Beyond Alton there are two villages with outsta literary connections. Chawton was the home of the n Jane Austen, and Selborne and its surroundings are f linked with Gilbert White. Across the Sussex border the follows the Rother valley through a string of appealing v to Petworth. Next comes Wisborough Green and Billingshurst, which is set on the line of Roman Stane Str

Shipley and Cowfold are on the edge of the wooded Weald, but at Albourne the country opens out once mo from Ditchling to Lewes the route sails along the edge Downs. From Lewes the River Ouse is accompanied journey to Newhaven, and then the route runs parallel coast through Seaford before dropping into the valley Cuckmere River. Tremendous downland landscapes op as the road climbs again, and for the last few miles to East the upland air is made bracing by the salty tang of the s

PLACES OF INTEREST: OPENING DETAILS

Henley-in-Arden
GUILDHALL open at all reasonable times on application to the Caretaker, Guild Cottage

Wilmcote
MARY ARDEN'S HOUSE open all year (except Good Fri, 24-26 Dec and Sun Nov to Mar); closed Sun am Apr to Oct

Stratford-upon-Avon
SHAKESPEARE'S BIRTHPLACE open all year (except Good Fri, 24-26 Dec); closed Sun am Nov to Mar

HALL'S CROFT open all year (except Good Fri, 24-26 Dec and Sun Nov to Mar); closed Sun am Apr to Oct

Mickleton
HIDCOTE MANOR GARDEN open Apr to end Oct daily (except Tue and Fri)

KIFTSGATE COURT GARDEN open Apr to end Sep Wed, Thu, Sun and Bank Holidays, pm only

Chipping Campden
WOOLSTAPLERS' HALL open Easter, then May to Sep

Broadway
BROADWAY TOWER COUNTRY PARK open Apr to end Sep

SNOWSHILL MANOR HOUSE open May to end Sep Wed to Sun and Bank Holidays; also open Apr and Oct Sat, Sun and Bank Holiday Mon

Guiting Power
COTSWOLD FARM PARK open May to end Sep

Bourton-on-the-Water
MODEL VILLAGE open all year

Wantage
WANTAGE MUSEUM open Wed, pm only, and Sat, am and pm

Donnington
DONNINGTON CASTLE open all year

Newbury
THE MUSEUM (OL CLOTH HALL) oper weekdays all year (except Wed pm ar Bank Holidays)

Chawton
JANE AUSTEN'S HOUSE open all ye daily (except Mon and Tue Nov to Ma and 25-26 Dec)

Selborne
THE WAKES open Mar to Oct Tue to S and Bank Holidays pm only

Petworth
PETWORTH HOUS open Apr to end Oc Tue, Wed, Thu, Sat Sun and Bank Holiday Mon, pm only

Shipley
KING'S MILL open conducted tours M to Oct, first weeken in month, pm only

Lewes
LEWES CASTLE ope all year: Mon to Sa all day, Sun pm on closed Sun Nov to Mar

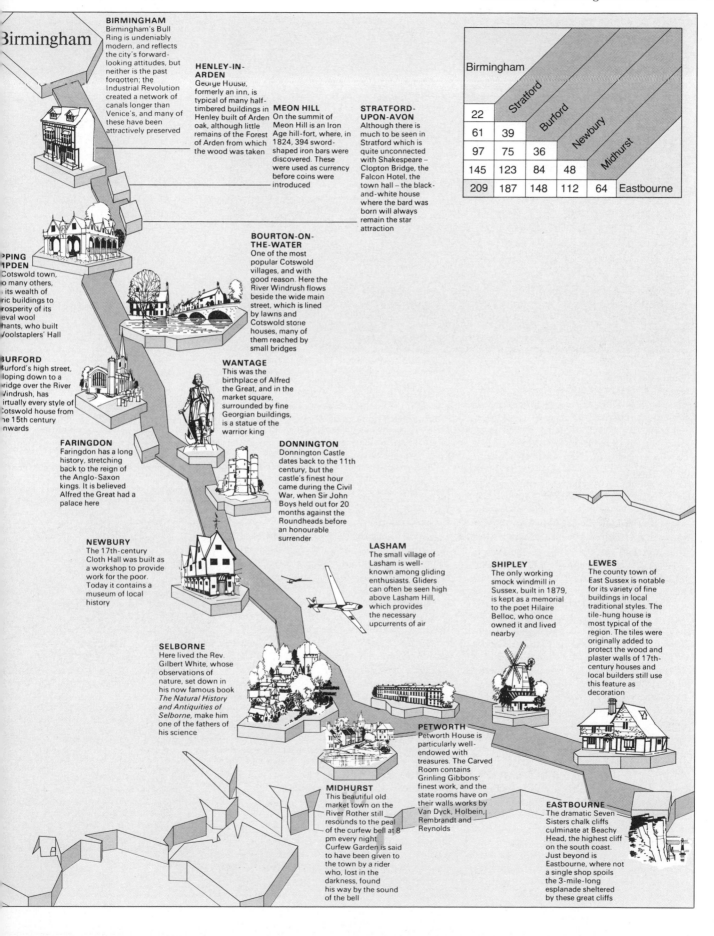

Birmingham

Birmingham	Stratford	Burford	Newbury	Midhurst	
22					
61	39				
97	75	36			
145	123	84	48		
209	187	148	112	64	Eastbourne

BIRMINGHAM
Birmingham's Bull Ring is undeniably modern, and reflects the city's forward-looking attitudes, but neither is the past forgotten; the Industrial Revolution created a network of canals longer than Venice's, and many of these have been attractively preserved

HENLEY-IN-ARDEN
George House, formerly an inn, is typical of many half-timbered buildings in Henley built of Arden oak, although little remains of the Forest of Arden from which the wood was taken

MEON HILL
On the summit of Meon Hill is an Iron Age hill-fort, where, in 1824, 394 sword-shaped iron bars were discovered. These were used as currency before coins were introduced

STRATFORD-UPON-AVON
Although there is much to be seen in Stratford which is quite unconnected with Shakespeare – Clopton Bridge, the Falcon Hotel, the town hall – the black-and-white house where the bard was born will always remain the star attraction

[CHI]PPING [CAM]PDEN
[A] Cotswold town, [like s]o many others, [owes] its wealth of [histo]ric buildings to [the pr]osperity of its [medie]val wool [merc]hants, who built [the W]oolstaplers' Hall

BURFORD
[B]urford's high street, [s]loping down to a [b]ridge over the River [W]indrush, has [v]irtually every style of [C]otswold house from [th]e 15th century [o]nwards

BOURTON-ON-THE-WATER
One of the most popular Cotswold villages, and with good reason. Here the River Windrush flows beside the wide main street, which is lined by lawns and Cotswold stone houses, many of them reached by small bridges

WANTAGE
This was the birthplace of Alfred the Great, and in the market square, surrounded by fine Georgian buildings, is a statue of the warrior king

FARINGDON
Faringdon has a long history, stretching back to the reign of the Anglo-Saxon kings. It is believed Alfred the Great had a palace here

DONNINGTON
Donnington Castle dates back to the 11th century, but the castle's finest hour came during the Civil War, when Sir John Boys held out for 20 months against the Roundheads before an honourable surrender

NEWBURY
The 17th-century Cloth Hall was built as a workshop to provide work for the poor. Today it contains a museum of local history

LASHAM
The small village of Lasham is well-known among gliding enthusiasts. Gliders can often be seen high above Lasham Hill, which provides the necessary upcurrents of air

SHIPLEY
The only working smock windmill in Sussex, built in 1879, is kept as a memorial to the poet Hilaire Belloc, who once owned it and lived nearby

LEWES
The county town of East Sussex is notable for its variety of fine buildings in local traditional styles. The tile-hung house is most typical of the region. The tiles were originally added to protect the wood and plaster walls of 17th-century houses and local builders still use this feature as decoration

SELBORNE
Here lived the Rev. Gilbert White, whose observations of nature, set down in his now famous book *The Natural History and Antiquities of Selborne*, make him one of the fathers of his science

PETWORTH
Petworth House is particularly well-endowed with treasures. The Carved Room contains Grinling Gibbons' finest work, and the state rooms have on their walls works by Van Dyck, Holbein, Rembrandt and Reynolds

MIDHURST
This beautiful old market town on the River Rother still resounds to the peal of the curfew bell at 8 pm every night. Curfew Garden is said to have been given to the town by a rider who, lost in the darkness, found his way by the sound of the bell

EASTBOURNE
The dramatic Seven Sisters chalk cliffs culminate at Beachy Head, the highest cliff on the south coast. Just beyond is Eastbourne, where not a single shop spoils the 3-mile-long esplanade sheltered by these great cliffs

BIRMINGHAM TO STRATFORD-UPON-AVON

From the Bull Ring in central Birmingham, follow the A41 (SP The South, Warwick) for 2 miles, then keep forward at a small roundabout to join the A34 (SP Stratford). The route passes through Hall Green and Shirley and, just beyond the last built-up area, reaches a roundabout which is the present southern end of the M42 motorway. Take the second exit to continue along the A34. (This roundabout is the obvious place to pick up the route if you are coming from further north or east of Birmingham.)

By now the route is running through open country, and two attractive old brick-and-timber barns on the right, with higgledy-piggledy roofs, are a fine introduction to rural Warwickshire. Follow the A34 through Hockley Heath and to Henley-in-Arden, whose antiquity is unmistakable. The church and adjoining guildhall* belong to the 15th century, as do many of the quaint timbered cottages, shops and inns which line the High Street. You need not look far for even older buildings. Barely 100 yards from the church, down the lane by its side, is the Norman church of Beaudesert, and on the hill behind it the earthworks of an 11th-century motte-and-bailey castle can be seen.

Continue south on the A34, which soon sweeps in a great curve around Wootton Wawen church, set on a hilltop site first chosen by the Saxons. Some of their masonry can still be seen today. As it leaves Wootton Wawen the road passes under a bridge which looks perfectly ordinary – unless you happen to see a boat gliding over it. It is in fact the Stratford-upon-Avon Canal, crossing the road here by an aqueduct built in 1813.

MARY ARDEN'S HOUSE, WILMCOTE
For a short detour to Mary Arden's house,* turn right 3 miles later on to an unclassified road (SP Wilmcote). A mile from the main road is the quaint old farmstead which was the girlhood home of Shakespeare's mother. The timber-framed house and farm buildings are the setting for a museum of English rural life, set up by the Shakespeare Birthplace Trust when they bought the property in 1930. Until then it had been a working farm for centuries and the collection of old country furniture, tools, farm implements and wagons looks perfectly at home.

Continue along the A34 to Stratford, where the Shakespeare industry is less subtle, though of course there is plenty to see. If you wish to by-pass the town centre, which lies just off to the right, follow signs to Oxford, crossing the Avon by 15th-century Clopton Bridge. Beside it is the canal basin, where bright barges huddle beneath a bronze statue of Shakespeare. The Memorial Theatre stands on the river bank nearby, and from there a path leads through peaceful riverside gardens to Holy Trinity Church, a fine Perpendicular building, where Shakespeare and some of his family lie buried. The Shakespeare Birthplace Trust maintains several old buildings associated with the playwright, among them the birthplace* itself, in Henley Street, and, in Old Town, Hall's Croft,* home of the doctor who married Shakespeare's daughter Susannah.

STRATFORD-UPON-AVON TO CHIPPING CAMPDEN

Follow signs out of Stratford for the A34 (SP Oxford), bearing right at the roundabout shortly past Clopton Bridge. A mile from the town centre, turn right on to the A46 (SP Cheltenham). This quiet, open road takes the

route through the last few miles of ro Warwickshire farmland into Gloucesters To the left rises Meon Hill, the first outpo the approaching Cotswolds. It is toppe clumps of trees and an Iron Age hill-fort.

Continue through Mickleton, the Gloucestershire village, set amid ma gardens. To the left of the village is Med House, its Renaissance style set off to pe tion by the lovely stone which is so typic Gloucestershire. At the end of the village left on to the B4081 (SP Chipping Campo

HIDCOTE BARTRIM AND KIFTSGATE COUR

One of the gazebos at Hidcote Bartrim

For a detour to Hidcote Manor Garden* tu immediately left again at this junction on an unclassified road, driving up a steep h with magnificent views behind. At the junction at the top, turn left (SP Hidco Bartrim, Quinton), then in ½ mile turn rigl The tiny lane leading to this picture-bo stone-and-thatch hamlet is guarded by 17 century Hidcote Manor, which is set beautiful formal gardens.*

Adjacent to Hidcote Bartrim are t gardens of Kiftsgate Court,* set in a co manding position overlooking a delight wooded valley. These gardens are not particularly for their magnificent displays rare rose bushes and shrubs.

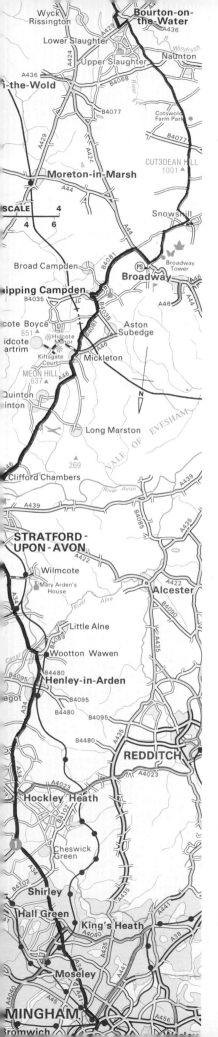

The route continues on the B4081, climbing steadily all the time and turning left on to the B4035 into Chipping Campden, the first true Cotswold village, dominated by the beautiful Perpendicular tower of its fine 'wool' church. One of the wealthy merchants who built it was William Grevel. He is remembered not only in the brass set into the chancel floor, but also in his fine house in the main street. It has a rare two-storeyed carved bay window of about 1380. Almost opposite is the old Woolstaplers' Hall,* now housing the tourist information office and a museum. The charming early 17th-century market hall further down the street now belongs to the National Trust. Turn left just past it (SP Stow-on-the-Wold), following the B4081 round to the right and out of the village.

CHIPPING CAMPDEN TO BOURTON-ON-THE-WATER

From Chipping Campden the B4081 climbs steadily, passing the quarries which provided the stone for its buildings. Turn right on to the A44 and in 1 mile, at a crossroads, turn left on to an unclassified road. This runs along the edge of the Cotswolds, giving magnificent views over the Vale of Evesham and passing Broadway Tower. Built in the 18th century, the tower houses an observation room and is set in a country park* which also has a countryside exhibition and a natural history centre. Bear right at each junction past the tower to reach the edge of Snowshill, where the main route turns left at the crossroads.

SNOWSHILL
Keep straight on at the crossroads for a detour into this beautiful village, hidden in a great combe and commanding wide views across the vale below. The Tudor manor house,* next to the pub at the foot of the steep slope on which the village lies, houses a unique collection of musical instruments, clocks, toys and Japanese armour.

From the crossroads mentioned above, follow the road for Stow and Bourton-on-the-Water, a narrow lane at first which soon becomes wider. The road rolls along the uplands, with enormous views to both sides. It reaches 1001 feet at Cutsdean Hill and 1 mile later crosses the B4077. After 1½ miles, on the right, is the entrance to the Cotswold Farm Park,* where visitors can see a fascinating working display of agriculture as our great-grandparents knew it. There are many rare breeds of farm animals no longer reared commercially, and traditional agricultural techniques can be seen in operation.

After 2½ miles the route crosses the B4068, then begins to drop, but there are still fine views over the Windrush valley to the right and the Eye valley to the left. At the foot of the hill turn left on to the A429 for ½ mile, then right into Bourton-on-the-Water. With its sprawling modern outskirts and industrial estate, Bourton lacks the unspoilt charm of many less popular Cotswold villages, but the centre is still attractive, and boasts a fine church with a domed Georgian tower.

Several breeds of hand-reared domestic goat are kept in Pets' Corner at the Cotswold Farm Park

BOURTON-ON-THE-WATER TO BURFORD

Follow signs through Bourton for The Rissingtons, The Barringtons and Burford, passing on the left the famous model village,* one-ninth the size of the real Bourton and faithful in almost every detail including little trees and running water. The River Windrush accompanies the route out of Bourton, then an unclassified road takes you through Little Rissington and climbs steeply to a crossroads where the route turns right (SP Great Rissington, The Barringtons).

The road passes Little Rissington airfield, then drops to rejoin the Windrush valley at Great Barrington, skirting Barrington Park. In Great Barrington turn left by the war memorial and continue through Taynton. Its quarries, no longer worked commercially, have in the past produced some of the most highly prized stone in the country. Many of Oxford's churches and colleges are built of Taynton stone, as is Blenheim Palace, and the village supplied Sir Christopher Wren not only with stone for the interior of St Paul's but also with a master mason.

Continue towards Burford, whose fine church spire shows the way. Turn right on to the A424 and right again on to the A361, crossing the ancient bridge to enter Burford's broad main street, lined with dignified buildings of fine stone. To the left at the foot of the hill is the large and beautiful church, where Cromwell imprisoned 400 rebels during the Civil War, relenting only after three of them had been shot. The present Lady Chapel was once completely separate from the church. Built as the Chapel of the Guild of Merchants of Burford, it was joined on to the main church in the 15th century.

BURFORD TO FARINGDON

Drive to the top of the hill, through the avenue of pollarded limes which shades the upper part of Burford's main street, and at the roundabout turn left on to the A40 (SP Witney, Oxford), then in ¼ mile turn right on to the B4020 (SP Faringdon). In 3 miles, at the roundabout on the outskirts of Carterton, take the third exit to continue along the B4020, following the same road (SP Faringdon) at the mini-roundabout 1 mile later. Just beyond Carterton is RAF Brize Norton, which often makes its presence felt by low-flying aircraft. Follow the B4020 through Alvescot, soon skirting Black Bourton.

BLACK BOURTON CHURCH

It is well worth making a short detour to the left here (SP Black Bourton), shortly turning left again, to visit Black Bourton's delightfully unspoilt church. The most notable feature of its exterior is the Norman doorway to the chancel, which has above it a tympanum decorated with a Maltese cross. Inside there are 13th-century wall paintings, one of them depicting, among other things, the coronation of the Virgin. The graceful north arcade is unaltered 12th-century work. There are several monuments to the Hungerford family, the best of which is a recumbent effigy of Eleanor Hungerford, dating from 1592.

The main route continues through [field], whose church, just off the road to [the] right, has an engaging statue of St Steph[en] in the tower above the south door. He h[olds a] book and a pile of stones, his emblems [as] preacher and martyr. The route keep[s] [west]ward in Clanfield to join the A4095 for [Rad]cot, approached through a landscape [of] meadowland divided by lines of poll[arded] willows. Radcot itself consists of little [more] than a large pub beside the Thames. O[ne of] the river's three channels is crossed [by a] bridge which has been here since at le[ast] early as 1387, when its central arch [was] broken during a battle between support[ers of] Richard II and his rebellious barons. [It is] probably the oldest bridge on the Tham[es.]

Continue on the A4095 to Faringdon [and] turn right at the T-junction for the [town] centre, passing the large parish church, w[hich] lost its spire during the Civil War. I[n the] centre of the market square, surround[ed by] an exceptionally attractive range of buil[dings] of many periods and styles, is the [17th-] century town hall. It stands on sturdy T[uscan] columns and is now the local library. B[ehind] the Georgian façade of the nearby C[rown] Hotel is a courtyard with some 14th-ce[ntury] details and a Jacobean staircase. In th[is] group of buildings is the Tudor Flower [Inn,] dated 1645, with part of its frontage [well] below street level.

Wantage was the birthplace of King Alfred, the gre[at] warrior-statesman who drove the Northmen from the [his] kingdom of Wessex. A statue of him stands in the at[tractive] market place

FARINGDON TO NEWBURY

From the market square follow the one-way system (SP All Traffic) to a mini-roundabout and take the first exit (SP Wantage, A417) to leave the town. Shortly, at the major T-junction, turn left on to the by-pass (SP Wantage), and in ½ mile turn right on to the A417 (SP Wantage, Stanford in the Vale). Ahead, views soon open up of the Vale of White Horse and the ridge of the Lambourn Downs. Continue across the Vale, passing through East Challow, where a handsome engineering works, dated 1840, stands to the left of the road. At the double junction in Wantage follow signs for the town centre, shortly branching right to enter the market square. A statue of King Alfred, who was born here in AD 849, looks over the square and the old buildings which cluster round it. The parish church, set in a peaceful and charming part of the town, can be glimpsed from one of the tiny streets leading off the square. The small museum* houses fascinating exhibits illustrating the prehistory of the area and mementoes of Wantage's more recent past.

To leave the town, follow signs for Newbury and the B4494, turning left into Ormond Road and shortly right. The road emerges into open downland country and climbs to cross the prehistoric Ridgeway, now a popular long-distance footpath. Beyond it attractive woodland – a delight at bluebell time – closes in around the road, and after 8 miles the route passes under the M4. Soon the route passes Snelsmore Common Country Park, a large expanse of birch-grown heath imaginatively set out with picnic and play areas. Continue to the outskirts of Donnington, where the B4494 turns right.

DONNINGTON CASTLE

Just beyond the Donnington Arms pub a detour can be made to Donnington Castle* by turning right and following the 'Ancient Monument' signs. Dramatically sited on a hilltop with commanding views, and guarding the main route from London to the West, the castle was always of great strategic importance since it was first built in the 11th century. Its splendid 14th-century gateway still stands intact. Around it can be seen the foundations of the rest of the walls, and the earthwork defences constructed during the Civil War when the castle was heroically defended by Royalist forces, who held out for 20 months before an honourable surrender.

From Donnington continue to a roundabout on the outskirts of Newbury and take the first exit (SP Basingstoke). (The second exit leads to the town centre, to which a detour can be made; see below.) At the next roundabout take the third exit to join the A34 (SP Winchester, Basingstoke), then follow signs for Basingstoke at subsequent roundabouts, climbing the hill on the south side of the town.

NEWBURY

The centre of Newbury has several handsome buildings, one of them – the Parish Church of St Nicholas – built by Newbury's most famous citizen, Jack O' Newbury, whose real name was John Smalwoode. He amassed a fortune from the wool trade, and entertained Henry VIII and Catherine of Aragon here. Not far from the church, a delicate-looking little bridge carries the main street over the Kennet and Avon Canal, which gives many of Newbury's back streets a pleasant waterside atmosphere. The restored Cloth Hall,* a fine example of Jacobean architecture, houses the town's museum.

NEWBURY TO SELBORNE

On the southern edge of Newbury, at the roundabout at the top of the hill, take the second exit, continuing on the A34 downhill to another roundabout where you take the first exit, the A339 (SP Basingstoke).

The route continues through pleasant woodland, soon passing RAF Greenham Common. Crossing the River Enborne to enter Hampshire, the road climbs to Headley and after 2½ miles winds its way through Kingsclere, whose attractive old buildings are grouped around a partly Norman church. As the route approaches Basingstoke, extensive views over the flatter lands of North Hampshire and Berkshire open up to the left, while to the right the chalk downs roll away into the distance. On the outskirts of Basingstoke join the ring road and follow signs all the way for the A339 Alton road, taking the second exit at each of the first three roundabouts and the third exit at the fourth. Keep forward at the fifth roundabout to pass under the M3 and emerge into wooded country. The landscape is well ordered, for much of the land belongs to two large parks, Hackwood and Herriard, both to the left of the road. Around Lasham, gliders may be seen circling above the fields, for the airfield here is one of the best-known gliding centres in the South. The route continues along an attractive wooded valley to the edge of Alton, where it turns right on to the B3006 (SP Liss). Pass under the railway bridge and at the mini-roundabout take the second exit, the B3006 (SP Liss, Selborne), which passes under the bridge carrying the A31 Winchester to Farnham road.

CHAWTON
Just past this bridge a detour can be made to Chawton by turning right. Opposite the Greyfriar Inn is the house where Jane Austen lived for the last eight years of her life and wrote *Mansfield Park, Emma* and *Persuasion*. The house now contains a museum.* In the Victorian church, down a lane to the left next to Elizabethan Chawton House, are the graves of the novelist's mother and sister. Her own is in Winchester Cathedral.

Right: A portrait of Jane Austen by her elder sister, Cassandra

Below: Chawton Cottage. The Austen family moved here from Southampton in 1809

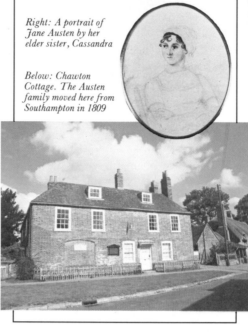

Appealing red-brick cottages line the main street at Kingsclere, a village set at the edge of the Hampshire Downs

A detail of the Gilbert White memorial window in Selborne church. It depicts St Francis feeding the recalling White's passionate interest in the area's w

Continue on the B3006 towards Selb passing through open downland and flo ing arable country. Several hop-fields to give the flavour of the south-east, and the road drops into the little hollow v shelters Selborne. Apart from being a de ful and beautifully situated village, Sell is famous as the home of Gilbert Whit was a clergyman who was born, and die Selborne in the 18th century and wro great detail about its wildlife in his now c book, *The Natural History and Antiquit Selborne*. His home was The Wakes,* n Gilbert White museum. From the ga there are fine views of Selborne Ha where White loved to walk among beeches. The footpaths among the dell hillocks and around the churchyard, wi massive yew, still delight visitors, an added pleasure is the excellent book which specializes in books on country lif natural history.

SELBORNE TO PETWORTH

Carry on along the B3006, skirting Emps and when you reach the A325, turn rig to it (SP Liss, Petersfield) and in 1½ miles left into Liss on the B3006. Cross the ra by the little station and follow the B3006 steep wooded valley. Cross the A3 by tu right and left (SP Rogate) on to an ur sified road which leads across the ple woodlands of Rogate Common. At th junction turn right (SP Midhurst) and fe the road down into Rogate, with sple views across the Rother valley toward South Downs. Country lanes are left be at Rogate, where you turn left, in the mi a cluster of whitewashed cottages gro around the church, on to the A272.

Trotton is the next village, and its ch should not be missed. The west wall is cov with an interesting and elaborate century mural, discovered in 1904, illu ing the seven deadly sins and the seven v of mercy. The church has two fine bra One is thought to be the oldest existing to a lady, dated 1310; the other is an unu ornate and well-preserved brass depicti knight and his wife.

Cross the Rother by the little medieval bridge, which still copes manfully with the demands of modern traffic, and drive on to Midhurst, passing roads to the left leading to the pleasant Rother valley villages of Chithurst and Woolbeding. Chithurst has an unrestored Norman church and a medieval manor, while Woolbeding has an elegant 17th-century hall.

Stop and explore Midhurst if you can: it is a charming country town, but hard to appreciate if you dash through in a car. The most attractive part lies off the main route, straight ahead as you enter the town, whereas the main route turns left (SP Petworth). Delightful buildings of all ages are dotted about the market place, and the street leading out of it slopes down past the 16th-century market house and the Spread Eagle Hotel to a pretty duckpond. Some of the little streets near the market place have overhanging houses of the 16th and 17th centuries, all adding up to a delightful townscape.

Leave Midhurst by the Petworth road, crossing the River Rother again to enter Easebourne, which is mentioned in Domesday Book while Midhurst is not. Its priory church still bears witness to its former importance, though it is heavily restored. The road bends sharply right and for a couple of miles runs right across Cowdray Park, famous for its polo ground – the Prince of Wales plays there. The road rolls on – still not far from the Rother – through Tillington, one of the estate villages of Petworth Park. The long stone wall of the park runs alongside the road all the way into Petworth. At the T-junction turn left (SP Billingshurst, A272) and follow the winding one-way system, past the gates of the house. Petworth House,* a National Trust property, was built in the 17th century but incorporates parts of a much earlier house. The state rooms contain many fine paintings. The largest room, richly decorated with intricate carvings in limewood by Grinling Gibbons, is outstanding. The west front of the house overlooks the huge landscaped park, where many acres of sheep-cropped turf, dotted with stately trees, surround a lake. This setting inspired some of Turner's most memorable landscape paintings.

To the right of the route is the town centre, a nest of quaint, winding streets leading from the market place. The one-way system brings the route past the church – an odd jumble of styles – to a junction where there is a curious Victorian lamp standard of stone and wrought iron. Turn left here and in ¼ mile right into North Street, at last leaving the great walls of Petworth Park and branching on to the A272 (SP Billingshurst), a road shaded by a mass of oaks and beeches.

The innovating landscape gardeners of the 18th century abandoned artificial, formal gardens in favour of a more natural look. Petworth Park, designed by Capability Brown, is among the finest examples of their work

PETWORTH TO COWFOLD
The A272 runs eastwards from Petworth through pleasant hilly country to Wisborough Green. The large tree-fringed green here is the perfect setting for a Sunday afternoon cricket match; a pub called the Cricketers' Arms completes the picture. Set on a hill above the little round pond is the interesting church. The west end is solid Norman work – so solid, in fact, that the 4½-foot-thick walls may be the remains of a castle that previously stood here. In the church's south wall is an attractive and unusual small lancet window made from fragments of glass found locally in recent years, the work of Huguenot glass-makers who were here in the 16th and 17th centuries.

The A272 leads to Billingshurst, crossing the River Arun at New Bridge. Turn left (SP Haywards Heath, A272) at the roundabout in Billingshurst, and for a few hundred yards follow the main street. Turn right with the A272 (SP Haywards Heath) by the church, which is perched on a hill in a quiet spot behind a row of cottages. Its 15th-century wagon roof has 126 intricately carved bosses.

Continue along the A272, which skirts the Wealden woodlands and runs through Coneyhurst Common, passing on the right the unusually named Blue Idol – not a pub, but a Friends' Meeting House where William Penn (1644–1718), the English religious leader who emigrated to found Pennsylvania, used to address Quaker meetings.

Ditchling Beacon, on the crest of the South Downs, offers some of the finest views in the South of England

The A272 crosses the A24 by turning right and left (SP Haywards Heath) and continues to Cowfold. Turn right by the Red Lion Inn. Opposite the pub stands the church, which is set in a picturesque, spacious churchyard surrounded by rows of old cottages of every shape and style. Unusually, they all face into the churchyard, almost giving it the appearance of a village green.

COWFOLD TO LEWES
Bear right at the next junction to Cowfold by the A281 (SP Henfield). A further on, hidden in the trees to the rig betrayed by its graceful slim spire, Hugh's Monastery. Two miles beyond i the River Adur and in ¾ mile turn left the B2116 (SP Albourne, Hurstpierp The tree-clad Wealden fringes begin t way to open country, and as you com Albourne the steep northern edge o South Downs is drawing near. Cross th by turning right and left (SP Hurstpier Hassocks, Lewes). At the junction is the grand King's Head Inn, complete with and pillars.

Drive along Hurstpierpoint's main then keep forward on the B2116 a crossroads to go through Hassock Keymer, both largely sprawling produ the railway age. Ditchling could not be different. It lies ½ mile further on, distanced by a short stretch of open co The village goes back to Saxon times mentioned in *Domesday Book*. The chu Early English, and some quaintly cr and bulging houses of the 16th centur enhance the streets.

SHIPLEY
Just over 1 mile past Coolham, turn right on to an unclassified road for a detour to the charming village of Shipley. Just past Butterstocks Farm turn left on to a little lane which goes down in a series of hills and bends to the village. To the right as you enter Shipley the sails of a windmill peep from behind the trees. This is King's Mill,* the last working smock-mill in Sussex. It still grinds corn once a year. Hilaire Belloc, the biographer, novelist and poet, perhaps most widely known for his *Cautionary Tales* for children, bought the mill in 1906 and lived in the house nearby until he died in 1953. The mill was restored in his memory after his death and now contains an exhibition of his life and work. It is still owned by his grandson.

Continue into the village. Shipley is a historic place; here the Knights Templars had a preceptory where knights were trained for the Crusades. The church, to the right, was built for them and features fine Norman work. From it there is a good view of the windmill, which is also depicted in one of the stained-glass windows. The composer John Ireland, who died in 1962, is buried in the churchyard, in a grave marked by fragments of prehistoric sarsen stones, recalling the love of antiquity which inspired much of his music.

Carry on through the village and turn left on to the B2224 (SP Southwater, Horsham), then in ½ mile turn right on to the A272 to rejoin the main route.

A plaque on King's Mill reads: 'Let this be a memorial to Hilaire Belloc, who garnered a harvest of wisdom and sympathy for young and old'

DITCHLING BEACON
For a spectacular detour to Ditchling Beac turn right at the crossroads in Ditchling then first left up the steep little road to Beacon. At 813 feet, this is one of the hig points of the South Downs. The views ar the sort usually seen only from an aeropla extending in every direction from the which is crossed by the South Downs W The hill was quite literally a beacon whe was the site of one of the chain of bonfires up across the country as a warning of approaching Spanish Armada in 1588.

The B2116 keeps forward in Ditchling for Westmeston, where it turns sharply left, coming closer and closer to the great northern wall of the Downs. Passing through Plumpton, the route hugs the edge of the Downs all the way to Lewes, turning right on to the A275 through Offham, and soon passing on the right the great white cliffs towering over a pub appropriately called the Chalk Pit. Many skeletons have been discovered in these quarries; they are thought to be of men killed in 1264 at the Battle of Lewes, when Henry III was defeated by Simon de Montfort. It is possible to by-pass Lewes by following signs for Eastbourne and the A27, but it would be a pity to miss this ancient and interesting town, traditionally the capital of Sussex, and now of East Sussex.

LEWES

Turn left off the A275 to make a detour to the town centre, better explored on foot because of its maze of steep, narrow one-way streets. Looking sternly down from the top of this hillside town is the keep of a Norman castle,* built by William de Warenne, with a barbican and gatehouse below. The castle overlooks the little round tower of St Michael's Church in the High Street, and almost opposite is the Bull House, dating from 1450 and the home for a while of Thomas Paine, author of *The Rights of Man*. Paine was an excise officer here in Lewes's heyday as a port. Further along the street is a 15th-century timbered house which has been most successfully turned into a bookshop. By its side, cobbled Keere Street leads down between old cottages to Southover, whose 16th-century Grange was once the home of the 17th-century diarist John Evelyn.

LEWES TO EASTBOURNE

From Lewes follow signs to join the A27 (SP Eastbourne). About 2 miles out of Lewes, shortly beyond a level crossing, turn right on to the B2109 (SP Newhaven). Here the River Ouse makes a wide corridor down to the sea; river, railway and two roads travel down it together. The busy docks of Newhaven are soon visible to the right; by-passing the town, the route turns left on to the A259 (SP Seaford). On the left, 1½ miles beyond this junction, the route passes a turning to Bishopstone, where there is a 1200-year-old church. There is little in the way of antiquities at Seaford; the road is lined by rows of seaside villas and flats.

The scenery from Lewes has been sober and flat, but suddenly a vast skyscape opens up as you climb out of Seaford before plunging down to cross the Cuckmere River. The huge meanders of the river's old course, now cut off from the main channel, are breathtaking in the sunshine when seen from the hilltops to either side. The South Downs here appear to be having a final fling before their dramatic plunge to the sea at Beachy Head: up again to Friston, with its duckpond and little church, and down to Eastdean, its flint cottages cosy in the valley. For a spectacular end to the journey, turn right 1½ miles beyond Eastdean on to the B2103 (SP Seafront, Beachy Head). The views are first to the right, across the downs to the sea, and then to the left, with the whole bay of Eastbourne and Pevensey stretching to the skyline, before the road winds its way down into the town to complete the journey. (For details and a town plan of Eastbourne, see p. 103.)

THE SOUTH DOWNS

RISING to 889 feet at Butser Hill, high above the A3 between Petersfield and Portsmouth, the 'blunt, bow-headed, whale-backed Downs' of Rudyard Kipling's poem 'Sussex' command exhilarating views over the English Channel and northwards across the Weald. The Downs start at St Catherine's Hill on the outskirts of Winchester and run roughly parallel to the coast for just over 70 miles. Downs and sea eventually meet at Beachy Head, where cliffs of gleaming white chalk dwarf the lofty lighthouse at their feet.

The hills are carved by rivers – Meon, Arun, Adur, Ouse and Cuckmere – whose tree-dappled valleys embrace short strings of attractive villages and small towns. Numerous roads cross the Downs, linking the seaside resorts to inland areas of Hampshire and Sussex, but the hills reveal their greatest riches to those who are prepared to leave the car and stretch their legs. There are countless opportunities for short strolls, and the South Downs Way attracts more serious hikers.

Intensive agriculture has brought man[y] changes to the South Downs since the [Second] World War. Slopes that were grazed [by] sheep for hundreds of years now produ[ce ...] and cereal crops. Landscapes like thos[e near] Alfriston (above and right) have a be[auty] and abstract symmetry that is enhance[d by] the clear light of high summer

WALKERS on the loneliest p[arts] of the South Downs relish what appears to be a timeless atmosph[ere,] but the landscape has been grad[ually] changing ever since the first settl[ers] arrived almost 6000 years ago. S[afer] and drier than the Wealden land [to] the north – then a vast forest roa[med] by ferocious beasts – the chalk hi[lls] provided a natural refuge for prehistoric farmers.

Neolithic and Bronze Age me[n] probably cleared many trees fro[m the] Downs – although there are still [over-] hanging beechwoods of great be[auty] – and cultivated the thin soil wit[h] primitive implements. Much lat[er] the Downs were roamed and cro[ssed] by vast flocks of sheep. The stock[y] Southdown, renowned for its me[at] and soft fleece, was first bred by [John] Ellman. A Wealden farmer's son[,] born at Hartfield in 1753, he wa[s] a small boy when his family mov[ed to] Glynde, near Lewes. One of the [great] men in the history of English far[ming,] Ellman died in 1832 and is burie[d in] Glynde churchyard.

The Long Man of Wilmington

BRONZE AGE burial mounds crown Bow Hill and Treyford Hill, but it was the Iron Age dwellers who gave the Downs their most outstanding prehistoric monuments. One such stronghold was Chanctonbury Ring, north of Worthing, where the ancient earthworks now surround a clump of beeches planted in 1760. Another magnificent Iron Age hill-fort is Cissbury Ring, near Worthing, where the defences enclose almost 80 acres dotted with Neolithic flint-mines.

Downland hill-forts can be dated with considerable accuracy, but the age of the Long Man of Wilmington has baffled experts for generations. Carved into the steep, north-facing slopes of the Downs between Lewes and Eastbourne, this mysterious figure is 226 feet high and clutches a slender staff in each hand.

BRICK, flint, chalk, timber and thatch combine to make the South Downs a fine area for those who appreciate traditional architecture. Many aspects of the area's architectural history can be seen at the fascinating Weald and Downland Open Air Museum at Singleton, near Goodwood, where buildings threatened with destruction elsewhere have been restored and preserved since 1967. The 40-acre site has farmhouses, barns, cattle-sheds, granaries, a charcoal-burners' camp and a great deal more.

Lovers of the quaint and whimsical should not miss Clayton, a village north of Brighton. Two 19th-century windmills, known as Jack and Jill, stand on a nearby hill, and trains on the London–Brighton line use a tunnel whose entrance resembles the lofty, twin-towered gatehouse of a castle. It was built in 1840 and ranks among the most delightful of England's many follies.

Above: A shepherd's crook is incorporated into the churchyard gate at Pyecombe Below: Bayleaf House is one of many superb buildings that have been reassembled at the Weald and Downland Museum

...e greatest changes followed hard ...e heels of the Second World ... Sheep still graze the downland ...but hundreds of acres are now ...by huge machines and treated ...chemical fertilizers to produce ...and lush grass suitable for hay ...ilage. Traditionalists regret such ...vations, but the long human ...ry of the South Downs is nothing ...evolutionary.

WILD FLOWERS thrive on the chalk soils of the Downs. Modern agricultural practices like spraying with weedkillers have meant that cornfields thick with poppies are virtually things of the past, but field edges and roadside verges still support an astonishing variety of plant life. Many other species, some rare, are found on the downland sheepwalks and unploughed slopes.

ROUTE 17   258 MILE

Manchester to Bournemouth

MANCHESTER's suburbs stretch across the River Bollin and into Cheshire, but this route breaks free of the commuter belt just beyond Wilmslow and begins to cross the verdant richness of the Cheshire Plain. During the Ice Ages an enormous sheet of ice covered the entire area. When it eventually retreated, great forests grew up over the Plain, later to supply the timber for the 'magpie' buildings which are such a distinctive feature of the Cheshire countryside.

The route continues past the dishes of Jodrell Bank radio telescope to reach the attractive old town of Sandbach. Avoiding Crewe, whose dull brick buildings are a sombre contrast to the traditional black-and-white of Cheshire, the route makes its way to Audlem, which has a remarkable flight of locks on the Shropshire Union Canal. Next come Market Drayton and Newport, which are also on the canal, and then the route passes through Shifnal and approaches the Severn Gorge and its rich legacy of industrial monuments.

The Coalbrookdale area has been called the Birthplace of the Industrial Revolution, perhaps something of an overstatement, but the discoveries made here certainly had a tremendous impact on the development of metal technology and manufacturing techniques.

In the early 18th century the Quaker ironmaster Abraham Darby purchased an old forge at Coalbrookdale and in 1709 succeeded in replacing charcoal with coke for the iron-smelting process. At first his revolutionary techniques were used to produce comparatively humble items like pots and pans; but his application, allied with Coalbrookdale's ideal situation near raw materials and water power, and with easy access via the Severn to the rest of the country, soon meant that the works were producing a wide range of items. Darby's son and grandson – both called Abraham – continued the pioneering work, and in 1777 Abraham Darby III designed and began to build the world's first iron bridge, which still spans the Severn.

All of the great industrial monuments in the area are now cared for by the Ironbridge Gorge Museum Trust, and include the original furnace where Abraham Darby I made his great breakthrough. The Blists Hill Open Air Museum covers 42 acres and not only displays exhibits and buildings related to the early ironworkings but also covers many other industrial innovations, including a restored canal, an exhibition of Telford's road-building techniques and an early printing shop.

The museums are all set in wooded scenery along the Severn – the gorge here is one of the most attractive reaches of the river – and the whole setting belies industry's reputation for dirt and noise. But at the height of Coalbrookdale's success the gorge was bright with furnace fires, loud with the sounds of hammers and machinery and crowded with workmen, pack animals and heavily laden barges.

From the Severn valley the route continues past Buildwas Abbey – a dramatic contrast with the cooling towers of the gigantic modern power station nearby – and makes its way along leafy lanes to Much Wenlock.

Next comes Wenlock Edge. At first the route follow: northern side of the Edge overlooking Ape Dale, but th crosses over to reach Ludlow along Corve Dale. The I Teme accompanies the route from Ludlow to Tenbury V and then a pleasant 'Leisure Drive' is followed to Brom through the orchards and hop-fields of Herefordshire.

Beyond Great Malvern the route runs beneath the rid the Malvern Hills, crowned by the 1394-foot Worcester Beacon to the west. Passing near Gloucestershire hamlets enchanting names like Snigs End and Nup End, the r continues through Gloucester and climbs into the Cotswo.

Beyond Malmesbury, limestone gives way to the ro chalklands of Wiltshire and the route follows the River / southwards, passing near the delightful village of Lacoc Melksham. Westbury and Warminster are situated on the of Salisbury Plain, beyond which, just inside Dorset, is th market town of Shaftesbury. The route reaches Bland Forum through a series of charming villages that overlooked by the Iron Age hill-forts of Hambledon Hill Hod Hill. Inside Hod Hill's ramparts can be traced the rem of hundreds of hut circles, as well as the outlines of a Roman built here after the future Emperor Vespasian captured the during the early phases of the Roman occupation.

Dramatic hill-forts are a Dorset speciality, and the another at Spetisbury, in which a mass grave containing skeletons was found in 1857. Badbury Rings, one of the famous hill-forts, lies to the east just beyond Spetisbury. T have grown inside its ramparts to make it a domi landmark. Bournemouth, with its golden sands, mild clir and tree-lined streets, marks the end of this route throu cross-section of England's natural, historic and industrial i

PLACES OF INTEREST: OPENING DETAILS

Jodrell Bank
JODRELL BANK RADIO TELESCOPES open Mar to Oct daily, Nov to Mar weekends (closed Christmas and New Year), pm only

Ironbridge Gorge
All places mentioned are part of the IRONBRIDGE GORGE MUSEUM TRUST and are open all yea

Buildwas
BUILDWAS ABBEY open all year

Much Wenlock
GUILDHALL open Apr to end Sep: Mon, Tue, Thu, Fri and Sat am and pm; Wed and Sun pm only

ST MILBURGA'S PRIORY open all year

Shipton
SHIPTON HALL open May to Sep Thu; also open Sun in Aug, and Spring and Summer Bank Holidays, pm only

Little Malvern
LITTLE MALVERN COURT open May to Sep Wed pm only

Cranham
PRINKNASH ABBEY: church open daily all year; pottery open Mon to Fri all day, Sat am, Sun pm

Lacock
LACOCK ABBEY open Apr, May and Oct Wed to Sun and Bank Holiday Mon; Jun to Sep daily, pm only

Shaftesbury
LOCAL HISTORY MUSEUM open Easter to end Sep: Mon to Sat all day, Sun pm only

Bournemouth
BRITISH TYPEWRITER MUSEUM open all year daily (except Sun)

RUSSELL-COTES ART GALLERY AND MUSEUM open all year daily (except Sun, Good Fri and 25-26 Dec)

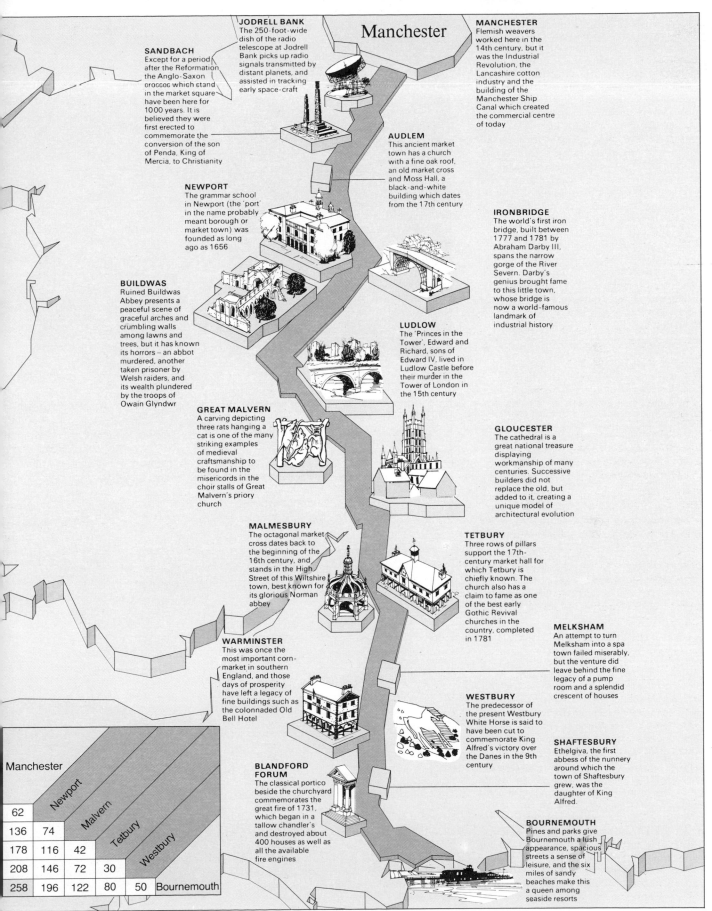

Manchester

JODRELL BANK
The 250-foot-wide dish of the radio telescope at Jodrell Bank picks up radio signals transmitted by distant planets, and assisted in tracking early space-craft

SANDBACH
Except for a period after the Reformation the Anglo-Saxon crosses which stand in the market square have been here for 1000 years. It is believed they were first erected to commemorate the conversion of the son of Penda, King of Mercia, to Christianity

MANCHESTER
Flemish weavers worked here in the 14th century, but it was the Industrial Revolution, the Lancashire cotton industry and the building of the Manchester Ship Canal which created the commercial centre of today

AUDLEM
This ancient market town has a church with a fine oak roof, an old market cross and Moss Hall, a black-and-white building which dates from the 17th century

NEWPORT
The grammar school in Newport (the 'port' in the name probably meant borough or market town) was founded as long ago as 1656

IRONBRIDGE
The world's first iron bridge, built between 1777 and 1781 by Abraham Darby III, spans the narrow gorge of the River Severn. Darby's genius brought fame to this little town, whose bridge is now a world-famous landmark of industrial history

BUILDWAS
Ruined Buildwas Abbey presents a peaceful scene of graceful arches and crumbling walls among lawns and trees, but it has known its horrors – an abbot murdered, another taken prisoner by Welsh raiders, and its wealth plundered by the troops of Owain Glyndwr

LUDLOW
The 'Princes in the Tower', Edward and Richard, sons of Edward IV, lived in Ludlow Castle before their murder in the Tower of London in the 15th century

GREAT MALVERN
A carving depicting three rats hanging a cat is one of the many striking examples of medieval craftsmanship to be found in the misericords in the choir stalls of Great Malvern's priory church

GLOUCESTER
The cathedral is a great national treasure displaying workmanship of many centuries. Successive builders did not replace the old, but added to it, creating a unique model of architectural evolution

MALMESBURY
The octagonal market cross dates back to the beginning of the 16th century, and stands in the High Street of this Wiltshire town, best known for its glorious Norman abbey

TETBURY
Three rows of pillars support the 17th-century market hall for which Tetbury is chiefly known. The church also has a claim to fame as one of the best early Gothic Revival churches in the country, completed in 1781

WARMINSTER
This was once the most important corn-market in southern England, and those days of prosperity have left a legacy of fine buildings such as the colonnaded Old Bell Hotel

MELKSHAM
An attempt to turn Melksham into a spa town failed miserably, but the venture did leave behind the fine legacy of a pump room and a splendid crescent of houses

WESTBURY
The predecessor of the present Westbury White Horse is said to have been cut to commemorate King Alfred's victory over the Danes in the 9th century

SHAFTESBURY
Ethelgiva, the first abbess of the nunnery around which the town of Shaftesbury grew, was the daughter of King Alfred.

BLANDFORD FORUM
The classical portico beside the churchyard commemorates the great fire of 1731, which began in a tallow chandler's and destroyed about 400 houses as well as all the available fire engines

BOURNEMOUTH
Pines and parks give Bournemouth a lush appearance, spacious streets a sense of leisure, and the six miles of sandy beaches make this a queen among seaside resorts

Manchester					
	Newport				
62		Malvern			
136	74		Tetbury		
178	116	42		Westbury	
208	146	72	30		
258	196	122	80	50	Bournemouth

MANCHESTER TO ALDERLEY EDGE

From the centre of Manchester (or from the ring road) first follow signs for Manchester Airport and the M6 (south), then join the A34 (SP Congleton). For the first 5 miles, as far as Cheadle, this road is a broad dual carriageway, bordered on either side by ribbons of pre-war suburban dwellings which stretch, almost unbroken, for another 5 miles into Wilmslow. Stay with the A34 to skirt Wilmslow, one of the string of Manchester 'dormitories' just across the Cheshire border. It retains little of the village character it once enjoyed and is, like its neighbour, Alderley Edge, very much a product of efficient road and rail access to Manchester.

As you leave Wilmslow, keeping forward with the A34 (SP Congleton) at the roundabout, the road begins to offer glimpses of the characteristic Cheshire countryside of small fields, hedges and trees. On the northern side of Alderley Edge, opposite a large garage, turn right on to the A535 (SP Chelford, Holmes Chapel).

Elaborate 'magpie' timbering is displayed on the 16th-century wing of Chorley Hall

ALDERLEY EDGE

By continuing along the A34 here you can make a detour to the Edge which gives Alderley a part of its name. For this detour, keep straight on along the High Street as far as St Hilary's School, and turn left on to the B5087 (SP Macclesfield). This road leads up a steep hill, lined with Victorian 'gothic' mansions in imposing grounds. After 1 mile it brings you to a short footpath on the left leading to the woods of the Edge, a dramatic sandstone bluff rising sheer out of the Cheshire Plain. The views are spectacular, and encompass almost the whole of the Plain, including the great gleaming disc of Jodrell Bank telescope. Many footpaths wind through the woods; one of them leads down from the Edge to the Wishing Well – simply a rough basin in the rock – which tradition associates with a wizard who once inhabited these woods. Some stories identify him with Merlin, and a local author, Alan Garner, has set two of his children's novels here: *The Weirdstone of Brisingamen* and *The Moon of Gomrath.*

ALDERLEY EDGE TO SANDBACH

A short distance from Alderley Edge along the A535 the main route passes Chorley Hall, set back on the left. It is a private house, but worth pausing for. The main hall is a stone-built, 14th-century moated house, with a small, square 16th-century timbered wing added on. The black-and-white decoration is typical of the Cheshire style. Indeed, the countryside along this part of the route gives the impression of having remained unchanged for centuries. Scattered with old farms and cottages, the landscape is flat but never boring, made up of varying tones of green, and supporting herds of black-and-white cows.

At Chelford roundabout take the second exit to continue along the A535 towards Holmes Chapel.

JODRELL BANK

About 2 miles beyond Chelford roundabout is a sharp left bend where a lane on the right offers a detour to Jodrell Bank.* This radio telescope, whose massive metal dish tracked the first satellites, is one of the technological wonders of the post-war decades and brings you with a jolt from contemplation of the rural past right into the space age.

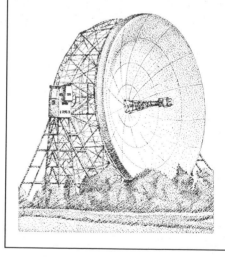

Carry on along the A535 into Holmes Chapel, where you should turn left on to the A50 (SP Kidsgrove), then in 2½ miles, at Brereton Green, turn right on to the A5022 (SP Sandbach, Crewe, Nantwich). After 1½ miles turn right at the T-junction on to the A534 and continue into Sandbach, crossing the M6. The A534 brings you into the centre of Sandbach and up to the traffic lights beside

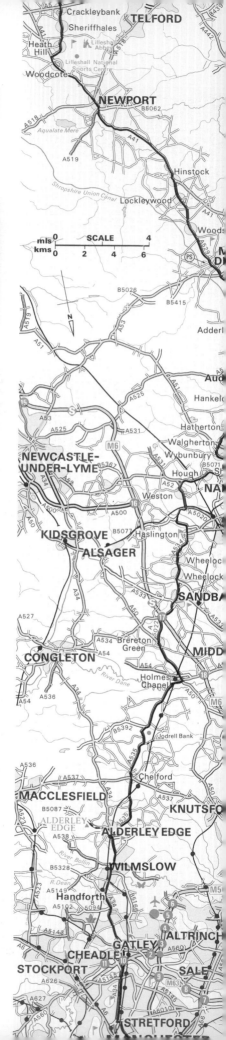

il of one of Sandbach's Saxon crosses. They were
ibled in 1816 after the pieces had been found
d throughout the town

wan Hotel, where you should bear right
Crewe, Nantwich) with the A534.
ndbach is a pleasant old market town
an arched, red-brick town hall and a
led market place. In it stand two
ately carved Saxon sandstone crosses,
1000 years old, the taller more than 15
igh. Their origin is unknown, but they
always been a pair and are unique in
hire. Also in the market square is the
ctive Black Bear pub, half-timbered
hatched.

BACH TO SHERIFFHALES
w signs for Nantwich to leave Sandbach
A534, passing through Wheelock and
lock Heath to reach Haslington. Just
he centre of this village, where the road
right, branch left on to an unclassified
(SP Alsager). Soon the route turns left
the B5077 and after 1 mile, on a sharp
and bend, keeps forward on to an
ssified road (SP Weston). The country-
here is so peaceful that it is hard to
nber that you are skirting Crewe with
mplex and busy railway junctions, and
he industrial conglomeration of Stoke-
ent is not far away. In 1 mile turn left to
e A5020, following it through Weston,
fter ¾ mile turn right on to the A52
ds Nantwich. At the edge of Shavington
left on to the B5071. Drive through
nbury, cross the A51 at Walgherton
ntinue through Hatherton to reach the
turning left on to it for Audlem.
approach to Audlem runs downhill
he church, built of dark red sandstone.
are traces of a medieval wall painting
ed during restoration work in 1885, and
17th-century benefaction boards, which

frame the north door. Turn right by the
church with the A529 (SP Market Drayton).
Beside the Bridge Inn is a pleasant stopping
place on the bank of the Shropshire Union
Canal, with a colourful prospect of narrow-
boats, a waterside pub and an attractive old
mill, now a craft shop. Nearby is a flight of 15
locks which lowers the canal by 100 feet as it
heads northwards on to the Cheshire Plain.
Branch left just past the Bridge Inn for
Market Drayton, continuing on the A529 and
crossing the border into Shropshire. The road
winds along between hedgerows, later crossing the A53 before passing through Market
Drayton, a pretty little market town with a
buttercross and several appealing black-and-
white buildings; the best one is now the
National Westminster Bank.

The route continues southwards on the
A529 through undulating country, with
views ahead now encompassing a distant bulk
of hills, notably the Wrekin, west of Telford.
At a T-junction 5 miles beyond Market
Drayton, turn left on to the A41 and drive
along it for 6 miles to Newport. The A41
forms the main street, and is lined with
handsome buildings; despite the traffic, it has
the air of belonging to a more leisurely age.
Yet here, although you would hardly know it,
you are approaching the Black Country, as
the signs for the vast 'new town' of Telford
remind you when you leave Newport, still on
the A41 (SP Wolverhampton). Continue past
the road to the Lilleshall National Sports
Centre on the right, and in 2 miles turn right
on to the B4379 Shifnal road.

Pleasure craft moor beside the converted mill on the Shropshire Union Canal at Audlem

SHERIFFHALES TO MUCH WENLOCK

Fringed with conifers, the route skirts Woodcote Park and passes through Sheriffhales, then crosses the A5 at a place quaintly named Crackleybank. Continue to Shifnal, where you should follow signs on to the A4169 (SP Bridgnorth). After 3 miles this road negotiates a series of roundabouts to the south of Telford new town. Keep forward on the A4169 at the first three roundabouts (taking the second, first and second exits respectively). At the fourth roundabout the main route takes the third exit to continue along the A4169.

BLISTS HILL AND COALPORT

At this roundabout a detour can be made down into the Severn Gorge; take the second exit on to an unclassified road (SP Coalport, Blists Hill). After 1 mile the detour passes the Blists Hill Open Air Museum.* Its buildings and machines illustrating the history of the Ironbridge area provide a fine introduction to this corner of Shropshire, which is itself a living museum of the Industrial Revolution.

At the foot of the hill you can turn left at the T-junction to extend the detour to Coalport, where the former works of the famous china company have been imaginatively turned into a museum.* Alternatively turn right on to the narrow road which runs along the deep, wooded gorge. After 1 mile keep forward on to the B4373 and ½ mile later join the A4169 and continue to Ironbridge to complete the detour.

The main route has followed the A4169 through two more roundabouts to descend into Ironbridge. Here the gorge is spanned by the world's first iron bridge, built by Abraham Darby III to advertise the quality of his ironworks at nearby Coalbrookdale. The bridge was completed in 1781. Half a mile past it, go forward on to the B4380 where the A4169 swings right.

COALBROOKDALE

At this point a second detour can be made, to Coalbrookdale, by continuing to the right on the A4169. This is the historic place where Abraham Darby, grandfather of the man who built the bridge, revolutionized iron-smelting in 1709 by using coke instead of charcoal as a fuel. Previously the industry had been confined to wooded areas such as the Weald of Sussex, and Darby's innovation enabled the industry to develop in many other places where coal was to be found, thus completely changing the face of Britain.

The Coalbrookdale Museum* has both outdoor and indoor exhibits tracing the history of the iron industry. Iron has been worked at Coalbrookdale for over 400 years. The monks of Wenlock Priory had a bloomery here in the 16th century, and Coalbrookdale still produces some cast-iron goods.

The peaceful ruins of Buildwas Abbey belie a turbulent past. In 1342 an abbot was murdered by renegade monks, and in 1350 another abbot was killed by Welsh marauders

The main route continues on the B4380, passing the huge Buildwas power station, on the south bank of the Severn. Shortly turn left on to the B4378, crossing the Severn and passing the ruins of 12th-century Buildwas Abbey* on the right. The road climbs steeply out of the gorge, between high banks crowned with trees whose branches at times meet overhead to form green tunnels. At the crest of the hill lies Much Wenlock, a well-preserved cluster of stone cottages encircling a fine Norman church and a half-timbered Tudor guildhall.* Behind the church are the impressive medieval ruins of St Milburga's Priory.* One of the walls of the chapter house displays a magnificent pattern of interlaced Norman arches.

Now a museum of iron, the former Great Warehouse in Coalbrookdale was built in 1838, at a time when the ironworks here was said to be the largest foundry in the world

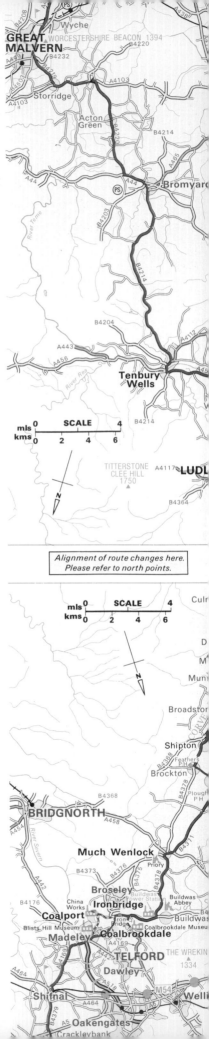

Alignment of route changes here. Please refer to north points.

CH WENLOCK TO TENBURY WELLS
e down Much Wenlock's main street,
osite the church, and at the end turn right
the A458 Shrewsbury road. After ¼ mile
left on to the B4371 for Church Stretton
ravel along the crest of Wenlock Edge.
r 5 miles, just past the Plough Inn, turn
nd rejoin the B4378 at the Feathers Inn,
ing right for Ludlow. Continue through
ton, which has a Norman church and an
abethan manor house, Shipton Hall,* in
lightful setting looking down Corve Dale.
t the junction shortly past Shipton Hall,
right (no sign) and continue to
dlebury (pronounced locally Delbury).
ut 1½ miles past the village, turn left on to
B4365 for Ludlow. Carry on through
nington, later crossing Ludlow race-
se – if a race is in progress motorists must
, as at a level crossing. On reaching the
turn left towards Ludlow. The A49 (SP
minster) by-passes the centre of Ludlow,
described as one of the best country
as in England. A detour to visit it can
ade by turning left in ½ mile on to the
51 (see p. 50). Otherwise follow signs for
minster along the by-pass. At Woofferton,
les beyond the second roundabout, turn
on to the A456 (SP Kidderminster),
wing the River Teme eastwards for 5
s to Tenbury Wells. Turn right here on to
A4112 (SP Leominster), crossing the
e and coming into the main street.
nbury Wells is a pretty little town, with
ctive timbered buildings. In 1839 saline
gs were discovered here, and an attempt

was made to establish Tenbury as a spa town,
though the baths are now long disused. The
church, reached by a right turn beside the
Royal Oak Hotel, contains an unusual
crusader's tomb. The figure is scarcely bigger
than a baby, and holds its heart in its hands.

TENBURY WELLS TO GREAT MALVERN
From Tenbury the route follows a signposted
'Leisure Drive' practically as far as Great
Malvern. As you leave Tenbury turn left, at
the point where the main road veers sharply
right, on to the B4214 (SP Bromyard) to
follow the Leisure Drive for 11 miles to
Bromyard. Turn left as you enter the town,
then almost immediately right (SP Worcester,
Stourport). At the end of the main street,
turn right for the A44 and at the bottom of
the hill turn left on to it (SP Worcester). In 1
mile turn right on to the B4220 (SP Malvern).
After several miles the route turns left on to
the A4103 (SP Worcester), and 2½ miles later,
at Storridge, turns right on to the B4219 to
continue into Great Malvern.

Turn left into North Malvern Road, then
at the T-junction turn right on to the A449,
which runs along the foot of the hills. Still
famous for its Malvern Water, the town was a
popular 19th-century spa. To the left of the
A449 is the town centre, dominated by the
massive Perpendicular tower of its priory
church. All that survives of the priory itself is
an arched Tudor gateway, at the top of
Church Street, but the fine church is ample
compensation for the lack of other remains. It
is particularly famous for its beautiful 15th-

*Victorian gothic architecture like the butcher's shop by the
priory gateway sprang up throughout Great Malvern after
the railway arrived in the mid 19th century*

century stained glass, especially impressive in
the huge east and west windows.

On the other side of the A449 is Bellevue
Terrace, where it is still possible to take the
waters at the Mount Pleasant Hotel. Beside it
a steep flight of steps leads to St Anne's Well
and up to the Worcestershire Beacon, the
highest point of the Malvern Hills.

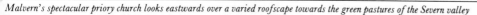

Malvern's spectacular priory church looks eastwards over a varied roofscape towards the green pastures of the Severn valley

GREAT MALVERN TO PAINSWICK

The route continues along the A449 to Malvern Wells. Here, shortly beyond the first turning to Welland, stands St Wulfstan's Roman Catholic church, where the composer Sir Edward Elgar and his wife are buried. Just past it turn left on to the A4104 (SP Upton upon Severn), passing on the right Little Malvern Priory and Little Malvern Court,* a house which incorporates some of the original priory buildings.

Follow the A4104 from Little Malvern to Welland, where the route turns right on to the B4208 (SP Gloucester). Cross the A438 and continue through Pendock to Staunton, where you turn right and immediately left on to the A417. Pass through Hartpury (where you can make a detour to Ashleworth; see p. 59), and continue through a landscape of low, wooded hills to Gloucester.

Approaching Gloucester, the A417 joins the A40. As you come into the city, follow signs for the city centre and the cathedral.

The cathedral dates from 1089 and is one of the most noble and awe-inspiring buildings in England. The tower was built around 1450 and, rising to 225 feet, gracefully dominates the city and the surrounding countryside. The east window is perhaps the single most remarkable feature. Bigger than any other in England, it measures 78 feet by 38 feet and is a memorial to local men who fought at Crécy in 1346 and in the siege of Calais a year later. Nearby is the tomb of King Edward II, who was cruelly murdered at Berkeley Castle in 1327. There is also a statue of Edward Jenner, the Gloucestershire doctor who pioneered vaccination against smallpox.

The 14th-century fan-vaulting in the cloisters at Gloucester Cathedral is the earliest of its kind known

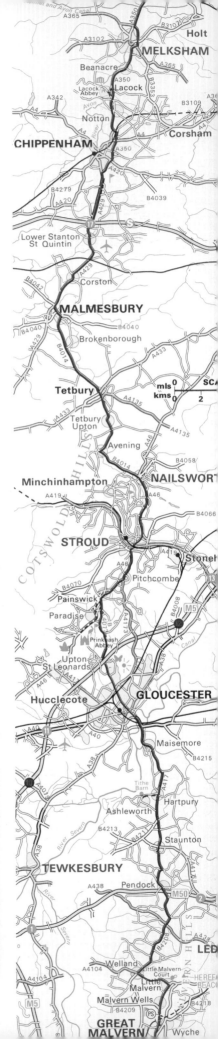

...e number of ornate tombs stand among the yew trees in the churchyard at Painswick. Many of them were carved ...cal family of masons during the 18th century

...ose by the cathedral, in College Court, is ...ouse immortalized by Beatrix Potter as ...ome of the Tailor of Gloucester in her ...ren's book of the same name. It is now a ...shop. (For Gloucester see also p. 59.)
...eep forward through the city, driving ...g Westgate, Eastgate and Barton Street ...in the B4073 for Painswick, keeping ...ard at the by-pass roundabout. The road ... passes under the M5 motorway, then ...bs steeply up the edge of the Cotswolds ...ugh fine beechwoods and descends into ...swick. The one-way system leads to a ...nction where the route turns right (SP ...d) into the main street, the A46.

...swick, Queen of the Cotswolds, is a glory ...lden stone, narrow streets and enviable ...es. Its churchyard contains 99 yew trees – ... is a tradition that the hundredth one ...never grow – and innumerable lavishly ...rated table tombs, some of them exuber-...monuments to 18th-century merchants.

...SWICK TO MALMESBURY

...A46 runs past the church and on down ...valley to Stroud, a busy little town ...ing to a hillside above the River Frome. ... right (SP Bath) at the roundabout at ...ot of the hill to by-pass the town centre, ...g the second exit at the roundabout ...e later. The A46 runs alongside the River

Frome, passing several old mill buildings. At Nailsworth turn left just before the church on to the B4014 and continue to the quiet hillside village of Avening.

On the far side of Avening the B4014 turns sharp right for Tetbury, whose graceful church spire can soon be seen ahead. Keep forward at the first crossroads in Tetbury to join the A433. Tetbury is the last Cotswold town on this route, and a place of great elegance. At its centre is the 17th-century market house, supported by 18 plump stone pillars and topped by a bell-tower. (For Tetbury see also p. 230.)

At the crossroads in the town centre bear left on to the B4014 Malmesbury road, following it round to the right to leave the town. Four miles beyond Tetbury the road bears right and 1 mile later turns left to enter Malmesbury, a prosperous centre of weaving in the heyday of the wool trade. It is now celebrated for the ruins of its abbey, of which only a magnificent fragment remains. If you follow signs for the town centre you will come right to the abbey doorway, with its elaborate and beautiful Romanesque carving, one of the finest survivals of Norman sculpture in Britain. Many of the figures are badly damaged, but enough remains to show the quality of these elongated figures and the meticulously carved drapery of their robes. The abbey was founded in the 7th century, but was twice burned down, and the present buildings date from the 12th century. A dubious tradition of an early attempt at aviation is connected with the building: a Saxon monk named Egelmer is said to have made a flying machine and launched himself from the top of the abbey tower. He failed.

The abbey is undoubtedly the finest sight in Malmesbury, but the whole town is extraordinarily pleasing and has many buildings dating from the 18th century or earlier.

MALMESBURY TO MELKSHAM

Keep forward (one-way) past the fine 16th-century octagonal market cross, then turn right (SP Chippenham) and shortly left. As you leave the town, turn right at the roundabout on to the A429 for Chippenham. Here a striking change takes place from the steeply wooded slopes of the Cotswolds to the rolling expanses of the Wiltshire countryside.

Chippenham, whose name derives from the Saxon word 'cheaping', a market, was a centre for the wool trade and also had one of the most important cheese-markets in the West of England, but there is little evidence now of either of these functions. On the outskirts of the town turn right on to the A350 (SP Warminster) to by-pass the centre. In 1 mile turn right then left to cross the A420, and in 1½ miles cross the A4. After ½ mile the A350 turns left under a railway bridge, then turns right to follow the Avon valley.

Continue along the A350 to Melksham, a pleasant stone-built town on the River Avon. Once a centre for the wool trade and, briefly, a spa, the town has now mostly been taken over by modern industries.

MELKSHAM TO WARMINSTER

The A350 skirts the centre of Melksham, and the route continues along it towards Warminster, taking the third exit at the roundabout on the southern outskirts of Melksham. The route crosses the Kennet and Avon Canal at Semington Bridge, the point where the canal begins its mammoth climb to Devizes by means of 29 locks. Keep forward to cross the A361 shortly past Semington, and at Yarnbrook crossroads turn left with the A350 for Westbury. On the approach to the town you cannot fail to notice, high on the hills ahead and to the left, the famous white horse carved in the chalk.

Follow the A350 (SP Warminster) through Westbury, a pleasant little country town of mainly 18th-century buildings, including some attractive old cloth mills. The church, which has a central tower, contains the fine tomb of the First Earl of Marlborough as well as a rare chained New Testament. Skirting the western edge of Salisbury Plain, the A350 runs on to Warminster, the fourth and last of the old Wiltshire market towns on this route. This one, overlooking the Wylye valley, was more concerned with grain than with wool, and was one of the most important wheat markets in the area. To the west of the town, off the A362 Frome road, is Longleat, Wiltshire's most famous stately home (see p. 71).

WARMINSTER TO BLANDFORD FORUM

From Warminster the A350 (SP Blandford Forum) follows the River Wylye as far as Longbridge Deverill before climbing on to the chalk downs, later turning right and then left to cross the A303. Soon it descends sharply into the pretty village of East Knoyle. On the little green here is a memorial to Sir Christopher Wren, who was born at East Knoyle in 1632. His father was rector here from 1623 until he lost his living in the Civil War. The chancel of the church still has the elaborate plasterwork, representing biblical scenes, which was planned by Dr Wren and used as evidence against him at his trial by the Commonwealth authorities in 1647.

The A350 continues southwards from East Knoyle, running for a while through flatter country before climbing to cross the border into Dorset and reaching the hilltop town of Shaftesbury. The A350 by-passes the town centre (SP Blandford).

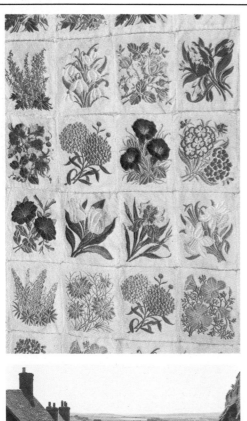

SHAFTESBURY

Shaftesbury is well worth a visit, and you can make a detour into the centre by keeping forward at the first roundabout. Set in a commanding position on a 700-foot-high spur overlooking Blackmoor Vale to the west, Shaftesbury was created a burgh by King Alfred and grew to become one of the chief towns of Wessex, with a castle, 12 churches and four market crosses, all now gone. To the west of the old market place once stood a great Benedictine abbey for women, founded by King Alfred in the 9th century. Only excavated ruins remain of what was once one of the richest and most important nunneries in England. It survived until the 16th century. A Saxon queen, Elgiva, was buried in the abbey; so was her grandson Edward, who was canonized as a saint. King Canute died here in 1035, but was buried at Winchester. After the Dissolution, the abbey gradually fell into ruins and by the 19th century, when the site was first excavated, the remains lay buried under five feet of earth. From the abbey gardens there are splendid views over the green plain below.

Another noteworthy feature of the town is the Local History Museum,* where there is an unusual display of buttons, the making of which was the principal industry here and at Blandford Forum. The museum is situated at the top of Gold Hill, a picturesque and much-photographed old cobbled street which curves steeply down the hillside.

Above: Embroidered motifs, at one time given away with cigarettes, were the forerunners of the later cigarette card. These examples have been made into a colourful wall-hanging, one of the exhibits in Shaftesbury's Local History Museum

Below: Gold Hill runs steeply down towards Blackmoor Vale past an array of charming old cottages

eave Shaftesbury by the A350 and follow
ns for Blandford through a string of
rming Dorset villages whose names –
mpton Abbas, Fontmell Magna, Sutton
ldron, Iwerne Minster – conjure up idyllic
ures of thatch and whitewash, country
s and village cricket. Reality is not so far
oved from the ideal, for this is in fact a
nquil, almost unspoilt stretch of English
ntryside. To the left of the road the rolling
sslands of Cranborne Chase stretch into
distance. Scattered with beechwoods
ical of chalk downland, the Chase covers
r 100 square miles. It was once a royal
ating-ground. The road sweeps in a huge
d round the grounds of Stepleton House,
sing on the left 622-foot-high Hambledon
l and then Hod Hill, crowned by the
ains of a 54-acre Iron Age hill-fort and a
man camp. Beyond Stourpaine the A350
s the Stour valley, following it through a
in the downs to the market town of
ndford Forum.

Blandford, the Shottesford Forum of
omas Hardy's Wessex novels, was almost
npletely destroyed in 1731 by a fire that
ted in a tallow chandler's shop and raged
ough the town centre. Architecturally, the
come was a happy one because the centre
replanned by two local architects, John
William Bastard, and most of this elegant
h-century rebuilding survives, including a
classical church. By it stands a small
tico commemorating the fact that the
n was raised 'like the Phoenix from its
es, to its present beautiful and flourishing
e'. The church overlooks the market
ce, with its bustling stalls and unpreten-
s shops. All around stand handsome
mples of Georgian architecture such as the
n hall, dated 1734, the Red Lion Inn and
Old Bank House, on a hill overlooking
churchyard.

NDFORD FORUM
BOURNEMOUTH
m Blandford, follow the A350 (SP Poole)
ng the Stour valley, passing through the
g village of Charlton Marshall, whose
inally Perpendicular church was
orginized' by the Bastard brothers of
ndford. Past the next village of Spetisbury,
ill across the valley to the north-east is
wned by Badbury Rings, one of the great
-forts of Wessex and the meeting point of
ral Roman roads.

he A350 skirts the village of Sturminster
rshall, then keeps forward at the rounda-
t to cross the A31. After 3½ miles, at the
t roundabout, take the first exit to join the
(SP Poole, Bournemouth). In ½ mile keep
ward on to the A3049, then in 3¾ miles, at
mini-roundabout, keep forward on to the
8. After 1 mile, at the next roundabout,
e the third exit to rejoin the A3049, and
follow signs to the town centre to
plete the journey.

BOURNEMOUTH
Until the middle of the last century Bournemouth was nothing more than a seaside village at the mouth of the River Bourne. But in the second half of the 19th century its growth was rapid, due to its south-facing position, warm climate and easy rail access from London. The famous golden sands extend for a good six miles and are sheltered by steep cliffs. There are lifts for those who cannot face the walk up and down. Other amenities that have contributed to Bournemouth's popularity range from two piers and a pavilion to a theatre, a famous symphony orchestra, and no less than five museums, including the world's only typewriter museum.* The Russell-Cotes Art Gallery and Museum* has a famous Oriental collection as well as a selection of works by local artists.

Right: Enhanced by a Regency-style façade and a glass tunnel-vaulted roof, the Arcade was built in the 1870s, and runs between Old Christchurch Road and Gervis Place

Below: Safe sea-bathing, golden sands and plenty of amenities for the holidaymaker make Bournemouth one of the most popular resorts on the south coast

ROUTE 18

187 MILE

Manchester to Cardiff

MODERN roads have revolutionized travel to such an extent that what used to be wearisome, day-long treks in heavy traffic can now be completed between breakfast and lunch. The journey from Manchester to Cardiff is a good example; it need take little more than three hours if you use the M6, M5 and M50, then follow the dual carriageway A40 and A449 down to Newport and the M4. This is a notably fast and efficient route – ideal for heavy lorries and clock-watching businessmen – but this alternative is infinitely more rewarding for the motorist who has time to enjoy the countryside. It uses good but remarkably quiet roads, visits many delightful places and takes in a broad range of splendid scenery.

The 'escape' from Manchester's sprawling conurbation is quick and easy. Shoulder-to-shoulder buildings are left behind once the route has left Bowden and crossed the River Bollin. At Tatton Park, 1000 acres of parkland surround one of England's finest stately homes; beyond the park's boundaries stretch the green dairy pastures of the Cheshire Plain.

To the south-west of Northwich, whose local salt-mining industry has created large meres or 'flashes' where the ground has subsided into the worked-out mines, is Delamere Forest. Now a fragment of its former size, it supplied much of the timber used in Cheshire's famous black-and-white buildings.

Rich, red farmland, drained by little rivers like the Roden at Wem, continues up to and beyond Shrewsbury, whose heart lies in a great loop of the River Severn. Outside Shrewsbury the route joins the Rea Brook for a while and passes through the villages of Minsterley and Pontesbury before climbing to nearly 1000 feet at the top of the wooded Hope valley. Away to the east are the distinctive rocky summits of the Stiperstones.

The route continues through the delightful border towns of Bishop's Castle and Clun before entering Knighton. Offa's Dyke, built in the late 8th century, runs through the centre of the town. It stretches for over 150 miles – with breaks where natural demarcations occurred – from the Bristol Channel near Chepstow up to the Dee Estuary.

English and Welsh names have become intertwined in the border country, as is demonstrated by three of the rivers on this part of the route. Knighton stands on the River Teme, the Lugg flows through Whitton, and Kington is watered by the Arrow. These all sound very English, but in fact they are derived from Welsh names: Tefeidiad, Llugwy and Arwy.

As the route enters Kington, Bradnor Hill – protected by the National Trust and crossed by Offa's Dyke – rises to the left, and Hergest Ridge stands on the right. At Willersley the route turns sharply westward and follows the looping Wye upstream through Hay-on-Wye to Glasbury. Below Talgarth the route enters the Brecon Beacons National Park and follows the Rhiangoll valley down towards the Usk.

At Tretower the Rhiangoll brook joins the Usk, and river and route sweep round to picturesque Crickhowell. From the little town's lovely 13-arched bridge there are views across the rooftops to aptly named Table Mountain.

North of Abergavenny is another distinctive hill, the 1⬚ foot Sugar Loaf. It looks just like a volcano – which it once ⬚ As the route follows the peaceful waters of the Monmouth ⬚ Brecon Canal from Abergavenny to Pontypool, the he⬚ slopes of 1833-foot Blorenge rise to the west.

Pontypool is situated on the edge of industrial South W⬚ and has been the site of ironworkings since possibly as earl⬚ Roman times. Newport stands at the mouth of the Usk ⬚ Ebbw rivers, and from here the route runs parallel with Se⬚ Mouth along Glamorgan's flat coastal plain to Cardiff.

Now the capital of Wales, Cardiff was a quiet seaside t⬚ until the great iron and coal boom of the 18th and ⬚ centuries. The Industrial Revolution took South Wales ⬚ storm – Cardiff became one of the world's busiest ports and ⬚ valleys to the north (regarded during the 18th century as s⬚ of the most picturesque beauty spots in Britain) ⬚ transformed by factories, coal-mines, spoil-heaps and end⬚ rows of workers' cottages. Though much natural beauty ⬚ lost, a surprising amount remains and a very special kin⬚ community emerged – exemplified by the Welsh choirs. Ca⬚ itself is a city of great character and dignity. It shares with ⬚ valleys a resilience and spirit that makes the singing at ⬚ famous rugby matches both heart-warming and stirring.

PLACES OF INTEREST: OPENING DETAILS

Tatton
TATTON PARK grounds open all year; house open Apr to Oct daily, also Mar and mid Oct to mid Nov Sun and Bank Holidays, pm only. All closed Mon except Aug and Bank Holidays

Beeston
BEESTON CASTLE open all year Mon to Fri

Cholmondeley
CHOLMONDELEY CASTLE GARDENS open Apr to Oct Sun and Bank Holidays, pm only

Shrewsbury
SHREWSBURY CASTLE open Easter to Oct daily, Oct to Easter Mon to Sat

BEAR STEPS open all year Mon to Sat

ROWLEY'S HOUSE open all year daily (except Sun and Bank Holidays)

CLIVE HOUSE open all year daily (except Sun and Bank Holidays)

Clun
CLUN TOWN TRUST MUSEUM open Easter to Nov, Tue and Sat, pm only

Kington
HERGEST CROFT open Easter, then May to mid Oct

Clifford
CLIFFORD CASTLE open at reasonable times on application at house by castle entrance

Tretower
TRETOWER COURT AND CASTLE open all year

Abergavenny
ABERGAVENNY CASTLE open all year

ABERGAVENNY MUSEUM open all year Mon to Sat; also Sun pm Mar to Oct

Newport
MUSEUM AND ART GALLERY open all year daily (except Sun and Bank Holidays)

TREDEGAR HOUSE grounds open all year; house and farm open Apr to end Sep Wed to Sun and Bank Holidays, pm only

Cardiff
CASTLE open all year for conducted tours

NATIONAL MUSEUM OF WALES open all year (except 24-26 Dec, 1 Jan, Good Fri and May Day): Mon to Sat all day, Sun pm only

WELSH INDUSTRIAL AND MARITIME MUSEUM open all year (except 24-26 Dec, 1 Jan, Good Fri and May Day): Mon to Sat all day, Sun pm only

WELSH FOLK MUSEUM, ST FAGANS, open all year (except 24-26 Dec, 1 Jan and May Day): Mon to Sat all day, Sun pm only

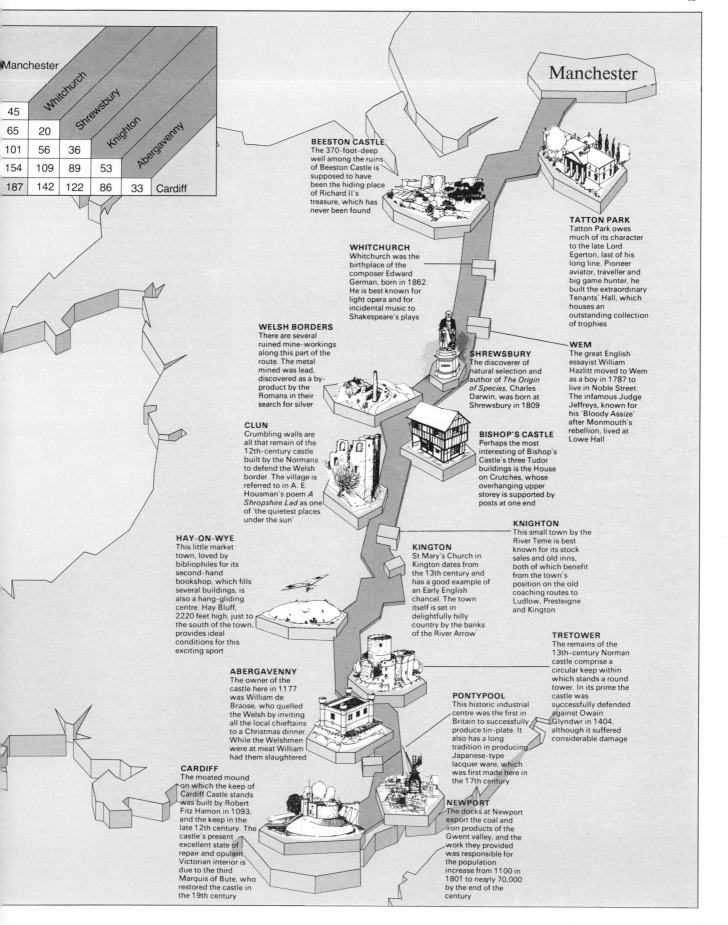

	Manchester				
45	Whitchurch				
65	20	Shrewsbury			
101	56	36	Knighton		
154	109	89	53	Abergavenny	
187	142	122	86	33	Cardiff

Manchester

BEESTON CASTLE
The 370-foot-deep well among the ruins of Beeston Castle is supposed to have been the hiding place of Richard II's treasure, which has never been found

TATTON PARK
Tatton Park owes much of its character to the late Lord Egerton, last of his long line. Pioneer aviator, traveller and big game hunter, he built the extraordinary Tenants' Hall, which houses an outstanding collection of trophies

WHITCHURCH
Whitchurch was the birthplace of the composer Edward German, born in 1862. He is best known for light opera and for incidental music to Shakespeare's plays

WELSH BORDERS
There are several ruined mine-workings along this part of the route. The metal mined was lead, discovered as a by-product by the Romans in their search for silver

SHREWSBURY
The discoverer of natural selection and author of *The Origin of Species*, Charles Darwin, was born at Shrewsbury in 1809

WEM
The great English essayist William Hazlitt moved to Wem as a boy in 1787 to live in Noble Street. The infamous Judge Jeffreys, known for his 'Bloody Assize' after Monmouth's rebellion, lived at Lowe Hall

CLUN
Crumbling walls are all that remain of the 12th-century castle built by the Normans to defend the Welsh border. The village is referred to in A. E. Housman's poem *A Shropshire Lad* as one of 'the quietest places under the sun'

BISHOP'S CASTLE
Perhaps the most interesting of Bishop's Castle's three Tudor buildings is the House on Crutches, whose overhanging upper storey is supported by posts at one end

KNIGHTON
This small town by the River Teme is best known for its stock sales and old inns, both of which benefit from the town's position on the old coaching routes to Ludlow, Presteigne and Kington

HAY-ON-WYE
This little market town, loved by bibliophiles for its second-hand bookshop, which fills several buildings, is also a hang-gliding centre. Hay Bluff, 2220 feet high, just to the south of the town, provides ideal conditions for this exciting sport

KINGTON
St Mary's Church in Kington dates from the 13th century and has a good example of an Early English chancel. The town itself is set in delightfully hilly country by the banks of the River Arrow

TRETOWER
The remains of the 13th-century Norman castle comprise a circular keep within which stands a round tower. In its prime the castle was successfully defended against Owain Glyndwr in 1404, although it suffered considerable damage

ABERGAVENNY
The owner of the castle here in 1177 was William de Braose, who quelled the Welsh by inviting all the local chieftains to a Christmas dinner. While the Welshmen were at meat William had them slaughtered

PONTYPOOL
This historic industrial centre was the first in Britain to successfully produce tin-plate. It also has a long tradition in producing Japanese-type lacquer ware, which was first made here in the 17th century

CARDIFF
The moated mound on which the keep of Cardiff Castle stands was built by Robert Fitz Hamon in 1093, and the keep in the late 12th century. The castle's present excellent state of repair and opulent Victorian interior is due to the third Marquis of Bute, who restored the castle in the 19th century

NEWPORT
The docks at Newport export the coal and iron products of the Gwent valley, and the work they provided was responsible for the population increase from 1100 in 1801 to nearly 70,000 by the end of the century

MANCHESTER TO NORTHWICH

Leave central Manchester on the A56 (SP Chester). The floodlights of Manchester United's football ground are landmarks on the right, while off to the left is the Old Trafford cricket ground, where England's Jim Laker made sporting history in 1956. Playing against Australia, he became the only bowler to take 19 wickets in one test match.

Immediately after going under an elevated section of the M63, the route crosses the River Mersey by an iron-railed bridge built along-side a considerably older one of stone. The river joins the Manchester Ship Canal a few miles downstream, at Irlam. Completed in 1894, the canal is navigable by vessels of up to 15,000 tons and links Manchester with the sea, 36 miles away.

Victorian and Edwardian houses, set back between high hedges and wooded gardens, line the road as it skirts Sale and Altrincham. Once small towns quite separate from Manchester, they evolved into commuter suburbs after the railway opened in 1849. Leaving Manchester's suburbs behind, the route drops gently down on to the Cheshire Plain beyond Bowdon. At the roundabout junction with the M56 keep straight ahead, taking the A556 towards Chester.

TATTON PARK

Two miles later, at Bucklow Hill, a detour can be made by turning left at the traffic lights on to the A5034 (SP Knutsford). The road leads to Tatton Park,* where 1000 acres of park-land and 50 acres of ornamental gardens surround one of England's finest stately homes, dating from the end of the 18th century. It contains a great wealth of period furniture, paintings and silver, and the Tenants' Hall Museum houses a collection of vintage cars.

On leaving the entrance to Tatton Park, turn left on to the A5034 and in $\frac{1}{4}$ mile turn right to join the A50 (SP Warrington). In $\frac{3}{4}$ mile, at Mere traffic lights, turn left to rejoin the A556 and the main route.

Continue towards Northwich, crossing M6 just west of Knutsford. A dual carri way by-pass sweeps the A556 ro Northwich, a bustling industrial town w huge underground deposits of salt are use ICI to make many chemical products.

NORTHWICH TO TILSTOCK

At the traffic lights just beyond Sandi turn left on to the A49 (SP Whitchurch long stretch of straight road runs betv Plover's Moss and Abbots Moss, expanses of wooded, lake-dappled land w form part of the Delamere Forest. I straight on across the A54, and in 1½ mile Cotebrook, turn left beyond the Alva Arms on to the B5152. The road pa through Eaton, a small village where tim framed cottages with thatched roofs leaded windows cluster round a sands smithy. A mile beyond Eaton bear following the B5152, then 1 mile later a traffic lights go straight on to rejoin the A

Views of the wooded Peckforton Hi part of Cheshire's sandstone 'spine' – de nate the horizon as the road drops dow cross the Shropshire Union Canal, a pop waterway bright with boats in the hol months. The lock on the left of the brid

The Shropshire Union Canal near Beeston. This stretch is part of the oldest section of the canal, constructed in the late 18th century and running from Chester to Nantwich

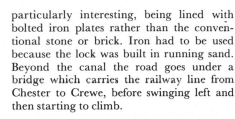

particularly interesting, being lined with bolted iron plates rather than the conventional stone or brick. Iron had to be used because the lock was built in running sand. Beyond the canal the road goes under a bridge which carries the railway line from Chester to Crewe, before swinging left and then starting to climb.

BEESTON CASTLE

It is well worth making a brief detour to the right where a sign points the way along unclassified roads to Beeston Castle.* This ruined fortress, built by a 13th-century earl of Chester, perches on the brink of a precipice facing towards Wales. A wall studded with towers guards the approach from the east. Richard II's treasure, lost during the 14th century, is said to be hidden down the well, which is more than 350 feet deep. Views from the castle embrace a dramatic sweep of North Wales and north-west England. The hill immediately to the south is dominated by Peckforton Castle; it looks like another full-blooded Norman stronghold, but was actually built for the Tollemache family in Victorian times.

The route follows the A49 southwards through rich farmland, typical of the Cheshire Plain, and after 4 miles passes on the right the entrance to Cholmondeley Castle Gardens.* The 19th-century castle, seat of the Marquess of Cholmondeley, remains private, but its 500-acre deer park, complete with lakeside picnic areas, is sometimes open to visitors. There is an ancient chapel in the park, and the farm has a collection of rare breeds of farm animals.

Just over 3 miles later the road crosses the Llangollen arm of the Shropshire Union Canal before climbing gently into Whitchurch. The town dates from Roman times and is dominated by the tower of St Alkmund's Church, which was built after its predecessor collapsed in 1711. Beneath the porch is buried the embalmed heart of John Talbot, the first Earl of Shrewsbury, 'who for 24 years fought his Country's battles against the French'. The doughty old warrior was 80 when he died fighting near Bordeaux in 1453. His tomb is inside the church.

Leave Whitchurch by the A41 (SP Shrewsbury), but turn right on the outskirts of the town to join the B5476 (SP Wem). The road runs towards Wem through flat farming country dotted with trees. On the left, 2 miles beyond Tilstock, is one of Shropshire's few surviving windmills. It has been converted into a private house and no longer has sails.

Beeston Castle was dismantled in 1646 after it had served as a Royalist stronghold during the Civil War

Thomas Telford at the end of the [...] century, and is now used for meetings [...] local council and other civic func[...] Nearby stands St Mary's Church, [...] around 1200 and crowned with a ma[...] spire. Fish Street's buildings include the [...] century Bear Steps* cottages, rescued [...] dereliction in the 1960s. Among the t[...] museums are Rowley's House,* notable [...] collection of Roman remains, and [...] House,* where a collection of china, s[...] costumes and militaria may be viewed. [...] House was the home of the first Lord [...] when he was mayor of Shrewsbury in [...] The town's most famous son, Ch[...] Darwin, is commemorated by a statu[...] posite the entrance to the castle.

SHREWSBURY TO KNIGHTON

Leave the town centre on the Welshpool [...] and cross the Severn by the Welsh Bridg[...] the roundabout beyond the bridge tak[...] first exit and then keep left at the [...] junction, joining the A488 (SP Bis[...] Castle). Cross the A5 at a roundabout. [...] road ahead leads into the lonely hi[...] southern Shropshire and the Welsh bo[...] passing through Pontesbury and Minst[...] where there is a most attractive little ch[...] before climbing the wooded Hope v[...]

Minsterley's unusual red-brick church dates from the late 17th century, a period in which very few churches were built. Above its west doorway is a frieze decorated with skulls, bones and an hour-glass

Roadside patches of pale-grey spoil, toge[...] with a few small ruins, are all that remai[...] what was once a prosperous lead-mi[...] industry. The workings date from Ro[...] times and were at their busiest in the mi[...] of the 19th century.

The statue of Clive of India in The Square at Shrewsbury is overlooked by the Old Plough, one of the town's many examples of elaborate half-timbered architecture

TILSTOCK TO SHREWSBURY

Wem, 6 miles beyond Tilstock, was devastated by fire in 1667, but the church's 14th-century tower still stands as a reminder of the little town's medieval history. An attractive house in Noble Street, opposite the Shrewsbury and Wem brewery, was the boyhood home of William Hazlitt, a famous 18th-century essayist and critic whose works included *Characters of Shakespeare's Plays*. His father was a local minister.

A more notorious inhabitant of Wem was Judge Jeffreys, who lived at 17th-century Lowe Hall. The judge gained eternal infamy following the 'Bloody Assize' of 1685, at which he tried the untrained troops of the Duke of Monmouth after their unsuccessful rebellion against James II. Over 300 people were executed as a result of the assize and

800 more were deported to the American colonies. Following the trial Jeffreys was made Lord Chancellor.

At the T-junction in the town centre turn right, then turn left by the church. In ½ mile pass under a railway bridge and turn right, continuing along the B5476 for 4 miles, then join the A528 (SP Shrewsbury). The ancient county town of Shropshire, Shrewsbury grew up on a steep hill almost islanded by a loop of the meandering Severn. It is a delightful place where picturesque black-and-white buildings line narrow streets rejoicing in such names as Dogpole, Mardol, Shoplatch, Grope Lane, Wyle Cop and Gullet Passage. The castle,* set on a sandstone bluff above the splendid Victorian railway station, was built by Roger de Montgomery shortly after the Norman Conquest. It was restored by

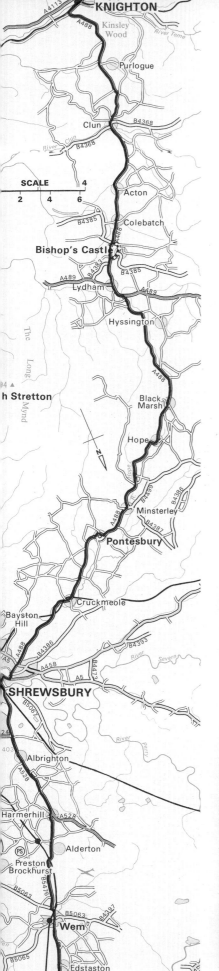

BISHOP'S CASTLE

The little town of Bishop's Castle, just off the A488 to the right, is well worth a brief detour. As a plaque on the town hall recalls, it was the smallest borough in England until local government was reorganized in 1967. As its name implies, it did once have a castle, dating from the 12th century, and a few remains of it can still be seen. In the town is an overhanging timbered building supported by posts. It was built in 1573 and is known as the 'House on Crutches'. Today many visitors to Bishop's Castle make for the Three Tuns, in Salop Street, where the landlord still makes his own beer in a Victorian brewhouse.

The A488 beyond this sleepy little township runs through wooded hills to Clun, another border community with more than its fair share of character. The gaunt ruins of a Norman castle stand on a grassy hillock as a reminder that the Welsh sacked Clun four times between 1195 and 1400. It is now, in A. E. Housman's words, one of the 'quietest places under the sun'.

The A488 passes the old town hall – once the court house to Clun Castle and now a museum* – then swings sharp right (SP Knighton) and crosses a narrow medieval bridge over the River Clun. It then climbs steeply past the church – notable for its massive Norman tower – and reaches almost 1200 feet on the way to Knighton. Before reaching the little valley town you pass Kinsley Wood, where the initials ER – Elizabeth Regina – are picked out in trees which contrast with their neighbours. They were planted in 1953 to commemorate the Queen's coronation.

The route has rarely strayed more than ten miles from the Welsh border since Beeston. Now it enters Wales for the first time, crossing the River Teme as the A488 runs into Knighton. The town stands on Offa's Dyke, the great ditch-and-rampart earthwork built by King Offa of Mercia in the 8th century AD to mark the boundary between his domain and Wales. Over the centuries a host of bloodthirsty stories has grown up around the Dyke; it is said that at certain periods during the Middle Ages any Welshman found on the wrong side of the Dyke risked having his hands cut off, or even death on the spot. In 1971 the Offa's Dyke long-distance footpath was officially opened at a ceremony in Knighton by Lord Hunt, leader of the first expedition to climb Everest. (For Knighton see also p. 141.) (Route continues on p. 196.)

Built in 1872, Knighton's handsome clock-tower watches over one of the most attractive townscapes in mid Wales. The little border town is well known for its livestock sales

SHROPSHIRE HILLS

THE Shropshire Hills have a tranquillity that belies a turbulent past. They witnessed great battles between local tribesmen and the Romans, and were later defended by King Offa of Mercia, whose 8th-century dyke is a remarkable tribute to the Saxons. The hills remained a battle-ground for Welsh and English until Owain Glyndwr's revolt lost momentum early in the 15th century. Ruined castles at Clun, Ludlow and elsewhere are poignant reminders of such troubled times.

Set between the River Severn and the Welsh border, the hills are spread out like the fingers of a giant hand. Quarry-scarred Titterstone Clee reaches 1750 feet above the Ludlow–Kidderminster road and looks northwards to Brown Clee, the highest point in Shropshire at 1772 feet. Corve Dale and Ape Dale flank the long limestone ridge of Wenlock Edge, while Caer Caradoc, the Lawley and others loom above the enchanting village of Cardington.

To the west, beyond Church Stretton, the heather-clad bulk of the Long Mynd reaches 1694 feet and has steep slopes from which graceful gliders are launched. Linley Hill, the eerie Stiperstones and tree-topped Corndon Hill are major landmarks close to the border defined by Henry VIII's officials in 1536.

One notable hill rises beyond the Severn, high above the new town of Telford. Known as the Wrekin, it is a great whale-back of volcanic rock, thickly wooded, which rises steeply to 1334 feet and is a welcome landmark for Shropshire people heading home through the Midlands.

THE mingling of Saxon, Celtic and Norman cultures has endowed the Shropshire Hills with a wealth of myths and legends. Some are not hard to believe when dark clouds brood over the peaks and the air grows heavy with the threat of thunder.

For instance, great storms are said to erupt if any mortal dares sit on the Devil's Chair, a tumbled mass of rock on the crest of the Stiperstones, a dozen miles south-west of Shrewsbury. Wild Edric, a Saxon earl who married a fairy princess and defied the Norman invaders, is believed to haunt the western hills. Mounted on a great white charger, he rides forth in warning when England's safety is threatened. One of the stones in the stone circle at Mitchell's Fold, on Stapeley Hill to the west of the Stiperstones, is said to be a witch who was turned to stone after she had milked dry a fairy cow that had previously supplied all the locals with milk during a famine.

Why is the Wrekin set apart from the rest of the hills? Geologists have their own theories, but folklore maintains that it was created by a giant who dumped a vast load of earth he was carrying to dam the Severn and drown Shrewsbury. He had been tricked by a quick-witted cobbler who told him the town was still many miles away. The Ercall, a small hill adjoining the Wrekin, was formed when the weary giant scraped mud from his boots before trudging home to Wales.

Right: Craggy outcrops of rock crown the Stiperstones

Below: The Wrekin

THE writings of Mary Webb and A. E. Housman have become as much a part of western Shropshire as the hills themselves.

Mary Webb was born at the foot of the Wrekin in 1881. Her first novel, *The Golden Arrow*, was inspired by a legend about a golden arrow said to have been dropped by a fairy on nearby Pontesford Hill. Other works were *Precious Bane* and *Gone to Earth*. Mary Webb died in 1927 and is buried at Meole Brace, on the outskirts of Shrewsbury.

A. E. Housman (1859–1936) was not born in the county, but he sang the praises of its hills in the 'Shropshire Lad' poems. They include such verses as:
On Wenlock Edge the wood's in trouble;
His forest fleece the Wrekin heaves;
The gale, it plies the saplings double,
And thick on Severn snow the leaves.
Housman's ashes rest beneath the lofty tower of Ludlow church.

IN return for keeping the Welsh at bay, Norman barons such as the Mortimers and Roger de Montgomery – founder of Shrewsbury Castle and of the delightful little town that still bears his name – were granted wide-ranging powers by William the Conqueror and his successors. Some became kings in all but name. They had private armies and drew up their own laws to govern what became known as the Welsh Marches. Helias de Say, Baron of Clun, actually declared independence in the 12th century and removed his 'buffer state' from English jurisdiction. Indeed, the king's writ did not run anywhere in the Marcher lands.

Many motte-and-bailey castles were built along the Welsh border immediately after the Norman Conquest. The ruined castle at Clun (above) is an impressive example of a motte-and-bailey which was later crowned by a stone keep

Most of the border towns and villages changed hands many times in the Middle Ages. Clun's history is typical. The Welsh burned the tiny township four times between 1195 and 1400, and it was also put to the torch by King John of England in 1216. Such events doubtless explain why many Marcher communities still have a strong sense of independence. Many people regard themselves as more 'border' than English or Welsh.

It was no coincidence that in 1644, during the Civil War, Clun and Bishop's Castle became part of the 'Clubmen' movement. They declared themselves to be for neither King nor Parliament, but 'to stand upon their own guard for the preservation of their lives and fortunes'.

[AC]TON SCOTT Working Farm [Muse]um, 4 miles south-east of [Chur]ch Stretton, provides a [delig]htful insight into life on a [Shro]pshire upland farm at the turn of [the c]entury. The museum uses the [buildi]ngs of the Home Farm of the [Acto]n Scott Estate, which supplied [food f]or Acton Scott Hall until 1950. [The f]armyard layout dates from 1769 [and m]ost of the buildings have been [erect]ed in the intervening years. [Lo]nghorn cattle graze in the [mead]ows and Shire horses are still [used] to pull ploughs and carts. Hens [and T]amworth pigs are kept in the [farmy]ard, and Shropshire sheep [wand]er at will in the park. As well as [anim]als the museum has displays of [agric]ultural equipment, and there are [frequ]ent demonstrations of butter-[and c]heese-making in the dairy.

[...]in the farmyard at Acton Scott [Work]ing Farm Museum

From the Wye valley near Hay-on-Wye the long ridge of the Black Mountains dominates the southern skyline

KNIGHTON TO HAY-ON-WYE

Leave Knighton on the A4113 (SP Bromfield), and in just over ¼ mile turn right on to the B4355 (SP Presteigne). The road climbs steadily for 2 miles to a junction where the route turns right on to the B4357 for Kington, and crosses Offa's Dyke. The ancient earthwork, crested with trees, is clearly visible on the right before the B4357 drops down to the hamlet of Whitton. Views ahead are dominated by the wooded slopes of Radnor Forest, a wild massif which reaches 2166 feet and is carved by steep, deep valleys. Keep straight on at the crossroads in Whitton and cross the River Lugg a few hundred yards later.

Follow the B4357 through Evenjobb and at Walton turn left on to the A44 for Kington. This road takes the route back into England and to Kington, another of the border country's enchanting little market towns, where timber-framed buildings rub shoulders with neighbours of grey-green stone. Their rooftops are overlooked by St Mary's Church, which dates from the early 13th century and, like many other border churches, was once used as a place of refuge. The tower walls are six feet thick and the door could be secured by sliding a massive bar into place. A lane near the church leads to Hergest Croft,* a large house whose gardens contain a fine collection of exotic trees and shrubs.

Follow the A44 round to the right in the centre of Kington, crossing the River Arrow and then turning right on to the A4111 (SP Hereford). As the road runs south towards Eardisley there are memorable views over the Wye valley to the Black Mountains and the distant Brecon Beacons. Eardisley itself is a very attractive little village whose single street is lined with many black-and-white buildings which nestle beneath roofs of mossy stone slabs. Just over a mile beyond Eardisley turn right on to the A438 (SP Brecon). The road follows the meandering Wye upstream to Whitney. Turn left ¾ mile past the Boat Inn on to the B4350, crossing the river by the old toll-bridge. The road runs through Clifford, where the remains of an 11th-century castle* stand on a cliff above the Wye, and continues to Hay-on-Wye.

This captivating little town stands on the edge of the Brecon Beacons National Park. It nestles beneath majestically steep hills – the northern outposts of the Black Mountains – which reach 2220 feet at Hay Bluff and rise to 2660 feet on the windswept summit of Waun Fach. Hay is a tight-knit maze of narrow streets hemmed in by buildings which span the centuries from black-and-white Tudor to dignified Victorian and Edwardian. Above them stands the castle, which has been in ruins since Owain Glyndwr's army ravaged Hay at the start of the 15th century. Since 1963 this old market town has become the home of the world's largest second-hand book business. It has spread into several buildings, including the former fire station and cinema.

HAY-ON-WYE TO CRICKHOWELL

Leave Hay on the B4350 for Brecon, keeping forward to join the A438 at the edge of Glasbury. Two miles later, turn left on to the A4078 (SP Talgarth) and continue to Talgarth, with the Brecon Beacons ri impressively to 2906 feet in the south-wes

Talgarth, now nothing more than a pe ful village, used to have eight cattle fa year and was important in the Middle A because it was strategically sited as routes from Brecon and Crickhowell. Ho Harris, one of the 'fathers' of Methodis Wales, is buried in the churchyard. The s a prosperous farmer, he was born at nearby village of Trefecca in 1714.

In the centre of Talgarth turn left on t A479 (SP Crickhowell, Abergavenny). route became a turnpike road in the 18 when it was built to link the Wye and valleys. It climbs to almost 1000 feet, wit highest peaks of the Black Mountains to left and the bracken-clad slopes of Myr Troed, 1997 feet high, rising steeply on right. The road then sweeps down Tretower. This tiny village, overlooke the limestone-capped summit of Pen Ce calch, is notable for two of the finest an monuments in the Brecon Beacons Nati Park – Tretower Court* and its neighbo ruined castle* known as Picard's Tower. original castle was built by a follower Bernard Newmarch, Lord of Brecon, sh after the Norman Conquest. A shell keep added around 1150, and substantial rem of it still partially enclose the tall round to built in the 13th century after the castle been wrested back from the Welsh. It fe off an assault by Glyndwr's army in 1403 was badly damaged in the fighting. Near Tretower Court, one of the finest fort manor houses in Wales, dating from the century. It was for many generations

Tretower Castle's circular keep was built in about 12

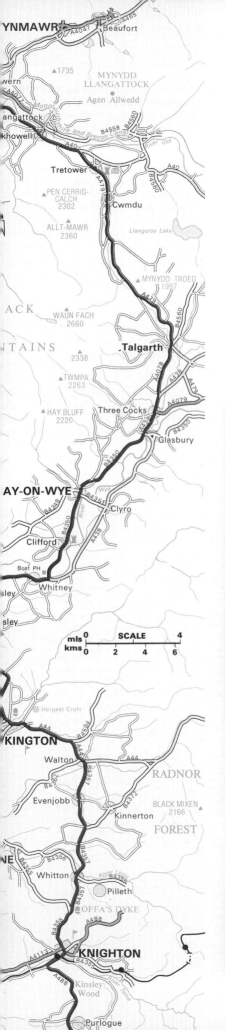

home of the Vaughan family, whose most famous member was Henry Vaughan, the 17th-century mystical poet.

One mile beyond Tretower, turn left on to the A40 (SP Abergavenny) and follow it to Crickhowell. The white-painted Manor Hotel is a landmark up the slope on the left, just before Crickhowell is reached. It was originally a private house, known as Gwernvale, where Sir George Everest lived. Sir George, born in 1790, became surveyor-general of India and gave his name to the world's highest mountain. He is buried in Crickhowell churchyard. A board on the White Hart, on the outskirts of Crickhowell, lists the tolls once paid by travellers to the Duke of Beaufort. They include 'For every score of cattle 10d' and 'For every cart drawn by one or two horses 3d'.

Crickhowell's attractive blend of Georgian and Victorian architecture reflects the years when this was an important resting-place on the road between London and West Wales. Stage-coaches carried travellers to and from the Irish ferries, and there is still a 'Post Horses' sign above the archway leading to what were once the stables of the Bear Hotel. Carts also rumbled along the turnpike, carrying farm produce to the booming industrial towns of South Wales. Crickhowell grew up around a Norman castle that was captured by the Welsh in 1172, changed hands again and was finally destroyed by Glyndwr's soldiers in 1403. Fragments of the castle, together with the large, grassy mound on which the keep stood, are features of the small park beside the A40. Much of Crickhowell's charm is derived from its setting. The little town looks southwards across the Usk valley to the limestone crags of Mynydd Llangattock, which rise to 1735 feet and are riddled with some of the most extensive cave systems in Britain. One cave, known as Agen Allwedd, has more then nine miles of passages.

Bright green pastures and thickly wooded slopes surround the road along the Usk valley from Tretower to Crickhowell

CRICKHOWELL TO NEWPORT

In Crickhowell, keep forward on the A40, following it down the Usk valley to Abergavenny, a bustling market town poised between the wild heart of rural Wales and the thickly populated valleys of the industrial south. It was known to the Romans as *Gobannium* and, like so many other border towns, was later fortified by the land-hungry Normans. Their castle,* in common with its counterpart in Crickhowell, fell to the Welsh in 1172. It was regained by William de Braose, who invited the local chieftains to a banquet in 1177, then had them slaughtered while they feasted. The castle was later captured by Llewelyn the Great, damaged in the Glyndwr uprising and finally 'slighted' by Parliamentary troops in 1645, during the Civil War. Ruined towers and other remains overlook the Usk immediately south of the town centre. In the castle grounds is a fascinating museum* complete with such imaginative exhibits as a traditional Welsh kitchen and a saddler's shop. The most unexpected item is a beer mat autographed by Rudolph Hess, Hitler's deputy, who made a flight to Scotland in 1941 and spent three years in a military hospital at Abergavenny.

The town centre has several interesting old buildings, the most notable being St Mary's Church. It originally formed part of a priory, founded in the 11th century, and its collection of medieval tombs is among the finest in Wales. It includes a rare wooden effigy, believed to depict George de Cantelupe, a young knight who died in 1273.

Signs for Newport take the route through Abergavenny and out on to the A4042, which is joined at a roundabout just outside the town. It runs southwards with rolling, wooded countryside to the left and steeper slopes marking the Brecon Beacons National Park's eastern boundary on the right. Also to the right is the Monmouthshire and Brecon Canal, which runs parallel with the route all the way to Pontypool. This town began its rise to industrial prominence during the 16th century when Richard Hanbury established what later became one of the world's most efficient ironworks. Pontypool was among the first places in Britain to produce tin-plate, and also became famous for the manufacture of japanware – metal goods covered with black lacquer and then decorated. Pontypool Park includes the town's rugby ground. The club's three front-row forwards – Graham Price, Bobby Windsor and Charlie Faulkener – played together for Wales on many occasions in the late 1970s and became a part of contemporary Welsh folklore.

At the roundabout on the outskir Pontypool, take the first exit and follov A4042 southwards towards Newport, ski the new town of Cwmbran. When you r the outskirts of Newport, several miles fu on, you can take either the A48 (via New town centre) or the M4 to Cardiff.

Newport is a product of the Indu Revolution – which changed the face of S Wales in the 18th century – althougl remains of a Norman castle are a remi that a town has stood at the mouth of the for many hundreds of years. Older s Caerleon, just north-east of the town. was the Roman legionary fortress of *Silurum*, occupied from about AD 75 t 400. Newport's museum and art gal illustrates much of the area's history includes Roman remains as well as exar of japanware from Pontypool. One secti the museum is devoted to the Chartist n ment – a militant forerunner of the t unions in South Wales.

Down by the docks is Newport's fa transporter bridge. Cables slung from a walk high above the muddy waters su a platform which glides along carrying and pedestrians. The 645-foot-long sp supported by two huge towers. Ships the docks through a large sea lock.

The Usk estuary at Newport is spanned by a transporter bridge, opened in 1906 and one of only two left in Britain

NEWPORT TO CARDIFF

On the town's western outskirts is Tredegar House,* dating from the 16th and 17th centuries and now the centre of a 58-acre country park beside the A48. Both the A48 and the M4 between Newport and Cardiff offer extensive views southwards over the 'Holland of Wales' to the chocolate-coloured waters of the Bristol Channel; in clear weather, the distant hills of Somerset can also be seen. The coastal plain, as flat as a billiard-table, is drained by a network of channels and sluices. Water flows into the Bristol Channel through a series of top-hinged doors, set in the sea wall, which close themselves as the tide rises. The wall itself is 24 miles long and runs from Cardiff towards the Severn Bridge.

Cardiff has been the official capital of Wales since 1955. Its history goes back to Roman times, and the moated castle* retains its Roman walls and a fine Norman keep, but the future capital was little more than a village until docks were built by the Marquis of Bute in the late 1830s. In the next 60 years the population increased from under 2000 to more than 160,000 and Cardiff became the world's greatest coal-exporting port. The city centre is remarkable for magnificent municipal buildings of white stone set among lawns, gardens and broad, tree-lined streets. Cardiff is the home of the National Museum of Wales* and the Welsh Industrial and Maritime Museum.* The Welsh Folk Museum,* in nearby St Fagans, occupies the grounds of a mansion and features a fascinating collection of buildings from all over the principality. They include farmhouses, a woollen mill, a tannery, a tollhouse, a quarryman's cottage and a chapel.

Cardiff is at its most lively and colourful when the Welsh rugby team is playing on the famous ground between Westgate Street and the River Taff. Singing fills the air and the streets are thronged with fans carrying giant leeks, daffodils and white-and-green banners emblazoned with the red dragon of Wales.

The ceiling of the 19th-century Arab room at Cardiff Castle is a riot of colour and pattern

Cardiff's City Hall was built in 1905 and forms part of a splendid complex of public buildings in Cathays Park

ROUTE 19   168 MILE

Buxton to Bath

THE waters of both Buxton and Bath were known to the Romans for their medicinal properties, but their fortunes over the centuries have been very different, the moorland town of Buxton never attaining the popularity enjoyed by Bath with its kinder climate and sheltered setting. The dukes of Devonshire took Bath as their model when trying to develop Buxton, but the town's fortunes declined throughout the 19th century. Now, however, great plans are under way for its rejuvenation; its hotels have been refurbished as conference centres, and a festival has recently been established in which the Pavilion and the elegant Opera House will play leading roles.

From Buxton the route leads across the western part of the Peak District National Park, passing Axe Edge, the summit of a moorland dome that is the source of many rivers, including the beautiful Dove. Across the county border, in Staffordshire, are Ramshaw Rocks and the Roaches, stupendous outcrops of millstone grit that have cracked and weathered into extraordinary shapes. Many of the houses in the area have walls of the same dark material, and isolated moorland farmhouses with low-pitched roofs of sandstone slabs are a distinctive feature of north Staffordshire.

Beyond Leek, a charming old town with vivid reminders of the textile industry, the route passes close to the Potteries and the 'Five Towns' immortalized by Arnold Bennett. The five towns are Tunstall, Burslem, Hanley, Stoke and Longton; however, tucked between Stoke and Longton is Fenton, certainly one of the group but usually forgotten – so the 'Five Towns' are really six.

The Potteries are situated on a geological mix of iron, coal, limestone and several sorts of clay, a bounty that has been appreciated since at least as early as Roman times. Pots have been made in the area ever since, but it was not until the 18th century, with new techniques and the introduction of sophisticated clay mixtures and glazes, that the industry really took off. The names of the great firms – Wedgwood, Spode and Minton – have become world-famous, and in the Wedgwood Museum at Barlaston there are thousands of examples of this beautiful and exacting craft.

Despite the proximity of the 'Five Towns' and the coming of the canals and railways, much of Staffordshire's countryside would still be familiar to Izaak Walton. This famous 17th-century angler was born in Stafford, and, as a boy, learned his craft in the streams and rivers of his home county. The cottage to which he retired (now a museum) lies a little way off the main route between Stone and Eccleshall. The quiet fields of Staffordshire merge imperceptibly with those of Shropshire just before Newport, and the route then travels through Shifnal to follow the Severn down to Bridgnorth, an ancient town that owes much of its character to the gorge carved by the river.

Winding through the thickly wooded country to the west of the Severn, the route reaches Bewdley. Once a flourishing inland port, it was by-passed by the Industrial Revolution, and its streets of Georgian houses – superimposed on a medieval

town plan – have been beautifully preserved. The Sever followed down to Stourport-on-Severn, a purpose-built ca town which retains many of the buildings, basins and l constructed by the engineer James Brindley in the late 1 century. Next comes Worcester, home of the famous sauce of the Royal Worcester China Company, whose hands 18th-century factory stands quite close to the great cathed

Still following the Severn, the route continues to U upon Severn. To the west, across the meadows of the Va Gloucester, rises the awesome bulk of the Malvern H Crossing the river at Haw Bridge, the route takes a little through water meadows before joining a major road to Gloucester. Immediately beyond Gloucester the route cli the steep west-facing escarpment of the Cotswolds and tra through many stone-built villages and towns whose s streets and solid houses have changed little over the centu Pitchcombe, Stroud, Nailsworth, Wotton-under-E Chipping Sodbury – the names alone suggest the charact this sheltered countryside of twisting lanes and hidden vall

Beyond Chipping Sodbury are two outstanding sta homes. The first is Dodington House, a Palladian man completed by James Wyatt in 1813 and surrounded by acres of parkland laid out by Capability Brown. The secor Dyrham Park, a lovely 17th-century house built partly of stone and partly of Cotswold stone. After climbing along edge of Charmy Down, crowned by Solsbury Hill, the r drops down to Bath, whose elegant squares, crescents terraces are unsurpassed showpieces of Georgian architect

---

PLACES OF INTEREST: OPENING DETAILS

Leek
BRINDLEY MILL open Apr to end Oct Sat, Sun and Bank Holiday Mon, pm only

Cheddleton
CHEDDLETON FLINT MILL open all year Sat and Sun, pm only

Barlaston
WEDGWOOD MUSEUM AND VISITOR CENTRE open all year Mon to Fri

Shallowford
IZAAK WALTON'S COTTAGE open all year Thu to Sun

Weston-under-Lizard
WESTON PARK open May to Aug daily (except Mon and Fri, but open Bank Holiday), pm only. Also open Apr and Sep, weekends only

Bridgnorth
SEVERN VALLEY RAILWAY open Mar to end Oct Sat and Sun; May to Sep usually daily. Also open Bank Holidays

Upper Broadheath
ELGAR'S BIRTHPLACE open all year daily (except Wed), pm only

Worcester
DYSON PERRINS MUSEUM OF WORCESTER PORCELAIN open all year Mon to Fri, also Sat Apr to Sep (closed Bank Holidays)

GUILDHALL open all year Mon to Fri

TUDOR HOUSE MUSEUM open all year daily (except Thu and Sun)

Wotton-under-Edge
REV. ROWLAND HILL'S TABERNACLE open Mar to end Oct Mon to Sat all day, Sun pm only

Dodington
DODINGTON HOUSE open Apr to Sep

Dyrham
DYRHAM PARK open Apr to Oct daily (except Fri, and Thu Apr, May and Oct), pm only

Bath
ROMAN BATHS AND PUMP ROOM open all year

Buxton

RAMSHAW ROCKS
Ramshaw Rocks are of the same geological structure as the Roaches, and thrust their jagged teeth eastwards over the road, the pinkish gritstone presenting a dramatic silhouette against the sky

LEEK
Steep streets, cobblestones, old mills and a friendly atmosphere make Leek a typical old-fashioned North Country town, set off to perfection by the magnificent wild moorland which surrounds it

BARLASTON
Just before the Second World War the Wedgwood family moved their factory to Barlaston, where there is now an excellent museum showing the history of this world-famous pottery

STONE
In the High Street is Joule's Old Brewery, which until 1974 had filled the town with the pleasant aroma of hops for almost 200 years. It is now a depot for Bass Charrington

NEWPORT
William Adam founded the grammar school in Cromwell's day, and the pleasant old building retains its original clock and cupola. Sir Oliver Lodge, who sent wireless telegrams before Marconi, was a pupil here

WESTON PARK
Weston Park is the remarkable achievement of an amateur architect, Lady Wilbraham, the wife of Thomas Wilbraham who bought the estate in the 17th century and built this great Renaissance house to his wife's design

BRIDGNORTH
The town hall in Bridgnorth was once a barn. It was brought from Much Wenlock and set up on stone arches during the Commonwealth to replace the old hall which was burnt down in a siege during the Civil War

WORCESTER
The cathedral was founded as a Saxon monastery in 983 by St Oswald. The earliest part of the present building is the crypt, built by St Wulstan, the only Saxon bishop to keep his post after the Norman Conquest

BEWDLEY
Telford's fine bridge over the River Severn was built in 1795. The town itself has a large number of 17th- and 18th-century houses, especially in elegant Load Street and beautiful Severnside

MALVERN HILLS
The composer Edward Elgar was born nearby at Upper Broadheath, and often walked the rough common land of these hills, which inspired many of his greatest works

GLOUCESTER
The cathedral, one of Britain's most beautiful buildings, houses the tomb of Edward II, murdered in 1327. It also has the largest stained-glass window in Britain, a memorial to the men who died at the Battle of Crécy in 1346

STROUD
Stroud has 18th-century mills, a 16th-century town hall and, in Church Street, a number of typical Cotswold cottages. In October the annual Festival of Religious Drama and the Arts takes place here

WOTTON-UNDER-EDGE
The 14th- to 15th-century church has among its treasures some fine brasses and an organ which was once housed in the Church of St Martin-in-the-Fields, London, and was played by Handel in the presence of George I

DYRHAM PARK
This 17th-century mansion was built for William Blathwayt, Secretary of State to William III, and was lived in by his descendants until 1958, when it was acquired by the National Trust

BATH
Pulteney Bridge, lined on both sides by shops, was designed by Robert Adam in 1770, inspired by the Ponte Vecchio in Florence

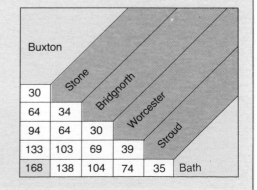

Buxton	Stone	Bridgnorth	Worcester	Stroud	
30					
64	34				
94	64	30			
133	103	69	39		
168	138	104	74	35	Bath

BUXTON TO LEEK

Leave Buxton town centre by the A53 (SP Leek), passing on the right the imposing Palace Hotel and the Royal Devonshire Hospital and, on the left, the famous Pavilion, behind which lie attractive formal gardens. The A53 keeps forward at the traffic lights, leaving the town and climbing steeply up Axe Edge to enter the Peak District National Park. At its highest point, Axe Edge rises to over 1800 feet, and the views across the wild moorland scenery are superb. About 5 miles from Buxton, the road passes a sign on the right pointing to the remote moorland settlement of Flash which, at 1518 feet, claims to be the highest village in England.

Shortly past this turning, the road begins its descent towards Leek. Ahead on the right rises the jagged outline of Ramshaw Rocks, a forbidding outcrop which forms one end of a more extensive ridge of exposed millstone grit known as the Roaches.

THE ROACHES

A short detour to the Roaches can be made by turning right on to an unclassified road (SP Upper Hulme) ¾ mile further down the hill past Ramshaw Rocks. This road leads down into a wooded valley at the bottom of which nestles the pretty hamlet of Upper Hulme. A sharp left turn over the bridge and past a collection of small workshops leads to the Roaches, about 1 mile further on. Their name is derived from the French *roches*, meaning 'rocks'. The gaunt rock faces rise sheer out of the barren moor, and have been eroded by wind and weather into strange shapes, making an impressive sight. From the path which leads along the top of the ridge you can see for miles – even as far as the Welsh mountains on a clear day. The rocks are popular as a practice ground for climbers.

Continue along the A53 to Leek, following signs for Macclesfield and Manchester as you enter the town. Formerly an important textile town, specializing in silk, Leek was once famous for its school of embroidery. Great Victorian mill buildings still dominate Mill Street. Here also stands Brindley Mill,* set by the River Churnet at the foot of the hill. A working water-powered corn mill, dating from 1752, it is named after the contemporary engineer, James Brindley, and houses a small museum of his life and work.

Despite its industrial character, Leek is a town of great individuality and charm, with an attractive old cobbled market place and a parish church with a beautiful oak-beamed roof and a fine brass depicting a 16th-century worthy, John Asshenhurst, together with his four wives and ten children.

LEEK TO STONE

Turn left, opposite the parish church, into St Edward's Street, and at the traffic lights go straight ahead on to the A520 (SP Stone). This road leads along a valley to the small town of Cheddleton where, by following a track on the right just over the river bridge, you can visit another interesting old mill.* This one is a flint mill, where natural flints, brought by barge up the Caldon Canal, were incinerated in kilns to make them brittle. They were then crushed by the mill to form a fine powder which was sent to the Potteries for use in the china industry.

The route follows the A520 for several miles, skirting the Potteries and passing through the village of Rough Close.

Towering above the road from Buxton to Leek are Ramshaw Rocks, part of a curiously weathered outcrop of millstone grit

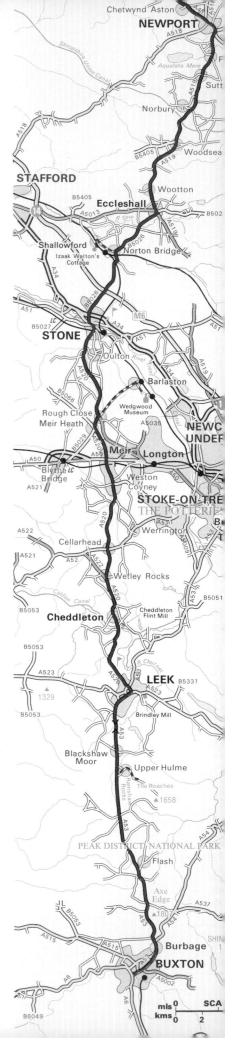

WEDGWOOD FACTORY AND MUSEUM

Rough Close, you can make a detour of
out 3 miles to the Wedgwood china factory
Barlaston. Turn right (SP Wedgwood) and
n, by the green at Barlaston, turn right
ain and follow the signs. In the factory's
eption area there is a large shop selling
ny 'seconds' as well as top-quality china,
d also a demonstration room where visitors
watch the craftsmen at work. The
ellent museum* contains some 6000 exits going back as far as 1754, when Josiah
dgwood established his first business. In
museum is the Portland Vase, which has
come the Wedgwood company symbol. It
k Josiah Wedgwood four years to make
faithful replica of a priceless Roman vase
t is now in the British Museum.

The A520 runs on into Stone, an attractive
town of mellow red brick. Bear left into the
main street, following signs for through
traffic. The outstanding building here is the
18th-century bow-fronted Crown Hotel.
Stone's traditional occupation was brewing,
first introduced by monks in medieval times.
The buildings of Joule's brewery still stand in
the main street, but local ale is no longer
made here. (For Stone see also p. 237.)

STONE TO NEWPORT
At the end of the main street turn right, then
follow signs for Eccleshall, keeping forward at
the A34 roundabout on to the B5026. After 2½
miles the road crosses a bridge and reaches
another roundabout, where the route turns
left (SP Eccleshall).

*Cheddleton Flint Mill's two huge wooden water-wheels
supplied power to crush flint for use in the pottery industry.
The powder was used in glazes or to strengthen the clay*

From Norton Bridge the route runs to
Eccleshall, a compact town with a pleasantly
village-like main street. Its castle (now a
private house) was for centuries the residence
of the bishops of Lichfield. At the crossroads
turn left on to the A519 (SP Newport), and
follow this road for 9 miles through pleasing
Staffordshire countryside. The route crosses
the Shropshire Union Canal, then enters
Shropshire just before reaching Newport and
turning left on to the A41 (SP
Wolverhampton, Telford). Newport is an
elegant little market town of dignified red-
brick houses; most of them were built after
1665, when the town was devastated by fire.

IZAAK WALTON'S COTTAGE
In ½ mile, at Norton Bridge, a detour can be
made to Izaak Walton's cottage and
museum* at Shallowford. Turn left just past
the railway bridge, crossing the railway again
after 1 mile to reach the house, an idyllic
black-and-white 17th-century cottage set
amid fields. The indefatigable angler was
born in Stafford in 1593, then went to London
to be apprenticed as an ironmonger. He
bought the cottage on his retirement from
business in London. Although he came to be
associated with more famous rivers, such as
the Dove in Derbyshire, and eventually
moved to Winchester, where he is buried,
Staffordshire was his home and its rivers were
the ones he knew most intimately. His book,
The Compleat Angler, written in 1653, remains
a classic to this day.

Bishop Percy's House is among the finest of Bridgnorth's ancient buildings

NEWPORT TO BRIDGNORTH

Follow the A41 through Newport, and 3 miles beyond it, shortly past Woodcote Hall, turn right on to the B4379 (SP Shifnal). This brings you through the village of Sheriffhales to a junction with the A5 at Crackleybank, where the route keeps forward for Shifnal.

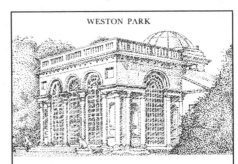

WESTON PARK

For a short detour to Weston Park, turn left on to the A5 (SP Cannock). Approximately 3 miles along the A5 is the village of Weston-under-Lizard and Weston Park,* seat of the earls of Bradford for over 300 years. The 17th-century hall contains a first-class collection of paintings, including some by Gainsborough and Reynolds. The park and gardens were landscaped by Capability Brown. They now include a woodland adventure playground, a pets' corner and an aquarium.

Follow the main road (SP Bridgnorth) in Shifnal and at the roundabout take the second exit (SP Bridgnorth) on to the A4169. At the next roundabout turn right. About 3 miles from Shifnal, branch left on to the B4379 Bridgnorth road. (By continuing here along the A4169 you can make a detour to Ironbridge and Coalbrookdale, often dubbed the birthplace of the Industrial Revolution; see p. 182 for directions and details.)

After 1½ miles, at the roundabout, take the second exit to join the A442 (SP Kidderminster) for Bridgnorth. The road runs gently downhill, later following the side of the steep, wooded valleys of the Worfe and Severn towards Bridgnorth, passing an extraordinary, mock-Gothic castle of pink sandstone, called Fort Pendlestone. It is the premises of a local dairy. Bridgnorth can now be seen, ahead and to the right, topping the crest of dramatic sandstone cliffs above the Severn. At the roundabout just outside the town, turn right (SP Shrewsbury) to cross the river, then turn left down Bridge Street.

Bridgnorth is in fact two towns in one – Low Town beside the Severn and High Town at the top of the cliffs. The two are connected by steep, winding lanes and steps, extremely

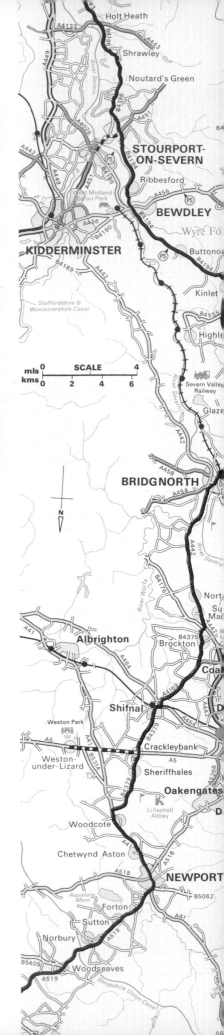

resque from the visitors' point of view,
nconvenient to the townsfolk. It was the
of them struggling up and down the hill
inspired a local 19th-century business-
to press for the installation of a cliff
ay by which one can travel effortlessly
een the two levels. Low Town, with its
ottages and steep twisting streets, has
of the character of a fishing village than
narket town. In former times it was the
t of bargees on their way up and down
River Severn, who frequented the many
side pubs, one of which, the Magpie
se (now a restaurant), still stands. Higher
he same street stands a lovely 16th-
ry black-and-white house known as
p Percy's House.
the centre of the wide High Street in
Town stands the 17th-century town
perched on an open arcade which allows
c to drive underneath. Church Street
off to the right beyond the town hall up
Leonard's Church, which stands en-
d by a miniature close of attractive old
es that lends it the dignity of a small
edral. At the other end of the High
t, East Castle Street leads up to Bridg-
h's second church, St Mary Magdalene,
endid neo-classical structure designed by
ngineer Thomas Telford. Beside it, lean-
t a perilous 17-degree angle, is a massive
nent of masonry – all that remains of the
astle, destroyed in Cromwell's day.
idgnorth is also known for its connection
the early history of the railways. The first
vay locomotive was built here for Trevi-
k in 1804 and also, a few years later, the
h-Me-Who-Can, another famous early
motive that was demonstrated in
don's Regent's Park. Bridgnorth station
w the terminus of the Severn Valley

Railway,* which maintains and runs a large
collection of preserved steam locomotives and
rolling-stock. A passenger service operates
between Bridgnorth and Bewdley.

BRIDGNORTH TO HOLT HEATH
Leave Bridgnorth by the B4363 (SP Cleobury
Mortimer). The road winds up and down for
9 miles through thickly wooded country to
Kinlet, where the route turns left by the
pub (SP Bewdley), then left again at the
T-junction on to the B4194. Soon the road
enters Wyre Forest, the remnant of a much
larger ancient woodland, now a favourite
recreation area for Midlanders. As you reach
Bewdley, turn left at the T-junction, then
almost immediately bear right with the

*Housed in The Shambles – once the butchers' market –
Bewdley's museum contains a fascinating exhibition of
country crafts*

B4194 (no sign) into the High Street. Just off
the route to the left at this junction is Load
Street, the main street of this attractive riverside town. Bewdley was for centuries a
flourishing inland port where heavily laden
craft stopped to transfer cargoes to smaller
vessels for the remainder of the voyage
upstream. (For Bewdley see also pp. 140–1.)

The B4194 climbs steeply out of the
sandstone gorge, then drops down again to
run beside the Severn, continuing through
woodland to reach the A451 Stourport road.
The main route crosses straight over for
Shrawley and Worcester.

STOURPORT-ON-SEVERN
By turning left at this crossroads on to the
A451 you can make a short detour into
Stourport, not so much a river town (although the Severn and the Stour meet here)
as a creation of the canal era. Bewdley refused
to let a canal come near it, so the Staffordshire
and Worcestershire Canal was constructed in
the 1770s to connect Kidderminster with the
Severn at Stourport. Many of the buildings
around the canal and in the town date from
this era; the Tontine Inn and Mart Lane are
of particular interest. The making of vinegar
and of the world-famous Worcestershire
Sauce are traditional industries here.

The B4194 ends at a T-junction where the
route turns right on to the B4196 (SP
Shrawley). Shortly past Shrawley, at Holt
Heath crossroads, turn left, then bear right on
to the A443 (SP Worcester). In the distance
ahead can be seen the imposing tower of
Worcester Cathedral.

*Wyre Forest now covers about 6000 acres – a fraction of its
former size. It remains one of the most peaceful and
unspoilt areas of the West Midlands*

HOLT HEATH TO UPTON
UPON SEVERN

ELGAR'S BIRTHPLACE

Five miles beyond Holt Heath, after entering Worcester's suburbs, a signposted detour can be made to the birthplace of Sir Edward Elgar. Turn right on to the B4204 (SP Lower Broadheath), and in 1½ miles, at Lower Broadheath, turn left on to an unclassified road for Upper Broadheath. Turn left into the village at the crossroads 1 mile later. The composer was born in 1857 in a small cottage in Crown East Lane. His father was organist of Worcester's Roman Catholic church, and kept a music shop in the city, but the composer received no formal musical education and was largely self-taught. He composed music for Queen Victoria's diamond jubilee, and was established as a British composer of outstanding talent by the turn of the century, gaining a knighthood in 1904. Today he is most widely remembered for his popular *Pomp and Circumstance* marches, one of which always features in the 'Last Night of the Proms'. But these show only one facet of his musical prowess; his other works include two symphonies, violin and cello concertos, *The Dream of Gerontius* and the *Enigma Variations*, each one of which is a musical portrayal of a friend or relative of the composer. Elgar died in 1934 and is buried in Little Malvern. His birthplace is now a museum* containing scores, photographs and personal effects.

The main route skirts Worcester, following signs for Great Malvern and the A449.

WORCESTER

For a detour to the city centre, follow signs to cross the Severn bridge. As a cathedral city, Worcester is rather disappointing at first sight, for much of the ancient centre has been redeveloped. The cathedral itself, however, is mainly in the Early English style and dates from the 12th to the 14th centuries. The crypt is even earlier, having been built by St Wulstan at the end of the 11th century. King John is buried in the cathedral, and his effigy is probably the earliest royal effigy in England.

East of the cathedral, a footpath leads to the attractive buildings of the Royal Worcester Porcelain Company. A local citizen, Dr Wall, founded the company in the 18th century as an alternative source of employment to the failing cloth trade, and it has flourished ever since. The porcelain works can be visited, and the Dyson Perrins Museum of Worcester Porcelain,* in Severn Street, has the finest collection of Worcester china in the world. There are also shops offering 'seconds' for sale.

To the north and west of the cathedral lies the main shopping centre, whose most notable building is the superb 18th-century guildhall,* recently cleaned and restored. The building was the work of a local sculptor and mason, Thomas White, and the statues on the lavish façade are of Queen Anne, Charles I and Charles II. The Tudor House Museum* in Friar Street is a 15th-century timber-framed house (formerly an inn) which displays interiors and furnishings from the Tudor and Stuart periods.

From the city centre follow signs for the A449 and Great Malvern, crossing the river and rejoining the main route.

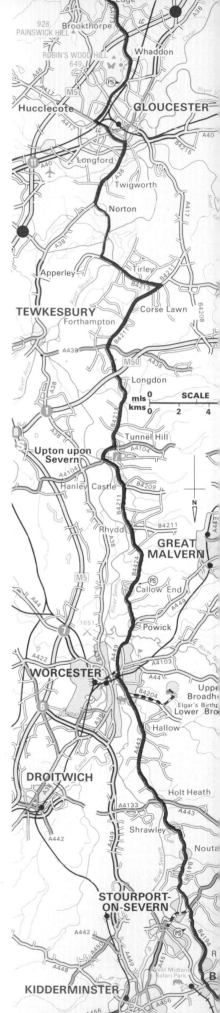

Beyond Worcester's outskirts, the route crosses the River Teme at Powick Bridge. To the left of the road, near the confluence of the Severn and Teme, is the spot where the Battle of Worcester took place in 1651. Cromwell's army crushed the Royalists, but the future King Charles II escaped and, after many hair-raising adventures, fled to exile in France. At Powick, turn left (SP Upton upon Severn) on to the B4424. From this road there are dramatic views of the bleak Malvern Hills – sometimes dubbed the English Alps – an impressive and, on a cloudy day, even a menacing sight. Pass through Callow End and in 3 miles keep forward to join the B4211.

At Upton upon Severn turn right on to the A4104 (SP Little Malvern), passing all that remains of the original parish church – a 14th-century square tower crowned by an 18th-century octagonal cupola, dome and lantern. The original steeple was demolished in 1745 and the rest of the church rebuilt shortly afterwards, only to be pulled down in 1937. In the unspoilt old town are a number of interesting houses and inns; the White Lion features in Fielding's novel *Tom Jones* and is one of the inns where his hero made merry.

UPTON UPON SEVERN TO EDGE

Half a mile beyond Upton turn left on to the B4211 (SP Gloucester). After 5 miles turn right then left to cross the A438. About 1 mile past Corse Lawn turn left on to the B4213 (SP Cheltenham, Tirley). The route crosses the Severn and then takes the next unclassified road on the right, crossing a cattle grid. This lane leads through a stretch of water meadows bordering the Severn, past a lonely fishermen's pub and a large apple orchard to a T-junction, where you turn right to reach the A38. Turn right on to it for Gloucester. This route by-passes Gloucester on the ring road (for the city centre see pp. 59 and 184). When you reach the ring road, join the A40 (SP Through Traffic). In 1 mile, keep forward at the roundabout and shortly bear left, then ½ mile later take the A38 (SP Bristol). Keep forward with the A38 at the next two roundabouts and after 1 mile take the A4173 (SP Stroud).

Soon the route is climbing gently out of the Vale of Gloucester and heading into lovely Cotswold countryside. Past Whaddon the road crosses the M5 and climbs more steeply, passing through the village of Edge.

Peaceful, lush countryside surrounds the route as it climbs from the Vale of Gloucester into the Cotswolds

EDGE TO WOTTON-UNDER-EDGE

From Edge the A4173 continues to Pitchcombe. The churchyard here, similar to the more famous one at nearby Painswick, has some handsome 18th-century table tombs and neatly clipped yew trees.

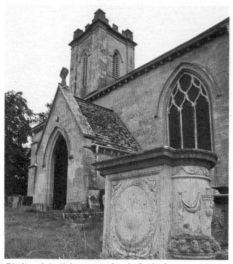

Pitchcombe's 19th-century church. In the foreground is one of several ornate table tombs, monuments to wealthy 18th-century merchants

As it leaves Pitchcombe, the route turns right on to the A46 for the descent into Stroud. Turn right (SP Bath) at the roundabout at the foot of the hill to by-pass the town centre. After 1 mile, at the next roundabout, take the second exit (SP Bath, Nailsworth). The road runs along the floor of a steep-sided valley as far as Nailsworth, an attractive old town whose small winding streets are a delight to explore. Turn right here on to the B4058 (SP Wotton-under-Edge), which leads across country for about 3 miles to a junction where the B4058 bears left. In 1¼ miles turn right to join the A4135 for a short stretch before bearing left on to the B4058 for Wotton-under-Edge.

On the outskirts of Wotton turn right at the roundabout, then left (SP Bristol), still following the B4058 and skirting the town centre. Founded in 1253 by Joan de Berkeley, Wotton is an ancient hill town of steep streets and picturesque old houses. Its Church of St Mary the Virgin contains two fine 14th-century brasses to Thomas Berkeley and his wife Margaret. The Berkeley family were the great landowners of the area in medieval times and their castle at Berkeley, not far away, is notorious as the place where King Edward II was cruelly murdered in 1327. An even earlier period is recalled in the Wotton Mosaic, to be seen in the Rev. Rowland Hill's Tabernacle,* to the right, off the B4058. This is a painstakingly faithful copy of the great Romano-British pavement from the Roman villa at nearby Woodchester. The original is hardly ever on view to the public. The mosaic, covering 2209 square feet, depicts the Greek legend of Orpheus charming the beasts with the music of his lyre.

A huge copper kettle – a former tradesman's sign – hangs outside one of the buildings in George Street, Nailsworth

[WOT]TON-UNDER-EDGE TO [CHIP]PING SODBURY

[Follo]w the B4058 out of Wotton and shortly [turn] left on to the B4060 (SP Wickwar, Yate) [for C]hipping Sodbury. This road skirts the [pleas]ant village of Kingswood, at the foot of [the e]scarp. For many years there was a [Cister]cian abbey at Kingswood, but only an [old g]ateway now remains. At the edge of [Wick]war, the B4060 turns left for Chipping [Sodb]ury. Wickwar is another place whose [prese]nt size belies its former importance; now [little] more than a village, it used to have a [mayo]r, a weekly market, two breweries and [three] malt-houses. About 2½ miles further on, [turn] left for the old market town of Chipping [Sodb]ury ('chipping' is derived from the [Saxo]n word for 'market'). The broad main [stree]t is lined with attractive houses, a [pleas]ing combination of Georgian red brick [and] Cotswold stone. The town hall dates [from] the 15th century, but its mock-Tudor [façad]e was added in 1858. Turn left by the [chur]ch and in ¾ mile, at the roundabout, take [the fi]rst exit, the A432, towards Old Sodbury.

[CHI]PPING SODBURY TO BATH

[In just] over 1 mile from the roundabout the [route] passes through the village of Old [Sodb]ury, whose church is up a lane to the left, [perch]ed on a hill overlooking the valley. [Insid]e is a crusader's tomb with a stone effigy, [but] there is also a life-sized wooden statue, [muc]h weathered, of the same knight. Such [effigi]es were often carried in the funeral [proc]ession, the permanent stone carving [bein]g made later, and it is unusual for these [woo]den effigies to survive.

[Co]ntinue along the A432, and at the [junc]tion with the A46 turn right for Bath. [Shor]tly past here, the A46 skirts the 700-acre [park], landscaped by Capability Brown, [whic]h surrounds 18th-century Dodington [Hou]se* (see p. 151).

[Ju]st beyond Dodington Park, cross the M4 [at a] roundabout, keeping straight ahead for [Bath], and after 1¾ miles pass the entrance to [Dyrh]am Park.* The name Dyrham is derived [from] *deorham*, meaning a deer enclosure; the [area] was recorded in early Anglo-Saxon [time]s as a deer park, and has remained so for [over] 1000 years. The hall was originally a [mano]r manor house, but was rebuilt in the [late] 17th century when it came into the [poss]ession of William Blathwayt, Secretary of [Stat]e to William of Orange. He married the [heir]ess of Dyrham in 1686 and began [rebu]ilding the house after her death five [year]s later. Many of the furnishings, [pain]tings and china in the house were [brou]ght from Holland by him.

[Sh]ortly after passing Dyrham, the A46 [cross]es the A420, then climbs to run along the [edge] of Charmy Down before descending [steep]ly to meet the A4 on the outskirts of [Bath]. Turn right on to the A4 and follow signs [for t]he city centre.

BATH

Bath has as much to offer the visitor as any English provincial city. One of its greatest claims to fame is the Roman Baths,* England's finest survival from the Roman period. The museum which has grown around them has a collection of Roman relics of all kinds: fragments of carved masonry, mosaics, jewellery, pottery and tools give a vivid impression of what life was like in Roman Bath. The Great Bath itself is almost exactly as it was 2000 years ago, and is lined with the original lead sheets which still prevent the water from leaking out. The Pump Room,* where the waters were piped for drinking, maintains its Georgian elegance, and offers meals and refreshments.

Queen Square, the Circus and Royal Crescent are the finest examples of Bath's perfectly proportioned Georgian streets. The Avon is spanned by Pulteney Bridge, its Adam design enhanced by the golden stone of which it is built.

Buildings in Bath which belong to a different era include Bath Abbey, noted particularly for its famous fan-vaulted roof and immense east window.

Above: A Georgian archway spans York Street, framing the graceful outlines of 15th-century Bath Abbey. On the corner is the Burrows Toy Museum, opened in 1976

Right: Tea, coffee and the famous waters from Bath's mineral springs can still be taken in the genteel surroundings of the Pump Room

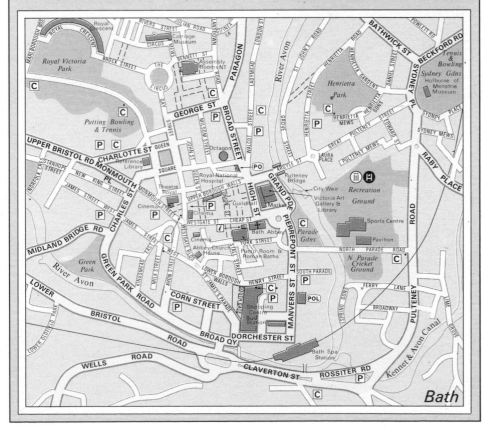

Bath

ROUTE 20

182 MILE

Buxton to Norwich

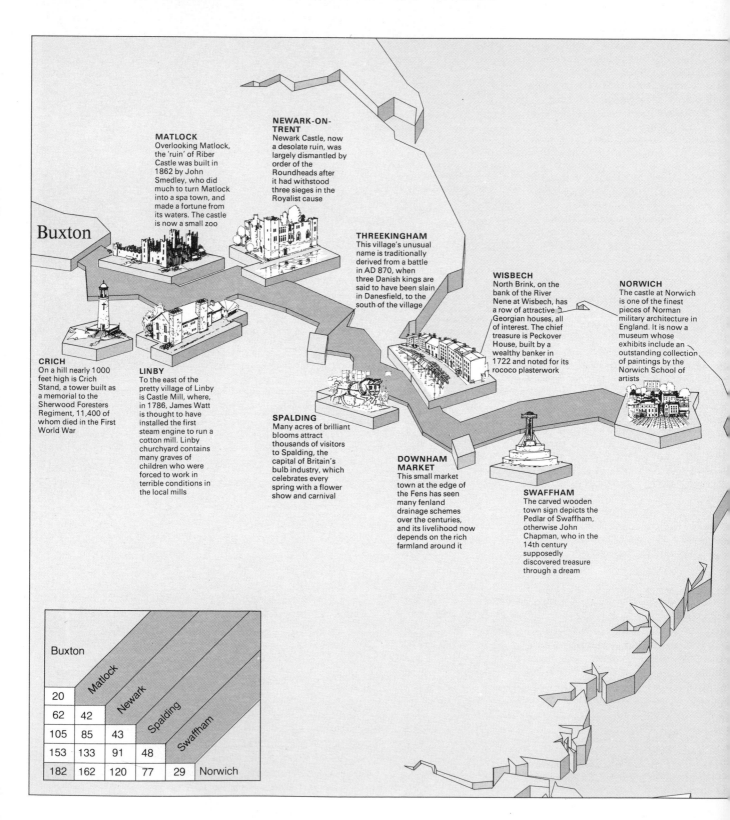

Buxton

MATLOCK
Overlooking Matlock, the 'ruin' of Riber Castle was built in 1862 by John Smedley, who did much to turn Matlock into a spa town, and made a fortune from its waters. The castle is now a small zoo

NEWARK-ON-TRENT
Newark Castle, now a desolate ruin, was largely dismantled by order of the Roundheads after it had withstood three sieges in the Royalist cause

THREEKINGHAM
This village's unusual name is traditionally derived from a battle in AD 870, when three Danish kings are said to have been slain in Danesfield, to the south of the village

WISBECH
North Brink, on the bank of the River Nene at Wisbech, has a row of attractive Georgian houses, all of interest. The chief treasure is Peckover House, built by a wealthy banker in 1722 and noted for its rococo plasterwork

NORWICH
The castle at Norwich is one of the finest pieces of Norman military architecture in England. It is now a museum whose exhibits include an outstanding collection of paintings by the Norwich School of artists

CRICH
On a hill nearly 1000 feet high is Crich Stand, a tower built as a memorial to the Sherwood Foresters Regiment, 11,400 of whom died in the First World War

LINBY
To the east of the pretty village of Linby is Castle Mill, where, in 1786, James Watt is thought to have installed the first steam engine to run a cotton mill. Linby churchyard contains many graves of children who were forced to work in terrible conditions in the local mills

SPALDING
Many acres of brilliant blooms attract thousands of visitors to Spalding, the capital of Britain's bulb industry, which celebrates every spring with a flower show and carnival

DOWNHAM MARKET
This small market town at the edge of the Fens has seen many fenland drainage schemes over the centuries, and its livelihood now depends on the rich farmland around it

SWAFFHAM
The carved wooden town sign depicts the Pedlar of Swaffham, otherwise John Chapman, who in the 14th century supposedly discovered treasure through a dream

Buxton					
20	Matlock				
62	42	Newark			
105	85	43	Spalding		
153	133	91	48	Swaffham	
182	162	120	77	29	Norwich

MUCH of Britain's appeal lies in the great variety of [scen]ery to be found in a small space, but seldom are the [con]trasts as great on a route less than 200 miles long as on this [on]e from the Peak District of Derbyshire to Broadland [Nor]folk. From a height of around 1000 feet the route drops to [lo]w sea level – taking in limestone gorges, moorland, rolling [farm]lands and peat fens on the way. The variety of architecture [i]s great: some of England's finest stately homes, such as [Cha]tsworth House, Haddon Hall and Newstead Abbey, lie on [or n]ear the route, and there are fine parish churches, a Norman [cath]edral and a wealth of pleasant villages which seem refresh[ingl]y unaware of their charm and are often to be found in the [mos]t unexpected places.

[F]rom Buxton the River Wye is accompanied to Wye Dale. [The]n, after leaving the valley to cross a stretch of open country [typi]cal of the White Peak, the route rejoins the Wye at [Ta]ddington Dale and makes its way through lush green [mea]dows to Ashford and Bakewell. At Rowsley, a few miles [bey]ond magnificent Haddon Hall, the Wye enters the [Der]went, which rushes through a dramatic limestone gorge [belo]w Matlock.

[M]atlock and neighbouring Matlock Bath owe their growth [to t]he 18th- and 19th-century fad for 'taking the waters'. [Peo]ple flocked here from all over the country in the hope that [the] mineral waters would bring them health and long life. [Tod]ay the waters are more likely to be used to turn such items [as] dolls, bottles and bowler hats to stone at the famous ['pet]rifying' wells.

[A]t Cromford the waters of the Derwent and its tributaries [sup]plied the motive power for the world's first mechanized [text]ile factories. Richard Arkwright, who had started his [wor]king life as a barber and wig-maker, chose this isolated spot [for t]he site of his factory in 1771 partly because it was far from [the] riots that greeted increased industrialization in the West [Mid]lands and the North Country. The original mill still stands, [alth]ough it is much altered and obscured by later building, and [a be]tter idea of how the early factories looked can be gained [fro]m Arkwright's Masson Mill, which stands beside the route [just] beyond Matlock Bath.

[A]t Crich the route leaves the Derwent and crosses the county [bor]der into Nottinghamshire to pass near Newstead Abbey and [thro]ugh the charming stone-built villages of Linby and [Pap]plewick. North of Oxton is Robin Hood Hill, a reminder [tha]t all of the area from Nottingham to Worksop, on the [Yor]kshire border, was once the royal hunting-ground of [She]rwood Forest. Set on a band of infertile sandstone soils, the [for]est was never an area of uninterrupted woodland, but [con]sisted largely of oak glades set in expanses of heathland. [Alth]ough many of the trees have long since gone, some of the [form]er character of the Forest has been preserved in [Shee]tstump Country Park. As to Robin Hood himself, he is [sup]posed to have been born at Lockesley Hall in about 1160, [but] there is no real proof that he existed at all. There is no [dou]bt, however, of the existence of his hated enemy, King [Joh]n. He died in 1216 in Newark, the next town on the route.

[N]ewark stands on the River Trent, which serves as a rough [bou]ndary between the rolling Nottinghamshire countryside [and] the flat plains of East Anglia. The River Witham, one of [fou]r great rivers that empty into the Wash, marks the actual [cou]nty boundary and once the route has crossed into [Lin]colnshire there is no mistaking the extraordinary man-[ma]de landscapes of the Fens.

PLACES OF INTEREST: OPENING DETAILS

Bakewell
HADDON HALL open Apr to end Sep daily (except Sun and Mon); also open Easter, Spring and Summer Bank Holidays

Rowsley
CHATSWORTH open end Mar to Oct Tue to Fri all day, Sat and Sun pm only; also open Bank Holiday Mon

Matlock
RIBER CASTLE FAUNA RESERVE open all year (except 25 Dec)

Matlock Bath
HEIGHTS OF ABRAHAM open all year; GREAT RUTLAND CAVERN open Easter to Oct;

GREAT MASSON CAVERN open Easter to end Sep Sun and Bank Holidays, also daily in Aug

Crich
TRAMWAY MUSEUM open Easter to end Oct Sat, Sun and Bank Holidays; also Tue, Wed and Thu Jun to Aug

South Wingfield
WINGFIELD MANOR open at reasonable times by permission from the neighbouring farm

Newstead
NEWSTEAD ABBEY house open Apr to end Sep, pm only; gardens open all year (except 25 Dec)

Spalding
AYSCOUGHFEE HALL AND GARDENS open all year Mon to Sat

SPRINGFIELDS spring gardens open Apr to mid May; summer gardens open mid Jun to end Sep

Wisbech
PECKOVER HOUSE open Apr to mid Oct daily (except Mon and Fri), pm only, and Bank Holiday Mon, pm only

Norwich
SAINSBURY CENTRE FOR THE VISUAL ARTS, open all year daily (except Mon), pm only

Once an area of swamps, lakes and reed-beds dotted with islands of gravel and clay, the Fens were transformed into some of the richest farmlands in the world by a series of land drainage schemes begun during the 17th century. Long before this, the Romans had realized the potential of the fenland soils, and drained some areas, but most of their work was inundated when the sea level rose by an inch or two.

Spalding, on the River Welland, lies at the centre of a large market-gardening area, and is the scene of a spectacular flower festival in spring, when floats covered in blooms from the surrounding bulb-fields make their way through the town.

Beyond Spalding the route crosses Whaplode Fen and Fleet Fen to reach the lovely old town of Wisbech. It was created as a seaport, and although the sea is now ten miles away across the Fens, ships still travel up the River Nene to its quays. Lining both sides of the river are some of England's finest Georgian houses, culminating in Peckover House, whose interior is decorated with beautifully moulded plasterwork and carved wood.

Following the Wisbech Canal, the route passes through Outwell and then continues past Salter's Lode, where the arrow-straight Bedford River enters the Great Ouse, to reach Downham Market. Carr Stone, probably quarried at nearby Bexwell (whose church tower is of the same material), lends Downham Market a singular charm and unity of character. The next town is Swaffham, whose town sign recalls the legend of the Pedlar of Swaffham. The story goes that John Chapman, a pedlar and native of the town, was standing on London Bridge one day when he was approached by a man who told him of a dream that he had had. In the dream the man went to a distant Norfolk town called Swaffham, dug in one of the gardens there and discovered treasure. Chapman recognized the garden as his own, rushed home, and found the treasure.

From Swaffham the route continues along quiet Norfolk roads to Shipdham, whose church has a more tangible treasure – one of the finest wooden lecterns in the world. Following the upper reaches of the River Yare, the route approaches Norwich through villages and hamlets that rest contentedly in the soft embrace of the East Anglian landscape.

BUXTON TO MATLOCK

Leave the centre of Buxton by following signs for Matlock, picking up the A6 which runs beside the infant River Wye. Once out of the town, the road starts to descend the Wye valley. The gorge of Ashwood Dale is barely wide enough to carry road and river side by side, and the railway is forced to run high above, carried back and forth across the valley by great ironwork bridges. Here and there between the trees huge limestone buttresses tower above the road.

Several miles out of Buxton the road swings to the right, clambering up towards the moor and leaving the Wye to go its own roundabout way through Chee Dale, Miller's Dale and Monsal Dale. The enclosed world of the dale gives way to an open green landscape, neatly divided by pale grey drystone walls and dotted with sheep to match. After descending through wooded Taddington Dale, road and river meet again, and the valley soon opens up, with cows grazing in flat, green meadows to the right and anglers making the most of the gentler waters here.

ASHFORD IN THE WATER

Ashford in the Water makes a pleasant detour, and is reached by turning left on to the A6020 (SP Chesterfield, Sheffield). One of three bridges across the River Wye here is the medieval Sheepwash Bridge, near the centre of the village. It has a stone enclosure where sheep were gathered to be washed in the Wye before shearing. The celebrated Derbyshire ceremony of well-dressing takes place at Ashford around Trinity Sunday.

From Ashford follow signs for Matlock, rejoining the A6 to reach Bakewell. On the hillside behind the Rutland Arms Hotel is a warren of charming little streets of unspoilt stone houses. Among them is All Saints' Church, where many ancient stone carvings can be seen, including an 8th-century sculptured cross. There are also several elaborate tombs of the Manners family of Haddon Hall. Perhaps more than anything, the town's name has been immortalized in Bakewell Tart, a local speciality – though the locals insist it be called 'pudding'.

Originally built in the 14th century, the octagonal tower and soaring spire of Bakewell's fine parish church were disma and carefully reconstructed in Victorian times

From Bakewell the A6 continues to follow the Wye, soon passing Haddon Hall,* one of the best preserved medieval manors in the country. For two centuries it was neglected and forgotten, to be lovingly restored in the 1920s by the Ninth Duke of Rutland. Haddon's finest features are the chapel, the banqueting hall and the splendid 16th-century Long Gallery, and it is famed for the romantic tale of Dorothy Vernon's elopement with John Manners in the 16th century.

Rowsley, dominated by its 17th-century Peacock Hotel, is where the route leaves the Peak District National Park, and where the Wye joins the Derwent on its way down from Chatsworth,* the palatial home of the dukes of Devonshire, 3 miles to the north. Follow the A6, passing through Darley Dale to reach Matlock. As you enter Matlock Bank, lofty Riber Castle,* now a fauna reserve, can be seen on the hilltop ahead. At the roundabout take the third exit (SP Derby) and cross the River Derwent. Towering above the A6 to the left as it runs along the limestone gorge are the High Tor rocks and later on, to the right, the Heights of Abraham, where cliffside gardens and caves* can be visited. Matlock Bath's popularity began in the 18th century when people came to visit the thermal springs which now supply the swimming pools of the New Bath Hotel.

Arkwright's mill at Cromford still stands as one of t great monuments to the Industrial Revolution

MATLOCK TO PAPPLEWICK

Shortly past Matlock Bath is Cromfor mecca for the industrial archaeologist Richard Arkwright, who revolutionized cotton industry, built the world's first me nized water-powered cotton mill her 1771. Another of his mills, the attra Masson Mill, stands beside the A6 on the

Continue along the A6, following Derwent and the Cromford Canal which beside it. High up on the left is Crich Sta a monument to the Sherwood Foresters Nottinghamshire and Derbyshire regin At 950 feet above sea level, the light on can be seen for many miles.

The Crich Tramway Museum is a unique collection of horse-drawn, steam-powered and electric trams. Many of the vehicles are in working order and some of them carry visitors along a mile of specially built tramway

Immediately after the A6 crosses the river, turn left on to the B5035 (SP Crich, Alfreton). The road climbs steeply, giving fine views along the Derwent valley, before turning away from it and dropping into Crich. The famous tramway museum,* signposted through the village, is to be found in the old quarry below Crich Stand. Its exhibits include not only trams from all over the world but also many pieces of old 'street furniture' such as lamp-posts and street signs.

Leave Crich by the B5035 Alfreton road. Approaching South Wingfield, the dramatic ruin of medieval Wingfield Manor,* where Mary, Queen of Scots, was four times a prisoner, can be seen on a hilltop to the right.

Continue along the B5035 through South Wingfield (taking care on the right-angled bend in the village), and ½ mile past South Wingfield church turn left then right, by the Butcher's Arms Inn, on to the A615. In 1¼ miles bear right, then at the T-junction turn right on to the A61 and at the roundabout take the first exit to join the A38. After 3 miles, at the motorway junction roundabout, take the fourth exit (SP The South) to join the M1. In 3¾ miles, at junction 27, branch left (SP Hucknall) to leave the motorway, and at the roundabout take the first exit, the A608 (SP Hucknall, Mansfield). In 1¼ miles, at the traffic lights, follow signs for Hucknall and Nottingham, joining the A611. After 2 miles, at the very edge of Hucknall, turn left on to the B6011 (SP Linby).

Linby, the next village, has cottages of golden stone, two roadside streams and two village crosses, and might almost belong to the Cotswolds. Go straight on to Papplewick, equally charming, though this time the old stone village lies off the route to the left at the crossroads by the Griffins Head pub.

NEWSTEAD ABBEY

By turning left in Papplewick on to the B683 a detour can be made to Newstead Abbey.* Turn left again when you reach the A60, and continue for ¾ mile. The abbey gates are on the left, opposite the Hutt Hotel. The abbey is set in pleasant grounds which include several lakes. Lawns and waterfalls make an enchanting setting for the magnificent 13th-century west front. Many ancient treasures have been recovered from the lakes, where they were thrown at the time of the Dissolution to keep them out of Henry VIII's hands. The abbey is perhaps most famous as the family home of the poet Byron, and his rooms are preserved much as he left them.

To rejoin the main route, take the A60 towards Nottingham for 3 miles as far as the left turn for Calverton.

PAPPLEWICK TO NEWARK

The main route keeps forward through Papplewick and turns right on to the A60 at a T-junction some 1½ miles further on. Follow the A60 for ¼ mile, then turn left (SP Calverton). Skirt Burntstump Country Park, following signs for Calverton and Woodborough, and cross the A614. After the road emerges from the woodland, turn left at the crossroads on to the B6386 (SP Oxton, Southwell) to pass Calverton colliery, and in 1½ miles keep forward with the B6386 at the roundabout.

OXTON

At the junction a few hundred yards later a detour may be made by turning left into Oxton village. Brick cottages and several elegant 17th- and 18th-century houses surround the church, which is half-hidden by an immense yew tree. Inside the church hangs an unusual decorated parchment, made in the 1950s, telling the history of the village in perfect copper-plate script.

Continue through the village and turn right, passing the Green Dragon Inn. At the T-junction turn left to rejoin the B6386.

The main route swings right and ¼ mile later sharp left to skirt Oxton before continuing through rolling Nottinghamshire farmland to Southwell, where the route keeps forward on to the A612 Newark road for the town centre. The Saracen's Head Hotel here is a historic inn which was visited by King Charles I and,

A summer landscape near Oxton village

Southwell Minster stands on the site of a Saxon chapel, and became a cathedral less than a century ago. Much of the original Norman work is remarkably well preserved, including fine examples of 11th-century arcading (right). The twin Norman towers (below) are crowned by pyramid-shaped spires, added in 1880

later, by Cromwell. It was reputedly [here] that, in 1647, King Charles threw hims[elf on] the protection of the Scottish army, [who] subsequently handed him over to [the] Parliamentarians for £400,000. The Ne[wark] road turns right to pass Southwell's prid[e and] joy – the minster – undoubtedly of cath[edral] proportions and splendour, though it [offi]cially became a cathedral only in 1884 w[hen] it was already nearly 800 years old. The [nave] and crossing are a magnificent sequen[ce of] Norman arches, and fine Early English [work] is to be seen at the east end and in [the] wonderful chapter house, noted for its [ex]quisite carvings and soaring roof. Behin[d the] minster stand the ruins of the 15th-cen[tury] palace of the archbishops of York, and a[t the] east end of the churchyard is Vicar's Cou[rt, a] group of five elegant Queen Anne houses.

Continue towards Newark-on-Trent [and] in 3¾ miles turn right on to the A617. Soo[n the] glowing red-and-cream spires and turre[ts of] Kelham Hall – formerly a theological col[lege]

SCALE

mls	0				4
kms	0	2	4	6	

Carre's Hospital in Eastgate, Sleaford, was founded in 1636. The present stone almshouses and chapel date from the mid 19th century

and now the offices of the local council – can be glimpsed through the trees to the right. The road loops right round the hall, crossing the Trent and heading into Newark, whose chief landmark is the 240-foot-high spire of its medieval church, one of the grandest parish churches in the country. The route turns right to cross the river, and Newark's other famous landmark, the castle, can be seen to the right on the river bank. The west front is one of the few parts that remain, but this one-time Royalist stronghold is nevertheless an impressive sight. On the right of the road, the cattle market tells of Newark's importance as an agricultural town, and it is a busy local centre with some old-fashioned shops and pleasing buildings. The large, cobbled market place is a delight, its buildings ranging from the dignified Palladian town hall to the timber-framed 14th-century White Hart Inn, which is one of the oldest domestic buildings in the Midlands.

NEWARK TO DONINGTON

Take the first exit at the roundabout after crossing the river and shortly turn right on to the A17 (SP Sleaford), climbing out of the Trent valley and crossing a flat agricultural landscape into Lincolnshire. The countryside soon begins to look just a little like the Fens; streams run in straight, man-made ditches between fields of dark, fertile soil, and Brant Broughton to the left displays the first typically fine Lincolnshire church spire, visible for miles across the plain. Soon afterwards, by complete contrast, a monolithic and gloomy disused windmill stands beside the road.

Leadenham displays a second splendid spire, set in trees to the right as the road snakes up a hill. This village is sadly chopped in two by the A17 which curls and twists through it, but the beautiful combination of rich gold and warm red in almost every building is most appealing; even the stone walls have little red-brick 'hats'.

Keep forward with the A17 at the traffic lights. After 3 miles the road bears right and left by a clump of trees, crossing the line of Ermine Street, the famous Roman road. Away to the left just past it are the buildings and airfield of the Royal Air Force Training College at Cranwell.

In 4 miles the route reaches the Sleaford by-pass roundabout, taking the third exit, the A15, to enter the town. A pleasing mixture mainly of Victorian and Georgian architecture, Sleaford is a busy little market town. Its square is overlooked by the west front of the magnificent parish church, which boasts one of the earliest stone spires in England, dating from the late 12th or early 13th century.

Keep forward through the town centre, following signs for Peterborough, then bear right over the level crossing and immediately turn left into Mareham Lane. An unclassified road – Roman in origin – leads out of the town, soon running dead straight across open fields, with church spires rising out of the landscape in every direction. A strip of woodland along the road serves as a welcome windbreak in this breezy countryside. Drainage ditches beside the road give a fenland touch; soon the Fens themselves begin. At the crossroads turn left on to the A52 (SP Boston, Spalding, Donington).

THREEKINGHAM
A short distance from this crossroads is the interesting little village of Threekingham, reached by turning right on to the A52 and then left into the village. Since Saxon times there has been a settlement here, near the crossing of two Roman roads: Mareham Lane and Salters' Way. The village pub, the Three Kings, is reputed to be one of the oldest in England. Past customers are said to have included King John, Henry VIII and Dick Turpin. An unusual carved inn sign is set into its wall. The long, low village church with its fine broach spire contains a large effigy of Sir Lambert de Trikingham, who died in 1280, and his wife. Two lions at his feet tell of his courage, two dogs at hers of her fidelity.

There is no mistaking the wide open spaces of Fenland now, punctuated only by isolated farmsteads, church spires and the occasional tree. Soon the route crosses the first of the great artificial watercourses of the Fens – the South Forty Foot Drain – and runs through a string of hard-working farming villages, their churches a legacy of agricultural wealth. The first is Donington; again a fine steeple is the village's chief boast, but this time it is detached from the church. (Route continues on p.218.)

THE FENLANDS

DRAINING the Fens created the finest, most fertile farmland in Britain complete with huge, perfectly flat fields that make life relatively easy for men and machines alike. The silt deposits nearest to the Wash are deep, free from stones and ideal for agriculture. A few miles inland, thick deposits of mineral-rich peat curl round from west of Boston to Ely and the borders of Norfolk.

The opening shots in man's titanic battle with nature in the Fens were fired by the Romans almost 2000 years ago. They dug drainage channels and built causeways, mainly in Lincolnshire, but the reedy wilderness crept back when the sea level rose after the engineers were called back to their homeland.

Small areas of the Fens were reclaimed during the Middle Ages, but it was not until the 17th century that the Duke of Bedford, backed by royal patronage, launched the long-running campaign that finally transformed the map of East Anglia. He employed Dutch experts, notably Cornelius Vermuyden, who straightened the meandering rivers and made them flow faster. He dug canals and built sluices to keep out the tides.

Nobody realized that the exposed peat would contract so dramatically as it dried out, making the lowest land in Britain lower than ever. Embankments were raised higher and higher, and many fenland rivers now flow about 15 feet above the surrounding fields. Windmills were built by the hundred to pump water up into the main waterways, but only the advent of steam power eventually saved the day. A splendid steam-driven pumping engine, capable of lifting 124 tons of water every minute, is preserved at Stretham, on the A10 south of Ely.

FIRST-TIME visitors to the East Anglian Fens tend to feel no more significant than a speck of dust in the middle of an enormous bowling-green. Sky seems to account for three-quarters of every view. The astonishing flatness is emphasized by large-scale maps: they have no contour lines for mile after mile, and it is almost impossible to find anything other than single-figure 'spot heights'.

Huge and hedgeless fields, criss-crossed by countless drainage ditches, now patchwork what was for centuries a treacherous wilderness of desolate marshland through which broad, sluggish rivers ambled towards the Wash. It is easy to appreciate that the

scattered settlements, raised a few modest vital feet above their waterlogged surroundings, were then lonely islands reached only by boats and causeways. The most famous of them all, Ely, is where Hereward the Wake defied the Normans their victory at Hastings. Ely means 'eel island' – a reminder that eels formed an important part of the fen-dwelling Saxon diet. Crowland, with its 13th-century brid and ruined abbey, was a typical commun before the Fens were drained. Farmers ha use small boats known as 'skerries' when t went to milk their cows, but their liveliho depended more on fish and wildfowl.

The Fourth Duke of Bedford, by Gainsborough

Beam engines like this one at Stretham, near Ely, once helped to drain the Fen

LIPS by the million make the
ng area Britain's answer to
d. Bulbs were first cultivated
n a commercial scale towards
d of the 19th century, when the
evolved around snowdrops. By
here were 300 acres of daffodils
lips planted near the town, but
elds now cover more than
gloriously colourful acres.
ng's annual Flower Parade, in
floats decorated with
nds of blooms are driven
h the streets, attracts visitors
l over the country. It is staged
aturday early in May.

Fenland orchards are also seen
best in spring and early
r when 'blossom trails' are
ted around Wisbech and other
rowing centres. It is all a far
m the time when Fenlanders
ded on eels, fish and wildfowl
ir meagre living.

Huge numbers of ducks, as well as swans and many other kinds of water-loving birds, congregate on the Fenland grasslands and waterways during the winter months. One of the best places to see them is in the Wildfowl Trust's refuge at Welney, off the A1101 south-west of Downham Market. The male ducks illustrated here are (left) pochard, (below left) shoveler and (below) wigeon

THE Fens' billiard-table flatness emphasizes the soaring splendour of two great medieval landmarks – Ely Cathedral and St Botolph's Church, across the Wash at Boston.

Ely Cathedral, built on the site of a Saxon abbey, was begun in 1083. The central tower collapsed in 1322, but was replaced by a magnificent octagonal structure, topped with a huge wooden 'lantern', that ranks among the finest examples of ecclesiastical architecture in Britain.

Boston, one of the busiest ports in England during the Middle Ages, stands on the banks of the River Witham. Its waters reflect the glories of a church whose size is an indication of the town's early importance. It was started in 1309, but the immense tower, 272 feet high and invariably known as 'Boston Stump', was not completed for another 150 years.

of flowers are a characteristic part of the Fenland countryside

The River Witham and Boston Stump

DONINGTON TO SPALDING

Continue from Donington along the A152 Spalding road through the fertile market-gardening country which surrounds Boston and Spalding. Glasshouses abound, and the fields are filled with succulent vegetables and, in spring, with masses of daffodils and tulips. The next village is Quadring, where a garage has an impromptu collection of traction engines; after that comes Gosberton, with its grand cruciform church. At the end of the village turn right on to the A16 for the last few miles into Spalding. Dotted alongside the road are vegetable and fruit stalls stacked high with the freshest of local produce. The string of villages continues with Surfleet, whose church steeple leans perilously towards the road. Pinchbeck's church has no spire, but its tower, not to be outdone, still serves very well as a landmark for miles around.

Bold stripes of colour near Spalding at tulip time

Soon a sign brightly painted with tulips welcomes you to Spalding. Turn right at the T-junction (SP Crowland, A1073) and continue to the town centre, which is well worth exploring. By following the signs (preferably on foot) from the market place to the tourist information office, you will cross the River Welland – on which the wealth of Spalding depended for many centuries – at High Bridge. Nearby is the White Horse Inn, one of the oldest buildings in Spalding. Upstream lies extraordinary Ayscoughfee Hall.* Some parts of the original house of 1429 survive, but much rebuilding over the intervening centuries has transformed it. It now houses a bird museum and the tourist information office. The attractive gardens have a huge and unruly yew hedge and a thatched wooden shelter. Nearby is the large and, as one might expect, magnificent church, set amid fine Georgian houses, and further down the street are Gamlyn's Almshouses, Victorian Gothic in style and very appealing in warm red brick.

For most of the year there is little evidence of Spalding's most famous 'trade-mark' – the tulip. But should you be passing this way in spring, at the time of the tulip festival, you will probably see little else. This is fiesta time, when the town and surrounding villages show off their famous crop in decorations and processions. Just outside the town is Springfields,* a unique 20-acre garden where the public can admire the profusion of spring blooms. But at tulip time do not expect to have Spalding to yourself, for many thousands of visitors converge here to see the world-famous spectacle.

SPALDING TO WISBECH

Leave Spalding by crossing High Bridge and follow signs to Wisbech and Sutton St James (B1165), turning left and later right. Cross the Coronation Channel, constructed in 1953 to carry the surplus waters of the Welland round Spalding to prevent flooding in the town.

The B1165 runs for 20 uneventful mil Wisbech, twisting and winding past lo farmsteads and through little farming h lets. Sutton St James, the first village of size, has an extraordinary church witho middle. Tower and chancel stand o separate, and grass grows where the once stood. The B1165 turns sharply rig miles past the village and continues thro Tydd St Giles (where, as at Donington church has an isolated tower) and thro Newton, before the route turns right on t A1101 for the last 3 miles into Wisbech. Newton the land is dotted with the orch that make Wisbech the hub of an impo fruit-growing district. It is also an area w large numbers of gypsies are still to be fo for livings are to be made, on an impro basis, in the fruit-picking season.

Wisbech displays all the trappings modern agricultural centre; in fact if drive straight through on the main road t

A stunning array of Georgian buildings lines both ba of the River Nene at Wisbech

is not much else to see. Yet the town has a fascinating history, and it is well worth turning right off the A1101 to see the centre of the old town.

Built as a seaport before the Fens were drained, Wisbech owes its many fine Georgian buildings to its days of maritime prosperity. The grand medieval church tells of earlier wealth, and even in Norman times Wisbech had a castle. It stood on the site behind the church where a Regency villa (still called the castle) stands now. Around it sweeps the Crescent, which, with the buildings lining the River Nene, makes up the finest of Georgian Wisbech. Peckover House,* on the North Brink, is the town's showpiece. It dates from the 1720s, and the dignified exterior is matched by the fine rococo plasterwork and intricately carved wood to be seen inside the house.

WISBECH TO DOWNHAM MARKET
Follow signs out of Wisbech on the A1101 for Downham Market, soon entering Norfolk. Skirting Outwell, and passing the first of many decorative Norfolk village signs, keep forward on to the A1122. Well Creek runs alongside, its level at times several feet above the surrounding fields, but firmly enclosed by its sturdy banks. Nordelph, the next village, sounds Dutch: many parts of the Fens are similar in names, in architecture and in general character to their counterparts across the North Sea, and it was a Dutchman, Vermuyden, who masterminded much of the fen drainage in the 17th century. Salter's Lode, the next hamlet, is a strategic point in his drainage system, for several of the man-made channels, controlled by huge sluices, run into the Great Ouse near here.

The Victorian cast-iron clock at Downham Market, a bustling little town at the edge of the Fens

Cross the Great Ouse – now quite vast – and the Flood Relief Channel, to enter Downham Market. The town's farming interests are betrayed by the rows of bright agricultural machinery, like pots of poster paint, lined up outside a farm supplier's premises beside the road. The A1122 runs through the town centre, passing market stalls stacked with fresh local produce. Beside them in the market place stands the ornate Gothic town clock, dated 1878, and bearing a plaque added in 1978 'thanking' it for 100 years' faithful service.

Many of the channels and rivers that drain the Bedford Levels empty into the Great Ouse at Salter's Lode

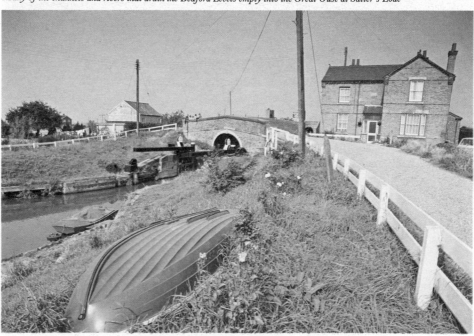

DOWNHAM MARKET TO SWAFFHAM

Turn left by Downham's clock and carry straight on along the Swaffham road at the crossroads by the church. The road starts to climb, and the hills are welcome, feeling positively mountainous after many miles of flat fen. At the roundabout junction with the A10 take the second exit, and continue past the hamlet of Bexwell. Its farm, hall and little church – whose Norman round tower has an octagonal top – cluster appealingly together among trees. The A1122 runs on through Stradsett and Fincham, where flint, the traditional East Anglian building stone, starts to appear in the buildings, including the fine Perpendicular church. The road at this point was the main Roman road in the area, a continuation of the Fen Causeway. After passing through a wood, turn right on to the A47 for the last 2 miles into Swaffham.

Looking more like a dignified spa than an East Anglian market town, Swaffham is a delightful place. Even the most mundane of shops and offices are housed in well-proportioned 18th- and 19th-century buildings set about the spacious market place, and the market cross – with its pillars, dome and figure of Ceres, the corn goddess – is remarkably elegant. It was built by the Earl of Oxford in 1783. The church has a wonderful

A figure of Swaffham's famous Pedlar is carved on one of the bench-ends in the parish church

The 15th-century hammer-beam roof of Swaffham church is adorned with 88 carved angels with outstretched wings

double-hammer-beam roof with 88 ca angels. The north aisle is said to have built by the Pedlar of Swaffham who, a brightly painted town sign relates, 'b dream found a great treasure'.

SWAFFHAM TO SHIPDHAM

Leave Swaffham by the A47 (SP Norw and at the bottom of the hill, past the chu turn right on to an unclassified road North Pickenham). The route is in heading for the Bradenhams, West and and Shipdham. In 2¾ miles keep forwar these villages, avoiding North Pickenha to the right. The lane has many twists turns, but is well signposted. Dotted alon roadside are large areas of concrete; thes not passing places, but dumps for sugar a staple crop in Norfolk. Over the fields t right can be seen a vast number of what like factory sheds; this is possibly where Christmas dinner comes from – one o mammoth, modern, scientifically equip turkey-farms for which Norfolk is also known. Here and there, flint-built cottag typical feature of East Anglia, are a welc reminder of older traditions. They are either of whole, or 'knapped' (halved) fli the knapping of local flints is a traditi craft in Norfolk.

The villages of West and East Braden merge into each other, and shortly the r reaches Shipdham, a pretty little place, w it turns left on to the A1075 (SP Dereham). Shipdham is famous for graceful, double-domed oriental-style cu which surmounts its square church tow dates from the 17th century and is of ca wood covered with lead. Inside the ch are two massive wooden chests where the parish registers and records coul securely kept. There is also an exceptio fine wooden lectern of about 1500, with appealing lions crouched about the foot.

On the green stands the village depicting an ancient custom, 'the drynk of church ales'. These 'drynkkings', recorded here in the early 16th century, the social gatherings, often simply calle church ales', of the parish, and correspo – in an age when home-brewed ale wa standard refreshment – to today's c mornings, garden fetes and village danc

SHIPDHAM TO NORWICH

Drive on past the green and turn right b the King's Head on to an unclassified (SP Reymerston). In 1¼ miles turn left 2½ miles later, at the T-junction, turn r Half a mile beyond the village of Reymer turn left (SP Garvestone, Dereham), right (SP Hardingham, Wymondham) a crossroads a few hundred yards furthe This leads to the B1135, where the turns right (SP Kimberley). Carry or nearly 3 miles and turn left on to the B for Norwich, passing through Barford

BAWBURGH

Almost 4 miles beyond Barford you can make a detour by taking the second signposted turning on the left to Bawburgh. This is a pretty village whose tiny church has an interesting legend attached to it. It is dedicated to St Walstan, a local farm-worker who was noted for his saintliness. When he died, in 1016, his body was placed on a bier drawn by his own oxen. They wandered off at will, stopping at nightfall to rest in nearby Costessey Woods. A well of holy water sprang up on the spot where they lay, and this has been called St Walstan's Well ever since. Over the centuries it became a place of pilgrimage, particularly for farm-workers, since Walstan is their patron saint. To this day one of the lodges of Bawburgh Hall is known as the Slipper House, for here the pilgrims would remove their shoes before visiting the shrine.

The main route passes through Colney and comes into Norwich past the University of East Anglia, one of the 'new' universities. It stands in Earlham Park, which retains its old hall, a lovely gabled building of red brick. The rest of the modernistic campus is in complete contrast. It was designed by Sir Denys Lasdun, architect of the South Bank complex of theatres, art gallery and concert hall in London, and the concept is similar. The buildings have a stark, geometrical outline, all in concrete. Down by the lake are some particularly eye-catching halls of residence in the form of stepped pyramids. The

The Sainsbury Centre at the University of East Anglia

latest addition to the university is the Sainsbury Centre for the Visual Arts.* This long, low building, looking rather like an aircraft hangar, is clad in aluminium panels and was donated by the head of the supermarket chain. With the building he also gave his own art collection, which includes paintings by Francis Bacon as well as African and South American sculpture. Not all the collection is on permanent display, but there are often good temporary exhibitions.

The B1108 leads all the way into Norwich, meeting the ring road at a roundabout. Ahead lies the city; to the left the roads to the north coast; to the right the roads to Ipswich, Great Yarmouth and the other east coast resorts. (For a town plan and description of Norwich, see p. 113.)

Norwich market is overlooked by the castle keep, which was refaced in Bath stone in the 19th century

ROUTE 21

164 MILE

Leicester to Taunton

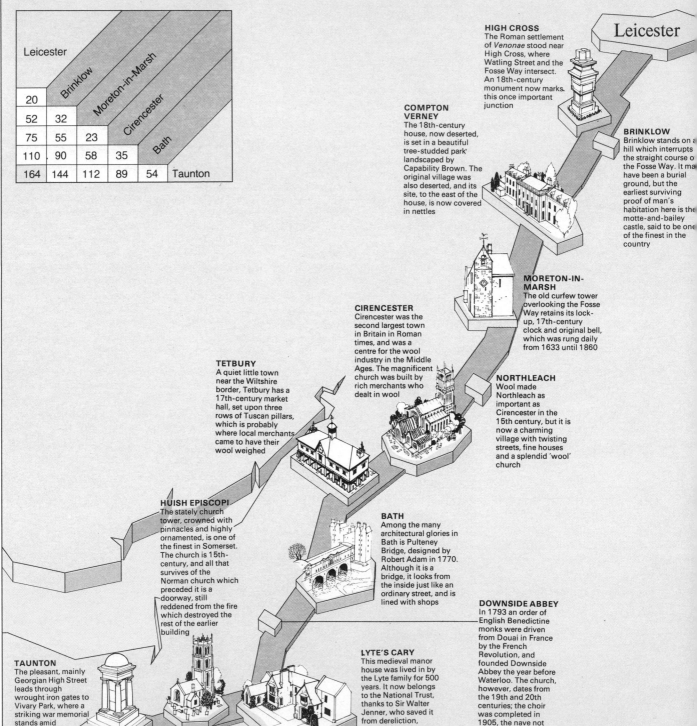

Leicester				
20	Brinklow			
52	32	Moreton-in-Marsh		
75	55	23	Cirencester	
110	90	58	35	Bath
164	144	112	89	54	Taunton

Leicester

HIGH CROSS
The Roman settlement of *Venonae* stood near High Cross, where Watling Street and the Fosse Way intersect. An 18th-century monument now marks this once important junction

BRINKLOW
Brinklow stands on a hill which interrupts the straight course of the Fosse Way. It may have been a burial ground, but the earliest surviving proof of man's habitation here is the motte-and-bailey castle, said to be one of the finest in the country

COMPTON VERNEY
The 18th-century house, now deserted, is set in a beautiful tree-studded park landscaped by Capability Brown. The original village was also deserted, and its site, to the east of the house, is now covered in nettles

MORETON-IN-MARSH
The old curfew tower overlooking the Fosse Way retains its lock-up, 17th-century clock and original bell, which was rung daily from 1633 until 1860

CIRENCESTER
Cirencester was the second largest town in Britain in Roman times, and was a centre for the wool industry in the Middle Ages. The magnificent church was built by rich merchants who dealt in wool

NORTHLEACH
Wool made Northleach as important as Cirencester in the 15th century, but it is now a charming village with twisting streets, fine houses and a splendid 'wool' church

TETBURY
A quiet little town near the Wiltshire border, Tetbury has a 17th-century market hall, set upon three rows of Tuscan pillars, which is probably where local merchants came to have their wool weighed

HUISH EPISCOPI
The stately church tower, crowned with pinnacles and highly ornamented, is one of the finest in Somerset. The church is 15th-century, and all that survives of the Norman church which preceded it is a doorway, still reddened from the fire which destroyed the rest of the earlier building

BATH
Among the many architectural glories in Bath is Pulteney Bridge, designed by Robert Adam in 1770. Although it is a bridge, it looks from the inside just like an ordinary street, and is lined with shops

DOWNSIDE ABBEY
In 1793 an order of English Benedictine monks were driven from Douai in France by the French Revolution, and founded Downside Abbey the year before Waterloo. The church, however, dates from the 19th and 20th centuries; the choir was completed in 1905, the nave not until 1925

TAUNTON
The pleasant, mainly Georgian High Street leads through wrought iron gates to Vivary Park, where a striking war memorial stands amid magnificent floral displays

LYTE'S CARY
This medieval manor house was lived in by the Lyte family for 500 years. It now belongs to the National Trust, thanks to Sir Walter Jenner, who saved it from dereliction, restored it, and collected the furniture

would be easy to find a descriptive title summarizing the
... of this route. It is the Fosse Way route. For, with the
...ption of the last 20 miles or so, the route follows this
...endous feat of Roman engineering along almost every
...on that remains open to traffic.

...hen the Romans arrived in Britain in AD 43 their first
...rity, after the worst of the fighting was over, was to establish
...k and easy communications from fort to fort. The Fosse
... was one of the earliest and most important of the Roman
...s, and marked the first boundary of the new Roman
...ince. Running from Lincoln down into Devon, it follows,
...uch of its length, the prehistoric Jurassic Way. To the west
... road was the highland region of Britain, much of it
...red by deep forests, where grain (the staple food of the
...naries) was in short supply, and peopled by fierce
...smen not yet under the Roman yoke. Eventually the
...ork of roads spread into Wales, Northern England and
...land, pushing the frontier into the tribal heartlands.

...oman roads were not conceived as ruler-straight for their
...e length, but were built as a series of stretches linking
...ninent topographical features by the straightest possible
...e. They were built to last and to carry heavy traffic – not
... troops and their equipment but, as the province became
... settled, all the essential and non-essential commodities of
...iving and peaceful society. After the Romans left, the roads
...nto gradual decay and were virtually forgotten. Not until
...8th century, with the coming of the turnpike roads, did
...in have a road system that could compare with the one
... by the ruthlessly methodical Romans.

...his route starts in Leicester, itself an important Roman
... It was called *Ratae* and was the capital of a large area
...hly equivalent to the Celtic kingdom of the Coritani tribe.
...s of the original Roman wall – called the Jewry Wall – still
...d to a height of 30 feet, and nearby are the remains of
...mportant baths.

...om Leicester the route travels southwards along the Fosse
..., leaving it for a while at the River Soar, and returning to it
...ligh Cross, where the Fosse Way and Watling Street
...sected. Watling Street here forms the boundary between
...estershire and Warwickshire, and the Fosse Way now runs
...ugh the peaceful Warwickshire countryside that lies to the
... of Coventry's enormous sprawl. For mile after mile the
...e Way takes the form of an unclassified road which leads
...ght across country, crossing the valleys of the Avon, Leam
...Dene. There are few villages on the line of the road, but just
... there are numerous little communities, almost all of which
...nhanced by an ancient church, an imposing manor house
...group of picturesque houses.

...aving crossed the River Dene, the route rises on to a long
..., then plunges dramatically down to Halford and the
...r Stour. Beyond the Vale of Red Horse and Stretton-on-
...osse is Moreton-in-Marsh, the first of this route's
...wold towns. Next comes Stow-on-the-Wold, built on a
...lswept hillside site that was crossed by prehistoric
...kways, Roman roads and stage-coach routes. To the south
...ow, and just off the main route, are some of the loveliest of
...Cotswold villages. The Fosse Way continues over the
...wold Hills, passing near Bourton-on-the-Water and
...hleach, to reach Cirencester.

...the valley of the River Colne, north of Cirencester, is
...lworth Roman Villa, one of the best preserved of its kind in
...ountry. It was begun in the first half of the 2nd century,

PLACES OF INTEREST: OPENING DETAILS

Upper Slaughter
MANOR HOUSE open May to end Sep Fri pm only

Chedworth
CHEDWORTH ROMAN VILLA open Mar to Oct Tue to Sun and Bank Holidays (except Good Fri); also open Feb and Nov to mid Dec Wed to Sun

Cirencester
CORINIUM MUSEUM open all year daily (except Sun am, Mon Oct to Apr, 25 and 26 Dec)

Westonbirt
WESTONBIRT ARBORETUM open all year

Badminton
BADMINTON HOUSE open Jun to Sep Wed pm only

Dodington
DODINGTON HOUSE open Apr to Sep

Dyrham
DYRHAM PARK open Apr to Oct daily (except Fri, and Thu Apr, May and Oct), pm only

Bath
ROMAN BATHS AND PUMP ROOM open all year

Oakhill
OAKHILL MANOR: WORLD OF MODELS open Apr to end Oct, pm only

Kingsdon
LYTE'S CARY open Mar to end Oct Wed and Sat, pm only

Muchelney
MUCHELNEY ABBEY open all year

Taunton
TAUNTON CASTLE, SOMERSET COUNTY MUSEUM, and SOMERSET MILITARY MUSEUM open all year (except Bank Holidays); closed Sun Apr to end Sep, Sun and Mon Oct to end Mar

POST OFFICE MUSEUM open all year Sat pm only

and was undoubtedly the home of some important personage –
perhaps one of the governors of nearby Cirencester. There were
four distinct building phases at Chedworth, each one of them
introducing additional comfort and luxury. Life on the Roman
pattern continued here well into the 5th century, after which
the precarious toe-hold kept on civilization by the Romano-
British citizens was broken by the relentless advances of
Germanic invaders. The villa was discovered quite by chance
in 1864, and is now preserved by the National Trust.

Cirencester, known to the Romans as *Corinium*, began life as a
military installation at the junction of the Fosse Way, Ermine
Street and Akeman Street. It grew to become the second largest
city in Roman Britain, first as the cantonal capital of the
Dobunnii tribal lands and then as the provincial capital of
Britannia Prima, which embraced the whole of Wales and the
West Country. Numerous villas have been found in the
Cirencester area, many of which have mosaics made by a
school of craftsmen which was probably based in the city.

Beyond Cirencester the Fosse Way marches across country
towards Bath as a track for much of its length, and the route
veers west to reach Bath via Tetbury. From Didmarton the
road follows a limestone finger that is a southward extension of
the Cotswolds, passing on the way the stately homes of
Dodington and Dyrham.

Created as a spa town by the Romans, Bath has preserved
much of the spirit of the province. The original bath is still
there, still lined with Roman lead from the Mendip mines and
still fed by Roman pipes. It is in Bath, perhaps more than
anywhere else in Britain, that the intimate aspects of life in the
Roman Empire come most vividly to life.

The Fosse Way is joined again on the other side of Bath and is
followed intermittently to a point some 12 miles beyond
Shepton Mallet, where the route turns westward, leaving the
Roman road to continue on its way deep into Devon.

Splendid churches are the highlight of the route around
Langport, beyond which are the flat lands of West Sedge Moor.
Taunton, set in a rich vale beneath the Quantocks and the
Blackdown Hills, also has Roman memories. In the local
museum is a mosaic from a nearby villa which tells in charming
pictures the story of Dido and Aeneas from Virgil's *Aeneid*.

A hilltop in Brinklow is the site of one of the finest motte-and-bailey castles in England

LEICESTER TO BRINKLOW

The route begins in central Leicester, and takes the A46 Coventry road to bring you out of the city along Narborough Road. There are few signs here that this Roman route has been in use for almost 2000 years: building sites, office blocks and mills are followed by rows of bright suburban shops and 'semis'; only the straightness of the road betrays its Roman origins.

The first major roundabout is where the spur road from M1 junction 21 joins the route. Travellers starting from points elsewhere in the area or further north can easily join the route here by taking the Leicester road from the motorway for ½ mile to reach this roundabout. Follow signs for Narborough and the B4114 at this roundabout and the next one, then, ignoring subsequent signs to Narborough, continue straight on for Sharnford. At Stoney Bridge the road begins to wind, leaving the course of the Fosse Way. Follow the one-way system (SP Wolvey) through Sharnford, still on the B4114.

About 2 miles beyond Sharnford turn left on to the A5, and in 1 mile, at the next junction, turn right on to an unclassified road (SP Monks Kirby, Fosse Way). The A5 here is Watling Street, most famous of British Roman roads, and the junction where you turn off it marked the centre of Roman Britain. Here, at High Cross, the Fosse Way – still visible as a grassy track to the north – crossed Watling Street, and the Roman settlement of *Venonae* was nearby. A monument in the garden of High Cross Farm, on the left-hand side of the A5, was erected in the 18th century by local landowners to commemorate this strategic crossing point.

From High Cross the Fosse Way takes the form of a true country lane, shaded by trees and running through rolling farmland, crossing the B4455 after 1¾ miles.

MONKS KIRBY

The Raising of Lazarus, a detail of the Victorian stained glass in St Edith's Church

Soon the imposing tower of St Edith's Church, Monks Kirby, comes into view in a hollow to the left, and a detour can be made by turning left to the village. The church is of rich, red sandstone and the interior, with its lofty arcading, is unusually impressive. The grand scale of the church (and the name of the village) is explained by the former existence of a priory here. In the Middle Ages this peaceful, pleasant village was quite a busy town; it not only had its monastic house, but also a weekly market and an annual fair.

The main route crosses the B4112 and the bridge over the M6, and at the T-junction turns right to join the A427. Approaching Brinklow, the road crosses the main railway line to the North-West and then the Oxford Canal – its wharf, to the right, lined with

...erton's unusual windmill was built in 1632 for the ... family, who held the local manor for 400 years

...htly painted barges. Brinklow itself has a ...example of castle earthworks, reached by ...ng the first turn left as you enter the ...ge, up Ell Lane. The 40-foot-high motte, ...astle mound, and two baileys can still be ... The castle stands on a steep hill, and ...e are splendid views over the Avon valley ...1 the top of the mound.

...NKLOW TO COMBROOK

...n left at the end of Brinklow's main street ...o the B4029. In 1½ miles, at Bretford, turn ...n to the A428 to cross the narrow bridge ... the Avon, then turn right on to the

B4029 (SP Wolston). In ½ mile, pass under the railway bridge and at the fork branch left (unclassified) to continue on the Fosse Way.

WOLSTON

The attractive village of Wolston is well worth a detour. To reach it, continue along the B4029 and turn right into Main Street. Beside the road runs a stream, spanned by several small bridges which lead to the cottages beyond. Further along on the left, just before you cross the river, is the church, which has a Norman south doorway and four fine Norman arches inside. Across the river from here can be seen the earthworks where Brandon Castle once stood.

After 2 miles the Fosse Way crosses the A45, which runs through a stately avenue of trees. Skirt Stretton-on-Dunsmore and 1 mile later, at Princethorpe, turn right on to the B4453, left on to the A423 and immediately right again on to an unclassified road (SP Eathorpe, Stow). Continue following signs for Stow. After 5½ miles cross the A425, and 2½ miles later, as you approach the second turning on the left to Harbury, look out for Chesterton Windmill on a hill to the left. It is an extraordinary building, domed and resting on six pillars. It dates from as long ago as 1632, and was probably originally built as an observatory. After the route crosses the A41, 2 miles later, wide views open up to the right over the valleys of the Avon and Dene.

COMPTON VERNEY AND COMBROOK

At the junction 3¾ miles later, where the Fosse Way crosses the B4086, you can make an attractive detour by turning left. The B4086 descends the hill past Compton Verney, on the left, a Palladian mansion set beside a tranquil lake which is spanned by a Georgian stone bridge. The house is partly the work of Robert Adam; the chapel, and possibly the grounds, that of Capability Brown. The house and grounds are privately owned and not open to the public, but much of the fine house and its cedar-shaded grounds can be seen from the road. At the foot of the hill the road crosses the long, narrow lake and rises up Spring Hill on the other side of the valley. Near the top, turn right on to an unclassified road for Combrook and follow a narrow lane which gives open views over this pleasing and little-known corner of Warwickshire.

Combrook is certainly no disappointment, nestling in a hollow and as lovely as many Cotswold villages without their self-conscious prettiness. The church is topped by a most curious steeple with all kinds of Gothic trimmings. To the west of the church a cul-de-sac leads down to a clutch of stone cottages – there is no mistaking that the Cotswolds are not far away now – and to the left two public footpaths offer a pleasant stroll down to the lower lake of Compton Verney. Drive through Combrook, climbing steeply up the valley side to return to the Fosse Way and turning left on to it at the top of the hill to complete the detour.

...osse Way near Combrook. This remarkable achievement in Roman road-building originally ran from Lincoln all the way down into Devon

COMBROOK TO STOW-ON-THE-WOLD

The Fosse Way continues along a ridge, with more wide views to right and left as it runs into much hillier country. Cross the A422 and descend a dramatic hill, keeping forward on to the B4451 before taking the first exit (A429) at the roundabout to enter Halford. The main part of this peaceful stone village lies just off the road to the right. Its church has a rare Norman tympanum above the north door, with a carving of a seated angel. The chancel arch is also Norman, and beside it is a niche with another Norman carving, uncovered in 1960 when local volunteers were helping to strip the stone walls of plaster. By the font are two fire hooks, once used for pulling burning thatch off cottages in the village. Continue on the main road and cross the Stour by the modern road bridge. Beside it, in great contrast, stands the narrow medieval bridge which carried the Fosse Way across the river until 1962. Cross the A34 at the roundabout ¾ mile later and continue along the A429. Rolling hill country accompanies the route into Gloucestershire and to Moreton-in-Marsh.

The Fosse Way forms the main street of this little country town, interrupted only by the Redesdale Market Hall with its fine windows and Cotswold stone roof, topped by a clock-tower and a tall chimney. The building dates from 1887. The curiosity on the corner opposite, cheek by jowl with petrol pumps and garage signs, is the stone curfew tower, which has a 17th-century clock and bell. Moreton has an array of shops, restaurants and banks along the broad main street – the first real signs of civilization for many miles.

The A429 leads from Moreton to Stow-on-the-Wold. The town's name is no joke, as you will discover as you climb the long hill on whose top the town sits; it has a reputation as one of the chilliest and windiest spots in the Cotswolds. The town centre is just off to the left. It is a historic place, for it lay on an early ridgeway long before the Romans came; then it became a coaching stop and finally a favourite stopping place for the modern motorist. Several interesting little streets lead out of the large market place – one to the fine church, where 1000 Royalists were imprisoned in the Civil War. (For Stow see also p. 48.)

THE SWELLS AND THE SLAUGHTERS

Cottages are reflected in the waters of the River Eye at the picture-postcard village of Lower Slaughter

By taking the B4077 Tewkesbury road from Stow you can make a circular detour which takes in four enchanting Cotswold villages. The first is Upper Swell, a gem of a place and quite unspoilt. As you enter the village you cross an old stone bridge, with a mill (complete with mill-wheel and mill-pond) on the right. Half-way up the hill on the right is a tiny Norman church, almost dwarfed by the solemn yews lining the churchyard path.

Continue through the village and turn left (SP Lower Swell, The Slaughters). A narrow country lane gives views over the tree-clad Dikler valley to the left before reaching Lower Swell. A stream winds its way around the village, emerging from a little culvert by the war memorial, designed by Sir Edwin Lutyens. At the memorial turn right on to the B4068 and then left (SP The Slaughters). Bear right at a fork (SP Upper Slaughter), and drop down into the valley of the River Eye, which winds through The Slaughters –

their name does not, as one might imagine, reflect a bloody past, but comes from the Saxon word *sloghtre* meaning 'muddy place'. Upper Slaughter, like Lower Swell, is a scattered village: houses with lovely old mullioned windows and Cotswold stone roofs peep from behind every clump of trees and every hill.

Cross the little bridge and follow signs to Lower Slaughter, turning left at the T-junction and passing Upper Slaughter's fine Elizabethan manor house* on the left, clearly visible as you round a left-hand bend.

Lower Slaughter is a different story, being very much on the tourist trail. But seen at its best, late on a spring or autumn afternoon, it is a peaceful, pretty and neat place – and a much-photographed one.

Turn right after crossing the stream, and when you reach the A429 turn right on to it to complete the detour, picking up the Fosse Way again.

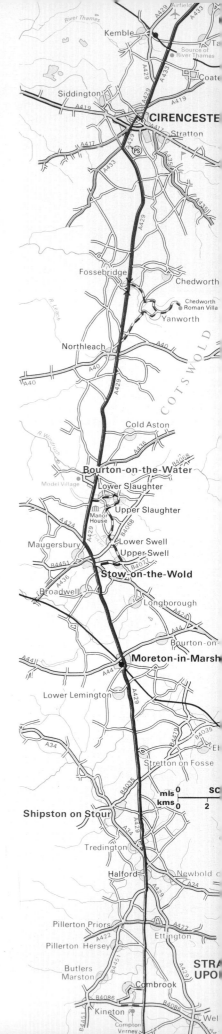

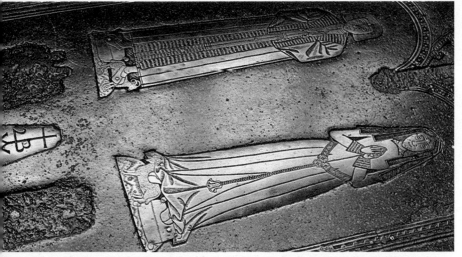

early 16th-century memorial to Thomas and Joan Bushe is one of many fine brasses in Northleach church

CHEDWORTH ROMAN VILLA

Within 3 miles of the A429 as it continues beyond Northleach lies Chedworth, site of probably the best-preserved Roman villa in the country. To reach it, turn right off the A429 at the first junction after the A40 crossroads and follow signs along unclassified roads to Yanworth and Roman Villa. The road leads through Yanworth, whose delightfully unspoilt Norman church is tucked away to the right, and along a secluded wooded valley to reach the villa.* It was excavated in the late 19th century, following the discovery of a fragment of Roman mosaic by a gamekeeper who was searching for a lost ferret. The plan of the villa is still distinct, and the remaining walls have been given miniature roofs to protect them from the weather. A museum houses many relics found on the site, including fine mosaic pavements.

Retrace your steps from the villa for almost 1½ miles; then, just before reaching Yanworth, turn right (SP Fossebridge). Follow unclassified roads to return to the A429, turning right on to it to rejoin the main route at Fossebridge.

OW-ON-THE-WOLD TO CIRENCESTER

main route continues from Stow along A429 (SP Cirencester), with open views ss the Cotswolds. Then comes a series of chback hills as the road dips to cross a ey and rises again, before dropping once e to cross the A40 at the edge of thleach. The town centre lies off to the left his junction. Here is one of the finest Cotswold 'wool' churches, built by wealthy merchants who owed their prosperity, like the Romans in the area before them, to the Cotswold sheep. The church possesses a rich collection of brasses, most of them depicting these woolmen of the 15th and 16th centuries and sometimes their individual 'woolmarks'. The gabled stone buildings in the market place include the old Wool Houses.

Six miles from Fossebridge, at the major crossroads, turn right into Cirencester, later following signs into the town centre. In Roman times, Cirencester was the second largest town in Britain after London. It stood at the junction of two great roads, the Fosse Way and Ermin Way – still important highways running almost arrow-straight over the Cotswolds. A fascinating collection of Roman relics, including spectacular mosaics and fragments of masonry, is housed in the Corinium Museum* in Park Street.

The town lapsed into obscurity during the Dark Ages that followed the return of the legions to Rome, but soared to new heights in the Middle Ages, when the wool trade made the Cotswolds one of the wealthiest parts of England. Prosperous merchants provided funds to build the superb church that towers above the market place. It is approached by a porch, built around 1500, that would not look out of place in front of a cathedral. From the top of the tower there is a magnificent view westwards over the 3000 acres of Cirencester Park. (Route continues on p. 230.)

iew from Cirencester's church tower extends beyond the town to Cirencester Park, screened by its enormous yew hedge

THE COTSWOLDS

Cottage architecture at Stow-on-the-

THE Cotswold Hills, long famous for their captivating buildings of honey-coloured stone, have enchanted generations of visitors. Even at the height of the holiday season, all but a few of the most popular villages – such as Bourton-on-the-Water and Broadway – have a degree of rustic charm and tranquillity rarely found elsewhere in southern England.

The hills are shaped like a huge wedge. The western escarpment, green with hanging woodlands, rises steeply above the broad, fertile vales of Berkeley, Gloucester and Evesham. The crest is just over 1000 feet high in places, but seems considerably higher because so much of the land below it is flat. Dover's Hill, Broadway Hill, Cleeve Common, Birdlip Hill and Haresfield Beacon are just a few of many vantage points from which there are immense views across the Severn valley to the Malverns, the uplands of southern Shropshire and the distant mountains of Wales.

Behind the escarpment the hills roll eastwards towards Malmesbury, Cirencester, Bibury, Burford and Chipping Norton. They run down towards the valley of the Cherwell in a series of soft undulations and are carved by several streams and rivers, notably the Windrush, Evenlode and Coln. A long finger of Cotswold stone stretches south towards Bath, and although less well known than the northern Cotswolds, its villages and rolling countryside of beech-shaded pastures are equally delightful.

COTSWOLD architecture achieves a harmony and unity that is rarely surpassed in Britain. This astonishing quality is mainly due to the oolitic limestone from which whole villages and towns are built. Some of the quarries which supplied the stone were opened more than 1000 years ago.

Such words as 'muffities', 'wivetts', 'tants' and 'cussems' could well have been invented by Lewis Carroll for one of his whimsical poems. In fact they denote different sizes of the roofing stones that contribute so much to the picture-postcard beauty of Cotswold buildings. Widespread use of the stones dates from the 14th century, when they replaced fire-prone thatch, and they were held in place by oak pegs, iron nails and, in some cases, sheep's bones. The stones are very heavy, which is why many old roofs undulate gently. Stones such as these should keep the weather at bay for at least 200 years, but those roofing the almshouses in

Chipping Campden are many still in excellent c after almost four centu

Cotswold stone is too used in towns with corr smoke-laden atmosphe here it weathers deligh the clean upland air. S makes it relatively easy so many buildings have attractive 'dripmoulds' their mullioned window blocks carved with date initials. Diamond-shap window panes, framed strips of lead, are anoth traditional feature.

Prizewinning sheep painted by Richard Whitford included the famous Northleach flock, which were shipped to America in the 19th century

WOOL made Stow-on-the-Wold one of the most prosperous places in England during the Middle Ages. As late as the 17th century, when Daniel Defoe chronicled his journeys through Britain, Stow Fair saw 20,000 sheep changing hands.

Sheep still play an important part in the economy of the Cotswolds, but the wool trade went into decline towards the end of the 18th century. Meat production became more important as the Industrial Revolution attracted country folk to the burgeoning towns of the Midlands and elsewhere.

Wool merchants left a rich legacy of superb churches – notably Fairford, with its magnificent stained glass, and the 15th-century delight at Northleach. John Fortey, builder of Northleach's nave, is buried in the church. Appropriately enough, a sheep and a sack of wool are featured on his commemorative brass.

Chipping Campden, one of the loveliest little towns in England, has retained an air of solid prosperity. William Grevel, a wealthy wool merchant whose 14th-century house still stands, is buried in Campden's notable 'wool' church. In Bibury, the quaint Arlington Row cottages where weavers once worked are now owned by the National Trust.

MAIN roads, many dating from Roman times, sweep through-traffic swiftly across the Cotswold Hills. But there are miles of little-used lanes and minor roads along which sleepy villages and hamlets are strung like jewels on a thread. They have such interesting names as Upper Slaughter and Guiting Power. 'Chipping', as in Chipping Campden and Chipping Norton, is the Old English word for 'market'. It recalls the golden days of the wool trade when wealthy merchants built many of the Cotswolds' superb houses and churches. The churches include Northleach and Painswick, where a 'tomb trail' takes in 75 fine examples of local craftsmanship in stone.

Many visitors are content just to stroll, pause and admire, but the Cotswolds have much to offer those who fancy something just a little more formal and organized. There are stately homes and gardens, wildlife parks, prehistoric and Roman remains, fish farms and motor museums. Bourton-on-the-Water has a delightful scale model of itself, fashioned from 200 tons of stone. Snowshill Manor, three miles south of Broadway, invariably delights lovers of the unexpected. Its many treasures include a room where Japanese warriors in ornate Samurai armour hold a 'council of war'. Roman remains include the splendid villa at Chedworth; and the Corinium Museum at Cirencester contains a memorable collection of Roman artefacts.

: A 17th-century gateway in Chipping Campden is all that remains of Campden House

Below: Snowshill is one of the most tranquil Cotswold villages

Wool was weighed and sold in Tetbury's 17th-century market hall when the town was a thriving centre for the wool trade

CIRENCESTER TO WESTONBIRT

Leave Cirencester on the A429 Chippenham road and keep forward to join the A433 1 mile beyond Cirencester's outskirts, where the Chippenham road goes left. Just past the railway bridge, 1½ miles later on the right, is a footpath which leads to the source of the River Thames. If you decide to make the short walk, do not expect to see a spring gushing spectacularly from the hillside: for most of the year the river runs underground, emerging on the other side of the Fosse Way. It is only during very wet spells that any trace of water can be seen at this hallowed spot.

Soon the road parts company with the Fosse Way, which continues across Kemble Airfield and beyond as a track, while the A433 goes to Tetbury. Follow signs through the town for Bristol and Bath, passing numerous antique shops, and turn right by the picturesque market hall, supported by three rows of stone pillars. The road out of Tetbury passes the church, an 18th-century Gothic masterpiece. Box pews, a gallery and slender wooden pillars grace its interior, and round three sides runs an enclosed corridor from which private doors lead to the pews. (For Tetbury see also p. 185.)

From Tetbury the A433 (SP Bath) is a wide road, bordered by stone walls and over-looking characteristic limestone scenery, which brings you after about 3 miles to the village of Westonbirt and its Arboretum,* whose entrance is signposted on the right.

The word 'arboretum' means a place devoted to the cultivation of trees.

Westonbirt, now managed by the Forestry Commission, was begun in 1829 by Robert Stayner Holford and his son, Sir George Holford. At the time when they began collecting and planting, many trees that we now take for granted as part of the scenery, such as the Douglas fir from North America, had not been established in this country. Both father and son were indefatigable collectors, and the trees they planted now form an unrivalled collection of specimens from all over Europe as well as parts of Asia and the Americas. In spring and early summer there are fine displays of flowering shrubs such as rhododendrons, magnolias and camellias. The visitor centre houses an exhibition explaining the history of the Arboretum and pointing out features of special interest.

WESTONBIRT TO BATH

Continue along the A433 through the attractive village of Didmarton and past Worcester Lodge, a rather grand gateway on the left which marks the boundary of Badminton Park. After 1½ miles, at the junction with the A46, turn left (SP Bath). About 3 miles down the road you will see, across a field on the right, the unmistakable rectangular outline of Sodbury Camp, an Iron Age hill-fort, and then, on the left approaching the crossroads with the B4040 and the A432, some curious miniature brick turrets sticking up out of the ground and looking like castles in a game of chess. These are ventilation shafts for the railway from South Wales to Swindon, which passes through a 2-mile-long tunnel here.

GREAT BADMINTON

At this crossroads a detour can be made to the village of Great Badminton. Turn left on to the B4040 (SP Malmesbury) and after about ½ miles turn left on to an unclassified road (SP Badminton), following it to a crossroads where you turn left into the village. Great Badminton is a most attractive cluster of stone-built model 'estate' cottages leading up to the entrance of Badminton Park. Badminton House,* home of the dukes of Beaufort, is a Palladian mansion dating from the 17th and 18th centuries. Every April the Park is the scene of the Badminton Horse Trials. This annual three-day event, started in 1949, is only the latest in a history of sporting events connected with Badminton. One earlier duke is said to have been instrumental in establishing fox-hunting as a field sport, and another named the game of badminton after his estate.

Barely a mile from the B4040 crossroads the main route passes on the right the entrance to Dodington Park* (see p. 151) and then about 2 miles beyond the M4 roundabout, the twin gate lodges of Dyrham Park,* also on the right (see p. 209).

If you do not want to stop in Bath, follow signs for Exeter and the A367, otherwise those for the city centre. Bath is a busy place, plagued by through-traffic as well as tourists and local bustle, but do not be put off, for it is a unique city and not one to be missed. It combines Britain's most impressive collection of Roman remains with the country's finest Georgian townscape. A visit to the Roman Baths* combines the city's two ages of magnificence perhaps better than anything.

The baths themselves now form part of a Roman museum, giving a penetrating insight into life in Britain almost 2000 years ago. Visitors can see the steaming mineral water – which rises at a constant temperature of 120°F – gushing out of the overflow from the main hot spring. The adjacent Pump Room was a focus of the social scene in Georgian Bath. A fine 18th-century longcase clock and two sedan chairs are among the items on display in the Pump Room. Here you can still take the waters in elegant surroundings, and afterwards stroll around the city's terraces and crescents, imagining the era when the wealthy and fashionable flocked to Bath in pursuit of the latest fad. (For more details and a town plan of Bath, see p. 209.)

BATH TO STRATTON-ON-THE-FOSSE

Take the A367 (SP Exeter) from Bath, following the Fosse Way again. Hills and small patchwork fields surround the A367, then it drops to pass through Radstock.

Several miles beyond Radstock, on a hill to the right, is an unusually imposing church tower. It belongs to Downside Abbey, which can be reached by turning right in Stratton-on-the-Fosse. The abbey was first founded in France in the 17th century, but the monks and their pupils fled to England during the French Revolution and eventually settled at Downside. The abbey church, begun in the last century and still not complete (the west front is only 'temporary'), has an austere but strikingly grand interior of pale stone.

The tower of Bath Abbey soars above the Roman Great Bath, which was rediscovered in 1880. It is fed by the original lead pipes, still intact after 2000 years

STRATTON-ON-THE-FOSSE TO HUISH EPISCOPI

OAKHILL MANOR

About 3 miles beyond Stratton-on-the-Fosse, at the edge of Oakhill, a detour can be made by turning right off the A367 and following signs to Oakhill Manor.* The manor itself is a pleasant country house set in 8 acres of gardens high in the Mendip Hills. It is best known for the 'World of Models', a collection of models of all kinds, covering the history of land, sea and air transport. One of the finest such collections in the world, it includes working models of steam locomotives, of ships such as Brunel's *Great Western* and the *Mauretania*, a steam-operated fire engine and a Vickers Vimy bomber. Visitors are carried from the car park on a ¾-mile-long model railway, travelling through a miniature Cheddar Gorge and passing attractive little stations built of Mendip stone.

Continue along the A367 to a T-junction, where you should turn left on to the A37 for Shepton Mallet. The town centre is by-passed by the main road, but those interested in church architecture should not miss Shepton's wonderful wagon roof, whose bosses are richly carved with over 300 different designs.

The Fosse Way also by-passes Shepton Mallet, rejoining the main road just south of the town, where you should take care not to miss a right turn (SP Yeovil, Exeter) to carry on along the A37. Continue for 12½ miles to the large roundabout where the A37 meets the A303 trunk road, and take the fourth exit, the A372, saying farewell to the Fosse Way for the last time.

LYTE'S CARY

Just past the roundabout, a lane on the right offers a detour to Lyte's Cary,* a little-known medieval manor house owned by the National Trust. It has been the home of the Lyte family for 500 years, and retains its 14th-century chapel and 15th-century great hall. There is also a small formal garden.

Superb 12th-century chevron decoration surrounds the south doorway of Huish Episcopi church

The A372 by-passes Kingsdon on the right and then Long Sutton on the left, its church tower – like so many in Somerset – heralding the village's position long before any signposts are seen. Later, Huish Episcopi church appears with the same effect. Another feature of this stretch of road, and by now as familiar as the mellow Cotswold cottages with their stone roofs were earlier on the route, are the cottages built of blue lias stone topped by red-tiled roofs. They are dotted along the road all the way to Langport and beyond.

When you reach Huish Episcopi church, turn left (SP Muchelney, Crewkerne) to take the 'back route' into Langport. The tower of Huish Episcopi church is quite a party-piece, richly carved and ornamented. The Norman doorway of the church was burnished to a rich reddish-brown colour in a fire.

HUISH EPISCOPI TO TAUNTON

MUCHELNEY

Almost opposite the church is a left turn (SP Muchelney), which offers an interesting detour to Muchelney. To the right, between a farmyard and the parish church as you enter sleepy Muchelney village, are the ruins of Muchelney Abbey.* Founded in the 7th century, the abbey was systematically demolished after the Dissolution and the stone used for other buildings. But parts of it survive, including the 16th-century abbot's lodgings. One of the upstairs rooms has a magnificent original fireplace. The shafts rising from the richly carved overmantel are topped by stone lions. A section of the cloisters also still stands, and the ground plan of the entire abbey can be clearly seen now that the foundations have been excavated.

The abbey is not Muchelney's only item of historic interest: opposite the small green by the church stands the thatched Priest's House, probably dating from the 14th century.

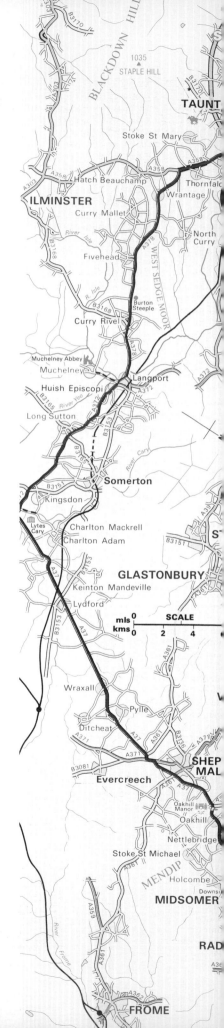

...ow shoots, called 'withies', grown on Sedgemoor are woven into baskets by craftsmen at Curry Rivel

The hilltop road through Langport leads beneath the unusual 'hanging chapel', a 15th-century stone gateway with a chapel above, and then past Langport's fine church, which dates from the same period.

At the foot of the hill, turn left on to the A378, which runs westwards along a ridge, offering extensive views southwards to the hill-country around Yeovil and sometimes northwards over West Sedge Moor. Curry Rivel boasts another fine medieval church, and 1 mile past the village, in the grounds of Burton Pynsent to the right, a Tuscan column known as Burton Steeple makes a prominent landmark. It was erected by Capability Brown in 1765 in memory of Sir William Pynsent, who owned the mansion. He left the house to the first Sir William Pitt, who lived here for a time.

Twelve miles beyond Langport, at Thornfalcon Garage, turn right on to the A358, dropping into the Vale of Taunton Deane and passing under the M5 to complete the journey into Taunton.

TAUNTON

Attractively set on the River Tone in the fertile Vale of Taunton Deane, Taunton is a historic market and county town with pleasant, tree-lined streets and several interesting old buildings.

Taunton first had a castle in the 8th century, but it was later rebuilt by the Normans. Some of their stonework survives in the present castle,* which was the headquarters of the Duke of Monmouth before the Battle of Sedgemoor – the last battle fought on English soil – in 1685. Many of the townsfolk supported Monmouth in his rebellion against James II. After Monmouth's defeat at the battle, Judge Jeffreys held his infamous 'Bloody Assize' in the Castle Hall, and many of the rebels were executed or deported as a result.

The Castle now houses the Somerset County Museum* and the Somerset Military Museum.* Taunton's other attractions include the unusual Post Office Museum,* in North Street, where the history of the telephone service is traced back over 100 years. The oldest telephone dates from 1877, and a section of the first trans-atlantic telephone cable, laid in 1857, is on display.

The Church of St Mary Magdalene is undoubtedly Taunton's finest building. It dates from the 15th century, but the magnificent 163-foot-high Perpendicular tower which dominates the town is a careful Victorian reconstruction.

Other buildings of interest include the fine black-and-white Tudor House, in Fore Street, and the thatched leper hospital, founded in the 12th century. It originally stood outside the town boundary. Gray's Almshouses and Huish's Almshouses both date from the 17th century.

Taunton Castle (below), which was probably founded in Saxon times, has been altered and extended several times in its long history. It now houses the Somerset County Museum. The rich variety of exhibits include a Roman mosaic floor depicting scenes from Virgil's 'Aeneid' (below right), discovered on the site of a Roman villa near Langport. One of the more unusual exhibits (right) is a glovemaker's last, once used by a local craftsman

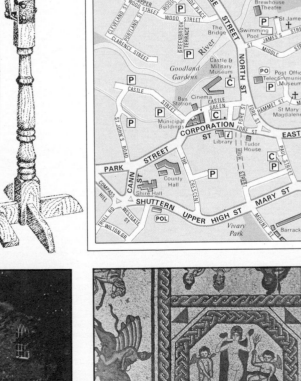

ROUTE 22

146 MILE[S]

Leicester to Llandudno

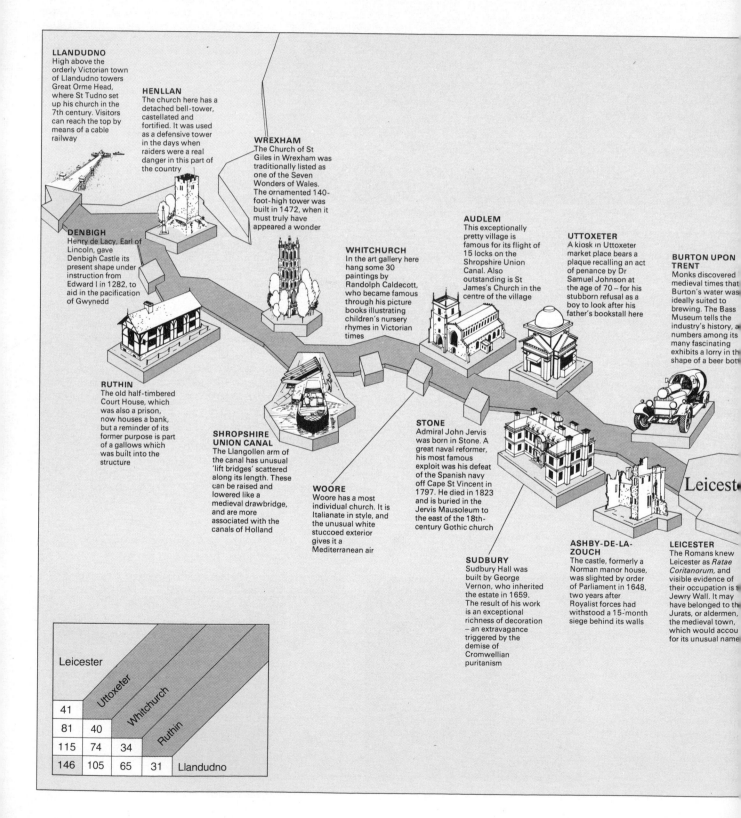

LLANDUDNO
High above the orderly Victorian town of Llandudno towers Great Orme Head, where St Tudno set up his church in the 7th century. Visitors can reach the top by means of a cable railway

HENLLAN
The church here has a detached bell-tower, castellated and fortified. It was used as a defensive tower in the days when raiders were a real danger in this part of the country

WREXHAM
The Church of St Giles in Wrexham was traditionally listed as one of the Seven Wonders of Wales. The ornamented 140-foot-high tower was built in 1472, when it must truly have appeared a wonder

AUDLEM
This exceptionally pretty village is famous for its flight of 15 locks on the Shropshire Union Canal. Also outstanding is St James's Church in the centre of the village

UTTOXETER
A kiosk in Uttoxeter market place bears a plaque recalling an act of penance by Dr Samuel Johnson at the age of 70 – for his stubborn refusal as a boy to look after his father's bookstall here

BURTON UPON TRENT
Monks discovered medieval times that Burton's water was ideally suited to brewing. The Bass Museum tells the industry's history, a numbers among its many fascinating exhibits a lorry in th shape of a beer bot[tle]

DENBIGH
Henry de Lacy, Earl of Lincoln, gave Denbigh Castle its present shape under instruction from Edward I in 1282, to aid in the pacification of Gwynedd

WHITCHURCH
In the art gallery here hang some 30 paintings by Randolph Caldecott, who became famous through his picture books illustrating children's nursery rhymes in Victorian times

RUTHIN
The old half-timbered Court House, which was also a prison, now houses a bank, but a reminder of its former purpose is part of a gallows which was built into the structure

SHROPSHIRE UNION CANAL
The Llangollen arm of the canal has unusual 'lift bridges' scattered along its length. These can be raised and lowered like a medieval drawbridge, and are more associated with the canals of Holland

WOORE
Woore has a most individual church. It is Italianate in style, and the unusual white stuccoed exterior gives it a Mediterranean air

STONE
Admiral John Jervis was born in Stone. A great naval reformer, his most famous exploit was his defeat of the Spanish navy off Cape St Vincent in 1797. He died in 1823 and is buried in the Jervis Mausoleum to the east of the 18th-century Gothic church

SUDBURY
Sudbury Hall was built by George Vernon, who inherited the estate in 1659. The result of his work is an exceptional richness of decoration – an extravagance triggered by the demise of Cromwellian puritanism

ASHBY-DE-LA-ZOUCH
The castle, formerly a Norman manor house, was slighted by order of Parliament in 1648, two years after Royalist forces had withstood a 15-month siege behind its walls

LEICESTER
The Romans knew Leicester as *Ratae Coritanorum*, and visible evidence of their occupation is t[he] Jewry Wall. It may have belonged to th[e] Jurats, or aldermen, the medieval town, which would accou[nt] for its unusual nam[e]

Leices[ter]

Leicester				
41	Uttoxeter			
81	40	Whitchurch		
115	74	34	Ruthin	
146	105	65	31	Llandudno

,OLLING green landscapes, watered by meandering rivers
the Soar, Trent and Dove emphasize central England's
t beauty on the early part of this route from Leicester to one
he most elegant seaside resorts in Wales. Modest hills
nge the mood in parts of Staffordshire, but the scenery does
change dramatically until the route has left Wrexham. The
l that runs north-westwards from the bustling old border
n soon reaches more than 1000 feet, then dips down before
bing again to cross the mountain range which guards the
utiful Vale of Clwyd. Wild hill scenery dotted with isolated
steads accompanies the route to the Vale of Conwy, from
re it is only a stone's throw to Llandudno.

rom Leicester the route travels westwards towards
rnwood Forest, passing through the villages of Groby and
kfield, both of which bear the scars of once extensive
rries. Charnwood covers a small area – little more than
n miles by five – but its scenery, in marked contrast to the
ssuming Midlands countryside that surrounds it, is
matic and unique.

is composed of extremely ancient rocks of several kinds,
e of them volcanic in origin, which have been exposed by
weathering away of the red marls that cover much of the
of the Midlands. During the Ice Ages Charnwood stood
ve the surrounding ice plain, and its rocks were shattered
splintered by the extreme cold. These pinnacles of rock,
n crowning bracken-covered slopes, are the most distinctive
ures of the area. Many of the delightful little valleys that
s-cross Charnwood have an infilling of softer rock, and as
e goes on more and more of this ancient landscape will be
aled. At one time Charnwood was a forest in the traditional
e of the word, and it is said that squirrels could travel from
to end of it without having to leave the treetops.

oalville – as its name suggests – stands above a substantial
field. Many of the houses in the mining towns and villages
d about have subsided through the collapse of old tunnels
are held together by iron bands or are propped up by
er baulks. Beyond Ashby-de-la-Zouch the route crosses
fly into Derbyshire before reaching Staffordshire and
ton upon Trent.

ver since an enterprising 11th-century monk discovered
the waters from the deep wells and springs in and around
ton were particularly good for making clear beer, the town
been engaged, to the exclusion of almost everything else, in
production of alcoholic beverages. Until well into the 20th
tury almost 90 per cent of the population were employed in
brewing industry, but increasing mechanization has
ced this figure in recent years. Beyond Burton the route
es its way past the ruins of Tutbury Castle – which has
n rebuilt several times during its long history and was
ually derelict when Mary, Queen of Scots, was imprisoned
e – and crosses the beautiful River Dove to enter Derby-
e once more. Running parallel to the Dove and the
fordshire–Derbyshire border, the route travels westwards
ugh Sudbury and Doveridge before re-entering
fordshire on the outskirts of Uttoxeter.

entle hills dotted with clumps of woodland lie on either side
e route between Uttoxeter and Stone which, like Burton,
ds beside the Trent. The manufacture of footwear is one of
ne's traditional industries. High-quality leather was avail-
e locally, for the rich pasturelands of the Trent (which
ders southwards in an enormous arc before turning north
each Burton) were ideal for cattle.

PLACES OF INTEREST: OPENING DETAILS

Ashby-de-la-Zouch
ASHBY-DE-LA-ZOUCH CASTLE open all year daily (except Wed and Thu)

Burton upon Trent
BASS MUSEUM open all year (except 25 and 26 Dec)

Tutbury
TUTBURY CASTLE open all year (except 25 and 26 Dec)

Sudbury
SUDBURY HALL open Apr to Oct Wed to Sun and Bank Holiday Mon, pm only

Elds Wood
WILLOUGHBRIDGE GARDEN TRUST open Mar to Nov

Wrexham
DOLL AND TOY MUSEUM open all year (except Nov)

ERDDIG open Apr to end Oct daily (except Mon, but open Bank Holiday), pm only

Denbigh
DENBIGH CASTLE open all year

LEICESTER'S CHURCH AND TOWN WALLS open all year

Prosperous farmland divided by little rivers stretches away in
all directions as the route passes through Woore and Audlem to
reach the old Shropshire market town of Whitchurch. The
clock set into the tower of St Alkmund's Church here was made
by J. B. Joyce and Co., who have been making clocks in Whitchurch through the reigns of 14 monarchs and proudly claim
in their catalogues to be the 'oldest clockmakers in the world'.

Beyond Whitchurch the route crosses an arm of the
Shropshire Union Canal and shortly enters what was once the
old county of Flintshire and now forms part of the Welsh
county of Clwyd. Bangor-is-y-coed, whose name means
'monastery under the wood', stands astride one of the
serpentine loops of the River Dee and was once the site of a
religious settlement of great size and importance. This was
destroyed by the Saxons after a battle fought in AD 615, and
nothing of it survives.

Although Wrexham is one of the fastest growing towns in
Wales and is surrounded by rapidly expanding suburbs, its
urban townscape lies remarkably close to wild countryside.
Quite suddenly the route has left factories, schools and houses
behind, and is in the moorland landscapes of the Clwydian
Hills. Several of the summits of the Clwydian range, notably
Foel Fenlli and Moel y Gaer, are crowned by hill-forts that are
lasting reminders of the Celtic tribesmen who lived in these
remote hills in late prehistoric times. As the route nears Ruthin
spectacular views open up across the Denbighshire Moors into
distant Snowdonia.

From Ruthin, a small country town with a tremendous
variety of handsome buildings, a fine old church and a
converted castle, the route follows the fertile Vale of Clwyd
northwards to Denbigh. North of Denbigh, whose ruined castle
looks across some of the richest farmland in North Wales, the
route climbs out of the Vale to reach Henllan. The beautiful
valley of the Afon Aled is accompanied from tiny Plasisaf to
Llansannan, and at Llanfair Talhaiarn, which was the birthplace of one of the most renowned 19th-century Welsh bards,
the road drops down into the valley of the Elwy.

Upland scenery, dominated by the limestone crags of Rhyd-
y-foel to the north, gives way to pastoral landscapes round
Dolwen, after which the route plummets down to the Conwy
estuary, with superb views across the water to Conwy Castle.
Two beautiful limestone headlands – Great Orme and Little
Orme – frame Llandudno's dignified sweep of seafront
buildings. Created as an early exercise in town planning in the
years after 1849, Llandudno quickly became known as the
'Queen of Welsh Resorts' – a title it has never lost.

The Jewry Wall is Leicester's most impressive survival from Roman times

LEICESTER TO BURTON UPON TRENT

Leave the centre of Leicester on the A50 (SP Burton upon Trent), following this road north-westwards through the suburbs, and passing the modern County Hall on the right. The road climbs very gradually, passing under the M1 and skirting Charnwood Forest. Coalville, as its name suggests, is the main town in the Leicestershire coalfield; shafts were first sunk here in the early 19th century. A colliery stands beside the A50 as it continues towards Ashby-de-la-Zouch.

Ashby is an interesting old market town – and was briefly a spa, when saline springs were discovered nearby in the early 19th century. The long main street has several attractive buildings; a bow-windowed shop on the north side is notably eye-catching.

St Helen's Church, a two-minute walk from the castle, has a chapel with effigies of the Hastings family, who for a long time held Ashby Castle.* Another chapel, on the opposite side of the building, has a 15th-century pilgrim's monument. The recumbent stone figure, dressed in a long cloak and clutching a staff, is believed to be of Thomas, the brother of Ashby's first Lord Hastings. (For Ashby see also p. 117.)

Follow the A50 (SP Burton) through Ashby, crossing into Derbyshire as the road runs through gently rolling country before dropping into the Trent valley at Burton. Almost islanded by the river and the Trent and Mersey Canal, Burton has long been famous as the 'beer capital' of Britain. Its air is often heady with beer fumes – locals joke that it is possible to get drunk just by walking through Burton's streets. Ale was brewed by the local abbey's monks in the 11th century, and by 1600 the town had almost 50 licensed victuallers brewing on a domestic scale. Burton's beers began to reach a wider market after the Trent Navigation Act was passed in 1698, while the opening of the canal in 1777 enabled exports to be shipped to the colonies by way of Liverpool. It was in the same year that William Bass started brewing in Burton,

and the Bass Museum* in Horninglow St illustrates the industry's story over centuries. Exhibits include a model brew a remarkable old Daimler truck shaped li beer bottle, and a directors' coach pulled an immaculate vintage steam locomot The entrance to the museum is on the le the A50 (SP Uttoxeter) as the route conti northwards towards Tutbury.

BURTON UPON TRENT TO SUDBUR

The road climbs gently beyond Bur providing good views eastwards along Trent valley with Repton's 212-foot-l church spire a major landmark to the ri The A50 then drops down into Tutb where the ruins of a medieval castle* do nate the skyline, looking northwards over River Dove to the distant heights of the P District National Park. The castle has longed to the Duchy of Lancaster since 1 and, like its counterpart at Ashby, was on the many strongholds where Mary, Quee Scots, was held prisoner before she beheaded in 1587. Another ill-starred m arch, Charles I, visited the castle after defeat at Naseby in 1646.

The church, set on a slope between castle and the centre of Tutbury, feat some of the finest Norman craftsmanship the Midlands. The western end is particula memorable for the carved birds, animals other details which embellish the doorwa series of six receding arches. Tutbury's ot eye-catcher is the Dog and Partridge

This extraordinary motorized beer-bottle is one of many fascinating exhibits in the Bass Museum at Burton upon Trent. Housed in the company's Victorian joiners' shop, the museum v illustrates the history of the brewing industry in Burton

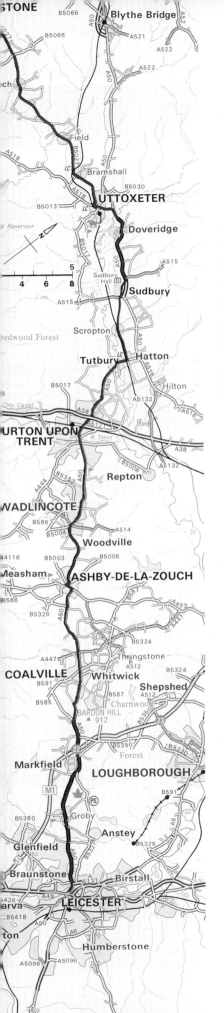

Sudbury Hall was begun in 1613 and completed towards the end of the 17th century. Its imposing exterior is matched by the sumptuous interior decorations, some of which are by the incomparable craftsman Grinling Gibbons

remarkably picturesque black-and-white pub in the main street, which carries the route down towards the River Dove in a series of sharp corners.

Follow the road over the river, and just after crossing the railway line turn left on to an unclassified road for Scropton. Two miles past Scropton turn right on to the A515, then almost immediately left on to an unclassified road which leads into the compact village of Sudbury. The Vernon Arms, an attractive blend of brick and stone, was built in 1671 and sets the mood for views of Sudbury Hall,* which George Vernon completed in 1695. It remained in the Vernon family until 1967 and now belongs to the National Trust. The Hall has a superb Long Gallery – it is more than twice the length of a cricket pitch – and its interior is a magnificently ornate treasure-house of paintings, carvings and elaborate plasterwork. A splendidly imaginative museum for children is now one of Sudbury Hall's chief attractions: young visitors can see a fully-furnished mousehole, feel what it was like to wear costumes of bygone days, or play with antique toys. There is even a climbable mock chimney, vividly recalling times when children were employed as sweeps.

SUDBURY TO STONE
The route runs along Sudbury's main street past the Hall and then turns left to rejoin the A50 Uttoxeter road. Four miles later it re-crosses the Dove just below a handsome old stone bridge. The river at this point marks the boundary between Derbyshire and Staffordshire. A few hundred yards later, turn left and follow the A518 into Uttoxeter, a small town best known for its unusual name and its National Hunt race-course. In the main square stands a curious little stone building, now a newsagent's kiosk, which carries a bas-relief carving depicting a famous incident connected with Dr Samuel Johnson. As a young man, Johnson once refused to attend Uttoxeter market to help his father, a bookseller from Lichfield. Fifty years later Johnson did penance for his disobedience by standing bareheaded in the rain for several hours on the site of his father's stall.

The B5027 (SP Stone) runs westwards from Uttoxeter through a landscape of low hills dappled with woodlands. The road was put in the charge of a turnpike trust in 1793, and the house where tolls were collected still stands just beyond the Green Man in Milwich, a pleasant little cluster of mellow brick cottages. Remain on the B5027, eventually turning right at a T-junction to follow the road into Stone.

This busy little town was the birthplace, in 1735, of John Jervis. He entered the Royal Navy as a boy of 13, was present at the capture of Quebec in 1759, and in 1797, aided by Nelson, destroyed the Spanish fleet off Cape St Vincent. His mausoleum stands outside the church, which was built in 1758 after the collapse of its predecessor. The Earl of St Vincent, as he became after his greatest victory, is commemorated inside the church by a plaque which outlines the story of his naval career. (For Stone see also p. 203.)

STONE TO WHITCHURCH

Signs for Newcastle-under-Lyme take the route through Stone, crossing the Trent and Mersey Canal, and in ½ mile turning right on to the A34 dual carriageway. At the big roundabout less than 1 mile later, take the first exit to join the A51 (SP Nantwich), soon crossing over the M6. The woodlands of Swynnerton Old Park and the Maer Hills overlook the road to the right as it heads westwards and crosses the A53. On the left, just over a mile beyond the A53 junction, is the Willoughbridge Garden Trust,* where old gravel workings have been transformed into a peaceful wonderland of trees, shrubs, flowers and streams.

At Woore, turn left (SP Audlem) on to the A525 for Whitchurch. Woore's Italianate church, built in 1832, faces the Swan Hotel, where stage-coaches travelling between Chester and London stopped to change horses.

Rich, flat farmland, typical of so much of Cheshire, flanks the road to Audlem. Here a quaint old building originally used as a butter-market stands below the impressive church. Canal enthusiasts know Audlem for a flight of 15 locks on the Shropshire Union Canal. Negotiating them involves more than two hours of energetic work, but the village has four pubs by way of compensation.

Follow the A525 through Audlem and on to Burleydam, bearing left and then turning left for Whitchurch at the junction with the road from Nantwich. A series of sweeping bends takes the route towards Whitchurch. This old town was the birthplace, in 1862, of E. G. Jones, better known as the composer Sir Edward German. There is a memorial to him in St Alkmund's Church (see p. 191).

An unusually modified narrow boat on the Trent and Mersey Canal near Stone

The classical lines and gleaming white stucco of Woore's unusual church give it a distinctly Italian appearance

Randolph Caldecott, the illustrator of some of our best-remembered Victorian picture-books for children, also lived in Whitchurch as a young man.

WHITCHURCH TO WREXHAM

Leave Whitchurch on the A525 (SP Wrexham), which passes 'the last public house in England'. Such geographical distinctions were very important to thirsty travellers when all Welsh pubs were forbidden by law to open on Sundays. The road soon crosses the Llangollen arm of Shropshire Union Canal. On the left is on the counterbalanced 'lift bridges' that ar feature of this attractive waterway. Beyo the canal the road drops down to a sm stone bridge over a stream which marks border between England and Wales. L gently undulating country sweeps the r north-westwards to Bangor-is-y-coed, wh a new by-pass carries the A525 across meandering River Dee. Also known Bangor-on-Dee, the village has one of o

two race-courses in the whole of Wales. The other is at Chepstow. The new bridge spans the river downstream from its predecessor, a medieval work of rich, red sandstone overlooked by the church. Nothing remains of the large Celtic monastery which once stood here. It came to an untimely end in AD 615 when Aethelfrith, King of Northumbria, ordered the slaughter of its 2400 monks after they had prayed for his defeat at the Battle of Chester.

The road runs through the hamlet of Cross Lanes and the village of Marchwiel before dropping down sharply to cross the River Clywedog and then climbing again to reach Wrexham, the largest town in North Wales.

As befits its status as the region's unofficial capital, Wrexham is a busy, expanding town. Relatively few tangible links with the past have survived 20th-century developments. The most notable exception is St Giles's Church, built in 1472. A splendid tower, richly sculpted with figures and almost 140 feet high, gives it the noble character of a small cathedral, and the churchyard is a peaceful oasis in the town centre. A replica of Wrexham's church tower is a feature of the buildings of Yale University in the USA, and inside St Giles's is the tomb of Elihu Yale, a much-travelled man who gave his name to the university after his handsome gift of books, Indian silks and other merchandise had enabled it to be founded early in the 18th century. He retired to his family's ancestral home near Wrexham.

One of Wrexham's chief attractions is the Doll and Toy Museum.* Its 3500 exhibits include a collection of period dolls, miniature furniture and mechanical toys.

These two 19th-century porcelain dolls are among the exhibits in the Doll and Toy Museum at Wrexham

ERDDIG

The Wrexham area's greatest delight is unquestionably Erddig,* 1½ miles south-west of the town centre off the A483. The house, set in a 2000-acre estate of farms, parkland and gardens, was given to the National Trust in 1973. Four years later, following extensive restoration work to repair subsidence damage caused by local coal-mines, it was officially opened by the Prince of Wales. Erddig dates from 1684 and was built for Joshua Edisbury shortly after he was appointed High Sheriff of Denbighshire. The work proved too much for his pocket, however, and the property was acquired by John Meller, a wealthy London lawyer involved in Edisbury's bankruptcy case. Meller died in 1733, leaving the estate to his nephew, Simon Yorke, whose successors – all christened Simon or Philip – lived at Erddig until the last of the line, Philip Yorke III, died in 1978.

The house has a charming 'family' atmosphere; it also provides a remarkable insight into the way in which great estates were run. It was almost self-sufficient, and the outbuildings include a joiner's shop, a sawpit, a blacksmith's forge and a wagon shed as well as stables, a laundry and a bakehouse. A typically homely touch is provided by a collection of portraits in the servants' hall, depicting various members of the Erddig staff over more than a century. Elsewhere are paintings of the Yorke family, including one by Gainsborough, a wealth of original furniture, superb 18th-century tapestries and a magnificent state bedroom. The state bed, badly damaged during Erddig's years of decline, was given to the Victoria and Albert Museum in London in 1968. A decade later it returned, beautifully restored, as a focal point in one of Wales's greatest showplaces.

WREXHAM TO RUTHIN

Wrexham is the point at which the route's scenic character suddenly changes. Signposted for Ruthin, the A525 climbs steadily through the straggling village of Coedpoeth – where it crosses the great 8th-century earthwork of Offa's Dyke – and skirts Esclusham Mountain, a flat-topped massif which reaches 1497 feet, with considerably higher ground to the south. Where the A525 swings to the right in Minera, keep straight ahead on to the B5430 (SP Gwynfryn). Two miles later, keep straight on at the crossroads for Rhydtalog, crossing the A525. Bleak moorland, patched with heather and marsh grass, stretches away to the left.

In 1½ miles, keep forward at the crossroads in Rhydtalog, and 1½ miles later, by the Rose and Crown pub, bear left with the B5430.

LLANARMON-YN-IAL

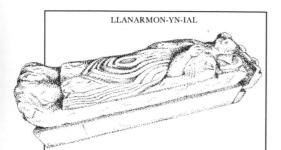

After 2 miles a very short detour can be made to the left along the B5431, across the valley of the River Alun to the small, isolated village of Llanarmon-yn-Ial. This is a delightfully peaceful place in the lee of the Clwydian Hills. Buildings of pale stone – some attractively whitewashed – are grouped round an 18th-century church, which stands on the site of a much earlier church and has a double nave that is typical of north-east Wales. Inside are several old monuments, including a stone effigy said to be of St Garmon.

The main route continues along the B5430, and in 1¾ miles bears left for Ruthin, then ¾ mile later turns left at a T-junction on to the A494. This road climbs steadily to almost 1000 feet as it crosses the steep Clwydian Hills. From the head of the pass there are spectacular views westwards over the Vale of Clwyd into the mountainous heart of North Wales. A sequence of sharp corners then sweeps the road down through Llanbedr-Dyffryn-Clwyd to Ruthin.

Although it was ravaged by Owain Glyndwr's army in 1400, during the last great Welsh bid for independence, this ancient town abounds in quaint timber-framed buildings. Among those in and near St Peter's Square, right in the heart of the town, are the Old Court House – built in 1401 and now occupied by the National Westminster Bank – and Exmewe Hall, which was built 100 years later for Sir Thomas Exmewe, a future Lord Mayor of London. The remains of a gallows beam can still be seen under the eaves at one end of the Old Court House; its last victim was a Jesuit priest, executed during Elizabeth I's reign.

St Peter's Church, on the opposite side of the square, dates from the 14th century. Its elaborate oak ceiling is said to have been presented by Henry VII to thank the many Welshmen who supported his successful bid to wrest the crown from Richard III at the Battle of Bosworth in 1485.

RUTHIN TO DENBIGH

Leave Ruthin on the A525 Denbigh road, which runs along the western side of the Vale of Clwyd. There are splendid views across the valley to the Clwydian Hills which reach 1818 feet at Moel Fammau. On the summit is

the distinctive ruin of the Jubilee To built in 1810 to commemorate the 50th of George III's reign.

At the roundabout on the outskir Denbigh, take the second exit for the centre and in ¾ mile turn left again, follo the A543 into the town. Denbigh is d nated by the battered limestone walls towers of a castle* which stands on the s the headquarters of Dafydd ap Gruffydd was, albeit briefly, the last native Prin Wales. The remains of the massive gateh are particularly impressive, and there interesting little museum inside the castl exhibits include reminders of Denbigh's famous son, Sir Henry Morton Stanley, was born near the castle in 1841. He sp miserable childhood in a workhouse, but achieved international fame after findin David Livingstone in the heart of Af supposedly uttering the immortal phrase Livingstone, I presume'.

A tall, square tower below the c gatehouse is all that remains of St Hila the old garrison church. Lower down the are parts of the medieval town walls a ruined church, known locally as Leices Folly,* which a 16th-century Earl of Leic intended to replace the cathedral at St As The building was never completed.

DENBIGH TO LLANDUDNO

The B5382 (SP Henllan) takes the route of Denbigh, offering fine views back to town and castle as it climbs out of the Va Clwyd and into the hills. A wonder 'secret' wooded valley, where rocks have I carved into caves and natural arches, northwards from Henllan. The village its notable for a sturdy medieval tower –

The view southwards across the quiet village of Llansannan towards the distant Denbigh Moors

An ornate Victorian puppet-theatre is the setting for a favourite seaside entertainment at Llandudno

---

unlike the defensive pele towers found along the Anglo-Scottish border – which stands on a knob of rock above the church. The Llindir Inn is one of the few thatched buildings in North Wales, a region characterized by its roofs of local slate.

The road climbs steadily to skirt Moel Fodiar before dropping down into the sleepy, sheltered valley of the Afon Aled. Follow the road round to the left, crossing one of the Aled's sparkling tributaries, and in $1\frac{3}{4}$ miles turn right on to the A544 to enter

Llansannan. The main road swings hard right on the far side of the village and immediately starts to climb. Looking back, there are memorable views southwards, over the wooded hills and open moorland of Mynydd Hiraethog, before the A544 winds down to Llanfair Talhaiarn, in the valley of the River Elwy.

At the T-junction on the far side of the river turn right on to the A548 (SP Abergele). Follow the road for $2\frac{1}{2}$ miles, than at the crossroads turn left on to the B5381, passing through Betws-yn-Rhos and Dolwen. After crossing the B5113 the road drops almost 800 feet in less than 3 miles to reach a roundabout little more than a stone's throw from the Afon Conwy's tidal waters. Take the second exit, the A55 (SP Conwy), and just over a mile later, at the roundabout in Llandudno Junction, take the second exit, the A546, for the drive alongside the estuary through Deganwy and into Llandudno. Superb views of Conwy's 13th-century castle, set against a backcloth of wooded hills, end the route on a memorable note.

Llandudno itself is one of the biggest seaside resorts in Wales and looks out over a broad bay flanked by impressive headlands known as the Great and Little Ormes. Despite its popularity, the town has retained a great deal of its original Victorian charm, epitomized by such features as the elegant promenade, the pier and the covered pavements in Mostyn Street. A statue of the White Rabbit on West Shore commemorates the fact that the Rev. Charles Lutwidge Dodgson – better known by his pen-name of Lewis Carroll – first met the little girl who inspired *Alice in Wonderland* during a visit to Llandudno in the 1860s.

Steamers travelling to and from Liverpool and Holyhead moor at Llandudno's fine pier, built in 1876

ROUTE 23

174 MILE

Chester to Tenby

Chester					
30	Oswestry				
60	30	Newtown			
93	63	33	Devil's Bridge		
119	89	59	26	Lampeter	
174	144	114	81	55	Tenby

OSWESTRY
Although the 1535 Act of Union finally laid down the nationality of Oswestry as English, many people here still speak Welsh. The double-headed eagle on Llwyd Mansion, awarded to the Lloyd family for services in the Crusades, seems an appropriate emblem for this two-sided town

HOLT
The red sandstone bridge over the River Dee here joins England and Wales, and was built shortly after 1400. Nearby is the site of *Bovium*, a sizeable Roman camp

Chester

OVERTON
A peaceful little to which seems more English than Wels its churchyard gro yews which are lis among the 'Seven Wonders of Wales

LLANDINAM
Llandinam was the birthplace of David Davies, whose statue stands near the bridge. The son of a small farmer, he began his career by buying an oak tree for £5 and selling it as planks for £80, and went on to become one of the great entrepreneurs of the Victorian age

WELSHPOOL
Some of the oak trees in the parkland around Powis Castle were probably growing when Owain ap Gruffydd built the castle here in 1250

DEVIL'S BRIDGE
Three bridges cross a deep, thickly wooded gorge here, the lowest of them known as the Devil's Bridge. Some say it was built by the Knights Hospitallers, others by the Cistercians from Strata Florida Abbey, but tradition has it that it was built by the Devil

NEWCASTLE EMLYN
The Afon Teifi makes a natural moat to the castle, named 'new castle' to distinguish it from the older one which stood at nearby Cilgerran. The last Welsh Royalist stronghold in the Civil War, the 'new castle' was slighted by Parliamentarian troops, who reduced it to the ruin that is seen today

YSBYTY CYNFYN
The church here lies within a stone circle of great antiquity. Many early Welsh churches were built on sites of pagan worship, which explains why Welsh churchyards are often circular in shape

LLANIDLOES
The old market hall in Llanidloes stands on arcades beneath which market stalls once sheltered. It is the only building of its kind to survive in Wales

NEWTOWN
Robert Owen was born and died her although he spent much of his life in United States. He remembered for h humanitarian principles and his beliefs on equality cooperation, whic anticipated those Karl Marx. His gra can be seen in the Churchyard

NARBERTH
Pwyll, Prince of Dyfed, who in legend met and exchanged places with the Lord of the Underworld, is said to have had his castle here, where a 13th-century castle stands today

LLANDEWI BREFI
St David preached on the spot where the church now stands, and its links with early Christianity are demonstrated by the five Saxon crosses which are kept here

LAMPETER
St David's College in Lampeter was founded in 1822 by Bishop Burgess of St David's for Welsh students who could not afford to attend Oxford or Cambridge. It became part of the University of Wales in 1970

CENARTH
The art of salmon-fishing using coracles, tiny boats whose ancestry stretches back to prehistoric times, is still practised in the pool below Cenarth bridge

TENBY
Tenby may have been a Norse settlement, but by the 9th century it was certainly a Welsh stronghold. It remained in Welsh hands until the Normans and their followers arrived in the early 12th century

ROM the historic town of Chester this route threads down
Welshpool through the northern Marcherlands. It then
ns into the heart of Wales, striking across the wild Cambrian
untains to reach Devil's Bridge. The Afon Teifi is followed
much of its course through the quiet countryside of old
rdiganshire, and finally the route turns southwards to reach
nby and the coastline of Carmarthen Bay.

'ollowing the Dee upstream from Chester, the route crosses
river at Holt to enter the Welsh county of Clwyd. Holt's
itegic position on the Dee lent it considerable importance in
dieval times, and it became a borough dominated by a
verful castle that is now reduced to a few overgrown ruins.
ore that the Romans were here; they established a
lement called *Bovium,* which supplied their town at Chester
h much of its pottery. The countryside along the Dee valley
the route continues towards Overton is very English in
pearance and character, but occasional glimpses may be
ight of the distant and unmistakable Welsh mountains.

Overton, like Holt, once had a castle beside the Dee, but
hing remains, for it was washed away centuries ago when
river changed course. Beyond Overton the route leaves
les for a while and travels through the peaceful countryside
orth Shropshire to reach Oswestry. Completely unaware of
inpretentious charms, the town, whose little streets are lined
h a remarkable diversity of old pubs, seems hardly to have
inged since the 1950s, and seems quite content to let the
rld go by.

At Llanymynech, where the Romans dug deep into
nymynech Hill for copper, the route crosses the Afon
rnwy and enters Wales once more. To the south the
idden Hills rise dramatically from the Severn valley.
rmed from hard igneous rocks, the three Breidden summits –
Breidden itself, Golfa and Middleton Hill – were natural
ensive sites, and on each one are the remnants of an Iron Age
-fort. They are crowned by an unlikely assortment of
ictures – a memorial to an 18th-century admiral who never
ne anywhere near here, the grave of a Romany prince, and
masts of a radio station. Following a branch of the
ropshire Union Canal, the route continues to Guilsfield,
ere the clock on the church tower bears the stern reminder:
diligent. Night cometh'.

Next comes Welshpool, which was known simply as Pool
il 1825 when its name was altered to avoid possible
ifusion with Poole in Dorset. South of the town is Powis
stle – one of the best preserved 13th-century castles in
tain, and equally famous for its beautiful terraced gardens.
e route accompanies the Montgomery branch of the
ropshire Union Canal into Newtown, passing the hamlet of
ermule, where there was a tragic railway disaster in 1921 in
ich 15 people were killed. Abermule is also said to be the
ting of a much earlier tragedy. Legend has it that this was
ere the fair maiden Sabrina – from whom the Severn takes
name – drowned herself to escape her wicked stepmother.
Newtown was new in 1279, when it received its charter, and
as become new all over again in the 20th century as the site
extensive planned development. The Severn valley and the
rounding scenery become increasingly wild and lovely as
route continues through Llandinam to reach the elegant
d-Wales town of Llanidloes. Here the Afon Clywedog joins
Severn. The Clywedog was dammed three miles to the
th-west of Llanidloes in 1968 to form Llyn Clywedog, one of
man-made lakes of central Wales.

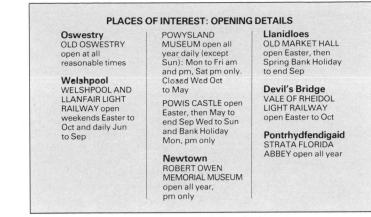

From Llangurig the route follows the infant Wye upstream
for a while before sweeping round the southern slopes of
Plynlimon. Once described, because of its boggy foothills, as a
'sodden weariness', the summit of Plynlimon gives some of the
finest and most far-reaching views in Wales, stretching from
Snowdonia in the north down to the Preseli Hills and the
Brecon Beacons in the south. Only on its western side does
Plynlimon appear appreciably different from the hills which
surround it, taking on a more mountainous character. Here
low crags rise towards the summit from the dark waters of the
Nant-y-moch Reservoir. Several stones marked 'WWW' are to
be found on the mountain. The initials are of Watkins William
Wynne, an 18th-century landowner whose vast estate stretched
from Aberystwyth right across central Wales to the family seat
at Ruabon, near Wrexham.

Plynlimon is the source of two of Britain's most beautiful
rivers – the Wye and the Severn – and of the Rheidol, which
tumbles through a justly famous series of falls at Devil's Bridge.
From Devil's Bridge the route wriggles through landscapes
of sedges and bleached grasses to cross the Ystwyth at
Pontrhydygroes and the Teifi at Pontrhydfendigaid.

The Teifi has its source some miles east of Strata Florida
Abbey in the bleak wastes of the 'great desert' of Wales – a
lonely landscape of low, rounded hills and barren moors dotted
with little pools. At Tregaron Bog the Teifi flows through one of
Wales's most important nature reserves, beyond which is the
tiny market town of Tregaron, birthplace of Twm Shon Catti,
a 16th-century Welsh equivalent of Robin Hood.

Neat patchworks of hedged fields that typify much of old
Cardiganshire line the route as it passes Llandewi Brefi and
approaches Lampeter. Beyond Lampeter the route leaves the
Teifi for a while and dips up and down from hill to hill to reach
Newcastle Emlyn. The route follows the Teifi from Newcastle
Emlyn to Cenarth, where coracle fishermen still ply their
ancient craft, and then finally leaves the river to head towards
the Preseli Hills.

Part of the Pembrokeshire Coast National Park, the gently
rounded moorland slopes of the Preselis are steeped in legends;
indeed all this part of Wales is traditionally known as *gwlad hud
a lledrith* – the 'land of magic and enchantment'. Many of the
legends are set round the large number of prehistoric
monuments – most of them still mysterious and awe-inspiring
– that are to be found throughout the Preselis. From Narberth,
called Arbeth in the *Mabinogion,* the great Welsh cycle of myth
and romance, it is a straight run to the ancient walls, winding
streets and sandy bays of Tenby.

CHESTER TO FARNDON

From Chester's ancient centre the route heads due east at first, following signs for Nantwich and Whitchurch for ¾ mile before keeping right in the one-way system, then turning left on to the B5130 for Farndon. Leaving the city behind, this road passes the Chester Sailing and Canoeing Club, on the bank of the River Dee, before heading out into open country.

The grounds of Eaton Hall, home of the Duke of Westminster, lie on the opposite bank of the River Dee as the route approaches Aldford. An ornate clock-tower can be seen through the trees on the far side of the river. Aldford itself deserves a short stop; the main part of the village lies to the right of the road. This neat 'estate' village of brick cottages with stone-framed windows is overlooked by the gargoyled tower of a sandstone church in whose grounds stands a medieval preaching-cross, restored in the 19th century by the First Duke of Westminster.

Continue along the Farndon road, passing through the leafy little village of Churton before going past an eye-catching roadside monument with four stone lions at its base. It commemorates Roger Barnston, a local land-owner who died of wounds received while leading an assault on Lucknow during the Indian Mutiny of 1857. He is buried in Cawnpore, India.

FARNDON TO OSWESTRY

At the T-junction in Farndon turn right on to the A534 Wrexham road. It crosses the Dee into Wales by a narrow, eight-arched bridge built at the beginning of the 15th century. Across the river is Holt, where the Romans had a base. At the far end of the village, where the road for Wrexham swings to the right, the route keeps straight on, following signs for Ridleywood and Isycoed along the B5130. Pass through these two hamlets and in 3 miles cross the A525, then 1¼ miles later turn left on to the A528 for Overton. There are beautiful views up the wooded Dee valley, and the route crosses the river before climbing through parkland into Overton. The village's broad main street runs past a terrace of attractive cottages, then swings right to pass the churchyard, whose yew trees are listed among the traditional 'Seven Wonders of Wales'. Follow the main street round to the left, then turn right (SP Ellesmere) just beyond the whimsically named Reading and Cocoa Rooms.

After ¾ mile turn right again, on to the B5069 for Oswestry. From this point there are superb views westwards over the Dee to the serried heights of North Wales. St Martin's, the next place of any size after Overton, used to be a mining village, but the pit closed in the 1960s and the old colliery site has been landscaped to blend in with its surroundings.

The Diamond Jubilee Clock above Eastgate is one of Chester's many fine examples of Victorian craftsmanship

and Margaret Yale are commemorated by this 17th-century monument in St Oswald's Church, Oswestry

f the road to the left in St Martin's is
rch Terrace – a charming row of alms-
es, built in 1810 and fronted by rose
ens – and the 13th-century church,
cated to St Martin of Tours. Continue
g the B5069, and at the end of the village,
osite the school, bear left towards
owen. The school was designed by Sir
Spence, the architect responsible for
entry Cathedral. The road drops steeply
oss the Llangollen arm of the Shropshire
on Canal. Often busy with pleasure craft
ng the holiday months, the waterway was
neered by Thomas Telford at the end of
8th century.
t the roundabout in Gobowen – where
5069 meets the A5, Telford's trunk road
een London and Holyhead – take the
nd exit and follow the A483 towards
estry. Old Oswestry,* one of Britain's
impressive Iron Age hill-forts, is a
ble feature of the landscape to the right of
oad, just before the town itself is reached.

Oswestry's name is derived from that of St
Oswald, a Northumbrian king who died on
the outskirts of the town in AD 642 while
fighting Penda, the pagan ruler of Mercia.
The main road passes Llwyd Mansion, a
handsome black-and-white building in Cross
Street. Its façade bears the double-headed
eagle emblem once carried by the Holy
Roman Emperor; it was granted to a member
of the Llwyd family for distinguished services
on a crusade to the Holy Land.

St Oswald's Church, at the far end of
Church Street, has effigies of members of the
Yale family whose cousin, Elihu Yale, provided funds to found the American university
that bears his name. Keep straight on for
Welshpool at the traffic lights by the church.
Half a mile later, on the outskirts of the town,
the Croeswylan Stone stands at the foot of
Croeswylan Lane. Markets were held there –
well beyond the town walls – when the plague
struck Oswestry in 1559. Some say money
was washed in the stone's hollow to avoid

contamination from the plague. Others
believe it formed the base of a cross – a theory
supported by the fact that Croeswylan is
Welsh for 'cross of weeping'. A hundred yards
further on, beyond the cricket field, is the
house where the First World War poet Wilfred
Owen was born. He was killed in action at
the age of 25, just before the Armistice.

OSWESTRY TO LLANYMYNECH

Views open out again beyond Morda, the
southern horizon dominated by the Breidden,
a hill which rises steeply above the Severn and
has been ravaged by quarrying. The monument on its summit is a landmark for many
miles. Known as Rodney's Pillar, it commemorates Admiral Rodney, the 18th-
century naval hero who defeated a Spanish
fleet off Cape St Vincent in 1780 and routed
the French off Dominica two years later. He
had no links with this area, but the pillar was
erected by local people who wished to pay
tribute to his seamanship, courage and
powers of leadership. A forest of lofty masts
stands at the foot of the hill, providing radio
links with ships all over the world.

Llanymynech Hill's limestone cliffs, carved
by Victorian quarrymen, tower above the
A483 as it climbs gently through the straggling village of Pant. Offa's Dyke, constructed
1200 years ago to mark the border between
England and Wales, runs along the top of the
hill. Llanymynech's slopes and summit are
riddled with caves where men once mined for
silver, lead, copper and zinc.

The route left Wales between Overton and
St Martins, but now re-enters the principality
at the village of Llanymynech. The border at
this point is nothing if not eccentric. It
wriggles up the main street to such an extent
that several of the buildings have some rooms
in England and some in Wales. They include
the Lion Inn, next to the pseudo-Norman
church built in 1845. When all Welsh pubs
were closed on Sundays it was legal to drink in
the Lion's 'English' bar, but not in the
'Welsh' lounge.

*Enclosed by vast earthen ramparts, Old Oswestry is the
finest Iron Age hill-fort in the Welsh Marches*

LLANYMYNECH TO WELSHPOOL

Just under 4 miles beyond Llanymynech, at Ardd-lin, turn right on to the B4392 for Guilsfield. Part of the old Montgomeryshire Canal can be seen on the left. Completed in 1821, this branch of the Shropshire Union network ran as far south as Newtown and was used by barges carrying such cargoes as coal, lime, timber and grain. Guilsfield has several picturesque black-and-white cottages and a handsome 14th-century church. A massive old oak chest stands on the ground floor of the two-storey porch, while the nave's lofty panelled roof is notable for its beautifully carved and painted bosses.

Follow the road round to the left in Guilsfield, and in 1 mile turn left on to the A490 for Welshpool. The road enters the town at Raven Square, where the roundabout is flanked by a new railway station, the terminus of the Welshpool and Llanfair Light Railway, a scenic narrow-gauge line that was opened in 1903 after plans had been discussed for 41 years. Passenger traffic ceased in 1931 and the last goods train ran in 1956. Seven years later, however, part of the line was revived by steam enthusiasts. It follows a beautiful valley from the headquarters,* at Llanfair Caereinion, to Sylfaen, 3 miles west of Welshpool on the A458. The newly restored section running between Sylfaen and Raven Square is due to be reopened in the near future.

Taking the second exit at the roundabout, the road from Raven Square into the centre of Welshpool runs past a medley of buildings, colour-washed in pinks, greens and blues, which rub shoulders with natural stone and timber-framed architecture. The handsome town hall and the Powysland Museum,* in Salop Street, both date from 1874. Welshpool is a thriving agricultural centre for this part of the border. Its weekly livestock market has been held every Monday, apart from Christmas Days, since 1406 and attracts farmers from a wide area. (For Welshpool see also p. 51.)

WELSHPOOL TO LLANDINAM

Turn right (SP Newtown) at the traffic lights in the centre of Welshpool, rejoining the A483, which runs alongside a restored stretch of the canal.

POWIS CASTLE

Just outside Welshpool a screen of trees up the slope on the right hides the noble sandstone façade of Powis Castle.* A detour to it can be made by turning right on to an unclassified road. Known in Welsh as Castell Coch – 'Red Castle' – it dates from the 13th century and is one of Wales's greatest treasures. It has been lived in ever since it was built, gradually and gracefully evolving from grim border fortress to stately home. Past owners include the second Lord Clive – son of Shropshire-born Clive of India – who became the Earl of Powis in 1804. The castle's terraced gardens look out over wooded parkland to the Long Mountain. Among the estate's timber is a Douglas fir almost 200 feet high, said to be the tallest tree in Britain.

High, rolling hills watch over the road as it continues southwards between the Severn and the old canal.

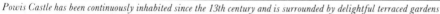

Powis Castle has been continuously inhabited since the 13th century and is surrounded by delightful terraced gardens

BERRIEW

ve miles beyond Welshpool a short detour
 the right, along the B4390, leads to Berriew.
his secluded riverside village is one of the
ost enchanting in Wales and has a wealth
 black-and-white buildings, mostly dating
om the 17th and 18th centuries. The church
 Victorian, but inside are marble effigies
om the Elizabethan period. They depict
rthur Price, Sheriff of Montgomeryshire in
78, and his two wives. On the edge of the
llage an impressive aqueduct carries the
nal over the Afon Rhiw as it races down to
 in the Severn.

 miles later, approaching the hamlet of
rmule, the route crosses the Severn for the
 and last time. Steep hills close in on the
ey as it approaches Newtown. This old
ving town was the birthplace, in 1771, of
ert Owen. A great philanthropist and
al reformer, he lived to be 87 and is buried
e shadow of the old parish church. Above
Midland Bank is a museum* dedicated to
. Follow the main road in Newtown,
tly bearing right on to the A489
ngurig road.

his road keeps forward at the level
sing near Caersws on to the A470 for
ndinam, where the hills close in again.
st of this attractive little village is tucked
y to the left, but a statue of David Davies
rd Davies of Llandinam – stands beside
road by an iron bridge over the Severn.
n in 1818, the son of a humble local
ner, Davies left school at the age of 11 but
t on to become one of the greatest
torian industrialists and entrepreneurs.
died in 1890, after he had changed Barry
n an insignificant South Wales fishing
age into the world's largest coal port.

NDINAM TO LLANGURIG

 scenery becomes steadily more impress-
beyond Llandinam, with hills towering
 above the Severn as its course is followed
Llanidloes. This friendly little town grew
 n a bowl of natural splendour at the point
re the Severn's waters are fed by those of
 Clywedog, one of its main tributaries.
ad, tree-lined streets give the town a
xed and peaceful atmosphere, but traffic
 to ease cautiously round the delightful old

market hall* in the centre. Timber-framed,
but with stone walls at either end, the
building dates from the 16th century and
shelters a cobbled area that used to echo to
the cries of traders. At the Newtown end is a
stone on which John Wesley, the 'father' of
Methodism, stood to preach in 1748. The hall
now houses a local-interest museum covering
many aspects of life in Llanidloes and the

The statue of David Davies at Llandinam

surrounding countryside. The church stands
near the Severn and has a low but massive
tower which served as a place of refuge in
troubled times. Forty shield-bearing angels
decorate the roof of the nave.

A crumpled landscape of wild and
frequently windswept splendour lies beyond
Llanidloes as the route delves into one of the
least-visited parts of Wales. Beyond
Llanidloes, just over 500 feet above sea level,
the road for Llangurig climbs gently but
steadily, skirting the hamlet of Cwmbelan
and reaching 960 feet beyond the head of a
narrow, wooded valley. Five miles beyond
Llanidloes, keep straight on along the A492
for Llangurig where the A470 branches off to
the left. On the right, across a field, can be
seen the low, grassy embankment of an ill-
fated railway line that was intended to link
Manchester to Milford Haven. Money ran
out when the track reached Llangurig.

The route turns right on to the A44
Aberystwyth road to pass through Llangurig,
a small village of considerable character on
the north bank of the infant Wye. Two inns,
the Blue Bell and the Black Lion, are
reminders that this isolated community
catered for weary travellers in the age of
horse-drawn transport, when crossing Wales
was a major adventure.

The church is said to have been founded by
St Curig in the 6th century, although the
present building, approached through a
sturdy lych-gate roofed with mossy slates, is
600 years younger. In 1878 it was restored by
Sir Gilbert Scott, the eminent Victorian
architect who designed the ornate Albert
Memorial in London.

Route 23

248

LLANGURIG TO DEVIL'S BRIDGE

Leaving Llangurig behind, the Aberystwyth road starts climbing westwards, tracing the Wye's course into wild, sheep-cropped mountains swathed by the regimented conifers of huge Forestry Commission plantations. The watershed, and the county boundary with Dyfed, is reached at Eisteddfa Gurig, a lonely farm 1400 feet above sea level. It huddles beneath the upper slopes of Plynlimon, a great hummock of peat-covered moorland, pitted with old lead mines. From the summit – a stiff walk from the farm – there are tremendous views in fine weather.

A small parking area on the left, shortly after the farm, provides another memorable viewpoint before the road sweeps down in a series of graceful bends with views over the Castell valley. Fork left beyond the Dyffryn Castell Hotel to join the B4343 (SP Devil's Bridge). Running between rowan trees, the road twists and climbs round the shoulder of a hill before joining the A4120 above the chasm-like, thickly wooded Rheidol gorge. The racing river rises from Nant-y-moch Reservoir, on Plynlimon's western slopes, and falls 1750 feet in its 28-mile dash to the sea at Aberystwyth.

Bear left at the junction with the A4120, but pause a mile later to visit a small church tucked away just off the road to the right at Ysbyty Cynfyn. The church itself is nothing special – a plain building, dating from 1827 – but the ground on which it stands has been used for religious ceremonies for 4000 years. Five great monoliths, part of a pagan circle of standing stones, have been built into the churchyard wall. By the wall, to the left of the porch, are the graves of Margaret, Elizabeth, Catherine and Isaac Hughes, the first quadruplets ever recorded in Britain. They were born on 17 February 1856, but all four died by the end of the month. Two more children, and the father of the family, had also died by 10 March and are buried in an adjoining grave. Behind the church, a short walk leads to Parson's Bridge, a narrow affair, suitable only for pedestrians, which spans the Rheidol. The original bridge was built for the benefit of priests who made their way to the church on foot.

Trees turn the road into a leafy tunnel when it reaches Devil's Bridge, a famous beauty spot above the Rheidol gorge. The iron-railed bridge which carries the road is, in fact, the uppermost of three and was built in 1901. Immediately below it is another, dating from the 18th century, while below that is the original span, probably built in the 12th century by monks from Strata Florida Abbey. The bridges, the gorge and its series of waterfalls – five cataracts with a combined drop of almost 300 feet – are best seen by going through a toll-gate and down a path, known as Jacob's Ladder, which starts from the road and makes the descent by means of 91 steps. (For Devil's Bridge see also p. 143.)

Legend has it that the oldest of the three bridges that span the Afon Mynach was built by the devil

At Devil's Bridge the Afon Mynach cascades down a spectacular series of falls to join the Afon Rheidol

DEVIL'S BRIDGE TO TREGARON

Continue for a short distance along the A4120, passing the terminus of the Vale of Rheidol Railway* (see p. 143). The station is delightfully set amid rhododendrons. Just beyond it, at the war memorial, turn left on to the twisting B4343 (SP Pontrhydygroes). The road soon climbs to almost 900 feet to give wide-ranging views over a rolling wilderness of high, green hills. After traversing an expanse of semi-moorland, the road plunges down through mixed woodland to cross the River Ystwyth at Pontrhydygroes. Continue southwards through Ysbyty Ystwyth and eventually bear left (SP Tregaron) into Pontrhydfendigaid.

STRATA FLORIDA ABBEY

On the far side of the stone-built village of Pontrhydfendigaid, just after the route crosses the upper waters of the Afon Teifi, an unclassified road on the left offers a detour to Strata Florida Abbey,* 1 mile away. An idyllically tranquil valley, hemmed in on three sides, is the unlikely but magical setting for what was hailed in the Middle Ages as the 'Westminster of Wales'. The abbey flourished from the end of the 12th century until the first half of the 16th, when it was closed by Henry VIII during his purge of the monastic houses. The only complete feature of the richly atmospheric ruins is the western doorway, a fine example of typical Norman architecture.

A Norman arch and beautifully decorated medieval tiles are the most striking survivals of ruined Strata Florida Abbey

...e main route continues along the B4343 ...th the watery wilderness of Tregaron Bog ... the right. The Bog, which is a national ...ture reserve and accessible only to permit ...lders, is rich in marsh plants, and is a haven ... many wild animals, including otters and ...lecats. The reserve also protects a great ...riety of bird and insect life.

On reaching Tregaron turn left, cross the ...idge and follow the B4343 as it swings right ...rough the square, towards Llanddewi Brefi. ...orge Borrow, the much-quoted author of ...ild Wales, walked here from Devil's Bridge ... the 1850s, when he was gathering material ... his book. He spent a night at the Talbot ...n, which still stands in the square and looks

out on a statue of Henry Richard. Born in 1812, the son of a local clergyman, Richard rose from the anonymity of a draper's apprentice to become a vociferous MP who championed Welsh causes and quickly gained recognition as the 'Apostle of Peace'.

TREGARON TO HOREB

Running between high hills and the meandering Teifi, the road from Tregaron makes its peaceful way to Llanddewi Brefi, a gem of a village. Colour-washed cottages huddle beneath a fascinating old church with an evocative statue of St David near its west door. The church stands on a grassy hillock said to have risen beneath the patron saint's feet when he addressed a large and turbulent gathering of Celtic clergymen here in the early years of the 6th century.

Hedge-topped banks shelter the B4343 as it runs on down the Teifi valley, where plump cattle graze contentedly on rich riverside pastures. Turn right on meeting the A482 and follow it into Lampeter. A population of little more than 2000 makes this one of the biggest and busiest towns in the 'wilderness'

of mid Wales, although it is little more than a village by English standards. A lively outdoor market is held in St Thomas's Square every other Tuesday, and a two-day livestock market fills the streets with visitors every alternate Monday and Tuesday. St David's College, founded with royal patronage in 1822, became part of the University of Wales in 1970. It has the distinction of being the smallest residential university college in Britain. A steep, grassy mound in the college grounds is all that remains of Lampeter's medieval castle.

Follow signs in the town centre for Newcastle Emlyn and the A475, bearing left past the 19th-century town hall in the High Street. The road climbs out of the Teifi valley and from several points there are splendid views back over Lampeter to the hills above Tregaron. This part of the route is an entertaining switchback, with the road reaching almost 900 feet in places before dropping into small valleys which cross it at right angles. They shelter small villages like Llanwnen, Drefach and Rhydowen as the route continues to Horeb.

In AD 519 St David addressed the Welsh bishops on the spot where Llanddewi Brefi's 13th-century church now stands

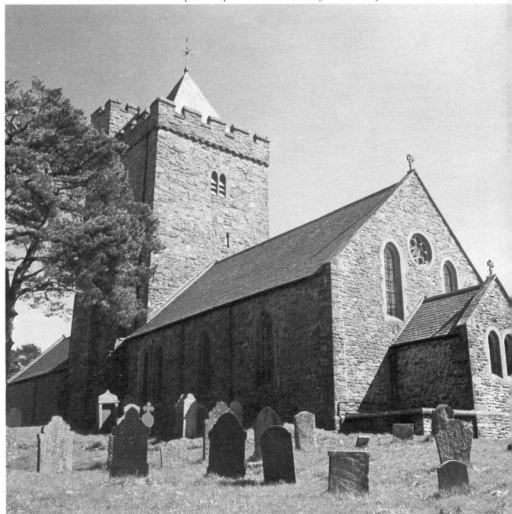

HOREB TO CENARTH

Cross the A486 at Horeb and gradually drop down to rejoin the Teifi near Llandyfriog. Just over 1 mile beyond the village, the route turns left into Newcastle Emlyn, crossing the old bridge across the Teifi, but there is something of interest to be seen before leaving the river's northern bank. On the right, opposite the Lamb Hotel, a tablet commemorates the setting up of the first Welsh printing press, by Isaac Carter, in 1718. The first book printed in Welsh was published the following year.

Newcastle Emlyn was 'new' in the 13th century when one of the local princes chose it as a site for a stronghold. The original castle repeatedly changed hands in skirmishes between the Welsh and the English, and was taken by Owain Glyndwr's troops in 1403, then fell into ruin. The romantic but fragmentary remains of its successor, 'slighted' by Cromwell's troops after the Civil War, stand on a hillock cradled by a huge loop in the Teifi. Other eye-catching buildings in the little market town include the town hall, built in 1892 and topped by a clock-tower, terraced cottages near the river, and the Emlyn Arms Hotel, which has iron railings enclosing a tiny verandah paved with local slate – a material that is also very much in evidence in the Victorian church. The floor and pillars are of slate, as is the font, and outside there is a slate sundial.

Turn right (SP Cardigan, A484) by the Plough Hotel, at the far end of the long main street, and then right again on to the A484 for Cenarth, 3 miles away. Here, having wandered placidly down from its remote source near Strata Florida, the Teifi is suddenly squeezed into a rocky gorge and foams down in a series of low but spectacular waterfalls where salmon may sometimes be seen leaping as they make their way upstream to spawn. Natural splendour is enhanced by the old mill, complete with waterwheel, and an 18th-century bridge whose spandrels are pierced by circular holes. Nearby, the White Hart's Old Coracle Bar is a reminder that at Cenarth these ancient craft – built to a design that was old in Roman times – are still used on the river by salmon fishermen.

CENARTH TO CRYMMYCH

Turn left before crossing the bridge and follow the unsigned B4332 south-westwards over another range of wooded hills to Boncath. The village's name is Welsh for 'buzzard'. Present in large numbers throughout most of Wales, buzzards are masters of the air, and can frequently be seen soaring

At Cenarth the Afon Teifi rushes past an old mill in a series of foaming cataracts

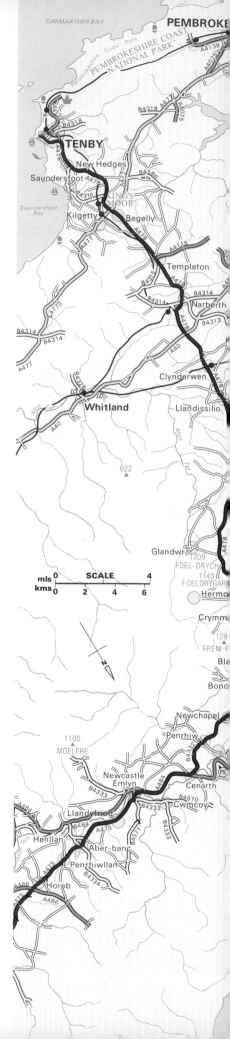

gliding above the woodlands and hill-es. Fork left just beyond the village, and in nile turn left on to the A478 for Tenby. The d skirts the eastern edge of the mbrokeshire Coast National Park, and re are superb views to be enjoyed just past enffos. Foeldrygarn, its 1140-foot-high nmit encircled by the ramparts of an Iron e hill-fort and crowned by three large onze Age cairns, is a prominent landmark the rim of the Preseli Hills, to the right. To south-west is Carn Meini, whose out-ps of white spotted dolerite were proved, 1923, to be one of the sources of the famous estones at Stonehenge. Throughout the nded Preseli Hills there is a wealth of ehistoric monuments, ranging from stone cles to the magnificent chambered tomb at ntre Ifan, 3 miles east of Newport, which is e of the finest of its kind in Britain.

The rest of the route is straightforward, lowing the A478 all the way down to nby. The village of Crymmych is sheltered the slopes of Freni-fawr, which rises to nost 1300 feet in the north-east.

RYMMYCH TO TENBY

e coming of the railway turned Crymmych m a tiny hamlet into a thriving agricul-al centre, and though the railway has now

Now a crumbling ruin, Narberth Castle once dominated much of south Pembrokeshire

gone, Crymmych is still a busy little farming village. As the route continues, crossing a prehistoric ridgeway, there are fine views to the left, while Preseli's heights still dominate the western horizon. Far away to the south, the skyline is punctuated by tall oil refinery towers and the huge power station chimney on the shores of Milford Haven.

After crossing the A40, the road curls through Narberth, a market town whose steep streets and colour-washed buildings of pink, green, grey, blue and yellow are overlooked from the south by the scanty remains of a 13th-century castle. The church tower dates from the same period, but the rest of the building is Victorian. Beyond the town, old milestones mark the distance to Tenby in yards as well as miles.

The great sweep of Carmarthen Bay comes into view near Templeton, which had a castle even before Narberth. It was built during the 11th century, but destroyed in 1215, and only the mound remains. The road dips and climbs again, passing through Begelly and crossing the A477 on King's Moor before finally running down to Tenby. The resort has retained its timeless and enchanting sea-side character despite its great popularity with summer visitors. (For details and a town plan of Tenby, see p. 65.)

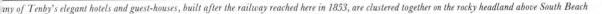

any of Tenby's elegant hotels and guest-houses, built after the railway reached here in 1853, are clustered together on the rocky headland above South Beach

252 *Alternative Routes in Britain*

ROUTE 24 163 MILE

Liverpool to Scarborough

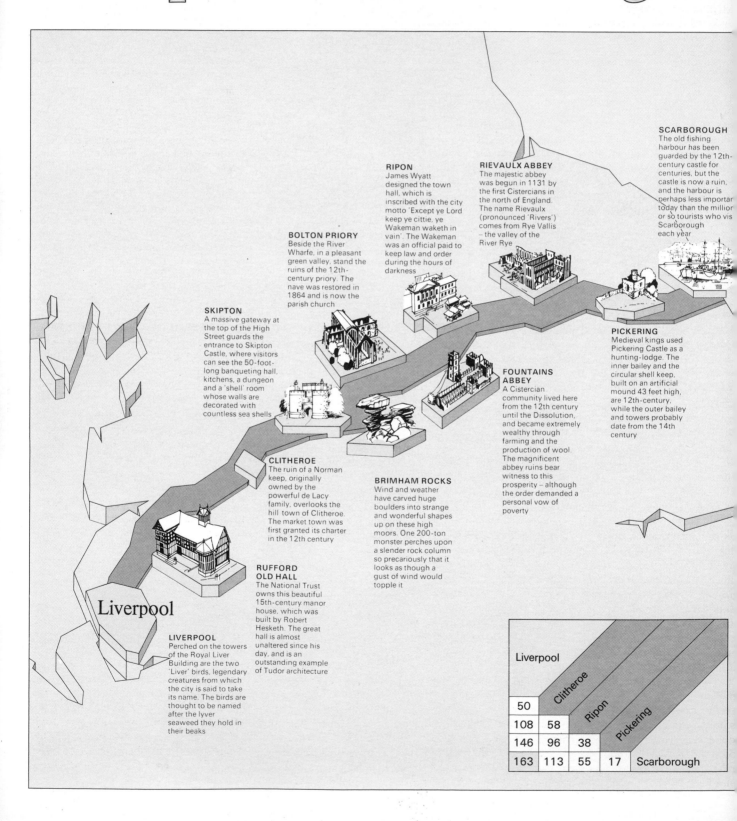

SCARBOROUGH
The old fishing harbour has been guarded by the 12th-century castle for centuries, but the castle is now a ruin, and the harbour is perhaps less important today than the million or so tourists who visit Scarborough each year

RIPON
James Wyatt designed the town hall, which is inscribed with the city motto 'Except ye Lord keep ye cittie, ye Wakeman waketh in vain'. The Wakeman was an official paid to keep law and order during the hours of darkness

RIEVAULX ABBEY
The majestic abbey was begun in 1131 by the first Cistercians in the north of England. The name Rievaulx (pronounced 'Rivers') comes from Rye Vallis – the valley of the River Rye

BOLTON PRIORY
Beside the River Wharfe, in a pleasant green valley, stand the ruins of the 12th-century priory. The nave was restored in 1864 and is now the parish church

SKIPTON
A massive gateway at the top of the High Street guards the entrance to Skipton Castle, where visitors can see the 50-foot-long banqueting hall, kitchens, a dungeon and a 'shell' room whose walls are decorated with countless sea shells

FOUNTAINS ABBEY
A Cistercian community lived here from the 12th century until the Dissolution, and became extremely wealthy through farming and the production of wool. The magnificent abbey ruins bear witness to this prosperity – although the order demanded a personal vow of poverty

PICKERING
Medieval kings used Pickering Castle as a hunting-lodge. The inner bailey and the circular shell keep, built on an artificial mound 43 feet high, are 12th-century, while the outer bailey and towers probably date from the 14th century

CLITHEROE
The ruin of a Norman keep, originally owned by the powerful de Lacy family, overlooks the hill town of Clitheroe. The market town was first granted its charter in the 12th century

BRIMHAM ROCKS
Wind and weather have carved huge boulders into strange and wonderful shapes up on these high moors. One 200-ton monster perches upon a slender rock column so precariously that it looks as though a gust of wind would topple it

RUFFORD OLD HALL
The National Trust owns this beautiful 15th-century manor house, which was built by Robert Hesketh. The great hall is almost unaltered since his day, and is an outstanding example of Tudor architecture

Liverpool

LIVERPOOL
Perched on the towers of the Royal Liver Building are the two 'Liver' birds, legendary creatures from which the city is said to take its name. The birds are thought to be named after the lyver seaweed they hold in their beaks

Liverpool	Clitheroe	Ripon	Pickering	
50				
108	58			
146	96	38		
163	113	55	17	Scarborough

BBEYS and castles are the outstanding architectural
ures of this route from Liverpool to the coast of east
kshire. It travels through Lancashire and Yorkshire –
litional rivals in sport and culture – crosses the great ridge of
Pennines and touches the edges of two exceptional upland
s: the Yorkshire Dales and the North York Moors.

he route begins in Liverpool, which Daniel Defoe, during
travels in the early 18th century, described as 'one of the
ders of Britain'. His enthusiasm for the port was almost
ounded, and he closed his account: 'In a word, there is no
n in England, London excepted, that can equal Liverpool
the fineness of the streets, and the beauty of the buildings.'
ough the city has changed dramatically since then, many
erpudlians would claim that his remarks still apply today.

rom the city the route threads northwards through the
urbs of Aintree and Maghull to the ancient town of
nskirk, which is the market centre for the surrounding
nlands. Now rich pasturelands, nearly all of the coastal
n to the west of Ormskirk consisted of featureless
shlands known as 'mosses' until the 18th century, when
e-scale drainage was undertaken.

wo worn stone pillars standing in a field at Burscough are
that remain of the first ancient religious foundation to be
sed on this route. They are the sole survivors of what was
e an important Augustinian priory. Following an arm of the
ds and Liverpool Canal, the route reaches Rufford, whose
Hall is one of the loveliest buildings in northern England.
rossing the River Douglas, the route passes through Much
ole, which has an unusual 17th-century church, and
worn, overlooked by the earthworks of a Norman castle
lt to defend the mouth of the Ribble. Preston's position at
lowest bridgeable point of the Ribble has meant that the
n has been important since at least as early as Roman times.
vas a prosperous spinning and weaving centre in the 16th
tury, and during the 18th-century cotton boom it grew
matically. In 1648 the Battle of Preston, at which a Royalist
ny from Scotland was soundly defeated by the
liamentarians, was fought on the town's doorstep.

ongridge Fell, beyond which stretches the wild countryside
the Forest of Bowland, rises to the north as the route
tinues through Hurst Green and across the River Hodder.
theroe Castle's little keep, standing high on a rocky outcrop
ove the Ribble, was built by the powerful de Lacy family in
12th century and commands extensive views of the valley.
kipton stands just outside the boundary of the Yorkshire
les National Park and is the capital of the district known as
aven. The national park covers some 700 square miles of
nery that ranges from the pastoral beauty of the dales
mselves to the immense landscapes of the remote moors.
kipton's lovely old castle owes its survival to Lady Anne
fford, who was born here in 1589. The daughter of the Third
rl of Cumberland, she inherited a vast estate which
compassed large parts of Yorkshire and Westmorland. She
d her household, which was considerable, divided their time
ween the estate's three principal castles – Skipton, Appleby
d Brougham. The entire retinue travelled by coach across
e moors in days when the country was very much wilder than
s now, and Lady Anne seems to have taken especial delight
choosing the wildest possible routes. She kept the castles in
od repair, virtually rebuilding them after the damage caused
ring the Civil War, and paid for repairs in churches
roughout the region as well as endowing almshouses.

PLACES OF INTEREST: OPENING DETAILS

Burscough Bridge
MARTIN MERE
WILDFOWL TRUST
open all year (except
24-25 Dec)

Rufford
RUFFORD OLD HALL
open Mar to Dec Tue
to Sun and Bank
Holiday Mon, pm
only; closed Wed in
Mar, Oct, Nov and
Dec

Ribchester
ROMAN MUSEUM
open Feb to Nov daily
(except Fri and Sun),
pm only; also open
Dec and Jan Sat
pm only

Clitheroe
CLITHEROE CASTLE
MUSEUM open
Easter to Sep Tue,
Thu , Sat and Sun,
pm only; open daily
last two weeks Jul
and all Aug

Skipton
SKIPTON CASTLE
open all year (except
Good Fri and 25 Dec):
Mon to Sat all day,
Sun pm only

Bolton Abbey
BOLTON PRIORY
open all year

Pateley Bridge
STUMP CROSS
CAVERNS open
Easter to end Oct

BRIMHAM ROCKS
open all year

Ripon
FOUNTAINS ABBEY
AND STUDLEY
ROYAL open all year
(except 25 Dec)

WAKEMAN'S HOUSE
open Spring Bank
Holiday to end Sep:
Mon to Sat all day,
Sun pm only; also
open Sat in winter

Helmsley
RIEVAULX ABBEY
open all year;
RIEVAULX TERRACE
open Apr to Oct
(except Good Fri)

HELMSLEY CASTLE
open all year

Pickering
PICKERING CASTLE
open all year

BECK ISLE MUSEUM
open Easter to Oct

NORTH YORKSHIRE
MOORS RAILWAY
open Easter to
end Oct

Scarborough
SCARBOROUGH
CASTLE open all year

ROTUNDA MUSEUM
open all year: Mon to
Sat am and pm, Sun
pm only; closed Sun
Oct to May

WOOD END MUSEUM
open all year: Mon to
Sat am and pm, Sun
pm only; closed Sun
Oct to May

Beyond Skipton the route follows Wharfedale into some of
the most enchanting and spectacular scenery in the national
park. The beauty of the setting was appreciated by the
Augustinian monks who built Bolton Priory in the late 12th
century, and by the Cliffords, whose medieval hunting-lodge
stands close to an awe-inspiring gorge. Near to the summit of
Greenhow Hill, on the eastern edge of Appletreewick Moor,
are two mine shafts that may be Roman in origin. They are
reminders that the dales, which now seem so idyllic and
peaceful, were once highly industrialized. Lead and iron mines
were opened up all over the moors, and many of the dales were
lined with smelt- and linen-mills. Remains of these old
industries can be found in abundance in Nidderdale, which
runs northwards from Pateley Bridge. One of the smelt-mills
here was run by monks from Fountains Abbey, now a beautiful
ruin which lies just off the route as it approaches Ripon.

Set at the meeting of the rivers Ure, Skell and Laver, Ripon is
a little cathedral city with a wealth of fine old buildings. Across
the River Swale is the old market town of Thirsk and the great
limestone shoulder of the Hambleton Hills, which form the
western boundary of the North York Moors National Park. Set
in the valley of the River Rye beyond the hills are the ruins of
Rievaulx Abbey and Helmsley Castle.

The route continues along the southern border of the park,
crossing numerous little tributaries of the Rye, before reaching
Pickering and its Norman castle. Moorland slopes stretch away
to the north beyond Pickering, while to the south are the fertile
lands of the Derwent and the Vale of Pickering.

At Ayton the route crosses the Derwent, which by an
extraordinary quirk of nature has its source barely ten miles
from the sea to the north of Scarborough. It flows parallel with
the coast, then heads inland before running down through
Yorkshire to become part of the Humber. Scarborough's
magnificent castle stands on a 300-foot headland overlooking
an ancient and historic seaside town that is now one of the most
popular resorts in the north of England.

LIVERPOOL TO PRESTON

Leave Liverpool on the A59 (SP Preston), driving northwards through Walton and passing Aintree station; the famous racecourse, home of the Grand National and associated, in recent years, with the immortal Red Rum, lies off the main road to the right. Follow signs for Preston at the large roundabout and stay with the A59, passing through Maghull.

The air becomes fresher and the skyline opens up as the road stretches ahead between flat agricultural lands. Ormskirk soon appears down the hill ahead, with a church tower looming like a beacon. The descent to the town, a market centre of some 700 years' standing, ends at a roundabout, where the route takes the second exit, the A59, bypassing the town centre to the right.

Modern houses, old cottages and farms border the switchback road through Burscough and Burscough Bridge, where the route crosses the Leeds and Liverpool Canal. Completed in 1816, the canal runs through the heart of the Pennines, and links the busy towns of industrial Yorkshire with Liverpool and the Humber estuary.

The pink-footed goose is a regular visitor to the Martin Mere reserve

MARTIN MERE WILDFOWL TRUST

By turning left on to an unclassified road immediately past Burscough Bridge station, you can make a detour to Martin Mere.* Opened in 1975 by the Wildfowl Trust, the reserve has a specially planned waterfowl garden and a 20-acre man-made lake set amid marshland which has been equipped with hides. Many species of wildfowl from all parts of the world can be seen here, and winter visitors include several thousand pink-footed geese, as well as pintails and teal. The visitor centre houses a large exhibition illustrating the work of the Wildfowl Trust.

The A59 continues through Rufford, w Rufford Old Hall* is signposted to the ri This is a fine timber-framed building n especially for its Tudor great hall, one of best in the country. It has a magnifice carved hammer-beam roof, and a mas and intricate Gothic screen.

Still on the A59, turn right at the tr lights on the outskirts of Tarleton and tinue through Much Hoole, Hutton Penwortham to Preston. Avoid the tov busy one-way system by turning left with ring road after crossing the Ribble Clitheroe, A59). This first crossing of Ribble is by no means the last, for the re meets it again several times on the riv 75-mile journey from the slopes of Wherns where it rises, to the Irish Sea.

PRESTON TO CLITHEROE

Follow signs for Clitheroe round the Pre ring road, but after 4 miles do not miss a turn at traffic lights into Ribbleton Ave (SP Longridge, B6243). Preston's resider belt soon gives way to open country. At edge of Longridge bear right (SP Clither still on the B6243.

Later additions to the magnificent 15th-century great hall at Rufford Old Hall include the elegant red-brick east wing, which dates from 1662

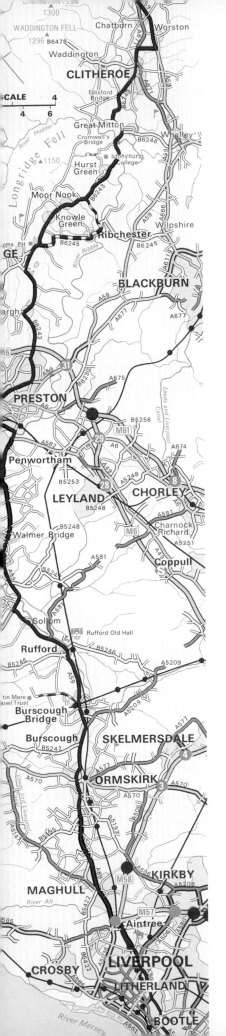

RIBCHESTER

In 1¼ miles, by the Corporation Arms pub, you can turn right on to the B6245 for a worthwhile detour to Ribchester. This historic and attractive village on the River Ribble originated as the Roman fort and staging-post of *Bremetennacum*. Among the buildings which have been excavated are two Roman granaries believed to have been constructed around AD 80. Several buildings in the village, including the 14th-century church, incorporate fragments of Roman pillars discovered in the river bed. A fine bronze ceremonial helmet, discovered here accidentally by a local boy in 1796, is in the British Museum. A replica of this important find is among the exhibits in Ribchester's Roman museum,* which is situated near the parish church. The museum also contains coins, pottery, jewellery and many other items discovered on the site, which is still being excavated.

Continue from Ribchester along the B6245 (SP Blackburn), cross the stone bridge and shortly turn left (SP Hurst Green) down winding Gallows Lane. Turn right after 1¾ miles at the T-junction (SP Clitheroe) picking up the B6243 again to rejoin the main route.

The main route has followed the B6243 through Knowle Green and Moor Nook. Hurst Green, the next village, is known as the home of Stonyhurst College, a famous Roman Catholic public school. Since it was founded in 1794 it has produced many famous names, among them cardinals, diplomats and authors – including Sir Arthur Conan Doyle. The college, which is off the main road to the left, is noted particularly for its spectacular façade, dominated by a gatehouse and twin-copper-domed towers.

Continuing along the B6243, cross the River Hodder after 2 miles. To the right of the road bridge is an old three-arched pack-horse bridge known as Cromwell's Bridge, which was crossed by him on 16 August 1648. The Parliamentary army camped near Stonyhurst on the night before they routed the Royalists at the Battle of Preston. Three miles further on, the road crosses Edisford Bridge, where the Ribble flows gently, and has seats on its grassy banks to enable visitors to relax in this pleasant spot.

Soon the B6243 enters Clitheroe, in the heart of the Ribble valley, and once a Saxon hamlet. It gained its charter in 1147 and the castle, which still dominates the town although only a shell, dates from the same century. From the castle grounds there are magnificent views over the Ribble valley, and an interesting local museum* is situated adjacent to the castle ruins. A hole that can still be seen in the wall of the castle keep is reputed to have been made by a Civil War cannon-ball in 1649. A more fanciful tale is that Old Nick – the devil himself – made the hole by hurling a rock from Pendle Hill, which rises to the east of the town.

This ruined medieval bridge over the River Hodder near Clitheroe has been known as Cromwell's Bridge since the Parliamentary troops crossed it in 1648 before the Battle of Preston

CLITHEROE TO SKIPTON

Clitheroe's links with the past are reflected by streets and shops which, though modernized, retain plenty of old-world charm, and the feel of this part of the country is maintained as you depart, following signs for Skipton (A59). Turn left on to the A59, which is overlooked by Pendle Hill. Seven-mile-long Pendle has known Roman legions, Norman invaders and the ill-famed 'Witches of Pendle'. In 1612 a number of local women were hanged following a trial at Lancaster Castle which found them guilty of bringing about by witchcraft the deaths of 16 people. Other tales of sorcery abound. The Wars of the Roses and the Civil War also cast their shadows across Pendle. Fires on its summit, 1832 feet above sea level, have beckoned yeomen to arms, and, in more recent times, signalled celebrations.

The route heads for Skipton via Gisburn, one of the villages reluctantly lost by Yorkshire and gained by Lancashire in the 1974 boundary changes. Approaching Skipton, the road runs beside the Leeds and Liverpool Canal, which follows the Aire valley here in its winding trek across the Pennines.

The road into Skipton leads past railway sidings and mills, leaving the visitor unprepared for the charm of a place which grew around a Norman castle. The parish church contains tombs of the Clifford family, who rebuilt the castle* in the early 14th century. The family motto *Desormais* (henceforth) is

carved in stone on the battlements. Lady Anne Clifford, born at the castle in 1589, was especially fond of her birthplace, and carefully restored it following Civil War damage. Skipton town centre is a delightful blend of new and old. A cobble-stone 'apron' on either side of the road has long provided a site for a busy little market, and modern shops now stand behind. (For Skipton see also p. 129.)

SKIPTON TO PATELEY BRIDGE

Following signs for Harrogate, branch right by the church with the A59, and in about 5 miles, by the Devonshire Arms at Bolton Bridge, turn left on to the B6160 (SP Bolton Abbey). Skipton lies just outside the huge and unspoilt area of the Yorkshire Dales National Park, and the B6160 leads into the park along an enchanting stretch of the River Wharfe written about by Wordsworth and painted by Turner. Less than a mile from the A59, beside the river and against a backdrop of dramatic moorland hills, stands 12th-century Bolton Priory.* One of over 80 important monastic houses in Yorkshire, it was founded in 1151, but even before that an Anglo-Saxon manor stood on the site. Upstream from the majestic ruins is the entrance to Strid Wood nature trails, where walkers can enjoy the natural beauty of the area. At the Strid gorge the Wharfe flows with great force through a deep, narrow ravine. The turbulent waters are terrifying after heavy rains, and the Strid has claimed lives – often when people have

The battlements of Skipton Castle's 14th-century gate are carved with the motto of the Clifford family

foolishly attempted to jump across, unaw[are] of the slipperiness of the rocks.

On the B6160 2¾ miles beyond Bo[lton] Abbey is the ruin of 15th-century Bar[den] Tower, a former hunting lodge of the Clif[ford] family of Skipton. Lady Anne trave[lled] widely in the Dales, and loved to visit [this] isolated place. Wordsworth wrote of [an] ancestor, the 'Shepherd Lord', who sp[ent] many years in hiding in the Dales and o[ften] stayed at Barden, where he studied the sta[rs.]

Turn right by the tower on to an uncla[ssi]fied road (SP Appletreewick) and cross [the] Wharfe by an old and narrow stone bri[dge.] The road weaves an undulating course t[o a] T-junction, where the route turns right [(SP] Pateley Bridge). Tight bends characte[rize] this steep little road at first, then the ro[ad] climbs on to the moors, reaching a T-junc[tion] where it turns right to join the B6265. J[ust] over a mile along this road, on the right, [are] Stump Cross Caverns,* where visitors [can] marvel at stalactites, stalagmites and glit[ter]ing crystal formations.

Continue to the former lead-mining to[wn] of Pateley Bridge, whose long, narrow m[ain] street leads uphill from the River Nidd t[o a] sharp right turn. Above this, stone steps l[ead] to Panorama Walk, where magnificent vi[ews] unfold of Nidderdale and the surround[ing] hills. From the viewpoint it is possible to [see] Gouthwaite Reservoir, higher up the val[ley,] and beyond it Great Whernside, where [the] Nidd rises.

PATELEY BRIDGE TO RIPON

Leave Pateley Bridge on the B6265, and t[urn] left after one mile (SP Felbeck, Brimh[am] Rocks, Ripon). After a short climb the ro[ad] levels out between the moors.

The distinctive outline of Pendle Hill rises above the Ribble valley between Clitheroe and Gisburn

BRIMHAM ROCKS

A lane on the right 3 miles beyond Pateley Bridge offers a detour to Brimham Rocks.* Here the bleak, heather-clad moor is capped by huge pieces of stone which, from their tops (for some can be scaled), give views which stretch for 40 miles on a clear day. The rocks are part of an outcrop of millstone grit, and have been sculpted into extraordinary shapes by millions of years of weathering. One is in the shape of a crocodile, another like a dancing bear, whilst yet another – said to weigh about 200 tons – looks as though it could be tipped by the touch of a hand.

FOUNTAINS ABBEY

Five miles further along the B6265, look out for a sign to Fountains Abbey* on the right. Here a detour can be made to the ruins of the great medieval abbey, set in the superb landscaped grounds of Studley Royal Park.* In 1132, 12 monks and their prior from St Mary's Abbey in York decided to break away and found a new community, choosing this spot in the tiny valley of the River Skell. The springs in the valley's rocky sides inspired the name 'Fountains'..The abbey grew from this humble beginning – aided by benefactors anxious to save their souls, and by income from wool production – to become the wealthiest Cistercian house in England by the end of the 13th century. The magnificent buildings have survived remarkably well, and the plan is almost intact, thanks to William Aislabie, Chancellor of the Exchequer in 1718 and owner of Studley Royal estate, who acquired the abbey and took a lively interest in its preservation. Near the abbey is Fountains Hall, a Jacobean country house built with stone taken from part of the abbey. The whole area, including deer park and period landscape, is perhaps one of Europe's most majestic settings – perfect for the occasional *son et lumière* performances which take place here in summer.

Continue along the B6265 to Ripon, a cathedral city which exudes history and possesses an air of quaint and quiet charm. The cathedral, surprisingly light and airy for its size, is a mixture of architectural styles and periods. The Early English west front is judged by many to be the finest in the country. The cathedral's patron saint and founder was St Wilfrid. The crypt dates from his time – around AD 670 – and is named after him. It now houses one of the largest collections of church plate in England. St Wilfrid is still remembered on the first Saturday in August in a traditional procession observed since medieval times.

The cathedral is five minutes' walk from the market square, and between the two is the tourist information office and museum, housed in an attractive half-timbered building dating from the 13th century and known as the Wakeman's House.* The title stems from the days when the chief official was the nightwatchman or Wakeman. Nightly at nine o'clock his modern counterpart marches into the square to set the watch by blowing a horn at the foot of the obelisk. This monument, erected in memory of William Aislabie of Studley Royal, is topped by a wind-vane in the shape of the Wakeman's horn. The tradition, which dates back almost 1000 years, is also remembered in the city motto, inscribed on the 19th-century town hall: 'Except ye Lord keep ye cittie, ye Wakeman waketh in vain'.

On mayor-making day in Ripon there is an unusual ceremony when the mayor elect goes 'into hiding'. A 'search' ensues, and when he is found he is escorted by two councillors to the council chamber, where he is finally installed. The custom dates back to the days when mayors sometimes had to be 'press-ganged' into service. Such ancient traditions seem quite at home in Ripon's medieval streets. For hundreds of years locals have come to Ripon market through streets with names like Kirkgate, Fishergate, Skellgate and St Agnesgate, and buildings of the 17th and 18th centuries still house shops selling craft goods, books and antiques.

Take the A61 (SP Thirsk) from Ripon, crossing the busy A1 trunk road at Baldersby Gate roundabout.

RIPON TO PICKERING

Pleasant countryside accompanies the route through Skipton-on-Swale and Carlton Miniott, and panoramic views of hills ahead open up as you cross the River Swale. Continue to Thirsk, a good old-fashioned market town whose cobbled square, packed with character, is once again a peaceful place now that most through traffic by-passes the town. Thirsk boasts an outstanding Perpendicular church, and nearby stands 18th-century Thirsk Hall. Several old coaching inns testify to Thirsk's history as a posting station at an important crossroads.

Leave Thirsk by the A170 (SP Scarborough) and head for Sutton-under-Whitestonecliffe. Watch for the picturesque house and garden on the left as you enter Sutton and also, on the left, the Whitestone Cliff itself, rearing skywards. Past Sutton the road makes one of the most famous road ascents in the north, climbing 500 feet in half a mile with gradients of up to 1 in 4 on the approach to Sutton Bank, 960 feet above sea level. The view from the top of Sutton Bank across the valley to the hills beyond is breathtaking. The small tarn to the left of the road is Gormire Lake, which local legend insists is bottomless.

RIEVAULX ABBEY

About a mile further on, a signpost invites a detour along an unclassified road to the left, to Rievaulx Abbey.* The winding lane reaches a narrow, hump-backed stone bridge across the River Rye; immediately past it, turn left to reach the abbey ruins. Rievaulx was founded in 1131, and is perfectly situated in thickly wooded country, giving an atmosphere of complete peace and seclusion. The land was given by Walter L'Espec, a Norman knight who later entered the community as a novice. He died and was buried here two years later. The finest views are from the long curve of Rievaulx Terrace,* landscaped in the 18th century for this purpose. It has two Grecian-style temples, and the panorama stretches across the abbey to the Hambleton Hills, which divide the North York Moors from the Dales country to the west.

Return to the junction by the hump-backed bridge and turn left, climbing out of the valley. In ½ mile turn right on to the B1257 to rejoin the route at Helmsley.

The A170 brings the main route into Helmsley. Not far from the picturesque market square is the medieval castle,* originally built by Walter L'Espec. It was altered and extended in subsequent centuries and the ruins stand within Norman earthworks.

The route continues from Helmsley along the A170 (SP Scarborough), passing through several unspoilt and charming hamlets. Beadlam has some attractive thatched cottages just off the main road; Kirkbymoorside is larger, with a market place, a tollbooth and, once, a castle, whose moat can still be seen. Middleton's church has a Saxon tower and houses parts of three Saxon crosses.

Immaculate cottages set beside a delightful beck help to make Thornton Dale one of the most beautiful villages in Engla

Pickering is the next town. Edward II rested in its 12th-century castle* after an unsuccessful campaign against the turbulent Scots in 1323, and Richard II was briefly imprisoned here before his murder at Pontefract. The parish church contains a whole series of wall paintings depicting the lives of the saints – one of the most complete sets in the country, and thought to date from the 15th century. Bible stories were often depicted in this way in the Middle Ages, to bring the scriptures to life for the many churchgoers who could not read. Yet when the paintings at Pickering were discovered in the 1850s, the vicar ordered them to be whitewashed over again immediately, lest they should distract his congregation from their worship.

Signs point the way from the town centre to the Beck Isle Museum,* an interesting collection conveying vivid glimpses of rural life in other eras. Also signposted from the town centre is the North Yorkshire Moors Railway.* This traverses the moors via Newton Dale and Goathland Moor to reach Grosmont, in Eskdale. The spectacular 18-mile journey, which can be made by steam train, affords views of countryside that is inaccessible by car, and the round trip takes about two hours.

PICKERING TO SCARBOROUGH

Continue from Pickering along the A170, which follows the north side of the Vale of Pickering. Stern moorland, punctuated by steep valleys, rises to the left, while the fertile lowlands of the vale offer a complete contrast to the right. Two miles beyond Pickering is

Thornton Dale, an enchanting vill situated at the foot of the dale whose nam bears. It is worth pausing here to admire green – complete with stocks and village c – and the stream, Thornton Beck, which r through the village. Several interesting ha lets mark the concluding stretch of journey. The Perpendicular church Allerston has a striking tower, and just bef the next village, Ebberston, is Ebbers Hall, built in 1718 for William Thomp MP, and once greatly famed for its extrav ant water garden, which included a ca 1200 feet long. In the church at Brompto few miles further on, William Wordswo was married on 4 October 1802. The poet a his sister Dorothy travelled to the wedd from Dove Cottage in Grasmere, and tonished the locals by walking much of way from Thirsk to Brompton. Wordswort bride was Mary Hutchinson, whose ho was Gallows Hill Farm, just east Brompton. The village is also noted as home of Sir George Cayley, the 'father aviation', who carried out many experime with early flying machines here at beginning of the 19th century. The n village is Wykeham, where a ruined abb stands off the road to the right.

Finally the route goes through the tv villages of West and East Ayton, divided the River Derwent and once guarded 14th-century Ayton Castle, now in rui After crossing the stone bridge, the ro makes its final climb up the valley side bef impressive views open up ahead as the ro descends into Scarborough.

SCARBOROUGH

Sea, sand and amusements are among Scarborough's more familiar attractions, but the old town has a great deal more to interest the visitor.

Its history began some 3000 years ago, when a headland projecting into the North Sea provided an ideal site for a Bronze Age settlement. It later became a Roman signal station, one of a chain along the Yorkshire coast. The Normans chose the same excellent spot to build a castle.* There are fine views of this historic site from Marine Drive, which runs right round the headland – an exciting place on a blustery day. Archaeological finds dating back to Scarborough's beginnings are displayed in the Rotunda Museum.* Additionally, there is a natural history museum* at Wood End, in the former seaside home of the famous literary family, the Sitwells. Two of the rooms are devoted to paintings, first editions and other exhibits connected with the family.

Scarborough's history as a resort began in the 17th century, when medicinal springs were discovered. The sedan chairs and fashionable carriages which were a familiar sight in those days were soon replaced by bathing machines when sea-bathing took over in the next century – and Scarborough has never looked back.

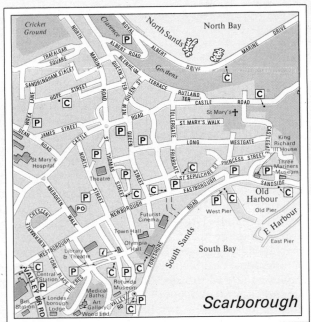

Scarborough

Right: Scarborough Castle's impressive keep was completed in 1158, and the mighty curtain walls were improved throughout the 13th century

Below: Elegant colour-washed buildings on the clifftop overlook the working boats in the harbour at Scarborough

ROUTE 25 191 MILE

Edinburgh to Inverness

FROM Scotland's capital city this route crosses the Firth of Forth into the ancient kingdom of Fife. It then makes its way over majestic hills and up lovely glens and breathtaking passes to Inverness, the 'capital' of the Highlands.

Edinburgh's wide streets and elegant buildings gradually give way to the soft farmlands of the old county of Midlothian as the route approaches the Firth of Forth and the Forth Road Bridge. For hundreds of years the Firth of Forth was the natural entrance into Scotland from Europe, and much Scottish history has been enacted near its waters.

Dunfermline has also played an important part in Scotland's complex and bloody history. Most of its ancient buildings have long since disappeared, but the great abbey church still stands, and is the burial place of Robert the Bruce, one of Scotland's most renowned monarchs. He died in 1329, just a year after he had negotiated a treaty with England that formally recognized Scotland's independence. However, within four years of the Bruce's death England once more claimed supremacy over Scotland. From Dunfermline the route continues northwards through the Cleish Hills, and at Yetts o' Muckhart it enters Glen Devon. This beautiful glen cuts through the rugged volcanic mass of the Ochil Hills to join Glen Eagles, which was gouged out of the unyielding rock by a great tongue of ice during the Ice Ages. It was the hummocks and hollows of sand and gravel left behind by the glaciers which brought fame to Glen Eagles, for although they were not suitable for agriculture they made superb golf courses. Near Auchterarder the route enters the wide and fertile vale of Strathearn and turns eastwards to reach Perth.

Across the Tay is Scone, the site of the ancient Pictish capital of Scotland and the place where all Scottish kings were crowned until the 17th century. From Scone the route runs on to Blairgowrie, which stands in a fertile agricultural district on the northern edge of Strath More and has become a popular holiday and retirement centre.

Following the River Ericht, the route continues through a landscape cloaked in silver birch and beech to reach Bridge of Cally and Glen Shee. One of the most important mountain passes in central Scotland, Glen Shee was used by English troops during the 18th century and was later the route taken by Queen Victoria on several of her visits to Balmoral. Above Spittal of Glenshee the scenery becomes increasingly wild as the route climbs to the Cairnwell Pass, the highest numbered road in Britain at 2199 feet. Away to the east is 3738-foot Lochnagar, its twin granite peaks forming the summit of the White Mounth range. Queen Victoria and Prince Albert climbed the mountain on ponies in 1848 while staying at Balmoral.

Bare mountain sides give way to tree-clad slopes as the route approaches Braemar and the River Dee. Now a peaceful holiday resort, Braemar was of great strategic importance during the Jacobite uprisings of the 18th century, and its castle was converted by English troops into a powerful fortress that is a splendid example of Hanoverian military engineering.

Balmoral, some six miles down the Dee from Braema famous for the imposing castle that is one of the Queen's priv residences. It stands on the site of an ancient royal hunt lodge called Bouchmorale, a Gaelic word that means 'maje dwelling', and was purchased by Prince Albert in 1852 after royal family had spent a number of holidays on Loch Lagg many miles to the west. Balmoral quickly became one of Qu Victoria's favourite houses, and it was here, perhaps more t anywhere else, that she was able to forget the cares of state.

North of Balmoral the route threads through heather-c moors and follows the line of the military road built by Gene Caulfield, who took over from General Wade, the most fam of the great military road-builders, in 1748. Caulfield reputed to have written the following lines in praise General Wade: 'If you'd seen these roads before they w made, You'd lift up your hands and bless General Wade'.

Descending alongside Conglass Water the route reac Tomintoul, which overlooks the beautiful scenery of Str Avon and Glenlivet Forest – famous for its malt whi distilleries. Beyond Tomintoul the route climbs on to op moorland once more, with views to the south-west of the lo Cairngorms and to the north of the Hills of Cromdale.

From the genteel streets of Grantown-on-Spey, which once a centre of the Highland linen industry, the route crosse great expanse of open moorland to reach the little commur of Ferness and the lovely meanders of the River Findhorn. the route approaches Nairn and the coast, the scenery becor more pastoral, laid out with neat fields and farms. Nairn the first place where Dr Johnson, travelling through Highlands with his friend and biographer Boswell, hea Gaelic spoken. From Nairn the route runs through the fer farmlands alongside the Moray Firth to reach Inverness, principal gateway to the lochs, mountains and emp wildernesses of the northern Highlands.

PLACES OF INTEREST: OPENING DETAILS

Dunfermline
DUNFERMLINE ABBEY open all year

ANDREW CARNEGIE'S BIRTH- PLACE open all year: Mon to Sat am and pm, Sun pm only

Auchterarder
STRATHALLAN AIRCRAFT COLLECTION open all year

Perth
MUSEUM AND ART GALLERY open all year: Mon to Sat am and pm, Sun pm only

BLACK WATCH REGIMENTAL MUSEUM open Apr to Nov Mon to Fri

FAIR MAID'S HOUSE open all year Mon to Sat

SCONE PALACE open Easter, then May to mid Oct: Mon to Sat all day, Sun pm only

Braemar
BRAEMAR CASTLE open May to end Sep

Crathie
BALMORAL CASTLE GROUNDS open May to end Jul daily (except Sun), when Royal Family are not in residence

Corgarff
CORGARFF CASTLE open Apr to Sep: Mon to Sat all day, Sun pm only

Ardclach
ARDCLACH BELL- TOWER open at reasonable times on application to key-keeper

Culloden Moor
CULLODEN BATTLE- FIELD open all year. VISITOR CENTRE open Easter to mid Oct: Mon to Sat all day, Sun pm only

NAIRN
A seaside resort on the traditional border between Highland and Lowland Scotland. It is said that at one time those who lived in the south-western part of the town spoke Gaelic, while the inhabitants of the north-eastern half spoke English

TOMINTOUL
The fountain presented to the village of Tomintoul in 1915 was given by Robert Grant MD as a memento of the happy boyhood he spent in the village

INVERNESS
The great red stone castle was built at the beginning of the Victorian era, but it occupies the site of an earlier castle in which Macbeth may once have lived

CORGARFF CASTLE
Since it was first built in the 16th century, Corgarff Castle has twice been burned by the Scottish Jacobites, but when last garrisoned in 1851 it was to suppress whisky smuggling

ARDCLACH
Here above the River Findhorn stands a curious detached bell-tower, built in 1655. It was used to summon the faithful to a church in the valley, and also as a watch-tower and fortification

GRANTOWN-ON-SPEY
This spacious Georgian town was planned and built by Sir James Grant in the second half of the 18th century, and has attracted tourists for over 100 years

BALMORAL
Balmoral Castle and its estate of some 24,000 acres is the holiday home of the Royal Family. It was bought by the Prince Consort in 1852 for £31,500

INVERCAULD HOUSE
Overlooking the River Dee from its northern bank is Invercauld House, the imposing home of the chief of the Clan Farquharson

BRAEMAR
After the 1715 Jacobite Rebellion, English troops were garrisoned in Braemar Castle. Later in the 18th century it was given its present form – that of a Hanoverian fortress

GLEN SHEE
Stretching from the Spittal of Glenshee to Bridge of Cally, this area is one of Scotland's three major skiing centres during the winter sports season

BLAIRGOWRIE
Blairgowrie is well known to sportsmen, for angling, golf and skiing can all be enjoyed in the area. The town is also the centre of a fertile district where soft fruits are cultivated

PERTH
It was in St John's Kirk, the only substantial survivor from Perth's medieval past, that John Knox preached a sermon which launched the Reformation in Scotland

GLENEAGLES
Golf began in Scotland, and Gleneagles is one of Scotland's leading golf resorts. This ancient sport was popular as long ago as 1457, the year James II banned the game in the interests of national security, when he found his subjects preferred golf to archery

SCONE
The present Palace of Scone was completed in 1808, but the site on which it stands is steeped in history, for here stood an abbey in which the kings of Scotland were crowned on the Stone of Destiny until 1296

RUMBLING BRIDGE
The noise caused by the River Devon as it tumbles in full spate down the chasm 120 feet below the road has given rise to the bridge's unusual name

DUNFERMLINE
Robert the Bruce was buried here in 1329, although for centuries the whereabouts of his tomb was unknown until excavations revealed his remains in the old choir. He was reburied in 1819 in a massive lead coffin in a vault now visible to all

FORTH RAIL BRIDGE
The famous Forth Rail Bridge was opened in 1890. The massive cantilever structure requires constant painting, a job which takes some 30 men three years or more to complete, using 7000 gallons of paint

Edinburgh

Edinburgh				
16	Dunfermline			
54	38	Perth		
105	89	51	Braemar	
152	136	98	47	Grantown-on-Spey
191	175	137	86	39	Inverness

EDINBURGH TO DUNFERMLINE

From central Edinburgh follow signs for the Forth Road Bridge. The route runs through some of the city's most handsome streets, which form part of the 'New Town'. This was new in the late 18th century, when much of it was laid out to the prizewinning designs of the young architect James Craig.

Join Queensferry Street (SP Forth Road Bridge) shortly past Charlotte Square, which boasts some of the finest Georgian buildings in northern Britain. The road soon crosses the Water of Leith, whose deep, wooded gorge is spanned by the Dean Bridge, built by Thomas Telford in 1832. This stretch of the A90 is bordered by elegant 18th- and early 19th-century houses.

Continue towards the Forth Road Bridge, which is clearly signposted all the way. Soon the Forth Rail Bridge comes briefly into view. This spectacular monument to Victorian engineering was opened in 1890 by the future King Edward VII after a mammoth construction project which involved 5000 men and cost just over £3 million. The 1½-mile-long cantilevered bridge really is painted continuously by a team of 30 men to protect it from rust.

The A90 runs westwards, bordered by gently undulating farmland, then veers north on the approach to the Forth Road Bridge. This elegant modern suspension bridge stands in dramatic contrast to its 19th-century neighbour. It took six years to build

Opened in 1890, the Forth Rail Bridge is one of the outstanding achievements of the Victorian age

The ancient town of Dunfermline played an important role in Scotland's history for many centuries, and is rich in royal connections. It was the birthplace of a number of Scottish kings, and nine of them, including Robert the Bruce, are buried here. Little survives of the royal palace which once stood here, but the foundations of the original abbey, established in the 11th century by Queen Margaret, can still be seen beneath the floor of the later church which occupies the same site. Much of it was restored and rebuilt in the 19th century, and the abbey church* is now Dunfermline's most outstanding building. It incorporates a magnificent Norman nave and some fine stained glass.

In more recent times Dunfermline has become known for its associations with Andrew Carnegie (1835–1919), who accrued a vast fortune in America's Industrial Revolution and became a great philanthropist. He was born in a modest house in Moodie Street which is now a museum* to his memory. In his lifetime he used his wealth to establish numerous libraries in many parts of the world. He also bought Pittencrieff Park in Dunfermline and presented it to the people of the town.

DUNFERMLINE TO GLENDEVON
To leave Dunfermline follow signs for Stirling, then Crieff, following the A823 out into open countryside. About 5 miles beyond Dunfermline are signs for the Knockhill Racing Circuit, a motorcycle racing venue where meetings are held on summer Sundays. Continue along the A823, which runs on to Powmill through the Cleish Hills.

At Powmill turn right on to the A977 (SP Crieff), and in 1 mile turn left to rejoin the A823 (SP Crieff). Just past this junction is Rumbling Bridge, named after the sounds made by boulders churning about in the spectacular gorge of the River Devon. The present 19th-century bridge, built 120 feet above the river, replaced a bridge of 1713 which still stands below it.

Beyond Rumbling Bridge, in Glen Devon, is the hamlet of Yetts o'Muckhart, whose name means 'gateway to Muckhart'. The name is derived from a toll-gate that stood at the entrance to the Muckhart estate. Tolls were charged on the many sheep and cattle that were brought down this road on their way to market at Falkirk.

Turn right on to the A91, then branch left to rejoin the A823 (SP Crieff, Glen Devon). Ahead, the Ochil Hills rise majestically from the plain as the route enters Glen Devon. The name of the glen is a corruption of the Gaelic *dubh abhainn*, meaning 'black river'. Glendevon village is beautifully set among high, sheep-cropped hills. To the left of the road, on the river bank, is the Castle Hotel, still looking like the baronial mansion it once was. Glendevon church, an attractive white-painted building, stands between the A823

and the narrow bed of the River Devon shortly beyond the village. A local man, John Brughe, is said to have met the devil three times in the churchyard in 1643. He was subsequently tried in Edinburgh for practising witchcraft.

GLENDEVON TO AUCHTERARDER
As the route continues to the top of Glen Devon, the distinctive 1591-foot peak of Steele's Knowe can be clearly seen to the north. Soon the A823 gradually changes direction, swinging northwards to enter beautifully wooded Glen Eagles, with impressive views of mountain scenery to the left as the route enters Gleneagles estate. Amid all this unspoilt scenery, the road suddenly crosses a main railway line and then a large dual carriageway, the A9. Turn right to join this road (SP Perth). About a mile to the north of the junction is the building that made the name of Gleneagles so famous: Gleneagles Hotel, now internationally known for its two championship golf courses.

After 1½ miles the route runs into Auchterarder. Although the town's history can be traced back more than 700 years, most of the buildings date from the 18th century or later, for Auchtertarder was burnt down in 1716 after the Battle of Sheriffmuir, an indecisive clash fought near Dunblane between Jacobites and English troops.

STRATHALLAN AIRCRAFT COLLECTION
At the northern end of Auchterarder a detour to the Strathallan Aircraft Collection* can be made by turning left on to the B8062 and following the signs for 4 miles. Exhibits in the main hangar include Second World War bombers and fighters such as Lancasters and Mosquitoes, and a number of unusual aircraft dating from the 1930s.

---

was opened by the Queen in 1964. From bridge there are excellent views of the h of Forth and the Forth Rail Bridge. The Forth bridges jointly sounded the death-l for what was probably one of the world's st ferry routes. Boats had carried passen- and cargo across the Firth of Forth at this nt possibly since Roman times, but certain-t least since the 11th century; it is known : at that time Queen Margaret, wife of lcolm III of Scotland, often used the te on her way from Edinburgh to her ourite palace at Dunfermline. The towns South and North Queensferry, at either of the crossing, are named after her.

At the northern end of the bridge the road ses through a cutting which had to be sted through solid rock, and 1½ miles later nches left (SP Kincardine Bridge). At the ndabout take the first exit, the A985. At edge of Rosyth keep forward at the ndabout, then at the next roundabout e the third exit, the B980 (SP nfermline). In 1 mile go forward on to the 23, soon entering Dunfermline.

AUCHTERARDER TO PERTH

The main route (A9) passes through Aberuthven, on Ruthven Water, and after 2½ miles crosses the River Earn. The road begins to climb out of Strathearn, bordered by fertile farming country with the mountains of Tayside in the distance to the left and the northernmost Ochil Hills, much closer and lower, to the right. Follow signs for The North, Perth, and Inverness. To the right of the road, on the outskirts of Perth, are the attractively landscaped gardens of the Bell's Distillery Company office. At the large roundabout take the first exit for Perth and approach this historic city by a pleasant road, passing the distinctive buildings of Dewar's whisky distillery on the right.

Perth is dominated by the spire of St John's Kirk; the city was once called St Johnstoun. It is an interesting and ancient city, with a written history going back to the 10th century. Although the Court actually moved from place to place, Perth was for many years virtually the capital of Scotland. This role came to an end in 1437, when King James I was assassinated at the former Blackfriars Monastery in Perth. His widow and son, James II, who was only six when his father was killed, moved the Court to Edinburgh soon afterwards.

Historic though Perth is, most of its buildings date only from the 18th and 19th centuries. St John's Kirk is the city's most venerable building, dating from the medieval period. The altars of the church were destroyed in 1559 following a famous sermon, condemning idolatry, preached here by John Knox, who led the Reformation in Scotland and went on to found the Church of Scotland. At one time divided into three separate churches, the building was restored in the 1920s as a memorial to local men killed in the First World War. The lovely modern stained glass dates from this restoration, and the carillon of 35 bells is even more recent; they were hung in 1936.

Perth's feeling of spaciousness is greatly enhanced by the Inches – two public parks, one at each end of the city, on the bank of the River Tay. On these, 500 years ago, golfers and archers competed for space against grazing cattle. There is still a golf course on the North Inch, and a more recent addition is the large, domed building of the Bell's Sports Centre. Perth's other attractions for the modern visitor include the fine Museum and Art Gallery* and the Black Watch Regimental Museum,* where the history of the famous Scottish regiment is traced back more than 250 years. A house* in North Port, restored in the 19th century, is said to have been the home of Catherine Glover – Scott's 'Fair Maid of Perth'. It now contains an exhibition of Scottish crafts and antiques.

---

*Scone's royal connections began in the **9th** century. This bedroom in the palace was used by Queen Victoria **1000** years later*

TH TO CRAY

e Perth by following signs for Braemar
the A93, crossing the handsome 18th-
ury bridge across the Tay. Large, elegant
es behind tall stone walls line the road
h leads out of Perth. Two miles beyond
bridge, on the left, is the entrance to Scone
ce,* which occupies a site that has played
mportant role in Scottish history for more
1000 years. Of the abbey buildings that
established here in the 12th century,
traces remain, and Scone's most famous
, the Stone of Destiny or Stone of Scone,
sits beneath the Coronation Chair in
tminster Abbey. The block of red
stone is thought originally to have been a
elling altar, perhaps from Iona, and was
ght to Scone in the 8th century. Scottish
s were crowned on it until 1296, when it
stolen by King Edward I of England and
r returned. However, coronations of
tish monarchs continued to take place at
e until 1651.

the 17th century the lands of Scone
e into the possession of the ancestors of the
of Mansfield, who still lives at Scone
y. The present Scone Palace, which
ds on the site of earlier mansions, was
t at the beginning of the 19th century. It
ses a fine collection of furniture, *objets d'art*
needlework, including bed hangings
ed by Mary, Queen of Scots. The park is

Pleasant gardens and wrought ironwork in Blairgowrie

known for its fine collection of rhododendrons
and azaleas, and there is a pinetum containing many rare species of conifer. At the edge
of Scone Park, off the A93, lies Perth National
Hunt Race-course. Originally, Perth Races
were run on the Inches, and it is said that the
Jacobite Rising of 1745 was planned at one of
the race-meetings.

The route continues for several miles with
occasional views of the Tay, and 5 miles
beyond Guildtown it crosses the tranquil
River Isla over a narrow stone bridge. Near
the village of Meikleour a remarkable beech
hedge dominates the left side of the road. It
was planted in about 1746 as the boundary of
Meikleour estate, and is 580 yards long with
an average height of 85 feet.

Crossing the A984, the route continues to
Blairgowrie. On the approach to the town
there are several hotels popular with skiers
and golfers; there is a winter sports centre and
a golf course close by. Blairgowrie stands
amid fertile farmland which has proved ideal
for raspberry-growing.

The route crosses the River Ericht to enter
Rattray, Blairgowrie's sister town on the
opposite bank. The A93 winds on, never far
from the River Ericht, and overshadowed by
beech and silver birch trees, with distant hills
beyond. At Bridge of Cally – a village set
amid delightful scenery at the point where
Strathardle meets Glen Shee – the route
turns right, after crossing the river, to begin
climbing Glen Shee.

Beyond Bridge of Cally the scenery becomes
increasingly mountainous, and distant views
open up on both sides of the road. On the
right is the valley of the River Black Water,
overshadowed to the north by peaks over
3000 feet high. (Route continues on p. 268.)

ridge of Cally the waters of the Rivers Ardle and Black Water combine to form the River Ericht

THE CAIRNGORM

HE CAIRNGORMS tower majestically
e the forests, fields, gleaming lochs and
e-built villages of the sinuous Spey valley
runs north-eastwards from Newtonmore.
re are memorable views from the A9, but
e who explore the mountains more closely
ewarded with some of the most awe-
iring scenery in Britain. Ben Nevis, away
e south-west, is the country's highest
ntain at 4406 feet – but the Cairngorms
d unchallenged as the greatest
centration of land above 3000 feet
where in the British Isles. Their summit is
Macdui (4296 feet), with Braeriach (4248
and Cairn Toul (4241 feet) not far
nd. Cairn Gorm itself is 4084 feet high.

LENTLESS GLACIERS
ted the mountains for hundreds
ousands of years during the Ice
finally retreating to reveal
endous cliffs and great cauldrons
k known as 'corries'. Loch
h is outstandingly impressive
ranks high among the scenic
ders of Britain. More than a mile
it is hemmed in by brooding
parts of rock and tumbled
ders that soar almost 2000 feet
e the dark, blue-green waters.
irg Ghru, the only pass through
ange, is one of the classic
land walks. Leaving the Spey
y, it climbs to 2733 feet to reach
ittle pools that are the source of
River Dee.
straight line drawn due north
the mountains from Blair Atholl
not cross a single public road in
e than 30 miles. As far as
orists are concerned, the only
e is the one carved into the northern flank of Cairn Gorm. It ends
ski lift which runs towards the
migan Restaurant, the highest in
ain at 3650 feet. Loch Morlich, far
w, is surrounded by sandy beaches
pine trees that in sunny weather
it an almost Mediterranean
earance. The road climbs through
2600-acre Glen More Forest Park,
re there are waymarked trails and
ic places. Immediately south of
park, the wildest and
t dramatic
s of the range
n a huge
ional nature
rve.

P INE FORESTS sweep up from
the Spey valley to the lower slopes of
the Cairngorms, their rich greens
contrasting sharply with the cliffs,
corries and almost barren slopes high
above. The trees, some more than 250
years old, are reminders of the great
Caledonian Forest, which once
swathed the region to a height of
about 2000 feet. They are the home of
such creatures as the crossbill, the red
squirrel, the tiny goldcrest and the
turkey-sized capercaillie that was
reintroduced to Scotland in 1837
after being hunted to extinction.
   A clearly marked nature trail
encircles Loch an Eilein, to the south
of Aviemore, and here walkers may
see many woodland and water-loving
creatures, including otters. Loch
Garten has been famous since 1954,
when ospreys – among Britain's rarest
birds of prey – returned to nest in
high trees near the loch after an
absence of many decades. Keen eyes
may see golden eagles soaring
majestically across the Highland sky.
One of the most distinctive birds is the
ptarmigan, a member of the grouse
family whose plumage
changes to white in
winter.

Hundreds of red deer roam the
mountains, occasionally visiting the
loch shores in winter. There are also
wildcats, and reindeer brought over
from Lapland in 1952.
   The upper slopes are speckled with
alpine speedwell, rose-root, curved
wood-rush, starry saxifrage and moss
campion — hardy plants that have
adapted themselves to survive in
sub-Arctic conditions.

The ptarmigan, illustrated here with two
lovely alpine flowers – moss campion (left)
and rose-root (right) – is one of the more
common Highland
birds and has a
distinctive rattling
call

Skiers on one of the nursery slopes below
the spectacular Cairngorm peaks

W INTER SPORTS have been
firmly established here since the mid-
1960s, when more than £3 million
was spent building the Aviemore
Centre, making the Cairngorms
Britain's main skiing area. Until then,
Aviemore was little more than a
village with a railway station on the
Perth to Inverness line. It now has
large hotels, restaurants, an indoor
swimming pool, a theatre and one of
the country's biggest skating and
curling rinks. These and other
facilities cater for *après-ski* relaxation
and also for holidaymakers at other
times of the year.
   White Lady, Coire na Ciste and
Coire Cas are among the most
popular slopes and have runs suitable
for beginners and experts. Conditions
are generally at their best in the three
.nonths immediately after Christmas,
but enough snow for skiing often
lingers on the upper slopes until
April, May and even June.
   Winter visitors who do not ski can
try their hand at the traditional
Scottish sport of curling. It is rather
like playing bowls on ice, but players
use heavy, cheese-shaped stones of
polished granite with a handle set
into the upper surface.

: Stands of Scots pine stretch down to the shores of Loch an Eilein

CRAY TO BRAEMAR

Beyond the turning to Cray, on the other side of the stream, the modern castle of Dalnaglar can be clearly seen as the route continues up Glen Shee. Until recent years Spittal of Glenshee was nothing more than a tiny hamlet in the wild heart of the Grampian Mountains. It is now a thriving ski centre, complete with hotel, ski school, and ski-hire shop. Its peculiar name is derived from 'hospital', in the sense of a hospice or travellers' lodge. Travellers of old on this route could shelter and rest here in the days when such a journey through desolate mountain country was the most gruelling of adventures. Spittal of Glenshee's little church stands on an even more ancient site; directly behind it is a standing stone, a memorial to a forgotten religion.

Continue on the A93 into the bleak and virtually treeless Cairnwell Pass. Five miles from Spittal of Glenshee, to the right of the road, is the once infamous Devil's Elbow, a series of steep hairpin bends which, until it was by-passed a few years ago, was often impassable in the winter. Beyond it, the road reaches the summit of its climb at an amazing 2199 feet, making this stretch of the A93 the highest numbered road in Britain. On the descent, the route passes the Glenshee ski centre, where beginners' slopes sweep down almost to the road. A chair-lift runs to the summit of 3059-foot Cairnwell Mountain. Altogether there are as many as nine lift systems operating in this area, which is one of Scotland's most popular skiing centres. The natural bowl in which the lifts are built protects them from the worst effects of the winter storms.

Beyond the ski centre the glen opens up and looks less menacing, with small homesteads tucked snugly away behind clumps of trees. To the left of the road is Clunie Water, a stream which races down alongside the road, on its way to join the Dee at Braemar. This little town is a pretty and unassuming place, with several hotels and guest-houses that remain open all year round to cater for winter sportsmen. One of them, the Invercauld Arms, stands on the hillock where the Jacobite standard was raised by the Earl of Mar in 1715. This was the start of the first of two unsuccessful rebellions, aimed at restoring the Stuarts to the Scottish throne after the Act of Union was passed in 1707.

During the autumn, at the time of the famous Braemar Highland Gathering, the population of the town swells considerably. For almost 150 years Highlanders have congregated here for the games and other events, and the Gathering now attracts visitors from all over the world. The Queen and other members of the Royal Family usually travel from nearby Balmoral to attend the ceremonies – a custom dating back to 1848, when Queen Victoria was guest of honour at the Gathering.

Surrounded by lofty peaks, Braemar is a thriving local centre and a popular Highland resort

BRAEMAR TO WELL OF THE LECHT

The route leaves Braemar by the A93 (SP Aberdeen). Less than a mile from the town a tower house of classic lines can be seen on the left through a screen of trees. This is Braemar Castle,* built in the 17th century by the Earl of Mar. After the Jacobite Rising of 1715 it became a barracks for English troops, who were moved here to keep the peace in the turbulent Highlands. During their occupation the castle was extended, and the result is one of the finest examples of a Hanoverian-style fortress to be seen in Britain today. The castle retains its underground pit, which was used as a prison, and some of the interior woodwork still has 'graffiti' carved by soldiers garrisoned here in the 18th century.

The road continues through an avenue of pines, with the river to the left and steep hillsides rising on the right. Presently Invercauld House comes into view on the far side of the river. This great mansion is the seat of the Clan Farquharson, and dates partly from the 15th century, though it has extensive Victorian additions. Shortly cross Invercauld Bridge, which was built on the instructions of Prince Albert to replace the Old Bridge of Dee, dating from 1752. The original bridge, now grass-covered and disused, can still be seen on the right. The A93 continues through pine forest, closely following the course of the lovely River Dee. Around the tiny, scattered hamlet of Inver you may catch a glimpse ahead of Balmoral Castle, which stands on the opposite bank of the river among the trees. Two miles beyond Inver turn left on to the B976 (SP Tomintoul), a single-track road with passing places.

CRATHIE AND BALMORAL

r a detour to Crathie and Balmoral con-
ue on the A93. Crathie's late 19th-century
rch is attended by the Royal Family when
y are in residence at Balmoral. Queen
ctoria worshipped at an earlier church on
same site. Appropriately, the church
tains several memorials to royalty. In the
rchyard stands a monument to Queen
ctoria's famous servant, John Brown,
ose house stands nearby.

The gateway to Balmoral Castle stands
side the B976 just across the Dee from
athie. Prince Albert purchased the
lmoral estate in 1852 for £31,500 and
uilt the older castle in the Scottish baronial
le. Queen Victoria first came here in 1848,
en the Royal Family held the lease, and
lmoral has remained the holiday home of
e Sovereign ever since. The estate covers
ne 24,000 acres, and the grounds* include
ne deer forest.

e main route climbs steadily through
odland out on to heather-covered grouse
or, reaching almost 1600 feet. The road is
rrow, with steep hills and sharp bends. It
ns part, as did the road through Glen
e, of an old military road, built during the
mpaigns of the 18th century. After a few
es the River Gairn runs beside the route on
approach to Rinloan, where the route
ns left on to the A939 (SP Tomintoul).
turesque Gairnshiel Bridge, which crosses
River Gairn just past the junction, should
approached with care, since it is very
rrow and has a steep hump-back.

ome 4 miles beyond Rinloan the road
ches a summit of 1750 feet and in $\frac{3}{4}$ mile,
the descent, a public footpath on the left
w marks the old course of the military road
Cock Bridge. Presently the route crosses
narrow, fast-flowing River Don, and
mediately bears sharp left to remain on the
39. Pass through the scattered village of
rgarff, and shortly cross the Don once
re. The grim outlines of Corgarff Castle*
now be seen ahead. Originally a medieval
er house, it suffered a turbulent history
was twice burned down before eventually
ng converted into a garrison post in 1748

Gairnshiel Bridge carries the old military road built by General Wade in the 18th century across the River Gairn

by General Wade. At first this important
fortress played its role in the disarming of the
Highlands, and troops were later stationed
here to suppress whisky smuggling.

The route crosses the Don once more at
Cock Bridge, and climbs steeply (1 in 5),
again following the course of the old military
road. This pass is the notorious Lecht Road.
Like Glen Shee, it was once notorious for its
hairpin bends and steep gradients. The main
pass reaches a height of 2114 feet, making this

the second highest numbered road in Britain.
On the descent, at the Well of the Lecht, an
inscription records the construction of the
military road across here in 1754.

In many of the little glens to the north, as
the route descends to Tomintoul, are distilleries connected with the name Glenlivet,
one of Scotland's most famous malt whiskies.
This area was chosen for Scotland's first
licensed distilleries early in the 19th century
because of the purity of the water.

WELL OF THE LECHT TO GRANTOWN-ON-SPEY

The route descends through increasingly wooded scenery which gradually opens out into an almost flat plain – dramatically different from the high hills around the Lecht. To the left can be seen the houses of Tomintoul, the highest village in the Highlands at 1150 feet. At the T-junction turn left to enter the village and shortly turn sharp right (still on the A939) to drive through the main street. Tomintoul, a planned village built from local limestone and slate, was conceived in 1779 by the Duke of Gordon. Its creation was possible only because of the military road; but even though the Duke also built mills to employ the inhabitants, his venture was a failure. Queen Victoria, who passed through here in 1869, described it as 'the most tumbledown, poor-looking place I ever saw – a long street with three inns, miserable, dirty-looking houses and a sad look of wretchedness about it'. It is now a spacious, pleasant little town with a neat square.

Views of the distant Cairngorms characterize the route from Tomintoul. The road runs for a short distance above the River Avon, which follows a serpentine course to the left of the road. Follow signs for Grantown-on-Spey on the A939, turning left over the Avon at Bridge of Avon. The road winds up across open moorland with superb views to the north of the Hills of Cromdale, and eventually descends to Strathspey to reach a junction with the A95. Turn left on to it (SP Grantown), and shortly cross the Spey to enter Grantown-on-Spey.

This handsome town, with its wide grass verges and elegant greystone buildings, was planned in 1765 by Sir James Grant, apparently because he considered that the original village, Castletown-of-Freuchie, was too near his home, Castle Grant. It was not uncommon for landlords to move whole communities lock, stock and barrel if they considered them an eyesore. The new town soon became a tourist resort, attracting the leisured classes when holidays in the Highlands became fashionable in the 19th century. Its healthy climate and well-appointed hotels still attract many visitors each year, and golf, skiing and salmon-fishing can all be enjoyed in the area.

GRANTOWN-ON-SPEY TO NAIRN

The route leaves Grantown on the A939 (SP Nairn) and after climbing through wooded country emerges on to Dava Moor.

LOCHINDORB

About 7½ miles from Grantown, an unclassified road to the left offers a detour to Lochindorb. The road runs right along the eastern shore of the loch, with views of the romantic island castle. Now in ruins, the castle was occupied both by Edward III of Scotland and by Edward I of England, but it is better known as the one-time stronghold of the notorious 'Wolf of Badenoch', the wayward son of King Robert II.

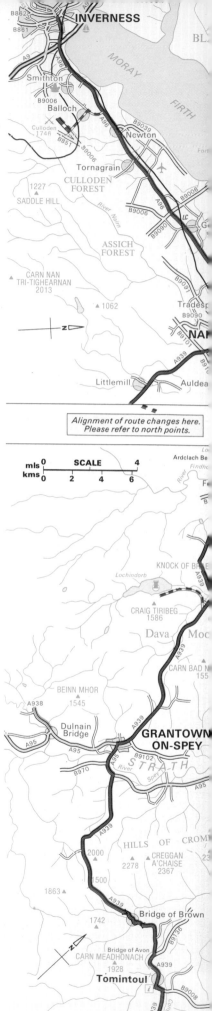

e A939 swings sharply left to cross the
ridge over the attractive Dorback Burn,
continues across wild, bare moorland.
e are long views, stretching to the distant
ntains, and the route eventually reaches
scattered community of Ferness. Less
a mile beyond Ferness cross the spark-
River Findhorn over an old three-arched
e bridge.

ARDCLACH BELL TOWER

ter ¾ mile an unclassified road on the left
P Dulsie Bridge, Ardclach, Ardclach Bell
ower) offers a delightful detour, clearly
gnposted along a forest-shaded lane and
en up a wooded glen, to the bell tower.*
erched high on a hill among the trees, the
wer is reached along a short lane unsuitable
r cars. Built in 1655, it has two storeys and is
feet square. The upper floor has a fireplace
d is also equipped with gun-loops, pre-
mably indicating that it was once fortified.
s chief purpose, however, was to call
orshippers to Ardclach church, which can
seen far below in a delightful setting beside
secluded stretch of the River Findhorn.

---

main route continues through country-
that becomes progressively more culti-
d as it nears the coast. Dense pinewoods
ually give way to a mixture of deciduous
dlands and farmland. Eventually the
dings of Nairn come into view and
ond them the waters of the Moray Firth.
the outskirts of the town, turn left to join
A96 (SP Inverness). A solid-looking town

Nairn's elegant ironwork bandstand typifies the dignified atmosphere of a resort that has been nicknamed 'the Brighton of the North'

Inverness became a popular touring centre for the Scottish Highlands in the 19th century. Many of the buildings that line the River Ness date from this period, giving the town a distinctly Victorian air

with a windswept, seaside air, Nairn has
been a market town and fishing port for
many centuries, though its harbour dates
only from 1829, when the course of the River
Nairn was altered to its present position
following a disastrous flood. After the railway
arrived here in the 1850s, Nairn became a
popular seaside resort, and was known as 'the
Brighton of the North'. Many of the
Victorian mansions that were built at that
time are now boarding-houses, catering for
the many tourists who still visit Nairn for its
beaches and its three golf-courses. The new
housing estates on the edge of the town have
been built to accommodate workers brought
in by the North Sea oil boom.

NAIRN TO INVERNESS

Leave Nairn by the A96 Inverness road, and
continue with views of the Moray Firth and
the low hills and bare cliffs of Black Isle, with
the peaks of Easter Ross in the distance. The
road runs through flat farmland bordered by
banks of pines that act as windbreaks, soon
passing Inverness Airport, to the right of the
road. Three miles beyond it a detour may be
made to Culloden Moor* – site of the famous
battle in 1746 – by following signs along
unclassified roads to the left (see p. 280). For
the last few miles the A96 runs ever closer to
the coast, with views to the right over the
Moray Firth, before reaching its destination,
a town long acknowledged as the capital of
the Highlands. (For details and a town plan
of Inverness, see p. 281.)

ROUTE 26

176 MILE

Glasgow to Inverness

MAGNIFICENT scenery begins on Glasgow's doorstep, and as this route travels northwards towards Inverness it passes through some of the most famous landscapes in Scotland. Upland scenery comes into its own once the route has entered Strath Blane, which lies beneath the moorland slopes of the Campsie Fells. Like most of the Highlands, the Campsie Fells were once cloaked in thick forest, but in Neolithic times man began to clear the trees for fuel and building purposes, and to make room for crops and domestic animals. Today's Highland landscapes of heather- and bracken-covered slopes and grassy mountains seem wild and untamed, but they owe nearly as much of their present character to the hand of man as do the neat fields and pastures of the glens and straths.

Well-tended farmland lies on either side of the route as it emerges from Strath Blane and, crossing the infant River Forth, runs through the Queen Elizabeth Forest Park to reach Aberfoyle. From here the route continues through Achray Forest – part of the Forest Park – and eventually descends, with breathtaking views, to Loch Achray and the Trossachs. Ever since Wordsworth and Sir Walter Scott celebrated the glory of the Trossachs in their poetry at the beginning of the 19th century the area has attracted countless thousands of tourists in search of quintessentially romantic scenery.

Beyond Loch Venachar the route turns northwards to follow the Pass of Leny up to Loch Lubnaig, which is overlooked by the stream-threaded slopes of Ben Ledi. At the far end of Strathyre, and to the west of the main route, is Balquhidder, the burial place of Rob Roy, perhaps the most famous of Scottish heroes. Born in about 1660, he was chief of the MacGregors and a dedicated Jacobite. A host of legends and tales grew up around his daring exploits and his adventures while on the run. Although he spent many years warring against the Dukes of Montrose, Atholl, and the English in the Jacobite cause, he eventually died peacefully in his bed.

At Lochearnhead the route enters Glen Ogle to reach Glen Dochart – both of which were gouged out of the mountain mass by glaciers during the Ice Ages. Long after the ice had retreated a way of life developed in the Highland glens which remained unaltered for centuries. Farmers cultivated the valley floors and glen sides and supported a warrior caste of leaders who ruled with an iron will but kept intruders at bay and preserved the clan traditions. This feudal way of life was destroyed by the disastrous rebellion of 1745, and further dramatic changes were brought to the Highlands by the notorious 'clearances' of the late 18th and early 19th centuries. Landlords realized that sheep – which could feed on the poor moorland grasses in summer and survive outdoors all winter – gave a high return for a comparatively small input of money and manpower. Whole glens were cleared of their populations, and Scotland, unlike the rest of Britain, saw a decrease in population throughout the 19th century.

Stretching northwards from Glen Dochart and Loch Tay are the wild expanses of the Breadalbane Mountains. Ben Lawers,

Tayside's highest peak, forms part of a vast National Trus Scotland property which has calcium-rich soil that supp the finest alpine flora in Britain.

The route continues along Loch Tay through Fearnan, then turns northwards to the delightful thatched villag Fortingall. From Coshieville, the route follows the Allt stream past the ruins of Garth Castle – one of many strongh in the area associated with the Wolf of Badenoch – and ur the glittering conical peak of Schiehallion. Beyond Tum Bridge the route runs along Glen Errochty to Calvine and A9, which follows the course of one of General Wade's g military roads. In the Drumochter Pass, parts of the old r can be seen near the present road.

Wild mountain scenery gives way to more pastoral la scapes as the route approaches Strath Spey. One of the important routeways in the Highlands, Strath Spey created by glaciers and is now a centre of the Highland to trade, making it one of the most populous areas of nortl Scotland. Its tree-dappled slopes contrast strongly with bleak undulations of the Monadhliath Mountains, wl stretch away to the west, and the mighty granite peaks of Cairngorms to the east. In the 14th century, Speyside subject to a reign of terror by the 'Wolf of Badenoch', so Robert II of Scotland, who had one of his strongholds at L an Eilein, under the shadow of the Cairngorm peaks. Cairngorms are now partly within the boundaries of the C More Forest Park, and partly set aside as a huge nature res that includes some of the wildest scenery in Britain.

From Carrbridge, where the Scottish Sculpture Trust assembled a superb collection of modern sculptures and pla them in the grounds of the fascinating Landmark visitor cer the route continues to the Slochd Summit. This once for part of a drove road, and later – in 1730 – became par General Wade's road from Dunkeld to Inverness. Bey Tomatin the route passes close to Loch Moy and its rui island castle, then crosses the plain of Drummossie Mui reach Inverness and the wide waters of the Moray Firth.

PLACES OF INTEREST: OPENING DETAILS

Lawers
BEN LAWERS
VISITOR CENTRE
open Easter to
end Sep

Newtonmore
CLAN MACPHERSON
MUSEUM open May
to Sep Mon to Sat

Kingussie
HIGHLAND FOLK
MUSEUM open all
year Mon to Fri; also
open Sat all day and
Sun pm only Apr
to Oct

Kincraig
KINCRAIG WILDLIFE
PARK open Mar to
end Oct

Aviemore
STRATHSPEY
RAILWAY open mid
May to end Sep Sat
and Sun; also open
Tue, Wed and Thu in
Jul and Aug

Carrbridge
LANDMARK open
all year

Culloden Moor
CULLODEN BATTLE-
FIELD open all year.
VISITOR CENTRE
open Easter to mid
Oct: Mon to Sat all
day, Sun pm only

Inverness
MUSEUM AND ART
GALLERY open all
year Mon to Sat

ABERTARFF HOUSE
open all year daily
(Wed and Sat,
pm only)

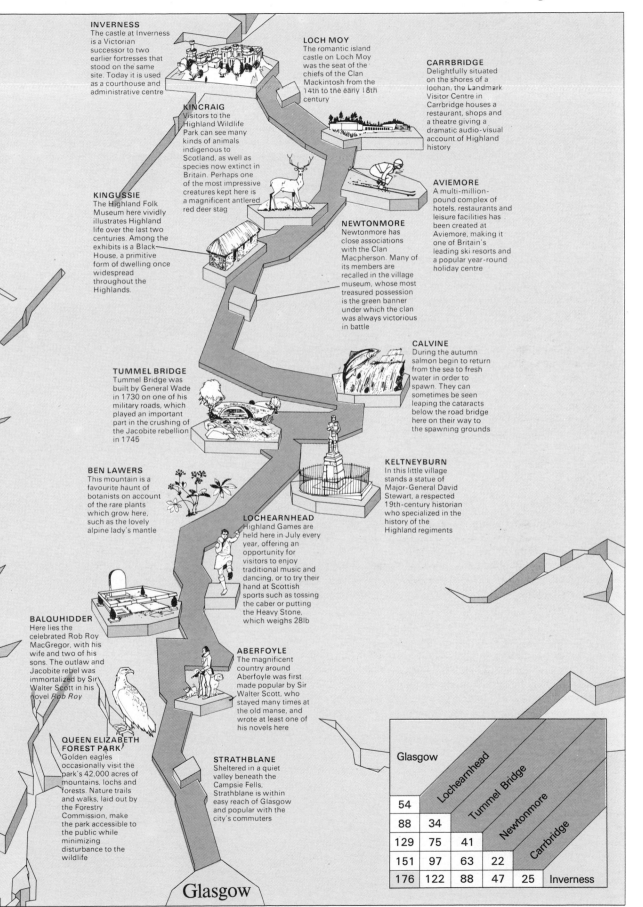

INVERNESS
The castle at Inverness is a Victorian successor to two earlier fortresses that stood on the same site. Today it is used as a courthouse and administrative centre

LOCH MOY
The romantic island castle on Loch Moy was the seat of the chiefs of the Clan Mackintosh from the 14th to the early 18th century

CARRBRIDGE
Delightfully situated on the shores of a lochan, the Landmark Visitor Centre in Carrbridge houses a restaurant, shops and a theatre giving a dramatic audio-visual account of Highland history

KINCRAIG
Visitors to the Highland Wildlife Park can see many kinds of animals indigenous to Scotland, as well as species now extinct in Britain. Perhaps one of the most impressive creatures kept here is a magnificent antlered red deer stag

KINGUSSIE
The Highland Folk Museum here vividly illustrates Highland life over the last two centuries. Among the exhibits is a Black-House, a primitive form of dwelling once widespread throughout the Highlands.

NEWTONMORE
Newtonmore has close associations with the Clan Macpherson. Many of its members are recalled in the village museum, whose most treasured possession is the green banner under which the clan was always victorious in battle

AVIEMORE
A multi-million-pound complex of hotels, restaurants and leisure facilities has been created at Aviemore, making it one of Britain's leading ski resorts and a popular year-round holiday centre

CALVINE
During the autumn salmon begin to return from the sea to fresh water in order to spawn. They can sometimes be seen leaping the cataracts below the road bridge here on their way to the spawning grounds

TUMMEL BRIDGE
Tummel Bridge was built by General Wade in 1730 on one of his military roads, which played an important part in the crushing of the Jacobite rebellion in 1745

KELTNEYBURN
In this little village stands a statue of Major-General David Stewart, a respected 19th-century historian who specialized in the history of the Highland regiments

BEN LAWERS
This mountain is a favourite haunt of botanists on account of the rare plants which grow here, such as the lovely alpine lady's mantle

LOCHEARNHEAD
Highland Games are held here in July every year, offering an opportunity for visitors to enjoy traditional music and dancing, or to try their hand at Scottish sports such as tossing the caber or putting the Heavy Stone, which weighs 28lb

BALQUHIDDER
Here lies the celebrated Rob Roy MacGregor, with his wife and two of his sons. The outlaw and Jacobite rebel was immortalized by Sir Walter Scott in his novel *Rob Roy*

ABERFOYLE
The magnificent country around Aberfoyle was first made popular by Sir Walter Scott, who stayed many times at the old manse, and wrote at least one of his novels here

QUEEN ELIZABETH FOREST PARK
Golden eagles occasionally visit the park's 42,000 acres of mountains, lochs and forests. Nature trails and walks, laid out by the Forestry Commission, make the park accessible to the public while minimizing disturbance to the wildlife

STRATHBLANE
Sheltered in a quiet valley beneath the Campsie Fells, Strathblane is within easy reach of Glasgow and popular with the city's commuters

Glasgow

Glasgow	Lochearnhead	Tummel Bridge	Newtonmore	Carrbridge	
54					
88	34				
129	75	41			
151	97	63	22		
176	122	88	47	25	Inverness

GLASGOW TO ABERFOYLE

From the centre of Glasgow follow the A81 (SP Aberfoyle, Strathblane) out through Milngavie and past Craigmaddie Reservoir, which is surrounded by attractive public parkland. Fields and banks of trees chequer the land on either side, but the countryside becomes less tamed by the minute as the Campsie Fells, the first taste of the Highlands, rise in front. Tucked beneath the steep southern slopes of the Fells, which reach 1897 feet at the summit of Earl's Seat, is the village of Strathblane, sited in an attractively wooded pass.

Farmland rises to wooded slopes and rough, heather-covered country on both sides of the A81 as it continues up Strath Blane – the valley of Blane Water, which runs to the left of the road. About 4 miles beyond Strathblane village, the route passes the Glengoyne whisky distillery, built in 1833. There is a tree near the distillery where the outlawed Rob Roy, the most famous member of the MacGregor clan, is said to have hidden from English soldiers.

Follow the A81 towards Aberfoyle. The road runs for several miles through pleasant farming country, then crosses the infant River Forth, which rises to the west of the road. Soon the route runs into the Queen Elizabeth Forest Park. Named in honour of the Queen's coronation in 1953, the park covers 42,000 acres, stretching from Loch Venachar to Loch Lomond. Many miles of well signposted walks and nature trails have been laid out to make the forest easily accessible to the public, and there are several picnic sites. The Forestry Commission has planted broad-leaved trees, as well as the more usual evergreens, to give variety and enhance the landscape. The forest is rich in bird life – larger species include buzzards, sparrow-hawks and owls – and is visited by golden eagles, though they do not nest here.

Approaching Aberfoyle, turn left on to the A821. A thickly wooded road leads into the little town, which has been a base for visitors to the Trossachs since Victorian times. To the right of the road is the ruined village church. In the churchyard stand two cast-iron mort-safes, built to protect corpses from the notori-ous 'body-snatchers' of the early 19th century.

ABERFOYLE TO BRIG O' TURK

Drive through Aberfoyle, bearing right (SP The Trossachs, Loch Katrine) and then climbing in a series of steep hairpin bends through Achray Forest. This part of the route is known as the Duke's Road; the pass was constructed in the early 19th century by the Duke of Montrose. Off to the right, about $\frac{3}{4}$ mile beyond Aberfoyle, is the David Marshall Lodge, a picnic pavilion and in-formation centre built in 1960. It commands superb views, taking in the upper Forth valley and the Fintry Hills in one direction and 3194-foot Ben Lomond in the other.

At the top of the climb, breathtaking views open up across the forest to the Trossachs – a classic Scottish scene of woodland, glens, lochans (small lochs) and distant, misty mountains, some of them 'Munroes' – that is, peaks over 3000 feet, named after the 18th-century Scottish mountaineer who charted them, Sir Hugh T. Munro. Soon the route is descending, still amid magnificent scenery, to the shores of Loch Achray.

LOCH KATRINE

At the junction at the north-west corner of Loch Achray, a detour can be made by turning left to reach the eastern end of Loch Katrine, 1 mile away. One of the loveliest Scottish lochs, Loch Katrine was the inspi-ration for Sir Walter Scott's long poem *The Lady of the Lake*. Ellen's Isle, at the eastern end of the loch, is named after his heroine, Ellen Douglas.

A boat trip is by far the best way to see the magnificent country which surrounds the inaccessible loch. In summer, visitors can make the 9-mile trip along the loch in an authentic Victorian steamer, the *Sir Walter Scott*. The boat was rebuilt and refurbished here, and now runs from Trossachs Pier, at the loch's eastern end, to Stronachlachar.

Overlooked by the rugged peak of Ben Venue, 2393 feet high, Loch Katrine and the land around it was for centuries the preserve of the warlike MacGregor clan – the 'children of the mist'. Near the head of the loch is their ancient graveyard, and Rob Roy himself was born around 1660 in nearby Glen Gyle.

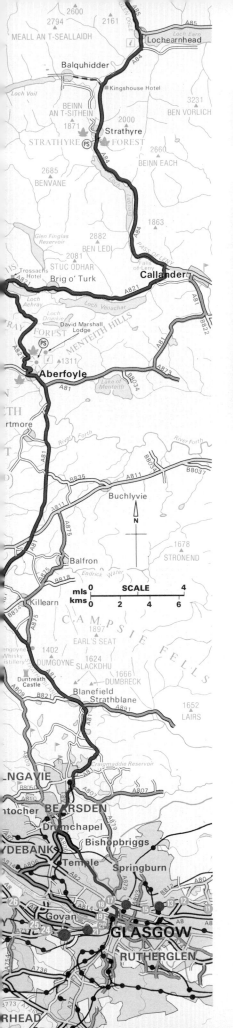

The Falls of Leny are a series of foaming cataracts in a narrow pass on the approach to Loch Lubnaig

The main route, the A821 (SP Callander) continues along the northern shore of Loch Achray, passing the astonishing Trossachs Hotel. Resembling a baronial hall, the great turreted building has stood here since the Victorian tourist boom in the area. Shortly past it, to the right on the loch shore, is the parish church of Trossachs. Built in 1849, it is a delightful little chapel in perfect surroundings. The A821 (SP Callander) continues through the tiny hamlet of Brig o' Turk, whose name, meaning 'bridge of the boar', is derived from the Gaelic.

BRIG O' TURK TO LOCHEARNHEAD

Continue along the northern shore of Loch Venachar, which is dramatically set between Ben Ledi to the north and the Menteith Hills to the south.

Beyond Loch Venachar, the country temporarily opens out and the buildings of Callander can be seen in the distance on the right. This was the setting for the village of Tannochbrae in the long-running television and radio series *Dr Finlay's Casebook*. One mile beyond the end of Loch Venachar, turn left on to the A84 (SP Lochearnhead), near the point where the road begins the gradual climb of the Pass of Leny. This narrow gorge is best known for the Falls of Leny, a series of white and swirling rapids.

Over the pass, Loch Lubnaig appears on the left; its name is Gaelic for 'loch of the bend'. At the southern end of the loch, by the roadside, is the ancient burial ground of St Bride, and the ruins of a pre-Reformation chapel. Several isolated houses on the far side are overlooked by the heights of Ben Ledi

above. The mountain is densely forested, with streams tumbling in waterfalls down its rocky faces. In clear conditions the loch mirrors beautifully the woods and hills that encroach so closely upon it.

North of Loch Lubnaig, the valley is clothed with the trees of the huge Strathyre Forest. In 1968 a hurricane blew down 80,000 of its trees – but another 8 million survived – an indication of the forest's vastness. Many of the foresters live in Strathyre, a village at the heart of the forest which is popular with tourists. At the southern end of the village is a nature trail and a Forestry Commission information centre.

BALQUHIDDER
Approximately 2 miles north of Strathyre, opposite the Kingshouse Hotel, an unclassified road on the left offers a detour to Balquhidder. After ½ mile the narrow lane passes an old chapel on the left. It is not open to the public, or identified in any way, but it is in fact a mausoleum for the MacGregor chiefs. Further along the road, at Balquhidder, is the grave of Rob Roy, dated 28 December 1734. His body lies in the shadow of a ruined 17th-century church, close to the Victorian one that replaced it. Nearby rest his wife and two of his sons.

Approximately 3 miles north of the Balquhidder turning, on the A84, lies the attractive village of Lochearnhead, a sailing and water-skiing resort. It is one of about 70 Scottish towns and villages which hold their own Highland Games every summer. Loch Earn, set amid hills over 2000 feet high, stretches away to the east of the village.

LOCHEARNHEAD TO KILLIN

From Lochearnhead the A85 (SP Crianlarich) climbs through the wild, bracken-clad country of Glen Ogle. The road reaches almost 1000 feet before descending into Glen Dochart, where the route turns right on to the A827 (SP Killin).

Beside the road runs the River Dochart, known for the spectacular Falls of Dochart, which are best seen from the old five-arched bridge as you enter Killin. Even in high summer or a dry autumn the river here seems full, and the rushing water swirls round islets in the middle of the river. Below the bridge is Inch Buie, a long, narrow, wooded island which is the ancient burial ground of the MacNab chiefs. Cross the old bridge and bear right, following signs for Aberfeldy.

FINLARIG CASTLE

A recommended short detour is to Finlarig Castle, described in Scott's *Fair Maid of Perth*. To reach it, turn right beyond the village centre just before the caravan site. This former seat of the Campbell clan is now a complete ruin, hidden in a small copse. It is well known for Black Duncan's beheading pit, which still exists. This was used only for the aristocracy, the common people being hanged from a neighbouring tree.

KILLIN TO KELTNEYBURN

Leaving Killin, the route runs along the northern shore of Loch Tay, one of Scotland's deepest lochs. It reaches a depth of 500 feet in places, and is sheltered to the north by Ben Lawers, the highest of Tayside's peaks at 3984 feet. Loch Tay is noted for a bloodthirsty tale of the MacNab clan. In the early 16th century, 12 of them rowed to the southern shore, then carried their boat over the hills to Loch Earn, where they rowed out to the island of the MacWeish, murdered the chief to settle an ancient feud and returned the same night to Loch Tay with his head.

The River Dochart becomes a rushing torrent at Killin, where it is forced through a rocky gorge before entering Loch Tay

BEN LAWERS
NATIONAL TRUST VISITOR CENTRE

A little under 5 miles from Killin an unclassified road on the left leads to the National Trust for Scotland Visitor Centre* on the flanks of Ben Lawers. This makes an enjoyable detour, with fine views of Loch Tay and the untamed high country to its north, where there are no fewer than ten peaks over 3000 feet. The visitor centre, established in 1950, is reached by a twisting road that quickly ascends to 1400 feet above sea level. The National Trust owns some 8000 acres of the lower slopes of Ben Lawers which are always open to the public. At the visitor centre the public can obtain information about the area as well as suggestions for mountain walks of varying length and difficulty. These are especially enjoyable in spring, since Ben Lawers is known for rare alpine plants that bloom early in the year.

Alpine lady's mantle, which has yellow flowers and silver-edged leaves, is among the rare plants that grow on the slopes of Ben Lawers

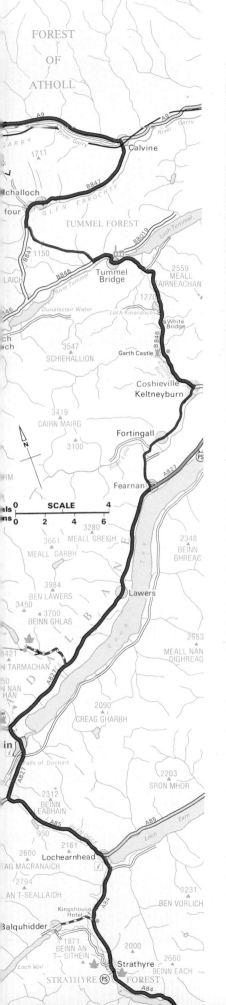

The conical peak of Schiehallion is one of the most distinctive landmarks in the Highlands

The main route continues through Lawers to the sleepy lochside hamlet of Fearnan, where you should turn left on to an unclassified road (SP Fortingall, Coshieville). In 1¼ miles, at the second junction, bear left and in ½ mile cross the River Lyon. At the edge of Fortingall the route passes the entrance to Glenlyon House, which can be seen clearly at the end of its long drive. Its present appearance is a result of 19th-century baronial additions to an older house built by the Campbell clan. (It is not open to the public.)

Fortingall is a very pretty village whose houses overlook green sheep pastures running down to the banks of the River Lyon. The village, whose thatched roofs are quite a rarity in Scotland, was laid out by Sir Donald Currie, a wealthy shipowner, at the end of the 19th century. The ancient yew in the churchyard has a circumference of over 50 feet, and was described even in 1769 as 'decrepit'. There is a strange legend that Fortingall was the birthplace of Pontius Pilate.

Continue for 2¾ miles to Keltneyburn, where there is a statue of Major-General David Stewart (1768–1869), historian of the Highlands and the Highland Regiments. The village is a delightful place, its peace disturbed only by the sound of rushing water coming from the Falls of Keltney, which are reached along a path at the side of the statue.

KELTNEYBURN TO CALVINE

Just past Keltneyburn, at Coshieville, turn left on to the B846 (SP Tummel). After 1 mile, 14th-century Garth Castle can be seen across the river on the left. It is said to have been built by the infamous 'Wolf of Badenoch', the rebellious great-grandson of

Robert the Bruce who was particularly notorious for his sacking and burning of Elgin Cathedral in 1390.

The soft, green countryside soon gives way to bleaker moorland, and the road rises to 1200 feet at White Bridge. Just past the turning for Kinloch Rannoch is a small loch near the road, and behind that the great peak of Schiehallion, 3547 feet high.

After crossing an expanse of wild moorland the road begins to descend, with many twists and turns, passing through forest on the way to Tummel Bridge, at the western end of Loch Tummel. The River Tummel flows swiftly into the loch, feeding the hydro-electric power station. The hydro-electric scheme is responsible for the loch's present shape. Once no more than a 3-mile-long swelling of the River Tummel, damming has more than doubled the length of the loch, which is now ¾ mile across at its widest point.

Turn left at the T-junction, continuing on the B846 (SP Kinloch Rannoch) for about 1 mile, then turn right on to an unclassified road (SP The North). The road climbs increasingly steeply through high, rugged country with Tummel Forest to the right and bare, barren country falling away to the left. Once over the summit, bear right on to the B847 and pass through the hamlets of Trinafour and Dalchalloch, dropping down into a sheltered valley, with farms and pastures to the right on the banks of Errochty Water.

At the junction with the A9 in the village of Calvine, turn left (SP Inverness). The road bridge over the River Garry just before this junction is a good vantage point for watching salmon leaping the cataracts during the spawning season.

CALVINE TO NEWTONMORE

This first stretch of the A9 is a new and very impressive cutting through solid rock. To the left is the old road, the River Garry and the Perth to Inverness railway line – all following a natural route corridor that was exploited in the 18th century by General Wade, whose military road to Inverness followed the same course. Wade was given the job of improving Scotland's roads after the 1715 Jacobite rebellion made it essential for troops to travel through the Highlands as easily as possible. This road, leading ultimately to the military fortifications at Inverness and the strategically important Moray Firth, is one of the 40 he built between 1726 and 1740. Between Dalnacardoch and Dalnaspidal, a 'Wade stone' stands to the right of the road, marking the point where workmen who had started at the northern end of the road met those coming from the south.

To the left of the road at Dalnaspidal there are good views of desolate Loch Garry, far below. The stretch of the A9 to the north of Dalnaspidal is the wild Pass of Drumochter, agreeable from the comfort of a car in summer, but a different matter in bad winter conditions. The road itself reaches 1516 feet above sea level, whilst the railway beside it reaches 1484 feet, the highest railway summit in Britain. The two mountains to the left of the pass are known as the Sow of Atholl and the Boar of Badenoch. Their peaks are snow-covered for several months of the year.

Leaving behind the austere landscapes of steep hills covered with scree and heather, the A9 descends into the flatter, green country of Glen Truim, which runs into the Spey valley. Here the route branches left on to the B9150 for Newtonmore, crossing the Spey to enter the town. Turn right on to the A86 (SP Kingussie), passing on the left the road which leads to the Clan Macpherson Museum.* Opened shortly after the Second World War, the museum contains many interesting mementoes of the clan, including the green banner under which, it is said, its members can never be defeated. This area has many associations with the Macphersons; a Clan Macpherson rally is still held in Newtonmore on the first Saturday in August. It is said that one of the chiefs of the clan once hid from the redcoats for nine years in one of the caves of Creag Dhubh, the 'black rock', to the south-west of the town. To the north are the wild Monadhliath ('Grey') Mountains, whose foothills are popular walking, canoeing and pony-trekking country.

Among the exhibits in the Clan Macpherson Museum Newtonmore is the banner said to protect the clan fro defeat in battle

Desolate countryside characterizes the route through Garry, where a newly built section of the A9 runs alo the old military road built by General Wade

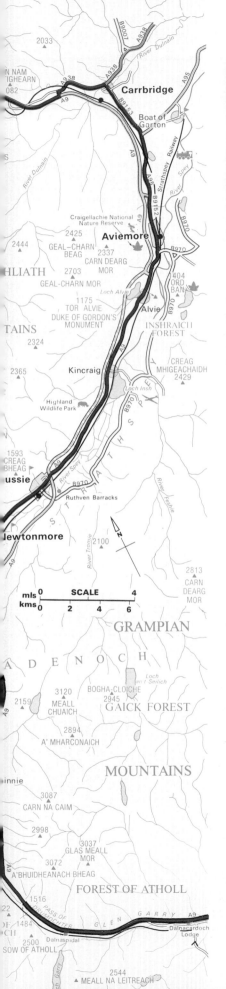

This reconstruction of a tinker encampment is one of many exhibits recalling traditional aspects of Highland life in Kingussie's Highland Folk Museum

NEWTONMORE TO AVIEMORE

From Newtonmore follow the A86 into Kingussie. This large village was laid out at the end of the 18th century by the Duke of Gordon. Kingussie is best known for its fascinating Highland Folk Museum,* whose exhibits include a reconstructed thatched Hebridean water-mill and a primitive 'Black House' – a crofter's cottage brought here from the Isle of Lewis and set in six acres of gardens. Across the Spey from Kingussie the remains of Ruthven Barracks can be seen to the right. The barracks were built in 1719 to control the Highlanders after the first Jacobite rebellion, and were later enlarged by General Wade. Castles have stood on the great mound for centuries and have witnessed the activities of many key figures in Scottish history from the 'Wolf of Badenoch' in the 14th century to Bonnie Prince Charlie in the 18th. His supporters were responsible for blowing up the barracks in 1746 after the Battle of Culloden, reducing them to the ruins that can be seen today.

Continue along the A86 from Kingussie, then follow signs for Aviemore and the A9 to continue down the Spey valley. After 3½ miles the road passes on the left the entrance to the Highland Wildlife Park,* where animals and birds native to Scotland may be seen at close quarters. They include animals now extinct in the wild, such as bears, wolves and bison. Wildcats, eagles, red deer and Soay sheep are among the many others that can be seen here. Some of the animals are kept in pens, while others roam free and can be watched from the safety of a car as you drive through.

Two miles further on is the village of Kincraig, in a lovely setting overlooking Loch Insh. On the loch shore is Insh church, which stands on a site said to have been used for worship for 1300 years. The present building, though charming, is a reconstruction of an older church, but inside is still kept the little bronze hand-bell of St Eunan, probably in use on this site in the 7th century.

Beyond Kincraig the country opens out further, into heathland enhanced by silver birch, with superb views of the Cairngorms to the right. Before reaching Aviemore the road passes the peaceful shores of Loch Alvie. On the opposite side of the road rises a hill topped by a 90-foot-high monument to the Fifth Duke of Gordon. On the same hill, Tor Alvie, is a cairn erected in memory of Highlanders killed at the Battle of Waterloo.

One mile further on, the route turns right on to the B9152 for Aviemore town centre. Although Aviemore had been a modest resort since the railway to Inverness opened in the mid 19th century, it has been completely transformed in recent years by the creation of the Aviemore Centre, a multi-million-pound complex of hotels, restaurants, shops and leisure facilities of all kinds. Aviemore is now one of the most comprehensively equipped leisure resorts in Britain, catering both for serious winter sports enthusiasts and for those who simply want a restful holiday. A theatre and a Highland craft centre are among the indoor attractions.

Above the town to the west is the Craigellachie National Nature Reserve, where there is a nature trail and several excellent viewpoints. At the southern end of Aviemore is a terminus of the privately owned Strathspey Railway,* which runs steam-hauled passenger trains in summer.

AVIEMORE TO TOMATIN

Continue northwards from Aviemore on the B9152 (SP Grantown-on-Spey), and in 1½ miles turn right on to the A95. After 2¾ miles keep forward to join the B9153 (SP Carrbridge), passing through densely wooded countryside to reach Carrbridge. This ski resort takes its name from the high-arched bridge across the River Dulnain, said to have been built in the 18th century after two men had drowned while carrying coffins across the river to a nearby churchyard. Carrbridge is perhaps best known for Landmark,* an award-winning visitor centre which provides an excellent audio-visual guide to the history of the Highlands from the Ice Ages to the present day. The centre was opened in 1970 and is situated at the southern end of the village.

Cross the River Dulnain, then turn left on to the A938 (SP Inverness). After 2¼ miles the route turns right to join the A9 for Inverness, beginning the long climb over the moors to the Slochd Summit, more than 1300 feet above sea level. Beyond the summit, road and railway descend side by side into the valley of the River Findhorn. To the left, just off the road as it crosses the wide and meandering river, the village of Tomatin can be clearly seen. Here there is a famous malt whisky distillery, one of the biggest in Scotland, where some 3 million gallons of light, rather 'peaty' whisky are produced each year.

TOMATIN TO INVERNESS

The country north of Tomatin (the name means 'juniper knoll') was once part of a royal forest belonging to Inverness Castle. The wide Findhorn valley lies to the right as the road curves attractively, climbing gradually all the time.

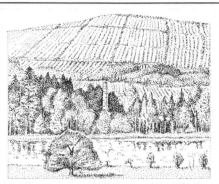

LOCH MOY

About 4 miles beyond Tomatin, just past the sign for Moy, a detour can be made along the B9154 on the right to Loch Moy. On an island in the middle of the loch is a 19th-century obelisk commemorating Sir Aeneas Mackintosh, and the ruin of Moy Castle. This was the stronghold of the Clan Mackintosh until, in about 1700, the clan's seat was moved to Moy Hall, which stood nearby on the mainland. The clan's chief still lives in a more recent house on the same site.

CULLODEN MOOR

Half a mile north of Daviot, the B851 on t right offers a detour to wooded Cullod Moor, site of the famous battle on 16 Ap 1746 – the last to be fought on British soil. represented a complete reversal of fortune the Jacobites, for Bonnie Prince Charli forces were routed, never to regroup. T supporters of the reigning monarch, Geor II, were led by his son the Duke Cumberland, nicknamed 'the Butcher' cause of his ruthlessness. In the battle quarter of Charles's 5000 men were kill within an hour, and many others crawl away to die slowly among the hills. Char himself escaped, and spent some mont disguised or in hiding in the Highlands – the government had offered a reward £30,000 for his capture. After many a ventures he eventually escaped to France.

The site of the battle, now owned by t National Trust, is commemorated by a visit centre,* and there is a museum in O Leanach cottage, which stood here while t battle raged. Scattered stones beside t cottage mark the site of a barn in whi Highland wounded were burned to death.

Further along the A9, the Moray Firth soon be seen ahead. This is said to be the point from which to see Inverness. The sweeps downhill, curving to the left. modern A9 passes over the A96, and following signs for the town centre the hea Inverness is quickly reached.

The old bridge across the River Dulnain at Carrbridge was built by the Earl of Seafield in 1715 for the use of funeral parties travelling from nearby Duthil

INVERNESS

Britain's northernmost city, Inverness has long been an important Highland crossroads. It occupies a commanding position at the point where the Beauly Firth joins the Moray Firth, and at the northern end of the remarkable geological fault-line – Glen More – that dramatically divides the central from the northern Highlands. Many generations of travellers to the far north-west or north-east of Scotland have passed through the city, and in Victorian times a steamer service ran to Inverness up the east coast of Britain. The 60-mile-long Caledonian Canal, opened in 1847, linked the city with the west coast, and now Inverness is served by a modern airport, which has really come into its own following the North Sea oil boom in the area.

Modern industry has made its mark on Inverness, and the city serves the present-day needs of a vast area of northern Scotland. Yet, despite this, Inverness preserves much of its colourful history. The museum* commemorates the city's strategic importance during the Jacobite rebellions of 1715 and 1745, and near the 19th-century castle – the successor to many earlier fortresses here – stands a statue of Flora Macdonald, who helped Bonnie Prince Charlie to escape the clutches of the Duke of Cumberland after Culloden. Outside the 18th-century High Parish Church stands a bullet-scarred stone, a reminder of 'Butcher' Cumberland's ruthless execution of his prisoners after the battle.

One of the city's oldest houses is Abertarff House* in Church Street, built in 1593 and now, appropriately, the headquarters of the Highland Association, which exists to preserve the Gaelic language and culture. The house contains an exhibition illustrating Highland history and crafts. Traditional handloom-weaving and spinning for tartans and tweeds can still be watched in workshops in Tomnahurich Street and Dores Road, and in summer pipe bands and Highland dancers perform in the Northern Meeting Park – vividly reminding the 20th-century visitor that Inverness retains its role as the capital of the Highlands.

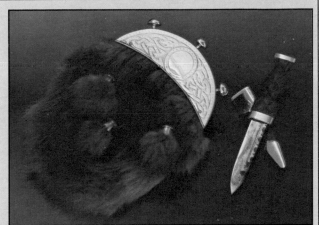

Above: The fine collection of locally made silver in Inverness Museum includes this silver-mounted sporran and 'sgian dhubh', or black knife – parts of the traditional Highland costume

Right: Inverness Castle overlooks a statue of Flora Macdonald, the famous Scottish heroine who helped Bonnie Prince Charlie escape to Skye after the Battle of Culloden

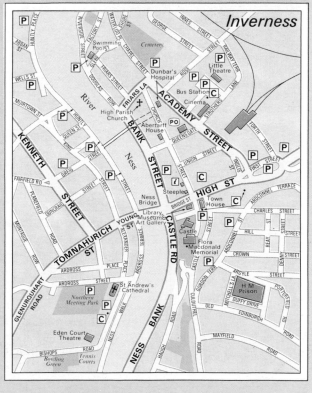

Additional Routes

The 32 additional routes listed here are compiled by linking sections of the basic routes

Route 27
London to Scarborough

Follow Route 2 from London to Lincoln (pp. 18–21), then Route 11 from Lincoln to Scarborough (pp. 120–3)

Route 28
London to Glasgow

Follow Route 3 from London to Lichfield (pp. 34–41), then Route 12 from Lichfield to Glasgow (pp. 126–37)

Route 29
London to Llandudno

Follow Route 3 from London to Uttoxeter (pp. 34–42), then Route 22 from Uttoxeter to Llandudno (pp. 237–41)

Route 30
London to Aberystwyth

Follow Route 4 from London to Ludlow (pp. 46–50), then Route 13 from Ludlow to Aberystwyth (pp. 141–3)

Route 31
London to Taunton

Follow Route 6 from London to Langport (pp. 68–72), then Route 21 from Langport to Taunton (p. 233)

Route 32
Birmingham to Edinburgh

Follow Route 12 from Birmingham to Skipton (pp. 126–9), then Route 24 from Skipton to Thirsk (pp. 256–8), then Route 2 from Thirsk to Edinburgh (pp. 25–31)

Route 33
Birmingham to Llandudno

Follow Route 12 from Birmingham to Sudbury (p. 126), then Route 22 from Sudbury to Llandudno (pp. 237–41)

Route 34
Birmingham to Caernarfon

Follow Route 13 from Birmingham to Ludlow (pp. 140–1), then Route 4 from Ludlow to Caernarfon (pp. 50–3)

Route 35
Birmingham to Tenby

Follow Route 13 from Birmingham to Devil's Bridge (pp. 140–3), then Route 23 from Devil's Bridge to Tenby (pp. 248–51)

Route 36
Birmingham to Cardiff

Follow Route 13 from Birmingham to Knighton (pp. 140–1), then Route 18 from Knighton to Cardiff (pp. 196–9)

Route 37
Birmingham to Bude

Follow Route 14 from Birmingham to the A38 west of Wellington (pp. 148–54), then Route 6 to Bude (pp. 73–5)

Route 38
Birmingham to Plymouth

Follow Route 14 from Birmingham to Exeter (pp. 148–55), then Route 7 from Exeter to Plymouth (pp. 84–5)

Route 39
Manchester to Aberystwyth

Follow Route 18 from Manchester to Knighton (pp. 190–3), then Route 13 from Knighton to Aberystwyth (pp. 142–3)

Route 40
Manchester to Tenby

Follow Route 18 from Manchester to Whitney (pp. 190–6), then Route 5 from Whitney to Tenby (pp. 61–5)

Route 41
Manchester to Bath

Follow Route 17 from Manchester to Nailsworth (pp. 180–5), then Route 19 from Nailsworth to Bath (pp. 208–9)

Route 42
Manchester to Bude

Follow Route 17 from Manchester to Nailsworth (pp. 180–5), then Route 14 from Nailsworth to the A38 west of Wellington (pp. 151–4), then Route 6 to Bude (pp. 73–5)

Additional Routes

Route 43
Manchester to Exeter

Follow Route 17 from Manchester to Nailsworth (pp. 180–5), then Route 14 from Nailsworth to Exeter (pp. 151–5)

Route 44
Manchester to Plymouth

Follow Route 17 from Manchester to Nailsworth (pp. 180–5), then Route 14 from Nailsworth to Exeter (pp. 151–5), then Route 7 from Exeter to Plymouth (pp. 84–5)

Route 45
Buxton to Aberystwyth

Follow Route 19 from Buxton to Newport (pp. 202–3), then Route 17 from Newport to Ludlow (pp. 181–3), then Route 13 from Ludlow to Aberystwyth (pp. 141–3)

Route 46
Buxton to Bude

Follow Route 19 from Buxton to Nailsworth (pp. 202–8), then Route 14 from Nailsworth to the A38 west of Wellington (pp. 151–4), then Route 6 to Bude (pp. 73–5)

Route 47
Buxton to Exeter

Follow Route 19 from Buxton to Nailsworth (pp. 202–8), then Route 14 from Nailsworth to Exeter (pp. 151–5)

Route 48
Buxton to Plymouth

Follow Route 19 from Buxton to Nailsworth (pp. 202–8), then Route 14 from Nailsworth to Exeter (pp. 151–5), then Route 7 from Exeter to Plymouth (pp. 84–5)

Route 49
Buxton to Bournemouth

Follow Route 19 from Buxton to Stroud (pp. 202–8), then Route 17 from Stroud to Bournemouth (pp. 185–7)

Route 50
Leicester to Glasgow

Follow Route 22 from Leicester to Sudbury (pp. 236–7), then Route 12 from Sudbury to Glasgow (pp. 126–37)

Route 51
Leicester to Buxton

Follow Route 22 from Leicester to Uttoxeter (pp. 236–7), then Route 3 from Uttoxeter to Buxton (pp. 42–3)

Route 52
Leicester to Tenby

Follow Route 21 from Leicester to Stow-on-the-Wold (pp. 224–6), then Route 4 from Stow-on-the-Wold to Ledbury (pp. 48–9), then Route 5 from Ledbury to Tenby (pp. 60–5)

Route 53
Leicester to Bude

Follow Route 21 from Leicester to Langport (pp. 224–33), then Route 6 from Langport to Bude (pp. 72–5)

Route 54
Leicester to Exeter

Follow Route 21 from Leicester to Taunton (pp. 224–33), then Route 14 from Taunton to Exeter (pp. 154–5)

Route 55
Leicester to Plymouth

Follow Route 21 from Leicester to Taunton (pp. 224–33), then Route 14 from Taunton to Exeter (pp. 154–5), then Route 7 from Exeter to Plymouth (pp. 84–5)

Route 56
Leicester to Bournemouth

Follow Route 21 from Leicester to Cirencester (pp. 224–7), then Route 15 from Cirencester to Bournemouth (pp. 160–5)

Route 57
Leicester to Eastbourne

Follow Route 21 from Leicester to the A429 south-west of Stow-on-the-Wold (pp. 224–7); turn left into Bourton-on-the-Water, then follow Route 16 to Eastbourne (pp. 170–5)

Route 58
Chester to Aberystwyth

Follow Route 23 from Chester to Devil's Bridge (pp. 244–8), then Route 13 from Devil's Bridge to Aberystwyth (p. 143)

The 32 additional routes listed here are compiled by linking sections of the basic routes

Index

This index lists towns, villages, places of interest in rural areas and certain natural features, with references to the pages where they are described in the text. The emphasis in the index is on places featured in the route commentaries, though major places which appear in the fourteen countryside features are also listed here.

The twenty-six basic routes described in detail in the book are indexed in italic type, followed by the route number. Additional routes 27–58 are not indexed here, but are listed on pages 282–3.

Acknowledgements

Most of the photographs which appear in 'Alternative Routes in Britain' were specially commissioned for the book; some, however, are from private individuals, picture libraries and other organizations. The publishers gratefully acknowledge the following for the use of photographs:

Title page Wherwell by Jon Wyand

Contents page Penshurst by S. & O. Mathews

Page 4 Chipping Campden by Trevor Wood

Page 5 Crich by Trevor Wood

Page 9 Broad Street, Ludlow, by Colin Molyneux

Route 1 (pp. 12–15): all photographs by **Trevor Wood** except Greensted church (p. 12) by Martyn J. Adelman

Route 2 (pp. 18–27 and 30–1): all photographs by **Martyn J. Adelman** except Durham view (p. 26) by Trevor Wood

Cheviots countryside feature (pp. 28–9): all photographs by **Martyn J. Adelman** except Battle of Otterburn (p. 29) from Mansell Collection

Route 3 (pp. 34–5 and 38–43): all photographs by **Martyn J. Adelman** except Warwick Castle (p. 40) by Colin Molyneux

Chiltern Hills countryside feature (pp. 36–7): Coombe Hill (p. 37), beechwoods and Stuart Linford (p. 36) by S. & O. Mathews; and Milton's Cottage (p. 37) by Martyn J. Adelman

Route 4 (pp. 46–53): all photographs by **S. & O. Mathews** except Tewkesbury (p.48) and Stokesay (p. 50) by Colin Molyneux

Route 5 (pp. 56–61 and 64–5): all photographs by **S. & O. Mathews** except Pen-y-crug hill-fort (p. 61), Paxton's Tower (p. 64), Tenby Bay and Laugharne (both on p. 65) by Colin Molyneux

Brecon Beacons countryside feature (pp. 62–3): all photographs by **Colin Molyneux** except Carreg Cennen Castle (p. 62) by Martyn J. Adelman; and log boat (p. 63) by S. & O. Mathews

Route 6 (pp. 68–75): all photographs by **Jon Wyand** except Marlow bridge (p. 68) by S. & O. Mathews; and Windsor Castle (p. 68) from BTA

Route 7 (pp. 78–85): all photographs by **Jon Wyand** except Abinger Hammer (p. 78) and Silent Pool (p. 79) by Martyn J. Adelman

Dartmoor countryside feature (pp. 86–7): all photographs by **Jon Wyand**

Route 8 (pp. 90–3): all photographs by **Jon Wyand** except Virginia Water (p. 90) by Martyn J. Adelman; and Stratfield Saye House (p. 91) by S. & O. Mathews

New Forest countryside feature (pp. 94–5): all photographs by **Robin Fletcher**

Route 9 (pp. 98–9 and 102–3): all photographs by **S. & O. Mathews**

Weald countryside feature (pp. 100–1): all photographs by **S. & O. Mathews** except hop pickers (p. 101) from Mary Evans Picture Library

Route 10 (pp. 106–13): all photographs by **Trevor Wood**

Route 11 (pp. 114–23): all photographs by **Colin Molyneux** except Melton Mowbray hunt scene (p. 118) by Philip Llewellin

Route 12 (pp. 126–9 and 132–7): all photographs by **Martyn J. Adelman**

Yorkshire Dales countryside feature (pp. 130–1): all photographs by **Colin Molyneux**

Route 13 (pp. 140–3): all photographs by **Colin Molyneux**

Cambrian Mountains countryside feature (pp. 144–5): all photographs by **Colin Molyneux** except Craig Goch Reservoir (p. 144) by Martyn J. Adelman

Route 14 (pp. 148–55): all photographs by **Jon Wyand** except Dodington House (p. 151) and Exeter Cathedral (p. 155) by Trevor Wood; and Taunton church (p. 154) by S. & O. Mathews

Route 15 (pp. 158–61 and 164–5): all photographs by **Jon Wyand**

Salisbury Plain countryside feature (pp. 162–3): Stonehenge by Colin Molyneux; Woodhenge (p. 162) by Robin Fletcher; Fovant Badges (p. 163) by courtesy of the Director, South Western Postal Region; and Stockton, Enford and the Breadstones (all on p. 163) by Jon Wyand

Route 16 (pp. 168–75): all photographs by **Trevor Wood**

South Downs countryside feature (pp. 176–7): all photographs by **S. & O. Mathews**

Route 17 (pp. 180–7): all photographs by **Richard Surman**

Route 18 (pp. 190–3 and 196–9): all photographs by **Colin Molyneux** except the Arab Room in Cardiff Castle (p. 199) by Peter Russell

Shropshire Hills countryside feature (pp. 194–5): Stiperstones (p. 194) and Clun Castle (p. 195) by Colin Molyneux; Wrekin (p. 194) and Acton Scott farmyard (p. 195) by S. & O. Mathews

Route 19 (pp. 202–9): all photographs by **Trevor Wood** except Wedgwood vase (p. 203) by S. & O. Mathews

Route 20 (pp. 212–15 and 218–21): all photographs by **Trevor Wood** except tulips near Spalding (p. 218) by S. & O. Mathews

Fenlands countryside feature (pp. 216–17): all photographs by **Trevor Wood**

Route 21 (pp. 224–7 and 230–3): all photographs by **S. & O. Mathews** except Brinklow Castle (p. 224) by Julia Craven; Great Bath at Bath (p. 231) by Trevor Wood; and basket-maker (p. 233) by Jon Wyand

Cotswolds countryside feature (pp. 228–9): Chipping Campden (p. 228) and Snowshill panorama by Trevor Wood; cottage exterior (p. 228) by S. & O. Mathews; and Richard Whitford painting (p. 229) from Museum of Rural Life, Reading

Route 22 (pp. 236–41): all photographs by **S. & O. Mathews**

Route 23 (pp. 244–51): all photographs by **S. & O. Mathews** except Old Oswestry hill-fort (p. 245) by Philip Llewellin; David Davies statue (p. 247) by Martyn J. Adelman; Mynach Falls, Devil's Bridge (p. 248) and Llandewi Brefi (p. 249) from BTA; and Tenby view (p. 251) by Colin Molyneux

Route 24 (pp. 254–9): all photographs by **S. & O. Mathews** except Scarborough (p. 259) by Colin Molyneux

Route 25 (pp. 262–5 and 268–71): all photographs by **Martyn J. Adelman**

Cairngorms countryside feature (pp. 266–7): Loch an Eilean (p. 266) and skiers (p. 267) from Scottish Tourist Board

Route 26 (pp. 274–81): all photographs by **Martyn J. Adelman** except Carrbridge view (p. 280) from Scottish Tourist Board

All portraits are from the National Portrait Gallery

DATE DUE
